WITH FIRE AND SWORD.

BY

HENRYK SIENKIKWICZ.

TRANSLATED BY JEREMIAH CURTIN.

INTRODUCTION.

The history of the origin and career of the two Slav States, Poland and Russia, is interesting not merely because it contains a vast number of surprising scenes and marvellous pictures of life, not merely because it gives us a kaleidoscope as it were of the acts of men, but because these acts in all their variety fall into groups which may be referred each to its proper source and origin, and each group contains facts that concern the most serious problems of history and political development.

The history of these two States should be studied as one, or rather as two parts of one history, if we are to discover and grasp the meaning of either part fully. When studied as a whole, this history gives us the life story of the greater portion of the Slav race placed between two hostile forces,--the Germans on the west, the Mongols and Tartars on the east.

The advance of the Germans on the Slav tribes and later on Poland presents, perhaps, the best example in history of the methods of European civilization. The entire Baltic coast from Lubeck eastward was converted to Christianity by the Germans at the point of the sword. The duty of rescuing these people from the errors of paganism formed the moral pretext for conquering them and taking their lands. The warrior was accompanied by the missionary, followed by the political colonist. The people of the country deprived of their lands were reduced to slavery; and if any escaped this lot, they were men from the higher classes who joined the conqueror in the capacity of assistant oppressors. The work was long and doubtful. The Germans made many failures, for their management was often very bad. The Slavs west of the Oder were stubborn, and under good leadership might have been invincible; but the leadership did not come, and to the Germans at last came the Hohenzollerns.

For the serious student there is no richer field of labor than the history of Poland and the Slavs of the Baltic, which is inseparable from the history of Mark Brandenburg and the two military orders, the Teutonic Knights and the Knights of the Sword.

The conquest of Russia by the Mongols, the subjection of Europeans to Asiatics,--not Asiatics of the south, but warriors from cold regions led by men of genius; for such were Genghis Khan, Tamerlane, and the lieutenants sent to the west,--was an affair of incomparably greater magnitude than the German wars on the Baltic.

The physical grip of the Mongol on Russia was irresistible. There was nothing for the Russian princes to do but submit if they wished to preserve their people from dissolution. They had to bow down to every whim of the conqueror; suffer indignity, insult, death,--that is, death of individuals. The Russians endured for a long time without apparent result. But they were studying their conquerors, mastering their policy; and they mastered it so well that finally the Prince of Moscow made use of the Mongols to complete the union of eastern Russia and reduce all the provincial princes of the country, his own relatives, to the position of ordinary landholders subject to himself.

The difference between the Poles and Russians seems to be this,--that the Russians saw through the policy of their enemies, and then overcame them; while the Poles either did not understand the Germans, or if they did, did not overcome them, though they had the power.

This Slav history is interesting to the man of science, it is interesting also to the practical statesman, because there is no country in the Eastern hemisphere whose future may be considered outside of Russian influence, no country whose weal or woe may not become connected in some way with Russia. At the same time there are no states studied by so few and misunderstood by so many as the former Commonwealth of Poland,--whose people, brave and brilliant but politically unsuccessful, have received more sympathy than any other within the circle of civilization,--and Russia, whose people in strength of character and intellectual gifts are certainly among the first of the Aryan race, though many men have felt free to describe them in terms exceptionally harsh and frequently unjust.

The leading elements of this history on its western side are Poland, the Catholic Church, Germany; on the eastern side they are Russia, Eastern Orthodoxy, Northern Asia.

Now let us see what this western history was. In the middle of the ninth century Slav tribes of various denominations occupied the entire Baltic coast west of the Vistula; a line drawn from Lubeck to the Elbe, ascending the river to Magdeburg, thence to the western ridge of the Bohemian mountains, and passing on in a somewhat irregular course, leaving Carinthia and Styria on the east, gives the boundary between the Germans and the Slavs at that period. Very nearly in the centre of the territory north of Bohemia and the Carpathians lived one of a number of Slav tribes, the Polyane (or men of the plain), who occupied the region afterwards called Great Poland by the Poles, and now called South Prussia by the Germans. In this Great Poland political life among the Northwestern Slavs began in the second half of the ninth century. About the middle of the tenth, Mechislav (Mieczislaw), the ruler, received Christianity, and the modest title of Count of the German Empire. Boleslav the Brave, his son and successor, extended his territory to the upper Elbe, from which region its boundary line passed through or near Berlin, whence it followed the Oder to the sea. Before his death, in 1025, Boleslav wished to be anointed king by the Pope. The ceremony was denied him, therefore he had it performed by bishops at home. About a century later the western boundary was pushed forward by Boleslav Wry-mouth (1132-1139) to a point on the Baltic about half-way between Stettin and Lubeck. This was the greatest extension of Poland to the west. Between this line and the Elbe were Slav tribes; but the region had already become marken (marches) where the intrusive Germans were struggling for the lands and persons of the Slavs.

The eastern boundary of Poland at this period served also as the western boundary of Russia from the head-waters of the western branch of the river San in the Carpathian Mountains at a point west of Premysl (in the Galicia of to-day) to Brest-Litovsk, from which point the Russian boundary continued toward the northeast till it reached the sea, leaving Pskoff considerably and Yurieff (now Dorpat) slightly to the east,--that is, on Russian territory. Between Russia, north of Brest-Litovsk and Poland, was the irregular triangle composing the lands of Lithuanian and Finnish tribes. From the upper San the Russian boundary southward coincided with the Carpathians, including the territory between the Pruth to its mouth and the Carpathians. This boundary between Poland and Russia, established at that period, corresponds as nearly as possible with the line of demarcation between the two peoples at the present day.

During the two centuries following 1139, Poland continued to lose on the west and the north, and that process was fairly begun through which the Germans finally excluded the Poles from the sea, and turned the cradle of Poland into South Prussia, the name which it bears to-day.

At the end of the fourteenth century a step was taken by the Poles through which it was hoped to win in other places far more than had been lost on the west. Poland turned now to the east; but by leaving her historical basis on the Baltic, by deserting her political birthplace, the only ground where she had a genuine mission, Poland entered upon a career which was certain to end in destruction, unless she could win the Russian power by agreement, or bend it by conquest, and then strengthened by this power, turn back and redeem the lost lands of Pomerania and Prussia.

The first step in the new career was an alliance with Yagello (Yahailo) of Lithuania, from which much was hoped. This event begins a new era in Polish history; to this event we must now give attention, for it was the first in a long series which ended in the great outburst described in this book,--the revolt of the Russians against the Commonwealth.

To reach the motives of this famous agreement between the Lithuanian prince and the nobles and clergy of Poland,--for these two estates had become the only power in the land,--we must turn to Russia.

Lithuania of itself was small, and a prince of that country, if it stood alone, would have received scant attention from Poland; but the Lithuanian Grand Prince was ruler over all the lands of western Russia as well as those of his own people.

What was Russia?

The definite appearance of Russia in history dates from 862, when Rurik came to Novgorod, invited by the people to rule over them. Oleg, the successor of this prince, transferred his capital from Novgorod to Kieff on the Dnieper, which remained the chief city and capital for two centuries and a half. Rurik's great-grandson, Vladimir, introduced Christianity into Russia at the end of the tenth century. During his long reign and that of his son Yaroslav the Lawgiver, the boundary was fixed between Russia and Poland through the places described above, and coincided very nearly with the watershed dividing the two river-systems of the Dnieper and the Vistula, and serves to this day as the boundary between the Russian and Polish languages and the Eastern and Catholic churches.

In 1157 Kieff ceased to be the seat of the Grand Prince, the capital of Russia. A new centre of activity and government was founded in the north,--first at Suzdal, and then at Vladimir, to be transferred later to Moscow.

In 1240 the conquest of Russia by the Tartars was complete. Half a million or more of armed Asiatics had swept over the land, destroying everything where they went. A part of this multitude advanced through Poland, and were stopped in Silesia and Moravia only by the combined efforts of central Europe. The Tartar dominion lasted about two hundred and fifty years (1240-1490), and during this period great changes took place. Russia before the Tartar conquest was a large country, whose western boundary was the eastern boundary of Poland; liberated Russia was a comparatively small country, with its capital at Moscow, and having interposed between it and Poland a large state extending from the Baltic to the Black Sea,--a state which was composed of two thirds of that Russia which was ruled before the Tartar conquest by the descendants of Rurik; a state which included Little, Red, Black, and White Russia, more than two thirds of the best lands, and Kieff, with the majority of the historic towns of pre-Tartar Russia.

How was this state founded?

This state was the Lithuanian Russian,--Litva í Rus (Lithuania and Russia), as it is called by the Russians,--and it rose in the following manner. In the irregular triangle on the Baltic, between Russia and Poland of the twelfth century, lived tribes of Finnish and Lithuanian stock, about a dozen in number. In the thirteenth and fourteenth centuries these were all conquered,--the Prussian Lithuanians from the Niemen to the Vistula, by the Teutonic Knights, aided by crusading adventurers from western Europe; the others, Lithuanian and Finnish, by the Knights of the Sword,--with the exception of two tribes, the Lithuanians proper, on the upper waters of the Niemen and its tributaries, and the Jmuds or Samogitians on the right bank of the same river, lower down and between the Lithuanians and the sea. These two small tribes were destined through their princes--remarkable men in the fullest sense of the word--to play a great part in Russian and Polish history. It is needless to say much of the Lithuanians, who are better known to scholars than any people, perhaps, of similar numbers in Europe. The main interest in them at present is confined to their language, which, though very valuable to the philologist and beautiful in itself, has never been used in government or law, and has but one book considered as belonging to literature,--"The Four Seasons" by Donaleitis.

Though small, the Lithuanian country, ruled by a number of petty princes, was as much given to anarchy as larger aggregations of men. United for a time under Mindog by reason of pressure from outside, the Lithuanians rose first to prominence under Gedimin (1315-1340), who in a quarter of a century was able to substitute himself for the petty princes of western Russia and extend his power to the south of Kieff. Gedimin was followed by Olgerd, who with his uncle Keistut ruled till 1377; during which time the domains of the Lithuanian prince were extended to the Crimea, and included the whole basin of the Dnieper with its tributaries, together with the upper Dvina. Gedimin and Olgerd respected in all places the clergy of the Eastern Church, and thus acquired rule over a great extent of country with comparative ease and rapidity.

Olgerd, who had completed a great state, left it to his sons and his brother Keistut. Yagello (Yahailo), one of these sons, had Keistut put to death; his brothers and cousins fled; Yagello became sole master. At this juncture the nobles and clergy of Poland effected an arrangement by which Yagello, on condition of becoming a Catholic, introducing the Catholic religion into Lithuania, and joining the state to Poland, was to marry the Queen Yadviga (the last survivor of the royal house) and be crowned king of Poland at Cracow. All these conditions were carried out, and with the reign of Yagello Polish history assumes an entirely new character.

With the establishment by Gedimin and Olgerd of the Lithuanian dynasty and its conquests, there were two Russias instead of one,--Western Russia, ruled by the house of Gedimin, and Eastern Russia, ruled by the house of Rurik. It had become the ambition of the Lithuanian princes to unite all Russia; it had long been the fixed purpose of the princes at Moscow to recover their ancient patrimony, the lands of Vladimir and Yaroslav; that is, all western Russia to the Polish frontier; consequently all the lands added by the Lithuanian princes to their little realm on the Niemen and its tributaries. This struggle between the two houses was very bitter, and more than once it seemed as though Moscow's day had come, and Vilna was to be the capital of reconstituted Russia.

When the question was at this stage, Yagello became King of Poland. The union, purely personal at first, became more intimate later on by means of the two elements of Polish influence, the Church and the nobility. Catholicism was made the religion of the Lithuanians at once; and twenty-seven years later, at Horodlo, it was settled that the Lithuanian Catholics of the higher classes should receive the same privileges as the Polish nobility, with whom they were joined by means of heraldry,--a peculiar arrangement, through which a number of Lithuanian families received the arms of some Polish house, and became thus associated, as the original inhabitants of America are associated under the same *totem* by the process of adoption.

Without giving details, for which there is no space here, we state merely the meaning of all the details. Lithuania struggled persistently against anything more than a personal union, while Poland struggled just as persistently for a complete union; but no matter how the Lithuanians might gain at one time or another, the personal union under a king influenced by Polish ideas joined to the great weight of the clergy and nobility was too much for them, and the end of the whole struggle was that under Sigismond Augustus, the last of the Yagellon kings, a diet was held at Lublin in which a union between Poland and Lithuania was proclaimed against the protest of a large number of the Lithuanians who left the diet. The King, who was hereditary Grand Duke of Lithuania, and childless, made a present to Poland of his rights,--made Poland his heir. The petty nobility of Lithuania were placed on the same legal footing as the princes and men of great historic families. Lithuania was assimilated to Poland in institutions.

The northern part of West Russia was attached to Lithuania, and all southern Russia merged directly in Poland. If the work of this diet had been productive of concord, and therefore of strength, Poland might have established herself firmly by the sea and won the first place in eastern Europe; but the Commonwealth, either from choice or necessity, was more occupied in struggling with Russians than in standing with firm foot on the Baltic. Sound statesmanship would have taught the Poles that for them it was a question of life and death to possess Pomerania and Prussia, and make the Oder at least their western boundary. They had the power to do that; they had the power to expel the two military orders from the coast; but they did not exert it,--a neglect which cost them dear in later times. Moscow would not have escaped the Poles had they been masters of the Baltic, and had they, instead of fighting with Cossacks and Russians, attached them to the Commonwealth by toleration and justice.

The whole internal policy of Poland from the coronation of Yagello to the reign of Vladislav IV. was to assimilate the nobility of Lithuania and Russia to that of Poland in political rights and in religious profession. The success was complete in the political sense, and practically so in the religious. The Polish nobility, who were in fact the state, possessed at the time of Yagello's coronation all the land, and owned the labor of the people; later on they ceased to pay taxes of any kind. It was a great bribe to the nobles of Lithuania and Russia to occupy the same position. The Lithuanians became Catholics at the accession of Yagello, or soon after; but in Russia, where all belonged to the Orthodox Church, the process was slow, even if sure. The princes Ostrorog and Dominik Zaslavski of this book were of Russian families which held their faith for a long time. The parents of Prince Yeremi Vishnyevetski were Orthodox, and his mother on her death-bed implored him to be true to the faith of his ancestors.

All had been done that could be done with the nobility; but the great mass of Russian people holding the same faith as the Russians of the East, whose capital was at Moscow, were not considered reliable; therefore a union of churches was effected, mainly through the formal initiative of the King Sigismond III. and a few ecclesiastics, but rejected by a great majority of the Russian clergy and people. This new or united church, which retained the Slav language with Eastern customs and liturgy, but recognized the supremacy of the Pope, was made the state church of Russia.

From this rose all the religious trouble.

The Russians, when Hmelnitski appeared, were in the following condition: Their land was gone; the power of life and death over them resided in lords, either Poles or Polonized Russians, who generally gave this power to agents or tenants, not infrequently Jews. All justice, all administration, all power belonged to the lord or to whomsoever he delegated his authority; there was no appeal. A people with an active communal government of their own in former times were now reduced to complete slavery. Such was the Russian complaint on the material side. On the moral side it was that their masters were filching their faith from them. Having stripped them of everything in this life, they were trying to deprive them of life to come.

The outburst of popular rage against Poland was without example in history for intensity and volume, and this would have made the revolt remarkable whatever its motives or objects. But the Cossack war was of world-wide importance in view of the issues. The triumph of Poland would have brought the utter subjection of the Cossacks and the people, with the extinction of Eastern Orthodoxy not only in Russia but in other lands; for the triumph of Poland would have left no place for Moscow on earth but a place of subjection. The triumph of the Cossacks would have brought a mixed government, with religious toleration and a king having means to curb the all-powerful nobles. This was what Hmelnitski sought; this was the dream of Ossolinski the Chancellor; this, if realized, might possibly have saved the Commonwealth, and made it a constitutional government instead of an association of irresponsible magnates.

It turned out that the Cossacks and the uprisen people were not a match for the Poles, and it was not in the interest of the Tartars to give the Cossacks the fruits of victory. It was the policy of the Tartars to bring the Poles into trouble and then rescue them; they wished the Poles to have the upper hand, but barely have it, and be in continual danger of losing it.

The battle of Berestechko, instead of giving peace to the Commonwealth, opened a new epoch of trouble. Hmelnitski, the ablest man in Europe at that time, could be conquered by nothing but death. Though beaten through the treachery of the Khan at Berestechko and perhaps also by treason in his own camp, he rallied, concluded the treaty of Bélaya Tserkoff, which reduced the Cossack army from forty to twelve thousand men, but left Hmelnitski hetman of the Zaporojians. That was the great mistake of the Poles; every success was for them a failure so long as Hmelnitski had a legal existence.

The Poles, though intellectual, sympathetic, brave, and gifted with high personal qualities that have made them many friends, have been always deficient in collective wisdom; and there is probably no more astonishing antithesis in Europe than the Poles as individuals and the Poles as a people.

After Berestechko the Poles entered the Ukraine as masters. Vishnyevetski went as the ruling spirit. To all appearance the time of his triumph had come; but one day after dinner he fell ill and died suddenly. The verdict of the Russian people was: The Almighty preserved him through every danger, saved him from every enemy, and by reason of the supreme wickedness of "Yarema," reserved him for his own holy and punishing hand.

The old order of things was restored in Russia,--landlords, garrisons, Jews; but now came the most striking event in the whole history.

Moldavia, the northern part of the present kingdom of Romania, was at that time a separate principality, owning the suzerainty of the Sultan. Formerly it had been a part of the Russian principality of Galich (Galicia), joined to Poland in the reign of Kazimir the Great, but connected, at the time of our story, with Turkey. The Poles had intimate relations with the country, and sought to bring it back. The Hospodar was Vassily Lupul, a man of fabulous wealth, according to report, and the father of two daughters, whose beauty was the wonder of eastern Europe. Prince Radzivil of Lithuania had married the elder; the younger, Domna (Domina) Rosanda, was sought in marriage by three men from Poland and by Timofei Hmelnitski, the son of Bogdan. The first of the Poles was Dmitry Vishnyevetski; the second was Kalinovski, the aged hetman of the Crown, captured by Hmelnitski at Korsún, but now free and more ambitons than any man in the Commonwealth of half his age, which was then near seventy.

Lupul, who had consented to the marriage of his daughter with young Hmelnitski, preferred Vishnyevetski; whereupon Bogdan exclaimed, "We will send a hundred thousand best men with the bridegroom." Thirty-six thousand Cossacks and Tartars set out for Yassy, the residence of Lupul. Kalinovski, the Polish hetman, with twenty thousand men, barred the way to young Hmelnitski at Batog on the boundary. It was supposed that Timofei was attended by a party of only five thousand, and Kalinovski intended to finish a rival and destroy the son of an enemy at a blow. This delusion of the hetman was probably caused, but in every case confirmed, by a letter from Bogdan, in which he stated that his son, with some attendants, was on his way to marry the daughter of the Hospodar; that young men are hot-headed and given to quarrels, blood might be spilled; therefore he asked Kalinovski to withdraw and let the party pass.

This was precisely what Kalinovski would not do; he resolved to stop Timofei by force. The first day, five thousand Cossacks and Tartars, while passing to the west, were attacked by the Poles, who pursued them with cavalry. When a good distance from the camp, a courier rushed to the hetman with news of a general attack on the rear of the Polish army. The Poles returned in haste, pursued in their turn.

Young Hmelnitski had fallen upon a division of the army in the rear of the camp, and almost destroyed it. Darkness brought an end to the struggle. No eye was closed on either side that night. One half of the Polish army resolved to escape in spite of the hetman. At daybreak they were marching. "They shall not flee!" said Kalinovski "Stop them with cavalry; open on the cowards with cannon!" One part of the Polish army hurried to stop the other; there was a discharge of artillery; some of the fugitives rushed on, but most of them stopped. Then a second discharge of artillery, and a battle began. The Cossacks gazed on this wonderful scene; when their amazement had passed, they attacked the enemy, and indescribable slaughter began. It was impossible for the Poles to re-form or make effective defence. At this moment the army-servants, many of whom were Russians, set fire to the camp. Outnumbered and panic-stricken, thousands of Poles rushed into the Bug and were drowned. The Cossacks, with Berestechko in mind, showed mercy to no man; and of the whole army of twenty thousand, less than five hundred escaped. The peasants in all the country about killed the fugitives with scythes and clubs. Those who crossed the river were slaughtered on the other bank; among them was Samuel Kalinovski, son of the hetman. Then Kalinovski himself, seeing that all was lost cried, "I have no wish to live; I am ashamed to look on the sun of this morning!" and rushed to the thick of the fight. He perished; and a Nogai horseman raced over the field, while from his saddle-bow depended the head of the hetman with its white streaming hair. After the battle the body was discovered; on it the portrait of Domna Rosanda and the letter of Bogdan.

Farther on, near the Bug, was a division of five thousand Germans under command of Marek Sobieski, the gifted chief who had fought at Zbaraj. Attacked in front by the Cossacks, they stood with manful persistence till Karach Murza, the Nogai commander, at the head of fourteen thousand men, descended upon them from the hills of Botog like a mighty rain from the clouds or a whirlwind of the desert, as the Ukraine chronicler phrases it. Split in the centre, torn through and through, the weapons dropped from their hands, they were ridden down and sabred by Nogais and Cossacks. Sobieski perished; Pshiyemski, commander of artillery, was killed.

A year later the Poles at Jvanyets were in greater straits than ever before. They were surrounded by Hmelnitski and the Khan so that no escape was possible; but they had more gold to give than had the Cossacks. They satisfied those in power, from the Khan downward, with gifts, and covenanted to let them plunder Russia and seize Russian captives during six weeks. On these conditions the Tartars deserted Hmelnitski, peace was concluded, and the Polish army and king were saved from captivity.

This was the last act of the Cossack-Tartar alliance. Hmelnitski now turned to Moscow; the Zaporojian army took the oath of allegiance to Alexis, father of Peter the Great. Lithuania and western Russia were overrun by the forces of Moscow and the Cossacks. The Swedes occupied Warsaw and Cracow. Karl Gustav, their king, became king of Poland. Yan Kazimir fled to Silesia.

Again the Polish king came back, but soon resigned, and ended his life in France.

The eastern bank of the Dnieper, with Kieff on the west, went to Russia; but it was not till the reign of Katherine II. that western Russia was united to the east, and Prussia and Austria received all the lands of Poland proper.

I feel constrained to ask kindly indulgence from the readers of this sketch. I am greatly afraid that it will seem indefinite and lacking in precision; but the field to be covered is so great that I wrote with two kinds of readers in view,--those who are already well acquainted with Slav history, and those who do not know this history yet, but who may be roused to examine it for themselves. I hope to give a sketch of this history in a future not too remote, with an account of the sources of original information; so that impartial students, as Americans are by position, may have some assistance in beginning a work of such commanding importance as the history of Poland and Russia.

Jeremiah Curtin.

Washington, D. C, April 4, 1890.

WITH FIRE AND SWORD.

CHAPTER I.

The year 1647 was that wonderful year in which manifold signs in the heavens and on the earth announced misfortunes of some kind and unusual events. Contemporary chroniclers relate that beginning with spring-time myriads of locusts swarmed from the Wilderness, destroying the grain and the grass; this was a forerunner of Tartar raids. In the summer there was a great eclipse of the sun, and soon after a comet appeared in the sky. In Warsaw a tomb was seen over the city, and a fiery cross in the clouds; fasts were held and alms given, for some men declared that a plague would come on the land and destroy the people. Finally, so mild a winter set in, that the oldest inhabitants could not remember the like of it. In the southern provinces ice did not confine the rivers, which, swollen by the daily melting of snows, left their courses and flooded the banks. Rainfalls were frequent. The steppe was drenched, and became an immense slough. The sun was so warm in the south that, wonder of wonders! in Bratslav and the Wilderness a green fleece covered the steppes and plains in the middle of December. The swarms in the beehives began to buzz and bustle; cattle were bellowing in the fields. Since such an order of things appeared altogether unnatural, all men in Russia who were waiting or looking for unusual events turned their excited minds and eyes especially to the Wilderness, from which rather than anywhere else danger might show itself.

At that time there was nothing unusual in the Wilderness,--no struggles there, nor encounters, beyond those of ordinary occurrence, and known only to the eagles, hawks, ravens, and beasts of the plain. For the Wilderness was of this character at that period. The last traces of settled life ended on the way to the south, at no great distance beyond Chigirin on the side of the Dnieper, and on the side of the Dniester not far from Uman; then forward to the bays and sea there was nothing but steppe after steppe, hemmed in by the two rivers as by a frame. At the bend of the Dnieper in the lower country beyond the Cataracts Cossack life was seething, but in the open plains no man dwelt; only along the shores were nestled here and there little fields, like islands in the sea. The land belonged in name to Poland, but it was an empty land, in which the Commonwealth permitted the Tartars to graze their herds; but since the Cossacks prevented this frequently, the field of pasture was a field of battle too.

How many struggles were fought in that region, how many people had laid down their lives there, no man had counted, no man remembered. Eagles, falcons, and ravens alone saw these; and whoever from a distance heard the sound of wings and the call of ravens, whoever beheld the whirl of birds circling over one place, knew that corpses or unburied bones were lying beneath. Men were hunted in the grass as wolves or wild goats. All who wished, engaged in this hunt. Fugitives from the law defended themselves in the wild steppes. The armed herdsman guarded his flock, the warrior sought adventure, the robber plunder, the Cossack a Tartar, the Tartar a Cossack. It happened that whole bands guarded herds from troops of robbers. The steppe was both empty and filled, quiet and terrible, peaceable and full of ambushes; wild by reason of its wild plains, but wild, too, from the wild spirit of men.

At times a great war filled it. Then there flowed over it like waves Tartar chambuls, Cossack regiments, Polish or Wallachian companies. In the night-time the neighing of horses answered the howling of wolves, the voices of drums and brazen trumpets flew on to the island of Ovid and the sea, and along the black trail of Kutchman there seemed an inundation of men. The boundaries of the Commonwealth were guarded from Kamenyets to the Dnieper by outposts and stanitsas; and when the roads were about to swarm with people, it was known especially by the countless flocks of birds which, frightened by the Tartars, flew onward to the north. But the Tartar, if he slipped out from the Black Forest or crossed the Dniester from the Wallachian side, came by the southern provinces together with the birds.

That winter, however, the birds did not come with their uproar to the Commonwealth. It was stiller on the steppe than usual. At the moment when our narrative begins the sun was just setting, and its reddish rays threw light on a land entirely empty. On the northern rim of the Wilderness, along the Omelnik to its mouth, the sharpest eye could not discover a living soul, nor even a movement in the dark, dry, and withered steppe grass. The sun showed but half its shield from behind the horizon. The heavens became obscured, and then the steppe grew darker and darker by degrees. Near the left bank, on a small height resembling more a grave-mound than a hill, were the mere remnants of a walled stanitsa which once upon a time had been built by Fedor Buchatski and then torn down by raids. A long shadow stretched from this ruin. In the distance gleamed the waters of the widespread Omelnik, which in that place turned toward the Dnieper. But the lights went out each moment in the heavens and on the earth. From the sky were heard the cries of storks in their flight to the sea; with this exception the stillness was unbroken by a sound.

Night came down upon the Wilderness, and with it the hour of ghosts. Cossacks on guard in the stanitsas related in those days that the shades of men who had fallen in sudden death and in sin used to rise up at night and carry on dances in which they were hindered neither by cross nor church. Also, when the wicks which showed the time of midnight began to burn out, prayers for the dead were offered throughout the stanitsas. It was said, too, that the shades of mounted men coursing through the waste barred the road to wayfarers, whining and begging them for a sign of the holy cross. Among these ghosts vampires also were met with, who pursued people with howls. A trained ear might distinguish at a distance the howls of a vampire from those of a wolf. Whole legions of shadows were also seen, which sometimes came so near the stanitsas that the sentries sounded the alarm. This was generally the harbinger of a great war.

The meeting of a single ghost foreboded no good, either; but it was not always necessarily of evil omen, for frequently a living man would appear before travellers and vanish like a shadow, and therefore might easily and often be taken for a ghost.

Night came quickly on the Omelnik, and there was nothing surprising in the fact that a figure, either a man or a ghost, made its appearance at the side of the deserted stanitsa. The moon coming out from behind the Dnieper whitened the waste, the tops of the thistles, and the distance of the steppe. Immediately there appeared lower down on the plain some other beings of the night. The flitting clouds hid the light of the moon from moment to moment; consequently those figures flashed up in the darkness at one instant, and the next they were blurred. At times they disappeared altogether, and seemed to melt in the shadow. Pushing on toward the height on which the first man was standing, they stole up quietly, carefully, slowly, halting at intervals.

There was something awe-exciting in their movements, as there was in all that steppe which was so calm in appearance. The wind at times blew from the Dnieper, causing a mournful rustle among the dried thistles, which bent and trembled as in fear. At last the figures vanished in the shadow of the ruins. In the uncertain light of that hour nothing could be seen save the single horseman on the height.

But the rustle arrested his attention. Approaching the edge of the mound, he began to look carefully into the steppe. At that moment the wind stopped, the rustling ceased; there was perfect rest.

Suddenly a piercing whistle was heard; mingled voices began to shout in terrible confusion, "Allah! Allah! Jesus Christ! Save! Kill!" The report of muskets re-echoed; red flashes rent the darkness. The tramp of horses was heard with the clash of steel. Some new horsemen rose as it were from beneath the surface of the steppe. You would have said that a storm had sprung up on a sudden in that silent and ominous land. The shrieks of men followed the terrible clash. Then all was silent; the struggle was over.

Apparently one of its usual scenes had been enacted in the Wilderness.

The horsemen gathered in groups on the height; a few of them dismounted, and examined something carefully. Meanwhile a powerful and commanding voice was heard in the darkness.

"Strike a fire in front!"

In a moment sparks sprang out, and soon a blaze flashed up from the dry reeds and pitch-pine which wayfarers through the Wilderness always carried with them.

Straightway the staff for a hanging-lamp was driven into the earth. The glare from above illuminated sharply a number of men who were bending over a form stretched motionless on the ground.

These men were soldiers, in red uniforms and wolf-skin caps. Of these, one who sat on a valiant steed appeared to be the leader. Dismounting, he approached the prostrate figure and inquired,--

"Well, Sergeant, is he alive yet, or is it all over with him?"

"He is alive, but there is a rattling in his throat; the lariat stifled him."

"Who is he?"

"He is not a Tartar; some man of distinction."

"Then God be thanked!"

The chief looked attentively at the prostrate man.

"Well, just like a hetman."

"His horse is of splendid Tartar breed; the Khan has no better," said the sergeant. "There he stands."

The lieutenant looked at the horse, and his face brightened. Two soldiers held a really splendid steed, who, moving his ears and distending his nostrils, pushed forward his head and looked with frightened eyes at his master.

"But the horse will be ours, Lieutenant?" put in, with an inquiring tone, the sergeant.

"Dog believer! would you deprive a Christian of his horse in the steppe?"

"But it is our booty--"

Further conversation was interrupted by stronger breathing from the suffocated man.

"Pour gorailka into his mouth," said the lieutenant, undoing his belt.

"Are we to spend the night here?"

"Yes. Unsaddle the horses and make a good fire."

The soldiers hurried around quickly. Some began to rouse and rub the prostrate man; some started off for reeds to burn; others spread camel and bear skins on the ground for couches.

The lieutenant, troubling himself no more about the suffocated stranger, unbound his belt and stretched himself on a burka by the fire. He was a very young man, of spare habit of body, dark complexion, very elegant in manner, with a delicately cut countenance and a prominent aquiline nose. In his eyes were visible desperate daring and endurance, but his face had an honest look. His rather thick mustache and a beard, evidently unshaven for a long time, gave him a seriousness beyond his years.

Meanwhile two attendants were preparing the evening meal. Dressed quarters of mutton were placed on the fire, a number of bustards and partridges were taken from the packs, and one wild goat, which an attendant began to skin without delay. The fire blazed up, casting out upon the steppe an enormous ruddy circle of light. The suffocated man began to revive slowly.

After a time he cast his bloodshot eyes around on the strangers, examining their faces; then he tried to stand up. The soldier who had previously talked with the lieutenant raised him by the armpits; another put in his hand a halbert, upon which the stranger leaned with all his force. His face was still purple, his veins swollen. At last, with a suppressed voice, he coughed out his first word, "Water!"

They gave him gorailka, which he drank repeatedly, and which appeared to do him good, for after he had removed the flask from his lips at last, he inquired in a clear voice, "In whose hands am I?"

The officer rose and approached him. "In the hands of those who saved you."

"It was not you, then, who caught me with a lariat?"

"No; the sabre is our weapon, not the lariat. You wrong our good soldiers with the suspicion. You were seized by ruffians, pretended Tartars. You can look at them if you are curious, for they are lying out there slaughtered like sheep."

Saying this, he pointed with his hand to a number of dark bodies lying below the height.

To this the stranger answered, "If you will permit me to rest."

They brought him a felt-covered saddle, on which he seated himself in silence.

He was in the prime of life, of medium height, with broad shoulders, almost gigantic build of body, and striking features. He had an enormous head, a complexion dried and sunburnt, black eyes, somewhat aslant, like those of a Tartar; over his thin lips hung a mustache ending at the tips in two broad bunches. His powerful face indicated courage and pride. There was in it something at once attractive and repulsive,--the dignity of a hetman with Tartar cunning, kindness, and ferocity.

After he had sat awhile on the saddle he rose, and beyond all expectation, went to look at the bodies instead of returning thanks.

"How churlish!" muttered the lieutenant.

The stranger examined each face carefully, nodding his head like a man who has seen through everything; then he turned slowly to the lieutenant, slapping himself on the side, and seeking involuntarily his belt, behind which he wished evidently to pass his hand.

This importance in a man just rescued from the halter did not please the young lieutenant, and he said in irony,--

"One might say that you are looking for acquaintances among those robbers, or that you are saying a litany for their souls."

"You are both right and wrong. You are right, for I was looking for acquaintances; and you are wrong, for they are not robbers, but servants of a petty nobleman, my neighbor."

"Then it is clear that you do not drink out of the same spring with that neighbor."

A strange smile passed over the thin lips of the stranger.

"And in that you are wrong," muttered he through his teeth. In a moment he added audibly: "But pardon for not having first given thanks for the aid and effective succor which freed me from such sudden death. Your courage has redeemed my carelessness, for I separated from my men; but my gratitude is equal to your good-will."

Having said this, he reached his hand to the lieutenant.

But the haughty young man did not stir from his place, and was in no hurry to give his hand; instead of that he said,--

"I should like to know first if I have to do with a nobleman; for though I have no doubt you are one, still it does not befit me to accept the thanks of a nameless person."

"I see you have the mettle of a knight, and speak justly, I should have begun my speech and thanks with my name. I am Zenovi Abdank; my escutcheon that of Abdank with a cross; a nobleman from the province of Kieff; a landholder, and a colonel of the Cossack regiment of Prince Dominik Zaslavski."

"And I am Yan Skshetuski, lieutenant of the armored regiment of Prince Yeremi Vishnyevetski."

"You serve under a famous warrior. Accept my thanks and hand."

The lieutenant hesitated no longer. It is true that armored officers looked down on men of the other regiments; but Pan Yan was in the steppe, in the Wilderness, where such things were less remembered. Besides, he had to do with a colonel. Of this he had ocular proof, for when his soldiers brought Pan Abdank the belt and sabre which were taken from his person in order to revive him, they brought at the same time a short staff with a bone shaft and ivory head, such as Cossack colonels were in the habit of using. Besides, the dress of Zenovi Abdank was rich, and his educated speech indicated a quick mind and social training.

Pan Yan therefore invited him to supper. The odor of roasted meats began to go out from the fire just then, tickling the nostrils and the palate. The attendant brought the meats, and served them on a plate. The two men fell to eating; and when a good-sized goat-skin of Moldavian wine was brought, a lively conversation sprang up without delay.

"A safe return home to us," said Pan Yan.

"Then you are returning home? Whence, may I ask?" inquired Abdank.

"From a long journey,--from the Crimea."

"What were you doing there? Did you go with ransom?"

"No, Colonel, I went to the Khan himself."

Abdank turned an inquisitive ear. "Did you, indeed? Were you well received? And what was your errand to the Khan?"

"I carried a letter from Prince Yeremi."

"You were an envoy, then! What did the prince write to the Khan about?"

The lieutenant looked quickly at his companion.

"Well, Colonel," said he, "you have looked into the eyes of ruffians who captured you with a lariat; that is your affair. But what the prince wrote to the Khan is neither your affair nor mine, but theirs."

"I wondered, a little while ago," answered Abdank, cunningly, "that his highness the prince should send such a young man to the Khan; but after your answer I am not astonished, for I see that you are young in years, but mature in experience and wit."

The lieutenant swallowed the smooth, flattering words, merely twisted his young mustache, and inquired,--

"Now do you tell me what you are doing on the Omelnik, and how you come to be here alone."

"I am not alone, I left my men on the road; and I am going to Kudák, to Pan Grodzitski, who is transferred to the command there, and to whom the Grand Hetman has sent me with letters."

"And why don't you go by water?"

"I am following an order from which I may not depart."

"Strange that the hetman issued such an order, when in the steppe you have fallen into straits which you would have avoided surely had you been going by water."

"Oh, the steppes are quiet at present; my acquaintance with them does not begin with to-day. What has met me is the malice and hatred of man."

"And who attacked you in this fashion?"

"It is a long story. An evil neighbor, Lieutenant, who has destroyed my property, is driving me from my land, has killed my son, and besides, as you have seen, has made an attempt on my life where we sit."

"But do you not carry a sabre at your side?"

On the powerful face of Abdank there was a gleam of hatred, in his eyes a sullen glare. He answered slowly and with emphasis,--

"I do; and as God is my aid, I shall seek no other weapon against my foes."

The lieutenant wished to say something, when suddenly the tramp of horses was heard in the steppe, or rather the hurried slapping of horses' feet on the softened grass. That moment, also, the lieutenant's orderly who was on guard hurried up with news that men of some kind were approaching.

"Those," said Abdank, "are surely my men, whom I left beyond the Tasmina. Not suspecting perfidy, I promised to wait for them here."

Soon a crowd of mounted men formed a half-circle in front of the height. By the glitter of the fire appeared heads of horses, with open nostrils, puffing from exertion; and above them the faces of riders, who, bending forward, sheltered their eyes from the glare of the fire and gazed eagerly toward the light.

"Hei! men, who are you?" inquired Abdank.

"Servants of God," answered voices from the darkness.

"Just as I thought,--my men," repeated Abdank, turning to the lieutenant. "Come this way."

Some of them dismounted and drew near the fire.

"Oh, how we hurried, batko! But what's the matter?"

"There was an ambush. Hvedko, the traitor, learned of my coming to this place, and lurked here with others. He must have arrived some time in advance. They caught me with a lariat."

"God save us! What Poles are these about you?"

Saying this, they looked threateningly on Pan Skshetuski and his companions.

"These are kind friends," said Abdank. "Glory be to God! I am alive and well. We will push on our way at once."

"Glory be to God for that! We are ready."

The newly arrived began to warm their hands over the fire, for the night was cool, though fine. There were about forty of them, sturdy men and well armed. They did not look at all like registered Cossacks, which astonished Pan Skshetuski not a little, especially since their number was so considerable. Everything seemed very suspicious. If the Grand Hetman had sent Abdank to Kudák, he would have given him a guard of registered Cossacks; and in the second place, why should he order him to go by the steppe from Chigirin, and not by water? The necessity of crossing all the rivers flowing through the Wilderness to the Dnieper could only delay the journey. It appeared rather as if Abdank wanted to avoid Kudák.

In like manner, the personality of Abdank astonished the young lieutenant greatly. He noticed at once that the Cossacks, who were rather free in intercourse with their colonels, met him with unusual respect, as if he were a real hetman. He must be a man of a heavy hand, and what was most wonderful to Skshetuski, who knew the Ukraine on both sides of the Dnieper, he had heard nothing of a famous Abdank. Besides, there was in the countenance of the man something peculiar,--a certain secret power which breathed from his face like heat from a flame, a certain unbending will, declaring that this man withdraws before no man and no thing. The same kind of will was in the face of Prince Yeremi Vishnyevetski; but that which in the prince was an inborn gift of nature special to his lofty birth and his position might astonish one when found in a man of unknown name wandering in the wild steppe.

Pan Skshetuski deliberated long. It occurred to him that this might be some powerful outlaw who, hunted by justice, had taken refuge in the Wilderness,--or the leader of a robber band; but the latter was not probable. The dress and speech of the man showed something else. The lieutenant was quite at a loss what course to take. He kept simply on his guard. Meanwhile Abdank ordered his horse.

"Lieutenant, 'tis time for him to go who has the road before him. Let me thank you again for your succor. God grant me to show you a service of equal value!"

"I do not know whom I have saved, therefore I deserve no thanks."

"Your modesty, which equals your courage, is speaking now. Accept from me this ring."

The lieutenant frowned and took a step backward, measuring with his eyes Abdank, who then spoke on with almost paternal dignity in his voice and posture,--

"But look, I offer you not the wealth of this ring, but its other virtues. When still in the years of youth, a captive among infidels, I got this from a pilgrim returning from the Holy Land. In the seal of it is dust from the grave of Christ. Such a gift might not be refused, even if it came from condemned hands. You are still a young man and a soldier; and since even old age, which is near the grave, knows not what may strike it before the last hour, youth, which has before it a long life, must meet with many an adventure. This ring will preserve you from misfortune, and protect you when the day of judgment comes; and I tell you that that day is even now on the road through the Wilderness."

A moment of silence followed; nothing was heard but the crackling of the fire and the snorting of the horses. From the distant reeds came the dismal howling of wolves. Suddenly Abdank repeated still again, as if to himself,--

"The day of judgment is already on the road through the Wilderness, and when it comes all God's world will be amazed."

The lieutenant took the ring mechanically, so much was he astonished at the words of this strange man. But the man was looking into the dark distance of the steppe. Then he turned slowly and mounted his horse. His Cossacks were waiting at the foot of the height.

"Forward! forward! Good health to you, my soldier friend!" said he to the lieutenant. "The times are such at present that brother trusts not brother. This is why you know not whom you have saved, for I have not given you my name."

"You are not Abdank, then?"

"That is my escutcheon."

"And your name?"

"Bogdan Zenovi Hmelnitski."

When he had said this, he rode down from the height, and his Cossacks moved after him. Soon they were hidden in the mist and the night. When they had gone about half a furlong, the wind bore back from them the words of the Cossack song,--

"O God, lead us forth, poor captives,
From heavy bonds,
From infidel faith,
To the bright dawn,
To quiet waters,
To a gladsome land,
To a Christian world.
Hear, O God, our prayers,--
The prayers of the hapless,
The prayers of poor captives."

The voices grew fainter by degrees, and then were melted in the wind sounding through the reeds.

CHAPTER II.

Reaching Chigirin next morning, Pan Skshetuski stopped at the house of Prince Yeremi in the town, where he was to spend some time in giving rest to his men and horses after their long journey from the Crimea, which by reason of the floods and unusually swift currents of the Dnieper had to be made by land, since no boat could make head against the stream that winter. Skshetuski himself rested awhile, and then went to Pan Zatsvilikhovski, former commissioner of the Commonwealth,--a sterling soldier, who, though he did not serve with the prince, was his confidant and friend. The lieutenant wanted to ask him if there were instructions from Lubni; but the prince had sent nothing special. He had ordered Skshetuski, in the event of a favorable answer from the Khan, to journey slowly, so that his men and horses might be in good health. The prince had the following business with the Khan; He desired the punishment of certain Tartar murzas, who had raided his estates beyond the Dnieper, and whom he himself had punished severely. The Khan had in fact given a favorable answer,--had promised to send a special envoy in the following April to punish the disobedient; and wishing to gain the good-will of so famous a warrior as the prince, he had sent him by Skshetuski a horse of noted stock and also a sable cap.

Pan Skshetuski, having acquitted himself of his mission with no small honor, the mission itself being a proof of the high favor of the prince, was greatly rejoiced at the permission to stop in Chigirin without hastening his return. But old Zatsvilikhovski was greatly annoyed by what had been taking place for some time in Chigirin. They went together to the house of Dopula, a Wallachian, who kept an inn and a wine-shop in the place. There they found a crowd of nobles, though the hour was still early; for it was a market-day, and besides there happened to be a halt of cattle driven to the camp of the royal army, which brought a multitude of people together. The nobles generally assembled in the square at Dopula's, at the so-called Bell-ringers' Corner. There were assembled tenants of the Konyetspolskis, and Chigirin officials, owners of neighboring lands, settlers on crown lands, nobles on their own soil and dependent on no one, land stewards, some Cossack elders, and a few inferior nobles,--some living on other men's acres and some on their own.

These groups occupied benches at long oaken tables and conversed in loud voices, all speaking of the flight of Hmelnitski, which was the greatest event of the place. Zatsvilikhovski sat with Skshetuski in a corner apart. The lieutenant began to inquire what manner of phœnix that Hmelnitski was of whom all were speaking.

"Don't you know?" answered the old soldier. "He is the secretary of the Zaporojian army, the heir of Subotoff,--and my friend," added he, in a lower voice. "We have been long acquainted, and were together in many expeditions in which he distinguished himself, especially under Tetera. Perhaps there is not a soldier of such military experience in the whole Commonwealth. This is not to be mentioned in public; but he has the brain of a hetman, a heavy hand, and a mighty mind. All the Cossacks obey him more than koshevoi and ataman. He is not without good points, but imperious and unquiet; and when hatred gets the better of him he can be terrible."

"What made him flee from Chigirin?"

"Quarrels with the Starosta Chaplinski; but that is all nonsense. Usually a nobleman bespatters a nobleman from enmity. Hmelnitski is not the first and only man offended. They say, too, that he turned the head of the starosta's wife; that the starosta carried off his mistress and married her; that afterward Hmelnitski took her fancy,--and that is a likely matter, for woman is giddy, as a rule. But these are mere pretexts, under which certain intrigues find deeper concealment. This is how the affair stands: In Chigirin lives old Barabash, a Cossack colonel, our friend. He had privileges and letters from the king. Of these it was said that they urged the Cossacks to resist the nobility; but being a humane and kindly man, he kept them to himself and did not make them known. Then Hmelnitski invited Barabash to a dinner in his own house, here in Chigirin, and sent people to Barabash's country-place, who took the letters and the privileges away from his wife and disappeared. There is danger that out of them such a rebellion as that of Ostranitsa may arise; for, I repeat, he is a terrible man, and has fled, it is unknown whither."

To this Skshetuski answered: "He is a fox, and has tricked me. He told me he was a Cossack colonel of Prince Dominik Zaslavski. I met him last night in the steppe, and freed him from a lariat."

Zatsvilikhovski seized himself by the head.

"In God's name, what do you tell me? It cannot have been."

"It can, since it has been. He told me he was a colonel in the service of Prince Dominik Zaslavski, on a mission from the Grand Hetman to Pan Grodzitski at Kudák. I did not believe this, since he was not travelling by water, but stealing along over the steppe."

"He is as cunning as Ulysses! But where did you meet him?"

"On the Omelnik, on the right bank of the Dnieper. It is evident that he was on his way to the Saitch."

"He wanted to avoid Kudák. I understand now. Had he many men?"

"About forty. But they came to meet him too late. Had it not been for me, the servants of the starosta would have strangled him."

"But stop a moment! That is an important affair. The servants of the starosta, you say?"

"That is what he told me."

"How could the starosta know where to look for him, when here in this place all were splitting their heads to know what he had done with himself?"

"I can't tell that. It may be, too, that Hmelnitski lied, and represented common robbers as servants of the starosta, in order to call more attention to his wrongs."

"Impossible! But it is a strange affair. Do you know that there is a circular from the hetman, ordering the arrest and detention of Hmelnitski?"

The lieutenant gave no answer, for at that moment some nobleman entered the room with a tremendous uproar. He made the doors rattle a couple of times, and looking insolently through the room cried out,--

"My respects, gentlemen!"

He was a man of forty years of age, of low stature, with peevish face, the irritable appearance of which was increased by quick eyes, protruding from his face like plums,--evidently a man very rash, stormy, quick to anger.

"My respects, gentlemen!" repeated he more loudly and sharply, since he was not answered at once.

"Respects! respects!" was answered by several voices.

This man was Chaplinski, the under-starosta of Chigirin, the trusted henchman of young Konyetspolski. He was not liked in Chigirin, for he was a terrible blusterer, always involved in lawsuits, always persecuting some one; but for all that he had great influence, consequently people were polite to him.

Zatsvilikhovski, whom all respected for his dignity, virtues, and courage, was the only man he regarded. Seeing him, he approached immediately, and bowing rather haughtily to Skshetuski, sat down near them with his tankard of mead.

"Well," inquired Zatsvilikhovski, "do you know what has become of Hmelnitski?"

"He is hanging, as sure as I am Chaplinski; and if he is not hanging yet, he will be soon. Now that the hetman's orders are issued, let me only get him in my hands!"

Saying this, he struck the table with his fist till the liquor was spilled from the glasses.

"Don't spill the wine, my dear sir!" said Skshetuski.

Zatsvilikhovski interrupted: "But how will you get him, since he has escaped and no one knows where he is?"

"No one knows? I know,--true as I am Chaplinski. You know Hvedko. That Hvedko is in his service, but in mine too. He will be Hmelnitski's Judas. It's a long story. He has made friends with Hmelnitski's Cossacks. A sharp fellow! He knows every step that is taken. He has engaged to bring him to me, living or dead, and has gone to the steppe before Hmelnitski, knowing where to wait for him."

Having said this, he struck the table again.

"Don't spill the wine, my dear sir!" repeated with emphasis Skshetuski, who felt an astonishing aversion to the man from the first sight of him.

Chaplinski grew red in the face; his protruding eyes flashed. Thinking that offence was given him, he looked excitedly at Pan Yan; but seeing on him the colors of Vishnyevetski, he softened. Though Konyetspolski had a quarrel with Yeremi at the time, still Chigirin was too near Lubni, and it was dangerous not to respect the colors of the prince. Besides, Vishnyevetski chose such people for his service that any one would think twice before disputing with them.

"Hvedko, then, has undertaken to get Hmelnitski for you?" asked Zatsvilikhovski again.

"He has, and he will get him,--as sure as I am Chaplinski."

"But I tell you that he will not. Hmelnitski has escaped the ambush, and has gone to the Saitch, which you should have told Pan Pototski to-day. There is no fooling with Hmelnitski. Speaking briefly, he has more brains, a heavier hand, and greater luck than you, who are too hotheaded. Hmelnitski went away safely, I tell you; and if perhaps you don't believe me, this gentleman, who saw him in good health on the steppe and bade good-by to him yesterday, will repeat what I have said."

"Impossible, it cannot be!" boiled up Chaplinski, seizing himself by the hair.

"And what is more," added Zatsvilikhovski, "this knight before you saved him and killed your servants,--for which he is not to blame, in spite of the hetman's order, since he was returning from a mission to the Crimea and knew nothing of the order. Seeing a man attacked in the steppe by ruffians, as he thought, he went to his assistance. Of this rescue of Hmelnitski I inform you in good season, for he is ready with his Zaporojians, and it is evident that you wouldn't be very glad to see him, for you have maltreated him over-much. Tfu! to the devil with such tricks!"

Zatsvilikhovski, also, did not like Chaplinski.

Chaplinski sprang from his seat, losing his speech from rage; his face was completely purple, and his eyes kept coming more and more out of his head. Standing before Skshetuski in this condition, he belched forth disconnected words,--

"How!--in spite of the hetman's orders! I will--I will--"

Skshetuski did not even rise from the bench, but leaned on his elbows and watched Chaplinski, darting like a hawk on a sparrow.

"Why do you fasten to me like a burr to a dog's tail?"

"I'll drag you to the court with me!--You in spite of orders!--I with Cossacks!"

He stormed so much that it grew quieter in other parts of the room, and strangers began to turn their faces in the direction of Chaplinski. He was always seeking a quarrel, for such was his nature; he offended every man he met. But all were astonished, then, that he began with Zatsvilikhovski, who was the only person he feared, and with an officer wearing the colors of Prince Yeremi.

"Be silent, sir!" said the old standard-bearer. "This knight is in my company."

"I'll take you to the court!--I'll take you to the court--to the stocks!" roared Chaplinski, paying no attention to anything or any man.

Then Skshetuski rose, straightened himself to his full height, but did not draw his sabre; he had it hanging low, and taking it by the middle raised it till he put the cross hilt under the very nose of Chaplinski.

"Smell that!" said he.

"Strike, whoever believes in God!--Ai! here, my men!" shouted Chaplinski, grasping after his sword-hilt.

But he did not succeed in drawing his sword. The young lieutenant turned him around, caught him by the nape of the neck with one hand, and with the other by the trousers below the belt raised him, squirming like a salmon, and going to the door between the benches called out,--

"Brothers, clear the road for big horns; he'll hook!"

Saying this, he went to the threshold, struck and opened the door with Chaplinski, and hurled the under-starosta out into the street. Then he resumed his seat quietly at the side of Zatsvilikhovski.

In a moment there was silence in the room. The argument used by Pan Yan made a great impression on the assembled nobles. After a little while, however, the whole place shook with laughter.

"Hurrah for Vislinyevetski's man!" cried some.

"He has fainted! he has fainted, and is covered with blood!" cried others, who had looked through the door, curious to know what Chaplinski would do. "His servants are carrying him off!"

The partisans of the under-starosta, but few in number, were silent, and not having the courage to take his part, looked sullenly at Skshetuski.

"Spoken truth touches that hound to the quick," said Zatsvilikhovski.

"He is a cur, not a hound," said, while drawing near, a bulky nobleman who had a cataract on one eye and a hole in his forehead the size of a thaler, through which the naked skull appeared,--"He is a cur, not a hound! Permit me," continued he, turning to Pan Yan, "to offer you my respects. I am Yan Zagloba; my escutcheon 'In the Forehead,' as every one may easily know by this hole which the bullet of a robber made in my forehead when I was on a pilgrimage to the Holy Land in penance for the sins of my youth."

"But leave us in peace," said Zatsvilikhovski; "you said yourself that that was knocked out of you with a tankard in Radom."

"As I live, the bullet of a robber! That was another affair in Radom."

"You made a vow to go to the Holy Land, perhaps; but that you have never been there is certain."

"I have not been there, for in Galáts I received the palm of martyrdom; and if I lie, I am a supreme dog and not a nobleman."

"Ah, you never stop your stories!"

"Well, I am a rogue without hearing. To you, Lieutenant!"

In the mean while others came up to make the acquaintance of Skshetuski and express their regard for him. In general Chaplinski was not popular, and they were glad that disgrace had met him. It is strange and difficult to understand at this day that all the nobility in the neighborhood of Chigirin, and the smaller owners of villages, landed proprietors, and agriculturists, even though serving the Konyetspolskis, all knowing in neighbor fashion the dispute of Chaplinski with Hmelnitski, were on the side of the latter. Hmelnitski had indeed the reputation of a famous soldier who had rendered no mean services in various wars. It was known, also, that the king himself had had communication with him and valued his opinion highly. The whole affair was regarded as an ordinary squabble of one noble with another; such squabbles were counted by thousands, especially in the Russian lands. The part of the man was taken who knew how to incline to his side the majority, who did not foresee what terrible results were to come from this affair. Later on it was that hearts flamed up with hatred against Hmelnitski,--the hearts of nobility and clergy of both churches in equal degree.

Presently men came up to Skshetuski with liquor by the quart, saying,--

"Drink, brother!"

"Have a drink with me too!"

"Long life to Vishnyevetski's men!"

"So young, and already a lieutenant with Vishnyevetski!"

"Long life to Yeremi, hetman of hetmans! With him we will go to the ends of the earth!"

"Against Turks and Tartars!"

"To Stamboul!"

"Long life to Vladislav, our king!"

Loudest of all shouted Pan Zagloba, who was ready all alone to out-drink and out-talk a whole regiment.

"Gentlemen!" shouted he, till the window-panes rattled, "I have summoned the Sultan for the assault on me which he permitted in Galáts."

"If you don't stop talking, you may wear the skin off your mouth."

"How so, my dear sir? Quatuor articuli judicii castrensis: stuprum, incendium, latrocinium et vis armata alienis ædibus illata. Was not that specifically vis armata?"

"You are a noisy woodcock, my friend."

"I'll go even to the highest court."

"But won't you keep quiet?"

"I will get a decision, proclaim him an outlaw, and then war to the knife."

"Health to you, gentlemen!"

Some broke out in laughter, and with them Skshetuski, for his head buzzed a trifle now; but Zagloba babbled on just like a woodcock, charmed with his own voice. Happily his discourse was interrupted by another noble, who, stepping up, pulled him by the sleeve and said in singing Lithuanian tones,--

"Introduce me, friend Zagloba, to Lieutenant Skshetuski,--introduce me, please!"

"Of course, of course. Most worthy lieutenant, this is Pan Povsinoga."

"Podbipienta," said the other, correcting him.

"No matter; but his arms are Zervipludry--"[2]

"Zervikaptur,"[3] corrected the stranger.

"All right. From Psikishki--"[4]

"From Myshikishki,"[5] corrected the stranger.

"It's all the same. I don't remember whether I said mouse or dog entrails. But one thing is certain: I should not like to live in either place, for it is not easy to get there, and to depart is unseemly. Most gracious sir," said he, turning to Skshetuski, "I have now for a week been drinking wine at the expense of this gentleman, who has a sword at his belt as heavy as his purse, and his purse is as heavy as his wit. But if ever I have drunk wine at the cost of such an original, then may I call myself as big a fool as the man who buys wine for me."

"Well, he has given him a description!"

But the Lithuanian was not angry; he only waved his hand, smiled kindly, and said: "You might give us a little peace; it is terrible to listen to you!"

Pan Yan looked with curiosity at the new figure, which in truth deserved to be called original. First of all, it was the figure of a man of such stature that his head was as high as a wall, and his extreme leanness made him appear taller still. His broad shoulders and sinewy neck indicated uncommon strength, but he was merely skin and bone. His stomach had so fallen in from his chest that he might have been taken for a man dying of hunger. He was well dressed in a gray closely fitting coat of sveboda cloth with narrow arms, and high Swedish boots, then coming into use in Lithuania. A broad and well-filled elk-skin girdle with nothing to support it had slipped down to his hips; to this girdle was attached a Crusader's sword, which was so long that it reached quite to the shoulder of this gigantic man.

But whoever should be alarmed at the sword would be reassured in a moment by a glance at the face of its owner. The face, lean like the whole person, was adorned with hanging brows and a pair of drooping, hemp-colored mustaches, but was as honest and sincere as the face of a child. The hanging mustaches and brows gave him an expression at once anxious, thoughtful, and ridiculous. He looked like a man whom people elbow aside; but he pleased Skshetuski from the first glance because of the sincerity of his face and his perfect soldierly self-control.

"Lieutenant," said he, "you are in the service of Prince Vishnyevetski?"

"I am."

The Lithuanian placed his hands together as if in prayer, and raised his eyes.

"Ah, what a mighty warrior, what a hero, what a leader!"

"God grant the Commonwealth as many such as possible!"

"But could I not enter his service?"

"He will be glad to have you."

At this point Zagloba interrupted the conversation.

"The prince will have two spits for his kitchen,--one in you, one in your sword,--or he will hire you as a cook, or he will order robbers to be hanged on you, or he will measure cloth with you to make uniforms! Tfu! why are you not ashamed as a man and a Catholic to be as long as a serpent or the lance of an infidel?"

"Oh, it's disgusting to hear you," said the Lithuanian, patiently.

"What is your title?" asked Skshetuski; "for when you were speaking Pan Zagloba interrupted so often that if you will pardon me--"

"Podbipienta."

"Povsinoga," added Zagloba.

"Zervikaptur of Myshikishki."

"Here, old woman, is fun for you. I drink his wine, but I'm a fool if these are not outlandish titles."

"Are you from Lithuania?" asked the lieutenant.

"Well, I'm two weeks now in Chigirin. Hearing from Pan Zatsvilikhovski that you were coming, I waited to present my request to the prince with his recommendation."

"Tell me, please,--for I am curious,--why do you carry such an executioner's sword under your arm?"

"It is not the sword of an executioner, Lieutenant, but of a Crusader, and I wear it because it is a trophy and has been long in my family. It served at Khoinitsi in Lithuanian hands, and that's why I wear it."

"But it's a savage machine, and must be terribly heavy. It's for two hands, I suppose?"

"Oh, it can be used in two hands or one."

"Let me have a look at it."

The Lithuanian drew the sword and handed it to him; but Skshetuski's arm dropped in a moment. He could neither point the weapon nor aim a blow freely. He tried with both hands; still it was heavy. Skshetuski was a little ashamed, and turning to those present, said,--

"Now, gentlemen, who can make a cross with it?"

"We have tried already," answered several voices. "Pan Zatsvilikhovski is the only man who raises it, but he can't make a cross with it."

"Well, let us see you, sir," said Skshetuski, turning to the Lithuanian.

Podbipienta raised the sword as if it were a cane, and whirled it several times with the greatest ease, till the air in the room whistled and a breeze was blowing on their faces.

"May God be your aid!" said Skshetuski. "You have sure service with the prince."

"God knows that I am anxious, and my sword will not rust in it."

"But what about your wits," asked Zagloba, "since you don't know how to use them?"

Zatsvilikhovski now rose, and with the lieutenant was preparing to go out, when a man with hair white as a dove entered, and seeing Zatsvilikhovski, said,--

"I have come here on purpose to see you, sir."

This was Barabash, the Colonel of Cherkasi.

"Then come to my quarters," replied Zatsvilikhovski. "There is such a smoke here that nothing can be seen."

They went out together, Skshetuski with them. As soon as he had crossed the threshold, Barabash asked,--

"Are there news of Hmelnitski?"

"There are. He has fled to the Saitch. This officer met him yesterday in the steppe."

"Then he has not gone by water? I hurried off a courier to Kudák to have him seized; but if what you say is true, 'tis useless."

When he had said this, Barabash covered his eyes with his hands, and began to repeat, "Oh, Christ save us! Christ save us!"

"Why are you disturbed?"

"Don't you know the treason he has wrought on me? Don't you know what it means to publish such documents in the Saitch? Christ save us! Unless the king makes war on the Mussulman, this will be a spark upon powder."

"You predict a rebellion?"

"I do not predict, I see it; and Hmelnitski is somewhat beyond Nalivaika and Loboda."

"But who will follow him?"

"Who? Zaporojians, registered Cossacks, people of the towns, the mob, cottagers, and such as these out here."

Barabash pointed to the market-square and to the people moving around upon it. The whole square was thronged with great gray oxen on the way to Korsún for the army; and with the oxen went a crowd of herdsmen (Chabani), who passed their whole lives in the steppe and Wilderness,--men perfectly wild, professing no religion, ("religionis nullius," as the Voevoda Kisel said). Among them were forms more like robbers than herdsmen,--fierce, terrible, covered with remnants of various garments. The greater part of them were dressed in sheepskin doublets or in untanned skins with the wool outside, open in front and showing, even in winter, the naked breast embrowned by the winds of the steppe. All were armed, but with the greatest variety of weapons. Some had bows and quivers on their shoulders; some muskets or "squealers" (so called by the Cossacks); some had Tartar sabres, some scythes; and finally, there were those who had only sticks with horse-jaws fastened on the ends. Among them mingled the no less wild, though better armed men from the lower country, taking to the camp for sale dried fish, game, and mutton fat. Farther on were the Chumaki (ox-drivers) with salt, bee-keepers from the steppes and forest, wax-bleachers with honey, forest-dwellers with tar and pitch, peasants with wagons, registered Cossacks, Tartars from Bélgorod, and God knows what tramps and "vampires" from the ends of the earth. The whole town was full of drunken men. Chigirin was the place of lodging, and therefore of a frolic before bedtime. Fires were scattered over the market-square, while here and there an empty tar-barrel was burning. From every point were heard cries and bustle. The shrill squeak of Tartar pipes and the sound of drums was mingled with the bellowing of cattle and the softer note of the lyre, to which old men sang the favorite song of the time,--

"Oh, bright falcon,
My own brother,
Thou soarest high,
Thou seest far."

And besides this went up the wild shouts "U-ha! u-ha!" of the Cossacks, smeared with tar and quite drunk, dancing the tropak on the square. All this was at once wild and frenzied. One glance was enough to convince Zatsvilikhovski that Barabash was right; that one breath was sufficient to let loose those chaotic elements, inclined to plunder and accustomed to violence, with which the whole Ukraine was filled. And behind these crowds stood the Saitch, the Zaporojie, recently bridled and put in curb after Masloff Stav, still gnawing the bit impatiently, remembering ancient privileges and hating commissioners, but forming an organized power. That power had also on its side the sympathy of a countless mass of peasants, less patient of control than in other parts of the Commonwealth, because near them was Chertomelik, and beyond lordlessness, booty, and freedom. The standard-bearer in view of this, though a Russian himself and a devoted adherent of Eastern orthodoxy, fell into gloomy thought.

Being an old man, he remembered well the times of Nalivaika, Loboda, and Krempski. He knew the robbers of the Ukraine better perhaps than any one in Russia; and knowing at the same time Hmelnitski, he knew that he was greater than twenty Lobodas and Nalivaikas. He understood, therefore, all the danger of his escape to the Saitch, especially with the letters of the king, which Barabash said were full of promises to the Cossacks and incitements to resistance.

"Most worthy colonel," said Zatsvilikhovski to Barabash, "you should go to the Saitch and neutralize the influence of Hmelnitski; pacify them, pacify them."

"Most worthy standard-bearer," answered Barabash, "I will merely say that in consequence of the news of Hmelnitski's flight with the papers of the king, one half of my men have followed him to the Saitch. My time has passed; not the baton awaits me, but the grave!"

Barabash was indeed a good soldier, but old and without influence.

Meanwhile they had come to the quarters of Zatsvilikhovski, who had regained somewhat the composure peculiar to his mild character; and when they sat down to half a gallon of mead, he said emphatically,--

"All this is nothing, if, as they say, war is on foot against the Mussulman; and it is likely that such is the case, for though the Commonwealth does not want war, and the diets have roused much bad blood in the king, still he may carry his point. All this fire may be turned against the Turk, and in every case we have time on our side. I will go myself to Pan Pototski, inform him, and ask that he, being nearest to us, should come with his army. I do not know whether I shall succeed, for though a brave man and a trained warrior, he is terribly confident in himself and his army. And you, Colonel of Cherkasi, keep the Cossacks in curb--and you, Lieutenant, the moment you arrive at Lubni warn the prince to keep his eyes on the Saitch. Even if they begin action, I repeat it, we have time. There are not many people at the Saitch now; they have scattered around, fishing and hunting, and are in villages throughout the whole Ukraine. Before they assemble, much water will flow down the Dnieper. Besides, the name of the prince is terrible, and if they know that he has his eye on Chertomelik, perhaps they will remain in peace."

"I am ready," said the lieutenant, "to start from Chigirin even in a couple of days."

"That's right. Two or three days are of no account. And do you, Colonel of Cherkasi, send couriers with an account of the affair to Konyetspolski and Prince Dominic. But you are asleep, as I see."

Barabash had crossed his hands on his stomach and was in a deep slumber, snoring from time to time. The old colonel, when neither eating nor drinking,--and he loved both beyond measure,--was sleeping.

"Look!" said Zatsvilikhovski quietly to the lieutenant; "the statesmen at Warsaw think of holding the Cossacks in curb through such an old man as that. God be good to them! They put trust, too, even in Hmelnitski himself, with whom the chancellor entered into some negotiations or other; and Hmelnitski no doubt is fooling them terribly."

The lieutenant sighed in token of sympathy. But Barabash snored more deeply, and then murmured in his sleep: "Christ save us! Christ save us!"

"When do you think of leaving Chigirin?" asked Zatsvilikhovski.

"I shall have to wait two days for Chaplinski, who will bring an action, beyond doubt, for what has happened to him."

"He will not do that. He would prefer to send his servants against you if you didn't wear the uniform of the prince; but it is ugly work to tackle the prince, even for the servants of the Konyetspolskis."

"I will notify him that I am waiting, and start in two or three days. I am not afraid of an ambush, either, having a sabre at my side and a party of men."

The lieutenant now took farewell of Zatsvilikhovski, and went out.

The blaze from the piles on the square spread such a glare over the town that all Chigirin seemed burning. The bustle and shouts increased with the approach of night. The Jews did not peep from their houses. In every corner crowds of Chabani howled plaintive songs of the steppe. The wild Zaporojians danced around the fires, hurling their caps in the air, firing from their "squealers," and drinking gorailka by the quart. Here and there a scuffle broke out, which the starosta's men put down. The lieutenant had to open a way with the hilt of his sabre. Hearing the shouts and noise of the Cossacks, he thought at times that rebellion was already beginning to speak. It seemed to him, also, that he saw threatening looks and heard low-spoken curses directed against his person. In his ears were still ringing the words of Barabash, "Christ save us! Christ save us!" and his heart beat more quickly.

But the Chabani sang their songs more loudly in the town; the Zaporojians fired from their muskets and swam in gorailka. The firing and the wild "U-ha! u-ha!" reached the ears of the lieutenant, even after he had lain down to sleep in his quarters.

CHAPTER III.

A few days later the lieutenant with his escort pressed forward briskly in the direction of Lubni. After the passage of the Dnieper, they travelled by a broad steppe road which united Chigirin with Lubni, passing through Juki, Semi Mogil, and Khorol. A similar road joined Lubni with Kieff. In times past, before the campaign of the hetman Jolkyevski against Solonitsa, these roads were not in existence. People travelled to Kieff from Lubni by the desert and the steppe; the way to Chigirin was by water, with return by land through Khorol. In general the country beyond the Dnieper, the ancient land of the Pólovtsi, was wild, scarcely more inhabited than the Wilderness, frequently visited by the Tartars, and exposed to Zaporojian bands.

On the banks of the Sula immense forests, which had never been touched by the foot of man, gave forth their voices; and in places also on the low shores of the Sula, the Ruda, Sleporod, Korovai, Orjavets, Psel, and other greater and smaller rivers and streams, marshes were formed, partly grown over with dense thickets and pine forests, and partly open in the form of meadows. In these pine woods and morasses wild beasts of every kind found commodious refuge; and in the deepest forest gloom lived in countless multitudes the bearded aurochs, bears, with wild boars, and near them wolves, lynxes, martens, deer, and wild goats. In the swamps and arms of rivers beavers built their dams. There were stories current among the Zaporojians that of these beavers were some a century old and white as snow from age.

On the elevated dry steppes roamed herds of wild horses, with shaggy foreheads and bloodshot eyes. The rivers were swarming with fish and water-fowl. It was a wonderful land, half asleep, but bearing traces of the former activity of man. It was everywhere filled with the ruins of towns of previous generations; Lubni and Khorol were raised from such ruins as these. Everywhere the country was full of grave-mounds, ancient and modern, covered already with a growth of pine. Here, as in the Wilderness, ghosts and vampires rose up at night. Old Zaporojians, sitting around their fires, told marvellous tales of what took place in those forest depths, from which issued the howling of unknown beasts,--cries half human, half brute,-- terrible sounds as of battle or the chase. Under water was heard the ringing of bells in submerged cities. The land was inhospitable, little accessible, in places too soft, in places suffering from lack of water,--parched, dry, and dangerous to live in; for when men settled down there anyhow and began to cultivate the land, they were swept away by Tartar raids. But it was frequently visited by Zaporojians while hunting--or, as they phrased it, while at "industry"--along all the rivers, ravines, forests, and reedy marshes, searching for beavers in places of which even the existence was known to few.

And still settled life struggled to cling to those regions, like a plant which seizes the ground with its roots wherever it can, and though torn out repeatedly, springs up anew. On desert sites rose towns, settlements, colonies, hamlets, and single dwellings. The earth was fruitful in places, and freedom was enticing. But life bloomed up first when these lands came into possession of the princes Vishnyevetski. Prince Michael, after his marriage with a Moldavian lady, began to put his domain beyond the Dnieper into careful order. He brought in people, settled waste regions, gave exemption from service for thirty years, built monasteries, and introduced his princely authority. Even a settler in that country from a time of unreckoned priority, who considered that he was on his own ground, was willing to descend to the status of a tribute-payer, since for his tribute he came under the powerful protection of the prince who guarded him,--defended him from the Tartars and the men from below, who were often worse than the Tartars. But real activity commenced under the iron hand of young Prince Yeremi. His possessions began immediately outside Chigirin, and ended at Konotóp and Komni. This did not constitute all the wealth of the prince, for beginning at Sandomir his lands lay in the voevodstvos of Volynia, Russia, and Kieff; but his domain beyond the Dnieper was as the eye in his head to the victor of Putívl.

The Tartar lay long in wait on the Oryól or the Vorskla, and sniffed like a wolf before he ventured to urge his horse to the north. The men from below did not attempt attack. The local disorderly bands entered service. Wild, plundering people, who had long subsisted by violence and raids, now held in check, occupied outposts on the borders, and lying on the boundaries of the state, were like a bull-dog on his chain, threatening intruders with his teeth.

Everything flourished and was full of life. Roads were laid out on the trace of ancient highways; rivers were blocked with dams, built by the captive Tartar or men from below caught robbing with armed hand. The mill now resounded where the wind used to play wildly at night in the reeds, and where wolves howled in company with the ghosts of drowned men. More than four hundred wheels, not counting the numerous windmills, ground grain beyond the Dnieper. More than forty thousand men were tributary to the prince's treasury. The woods swarmed with bees. On the borders new villages, hamlets, and single dwellings were rising continually. On the steppes, by the side of wild herds, grazed whole droves of domestic cattle and horses. The endless monotony of pine groves and steppes was varied by the smoke of cottages, the gilded towers of churches,--Catholic and orthodox. The desert was changed into a peopled land.

Lieutenant Skshetuski travelled on gladly, and without hurry, as if going over his own ground, having plenty of leisure secured to him on the road. It was the beginning of January, 1648; but that wonderful, exceptional winter gave no sign of its approach. Spring was breathing in the air; the earth was soft and shining with the water of melted snow, the fields were covered with green, and the sun shone with such heat on the road at midday that fur coats burdened the shoulders as in summer.

The lieutenant's party was increased considerably in Chigirin, for it was joined by a Wallachian embassy which the hospodar sent to Lubni in the person of Pan Rozvan Ursu. The embassy was attended by an escort, with wagons and servants. Our acquaintance, Pan Longin Podbipienta, with the shield of Zervikaptur, his long sword under his arm, and with a few servants, travelled with Pan Yan.

Sunshine, splendid weather, and the odor of approaching spring filled the heart with gladness; and the lieutenant was the more rejoiced, since he was returning from a long journey to the roof of the prince, which was at the same time his own roof. He was returning having accomplished his mission well, and was therefore certain of a good reception.

There were other causes, also, for his gladness. Besides the good-will of the prince, whom the lieutenant loved with his whole soul, there awaited him in Lubni certain dark eyes. These eyes belonged to Anusia Borzobogata Krasenska, lady-in-waiting to Princess Griselda, the most beautiful maiden among all her attendants; a fearful coquette, for whom every one was languishing in Lubni, while she was indifferent to all. Princess Griselda was terribly strict in deportment and excessively austere in manner, which, however, did not prevent young people from exchanging ardent glances and sighs. Pan Yan, in common with the others, sent his tribute to the dark eyes, and when alone in his quarters he would seize a lute and sing,--

"Thou'rt the daintiest of the dainty;"

or,

"The Tartar seizes people captive;
Thou seizest captive hearts."

But being a cheerful man, and, besides, a soldier thoroughly devoted to his profession, he did not take it too much to heart that Anusia smiled on Pan Bykhovets of the Wallachian regiment, or Pan Vurtsel of the artillery, or Pan Volodyovski of the dragoons, as well as on him, and smiled even on Pan Baranovski of the huzzars, although he was already growing gray, and lisped since his palate had been wounded by a musket-ball. Our lieutenant had even had a sabre duel with Volodyovski for the sake of Anusia; but when obliged to remain too long at Lubni without an expedition against the Tartars, life was tedious there, even with Anusia, and when he had to go on an expedition, he went gladly, without regret or remembrance.

He returned joyfully, however, for he was on his way from the Crimea after a satisfactory arrangement of affairs. He hummed a song merrily, and urged his horse, riding by the side of Pan Longin, who, sitting on an enormous Livonian mare, was thoughtful and serious as usual. The wagons of the embassy escort remained considerably in the rear.

"The envoy is lying in the wagon like a block of wood, and sleeps all the time," said the lieutenant. "He told me wonders of his Wallachian land till he grew tired. I listened, too, with curiosity. It is a rich country,--no use in denying that,--excellent climate, gold, wine, dainties, and cattle in abundance. I thought to myself meanwhile: Our prince is descended from a Moldavian mother, and has as good a right to the throne of the hospodar as any one else; which rights, moreover, Prince Michael claimed. Wallachia is no new country to our warriors; they have beaten the Turks, Tartars, Wallachians, and Transylvanians."

"But the people are of weaker temper than with us, as Pan Zagloba told me in Chigirin," said Pan Longin. "If he is not to be believed; confirmation of what he says may be found in prayer-books."

"How in prayer-books?"

"I have one myself, and I can show it to you, for I always carry one with me."

Having said this, he unbuckled the saddle-straps in front of him, and taking out a small book carefully bound in calfskin, kissed it reverentially; then turning over a few leaves, said, "Read."

Skshetuski began: "'We take refuge under thy protection, Holy Mother of God--' Where is there anything here about Wallachia? What are you talking of? This is an antiphone!"

"Read on farther."

"'That we may be worthy of the promises of Christ our Lord. Amen.'"

"Well, here we've got a question."

Skshetuski read: "'Question: Why is Wallachian cavalry called light? Answer: Because it is light-footed in flight. Amen.' H'm! this is true. Still, there is a wonderful mixture of matters in this book."

"It is a soldiers' book, where, side by side with prayers, a variety of military information is given, from which you may gain knowledge of all nations,--which of them is noblest, and which mean. As to the Wallachians, it appears that they are cowardly fellows, and terrible traitors besides."

"That they are traitors is undoubted, for that is proven by the adventures of Prince Michael. I have heard as a fact that their soldiers are nothing to boast of by nature. But the prince has an excellent Wallachian regiment, in which Bykhovets is lieutenant; but to tell the truth, I don't think it contains even two hundred Wallachians."

"Well, Lieutenant, what do you think? Has the prince many men under arms?"

"About eight thousand, not counting the Cossacks that are at the outposts. But Zatsvilikhovski tells me that new levies are ordered."

"Well, may God give us a campaign under the prince!"

"It is said that a great war against Turkey is in preparation, and that the king himself is going to march with all the forces of the Commonwealth. I know, too, that gifts are withheld from the Tartars, who, I may add, are afraid to stir. I heard of this even in the Crimea, where on this account, I suppose, I was received with such honor; for the report is, that if the king moves with the hetmans, Prince Yeremi will strike the Crimea and wipe out the Tartars. It is quite certain they will not confide such an undertaking to any one else."

Pan Longin raised his hands and eyes to heaven.

"May the God of mercy grant such a holy war for the glory of Christianity and our nation, and permit me, sinful man, to fulfil my vow, so that I may receive joy in the struggle or find a praiseworthy death!"

"Have you made a vow, then, concerning the war?"

"I will disclose all the secrets of my soul to such a worthy knight, though the story is a long one; but since you incline a willing ear I will begin. You are aware that the motto on my shield is 'Tear cowl;' and this has the following origin: When my ancestor, Stoveiko Podbipienta, at the battle of Grünwald saw three knights in monks' cowls riding in a row, he dashed up to them and cut the heads off all three with one blow. Touching this glorious deed, the old chroniclers write in great praise of my ancestor."

"Your ancestor had not a lighter hand than you, and he was justly 'Tear cowl.'"

"To him the king granted a coat of arms, and upon it three goat-heads on a silver field in memory of those knights, because the same heads were depicted on their shields. Those arms, together with this sword, my ancestor, Stoveiko Podbipienta, left to his descendants with the injunction to strive to uphold the glory of their race and sword."

"It is not to be denied that you come of gentle stock."

Here Pan Longin began to sigh earnestly; and when he had comforted himself somewhat he continued:--

"Being the last of my race, I made a vow in Troki to the Most Holy Lady to live in continence and not marry till, in emulation of my ancestor Stoveiko Podbipienta, I should sweep off with this same sword three heads at one blow. Oh, merciful God, thou seest that I have done all in my power. I have preserved my purity to this day; I have commanded a tender heart to be still; I have sought war and I have fought, but without good fortune."

The lieutenant smiled under his mustache. "And you have not taken off three heads?"

"'No! it has not come to pass! No luck! Two at a blow I have taken more than once, but never three. I've never been able to come up to them, and it would be hard to ask enemies to stand in line for a blow. God knows my grief. There is strength in my bones, I have wealth, youth is passing away, I am approaching my forty-fifth year, my heart rushes forth in affection, my family is coming to an end, and still the three heads are not there! Such a Zervikaptur am I. A laughing-stock for the people, as Pan Zagloba truly remarks. All of which I endure patiently and offer to the Lord."

The Lithuanian began again to sigh, noticing which his Livonian mare from sympathy for her master fell to groaning and snorting.

The whole caravan pushed on briskly, and quiet was broken only by the snorting of the horses or the clank of stirrup against stirrup. After a time the escort at the rear wagons began a plaintive Wallachian song; soon, however, they stopped, and immediately the nasal voice of Pan Longin was heard singing piously,--

"In heaven I caused an endless light to dwell,
And mist I spread o'er all the earth."

That moment it grew dark, the stars twinkled in the sky, and from the damp plains white mists rose, boundless as the sea.

They entered a forest, but had gone only a few furlongs when the sound of horses' feet was heard and five riders appeared before the caravan. They were the young princes, who, informed by the driver of the accident which had happened to their mother, were hurrying to meet her, bringing a wagon drawn by four horses.

"Is that you, my sons?" called out the old princess.

The riders approached the carriage. "We, mother!"

"Come this way! Thanks to these gentlemen, we need no more assistance. These are my sons, whom I commend to your favor, gentlemen,--Simeon, Yury, Andrei, Nikolai-- And who is the fifth?" asked she, looking around attentively. "Oh! if my old eyes can see in the darkness, it is Bogun."

The princess drew back quickly to the depth of the carriage.

"Greetings to you, Princess, and to you, Princess Helena!" said the fifth.

"Ah, Bogun! You have come from the regiment, my falcon? And have you brought your lute? Welcome, welcome! Well, my sons, I have asked these gentlemen to spend the night with us at Rozlogi; and now greet them! A guest in the house is God in the house. Be gracious to our house, gentlemen!"

The young men removed their caps. "We entreat you most respectfully to cross our lowly threshold."

"They have already promised me,--the envoy has promised and the lieutenant. We shall receive honorable guests, but I am not sure that our poor fare will be savory for men accustomed to castle dainties."

"We are reared on the fare of soldiers, not of castles," said Skshetuski.

And Pan Rozvan added: "I have tried the hospitality of country-houses, and know that it is better than that of castles."

The carriages moved on, and the old princess continued: "Our best days have passed long ago. In Volynia and Lithuania there are still members of the Kurtsevich family who have retinues of attendants and live in lordly fashion, but they do not recognize their poor relations, for which God punish them. We live in real Cossack poverty, which you must overlook, and accept with a good heart what we offer with sincerity. I and my five sons live on one village and a few hamlets, and in addition we have this young lady to care for."

These words astonished the lieutenant not a little, for he had heard in Lubni that Rozlogi was no small estate, and also that it belonged to Prince Vassily, the father of Helena. He did not deem it proper, however, to inquire how the place had passed into the hands of Constantine and his widow.

"Then you have five sons, Princess?" asked Pan Rozvan Ursu.

"I had five, all like lions," answered she; "but the infidels in Bélgorod put out the eyes of the eldest, Vassily, with torches, wherefore his mind has failed him. When the young men go on an expedition I stay at home with him and this young lady, with whom I have more suffering than comfort."

The contemptuous tone with which the princess spoke of her niece was so evident that it did not escape the attention of the lieutenant. His breast boiled up in anger, and he had almost allowed an unseemly oath to escape him; but the words died on his lips when he looked at the young princess, and in the light of the moon saw her eyes filled with tears.

"What has happened? Why do you weep?" asked he, in a low voice.

She was silent.

"I cannot endure to see you weep," said Pan Yan, and bent toward her. Seeing that the old princess was conversing with the envoy and not looking toward him, he continued: "In God's name, speak but one word, for I would give blood and health to comfort you!"

All at once he felt one of the horsemen press against him so heavily that the horses began to rub their sides together. Conversation with the princess was interrupted. Skshetuski, astonished and also angered, turned to the intruder. By the light of the moon he saw two eyes, which looked at him insolently, defiantly, sneeringly. Those terrible eyes shone like those of a wolf in a dark forest.

"What devil is that?" thought the lieutenant,--"a demon or who?" And then, looking closely into those burning eyes, he asked: "Why do you push on me with your horse, and dig your eyes into me?"

The horseman did not answer, but continued to look with equal persistence and insolence.

"If it is dark, I can strike a light; and if the road is too narrow, then to the steppe with you!" said the lieutenant, in a distinct voice.

"Off with you from the carriage, Pole, if you see the steppe!" answered the horseman.

The lieutenant, being a man quick of action, instead of an answer struck his foot into the side of his enemy's horse with such force that the beast groaned and in a moment was on the very edge of the road.

The rider reined him in on the spot, and for a moment it seemed that he was about to rush on the lieutenant; but that instant the sharp, commanding voice of the old princess resounded.

"Bogun, what's the matter?"

These words had immediate effect. Bogun whirled his horse around, and passed to the other side of the carriage to the princess, who continued: "What is the matter? You are not in Pereyasláv nor the Crimea, but in Rozlogi. Remember this! But now gallop ahead for me, conduct the carriages; the ravine is at hand, and it is dark. Hurry on, you vampire!"

Skshetuski was astonished, as well as vexed. Bogun evidently sought a quarrel and would have found it; but why did he seek it,--whence this unexpected attack? The thought flashed through the lieutenant's mind that Princess Helena had something to do with this; and he was confirmed in the thought, for, looking at her face, he saw, in spite of the darkness, that it was pale, and evident terror was on it.

Bogun spurred forward immediately in obedience to the command of the princess, who, looking after him, said half to herself and half to Pan Yan,--

"That's a madcap, a Cossack devil."

"It is evident that he is not in his full mind," answered the lieutenant, contemptuously. "Is that Cossack in the service of your sons?"

The old princess threw herself back in the seat.

"What do you mean? Why, that is Bogun, lieutenant-colonel, a famous hero, a friend of my sons, and adopted by me as a sixth son. Impossible that you have not heard his name, for all know of him."

This name was, in fact, well known to Pan Yan. From among the names of various colonels and Cossack atamans this one had come to the top, and was on every lip on both banks of the Dnieper. Blind minstrels sang songs of Bogun in market-places and shops, and at evening meetings they told wonders about the young leader. Who he was, whence he had come, was known to no man. This much was certain,--the steppes, the Dnieper, the Cataracts, and Chertomelik, with its labyrinth of narrows, arms, islands, rocks, ravines, and reeds, had been his cradle. From childhood he had lived and communed with that wild world.

In time of peace he went with others to fish and hunt, battered through the windings of the Dnieper, wandered over swamps and reeds with a crowd of half-naked comrades; then again he spent whole months in forest depths. His school was in raids to the Wilderness on the herds of the Tartars, in ambushes, battles, campaigns against Tartar coast towns, against Bélgorod, Wallachia, or with boats on the Black Sea. He knew no days but days on his horse, no nights but nights at a steppe fire.

Soon he became the favorite of the entire lower country, a leader of others, and surpassed all men in daring. He was ready to go with a hundred horse even to Bagche Sarai, and start up a blaze under the very eyes of the Khan; he burned Tartar towns and villages, exterminated the inhabitants, tore captive murzas to pieces with horses, came down like a tempest, passed by like death. On the sea he fell upon Turkish galleys with frenzy, swept down upon the centre of Budjak,--rushed into the lion's mouth, as 'tis said. Some of his expeditions were simple madness. Men less daring, less fond of danger, perished impaled on stakes in Stamboul, or rotted at the oar on Turkish galleys; he always escaped unhurt, and with rich booty. It was said that he had collected immense treasures, which he had hidden in the reeds of the Dnieper; but it was also seen more than once how with muddy boots he had stamped upon cloth of gold, and spread carpets under the hoofs of his horse,--how, dressed in satin, he had spotted himself with tar, on purpose to show Cossack contempt for these lordly stuffs.

He never warmed any place long. Caprice was the motive of his deeds. At times, when he came to Chigirin, Cherkasi, or Pereyaslâv, he had terrible frolics with other Zaporojians; at times he lived like a monk, spoke to no man, escaped to the steppe. Then again he surrounded himself with blind minstrels, and listened to their songs and stories for days at a time, heaping gold on them. Among nobles he knew how to be a polished cavalier; among Cossacks he was the wildest of Cossacks. In knightly company he was a knight; among robbers, a robber. Some held him to be insane; for he was an unbridled, mad spirit. Why he was living in the world, what he wanted, whither he was tending, whom he served, he knew not himself. He served the steppes, the whirlwinds, war, love, his own fancy. This fancy of his distinguished him from all the other rude leaders, and from the whole robber herd who had only plunder as an object, and for whom it was the same whether they plundered Tartars or their own. Bogun took plunder, but preferred war to pillage; he was in love with peril for its own charm; he gave gold for songs; he hunted for glory, and cared for no more.

Of all leaders, he alone personified best the Cossack knight; therefore songs had sought him out as a favorite, and his name was celebrated throughout the whole Ukraine.

He had recently become the Pereyaslâv lieutenant-colonel, but he exercised the power of colonel; for old Loboda held the baton feebly in his stiffening hand.

Pan Yan, therefore, knew well who Bogun was, and if he asked the old princess whether the Cossack was in the service of her sons, he did it through studied contempt; for he felt in him an enemy, and in spite of all the reputation of Bogun, his blood boiled up because the Cossack had begun with him so insolently. He understood, too, that what had been begun would not end in a trifle. But Skshetuski was as unbending as an axle, self-confident to excess, yielding before nothing, and really eager for danger. He was ready even that moment to urge his horse after Bogun, but he rode near the princess. Besides, the wagon had already passed the ravine, and lights were gleaming in Rozlogi.

CHAPTER IV.

The Kurtsevichi Bulygi were of an ancient princely stock which used the escutcheon of Kurts, claimed to be from Koryat, but was really from Rurik. Of the two main lines, one lived in Lithuania, the other in Volynia, till Prince Vassily, one of the numerous descendants of the Volynian line, settled beyond the Dnieper. Being poor, he did not wish to remain among his powerful relatives, and entered the service of Prince Michael Vishnyevetski, father of the renowned "Yarema."[6]

Having covered himself with glory in that service, he received from the latter, as a permanent possession, Krasnie Rozlogi, which subsequently, by reason of its vast number of wolves, was called Volchie Rozlogi; and there he settled for good. He went over to the Latin rite in 1629, and married a lady of a distinguished Austrian family of Italian descent. From that marriage a daughter, Helena, came into the world a year later, her mother dying at her birth. Prince Vassily, without thinking of a second marriage, gave himself up altogether to the management of his land and the rearing of his only daughter. He was a man of great character and uncommon virtue. Having acquired a moderate fortune rather rapidly, he remembered at once his eldest brother Constantine, who, rejected by his powerful family, remained in Volynia, and was obliged to live on rented land. He brought him, with his wife and five sons, to Rozlogi, and shared every bit of bread with him.

The two Kurtsevichi lived in this way quietly till the end of 1634, when Vassily went with King Vladislav to the siege of Smolensk, where that unfortunate event took place which caused his ruin. In the royal camp was intercepted a letter written to Sheyin (the Russian commander), signed with the name of the prince, with the seal of Kurts added. Such a clear proof of treason on the part of a knight who till then had enjoyed an unspotted fame, astonished and confounded every one. It was in vain that Vassily called God to witness that neither the hand nor the signature on the paper was his; the arms of Kurts on the seal removed every doubt, no one believed that the seal had been lost,--which was the prince's explanation,-- and finally the unfortunate prince, sentenced *pro crimine perduelionis* to the loss of his honor and his head, was forced to seek safety in flight.

Arriving at Rozlogi in the night, Vassily implored his brother Constantine, by all that was holy, to care for Helena as his own daughter, and then he disappeared forever. It was said that he wrote a letter from Bar to Vishnyevetski, entreating the prince not to take the bread out of Helena's mouth, and to leave her in peace at Rozlogi under the care of Constantine; after that there was no more word of him. There was a report that he had died suddenly, also that he had joined the imperial army and had perished in battle in Germany. No one, however, had certain knowledge of him; but he must have died, since he inquired no further for his daughter. Soon mention of his name ceased, and he was only remembered when his innocence became evident. A certain Kuptsevich from Vytebsk confessed on his death-bed that he had written, at the siege of Smolensk, the letter to Sheyin, and sealed it with the seal found in camp. In the face of such testimony, pity and confusion seized all hearts. The sentence was revoked, the name of Prince Vassily restored to honor, but for Vassily himself the reward for his sufferings came too late. As to Rozlogi, Yeremi did not think of confiscating that; for the Vishnyevetskis, knowing Vassily better than others, were never entirely convinced of his guilt. He might even have remained under their powerful protection and laughed at the sentence; and if he fled, it was because he was unable to endure disgrace.

Helena grew up quietly at Rozlogi under the tender care of her uncle, and only after his death did painful times begin for her. The wife of Constantine, from a family of dubious origin, was a stern, impulsive, and energetic woman, whom her husband alone was able to keep within bounds. After his death she gathered into her iron hand the management of Rozlogi. The serving-men trembled before her, the house-servants feared her as fire, and soon she made herself known to the neighbors. During the third year of her management she attacked the Sivinskis of Brovarki twice with armed hand, dressed in male attire and on horseback, leading her servants with hired Cossacks. Once when the regiments of Prince Yeremi scattered Tartar bands, plundering in the neighborhood of Semi Mogil, the princess at the head of her people cut to pieces the remnant that had escaped as far as Rozlogi. She had settled for good in Rozlogi, and began to consider the place as the property of herself and her sons. She loved these sons as the wolf loves her young, but being rude she had no thought of a proper education for them. A monk of the Greek rite from Kieff taught them to read and write; here their education ended. It was not far to Lubni, where Vishnyevetski's court was, at which the young princes might have acquired polish and trained themselves to public business in the Chancery, or entered the school of knighthood under his banners. The princess, however, had reasons of her own for not sending the young men to Lubni.

Prince Yeremi might remember to whom Rozlogi belonged, and might look into the guardianship of Helena, or in memory of Vassily might take that guardianship upon himself; then she would undoubtedly have to move away from Rozlogi. The princess preferred, therefore, that in Lubni they should forget there were Kurtsevichi on earth. So the young princes were reared half wild, more as Cossacks than as nobles. While still young, they took part in the quarrels of the old princess, in attacks on the Sivinskis, and in her expeditions against Tartars. Feeling an innate aversion to books and letters, they fired arrows from bows for whole days, or took exercise in the management of their fists or sabres and lariats. They never occupied themselves with the estate, for their mother would not let that out of her own hands. It was sad to look at those descendants of a noted stock in whose veins princely blood was flowing, but whose manners were harsh and rude, and whose ideas and dull hearts reminded one of the uncultivated steppe. Meanwhile they were growing up like young oaks; seeing their own ignorance, they were ashamed to live with the nobility; on the contrary, the companionship of wild Cossack leaders was more agreeable. When old enough, therefore, they went with companies to the lower country, where they were considered as comrades. Sometimes they stayed half a year in the Saitch; went to "industry" with the Cossacks, took part in campaigns against the Turks and Tartars, which finally became their chief and favorite occupation.

Their mother was not opposed to this, for they often brought back abundant booty. But in one of these campaigns the eldest, Vassily, fell into pagan hands. His brothers, it is true, with the aid of Bogun and the Zaporojians, rescued him, but without his eyes. From that time Vassily was forced to remain at home; as formerly he had been the wildest of all, so then he became very mild and was sunk in meditation and religious exercises. The young men continued their warlike occupations, which at last obtained for them the surname of Prince-Cossacks.

A glance at Rozlogi-Siromakhi was enough to enable one to guess what kind of people lived there. When the envoy and Pan Yan drove through the gate with their wagons, they saw, not a castle, but rather a roomy shed built of enormous oak planks, with narrow windows like port-holes. Dwellings for servants and Cossacks, the stables, the granaries, and store-rooms were attached directly to the house, composing an irregular building made up of many parts, some high and some low. It would have been difficult to consider such a poor and rude exterior as a human dwelling, but for the lights in the windows. On the square in front of the house were two well-cranes; nearer the gate was a post with a ring on the top, to which was chained a bear. A strong gate of the same kind of planks as the house afforded entrance to the square, which was surrounded by a ditch and a palisade.

Evidently it was a fortified place, secure against attacks and incursions. It recalled in every regard the Cossack posts of the frontier; and though the majority of nobles on the border had no houses of fashion different from this, still this was more like some species of robber's nest than any of them. The attendants who came out with torches to meet the guests were bandits in appearance, rather than servants. Great dogs on the square tugged at their chains as if to break away and rush at the newly arrived. From the stable was heard the neighing of horses. The young Bulygi and their mother began to call to the servants with commands and curses.

In the midst of this hurly-burly the guests entered the house. But now Pan Rozvan Ursu, who had almost regretted his promise to pass the night there when he saw the wildness and wretchedness of the place, was really astonished at the sight that met his eyes. The inside of the house answered in no way to the unseemly exterior. First they entered a broad ante-room, the walls of which were almost entirely covered with armor, weapons, and skins of wild beasts. Logs of wood were blazing in two enormous fireplaces, and by their bright light were to be seen, on one wall, horse-trappings, shining armor, Turkish steel shirts on which here and there were glittering precious stones; chain-mail with gilt knobs on the buckles, half armor, breast-pieces, neck-pieces, steel armor of great value, Polish and Turkish helmets, steel caps with silver tips. On the opposite wall hung shields, no longer used in that age; near them Polish lances and Oriental javelins, also edged weapons in plenty,--from sabres to daggers and yatagans,--the hilts of which glittered in the firelight with various colors, like stars. In the corners hung bundles of skins of bears, wolves, foxes, martens, and ermine, gained by the hunting of the princes. Farther away, near the walls, dozing on their rings were hawks, falcons, and great golden eagles; the last, brought from the distant steppes of the East, were used in the wolf-hunt.

From that antechamber the guests passed to a spacious reception-room, and here in a chimney with a depression in front burned a brisk fire. In this room there was still greater luxury than in the antechamber. The bare planks of the walls were covered with woven stuffs. On the floor lay splendid Oriental carpets. In the centre of the room stood a long, cross-legged table, made of common planks, on which were goblets, gilt or cut from Venetian glass. At the walls were smaller tables, bureaus, and shelves on which were caskets, bottle-cases inlaid with bronze, brass candlesticks and clocks, taken in their time by the Turks from the Venetians and by the Cossacks from the Turks. The whole room was crowded with superfluous objects, of a use very often unknown to the possessor. Everywhere was luxury blended with the extreme rudeness of the steppe. Costly Turkish bureaus, inlaid with bronze, ebony, mother-of-pearl, were standing at the side of unplaned shelves; simple wooden chairs at the side of soft sofas. Cushions lying in Eastern fashion on sofas had covers of brocade or silk stuff, but were rarely filled with down, oftener with hay or pea-stalks. Costly stuffs and superfluous objects were the so-called Turkish or Tartar goods, partly bought for a trifle from the Cossacks, partly obtained in numerous wars by old Prince Vassily, partly during expeditions with men of the lower country by the young Bulygi, who chose rather to go with boats to the Black Sea than to marry or manage the land.

All this roused no surprise in Skshetuski, who was well acquainted with houses on the border; but the Wallachian boyar was astonished to see in the midst of all this luxury the Kurtsevichi in leather boots and fur coats not much better than those worn by the servants. Pan Longin Podbipienta, accustomed to a different order of things in Lithuania, was equally astonished.

Meanwhile the young princes received the guests heartily and with great welcome. Being little trained in society, they did this in so awkward a manner that the lieutenant was scarcely able to restrain his laughter. The eldest, Simeon, said,--

"We are glad to see you, and are thankful for your kindness. Our house is your house; therefore make yourselves at home. We bow to you, gentlemen, at our lowly thresholds."

And though no humility was observable in the tone of his speech, nor a recognition that he received persons superior to himself, he bowed in Cossack fashion to the girdle; and after him bowed the younger brothers, thinking that politeness required it.

"The forehead to you, gentlemen, the forehead."

Just then the princess, seizing Bogun by the sleeve, led him to another room.

"Listen, Bogun," said she, hurriedly, "I've no time for long speeches: I saw you attack that young noble. You are seeking a quarrel with him."

"Mother," answered the Cossack, kissing the old woman's hand, "the world is wide,--one road to him, another to me. I have not known him, nor heard of him; but let him not draw near the princess, or as I live I'll flash my sabre in his eyes."

"Oh! are you mad? Where, Cossack, is your head? What has come upon you? Do you want to ruin yourself and us? He is a soldier of Prince Yeremi, a lieutenant, a person of distinction, for he was sent as envoy from the prince to the Khan. Let a hair fall from his head while under our roof, do you know what will happen? The prince will turn his eyes to Rozlogi, will avenge this man, send us to the four winds, take Helena to Lubni,--and then what? Will you quarrel with Vishnyevetski, or attack Lubni? Try it if you want to taste an impaling stake, lost Cossack! Whether he comes near the girl or not, he will leave here as he came, and there will be peace. But restrain yourself! If not, then be off to where you came from, for you will bring misfortune to us if you stay."

The Cossack gnawed his mustache, frowned, but saw that the princess was right.

"They will go away in the morning, mother, and I will restrain myself; only let the princess stay in her own rooms."

"Why do you ask this? So that they should think I keep her in confinement? She will appear, because I wish it. Give no orders to me in this house, for you are not master here!"

"Be not angry. Princess! Since it cannot be otherwise, I will be as sweet to them as Turkish tidbits. I'll not grind my teeth nor touch my head, even though anger were consuming me, though my soul were ready to groan. Let your will be done."

"Oh, that's your talk! Take your lyre, play, sing; then you will feel easier. But now meet the guests."

They returned to the reception-room, in which the princes, not knowing how to entertain the guests, continued to ask them to make themselves at home, and were bowing to the girdle before them.

Skshetuski looked sharply and haughtily into the eyes of Bogun as soon as he came, but he saw in them neither quarrel nor defiance. The face of the youthful leader was lighted up with good-humor, so well simulated that it might have deceived the most experienced eye. The lieutenant looked at him carefully, for previously he had been unable to distinguish his features in the darkness. He saw now a young hero, straight as a poplar, with splendid brunette face, and rich, dark, drooping mustache. On that face gladness burst through the pensive mood of the Ukraine, as the sun through a mist. The leader had a lofty forehead, on which his dark hair drooped as a mane above his powerful brow. An aquiline nose, dilated nostrils, and white teeth, shining at every smile, gave the face a slight expression of rapacity; but on the whole it was a model of Ukraine beauty, luxuriant, full of character and defiance. His splendid dress also distinguished this hero of the steppe from the princes dressed in skins. Bogun wore a tunic of silver brocade and a scarlet kontush, which color was worn by all the Pereyaslàv Cossacks. His loins were girt with a silken sash from which depended a rich sabre; but the sabre and the dress paled before the Turkish dagger at his belt. This dagger was so thickly studded with jewels that sparks flew from it. Arrayed in this fashion, he would have been easily taken by any one for a scion of some great house; rather than a Cossack, especially since his freedom and his lordly manners betrayed no low descent.

Approaching Pan Longin, he listened to the story of his ancestor Stoveiko and the cutting off of the three heads. He turned to the lieutenant, and said with perfect indifference, just as if nothing had happened between them,--

"You are on your way from the Crimea, I hear."

"From the Crimea," answered the lieutenant, dryly.

"I have been there too, though I did not go to Baktche Serai; but I think I shall be there if the favorable news we hear comes true."

"Of what news are you speaking?"

"It is said that if the king opens war against the Turks, Prince Vishnyevetski will visit the Crimea with fire and sword. This report brings great joy through the whole Ukraine and the lower country, for if under such a leader we do not frolic in Baktche Serai, then under none."

"We will frolic, as God is in heaven!" cried the young princes.

The respect with which Bogun spoke of the prince captivated the lieutenant; so he smiled and said in a more friendly voice,--

"I see that you are not satisfied yet with the expeditions which you have had with men of the lower country, which however have covered you with glory."

"Small war, small glory! Konashevich Sahaidachni did not win it on boats, but in Khotím."

At that moment a door opened, and Vassily, the eldest of the Kurtsevichi, came slowly into the room, led by Helena. He was a man of ripe years, pale and emaciated, with a sad ascetic countenance, recalling the Byzantine pictures of saints. His long hair, prematurely gray from misfortune and pain, came down to his shoulders, and instead of his eyes were two red depressions. In his hand he held a bronze cross, with which he began to bless the room and all present.

"In the name of God the Father, in the name of the Saviour and of the Holy Most Pure," said he, "if you are apostles and bring good tidings, be welcome on Christian thresholds!"

"Be indulgent, gentlemen," muttered the princess; "his mind is disturbed."

But Vassily continued to bless them with the cross, and added: "As it is said in the 'Dialogues of the Apostles,' 'Whoso sheds his blood for the faith will be saved; he who dies for gain or booty will be damned.' Let us pray! Woe to you, brothers, woe to me, since we made war for booty! God be merciful to us, sinners! God be merciful! And you, men who have come from afar, what tidings do you bring? Are you apostles?"

He was silent, and appeared to wait for an answer; therefore the lieutenant replied,--

"We are far from such a lofty mission. We are only soldiers ready to lay down our lives for the faith."

"Then you will be saved," said the blind man; "but for us the hour of liberation has not come. Woe to you, brothers! woe to me!"

He uttered the last words almost with a groan, and such deep despair was depicted on his countenance that the guests were at a loss what to do. Helena seated him straightway on a chair, and hastening to the anteroom, returned in a moment with a lute in her hand.

Low sounds were heard in the apartment, and the princess began to sing a hymn as accompaniment,--

"By night and by day I call thee, O Lord!
Relieve thou my torment, and dry my sad tears;
Be a merciful Father to me in my sins;

Oh, hear thou my cry!"

The blind man threw his head back and listened to the words of the song, which appeared to act as a healing balm, for the pain and terror disappeared by degrees from his face. At last his head fell upon his bosom, and he remained as if half asleep and half benumbed.

"If the singing is continued, he will become altogether pacified. You see, gentlemen, his insanity consists in this, that he is always waiting for apostles; and if visitors appear, he comes out immediately to ask if they are apostles."

Helena continued:--

"Show me the way, Lord above Lords!
I'm like one astray in a waste without end,
Or a ship in the waves of a measureless sea,

Lost and alone."

Her sweet voice grew louder and louder. With the lute in her hands, and eyes raised to heaven, she was so beautiful that the lieutenant could not take his eyes from her. He looked, was lost in her, and forgot the world. He was roused from his ecstasy only by the words of the old princess,--

"That's enough! He will not wake soon. But now I request you to supper, gentlemen."

"We beg you to our bread and salt," said the young princes after their mother.

Pan Rozvan, as a man of polished manners, gave his arm to the lady of the house. Seeing this, Skshetuski hurried to the Princess Helena. His heart grew soft within him when he felt her hand on his arm, till fire flashed in his eyes, and he said,--

"The angels in heaven do not sing more beautifully than you."

"It is a sin for you to compare my singing to that of angels," answered Helena.

"I don't know whether I sin or not; but one thing is sure,--I would give my eyes to hear your singing till death. But what do I say? If blind, I could have no sight of you, which would be the same as torture beyond endurance."

"Don't say that, for you will leave here to-morrow, and to-morrow forget me."

"That will not be. My love is such that to the end of life I can love no one else."

The face of the princess grew scarlet; her breast began to heave. She wished to answer, but her lips merely trembled. Then Pan Yan continued,--

"But you will forget me in the presence of that handsome Cossack, who will accompany your singing on a balalaika."

"Never, never!" whispered the maiden. "But beware of him; he is a terrible man."

"What is one Cossack to me? Even if the whole Saitch were behind him, I should dare everything for your sake. You are for me like a jewel without price,--you are my world. But tell me, have you the same feeling for me?"

A low "Yes" sounded like music of paradise in the ears of Pan Yan, and that moment it seemed to him as if ten hearts, at least, were beating in his breast; in his eyes all things grew bright, as if a ray of sunlight had come to the world; he felt an unknown power within himself, as if he had wings on his shoulders.

During supper Bogun's face, which was greatly changed and pale, glared several times. The lieutenant, however, possessing the affection of Helena, cared not for his rival. "The devil take him!" thought he. "Let him not get in my way; if he does, I'll rub him out."

But his mind was not on Bogun. He felt Helena sitting so near that he almost touched her shoulder with his own; he saw the blush which never left her face, from which warmth went forth; he saw her swelling bosom, and her eyes, now drooping and covered with their lids, now flashing like a pair of stars,--for Helena, though cowed by the old princess and living in orphanhood, sadness, and fear, was still of the Ukraine and hot-blooded. The moment a warm ray of love fell on her she bloomed like a flower, and was roused at once to new and unknown life. Happiness with courage gleamed in her eyes, and those impulses struggling with her maiden timidity painted her face with the beautiful colors of the rose.

Pan Yan was almost beside himself. He drank deeply, but the mead had no effect on him; he was already drunk from love. He saw no one at the table save her who sat at his side. He saw not how Bogun grew paler each moment, and, touching the hilt of his dagger, gave no ear to Pan Longin, who for the third time told of his ancestor Stoveiko, nor to Kurtsevich, who told about his expedition for "Turkish goods."

All drank except Bogun; and the best example was given by the old princess, who raised a goblet, now to the health of her guests, now to the health of Vishnyevetski, now to the health of the hospodar Lupul. There was talk, too, of blind Vassily and his former knightly deeds, of his unlucky campaign and his present insanity, which Simeon, the eldest, explained as follows:--

"Just think! the smallest bit of anything in the eye prevents sight; why should not great drops of pitch reaching the brain cause madness?"

"Oh, it is a very delicate organ," said Pan Longin.

At this moment the old princess noticed the changed face of Bogun.

"What is the matter, my falcon?"

"My soul is suffering, mother," said he, gloomily; "but a Cossack word is not smoke. I will endure."

"Hold out, my son; there will be a feast."

Supper came to an end, but mead was poured into the goblets unsparingly. Cossacks called to the dance came, therefore, with greater readiness. The balalaikas and drums, to which the drowsy attendants were to dance, began to sound. Later on, the young princes dropped into the prisyadka. The old princess, putting her hands on her sides, began to keep time with her foot and hum. Pan Yan, seeing this, took Helena to the dance. When he embraced her with his arm it seemed to him that he was drawing part of heaven toward his breast. In the whirl of the dance her long tresses swept around his neck, as if she wished to bind him to herself forever. He did not restrain himself; and when he saw that no one was looking, he bent and kissed her lips with all his might.

Late at night, when alone with Longin in their sleeping-room, the lieutenant, instead of going to rest, sat on the wooden bedstead and began: "You will go to Lubni tomorrow with another man."

Podbipienta, who had just finished his prayers, opened wide his eyes and asked: "How is that? Are you going to stay here?"

"I shall not stay, but my heart will remain, and only the *dulcis recordatio* will go with me. You see in me a great change, since from tender desires I am scarcely able to listen to a thing."

"Then you have fallen in love with the princess?"

"Nothing else, as true as I am alive before you. Sleep flees from my lids, and I want nothing but sighs, from which I am ready to vanish into vapor. I tell you this, because, having a tender heart famishing for love, you will easily understand my torture."

Pan Longin began to sigh, in token that he understood the torments of love, and after a time he inquired mournfully: "Maybe you have also made a vow of celibacy?"

"Your inquiry is pointless, for if all made such vows the *genus humanum* would soon be at an end."

The entrance of a servant interrupted further conversation. It was an old Tartar, with quick black eyes and a face as wrinkled as a dried apple. After he came in he cast a significant look at Pan Yan and asked,--

"Don't you wish for something? Perhaps a cup of mead before going to bed?"

"No, 'tis not necessary."

The Tartar approached Skshetuski and muttered: "I have a word from the young princess for you."

"Then be my gift-giver! You may speak before this knight, for he knows everything."

The Tartar took a ribbon from his sleeve, saying, "The lady has sent you this scarf, with a message that she loves you with her whole soul."

The lieutenant seized the scarf, kissed it with ecstasy, and pressed it to his bosom. After he had become calmer, he asked: "What did the princess tell you to say?"

"That she loved you with her whole soul."

"Here is a thaler for your message. She said, then, that she loved me?"

"Yes."

"Here is another thaler for you. May God bless her, for she is most dear to me. Tell her, too-- But wait, I'll write to her. Bring me ink, pen, and paper."

"What?" asked the Tartar.

"Ink, pen, and paper."

"We have none in the house. In the time of Prince Vassily we had, and afterward when the young princes learned to write from the monk; but that is a long time ago."

Pan Yan clasped his hands. "Haven't you ink and pen?" asked he of Podbipienta.

The Lithuanian opened his hands and raised his eyes to heaven.

"Well, plague take it!" said the lieutenant; "what can I do?"

The Tartar had squatted before the fire. "What is the use of writing?" said he, gathering up the coals. "The young lady has gone to sleep. And what you would write to her now, you can tell her in the morning."

"In that case I need no ink. You are a faithful servant to the young lady, as I see. Here is a third thaler for you. Are you long in her service?"

"It is now fourteen years since Prince Vassily took me captive, and since that time I have served faithfully. The night he went away through losing his name he left his little child to Constantine, and said to me: 'You will not desert the little girl, and you will be as careful of her as the eye in your head."

"Are you doing what he told you?"

"Yes, I am; I will care for her."

"Tell me what you see. How is she living here?"

"They have evil designs against her, for they wish to give her to Bogun, and he is a cursed dog."

"Oh, nothing will come of that! A man will be found to take her part."

"Yes!" said the old man, pushing the glowing coals. "They want to give her to Bogun, to take and bear her away as a wolf bears a lamb, and leave them in Rozlogi; for Rozlogi is not theirs, but hers from her father, Prince Vassily. Bogun is willing to do this, for he has more gold and silver in the reeds than there is sand in Rozlogi; but she holds him in hatred from the time he brained a man before her face. Blood has fallen between them, and hatred has sprung up. God is one!"

"But won't you betray me?"

"If we only could; but we cannot, as you see yourself. Give your word that you will keep the secret."

"If I give it, will you give the girl?"

"Yes, for we are unable not to give her, though we are sorry for Bogun."

"Pshaw!" said the lieutenant, turning to the princes, "There are four of you, like oaks, and afraid of one Cossack, and you wish to overcome him by treason! Though I am obliged to thank you, still I say that it is not the thing for men of honor."

"Do not interfere in this," cried the princess. "It is not your affair. What can we do? How many soldiers have you against his hundred and fifty Cossacks? Will you protect us? Will you protect Helena herself, whom he is ready to bear away by force? This is not your affair. Go your way to Lubni. How we must act is for us to judge, if we only bring Helena to you."

"Do what you like; but one thing I repeat: If any wrong comes to Helena, woe to you!"

"Do not treat us in this fashion, you might drive us to desperation."

"You wished to bend her to your will, and now, when selling her for Rozlogi, it has never entered your heads to ask whether my person is pleasing to her."

"We are going to ask her in your presence," said the princess, suppressing the rage which began to seethe up again in her breast, for she felt clearly the contempt in these words of Skshetuski.

Simeon went for Helena, and soon entered the room with her. Amidst the rage and threats which still seemed to quiver in the air like the echoes of a tempest that has passed, amidst those frowning brows, angry looks, and threatening scowls, her beautiful face shone like the sun after a storm.

"Well, young lady!" said the princess sullenly, pointing to Pan Yan; "if you choose this man, he is your future husband."

Helena grew pale, and with a sudden cry covered her eyes with her two hands; then suddenly stretched them toward Skshetuski.

"Is this true?" whispered she, in transport.

An hour later the retinue of the envoy and the lieutenant moved slowly along the forest road toward Lubni. Skshetuski with Pan Longin Podbipienta rode in front; after them came the wagons of the envoy in a long line. The lieutenant was completely sunk in thought and longing, when suddenly he was roused from his pensiveness by the words of the song,--

"I grieve, I grieve, my heart is sore."

In the depth of the forest appeared Bogun on a narrow path trodden out by the peasants. His horse was covered with foam and mud. Apparently the Cossack, according to habit, had gone out to the steppes and the forest to dissipate with the wind, destroy, and forget in the distance that which over-pained his heart. He was returning then to Rozlogi.

Skshetuski answered: "This is no time for me to speak of my nobility. I think, however, that your rank might well bear the sword and shield behind mine. But for that matter, since a peasant was good in your eyes, I am better. As to my fortune, that too may be compared with yours; and since you say that you will not give me Helena, then listen to what I tell you: I will leave you in Rozlogi, and ask no account of guardianship."

"Do not give that which is not yours."

"I give nothing but my promise for the future. I give it, and strengthen it with my knightly word. Now choose, either to render account to the prince of your guardianship and leave Rozlogi, or give me Helena and you may keep the land."

The dart dropped slowly from the hand of the princess, and after a moment fell on the floor with a rattle.

"Choose," repeated Skshetuski,--"either peace or war!"

"It is lucky," said she, more mildly, "that Bogun has gone out with the falcon, not wishing to look at you; for he had suspicions even yesterday. If he were here, we should not get on without bloodshed."

"I do not wear a sword, madam, to have my belt cut off."

"But think, is it polite on the part of such a knight as you, after entering a house by invitation, to force people in this way, and take a maiden by assault, as if from Turkish slavery?"

"It is right, since she was to be sold against her will to a peasant."

"Don't say that of Bogun, for though of unknown parentage, he is a famous warrior and a splendid knight; known to us from childhood, he is like a relative in the house. To take the maiden from him is the same as to stab him with a knife."

"Well, Princess, it is time for me to go. Pardon me, then, if I ask you once more to make your choice."

The princess turned to her sons. "Well, my sons, what do you say to such an humble request from this cavalier?"

The young men looked down, nudged each other with their elbows, and were silent. At last Simeon muttered: "If you tell us, mother, to slay him, we will slay; if you say give the girl, we will give her."

"To give is bad, and to slay is bad." Then turning to Skshetuski, she said: "You have pushed us to the wall so closely that there is no escape. Bogun is a madman, ready for anything. Who will save us from his vengeance? He will perish himself through the prince, but he will destroy us first. What are we to do?"

"That is your affair."

The princess was silent for a time, then said: "Listen to me. All this must remain a secret. We will send Bogun to Pereyasláv, and will go ourselves with Helena to Lubni, and you will ask the prince to send us a guard at Rozlogi. Bogun has a hundred and fifty Cossacks in the neighborhood; part of them are here. You cannot take Helena immediately, for he would rescue her. It cannot be arranged otherwise. Go your way, therefore; tell the secret to no man, and wait for us."

"Forgive me, sir," said she, coughing; and her voice became dry and sharp. "The proposal of such a knight is no small honor for us; but nothing can come of it, since I have already promised Helena to another."

"But be pleased to consider, as a careful guardian, whether that promise was not made against the will of the princess, and if I am not better than he to whom you have promised her."

"Well, sir, it is for me to judge who is better. You may be the best of men; but that is nothing to us, for we do not know you."

The lieutenant straightened himself still more proudly, and his glances, though cold, became sharp as knives.

"But I know you, you traitors!" he burst forth. "You wish to give your relative to a peasant, on condition that he leaves you property unjustly acquired."

"You are a traitor yourself!" shouted the princess. "Is this your return for hospitality? Is this the gratitude you cherish in your heart? Oh, serpent! What kind of person are you? Whence have you come?"

The fingers of the young princes began to quiver, and they looked along the walls for weapons; but the lieutenant cried out,--

"Wretches! you have seized the property of an orphan, but to no purpose. In a day from now Vishnyevetski will know of this."

At these words the princess rushed to the end of the room, and seizing a dart, went up to the lieutenant. The young men also, having seized each what he could lay hands on,--one a sabre, another a knife,--stood in a half-circle near him, panting like a pack of mad wolves.

"You will go to the prince, will you?" shouted the old woman; "and are you sure that you will go out of here alive, and that this is not your last hour?"

Skshetuski crossed his arms on his breast, and did not wink an eye.

"I am on my way from the Crimea," said he, "as an envoy of Prince Yeremi. Let a single drop of my blood fall here, and in three days the ashes of this house will have vanished, and you will rot in the dungeons of Lubni. Is there power in the world to save you? Do not threaten, for I am not afraid of you."

"We may perish, but you will perish first."

"Then strike! Here is my breast."

The princes, with their mother near them, held weapons pointed at the breast of the lieutenant; but it seemed as if invisible fetters held their hands. Panting, and gnashing their teeth, they struggled in vain rage, but none of them struck a blow. The terrible name of Vishnyevetski deprived them of strength. The lieutenant was master of the position.

The weak rage of the princess was poured out in a mere torrent of abuse: "Trickster! beggar! you want princely blood. But in vain; we will give her to any one, but not to you. The prince cannot make us do that."

The lieutenant was unable to sleep that night. He paced the apartment, gazed at the moon, and had many thoughts on his mind. He penetrated the game of the Bulygi. If a nobleman of the vicinity were to marry the princess, he would remember Rozlogi, and justly, for it belonged to her; and he might demand also an account of the guardianship. Therefore the Bulygi, already turned Cossacks, decided to give the young woman to a Cossack. While thinking of this, Skshetuski clinched his fists and sought the sword at his side. He resolved to baffle these plots, and felt that he had the power to do so. Besides, the guardianship of Helena belonged to Prince Yeremi,--first, because Rozlogi was given by the Vishnyevetskis to old Vassily; secondly, because Vassily himself wrote a letter to the prince from Bar, requesting this guardianship. The pressure of public business alone--wars and great undertakings--could have prevented the prince from looking into the guardianship. But it would be sufficient to remind him with a word, and he would have justice done.

The gray of dawn was appearing when Skshetuski threw himself on the bed. He slept soundly, and in the morning woke with a finished plan. He and Pan Longin dressed in haste, all the more since the wagons were ready and the soldiers on horseback waiting to start. He breakfasted in the reception-room with the young princes and their mother, but Bogun was not there; it was unknown whether he was sleeping yet or had gone.

After he had refreshed himself Skshetuski said: "Worthy princess! time flies, and we must be on horseback in a moment; but before we thank you with grateful hearts for your entertainment, I have an important affair on which I should like to say a few words to you and your sons apart."

Astonishment was visible on the face of the princess. She looked at her sons, at the envoy, and Pan Longin, as if trying to divine from their faces what the question might be; and with a certain alarm in her voice she said: "I am at your service."

The envoy wished to retire, but she did not permit him. They went at once to the room which was hung with armor and weapons. The young princes took their places in a row behind their mother, who, standing opposite Skshetuski, asked: "Of what affair do you wish to speak, sir?"

The lieutenant fastened a quick and indeed severe glance on her, and said: "Pardon me, Princess, and you, young Princes, that I act contrary to custom, and instead of speaking through ambassadors of distinction, I am the advocate in my own cause. But it cannot be otherwise; and since no man can battle with necessity, I present my humble request to you as guardians to be pleased to give me Princess Helena as wife."

If at that moment of the winter season lightning had descended in front of the house at Rozlogi, it would have caused less astonishment to the princess and her sons than those words of the lieutenant. For a time they looked with amazement on the speaker, who stood before them erect, calm, and wonderfully proud, as if he intended not to ask, but to command; and they could not find a word of answer, but instead, the princess began to ask,--

"How is this? Are you speaking of Helena?"

"I am, Princess, and you hear my fixed resolve."

A moment of silence followed.

"I am waiting for your answer, Princess."

Looking on that splendid, genuine knightly form, which only flashed up before him and vanished, Skshetuski murmured involuntarily,--

"It is lucky in every case that he brained a man in her presence."

All at once an undefined sorrow pressed his heart. He was sorry as it were for Bogun, but still more sorry that having bound himself by word to the princess, he was unable that moment to urge his horse after him and say,--

"We love the same woman; there is one of us, therefore, who cannot live in the world. Draw your sword, Cossack!"

CHAPTER V.

When he arrived at Lubni, Pan Yan did not find the prince, who had gone to a christening at the house of an old attendant of his, Pan Sufchinski, at Senchy, taking with him the princess, two young princesses Zbaraskie, and many persons of the castle. Word was sent to Senchy of the lieutenant's return from the Crimea, and of the arrival of the envoy.

Meanwhile Skshetuski's acquaintances and comrades greeted him joyfully after his long journey; and especially Pan Volodyovski, who had been the most intimate of all since their last duel. This cavalier was noted for being always in love. After he had convinced himself of the insincerity of Anusia Borzobogata, he turned his sensitive heart to Angela Lenska, one of the attendants of the princess; and when she, a month before, became engaged to Pan Stanishevski, Volodyovski, to console himself, began to sigh after Anna, the eldest princess Zbaraska, niece of Prince Yeremi.

But he understood himself that he had raised his eyes so high that he could not strengthen himself with the least hope, especially since Pan Bodzynski and Pan Lyassota came to make proposals for the princess in the name of Pan Pshiyemski, son of the voevoda of Lenchitsk. The unfortunate Volodyovski therefore told his new troubles to the lieutenant, initiating him into all the affairs and secrets of the castle, to which he listened with half an ear, since his mind and heart were otherwise occupied. Had it not been for that mental disquiet which always attends even mutual love, Skshetuski would have felt himself happy on returning, after a long absence, to Lubni, where he was surrounded by friendly faces and that bustle of military life to which he had long grown accustomed. Though Lubni, as a lordly residence, was equal in grandeur to any of the seats of the "kinglets," still it was different from them in this,--that its life was stern, really of the camp. A visitor unacquainted with its usages and order, and coming, even in time of profoundest peace, might suppose that some military expedition was on foot. The soldier there was above the courtier, iron above gold, the trumpet-call louder than sounds of feasts and amusements. Exemplary order reigned in every part, and a discipline elsewhere unknown. On all sides were throngs of knights of various regiments, armored cavalry dragoons, Cossacks, Tartars, and Wallachians, in which served not only the whole Trans-Dnieper, but volunteers, nobles from every part of the Commonwealth. Whoever wished training in a real school of knighthood set out for Lubni; therefore neither the Mazur, the Lithuanian, the man of Little Poland, nor even the Prussian, was absent from the side of the Russian. Infantry and artillery, or the so-called "fire people," were composed, for the greater part, of picked Germans engaged for high wages. Russians served principally in the dragoons, Lithuanians in the Tartar regiments; the men of Little Poland rallied most willingly to the armored regiments. The prince did not allow his men to live in idleness; hence there was ceaseless movement in the camp. Some regiments were marching out to relieve the stanitsas and outposts, others were entering the capital,--day after day drilling and manœuvres. At times, even when there was no trouble from Tartars, the prince undertook distant expeditions into the wild steppes and wildernesses to accustom the soldiers to campaigning, to push forward where no man had gone before, and to spread the glory of his name. So the past spring he had descended the left bank of the Dnieper to Kudák, where Pan Grodzitski, in command of the garrison, received him as a monarch; then he advanced farther beyond the Cataracts to Hortitsa; and at Kuchkasy he gave orders to raise a great mound of stones as a memorial and a sign that no other lord had gone so far along that shore.

Pan Boguslav Mashkevich--a good soldier, though young, and also a learned man, who described that expedition as well as various campaigns of the prince--told Skshetuski marvels concerning it, which were confirmed at once by Volodyovski, for he had taken part in the expedition. They had seen the Cataracts and wondered at them, especially at the terrible Nenasytets, which devoured every year a number of people, like Scylla and Charybdis of old. Then they set out to the east along the parched steppes, where cavalry were unable to advance on the burning ground and they had to cover the horses' hoofs with skins. Multitudes of reptiles and vipers were met with,--snakes ten ells long and thick as a man's arm. On some oaks standing apart they inscribed, in eternal memory of the expedition, the arms of the prince. Finally, they entered a steppe so wild that in it no trace of man was found.

"I thought," said the learned Pan Mashkevich, "that at last we should have to go to Hades, like Ulysses."

To this Volodyovski added: "The men of Zamoiski's vanguard swore that they saw those boundaries on which the circle of the earth rests."

The lieutenant told his companions about the Crimea, where he had spent almost half a year in waiting for the answer of the Khan; he told of the towns there, of present and remote times, of Tartars and their military power, and finally of their terror at reports of a general expedition to the Crimea, in which all the forces of the Commonwealth were to engage.

Conversing in this way every evening, they waited the return of the prince. The lieutenant presented to his most intimate companions Pan Longin Podbipienta, who as a man of mild manners gained their hearts at once, and by exhibiting his superhuman strength in exercises with the sword acquired universal respect. He did not fail to relate to each one the story of his ancestor Stoveiko and the three severed heads; but he said nothing of his vow, not wishing to expose himself to ridicule. He pleased Volodyovski, especially by reason of the sensitive hearts of both. After a few days they went out together to sigh on the ramparts,--one for a star which shone above his reach, that is, for Princess Anna; the other for an unknown, from whom he was separated by the three heads of his vow.

Volodyovski tried to entice Longin into the dragoons; but the Lithuanian decided at last to join the armored regiment, so as to serve with Skshetuski, whom, as he learned in Lubni, to his delight, all esteemed as a knight of the first degree, and one of the best officers in the service of the prince. And precisely in Skshetuski's regiment there was a vacancy in prospect. Pan Zakshevski, nicknamed "Miserere Mei," had been ill for two weeks beyond hope of recovery, since all his wounds had opened from dampness. To the love-cares of Skshetuski was now added sorrow for the impending loss of his old companion and tried friend. He did not go a step, therefore, from Zakshevski's pillow for several hours each day, comforting him as best he could, and strengthening him with the hope that they would still have many a campaign together.

But the old man needed no consolation; he was closing life joyfully on the hard bed of the soldier, covered with a horse-skin. With a smile almost childlike, he gazed on the crucifix above his bed, and answered Skshetuski,--

"Miserere mei! Lieutenant, I am on my way to the heavenly garrison. My body has so many holes from wounds that I fear Saint Peter, who is the steward of the Lord and must look after order in heaven, won't let me in with such a rent body; but I'll say: 'Saint Peter, my dear, I implore you, by the ear of Malchus, make no opposition, for it was pagans who injured my mortal coil,' miserere mei. And if Saint Michael shall have any campaigning against the powers of hell, old Zakshevski will be useful yet."

The lieutenant, though he had looked so often upon death as a soldier and inflicted it himself, could not restrain his tears while listening to the old man, whose departure was like a quiet sunset.

At last, one morning the bells tolled in all the churches of Lubni, announcing the death of Pan Zakshevski. That same day the prince came from Senchy, and with him Bodzynski and Lyassota, with the whole court and many nobles in a long train of carriages, for the company at Pan Sufchinski's was very large. The prince arranged a great funeral, wishing to honor the services of the deceased and to show how he loved brave men. All the regiments at Lubni took part in the procession; from the ramparts guns and cannon were fired; the cavalry marched from the castle to the parish church in battle-array, but with furled banners; after them the infantry, with muskets reversed. The prince himself, dressed in mourning, rode behind the hearse in a gilded carriage, drawn by eight milk-white horses with purple-stained manes and tails, and tufts of black ostrich feathers on their heads. In front of the carriage marched a detachment of janissaries, the body-guard of the prince. Behind the carriage, on splendid steeds, rode pages in Spanish costume; farther on, high officials of the castle, attendants, lackeys; finally, haiduks and guards.

The cortége stopped before the church door, where the priest, Yaskolski, made a speech beginning with the words: "Whither art thou hastening, O Zakshevski!" Then speeches were made by some of his comrades, and among them by Skshetuski, as the superior and friend of the deceased. Then his body was borne into the church, and there was heard the voice of the most eloquent of the eloquent, the Jesuit priest Mukhovetski, who spoke with such loftiness and grace that the prince himself wept; for he was a man of rare tenderness of heart and a real father to the soldiers. He maintained an iron discipline, but was unequalled in liberality and kindly treatment of people, and in the care with which he surrounded not only them, but their children and wives. Terrible and pitiless to rebels, he was a real benefactor, not only to the nobility, but to all his people. When the locusts destroyed the crops in 1646 he remitted the rent for a year, and ordered grain to be given from the granaries to his subjects; and after the fire in Khorol he supported all the townspeople at his own expense for two months. Tenants and managers of crown estates trembled lest accounts of any of the abuses or wrongs inflicted by them on the people should come to the ears of the prince. His guardianship over orphans was so good that these orphans were called, in the country beyond the Dnieper, "the prince's children." Princess Griselda herself watched over this, aided by Father Mukhovetski.

Order reigned in all the lands of the prince, with plenty, justice, peace, but also terror,--for in case of the slightest opposition the prince knew no bounds to his anger and to the punishments he inflicted; to such a degree was magnanimity joined with severity in his nature. But in those times and in those regions that severity alone permitted life and the labor of men to thrive and continue. Thanks to it alone, towns and villages rose, the agriculturist took the place of the highwayman, the merchant sold his wares in peace, bells called the devout in safety to prayer, the enemy dared not cross the boundaries, crowds of thieves perished, empaled on stakes, or were changed into regular soldiers, and the wilderness bloomed.

A wild country and its wild inhabitants needed such a hand; for to the country beyond the Dnieper went the most restless elements of the Ukraine. Settlers came in, allured by the land and the fatness of the soil; runaway peasants from all lands of the Commonwealth; criminals escaping from prison,--in one word, as Livy said, "Pastorum convenarumque plebs transfuga ex suis populis." Only a lion at whose roar everything trembled could hold them in check, make them peaceable inhabitants, and force them into the bonds of settled life.

Pan Longin Podbipienta, seeing the prince for the first time at the funeral, could not believe his own eyes. Having heard so much of his glory, he imagined that he must be a sort of giant, a head above the race of common men; while the prince was really of small stature, and rather delicate. He was still young,--in the thirty-sixth year of his age,--but on his countenance military toil was evident; and as he lived in Lubni like a real king, so did he share in time of campaign and expedition the hardships of the common soldier. He ate black bread, slept on the ground in a blanket; and since the greater part of his life was spent in labors of the camp, the years left their marks on his face. But that countenance revealed at the first glance an extraordinary man. There was depicted on it an iron, unbending will, and a majesty before which all involuntarily inclined. It was evident that this man knew his own power and greatness; and if on the morrow a crown were placed on his head, he would not feel astonished or oppressed by its weight. He had large eyes, calm, and indeed mild; still, thunders seemed to slumber in them, and you felt that woe would follow him who should rouse them. No man could endure the calm light of that look; and ambassadors trained at courts on appearing before Yeremi were seen to grow confused and unable to begin their discourse. He was, moreover, in his domain beyond the Dnieper a genuine king. There went out from his chancery privileges and grants headed, "We, by the grace of God Prince and Lord," etc. There were few magnates whom he considered equal to himself. Princes of the blood of ancient rulers were his stewards. Such in his day was the father of Helena, Vassily Bulyga Kurtsevich, who counted his descent, as already mentioned, from Koryat; but really he was descended from Rurik.

There was something in Prince Yeremi which, in spite of his native kindness, kept men at a distance. Loving soldiers, he was familiar with them; with him no one dared to be familiar; and still, if he should ask mounted knights to spring over the precipices of the Dnieper, they would do so without stopping to think. From his Wallachian mother he inherited a clearness of complexion like the color of iron at a white glow, from which heat radiates, and hair black as a raven's wing, which, shaven closely at the sides of his head, was cut square above the brows, covering half his forehead. He wore the Polish costume, and was not over-careful of his dress. Only on great occasions did he wear costly apparel; but then he was all glitter from gold and jewels.

Pan Longin, a few days later, was present at such a solemnity, when the prince gave audience to Rozvan Ursu. The reception of ambassadors always took place in a Heavenly Hall, so called because on its ceiling was depicted the firmament of heaven with the stars, by the pencil of Helm of Dantzig. On that occasion the prince sat under a canopy of velvet and ermine on an elevated seat like a throne, the footstool of which was bound with a gilded circle. Behind the prince stood the priest Mukhovetski, his secretary, the steward prince Voronich, and Pan Boguslav Mashkevich; farther on, pages and twelve body-guards, in Spanish costume, bearing halberts. The depths of the hall were filled with knights in splendid dress and uniforms. Pan Rozvan asked, in the name of the hospodar, that the prince by his influence and the terror of his name should cause the Khan to prohibit the Budjak Tartars from attacking Wallachia, where they caused fearful losses and devastation every year. The prince answered in elegant Latin that the Budjak Tartars were not over-obedient to the Khan himself; still, since he expected to receive an envoy of the Khan during the coming April, he would remind the Khan through him of the injury done the Wallachians.

Pan Yan had already given a report of his embassy and his journey, together with all he had heard of Hmelnitski and his flight to the Saitch. The prince decided to despatch a few regiments to Kudák, but did not attach great importance to this affair. Since nothing appeared therefore to threaten the peace and power of his domain beyond the Dnieper, festivals and amusements were begun in Lubni by reason of the presence of the envoy Rozvan, also because Bodzynski and Lyassota on the part of the son of the voevoda Pshiyemski had made a formal proposal for the hand of Anna, the elder princess, and had received a favorable answer from the prince and the Princess Griselda.

Volodyovski suffered not a little from this; and when Skshetuski tried to pour consolation into his heart, he answered,--

"It is easy for you to talk; you have but to wish and Anusia Borzobogata will not avoid you. She spoke of you very handsomely all the time. I thought at first that she was rousing the jealousy of Bykhovets; but I see that she was ready to put him on a hook, feeling living sentiment in her heart for you alone."

"Oh! what is Anusia to me? Return to her; I have no objection. But forget Princess Anna, since thinking of her is like wishing to cover the phœnix on its nest with your cap."

"I know she is a phœnix, and therefore I shall surely die of grief for her."

"You'll live and straightway be in love again; but don't fall in love with Princess Barbara, for another son of a voevoda will snatch her away from under your nose."

"Is the heart a servant at command, or can the eyes be stopped from looking at such a wonderful being as Princess Barbara, the sight of whom would be enough to move wild beasts themselves?"

"Well, devil, here is an overcoat for you!" cried Pan Yan. "I see you will console yourself without my help. But I repeat. Go back to Anusia; you will meet with no hindrance from me."

But Anusia was not thinking, in fact, of Volodyovski. Instead of that, her curiosity was roused. She was angry at the indifference of Skshetuski, who on his return from so long an absence did not even look at her. In the evening, when the prince with his chief officers and courtiers came to the drawing-room of the princess to converse, Anusia, looking from behind the shoulder of her mistress (for the princess was tall and Anusia was short), peered with her black eyes into the lieutenant's face, wishing to get at the solution of this riddle. But the eyes of Skshetuski, like his mind, were elsewhere; and when his glance fell on the maiden it was as preoccupied and glassy as if he had never looked upon her, of whom he had once sung,--

"The   Tartar   seizes   people   captive;
Thou seizest captive hearts!"

"What has happened to him?" asked of herself the petted favorite of the whole castle; and stamping with her little foot, she determined to investigate the matter. She didn't love Skshetuski; but accustomed to homage, she was unable to endure neglect, and was ready from very spite to fall in love with the insolent fellow.

Once, when running with skeins of thread for the princess, she met Pan Yan coming out of the bedchamber of the prince. She ran against him like a storm, striking him full in the breast; then springing back, she exclaimed,--

"Oh, how you have frightened me! Good-day, sir!"

"Good-day. Am I such a monster as to terrify you?"

She stood with downcast eyes, began to twist the end of her tresses, and standing first on one foot and then on the other, as if confused, she answered with a smile: "Oh, no! not at all,--sure as I love my mother!" She looked quickly at the lieutenant and dropped her eyes a second time. "Are you angry with me?" asked she.

"I? But could Panna Anna care for my anger?"

"Well, to tell the truth, no. Maybe you think that I would fall to crying at once? Pan Bykhovets is more polite."

"If that is true, there is nothing for me but to leave the field to Pan Bykhovets and vanish from the eyes of Panna Anna."

"Do I prevent you?" Having said this, Anusia blocked the way before him. "You have just returned from the Crimea?" asked she.

"From the Crimea."

"And what have you brought back from the Crimea?"

"I've brought back Pan Podbipienta. You have seen him, I think? A very amiable and excellent cavalier."

"It is sure he is more amiable than you. And why has he come?"

"So there might be some one on whom Panna Anna might try her power. But I advise great care, for I know a secret which makes this cavalier invincible, and Panna Anna can do nothing with him."

"Why is he invincible?"

"He cannot marry."

"What do I care for that? Why can he not marry?"

Skshetuski bent to the ear of the young woman, but said very clearly and emphatically: "He has made a vow of celibacy."

"Oh, you stupid!" cried Anusia, quickly; and at the same moment she shot away like a frightened bird.

That evening, however, she looked for the first time carefully at Pan Longin. The guests were numerous, for the prince gave a farewell dinner to Pan Bodzynski. Our Lithuanian, dressed with care in a white satin tunic and a dark blue velvet coat, had a grand appearance, especially since a light curved sabre hung at his side in a gilded sheath, instead of his death-dealing long sword.

The eyes of Anusia shot their darts at Pan Longin, somewhat on purpose to spite Skshetuski. The lieutenant would not have noticed them, however, had it not been for Volodyovski, who, pushing him with his elbow, said,--

"May captivity strike me if Anusia isn't making up to that Lithuanian hop-pole!"

"Tell him so."

"Of course I will. They will make a pair."

"Yes, he might wear her in place of a button in his coat, such is the proportion between them, or instead of a plume in his cap."

Volodyovski went up to the Lithuanian and said: "It is not long since you arrived, but I see you are getting to be a great rogue."

"How is that, brother? how is that?"

"You have already turned the head of the prettiest girl among the ladies in waiting."

"Oh, my dear friend!" said Podbipienta, clasping his hands together, "what do you tell me?"

"Well, look for yourself at Panna Anusia Borzobogata, with whom we have all fallen in love, and see how she fixes you with her eyes. But look out that she doesn't fool you as she has us!"

When he had said this, Volodyovski turned on his heel and walked off, leaving Podbipienta in meditation. He did not indeed dare to look in the direction of Anusia at once. After a time, however, he cast a quick glance at her, but he trembled. From behind the shoulder of Princess Griselda two shining eyes looked on him steadfastly and curiously. "Avaunt, Satan!" thought the Lithuanian; and he hurried off to the other end of the hall, blushing like a schoolboy.

Still, the temptation was great. That imp, looking from behind the shoulder of the princess, possessed such charm, those eyes shone so clearly, that something drew Pan Longin on to glance at them even once more. But that moment he remembered his vow. Zervikaptur stood before him, his ancestor Stoveiko Podbipienta, the three severed heads,--and terror seized him. He made the sign of the cross, and looked at her no more that evening. But next morning, early, he went to the quarters of Pan Yan.

"Well, Lieutenant, are we going to march soon? What do you hear about the war?"

"You are in great straits. Be patient till you join the regiment."

Pan Podbipienta had not yet been enrolled in the place of the late Zakshevski; he had to wait till the quarter of the year had expired,--till the first of April. But he was in a real hurry; therefore he asked,--

"And has the prince said nothing about this matter?"

"Nothing. The king won't stop thinking of war while he lives, but the Commonwealth does not want it."

"But they say in Chigirin that a Cossack rebellion is threatened."

"It is evident that your vow troubles you greatly. As to a rebellion, you may be sure there will be none till spring; for though the winter is mild, winter is winter. It is now the 15th of February, and frost may come any day. The Cossacks will not take the field till they can intrench themselves behind earthworks; they fight terribly, but in the field they cannot hold their own."

"So one must wait for the Cossacks?"

"Think of this, too, that although you should find your three heads in time of rebellion, it is unknown whether you would be released from your vow; for Crusaders or Turks are one thing, and your own people are another,--children of the same mother, as it were."

"Oh, great God! what a blow you have planted on my head! Here is desperation! Let the priest Mukhovetski relieve me from this doubt, for otherwise I shall not have a moment's rest."

"He will surely solve your doubt, for he is a learned and pious man; but he will not tell you anything else. Civil war is a war of brothers."

"But if a foreign power should come to the aid of the rebels?"

"Then you would have a chance. Meanwhile I can recommend but one thing to you,--wait, and be quiet."

But Skshetuski was unable to follow this advice himself. His melancholy increased continually. He was annoyed by the festivals at the castle, and by those faces on which some time before he gazed with such pleasure. Bodzynski and Rozvan Ursu departed at last, and after their departure profound quiet set in. Life began to flow on monotonously. The prince was occupied with the review of his enormous estates, and every morning shut himself in with his agents, who were arriving from all Rus and Sandomir, so that even military exercises took place but rarely. The noisy feasts of the officers, at which future wars were discussed, wearied Skshetuski beyond measure; so he used to go out with a gun on his shoulder to Solonitsa, where Jolkefski had inflicted such terrible defeats on Nalivaika, Loboda, and Krempski. The traces of these battles had already disappeared from the memory of men, and the field of conflict; but from time to time the earth cast up from its bosom whitened bones, and beyond the water was visible the Cossack breastwork from behind which the Zaporojians of Loboda and the volunteers of Nalivaika had made such a desperate defence. But a dense grove had already spread its roots over the breastwork. That was the place where Skshetuski hid himself from the noise of the castle; and instead of shooting at birds he fell into meditation, and before the eyes of his spirit stood the form of the beloved maiden called hither by his memory and his heart. There in the mist, the rustle of the reeds, and the melancholy of those places he found solace in his own yearning.

But later on began abundant rains, the harbinger of spring. Solonitsa became a morass; it was difficult to put one's head from under the roof. The lieutenant was deprived, therefore, even of the comfort which he had found in wandering about alone; and immediately his disquiet began to increase, and justly. He had hoped at first that the princess would come immediately with Helena to Lubni, if she could only succeed in sending Bogun away; but now that hope vanished. The wet weather had destroyed the roads; the steppe for many miles on both sides of the Sula had become an enormous quagmire, which could not be crossed till the warm sun of spring should suck out the superfluous water.

All this time Helena would have to remain under guardianship in which Skshetuski had no trust, in a real den of wolves, among wild, uncouth people, ill disposed to him. They had, it is true, to keep faith for their own sake, and really they had no other choice; but who could guess what they might invent, what they might venture upon, especially when they were pressed by the terrible Bogun, whom they seemed both to love and fear? It would be easy for Bogun to force them to yield up the girl, for similar deeds were not rare. In this way Loboda, the comrade of the ill-starred Nalivaika, had forced Pani Poplinska to give him her foster-daughter as wife, although she was of good family and hated the Cossack with her whole soul. And if what was said of the immeasurable wealth of Bogun were true, he might remunerate them for the girl and the loss of Rozlogi. And then what? "Then," thought Pan Yan, "they will tell me with a sneer, 'Your lash is lost,' they will vanish into some Lithuanian or Mazovian wilderness, where even the hand of the prince cannot reach them."

Skshetuski shook as if in a fever at the thought, and was impatient as a chained wolf, regretted the word of honor he had given the princess, and knew not what to do. He was a man who was unwilling to let chance pull him on by the beard. There was great energy and enterprise in his nature. He did not wait for what fate would give, he chose to take fate by the shoulder and force it to give him good fortune; hence it was more difficult for him than any other man to sit with folded hands in Lubni. He resolved, therefore, to act. He had a young lad in waiting, Jendzian, from Podlesia,--sixteen years old, but a most cunning rogue, whom no old fox could out-trick,--and he determined to send him to Helena at once to discover everything.

February was at an end; the rains had ceased. March appeared rather favorable, and the roads must have improved a little. Jendzian got ready for the journey, Skshetuski provided him with paper, pens, and a bottle of ink, which he commanded him to guard as the eye in his head, for he remembered that those things were not to be had at Rozlogi. The young fellow was not to tell from whom he came, but to pretend that he was going to Chigirin, to keep a sharp eye on everything, and especially to find out carefully where Bogun was, and what he was doing. Jendzian did not wait to have his instructions repeated; he stuck his cap on the side of his head, cracked his whip, and was off.

Dreary days of waiting set in for Skshetuski. To kill time, he occupied himself in sword exercise with Volodyovski, who was a great master in this art, or hurled javelins at a ring. There happened in Lubni also something which came near costing the lieutenant his life. One day a bear, having broken away from his chain, wounded two stable-boys, frightened the horse of Pan Hlebovski, the commissary, and finally rushed on the lieutenant, who was on his way to the prince at the armory without a sabre, and had only a light stick with a brass knob in his hand. He would have perished undoubtedly, had it not been for Pan Longin, who, seeing from the armory what was passing, rushed for his long sword, and hurried to the rescue. Pan Longin showed himself a worthy descendant of his ancestor Stoveiko in the full sense, for with one blow he swept off the front half of the bear's head, together with his paw, before the eyes of the whole court. This proof of extraordinary strength was seen from the window by the prince himself, who took Pan Longin afterward to the apartments of the princess, where Anusia Borzobogata so tempted him with her eyes that next morning he had to go to confession, and for three days following he did not show himself in the castle until by earnest prayer he had expelled every temptation.

Ten days had passed, and no sign of Jendzian. Skshetuski had grown so thin from waiting and so wretched-looking that Anusia began to ask, through messengers, what the matter was, and Carboni, physician of the princess, prescribed an herb for melancholy. But he needed another remedy; for he was thinking of his princess day and night, and with each moment he felt more clearly that no trivial feeling had nestled in his heart, but a great love which must be satisfied, or his breast would burst like a weak vessel.

It is easy to imagine, then, the gladness of Pan Yan when one morning about daybreak Jendzian entered his room covered with mud, weary, thin, but joyful, and with good news written on his forehead. The lieutenant tore himself from the bed, rushed to the youth, caught him by the shoulder, and cried,--

"Have you a letter?"

"I have. Here it is."

The lieutenant tore it open and began to read. For a long time he had been in doubt whether in the most favorable event Jendzian would bring a letter, for he was not sure that Helena knew how to write. Women in the country were uneducated, and Helena was reared among illiterate people. It was evident now that her father had taught her to write, for she had sent a long letter on four pages of paper. The poor girl didn't know how to express herself elegantly or rhetorically, but she wrote straight from the heart, as follows:--

"Indeed I shall never forget you. You will forget me sooner, for I hear that there are deceivers among you. But since you have sent your lad on purpose so many miles, it is evident that I am dear to you as you are to me, for which I thank you with a grateful heart. Do not think that it is not against my feeling of modesty to write thus to you about loving; but it is better to tell the truth, than to lie or dissemble when there is something altogether different in the heart. I have asked Jendzian what you are doing in Lubni, and what are the customs at a great castle; and when he told me about the beauty and comeliness of the young ladies there, I began to cry from sorrow "--

Here the lieutenant stopped reading and asked Jendzian: "What did you tell her, you dunce?"

"Everything good," answered Jendzian.

The lieutenant read on:--

--"for how could I, ignorant girl, be equal to them? But your servant told me that you wouldn't look at any of them"--

"You answered well," said the lieutenant.

Jendzian didn't know what the question was, for the lieutenant read to himself; but he put on a wise look and coughed significantly. Skshetuski read on:--

--"and I immediately consoled myself, begging God to keep you for the future in such feeling for me and to bless us both,--Amen. I have also yearned for you as if for my mother; for it is sad for me, orphan in the world, when not near you. God sees that my heart is clean; anything else comes from my want of experience, which you must forgive."

Farther on in the letter, the charming princess wrote that she and her aunt would come to Lubni as soon as the roads were better, and that the old princess herself wanted to hasten the journey, for tidings were coming from Chigirin of Cossack disturbances. She was only waiting for the return of her sons, who had gone to Boguslav to the horse-fair.

"You are a real wizard [wrote Helena] to be able to win my aunt to your side."

Here the lieutenant smiled, for he remembered the means which he was forced to use in winning her aunt. The letter ended with assurances of unbroken and true love such as a future wife owed her husband. And in general a genuine good heart was evident in it. Therefore the lieutenant read the affectionate letter several times from beginning to end, repeating to himself in spirit, "My dear girl, may God forsake me if I ever abandon you!"

Then he began to examine Jendzian on every point.

The cunning lad gave him a detailed account of the whole journey. He was received politely. The old princess made inquiries of him concerning the lieutenant, and learning that he was a famous knight, a confidant of the prince, and a man of property besides, she was glad.

"She asked me, too," said Jendzian, "if you always keep your word when you make a promise, and I answered, 'My noble lady, if the Wallachian horse on which I have come had been promised me, I should be sure he wouldn't escape me.'"

"You are a rogue," said the lieutenant; "but since you have given such bonds for me, you may keep the horse. You made no pretences, then,--you said that I sent you?"

"Yes, for I saw that I might; and I was still better received, especially by the young lady, who is so wonderful that there isn't another like her in the world. When she knew that I came from you, she didn't know where to seat me; and if it hadn't been a time of fast, I should have been really in heaven. While reading your letter she shed tears of delight."

The lieutenant was silent from joy, too, and after a moment asked again: "But did you hear nothing of that fellow Bogun?"

"I didn't get to ask the old lady or the young princess about him, but I gained the confidence of Chehly, the old Tartar, who, though a pagan, is a faithful servant of the young lady. He said they were all very angry at you, but became reconciled afterward, when they discovered that the reports of Bogun's treasures were fables."

"How did they discover that?"

"Well, you see, this is how it was. They had a dispute with the Sivinskis which they bound themselves to settle by payment. When the time came, they went to Bogun with, 'Lend us money!' 'I have some Turkish goods,' said he, 'but no money; for what I had I squandered.' When they heard this, they dropped him, and their affection turned to you."

"It must be said that you have found out everything well."

"If I had found out one thing and neglected another, then you might say that you would give me the horse, but not the saddle; and what is the horse without a saddle?"

"Well, well, take the saddle too."

"Thank you most humbly. They sent Bogun off to Pereyasláv immediately. When I found that out, I thought to myself, 'Why shouldn't I push on to Pereyasláv? My master will be satisfied with me, and a uniform will come to me the sooner.'"

"You'll get it next quarter. So you were in Pereyasláv?"

"I was, but didn't find Bogun. Old Colonel Loboda is sick. They say Bogun will succeed him soon. But something strange is going on. Hardly a handful of Cossacks have remained in the regiment; the others, they say, have gone after Bogun, or run away to the Saitch; and this is very important, for some rebellion is on foot. I wanted to know something certain about Bogun, but all they told me was that he had crossed to the Russian bank, [7] 'Well,' thought I, 'if that is true, then our princess is safe from him;' and I returned."

"You did well. Had you any adventures on the road?"

"No, but I want awfully to eat something."

Jendzian went out; and the lieutenant, being alone, began to read Helena's letter again, and to press to his lips those characters that were not so shapely as the hand that had penned them. Confidence entered his heart, and he thought,--

"The road will soon dry, if God gives good weather. The Kurtsevichi, too, knowing that Bogun has nothing, will be sure not to betray me. I will leave Rozlogi to them, and add something of my own to get that dear little star."

He dressed with a bright face, and with a bosom full of happiness went to the chapel to thank God humbly for the good news.

CHAPTER VI.

Over the whole Ukraine and beyond the Dnieper strange sounds began to spread like the heralds of a coming tempest; certain wonderful tidings flew from village to village, from farmhouse to farmhouse,--like those plants which the breezes of spring push along the steppes, and which the people call field-rollers. In the towns there were whispers of some great war, though no man knew who was going to make war, nor against whom. Still the tidings were told. The faces of people became unquiet. The tiller of the soil went with his plough to the field unwillingly, though the spring had come early, mild and warm, and long since the larks had been singing over the steppes. Every evening people gathered in crowds in the villages, and standing on the road, talked in undertones of terrible things. Blind men wandering around with lyres and songs were asked for news. Some persons thought they saw in the night-time reflections in the sky, and that a moon redder than usual rose from behind the pine woods. Disaster or the death of the king was predicted. And all this was the more wonderful, since fear found no easy approach to those lands, long accustomed to disturbances, conflicts, and raids. Some exceptionally ominous currents must have been playing in the air, since the alarm had become universal.

It was the more oppressive and stifling, because no one was able to point out the danger. But among the signs of evil omen, two especially seemed to show that really something was impending. First, an unheard-of multitude of old minstrels appeared in all the villages and towns, and among them were forms strange, and known to no one; these, it was whispered, were counterfeit minstrels. These men, strolling about everywhere, told with an air of mystery that the day of God's judgment and anger was near. Secondly, the men of the lower country began to drink with all their might.

The second sign was the more serious. The Saitch, confined within too narrow limits, was unable to feed all its inhabitants; expeditions were not always successful; besides, the steppes yielded no bread to the Cossacks. In time of peace, therefore, a multitude of Zaporojians scattered themselves yearly over the inhabited districts. The Ukraine, and indeed all Russia, was full of them. Some rose to be land stewards; some sold liquor on the highways; some labored in hamlets and towns, in trade and industry. In every village there was sure to be a cottage on one side, at a distance from the rest, in which a Zaporojian dwelt. Some of them had brought their wives with them, and kept house in these cottages. But the Zaporojian, as a man who usually had passed through every experience, was generally a benefactor to the village in which he lived. There were no better blacksmiths, wheelwrights, tanners, wax-refiners, fishermen, and hunters than they. The Cossack understood everything, did everything; he built a house, he sewed a saddle. But the Cossacks were not always such quiet inhabitants, for they lived a temporary life. Whoever wished to carry out a decision with armed hand, to make an attack on a neighbor, or to defend himself from an expected attack, had only to raise the cry, and straightway the Cossacks hurried to him like ravens to a ready spoil. The nobility and magnates, involved in endless disputes among themselves, employed the Cossacks. When there was a lack of such undertakings the Cossacks stayed quietly in the villages, working with all diligence, earning their daily bread in the sweat of their brows.

They would continue in this fashion for a year or two, till sudden tidings came of some great expedition, either of an ataman against the Tartars or the Poles, or of Polish noblemen against Wallachia; and that moment the wheelwrights, blacksmiths, tanners, and wax-refiners would desert their peaceful occupations, and begin to drink with all their might in every dram-shop of the Ukraine. After they had drunk away everything, they would drink on credit,--not on what they had, but on what they would have. Future booty must pay for the frolic.

This phenomenon was repeated so regularly that after a while people of experience in the Ukraine used to say; "The dram-shops are bursting with men from below; something is on foot in the Ukraine."

The starostas strengthened the garrisons in the castles at once, looking carefully to everything; the magnates increased their retinues; the nobility sent their wives and children to the towns.

That spring the Cossacks began to drink as never before, squandering at random all they had earned, not in one district, not in one province, but throughout all Russia,--the length and the breadth of it.

Something was on foot, indeed, though the men from below had no idea of what it was. People had begun to speak of Hmelnitski, of his flight to the Saitch, of the men from Cherkasi, Boguslav, Korsún, and other places who had followed him; but something else was talked of too. For years reports had been current of a great war with the Pagans,--a war desired by the king to give booty to the Cossacks, but opposed by the Poles. This time all reports were blended, and roused in the brains of men uneasiness and the expectation of something uncommon.

This uneasiness penetrated the walls of Lubni also. It was not proper to shut one's eyes to such signs, and Prince Yeremi especially had not that habit. In his domain the disturbance did not really come to an outbreak, fear kept all within bounds; but for some time reports had been coming from the Ukraine, that here and there peasants were beginning to resist the nobles, that they were killing Jews, that they wished to force their own enrolment for war against the Pagans, and that the number of deserters to the Saitch was increasing continually.

The prince sent envoys in various directions,--to Pan Pototski, to Pan Kalinovski, to Loboda in Pereyasláv,--and collected in person the herds from the steppes and the troops from the outposts. Meantime peaceful news was brought. The Grand Hetman communicated all that he knew concerning Hmelnitski; he did not think, however, that any storm could rise out of the affair. The full hetman wrote that the rabble were accustomed "to bustle in spring like bees," Zatsvilikhovski was the only man who sent a letter imploring the prince to underestimate nothing, for a mighty storm was coming on from the Wilderness. He wrote that Hmelnitski had hurried to the Crimea to ask assistance of the Khan.

"And as friends from the Saitch inform me," wrote he, "the koshevoi is collecting the army, horse and foot, from all the meadows and streams, telling no one why he does it. I think, therefore, that this storm will come on us. If it comes with Tartar aid, then God save all Russian lands from ruin!"

The prince had more confidence in Zatsvilikhovski than in the hetmans, for he knew that no one in all Russia had such knowledge of the Cossacks and their devices as he. He determined, therefore, to concentrate as many troops as possible, and also to get to the bottom of the truth.

One morning he summoned to his presence the lieutenant of the Wallachian regiment, Pan Bykhovets, to whom he said,--

"You will go for me to the Saitch on a mission to the koshevoi, and give him this letter with the seal of my lordship. But that you may know what plan of action to follow, I tell you this letter is a pretext, and the whole meaning of the mission lies in your own wit. You are to see everything that is done there,--what troops they have assembled, and whether they are assembling more. I enjoin you specially to win some people to your person, and find out for me carefully all about Hmelnitski,--where he is, and if it is true that he has gone to the Crimea to ask aid of the Tartars. Do you understand what I say?"

"As if it had been written on the palm of my hand."

"You will go by Chigirin. Rest but one night on the way. When you arrive, go to Zatsvilikhovski for letters, which you will deliver secretly to his friends in the Saitch. They will tell you all they know. From Chigirin you will go by water to Kudák. Give my respects with this letter to Pan Grodzitski. He will issue orders to convey you over the Cataracts by proper guides. Be fearless in the Saitch, keep your eyes and ears open, and come back if you survive, for the expedition is no easy one."

"Your Highness is the steward of my blood. Shall I take many men?"

"You will take forty attendants. Start to-day; before evening come for further instructions. Your mission is important."

Pan Bykhovets went out rejoicing. In the antechamber he met Skshetuski with some artillery officers.

"Well, what is going on?" asked they.

"I take the road to-day."

"Where, where?"

"To Chigirin, and from there farther on."

"Then come with me," said Pan Yan.

And taking him to his quarters, he began to tease him to transfer his mission to him.

"As my friend," said he, "ask what you like,--a Turkish horse, an Arab steed,--you shall have one. I'll spare nothing if I can only go, for my soul is rushing out in that direction. If you want money I'll give it, if you will only yield. The trip will bring you no glory; for if war breaks out it will begin here, and you may be killed in the Saitch. I know, too, that Anusia is as dear to you as to others; if you go they will get her away from you."

This last argument went home to the mind of Pan Bykhovets more than any other, but still he resisted. What would the prince say if he should withdraw? Wouldn't he take it ill of him? An appointment like this was such a favor.

Hearing this, Skshetuski rushed off to the prince and directed the page at once to announce him.

The page returned soon with the answer that the prince permitted him to enter.

The lieutenant's heart beat like a hammer, from fear that he should hear a curt "No!" after which he would be obliged to let the matter drop entirely.

"Well, what have you to say?" asked the prince, looking at the lieutenant.

Skshetuski bent down to his feet.

"Mighty prince, I have come to implore you most humbly to intrust me with the expedition to the Saitch. Bykhovets would give it up, perhaps, for he is my friend, and to me it is as important as life. Bykhovets' only fear is that you may be angry with him for yielding the place."

"As God lives!" said the prince, "I should have sent no one else, but I thought you would not like to go just after returning from a long journey."

"I should rejoice to be sent even every day in that direction."

The prince looked at him very attentively with his black eyes, and after a while inquired: "What have you got there?"

The lieutenant grew confused, like a culprit unable to bear a searching glance.

"I must tell the truth, I see," said he, "since no secret can stand before your reason. Of one thing I am not sure,--your favorable hearing."

Thereupon he began to tell how he had become acquainted with the daughter of Prince Vassily, had fallen in love with her and would like to visit her, and on his return from the Saitch to Lubni to remove and save her from Cossack turmoil and the importunities of Bogun. But he said nothing of the machinations of the old princess, for in this he was bound by his word. He began then to beg the prince so earnestly to give him the mission confided to Bykhovets, that Vishnyevetski said,--

"I should permit you to go on your own account and give you men; but since you have planned everything so cleverly that your personal affection agrees with your office, I must arrange this affair for you."

Then he clapped his hands and commanded the page to call Pan Bykhovets.

The lieutenant kissed the prince's hand with joy. Yeremi took him by the head and commanded him to be quiet. He loved Skshetuski beyond measure as a splendid soldier and officer whom he could trust in all things. Besides, there was between them that bond which is formed between a subordinate reverencing his chief with his whole soul and a chief who feels this clearly. There were not a few courtiers and flatterers who circled around the prince for their own profit; but the eagle eye of Yeremi knew well whom to choose. He knew that Pan Yan was a man without blemish; he valued him, and was grateful to him for his feelings. He rejoiced, too, that his favorite had fallen in love with the daughter of the old servant of the Vishnyevetskis, Vassily Kurtsevich, whose memory was the dearer because of its sadness.

"It was not from ungratefulness to the prince," said he, "that I made no inquiry concerning his daughter. Since the guardians did not visit Lubni, and I received no complaint against them, I supposed they were good people. But as you have put me in mind of the lady, I will care for her as for my own daughter."

Skshetuski, hearing this, could not admire sufficiently the kindness of the prince, who reproached himself, notwithstanding the multitude of his occupations, with inattention to the child of his former soldier and official.

Bykhovets now came in.

"Well," said the prince, "my word is given, and if you wish to go you will go; but I ask you to do this for me: yield your mission to Skshetuski,--he has his own special and solid reasons for wanting it,--and I will think of another reward for you."

"Oh, your Highness," said Bykhovets, "your favor is great; for while able to command, you ask that which if I refused to give I should be unworthy of your favor."

"Thank your friend," said the prince, turning to Pan Yan, "and prepare for the road."

Skshetuski thanked Bykhovets heartily indeed, and in a few hours he was ready. For some time it had been irksome for him in Lubni, and this expedition accorded with all his wishes. First, he was to see Helena. True, he had to go from her for a long time; but just such an interval was needed to make the roads passable for wheels, after such measureless rains. The princess and Helena could not come earlier to Lubni. Skshetuski therefore must either wait in Lubni or live at Rozlogi,--which would be against his covenant with the princess, and, what was more, rouse the suspicions of Bogun. Helena could be really safe against his attacks only in Lubni; but since she must in every case wait some time yet in Rozlogi, it appeared best to Pan Yan to depart, and on his return take her under the protection of the armed power of the prince. Having settled the matter thus, the lieutenant hastened his journey,--got everything ready, took letters and instructions from the prince, money for expenses from the treasurer, and made a good start over the road before night, having with him Jendzian and forty horsemen from the Cossack regiment.

CHAPTER VII.

It was now the second half of March; the grass was growing luxuriantly, the field-roller was blooming, the steppe was stirring with life. In the morning the lieutenant, travelling at the head of his men, rode as if over a sea whose moving wave was the wind-stirred grass. Every place was filled with joy and the voices of spring,--chirruping, whistling, clattering, the shaking of wings, the glad hum of insects; the steppe sounded like a lyre touched by the hand of the Lord. Above the heads of the horsemen floated falcons motionless in the blue ether, like suspended crosses, triangles of wild geese, lines of storks; and on the ground the coursing of flocks run wild. Behold, a herd of steppe horses rush on! They move like a storm, stop before the mounted men in a half-circle suddenly, as if spiked to the earth, their manes spread to the wind, their nostrils dilated, their eyes full of wonder. You would say they are here to trample the unbidden guests. But a moment more they are gone, vanishing as suddenly as they came. Now we have only the sound of the grass and the gleam of the flowers; the clatter is still. Again nothing is heard save the play of birds. The land seems full of joy; yet a kind of sadness is in that joy. It seems crowded, and it is an empty land. Oh, it is wide, and it is roomy! With a horse you cannot surround it; in thought you cannot grasp it,--unless you love the sadness, the desert, and the steppes, and with yearning soul circle above them, linger upon their gravemounds, hearken to their voices, and give answer.

It was early morning. Great drops glittered on the grass and reeds; the quick movement of the wind dried the ground, on which after the rains broad ponds were spread, like lakes shining in the sun. The retinue of the lieutenant moved on slowly, for it was difficult to hasten when the horses sank to their knees at times in the soft earth; and he gave them only short resting-spells on the grave-mounds, for he was hastening to a greeting and a parting.

The second day, about noon, after he had passed a strip of forest, he saw the windmills of Rozlogi scattered on the hillsides and mounds. His heart beat like a hammer. No one there expected him; no one knew he was coming. What will she say when she sees him? Now he beholds the cottages of the neighbors, nearly hidden, covered in the cherry-orchards; farther on is a straggling village of cottages; and still farther is seen the well-sweep on the square in front of the house. The lieutenant, putting spurs to his horse, galloped swiftly; and after him flew his suite through the village with a clatter and a noise. Here and there a peasant, rushing out of his cottage, made a sign of the cross. Devils!--not devils? Tartars!--not Tartars? The mud spatters from under their hoofs so that you don't know who is hurrying on. Meanwhile they are at the square, and have halted before the closed gate.

"Hallo there! Who lives, open!"

The bustle and pounding, the barking of dogs, called out the people from the house. They hurried to the gate frightened, thinking it was an attack.

"Who goes?"

"Open!"

"The princes are not at home."

"But open, you son of an infidel! We are from the prince at Lubni."

The servants at last recognized Skshetuski. "Oh, that is you! Right away! right away!"

The gate was thrown open. Then the princess herself appeared before the entrance, and shading her eyes with her hand, looked at the new-comers.

Skshetuski sprang from his horse, and coming up to her said: "Don't you know me?"

"Oh! that is you. Lieutenant. I thought it was a Tartar raid. I salute you and beg you to enter."

"You wonder, no doubt," said Pan Yan, "at seeing me in Rozlogi. Still I have not broken my word, for the prince sends me to Chigirin and farther. He asked me also to stop at Rozlogi and inquire for your health."

"I am thankful to his Highness. Does he think of driving us from Rozlogi soon?"

"He doesn't think of it at all, for he knows of no cause to drive you out; and what I have said will take place. You will remain in Rozlogi; I have bread enough of my own."

Hearing this, the princess grew good-humored at once, and said: "Be seated, and be as glad as I am to see you."

"Is Princess Helena well? Where is she?"

"I know you. You have not come to see me, my cavalier. She is in good health, she is well; the girl has improved in appearance. But I'll call her to you this minute, and I'll dress a little myself, for I am ashamed to receive guests in this gown."

The princess was wearing a faded dress, with a fur coat outside, and heavy boots.

At this moment Helena, though not called, rushed into the room; for she had heard from the old Tartar, Chehly, who the visitor was. She ran in panting, and red as a cherry, barely able to catch her breath, but her eyes were laughing from happiness and joy. Skshetuski sprang to her hand, and when the princess had withdrawn discreetly, kissed her on the lips, for he was an impulsive man. She did not defend herself vigorously, feeling that weakness had come upon her from an overflow of happiness and joy.

"I did not expect to see you," whispered she, half closing her eyes. "But don't kiss me that way, for it isn't proper."

"Why shouldn't I kiss when honey is not half so sweet? I thought I should wither away without you, till the prince himself sent me here."

"What does the prince know?"

"I told him all, and he was glad when he remembered your father. Oh, you must have given me some herb, my girl, for I cannot see the light of day on account of you."

"Your blindness is a favor from God."

"But do you remember that omen which the falcon gave when she drew our hands together? It was destiny beyond a doubt."

"I remember."

"When at Lubni I used to go from sadness to Solonitsa and see you there just as if present, if I stretched forth my hand you disappeared; but you will not escape me again, for I think that nothing will stand in our way now."

"If anything does, it will not be my will."

"Tell me again that you love me."

Helena dropped her eyes, but answered with dignity and decision: "As nobody in the world."

"If any one should surround me with honor and gold, I should prefer those words of yours; for I feel that you speak the truth, though I do not know why I deserve such favor from you."

"Because you had pity on me, drew me to you, took my part, and spoke words such as I had never heard before."

Helena was silent from emotion, and the lieutenant began again to kiss her hand.

"You will be my ruler, not my wife."

They were silent for a while, but he did not take his eyes from her, wishing to make up for the long time in which he had not seen her. She seemed to him more beautiful than before. In that dim room, in the sunlight broken into rays by the glass window-panes, she looked like those pictures of holy virgins in dusky chapels. At the same time such warmth and life surrounded her, so many splendid womanly graces and charms were pictured in her face and whole form, that it was possible to lose one's head, fall desperately in love with her, and love forever.

"I shall lose my sight from your beauty," said the lieutenant.

The white teeth of the princess glittered joyously in a smile. "Undoubtedly Anusia Borzobogata is a hundred times better looking than I!"

"She is to you as a pewter plate to the moon."

"But Jendzian told me a different story."

"Jendzian deserves a slap on the mouth. What do I care for her? Let other bees take honey from that flower, and there are plenty of them there."

Further conversation was interrupted by the entrance of old Chehly, who came to greet the lieutenant. He looked on him already as his future master, and he bowed to him at the threshold, giving the salaam in Oriental fashion.

"Well, old Chehly, I take you too with your mistress. You will serve her till you die."

"She won't have long to wait for my death; but while I live I will serve her. God is one!"

"In a month or so, when I return from the Saitch, we will go to Lubni," said the lieutenant, turning to Helena; "and there Mukhovetski is ready with his robes."

Helena was startled. "Then you are going to the Saitch?"

"The prince sends me with letters. But have no fear; the person of an envoy is sacred, even among pagans. I should send you and the princess immediately to Lubni, but the roads are fearful. Even on horseback it is hard to get along."

"Will you stay long in Rozlogi?"

"I leave this evening for Chigirin. The sooner I go the sooner I shall return. Besides, it is the prince's service; neither my time nor will is at my disposal."

"Will you come to dinner, if you have had enough of billing and cooing?" said the princess, coming in. "Ho! ho! the young woman's cheeks are red; 'tis evident you have not been idle, sir! Well, I'm not surprised at you."

Saying this, she stroked Helena affectionately on the shoulder, and they went to dinner. The princess was in perfectly good humor. She had given up Bogun long ago, and all was arranged now, owing to the liberality of the lieutenant, so that she could look on Rozlogi, "with its pine woods, forests, boundaries, and inhabitants," as belonging to her and her sons,--no small property, indeed.

The lieutenant asked for the princes,--whether they would return soon.

"I expect them every day. They were angry at first with you, but afterward, when they scrutinized your acts, they conceived a great affection for you as their future relative; for in truth it is difficult in these mild times to find a man of such daring."

After dinner the lieutenant and Helena went to the cherry orchard, which came up to the ditch beyond the square. The orchard was covered with early white blossoms as if with snow; beyond the orchard was a dark oak grove in which a cuckoo was heard.

"That is a happy augury for us," said Skshetuski, "but we must make the inquiry." And turning to the oak grove, he asked: "Good cuckoo, how many years shall I live in marriage with this lady?"

The cuckoo began to call, and counted fifty and more.

"God grant it!"

"The cuckoo always tells the truth," remarked Helena.

"If that's the case, I'll ask another question," said the enamoured lieutenant.

"No, it is not necessary."

In converse and merriment like this the day passed as a dream. In the evening came the moment of tender and long parting, and the lieutenant set out for Chigirin.

CHAPTER VIII.

In Chigirin, Skshetuski found the old man Zatsvilikhovski in great excitement and fever. He looked impatiently at the prince's envoy, for tidings more and more terrible kept coming from the Saitch. There was no doubt that Hmelnitski was preparing to demand with armed hand justice for himself and the ancient rights of the Cossacks. Zatsvilikhovski had news that he had been with the Khan in the Crimea to beg Tartar aid, with which he was expected every day in the Saitch. Then there would be a general campaign from the lower country against the Commonwealth, which with Tartar assistance might be destructive. The storm drew nearer and nearer, more definite and more terrible. It was no longer vague undefined alarm that swept over the Ukraine, but clear certainty of slaughter and war. The Grand Hetman, who at first had made light of the whole affair, was pushing forward with his troops to Cherkasi. The advance guard of the royal armies was advancing mainly to prevent desertion; for the Cossacks of the towns, and the mob had begun to flee to the Saitch in masses. The nobility assembled in the towns. It was said that the general militia were to be called out in the southern provinces. Some, not waiting for the call, sent their wives and children to castles, and assembled in person at Cherkasi. The ill-fated Ukraine was divided into two parties,--one of these hastened to the Saitch, the other to the royal camp; one declared for the existing order of affairs, the other for wild freedom; one desired to keep possession of that which was the fruit of ages of labor, the other desired to deprive these possessors of that property. Both were to imbrue fraternal hands in the blood of each other. The terrible dispute, before it found religious rallying-cries which were completely foreign to the lower country, was breaking out as a social war.

But though black clouds were gathering on the heaven of the Ukraine, though a dark and ominous night was descending from these clouds, though within them it rumbled and roared and thunder-claps rolled from horizon to horizon, people still could not tell to what degree the storm would burst forth. Perhaps even Hmelnitski himself could not,--Hmelnitski, who had just sent letters to Pan Pototski, to the Cossack commissioner, and to the royal standard-bearer, full of accusation and complaints, and at the same time of assurances of loyalty to Vladislav IV. and the Commonwealth. Did he wish to win time, or did he suppose that some agreement might yet end the dispute? On this there was a variety of opinions. There were only two men who did not deceive themselves for a single moment. These men were Zatsvilikhovski and Barabash.

The old colonel had also received a letter from Hmelnitski. The letter was sarcastic, threatening, and full of abuse. Hmelnitski wrote:--

"We shall begin, with the whole Zaporojian army, to beg most fervently and to ask for that charter of rights which you secreted. And because you secreted it for your own personal profit and advantage, the whole Zaporojian army creates you a colonel over sheep or swine, but not over men. I beg pardon if in any way I failed to please you in my poor house in Chigirin on the feast-day of Saint Nicholas, and that I went off to the Zaporojie without your knowledge or permission."

"Do you see," said Barabash to Zatsvilikhovski and Pan Yan, "how he ridicules me? Yet it was I who taught him war, and was in truth a father to him."

"He says, then, that the whole Zaporojian army will demand their rights," said Zatsvilikhovski. "That is simply a civil war, of all wars the most terrible."

"I see that I must hasten," said Skshetuski. "Give me the letters to those men with whom I am to come in contact."

"You have one to the koshevoi ataman?"

"I have, from the prince himself."

"I will give you a letter to one of the kuren atamans. Barabash has a relative there,--Barabash also. From these you will learn everything. Who knows, though, but it is too late for such an expedition? Does the prince wish to hear what is really to be heard there? The answer is brief: 'Evil!' And he wants to know what to do? Short advice: 'Collect as many troops as possible and join the hetmans.'"

"Despatch a messenger, then, to the prince with the answer and the advice," said Skshetuski. "I must go; for I am on a mission, and I cannot alter the decision of the prince."

"Are you aware that this is a terribly dangerous expedition?" asked Zatsvilikhovski. "Even here the people are so excited that it is difficult for them to keep still. Were it not for the nearness of the army of the crown, the mob would rush upon us. But there you are going into the dragon's mouth."

"Jonah was in the whale's belly, not his mouth, and with God's aid he came out in safety."

"Go, then! I applaud your courage. You can go to Kudák in safety, and there you will see what is to be done further. Grodzitski is an old soldier; he will give you the best of advice. And I will go to the prince without fail. If I have to fight in my old age, I would rather fight under him than any one else. Meanwhile I will get boats for you, and guides who will take you to Kudák."

Skshetuski slipped out, and went straight to his quarters on the square, in the prince's house, to make his final preparations. In spite of the dangers of the journey mentioned by Zatsvilikhovski, the lieutenant thought of it not without a certain satisfaction. He was going to behold the Dnieper in its whole length, almost to the lower country and the Cataracts; and for the warrior of that time it was a sort of enchanted and mysterious land, to which every adventurous spirit was drawn. Many a man had passed his whole life in the Ukraine, and still was unable to say that he had seen the Saitch,--unless he wished to join the Brotherhood, and there were fewer volunteers among the nobility than formerly. The times of Samek Zborovski had passed never to return. The break between the Saitch and the Commonwealth which began in the time of Nalivaika and Pavlyuk had not lessened, but, on the contrary, had increased continually; and the concourse of people of family, not only Polish, but Russian, differing from the men of the lower country neither in speech nor faith, had greatly decreased. Such persons as the Bulygi Kurtsevichi did not find many imitators. In general, nobles were forced into the Brotherhood at that time either by misfortune or outlawry,--in a word, by offences which were inconvenient for repentance. Therefore a certain mystery, impenetrable as the fogs of the Dnieper, surrounded the predatory republic of the lower country. Concerning it men related wonders, which Pan Yan was curious to see with his own eyes. To tell the truth, he expected to come out of it safely; for an envoy is an envoy, especially from Prince Yeremi.

While meditating in this fashion he gazed through the windows into the square. Meanwhile one hour had followed another, when suddenly it appeared to Pan Yan that he recognized a couple of figures going toward the Bell-ringers' Corner to the wine-cellar of Dopula, the Wallachian. He looked more carefully, and saw Zagloba with Bogun. They went arm in arm, and soon disappeared in the dark doorway over which was the sign denoting a drinking-place and a wine-shop.

The lieutenant was astonished at the presence of Bogun in Chigirin and his friendship with Zagloba.

"Jendzian! are you here?" called he to his attendant.

Jendzian appeared in the doorway of the adjoining room.

"Listen to me, Jendzian! Go to the wine-shop where the sign hangs. You will find a fat nobleman with a hole in his forehead there. Tell him that some one wants to see him quickly. If he asks who it is, don't tell him."

Jendzian hurried off, and in a short time Skshetuski saw him returning in company with Zagloba.

"I welcome you," said Pan Yan, when the noble appeared in the door of the room. "Do you remember me?"

"Do I remember you? May the Tartars melt me into tallow and make candles of me for the mosques if I forget you! Some months ago you opened the door at Dopula's with Chaplinski, which suited my taste exactly, for in the selfsame way I got out of prison once in Stamboul. And what is Pan Povsinoga, with the escutcheon Zervipludry, doing with his innocence and his sword? Don't the sparrows always perch on his head, taking him for a withered tree?"

"Pan Podbipienta is well, and asked to be remembered to you."

"He is a very rich man, but fearfully dull. If he should cut off three heads like his own, it would be only a head and a half, for he would cut off three half-heads. Pshaw! how hot it is, though it is only March yet! The tongue dries up in one's throat."

"I have some excellent triple mead; maybe you would take a glass of it?"

"It is a fool who refuses when a wise man offers. The barber has enjoined me to drink mead to draw melancholy from my head. Troublesome times for the nobility are approaching,--*dies iræ et calamitatis.* Chaplinski is breathless from fear; he visits Dopula's no longer, for the Cossack elders drink there. I alone set my forehead bravely against danger, and keep company with those colonels, though their dignity smells of tar. Good mead! really very excellent! Where do you get it?"

"I got this in Lubni. Are there many Cossack elders here?"

"Who is not here? Fedor Yakubovich, Old Filon Daidyalo, Danilo Nechai, and their eye in the head, Bogun, who became my friend as soon as I outdrank him and promised to adopt him. Chigirin is filled with the odor of them. They are looking which way to turn, for they do not dare yet to take the side of Hmelnitski openly. But if they do not declare for him, it will be owing to me."

"How is that?"

"While drinking with them I bring them over to the Commonwealth and argue them into loyalty. If the king does not give me a crown estate for this, then believe me there is no justice in the Commonwealth, nor reward for services; and in such a case it would be better to breed chickens than to risk one's head *pro bono publico*."

"It would be better for you to risk your head fighting with them; but it appears to me you are only throwing away your money for nothing in treating them, for in that way you will never win them."

"I throw money away! For whom do you take me? Isn't it enough for me to hobnob with trash, without paying their scores? I consider it a favor that I allow them to pay mine."

"And that fellow Bogun, what is he doing here?"

"He? He keeps his ears open to hear reports from the Saitch, like the rest. That is why he came here. He is the favorite of all the Cossacks. They are after him like monkeys, for it is certain that the Pereyasláv regiment will follow him, and not Loboda. And who knows, too, whom Krechovski's registered Cossacks will follow? Bogun is a brother to the men of the lower country when it is a question of attacking the Turks or the Tartars; but this time he is calculating very closely, for he confessed to me, in drink, that he was in love with a noblewoman, and intended to marry her. On this account it would not befit him, on the eve of marriage, to be a brother to slaves. He wishes, too, that I should adopt him and give him my arms. That is very excellent triple mead!"

"Take another drink of it."

"I will, I will. They don't sell such mead as that behind tavern-signs."

"You did not ask, perhaps, the name of the lady whom Bogun wants to marry?"

"Well, my dear sir, what do I care about her name? I know only that when I put horns on Bogun, she will be Madame Deer. In my youthful years I was a fellow of no ordinary beauty. Only let me tell you how I carried off the palm of martyrdom in Galáts. You see that hole in my forehead? It is enough for me to say that the eunuchs in the harem of the local pasha made it."

"But you said the bullet of a robber made it."

"Did I? Then I told the truth; for every Turk is a robber, as God is my aid!"

Further conversation was interrupted by the entrance of Zatsvilikhovski.

"Well, my dear lieutenant," said the old man, "the boats are ready, you have trusty men for attendants; you can start, in God's name, this moment, if you like. And here are the letters."

"Then I'll tell my people to be off for the shore at once."

"But where are you going?" asked Zagloba.

"To Kudák."

"It will be hot for you there."

The lieutenant did not hear his prophecy, for he went out of the room into the court, where the Cossacks with horses were almost ready for the road.

"To horse and to the shore!" commanded Pan Yan. "Put the horses on the boats, and wait for me."

Meanwhile the old man said to Zagloba: "I hear that you court the Cossack colonels, and drink with them."

"For the public good, most worthy standard-bearer."

"You have a nimble mind, but inclining rather to disgrace. You wish to bring the Cossacks to your side in their cups, so they may befriend you in case they win."

"Even if that were true, having been a martyr to the Turks, I do not wish to become one to the Cossacks; and there is nothing wonderful in that, for two mushrooms would spoil the best soup. And as to disgrace, I ask no one to drink it with me,--I drink it alone; and God grant that it taste no worse than this mead. Merit, like oil, must come to the top."

At that moment Skshetuski returned. "The men have started already," said he.

Zatsvilikhovski poured out a measure. "Here is to a pleasant journey!"

"And a return in health!" added Zagloba.

"You will have an easy journey, for the water is tremendous."

"Sit down, gentlemen, and drink the rest. It is not a large vessel."

They sat down and drank.

"You will see a curious country," said Zatsvilikhovski. "Greet Pan Grodzitski in Kudák for me. Ah, that is a soldier! He lives at the end of the world, far from the eyes of the hetman, and he maintains such order that God grant its like might be in the whole Commonwealth. I know Kudák and the Cataracts well. Years ago I used to travel there, and there is gloom on the soul when one thinks of what is past and gone; but now--"

Here the standard-bearer rested his milk-white head on his hand, and fell into deep thought. A moment of silence followed, broken only by the tramp of horses heard at the gate; for the rest of Skshetuski's men were going to the boats at the shore.

"My God!" said Zatsvilikhovski, starting from his meditation; "and there were better times formerly, though in the midst of turmoil. I remember Khotím, twenty-seven years ago, as if it were to-day! When the hussars under Lyubomirski moved to attack the janissaries, then the Cossacks in the trenches threw up their caps and shouted to Sahaidachny, till the earth trembled, 'Let us die with the Poles!' And what do we see to-day? To-day the lower country, which should be the first bulwark of Christendom, lets Tartars into the boundaries of the Commonwealth, to fall upon them when they are returning with booty. It is still worse; for Hmelnitski allies himself directly with Tartars, with whom he will murder Christians."

"Let us drink by reason of this sorrow!" said Zagloba. "What triple mead this is!"

"God grant me the grave as soon as possible!" said the old man, continuing. "Mutual crimes will be washed out in blood, but not blood of atonement, for here brother will murder brother. Who are in the lower country? Russians. Who in the army of Prince Yeremi? Russians. Who in the retinues of the magnates? Russians. And are there few of them in the king's camp? And I myself,--who am I? Oh, unhappy Ukraine! pagans of the Crimea will put the chain upon thy neck, and thou wilt pull the oar in the galley of the Turk!"

"Grieve not so, worthy standard-bearer," said Pan Yan; "if you do, tears will come to our eyes. A fair sun may shine upon us yet!"

In fact, the sun was going down that very moment, and its last rays fell with a red gleam on the white hair of the old man. In the town the bells began to ring "Ave Maria" and "Praise to God."

They left the house. Skshetuski went to the Polish church, Zatsvilikhovski to the Russian, and Zagloba to Dopula's at the Bell-ringers' Corner.

It was dark when they met again at the shore by the landing. Skshetuski's men were sitting already in the boats. The ferrymen were still carrying in packages. The cold wind blew from the neighboring point where the river entered the Dnieper, and the night gave no promise of being very pleasant. By the light of the fire burning on the bank, the water of the river looked bloody, and seemed to be running with immeasurable speed somewhere into the unknown gloom.

"Well, happy journey to you!" said the old man, pressing the lieutenant's hand heartily; "but be careful of yourself!"

"I will neglect nothing. God grant us soon to meet!"

"Either in Lubni or the prince's camp."

"Then you will go without fail to the prince?"

Zatsvilikhovski shrugged his shoulders. "What am I to do? If there is war, then war!"

"Be in good health."

"God guard you!"

"Vive, valeque!" said Zagloba. "And if the water bears you all the way to Stamboul, then give my respects to the Sultan. Or rather, let the devil take him! That was very respectable triple mead. Brr! how cold it is!"

"Till we meet again!"

"Till we see each other!"

"May God conduct you!"

The oar creaked and plashed against the water, the boats moved on. The fire burning on the shore began to recede quickly. For a long time Skshetuski saw the gray form of the standard-bearer lighted up by the flame of the fire, and a certain sadness pressed his heart. The water is bearing him on, but far away from well-wishing hearts and from the loved one; from known lands it is bearing him as mercilessly as fate, but into wild places and into darkness.

They sailed through the mouth of the Tasma into the Dnieper. The wind whistled; the oars plashed monotonously and sadly. The oarsmen began to sing.

Skshetuski wrapped himself in a burka, and lay down on the bed which the soldier had fixed for him. He began to think of Helena,--that she was not yet in Lubni, that Bogun was behind, and he departing. Fear, evil presentiments, care, besieged him like ravens. He began to struggle with them, struggled till he was wearied; thoughts tormented him; something wonderful was blended with the whistle of the wind, the plash of the oars, and the songs of the oarsmen,--he fell asleep.

CHAPTER IX.

Next morning Pan Yan woke up fresh, in good health, and cheerful. The weather was wonderful. The widely overflowed waters were wrinkled into small ripples by the warm, light breeze. The banks were in a fog, and were merged in the plain of waters in one indistinguishable level.

Jendzian, when he woke, rubbed his eyes and was frightened. He looked around with astonishment, and seeing shore nowhere, cried out,--

"Oh, for God's sake! my master, we must be out on the sea."

"It is the swollen river, not the sea," answered Pan Yan; "you will find the shores when the fog rises."

"I think we shall be travelling before long in the Turkish land."

"We shall travel there if we are ordered, but you see we are not sailing alone."

And in the twinkle of an eye were to be seen many large boats and the narrow Cossack craft, generally called chaiki, with bulrushes fastened around them. Some of these were going down the river, borne on by the swift current; others were being urged laboriously against the stream with oars and sail. They were carrying fish, wax, salt, and dried cherries to towns along the river, or returning from inhabited neighborhoods laden with provisions for Kudák, and goods which found ready sale in the bazaar at the Saitch. From the mouth of the Psel down the banks of the Dnieper was a perfect desert, on which only here and there wintering-posts of the Cossacks whitened. But the river formed a highway connecting the Saitch with the rest of the world; therefore there was a considerable movement on it, especially when the increase of water made it easy for vessels, and when the Cataracts, with the exception of Nenasytets, were passable for craft going with the current.

The lieutenant looked with curiosity at that life on the river. Meanwhile his boats were speeding on quickly to Kudák. The fog rose, and the shore appeared in clear outline. Over the heads of the travellers flew millions of water-birds,--pelicans, wild geese, storks, ducks, gulls, curlews, and mews. In the reeds at the side of the river was heard such an uproar, such a plashing of water, such a sound of wings, that you would have said there was either a war or a council of birds. Beyond Kremenchug the shores became lower and open.

"Oh, look, my master!" cried Jendzian, suddenly; "the sun is roasting, but snow lies on the fields."

Skshetuski looked, and indeed on both sides of the river, as far as the eye could reach, some kind of a white covering glittered in the rays of the sun.

"Hallo! what is that which looks white over there?" asked he of the pilot.

"Cherry-trees!" answered the old man.

In fact there were forests of dwarf cherry-trees, with which both shores were covered from beyond the mouth of the Psel. In autumn the sweet and large fruit of these trees furnished food to birds and beasts, as well as to people losing their way in the Wilderness. This fruit was also an article of commerce which was taken in boats to Kieff and beyond. When they went to the shore, to give the oarsmen time to rest, the lieutenant landed with Jendzian, wishing to examine the bushes more closely. The two men were surrounded by such an intoxicating odor that they were scarcely able to breathe. Many branches were lying on the ground. In places an impenetrable thicket was formed. Among the cherry-trees were growing, also luxuriantly, small wild almond-trees covered with rose-colored blossoms, which gave out a still more pungent odor. Myriads of black bees and yellow bees, with many-colored butterflies, were flitting over this variegated sea of blossoms, the end of which could not be seen.

"Oh, this is wonderful, wonderful!" said Jendzian. "And why do not people live here? I see plenty of wild animals too."

Among the cherry-trees gray and white rabbits were running, and countless flocks of large blue-legged quails, some of which Jendzian shot; but to his great distress he learned from the pilot that their flesh was poisonous. On the soft earth tracks of deer and wild goats were to be seen, and from afar came sounds like the grunting of wild boars.

When the travellers had sated their eyes and rested, they pushed on farther. The shores were now high, now low, disclosing views of fine oak forests, fields, mounds, and spacious steppes. The surrounding country seemed so luxuriant that Skshetuski involuntarily repeated to himself the question of Jendzian: "Why do not people live here?" But for this there was need of some second Yeremi Vishnyevetski to occupy those desert places, bring them to order, and defend them from attacks of Tartars and men from the lower country. At points the river made breaches and bends, flooded ravines, struck its foaming wave against cliffs on the shore, and filled with water dark caverns in the rocks. In such caverns and bends were the hiding-places and retreats of the Cossacks. The mouths of rivers were covered with forests of rushes, reeds, and plants, which were black from the multitude of birds; in a word, a wild region, precipitous, in places sunken, but waste and mysterious, unrolled itself before the eyes of our travellers. Movement on the water became disagreeable; for by reason of the heat swarms of mosquitoes and insects unknown in the dry steppe appeared,--some of them as large as a man's finger, and whose bite caused blood to flow in a stream.

In the evening they arrived at the island of Romanovka, the fires of which were visible from a distance, and there they remained for the night. The fishermen who had hurried up to look at the escort of the lieutenant had their shirts, their faces, and their hands entirely covered with tar to save them from insect bites. These were men of rude habits and wild. In spring they assembled here in crowds to catch and dry fish, which afterward they took to Chigirin, Cherkasi, Pereyasláv, and Kieff. Their occupation was difficult, but profitable, by reason of the multitude of fish that in the summer became a misfortune to that region; for, dying from lack of water in the bays and so-called "quiet corners," they infected the air with putrefaction.

The lieutenant learned that all the Zaporojians occupied there in fishing had left the island some days before and returned at the call of the koshevoi ataman. Every night, too, from the island were seen fires kindled on the steppe by people hastening to the Saitch. The fishermen knew that an expedition against the Poles was in preparation, and they made no secret of this from the lieutenant. Skshetuski saw that his journey might indeed be too late; perhaps before he could reach the Saitch the Cossack regiments would be moving to the north; but he had been ordered to go, and like a true soldier he did not argue, but resolved to push on, even to the centre of the Zaporojian camp.

Early next morning they kept on their way. They passed the wonderful Tarenski Corner, Sukhaya Gora, and Konski Ostrog, famous for its swamps and myriads of insects, which rendered it unfit for habitation. Everything about them--the wildness of the region, the increased rush of the water--announced the vicinity of the Cataracts. At last the tower of Kudák was outlined on the horizon; the first part of their journey was ended.

The lieutenant, however, did not reach the castle that night; for Pan Grodzitski had established the order that after the change of guard, just before sunset, no one would be permitted to enter the fortress or leave it. Even if the king himself were to arrive after that hour, he would be obliged to pass the night in the village under the walls of the castle.

And this is what the lieutenant did. His lodgings were not very commodious; for the cabins in the village, of which there were about sixty, built of clay, were so small that it was necessary to crawl into some of them on hands and knees. It was not worth while to build any other; for the fortress reduced them to ruins at every Tartar attack, so as not to give the assailants shelter or safe approach to the walls. In that village dwelt "incomers,"--that is, wanderers from Poland, Russia, the Crimea, and Wallachia. Almost every man had a faith of his own, but of that no one raised a question. They cultivated no land because of danger from the horde. They lived on fish and grain brought from the Ukraine; they drank spirits distilled from millet, and worked at handicraft for which they were esteemed at Kudák.

The lieutenant was scarcely able to close his eyes that night from the odor of horse-skins, of which straps were made in the village. Next morning at daybreak, as soon as the bell rang and the tattoo was sounded, he gave notice at the fortress that an envoy of the prince had arrived.

Grodzitski, who had the visit of the prince fresh in mind, went out to meet him in person. He was a man fifty years of age, one-eyed like a Cyclops, sullen; for, seated in a desert at the end of the world and not seeing people, he had become wild, and in exercising unlimited power had grown stern and harsh. Besides, his face was pitted with small-pox, and adorned with sabre-cuts and scars from Tartar arrows, like white spots on a tawny skin. But he was a genuine soldier, watchful as a stork; he kept his eye strained in the direction of Tartars and Cossacks. He drank only water, and slept but seven hours in twenty-four; often he would spring up in the night to see if the guards were watching the walls properly, and for the least carelessness condemned soldiers to death. Though terrible, he was indulgent to the Cossacks, and acquired their respect. When in winter they were short of provisions in the Saitch, he helped them with grain. He was a Russian like those who in their day campaigned in the steppes with Psheslav, Lantskoronski, and Samek Zborovski.

"Then you are going to the Saitch?" asked he of Skshetuski, conducting him first to the castle and treating him hospitably.

"To the Saitch. What news have you from there?"

"War! The koshevoi ataman is concentrating the Cossacks from all the meadows, streams, and islands. Fugitives are coming from the Ukraine, whom I stop when I can. There are thirty thousand men or more in the Saitch at present. When they move on the Ukraine and when the town Cossacks and the crowd join them, there will be a hundred thousand."

"And Hmelnitski?"

"He is looked for every day from the Crimea with the Tartars; he may have come already. To tell the truth, it is not necessary for you to go to the Saitch; in a little while you will see them here, for they will not avoid Kudák, nor leave it behind them."

"But will you defend yourself?"

Grodzitski looked gloomily at the lieutenant and said with a calm, emphatic voice: "I will not defend myself."

"How is that?"

"I have no powder. I sent twenty boats for even a little; none has been sent me. I don't know whether the messengers were intercepted or whether there is none. I only know that so far none has come. I have powder for two weeks,--no longer. If I had powder enough, I should blow Kudák and myself into the air before a Cossack foot should enter. I am commanded to lie here,--I lie; commanded to watch,--I watch; commanded to be defiant,--I am defiant; and if it comes to dying, since my mother gave me birth, I shall know how to die too."

"And can't you make powder yourself?"

"For two months the Cossacks have been unwilling to let me have saltpetre, which must be brought from the Black Sea. No matter! if need be I will die!"

"We can all learn of you old soldiers. And if you were to go for the powder yourself?"

"I will not and cannot leave Kudák; here was life for me, let my death be here. Don't you think, either, that you are going to banquets and lordly receptions, like those with which they welcome envoys in other places, or that the office of envoy will protect you there. They kill their own atamans; and since I have been here I don't remember that any of them has died a natural death. And you will perish also."

Skshetuski was silent.

"I see that your courage is dying out; you would better not go."

"My dear sir," said the lieutenant, angrily, "think of something more fitted to frighten me, for I have heard what you have told me ten times, and if you counsel me not to go I shall see that in my place you would not go. Consider, therefore, if powder is the only thing you need, and not bravery too, in the defence of Kudák."

Grodzitski, instead of growing angry, looked with clear eyes at the lieutenant.

"You are a biting dog!" muttered he in Russian. "Pardon me. From your answer I see that you are able to uphold the dignity of the prince and the rank of noble. I'll give you a couple of Cossack boats, for with your own you will not be able to pass the Cataracts."

"I wished to ask you for them."

"At Nenasytets you will have them drawn overland; for although the water is deep, it is never possible to pass,--scarcely can some kind of small boat slip through. And when you are on the lower waters guard against surprise, and remember that iron and lead are more eloquent than words. There they respect none but the daring. The boats will be ready in the morning; but I will order a second rudder to be put on each, for one is not enough on the Cataracts."

Grodzitski now conducted the lieutenant from the room, to show him the fortress and its arrangements. It was a model of order and discipline throughout. Night and day guards standing close to one another watched the walls, which Tartar captives were forced to strengthen and repair continually.

"Every year I add one ell to the height of the walls," said Grodzitski, "and they are now so strong that if I had powder enough even a hundred thousand men could do nothing against me; but without ammunition I can't defend myself when superior force appears."

The fortress was really impregnable; for besides the guns it was defended by the precipices of the Dnieper and inaccessible cliffs rising sheer from the water, and did not require a great garrison. Therefore there were not more than six hundred men in the fortress; but they were the very choicest soldiers, armed with muskets. The Dnieper, flowing in that place in a compressed bed, was so narrow that an arrow shot from the walls went far on to the other bank. The guns of the fortress commanded both shores and the whole neighborhood. Besides, about two miles and a half from the fortress was a lofty tower, from which everything was visible for forty miles around, and in which were one hundred soldiers whom Pan Grodzitski visited every day. Whenever they saw people in the neighborhood they gave signal to the fortress immediately, the alarm was rung, and the whole garrison stood under arms at once.

"In truth," said Grodzitski, "there is no week without an alarm; for the Tartars, sometimes several thousands strong, wander around like wolves. We strike them as well as we can with the guns, and many times wild horses are mistaken for Tartars."

"And are you not weary of living in such a wild place?" asked Skshetuski.

"Even if a place were given me in the chambers of the king, I would not take it. I see more of the world from this place than the king does from his windows in Warsaw."

In truth, from the walls an immense stretch of steppes was to be seen, which at that time seemed one sea of green,--to the north the mouth of the Samara; and on the south the whole bank of the Dnieper, rocks, precipices, forests, as far as the foam of the second Cataract, the Sur.

Toward evening they visited the tower again, since Skshetuski, seeing for the first time that fortress in the steppe, was curious about everything. Meanwhile in the village boats were being prepared for him, which, provided with rudders at both ends, could be turned more easily. He was to start early in the morning; yet during the night he did not lie down to sleep at all, but pondered what was to be done in face of the inevitable destruction with which his mission to the terrible Saitch was threatened. Life smiled on him indeed; for he was young and in love, and a future at the side of a loved one was promised him. Still honor and glory were dearer. But he remembered that war was near; that Helena, waiting for him in Rozlogi, might be seized by the most terrible misfortune,--exposed to the violence, not of Bogun alone, but of the wild and unbridled mob. Alarm for her and pain had seized his spirits. The steppes must have become dry already; it was surely possible to go from Rozlogi to Lubni. But he had told Helena and the old princess to wait for him; for he had not expected that the storm would burst so soon, he did not know the danger in the journey to the Saitch. He walked therefore with quick steps in his room in the fortress, twisted his beard, and wrung his hands. What was he to do? How was he to act? In his mind he saw Rozlogi already in flames, surrounded by a howling mob, more like devils than men. His own steps were answered by a gloomy echo under the vault of the castle; and it seemed to him that an evil power was already approaching Helena. On the walls the quenching of the lights was signalled, and that seemed to him the echo of Bogun's horn. He gnashed his teeth, and grasped after the hilt of his sword. Oh! why did he insist on this expedition, and get it away from Bykhovets?

Jendzian, who was sleeping on the threshold, noticed the change in his master, rose therefore, wiped his eyes, snuffed the torch burning in the iron candlestick, and began to walk around in the room, wishing to arrest the attention of his master.

But the lieutenant, buried completely in his own painful thoughts, kept walking on, rousing with his steps the slumbering echoes.

"Oh, my master!" said Jendzian.

Skshetuski gazed at him with a glassy look. Suddenly he woke up from his revery.

"Jendzian, are you afraid of death?" asked he.

"How death? What are you saying?"

"For who goes to the Saitch does not return."

"Then why do you go?"

"That is my affair; do not meddle with it. But I am sorry for you; you are a stripling, and though a cunning fellow, cunning cannot save you in the Saitch. Return to Chigirin, and then to Lubni."

Jendzian began to scratch his head.

"My master, I fear death; for whoever would not fear death would not fear God; for it is his will either to keep a man alive or to put him to death. But if you run to death of your own will, then it is your sin as a master, not mine as a servant. I will not leave you; for I am not a serf, but a nobleman; though poor, still I am not without pride."

"I see that you are a good fellow; but I will tell you, if you do not wish to go willingly, you will go by command, since it cannot be otherwise."

"Though you were to kill me, I will not go. Do you think that I am a Judas, to give you up to death?"

Here Jendzian raised his hands to his eyes, and began to sob audibly. Skshetuski saw that he could not reach him in that way, and he did not wish to command him threateningly, for he was sorry for the lad.

"Listen!" said he to him. "You can give me no assistance, and I shall not put my head under the sword voluntarily. You will take letters to Rozlogi, which are of more importance to me than my own life. You will tell the old princess to take the young lady to Lubni at once, without the least delay, otherwise rebellion will catch them; and do you watch to see they go. I give you an important mission, worthy of a friend, not a servant."

"You can send somebody else with the letter,--anybody will go."

"And what trusted person have I here? Have you lost your senses? I repeat to you: Doubly save my life, and still you do not wish to render me such service, while I am living in torment, thinking what may happen, and my skin is sweating from pain."

"Well, as God lives, I see I must go! But I grieve for you; so if you were even to give me that spotted belt, I should take no comfort in it at all."

"You shall have the belt; but do your work well."

"I do not want the belt, if you will only let me go with you."

"To-morrow you will return with the boat which Pan Grodzitski is sending to Chigirin. From there you will go, without delay or rest, straight to Rozlogi. Here is a purse for the road. I will write letters immediately."

Jendzian fell at the feet of the lieutenant, "Oh, my master, shall I never see you again?"

"As God gives, as God gives," said Skshetuski, raising him up. "But show a glad face in Rozlogi. Now go to sleep."

The remainder of the night passed for Skshetuski in writing letters and ardent prayer, after which the angel of rest came to him. Meanwhile the night was growing pale; light whitened the narrow windows from the east; day was coming. Then rosy gleams stole into the room; on the tower and fortress they began to play the morning "tattoo." Shortly after Grodzitski appeared in the room.

"The boats are ready."

"And I am ready," said Skshetuski, calmly.

CHAPTER X.

The swift boats bearing the knight and his fortunes shot down the current with the speed of swallows. By reason of high water the Cataracts presented no great danger. They passed Surski and Lokhanny; a lucky wave threw them over the Voronoff bar; the boats grated a little on the Knyaji and Streletski, but they were scratched, not broken. At length they beheld in the distance the foaming and whirling of the terrible Nenasytets. There they were obliged to land and drag the boats along the shore,--a tedious and difficult labor, usually occupying an entire day. Fortunately a great many blocks, apparently left by previous travellers, lay along the whole way; these were placed under the boats to ease them over the ground. In all the region about and on the steppes not a living soul was to be seen, nor a single boat; for none could sail to the Saitch excepting those alone whom Pan Grodzitski permitted to pass Kudák, and Pan Grodzitski cut off the Zaporojie from the rest of the world on purpose. Only the splash of the waves on the cliff of Nenasytets broke the silence.

While the men were dragging the boats, Skshetuski examined this wonder of Nature. An awful sight met his eyes. Through the entire width of the river extended crosswise seven rocky ridges, jutting out above the water, black, rent by waves which broke through them gaps and passages after their fashion. The river pressed with the whole weight of its waters against those ridges, and was broken on them; then wild and raging, lashed into white foaming pulp, it sought to spring over like an infuriated horse, but, pushed back again before it could sweep through the passage, it seemed to gnaw the rocks with its teeth, making enormous circles in impotent wrath; it leaped up toward the sky, raging like a monster, panting like a wild beast in pain. And then again a roar from it as from a hundred cannon, howls as from whole packs of wolves, wheezing, struggling, and at every ridge the same conflict. Over the abyss were heard screams of birds, as if terrified by the sight. Between the ridges the gloomy shadows of the cliff quivered like spirits of evil.

The men, though accustomed to the place, crossed themselves devoutly while dragging the boats, warning the lieutenant not to approach too near the shore; for there were traditions that whoever should gaze too long on Nenasytets would at last see something at which his mind would be disturbed. They asserted, also, that at times there rose from the whirlpool long black hands which caught the unwary who approached too near, and then terrible laughter was heard through the precipices. The Zaporojians did not dare to drag boats along in the night-time.

No man could be received into the Brotherhood of the Saitch who had not crossed the Cataracts alone in a boat; but an exception was made of Nenasytets, since its rocks were never under water. Of Bogun alone blind minstrels sang as if he had stolen through Nenasytets; still belief was not given to the song.

The transfer of the boats occupied nearly all the day, and the sun had begun to set when the lieutenant resumed his place in the boat. But to make up for this the succeeding Cataracts were crossed with ease, for the rocks were covered entirely, and after that they sailed out into the quiet waters of the lower country.

Along the way Skshetuski saw on the field of Kuchkasi the enormous mound of white stone raised at command of Prince Yeremi as a memorial of his visit, and of which Pan Boguslav Mashkevich had spoken in Lubni. From there it was not far to the Saitch. But the lieutenant did not wish to enter the Chertomelik labyrinth in the dark; he determined therefore to pass the night at Hortitsa.

He wished to meet some Zaporojians and announce himself, so that it should be known that an envoy and no one else was coming. Hortitsa, however, appeared to be empty; which surprised the lieutenant not a little, for he had learned from Grodzitski that a Cossack garrison was always stationed there against Tartar attacks. He went himself with some of the men a considerable distance from the shore to reconnoitre; but he could not go over the whole island, for it was more than five miles long, and the night was coming down dark and not very clear. He returned then to the boats, which meanwhile had been dragged up on the sand, and a fire had been made as protection against mosquitoes.

The greater part of the night passed quietly. The Cossacks and the guides slept by the fire. Only the guards were awake, and the lieutenant, who had been tormented by a terrible sleeplessness since he left Kudák. He felt also that fever was wearing him. At times he fancied he heard steps approaching from the interior of the island, then again certain strange sounds like the distant bleating of goats. But he thought that his hearing deceived him. Suddenly, when it was near daybreak, a dark figure stood before him. It was a servant from the guard.

"People are coming!" said he, hastily.

"Who are they?"

"Undoubtedly Zaporojians. There are forty of them."

"Very well. That is not a great number. Rouse the men! Stir the fire!"

The Cossacks sprang to their feet at once. The replenished fire blazed high, and lighted the boats and the handful of soldiers under the lieutenant. The guards ran up also to the circle.

Meanwhile the irregular steps of a crowd became distinctly audible. The steps stopped at a certain distance. Immediately some voice inquired in threatening accents,--

"Who is on shore?"

"And who are you?" answered the sergeant.

"Answer, son of the enemy! if not, we will inquire with a musket."

"His Highness, the envoy of Prince Yeremi Vishnyevetski, going to the koshevoi ataman," said the sergeant, with emphasis.

The voices in the crowd were silent; evidently there was a short consultation.

"But come here yourself," cried the sergeant; "don't be afraid! People do not fall upon envoys, and envoys do not attack."

Steps were heard again, and after a while a number of figures came out of the shadow. By the swarthy complexion, low stature, and skin coats with wool outside, the lieutenant knew from the first glance that most of them were Tartars; there were only a few Cossacks among them. The idea flashed like lightning through Skshetuski's brain that if the Tartars were in Hortitsa Hmelnitski had returned from the Crimea.

In front of the crowd stood an old Zaporojian of gigantic size, with a wild and savage face. Approaching the fire, he asked,--

"Who is the envoy here?" A strong smell of spirits came from him; the Zaporojian was evidently drunk. "Who is envoy here?" repeated he.

"I am," said Skshetuski, haughtily.

"Thou!"

"Am I a brother to thee that thou sayest 'Thou' to me?"

"Learn politeness, you ruffian!" interrupted the sergeant. "You must say, 'Serene great mighty lord envoy.'"

"Destruction to you, devils' sons! May the death of Serpyagoff strike you, serene great mighty sons! And what business have you with the ataman?"

"It is not thy affair! Know only that thy life depends upon my reaching the ataman as quickly as possible."

At that moment another Zaporojian came out from the crowd.

"We are here at the command of the ataman," said he, "on guard so that no one from the Poles may approach; and if any man approaches, we are to bind him and deliver him bound, and we will do that."

"Whoever goes voluntarily, you will not bind."

"I will, for such is the order."

"Do you know, clown, what the person of an envoy means? Do you know whom I represent?"

Then the old giant interrupted: "We will lead in the envoy, but by the beard,--in this fashion!"

Saying this, he reached his hand to the lieutenant's beard. But that moment he groaned, and as if struck by lightning dropped to the earth. The lieutenant had shivered his head with a battle-hammer.

"Slash! slash!" howled enraged voices from the crowd.

The Cossacks of the prince hurried to the rescue of their leader; muskets roared. "Slash! slash!" was mingled with the clash of steel. A regular battle began. The fire, trampled in the disturbance, went out, and darkness surrounded the combatants. Soon both sides had grappled each other so closely that there was no room for blows and knives; fists and teeth took the place of sabres.

All at once, in the interior of the island, were heard numerous fresh shouts and cries. Aid was coming to the attacking party. Another moment and they would have come too late, for the disciplined Cossacks were getting the upper hand of the crowd.

"To the boats!" cried the lieutenant, in a thundering voice.

The escort executed the command in a twinkle. Unfortunately the boats had been dragged too far on the sand, and could not be pushed at once into the water. That moment the enemy sprang furiously toward the shore.

"Fire!" commanded Pan Yan.

A discharge of musketry restrained the assailants, who became confused, crowded together, and retreated in disorder, leaving a number of bodies stretched upon the sand. Some of these bodies squirmed convulsively, like fish snatched from the water and thrown on shore.

The boatmen, assisted by a number of the Cossacks, planting their oars in the ground, pushed with all their might to get the boats into the water; but in vain.

The enemy began their attack from a distance. The splashing of balls on the water was mingled with the whistling of arrows and the groans of the wounded. The Tartars, shouting "Allah!" with increased shrillness, urged one another on. The Cossack cries: "Cut! cut!" answered them; and the calm voice of Skshetuski, repeating faster and faster the command, "Fire!"

The dawn was beginning to shine with pale light on the struggle. From the land side was to be seen a crowd of Cossacks and Tartars, some with their muskets held ready to aim, others stooping in the rear and drawing their bowstrings; from the side of the water two boats smoking and flashing with the continual discharges of musketry. Between them lay bodies stretched quietly on the sand.

In one of these boats stood Pan Yan, taller than the others, haughty, calm, with the lieutenant's staff in his hand and with uncovered head,--for a Tartar arrow had swept away his cap. The sergeant approached him and whispered,--

"We cannot hold out; the crowd is too great!"

But the lieutenant's only thought was to seal his mission with his blood, to prevent the disgrace of his office, and to perish not without glory. Therefore, when the Cossacks made a sort of breastwork for themselves of the provision bags, from behind which they struck the enemy, he remained visible and exposed to attack.

"Good!" said he; "we will die to the last man."

"We will die, father!" cried the Cossacks.

"Fire!"

Again the boats smoked. From the interior of the island new crowds came, armed with pikes and scythes. The assailants separated into two parties. One party kept up the fire; the other, composed of more than two hundred Cossacks and Tartars, only waited the proper moment for a hand-to-hand encounter. At the same time from the reeds of the island came out four boats, which were to attack the lieutenant from the rear and from both sides.

It was clear daylight now. The smoke stretched out in long streaks in the quiet air, and covered the scene of conflict.

The lieutenant commanded his twenty Cossacks to turn to the attacking boats, which, pushed with oars, moved on swiftly as birds over the quiet water of the river. The fire directed against the Tartars and Cossacks approaching from the interior of the island, was notably weakened on that account. They seemed, too, to expect this.

The sergeant approached the lieutenant again.

"The Tartars are taking their daggers between their teeth; they will rush on us this minute."

In fact, almost three hundred of the horde, with sabres in hand and knives in their teeth, prepared for the attack. They were accompanied by some tens of Zaporojians armed with scythes.

The attack was to begin from every direction, for the assailing boats were within gunshot; their sides were already covered with smoke.

Bullets began to fall like hail on the lieutenant's men. Both boats were filled with groans. In a few moments half of the Cossacks were down; the remainder still defended themselves desperately. Their faces were black, their hands wearied, their sight dim, their eyes full of blood; their gun-barrels began to burn their hands. Most of them were wounded.

At that moment a terrible cry and howl rent the air. The Tartars rushed to the attack.

The smoke, pushed by the movement of the mass of bodies, separated suddenly and left exposed to the eye the two boats of the lieutenant covered with a dark crowd of Tartars, like two carcasses of horses torn by a pack of wolves. Some Cossacks resisted yet; and at the mast stood Pan Yan, with bleeding face and an arrow sunk to the shaft in his left shoulder, but defending himself furiously. His form was like that of a giant in the crowd surrounding him. His sabre glittered like lightning; groans and howls responded to his blows. The sergeant, with another Cossack, guarded him on both sides; and the crowd swayed back at times in terror before those three, but, urged from behind, pushed on, and died under the blows of the sabre.

"Take them alive to the ataman!" was called out in the crowd. "Surrender!"

But Skshetuski was surrendering only to God; for he grew pale in a moment, tottered, and fell to the bottom of the boat.

"Farewell, father!" cried the sergeant, in despair.

But in a moment he fell also. The moving mass of assailants covered the boats completely.

CHAPTER XI.

At the house of the inspector of weights and measures, in the outskirts of Hassan Pasha, at the Saitch, sat two Zaporojians at a table, fortifying themselves with spirits distilled from millet, which they dipped unceasingly from a wooden tub that stood in the middle of the table. One of them, already old and quite decrepit, was Philip Zakhar. He was the inspector. The other, Anton Tatarchuk, ataman of the Chigirin kuren, was a man about forty years old, tall, with a wild expression of face and oblique Tartar eyes. Both spoke in a low voice, as if fearing that some one might overhear them.

"But it is to-day?" asked the inspector.

"Yes, almost immediately," answered Tatarchuk. "They are waiting for the koshevoi and Tugai Bey, who went with Hmelnitski himself to Bazaluk, where the horde is quartered. The Brotherhood is already assembled on the square, and the kuren atamans will meet in council before evening. Before night all will be known."

"It may have an evil end," muttered old Philip Zakhar.

"Listen, inspector! But did you see that there was a letter to me also?"

"Of course I did, for I carried the letters myself to the koshevoi, and I know how to read. Three letters were found on the Pole,--one to the koshevoi himself, one to you, the third to young Barabash. Every one in the Saitch knows of this already."

"And who wrote? Don't you know?"

"The prince wrote to the koshevoi, for his seal was on the letter; who wrote to you is unknown."

"God guard us!"

"If they don't call you a friend of the Poles openly, nothing will come of it."

"God guard us!" repeated Tatarchuk.

"It is evident that you have something on your mind."

"Pshaw! I have nothing on my mind."

"The koshevoi, too, may destroy all the letters, for his own head is concerned. There was a letter to him as well as to you."

"He may."

"But if you have done anything, then--" here the old inspector lowered his voice still more--"go away!"

"But how and where?" asked Tatarchuk, uneasily. "The koshevoi has placed guards on all the islands, so that no one may escape to the Poles and let them know what is going on. The Tartars are on guard at Bazaluk. A fish couldn't squeeze through, and a bird couldn't fly over."

"Then hide in the Saitch, wherever you can."

"They will find me,--unless you hide me among the barrels in the bazaar? You are my relative."

"I wouldn't hide my own brother. If you are afraid of death, then drink; you won't feel it when you are drunk."

"Maybe there is nothing in the letters."

"Maybe."

"Here is misfortune, misfortune!" said Tatarchuk. "I don't feel that I have done anything. I am a good fellow, an enemy to the Poles. But though there is nothing in the letter, the devil knows what the Pole may say at the council. He may ruin me."

"He is a severe man; he won't say anything."

"Have you seen him to-day?"

"Yes; I rubbed his wounds with tar, I poured spirits and ashes into his throat. He will be all right. He is an angry fellow! They say that at Hortitsa he slaughtered the Tartars like swine, before they captured him. Set your mind at rest about the Pole."

The sullen sound of the kettledrums which were beaten on the Koshevoi's Square interrupted further conversation. Tatarchuk, hearing the sound, shuddered and sprang to his feet. Excessive fear was expressed by his face and movements.

"They are beating the summons to council," said he, catching his breath. "God save us! And you, Philip, don't speak of what we have been saying here. God save us!"

Having said this, Tatarchuk, seizing the tub with the liquor, brought it to his mouth with both hands, and drank,--drank as though he wished to drink himself to death.

"Let us go!" said the inspector.

The sound of the drums came clearer and clearer.

They went out. The field of Hassan Pasha was separated from the square by a rampart surrounding the encampment proper, and by a gate with lofty towers on which were seen the muzzles of cannon fixed there. In the middle of the field stood the house of the inspector of weights and measures, and the cabins of the shop atamans, and around a rather large space were shops in which goods were stored. These shops were in general wretched structures made of oak planks, which Hortitsa furnished in abundance, fastened together with twigs and reeds. The cabins, not excepting that of the inspector, were mere huts, for only the roofs were raised above the ground. The roofs were black and smoked; for when there was fire in the cabin the smoke found exit, not only through the smoke-hole, but through every cranny in the roof, and one might suppose that it was not a cabin at all, but a pile of branches and reeds covering a tar-pit. No daylight entered these cabins; therefore a fire of pitch pine and oak chips was kept up. The shops, a few dozen in number, were divided into camp-shops which belonged to individual camps, and those of strangers in which during time of peace Tartars and Wallachians traded,--the first in skins, Eastern fabrics, arms, and every kind of booty; the second, chiefly in wine. But the shops for strangers were rarely occupied, since in that wild nest trade was changed most frequently to robbery, from which neither the inspectors nor the shop atamans could restrain the crowds.

Among the shops stood also thirty-eight camp-drinking shops; and before them always lay, on the sweepings, shavings, oak-sticks, and heaps of horse-manure, Zaporojians, half dead from drinking,--some sunk in a stony sleep; others with foam in their mouths, in convulsions or delirium-tremens; others half drunk, howling Cossack songs, spitting, striking, kissing, cursing Cossack fate or weeping over Cossack sorrow, walking upon the heads and breasts of those lying around. Only during expeditions against the Tartars or the upper country was sobriety enforced, and at such times those who took part in an expedition were punished with death for drunkenness. But in ordinary times, and especially in the bazaar, all were drunk,--the inspector, the camp ataman, the buyers, and the sellers. The sour smell of unrectified spirits, mixed with the odor of tar, fish, smoke, and horse-hides, filled the air of the whole place, which in general, by the variety of its shops, reminded one of some little Turkish or Tartar town. Everything was for sale that at any time had been seized as plunder in the Crimea, Wallachia, or on the shores of Anatolia,--bright fabrics of the East, satins, brocades, velvets, cotton cloths, ticking, linen, iron and brass guns, skins, furs, dried fish, cherries, Turkish sweetmeats, church vessels, brass crescents taken from minarets, gilded crosses torn from churches, powder and sharp weapons, spear-staffs, and saddles. In that mixture of objects and colors moved about people dressed in remnants of the most varied garments, in the summer half-naked, always half-wild, discolored with smoke, black, rolled in mud, covered with wounds, bleeding from the bites of gigantic gnats which hovered in myriads over Chertomelik, and eternally drunk, as has been stated above.

At that moment the whole of Hassan Pasha was more crowded with people than usual; the shops and drinking-places were closed, and all were hastening to the Square of the Saitch, on which the council was to be held. Philip Zakhar and Anton Tatarchuk went with the others; but Tatarchuk loitered, and allowed the crowd to precede him. Disquiet grew more and more evident on his face. Meanwhile they crossed the bridge over the fosse, passed the gate, and found themselves on the broad fortified square, surrounded by thirty-eight large wooden structures. These were the kurens, or rather the buildings of the kurens,--a kind of military barracks in which the Cossacks lived. These kurens were of one structure and measure, and differed in nothing unless in the names, borrowed from the various towns of the Ukraine from which the regiments also took their names. In one corner of the square stood the council-house, in which the atamans used to sit under the presidency of the koshevoi. The crowd, or the so-called "Brotherhood," deliberated under the open sky, sending deputations every little while, and sometimes bursting in by force to the council-house and terrorizing those within.

The throng was already enormous on the square, for the ataman had recently assembled at the Saitch all the warriors scattered over the islands, streams, and meadows; therefore the Brotherhood was more numerous than on ordinary occasions. Since the sun was near its setting, a number of tar-barrels had been ignited already; and here and there were kegs of spirits which every kuren had set out for itself, and which added no small energy to the deliberations. Order between the kurens was maintained by the essauls, armed with heavy sticks to restrain the councillors, and with pistols to defend their own lives, which were frequently in danger.

Philip Zakhar and Tatarchuk went straight to the council-house; for one as inspector, and the other as kuren ataman, had a right to a seat among the elders. In the council-room there was but one small table, before which sat the army secretary. The atamans and the koshevoi had seats on skins by the walls; but at that hour their places were not yet occupied. The koshevoi walked with great strides through the room; the kuren atamans, gathering in small groups, conversed in low tones, interrupted from time to time by more audible oaths. Tatarchuk, noticing that his acquaintances and even friends pretended not to see him, at once approached young Barabash, who was more or less in a position similar to his own. Others looked at them with a scowl, to which young Barabash paid no attention, not understanding well the reason. He was a man of great beauty and extraordinary strength, thanks to which he had the rank of kuren ataman. He was notorious throughout the whole Saitch for his stupidity, which had gained him the nickname of "Dunce Ataman" and the privilege of being laughed at by the elders for every word he uttered.

"Wait awhile; maybe we shall go in the water with a stone around the neck," whispered Tatarchuk to him.

"Why is that?" asked Barabash.

"Don't you know about the letters?"

"The plague take his mother! Have I written any letters?"

"See how they frown at us!"

"If I give it to one of them in the forehead, he won't look that way, for his eyes will jump out."

Just then shouts from the outside announced that something had happened. The doors of the council-house opened wide, and in came Hmelnitski with Tugai Bey. They were the men greeted so joyfully. A few months before Tugai Bey, as the most violent of the Tartars and the terror of the men from below, was the object of extreme hatred in the Saitch. Now the Brotherhood hurled their caps in the air at the sight of him, as a good friend of Hmelnitski and the Zaporojians.

Tugai Bey entered first, and then Hmelnitski, with the baton in his hand as hetman of the Zaporojian armies. He had held that office since his return from the Crimea with reinforcements from the Khan. The crowd at that time raised him in their hands, and bursting open the army treasury, brought him the baton, the standard, and the seal which were generally borne before the hetman. He had changed, too, not a little. It was evident that he bore within himself the terrible power of the whole Zaporojie. This was not Hmelnitski the wronged, fleeing to the steppe through the Wilderness, but Hmelnitski the hetman, the spirit of blood, the giant, the avenger of his own wrongs on millions of people.

Still he did not break the chains; he only imposed new and heavier ones. This was evident from his relations with Tugai Bey. This hetman, in the heart of the Zaporojie, took a place second to the Tartar, and endured with submission Tartar pride and treatment contemptuous beyond expression. It was the attitude of a vassal before his lord. But it had to be so. Hmelnitski owed all his credit with the Cossacks to the Tartars and the favor of the Khan, whose representative was the wild and furious Tugai Bey. But Hmelnitski knew how to reconcile with submission the pride which was bursting his own bosom, as well as to unite courage with cunning; for he was a lion and a fox, an eagle and a serpent. This was the first time since the origin of the Cossacks that the Tartar had acted as master in the centre of the Saitch; but such were the times that had come. The Brotherhood hurled their caps in the air at sight of the Pagan. Such were the times that had been accepted.

The deliberations began. Tugai Bey sat down in the middle of the room on a large bundle of skins, and putting his legs under him, began to crack dry sunflower-seeds and spit out the husks in front of himself. On his right side sat Hmelnitski, with the baton; on his left the koshevoi; but the atamans and the deputation from the Brotherhood sat farther away near the walls. Conversation had ceased; only from the crowd outside, debating under the open sky, came a murmur and dull sound like the noise of waves. Hmelnitski began to speak:--

"Gentlemen, with the favor, attention, and aid of the serene Tsar of the Crimea, the lord of many peoples and relative of the heavenly hosts; with the permission of his Majesty the gracious King Vladislav, our lord, and the hearty support of the brave Zaporojian armies,--trusting in our innocence and the justice of God, we are going to avenge the terrible and savage deeds of injustice which, while we had strength, we endured like Christians, at the hands of the faithless Poles, from commissioners, starostas, crown agents, from all the nobility, and from the Jews. Over these deeds of injustice you, gentlemen, and the whole Zaporojian army have shed many tears, and you have given me this baton that I might find the speedy vindication of our innocence and that of all our people. Esteeming this appointment as a great favor from you, my well-wishers, I went to ask of the serene Tsar that aid which he has given. But being ready and willing to move, I was grieved not a little when I heard that there could be traitors in the midst of us, entering into communication with the faithless Poles, and informing them of our work. If this be true, then they are to be punished according to your will and discretion. We ask you, therefore, to listen to the letters brought from our enemy. Prince Vishnyevetski, by an envoy who is not an envoy but a spy, who wants to note our preparations and the good-will of Tugai Bey, our friend, so as to report them to the Poles. And you are to decide whether he is to be punished as well as those to whom he brought letters, and of whom the koshevoi, as a true friend of me, of Tugai Bey, and of the whole army, gave prompt notice."

Hmelnitski stopped. The tumult outside the windows increased every moment. Then the army secretary began to read, first, the letter of the prince to the koshevoi ataman, beginning with these words: "We, by the grace of God, prince and lord in Lubni, Khorol, Pryluki, Gadyatch, etc., voevoda in Russia, etc., starosta, etc." The letter was purely official. The prince, having heard that forces were called in from the meadows, asked the ataman if that were true, and summoned him at once to desist from such action for the sake of peace in Christian lands; and in case Hmelnitski disturbed the Saitch, to deliver him up to the commissioners on their demand. The second letter was from Pan Grodzitski, also to the chief ataman; the third and fourth from Zatsvilikhovski and the old colonel of Cherkasi to Tatarchuk and Barabash. In all these there was nothing that could bring the persons to whom they were addressed into suspicion. Zatsvilikhovski merely begged Tatarchuk to take the bearer of his letter in care, and to make everything he might want easy for him.

Tatarchuk breathed more freely.

"What do you say, gentlemen, of these letters?" inquired Hmelnitski.

The Cossacks were silent. All their councils began thus, till liquor warmed up their heads, since no one of the atamans wished to raise his voice first. Being rude and cunning people, they did this principally from a fear of being laughed at for folly, which might subject the author of it to ridicule or give him a sarcastic nickname for the rest of his life; for such was the condition in the Saitch, where amidst the greatest rudeness the sense of the ridiculous and the dread of sarcasm were wonderfully developed.

The Cossacks remained silent. Hmelnitski raised his voice again.

"The koshevoi ataman is our brother and sincere friend. I believe in the koshevoi as I do in my own soul. And if any man were to speak otherwise, I should consider him a traitor. The koshevoi is our old friend and a soldier."

Having said this, he rose to his feet and kissed the koshevoi.

"Gentlemen," said the koshevoi, in answer, "I bring the forces together, and let the hetman lead them. As to the envoy, since they sent him to me, he is mine; and I make you a present of him."

"You, gentlemen of the delegation, salute the koshevoi," said Hmelnitski, "for he is a just man, and go to inform the Brotherhood that if there is a traitor, he is not the man; he first stationed a guard, he gave the order to seize traitors escaping to the Poles. Say, gentlemen, that the koshevoi is not the traitor, that he is the best of us all."

The deputies bowed to their girdles before Tugai Bey, who chewed his sunflower-seeds the whole time with the greatest indifference; then they bowed to Hmelnitski and the koshevoi, and went out of the room.

After a while joyful shouts outside the windows announced that the deputies had accomplished their task.

"Long life to our koshevoi! long life to our koshevoi!" shouted hoarse voices, with such power that the walls of the building seemed to tremble to their foundations.

At the same time was heard the roar of guns and muskets. The deputies returned and took their seats again in the corner of the room.

"Gentlemen," said Hmelnitski, after quiet had come in some degree outside the windows, "you have decided wisely that the koshevoi is a just man. But if the koshevoi is not a traitor, who is the traitor? Who has friends among the Poles, with whom do they come to an understanding, to whom do they write letters, to whom do they confide the person of an envoy? Who is the traitor?"

While saying this, Hmelnitski raised his voice more and more, and directed his ominous looks toward Tatarchuk and young Barabash, as if he wished to point them out expressly.

A murmur rose in the room; a number of voices began to cry, "Barabash and Tatarchuk!" Some of the kuren atamans stood up in their places, and among the deputies was heard the cry, "To destruction!"

Tatarchuk grew pale, and young Barabash began to look with astonished eyes at those present. His slow mind struggled for a time to discover what was laid to his charge; at length he said,--

"The dog won't eat meat!"

Then he burst out into idiotic laughter, and after him others. And all at once the majority of the kuren atamans began to laugh wildly, not knowing themselves why. From outside the windows came shouts, louder and louder; it was evident that liquor had begun to heat their brains. The sound of the human wave rose higher and higher.

But Anton Tatarchuk rose to his feet, and turning to Hmelnitski, began to speak:--

"What have I done to you, most worthy hetman of the Zaporojie, that you insist on my death? In what am I guilty before you? The commissioner Zatsvilikhovski has written a letter to me,-- what of that? So has the prince written to the koshevoi. Have I received a letter? No! And if I had received it, what should I do with it? I should go to the secretary and ask to have it read; for I do not know how to write or to read. And you would always know what was in the letter. The Pole I don't know by sight. Am I a traitor, then? Oh, brother Zaporojians! Tatarchuk went with you to the Crimea; when you went to Wallachia, he went to Wallachia; when you went to Smolensk, he went to Smolensk,--he fought with you, brave men, lived with you, and shed his blood with you, was dying of hunger with you; so he is not a Pole, not a traitor, but a Cossack,--your own brother; and if the hetman insists on his death, let the hetman say why he insists. What have I done to him? In what have I shown my falsehood? And do you, brothers, be merciful, and judge justly."

"Tatarchuk is a brave fellow! Tatarehuk is a good man!" answered several voices.

"You, Tatarchuk, are a brave fellow," said Hmelnitski; "and I do not persecute you, for you are my friend, and not a Pole,--a Cossack, our brother. If a Pole were the traitor, then I should not be grieved, should not weep; but if a brave fellow is the traitor, my friend the traitor, then my heart is heavy, and I am grieved. Since you were in the Crimea and in Wallachia and at Smolensk, then the offence is the greater; because now you were ready to inform the Poles of the readiness and wishes of the Zaporojian army. The Poles wrote to you to make it easy for their man to get what he wanted; and tell me, worthy atamans, what could a Pole want? Is it not my death and the death of my good friend Tugai Bey? Is it not the destruction of the Zaporojian army? Therefore you, Tatarchuk, are guilty; and you cannot show anything else. And to Barabash his uncle the colonel of Cherkasi wrote,--his uncle, a friend to Chaplinski, a friend to the Poles, who secreted in his house the charter of rights, so the Zaporojian army should not obtain it. Since it is this way,--and I swear, as God lives, that it is no other way,-- you are both guilty; and now beg mercy of the atamans, and I will beg with you, though your guilt is heavy and your treason clear."

From outside the windows came, not a sound and a murmur, but as it were the roar of a storm. The Brotherhood wished to know what was doing in the council-room, and sent a new deputation.

Tatarchuk felt that he was lost. He remembered that the week before he had spoken in the midst of the atamans against giving the baton to Hmelnitski, and against an alliance with the Tartars. Cold drops of sweat came out on his forehead; he understood that there was no rescue for him now. As to young Barabash, it was clear that in destroying him Hmelnitski wished to avenge himself on the old colonel of Cherkasi, who loved his nephew deeply. Still Tatarchuk did not wish to die. He would not have paled before the sabre, the bullet, or the stake; but a death such as that which awaited him pierced him to the marrow of his bones. Therefore, taking advantage of a moment of quiet which reigned after the words of Hmelnitski, he screamed in a terrified voice,--

"In the name of Christ, brother atamans, dear friends, do not destroy an innocent man! I have not seen the Pole, I have not spoken with him! Have mercy on me, brothers! I do not know what the Pole wanted of me; ask him yourselves! I swear by Christ the Saviour, the Holy Most Pure, Saint Nicholas the wonder-worker, by Michael the archangel, that you are destroying an innocent man!"

"Bring in the Pole!" shouted the chief inspector.

"The Pole this way! the Pole this way!" shouted the kuren atamans.

Confusion began. Some rushed to the adjoining room in which the prisoner was confined, to bring him before the council. Others approached Tatarchuk and Barabash with threats. Gladki, the ataman of the Mirgorod kuren, first cried, "To destruction!" The deputies repeated the cry. Chernota sprang to the door, opened it, and shouted to the assembled crowd,--

"Worthy Brotherhood, Tatarchuk is a traitor, Barabash is a traitor; destruction to them!"

The multitude answered with a fearful howl. Confusion continued in the council-room; all the atamans rose from their places; some cried, "The Pole! the Pole!" others tried to allay the disturbance. But while this was going on the doors were thrown wide open before the weight of the crowd, and to the middle of the room rushed in a mass of men from the square outside. Terrible forms, drunk with rage, filled the space, seething, waving their hands, gnashing their teeth, and exhaling the smell of spirits. "Death to Tatarchuk, and Barabash to destruction! Give up the traitors! To the square with them!" shouted the drunken voices. "Strike! kill!" And hundreds of hands were stretched out in a moment toward the hapless victims.

Tatarchuk offered no resistance; he only groaned in terror. But young Barabash began to defend himself with desperate strength. He understood at last that they wanted to kill him. Terror, despair, and madness were seen on his face; foam covered his lips, and from his bosom came forth the roar of a wild beast. Twice he tore himself from the hands of his executioners, and twice their hands seized him by the shoulders, by the breast, by the beard and hair. He struggled, he bit, he bellowed, he fell on the ground, and again rose up bleeding and terrible. His clothes were torn, his hair was pulled out of his head, an eye knocked out. At last, pressed to the wall, his arm was broken; then he fell. His executioners seized his feet, and dragged him with Tatarchuk to the square. There, by the light of tar-barrels and the great fires, the final execution began. Several thousand people rushed upon the doomed men and tore them, howling and struggling among themselves to get at the victims. They were trampled under foot; bits of their bodies were torn away. The multitude struggled around them with that terrible convulsive motion of furious masses. For a moment bloody hands raised aloft two shapeless lumps, without the semblance of human form; then again they were trampled upon the earth. Those standing farther away raised their voices to the sky,--some crying out to throw the victims into the water, others to beat them into a burning tar-barrel. The drunken ones began to fight among themselves. In the frenzy two tubs of alcohol were set on fire, which lighted up the hellish scene with trembling blue flames; from heaven the moon looked down on it also,--the moon calm, bright, and mild. In this way the Brotherhood punished its traitors.

In the council-chamber, the moment the Cossacks dragged Tatarchuk and young Barabash through the doors there was quiet, and the atamans occupied their former places near the wall; for a prisoner was led forth from the adjoining closet.

The shade fell upon his face; in the half-light could be seen only the tall figure, with simple and haughty bearing, though with hands bound together. But Gladki threw a bundle of twigs on the fire, and in a moment a bright flame shot up and covered with a clear light the face of the prisoner, who turned to Hmelnitski.

When he saw him Hmelnitski started. The prisoner was Pan Yan.

Tugai Bey spat out husks of sunflower-seeds, and muttered in Russian,--

"I know that Pole; he was in the Crimea."

"Destruction to him!" cried Gladki.

"Destruction!" repeated Chernota.

Hmelnitski mastered his surprise, but turned his eyes to Gladki and Chernota, who under the influence of that glance grew quiet; then turning to the koshevoi, he said: "And I know him too."

"Whence do you come?" asked the koshevoi of Pan Yan.

"I was coming with an embassy to you, kosheroi ataman, when robbers fell upon me at Hortitsa, and, in spite of customs observed among the wildest people, killed my men, and, regarding neither my office of envoy nor my birth, wounded me, insulted me, and brought me here as a prisoner; for which my lord, Prince Yeremi Vishnyevetski, will know how to demand of you account, koshevoi ataman."

"And why did you dissemble? Why did you crush the head of a brave man? Why did you kill four times as many people as your own number? And you came with a letter to me to observe our preparations and report them to the Poles! We know also that you had letters to traitors in the Zaporojian army, so as to plan with them the destruction of that whole army; therefore you will be received, not as an envoy, but as a traitor, and punished with justice."

"You deceive yourself, koshevoi, and you, self-styled hetman," said the lieutenant, turning to Hmelnitski. "If I brought letters, every envoy does the same when he goes to strange places; for he takes letters from acquaintances to acquaintances, so that through them he may have society. And I came here with a letter from the prince, not to contrive your destruction, but to restrain you from deeds which are an unendurable outrage to the Commonwealth, and which in the end will bring ruin on you and the whole Zaporojian army. For on whom do you raise your godless hands? Against whom do you, who call yourselves defenders of Christianity, form an alliance with Pagans? Against the king, against the nobility, and the whole Commonwealth. You therefore, not I, are traitors; and I tell you that unless you efface your crimes with obedience and humility, then woe to you! Are the times of Pavlyuk and Nalivaika so remote? Has their punishment left your memory? Remember, then, that the patience of the Commonwealth is exhausted, and the sword is hanging over your heads."

"Oh, you son of Satan!" shouted the koshevoi. "You bark to squeeze out and escape death; but your threatening and your Polish Latin won't help you."

Other atamans began to gnash their teeth and shake their sabres; but Skshetuski raised his head still higher, and said,--

"Do not think, atamans, that I fear death, or that I defend my life, or that I am exhibiting my innocence. Being a noble, I can be tried only by equals. Here I am standing, not before judges, but before bandits,--not before nobility, but before serfdom,--not before knighthood, but before barbarism; and I know well I shall not escape my death, with which you will fill the measure of your iniquity. Before me are death and torment; but behind me the power and vengeance of the Commonwealth, in presence of which you are all trembling."

Indeed the lofty stature, the grandeur of his speech, and the name of the Commonwealth made a deep impression. The atamans looked at one another in silence. After a while it seemed to them that not a prisoner, but the terrible messenger of a mighty people, was standing before them.

Tugai Bey murmured: "That is an angry Pole!"

"An angry Pole!" said Hmelnitski.

A violent knocking at the door stopped further conversation. On the square the remains of Tatarchuk and Barabash had been disposed of; and the Brotherhood sent a new deputation. A number of Cossacks, bloody, panting, covered with sweat, drunk, entered the room. They stood near the door, and stretching forth their hands still steaming with blood, began to speak.

"The Brotherhood bow to the elders,"--here they bowed to their girdles,--"and ask that the Pole be given them to play with, as they played with Barabash and Tatarchuk."

"Let them have the Pole!" cried Chernota.

"No," cried others, "let them wait! He is an envoy!"

"To destruction with him!" answered a number of voices.

Then all were silent, waiting for the answer of the koshevoi and Hmelnitski.

"The Brotherhood ask; and if he is not given, they will take him themselves," said the deputies.

Skshetuski seemed lost beyond redemption, when Hmelnitski inclined to the ear of Tugai Bey and whispered,--

"He is your captive. The Tartars took him, he is yours. Will you let him be taken from you? He is a rich nobleman, and besides Prince Yeremi will ransom him with gold."

"Give up the Pole!" cried the Cossacks, with increasing violence.

Tugai Bey straightened himself in his seat and stood up. His countenance changed in a moment; his eyes dilated like the eyes of a wildcat, they began to flash fire. Suddenly he sprang like a tiger in front of the Cossacks who were demanding the prisoner.

"Be off, clowns, infidel dogs, slaves, pig-eaters!" bellowed he, seizing by the beard two of the Zaporojians and pulling them with rage. "Be off, drunkards, brutes, foul reptiles! You have come to take my captive, but this is the way I'll treat you." So saying, he pulled some by the beard; at last he threw one down and began to stamp on him with his feet. "On your faces, slaves! I will send you into captivity, I will trample the whole Saitch under foot as I trample you! I will send it up in smoke, cover it with your carcasses."

The deputies drew back in fear; their terrible friend had shown what he could do.

And, wonderful thing in Bazaluk, there were only six thousand of the horde! It is true that behind them stood the Khan and all the power of the Crimea; but in the Saitch itself there were several thousand Cossacks besides those whom Hmelnitski had already sent to Tomakovka,-- but still not one voice was raised in protest against Tugai Bey. It might be that the method with which the terrible murza had defended his captive was the only one practicable, and that it brought conviction at once to the Zaporojians, to whom the aid of the Tartars was at that time indispensable.

The deputation went out on the square, shouting to the crowd that they would not play with the Pole, for he was Tugai Bey's captive and Tugai Bey said he himself was wild! "He has pulled our beards!" cried they. On the square they began immediately to repeat: "Tugai Bey is wild!" "Is wild!" cry the crowd, plaintively,--"is wild, is wild!" In a few minutes a certain shrill voice began to sing near the fire,--

"Hei, hei!
Tugai Bey

Is wild, roaring wild.

Hei, hei!
Tugai Bey,

Don't get wild, my friend!"

Immediately thousands of voices repeated: "Hei, hei! Tugai Bey!" And at once rose one of those songs which afterward spread over the whole Ukraine, as if the wind had carried it, and was sung to the sound of lyre and teorban.

But suddenly the song was interrupted; for through the gates, from the side of Hassan Pasha, rushed a number of men who broke through the crowd, shouting, "Out of the way! out of the way!" and hastened with all speed to the council-house. The atamans were preparing to go out when these new guests fell into the room.

"A letter to the hetman!" shouted an old Cossack. "We are from Chigirin. We have rushed on night and day with the letter. Here it is!"

Hmelnitski took the letter from the hands of the Cossack, and began to read. Suddenly his face changed; he stopped the reading, and said with a piercing voice,--

"Atamans! The Grand Hetman Pototski sends his son Stephen with his army against us. War!"

In the room there rose a wonderful sound,--uncertain whether of joy or amazement. Hmelnitski stepped forward into the middle of the room, and put his hand on his hip; his eyes flashed lightning, his voice was awful and commanding,--

"Atamans, to the kurens! Fire the cannon from the tower! Break the liquor-barrels! We march at daybreak to-morrow!"

Prom that moment the common council ceased, the rule of atamans and the preponderance of the Brotherhood were at an end. Hmelnitski assumed unlimited power. A little while before, through fear that his voice might not be obeyed, he was forced to destroy his opponents by artifice, and by artifice defend the prisoner. Now he was lord of life and death for them all.

So it was ever. Before and after expeditions, even if the hetman was chosen, the multitude still imposed its will on the atamans and the koshevoi for whom opposition was coupled with danger. But when the campaign was declared, the Brotherhood became an army subject to military discipline, the atamans officers, and the hetman a dictator in command. Therefore, when they heard the orders of Hmelnitski, the atamans went at once to their kurens. The council was at an end.

Soon the roar of cannon from the gates leading from Hassan Pasha to the square of the Saitch shook the walls of the room, and spread with gloomy echoes through all Chertomelik, giving notice of war.

It opened also an epoch in the history of two peoples; but that was unknown to the drunken Cossacks as well as to the Zaporojian hetman himself.

CHAPTER XII.

Hmelnitski and Skshetuski went to spend the night at the house of the koshevoi, and with them Tugai Bey, for whom it was too late to return to Bazaluk. The wild bey treated the lieutenant as a captive who was to be ransomed for a large sum, and therefore not as a slave; and with greater respect indeed than he would have shown perhaps to Cossacks, for he had seen him formerly as an envoy at the court of the Khan. In view of this the koshevoi asked Pan Yan to his own house, and also changed his bearing toward him. The old koshevoi was a man devoted body and soul to Hmelnitski, who had conquered and taken possession of him. He had observed that Hmelnitski seemed anxious to save the life of the captive at the time of the council; but he was more astonished when, after having barely entered the room, Hmelnitski turned to Tugai Bey.

"Tugai Bey," said he, "how much ransom do you think of getting for this captive?"

Tugai Bey looked at Skshetuski and answered: "You said this was a man of distinction, and I know that he was an envoy of the terrible prince, and the terrible prince is fond of his own men. Bismillah! one pays and the other pays--together--" here Tugai Bey stopped to think--"two thousand thalers."

Hmelnitski answered: "I will give you two thousand thalers."

The Tartar was silent for a moment. His black eyes appeared to pierce Hmelnitski through and through. "You will give three," said he.

"Why should I give three when you asked two yourself?"

"For if you wish to have him, it is important for you; and if it is important, you will give three."

"He saved my life."

"Allah! that is worth a thousand more."

Here Skshetuski interfered in the bargain. "Tugai Bey," said he, with anger, "I can promise you nothing from the prince's treasury; but even if I had to injure my own fortune, I would give you three. I have almost that much saved in the prince's hands, and a good village, which will be sufficient. And I do not want to thank this hetman for my freedom and life."

"And whence dost thou know what I shall do with thee?" asked Hmelnitski; and then turning to Tugai Bey, he said: "The war will begin. You will send to the prince, and before the return of your messenger much water will flow down the Dnieper, but I will take you the money myself to Bazaluk to-morrow."

"Give four, and I will not say another word to the Pole," answered Tugai, impatiently.

"I will give four, on your word."

"Hetman," said the koshevoi, "I will count it out this minute. I have it here under the wall, maybe more."

"To-morrow you will take it to Bazaluk," said Hmelnitski.

Tugai Bey stretched himself and yawned. "I am sleepy," said he. "To-morrow before daylight I must start for Bazaluk. Where am I to sleep?"

The koshevoi showed him a pile of sheepskins against the wall. The Tartar threw himself on this bed, and a little later was snorting like a horse.

Hmelnitski walked a number of times across the room, and said: "Slumber escapes my eyelids; I cannot sleep. Give me something to drink, most worthy koshevoi."

"Gorailka or wine?"

"Gorailka. I cannot sleep."

"It is cockcrow already," said the koshevoi.

"It is late. Go you to sleep, old friend! Drink and go!"

"Here is to fame and success!"

"To success!"

The koshevoi wiped his lips with his sleeve, then gave his hand to Hmelnitski, and going to the other corner of the room buried himself almost in sheepskins, for his blood had grown cold through age. Soon his snoring answered the snoring of Tugai Bey.

Hmelnitski sat at the table, sunk in silence. Suddenly he started up, looked at Skshetuski, and said: "Well, worthy lieutenant, you are free."

"I am thankful to you, Zaporojian hetman, though I do not conceal from you that I should prefer to thank some one else for my freedom."

"Then do not thank. You saved my life, I return you good; now we are even. And I must tell you also that I will not let you go immediately unless you give me the word of a knight that when you have returned you will say nothing of our preparation or power or of anything you have seen in the Saitch."

"I see only this, that you offer me useless fruit of freedom to taste. I will not give you such a word; for by giving it, I should act precisely as those who go over to the enemy."

"My life and the safety of the Zaporojian army lie in this, that the Grand Hetman should not move on us with all his forces, which he would not be slow to do should you inform him of our power. Be not surprised, then, if I detain you until I find myself out of danger, unless you give your word. I know what I have undertaken; I know how formidable is the power opposed to me,--the two hetmans, your terrible prince (who is a whole army himself), the Zaslavskis and Konyetspolskis and all those kinglets who keep their feet on the Cossack neck! Not small was my labor, nor few the letters I wrote before I succeeded in putting their watchfulness to sleep; now I cannot allow you to rouse it. Since the masses of the people, with the Cossacks of the towns, and all who are oppressed in faith and freedom will take my side, as well as the Zaporojian army and the Khan of the Crimea, I expect to manage the enemy, for my power will be considerable; but most of all do I trust in God, who has beheld the injustice done, and who sees my innocence."

Here Hmelnitski drank a glass of vudka, and began to walk unquietly around the table. Skshetuski measured him with his eyes, and spoke with power,--

"Do not blaspheme, Zaporojian hetman, by calling upon God and his divine protection; for in truth you will only bring down upon yourself his anger and swift punishment. Is it right for you to call the Highest to your defence,--you, who for the sake of your private squabbles and the injustice done you raise such a terrible storm, kindle the flame of civil war, and join yourself with Pagans against Christians? For what will happen? Whether victorious or vanquished, you will shed a sea of human blood and tears, you will desolate the land worse than locusts, you will shake the Commonwealth, you will raise your hand against majesty, you will desecrate the altars of the Lord; and all this because Chaplinski took some land from you, and threatened you when he was drunk! What do you not attempt? What do you not devote to your private interests? You call upon God; and though I am in your power, though you can take my life and freedom, I tell you that you are a Satan. Call not God to your assistance, for hell alone can give you aid!"

Hmelnitski grew purple and reached for his sword. He looked at the lieutenant like a lion about to roar and spring on his victim, but he restrained himself. Fortunately, he was not drunk yet. Perhaps, also, disquiet had seized him, maybe certain voices called from his soul to turn from the road; for suddenly, as if wishing to defend himself before his own thoughts, he said,--

"From another I should not have endured such speech, but do you have a care that your boldness does not exhaust my patience. You frighten me with hell, you speak to me of private interests and of treason. And from whence do you know that I have risen to avenge private wrongs alone? Where should I find assistance, where those thousands who have, already taken my side and who are taking it, if I wished merely to redress wrongs of my own? Look around at what is going on in the Ukraine. Oh, rich land, motherland, native land! And who in her is sure of to-morrow, who in her is happy, who is not robbed of his faith, spoiled of his freedom; who in her is not weeping and sighing?--save only the Vishnyevetskis, the Pototskis, the Zaslavskis, Kalinovskis, Konyetspolskis, and a handful of nobles! For them are crown estates, dignities, land, and people,--for them happiness and golden freedom; and the rest of the nation in tears stretch forth their hands to heaven waiting for the pity of God, since the pity of the king cannot help them. How many, even of the nobility, unable to bear this intolerable oppression, have fled to the Saitch, as I myself have fled? I want no war with the king, I want no war with the Commonwealth! It is the mother, and he is the father. The king is a merciful lord; but the kinglets!--with them it is impossible for us to live; their extortions, their rents, meadow-taxes, mill-taxes, eye and horn taxes, their tyranny and oppression exercised through the agency of Jews, cry for vengeance. What thanks has the Zaporojian army received for great services rendered in numerous wars? Where are the Cossack rights? The king gave them, the kinglets took them away. Nalivaika quartered! Pavlyuk burned in a brazen bull! The blood is not dry on the wounds inflicted by the sabres of Jolkevski and Konyetspolski! The tears have not dried for those killed and empaled an stakes; and now look! What is gleaming in the sky?"--here Hmelnitski pointed through the window at the flaming comet,--"The anger of God, the scourge of God! And if I have to be the scourge of God on earth, then let the will of God be done! I will take the burden on my shoulders."

Having said this, he raised his hand above his head and seemed to flame up like a great torch of vengeance, and began to tremble; and then he dropped on the bench, as if bent down by the weight of his destiny.

Silence followed, interrupted only by the snoring of Tugai Bey and the koshevoi, and by the plaintive chirp of the cricket in one corner of the cabin.

The lieutenant sat with drooping head, as if seeking answers to the words of Hmelnitski, as weighty as blocks of granite; at length he began to speak in a quiet and sad voice,--

"Alas! even if that were true, who art thou, Hetman, to create thyself judge and executioner? With what tyranny and pride art thou carried away? Why dost thou not leave judgment and punishment to God? I do not defend the wicked, I do not praise injustice, I do not call oppression right; but, dost thou believe in thyself, Hetman? Thou complainest of oppression from the kinglets,--that they listen neither to the king nor justice. Thou condemnest their pride, but art thou free of it thyself? Do you not raise your hand upon the Commonwealth, on right and majesty? You see the tyranny of lordlets and nobility, but you do not see that were it not for their breasts, their bosoms, their breastplates, their power, their castles, their cannon, and their legions, this land, flowing with milk and honey, would groan under the hundred times heavier yoke of the Turk and the Tartar! For who would defend it? By whose care and power is it that your children are not serving as janissaries, and your women dragged off to infamous harems? Who settled the desert, founded villages and towns, and raised up the sanctuary of God?"

Here the voice of Skshetuski grew stronger and stronger; and Hmelnitski looked with gloomy eyes into the bottle of vudka,[9] put his clinched fists on the table, and was silent as if struggling with himself.

"And who are they?" continued Skshetuski. "Have they come from Germany or from Turkey? Is it not the blood of your blood, and the bone of your bone? Are not the nobility yours, and the princelets yours? If that is true, then woe to thee, Hetman; for thou art raising up the younger brothers against the elder, and making parricides of them. Oh, in God's name, even if they were wicked,--even if all of them, as many as there are, have trampled upon justice, violated rights,--let God judge them in heaven, and the Diet on earth, but not you, O Hetman! Are you able to say that among yours there are only just men? Have yours never been guilty, that you have a right to cast a stone at another for his guilt? And if you ask me, Where are the rights of the Cossacks, I answer: Not kinglets betrayed them, but Zaporojians,--Loboda, Sasko, Nalivaika, and Pavlyuk, of whom you falsely say that he was roasted in a brazen bull, for you know well that this is not true! Your seditions, your disturbances and attacks, made like attacks of Tartars, were put down. Who let the Tartars into the boundaries of the Commonwealth, so that when they were coming back laden with booty, they might be attacked? You! Who--God guard us!--gave their own Christian people into captivity? Who raised the greatest disturbances? You! Before whom is neither noble nor merchant nor village safe? Before you! Who has inflamed domestic war, who has sent up in smoke the villages and towns of the Ukraine, plundered the sanctuaries of God, violated women? You! you! What do you want, then? Do you want that the rights of making civil war and of robbing and plundering should be granted you? In truth, more has been forgiven you than taken away! We wished to cure putrid members instead of cutting them off, and I know no power in the world but the Commonwealth that would exhibit equal patience and clemency by permitting such an ulcer in its own bosom. But what is your gratitude in response? There sleeps your ally, but the raging enemy of the Commonwealth,--your friend, but the foe of the cross and Christianity,--not a kinglet of the Ukraine, but a murza of the Crimea; and with him you will go to burn your own home, and with him to judge your own brother. But he will lord it over you, and you will be forced to hold his stirrup."

Hmelnitski emptied another glass of vudka. "When we, with Barabash, were with his Majesty the King, and when we wept over the oppression and injustice practised on us, he said, 'But have you not muskets, and have you not sabres at your side?'"

"If you were standing before the King of kings, he would say, 'Forgive your enemies, as I forgive mine.'"

"I do not wish to war with the Commonwealth."

"But you put your sword to its throat."

"I go to free the Cossacks from your fetters."

"To tie them in Tartar bonds!"

"I wish to defend the faith."

"In company with the Pagan."

"Stop! You are not the voice of my conscience. Stop, I tell you!"

"Blood will weigh you down, the tears of men will accuse you, death awaits you, judgment awaits you!"

"Screech-owl!" shouted Hmelnitski in rage, and flashed a knife before the breast of Skshetuski.

"Strike!" said Skshetuski.

Again came a moment of silence; again there was nothing to be heard but the snore of the sleeping men and the plaintive chirp of the cricket.

Hmelnitski stood for a time with the knife at Skshetuski's breast; suddenly he trembled, he bethought himself, dropped the knife, and seizing the decanter of vudka, began to drink. He emptied it, and sat heavily on the bench.

"I cannot stab him," he muttered,--"I cannot. It is late--is that daylight?--but it is late to turn from the road. Why speak to me of judgment and blood?"

He had already drunk much; the vudka was rising to his head. He went on, gradually losing consciousness: "What judgment? The Khan promised me reinforcements. Tugai Bey is sleeping here! To-morrow the Cossacks march. With us is Saint Michael the victorious! But if--if--I ransomed thee from Tugai Bey--remember it, and say--Oh, something pains--pains! To turn from the road--'tis late!--judgment--Nalivaika--Pavlyuk--"

Suddenly he straightened himself, strained his eyes in fright, and cried: "Who is there?"

"Who is there?" repeated the half-roused koshevoi.

But Hmelnitski dropped his head on his breast, nodded a couple of times, muttered, "What judgment?" and fell asleep.

Skshetuski grew very pale and weak from recent wounds and from the excitement of talking. He thought therefore that perhaps death was coming, and began to pray aloud.

CHAPTER XIII.

Next morning early the Cossacks marched out of the Saitch, foot and horse. Though blood had not yet stained the steppes, the war had begun. Regiment followed regiment; just as if locusts, warmed by the spring sun, had swarmed in the reeds of Chertomelik, and were flying to the fields of the Ukraine. In the woods behind Bazaluk the warriors of the horde were waiting, ready for the march. Six thousand chosen men, armed incomparably better than ordinary partisan robbers, composed the contingent which the Khan sent to the Zaporojians and to Hmelnitski. At the sight of them the Cossacks hurled their caps into the air. The guns and muskets rattled. The shouts of the Cossacks, mingling with the "Allah" of the Tartars, struck the dome of heaven. Hmelnitski and Tugai Bey, both under their banners, galloped toward each other on horseback, and exchanged formal greetings.

The order of march was formed with the rapidity peculiar to Tartars and Cossacks; then the troops moved on. The horde occupied both Cossack wings; the centre was formed by Hmelnitski and his cavalry, behind which marched the terrible Zaporojian infantry. Farther in the rear were the gunners, with their cannon; still farther the tabor-wagons, in them camp-servants and stores of provisions; finally, the herdsmen, with reserve herds and cattle.

After they had passed the forest of Bazaluk the regiments flowed out on the level country. The day was clear, the field of heaven unspotted by a cloud. A light breeze blew from the north to the sea; the sun played on the lances, and on the flowers of the plain. The primeval steppes were spread before the Zaporojians like a boundless sea, and at this sight joy embraced the Cossack hearts. The great red standard, with the archangel, was inclined repeatedly in greeting to the native steppe; and following its example, every bunchuk and regimental standard was lowered. One shout sprang from all breasts.

The regiments deployed freely on the plain. The drummers and buglers went to the van of the army; the drums thundered, trumpets and bugles sounded, and in concert with them a song, sung by thousands of voices, reverberated through the air and the earth,--

"O steppes, our native steppes,
Ye are painted with beautiful flowers,
Ye are broad as the sea!"

The teorbanists dropped the reins, and bending back in the saddles, with eyes turned to the sky, struck the strings of their teorbans; the cymbalists, stretching their arms above their heads, struck their brazen disks; the drummers thundered with their kettledrums; and all these sounds, together with the monotonous words of the song and the shrill whistle of the tuneless Tartar pipes, mingled in a kind of mighty note, wild and sad as the Wilderness itself. Delight seized all the regiments; the heads bent in time with the song, and at last it seemed as if the entire steppe, infected with music, trembled together with the men and the horses and the standards.

Frightened flocks of birds rose from the steppe and flew before the army like another army,-- an army of the air. At times the song and music stopped; then could be heard the rustling of banners, the tramping and snorting of horses, the squeak of the tabor-wagons,--like the cry of swans or storks.

At the head of the army, under a great red standard and the bunchuk, rode Hmelnitski, in a red uniform, on a white horse, holding a gilded baton in his hand.

The whole body moved on, slowly marching to the north, covering like a terrible wave the rivers, groves, and grave-mounds, filling with its noise and sound the space of the steppe.

But from Chigirin, from the northern rim of the Wilderness, there moved against this wave a wave of the armies of the crown, under the leadership of young Pototski. Here the Zaporojians and the Tartars went as if to a wedding, with a joyful song on their lips; there the serious hussars advanced in grim silence, going unwillingly to that struggle without glory. Here, under the red banner, an old experienced leader shook his threatening baton, as if certain of victory and vengeance; there in front rode a youth with thoughtful countenance, as if knowing, his sad and approaching fate. A great expanse of steppe still divided them.

Hmelnitski did not hurry, for he calculated that the farther young Pototski went into the Wilderness, the farther he went from the two hetmans, the more easily could he be conquered. Meanwhile new fugitives from Chigirin, Povolochi, and all the shore towns of the Ukraine gave daily increase to the Zaporojian power, bringing also news from the opposite camp. From them Hmelnitski learned that the old hetman had sent his son with only two thousand cavalry by land and six thousand Cossacks, with one thousand German infantry in boats by the Dnieper. Both these divisions were ordered to maintain communication with each other, but the order was violated from the first day; for the boats, borne on by the current of the Dnieper, went considerably in advance of the hussars going along the shore, whose march was greatly delayed by the crossings at all the rivers falling into the Dnieper.

Hmelnitski, wishing that the distance between them should be increased still more, did not hurry. On the third day of his march he disposed his camp around Komysha Water, and rested.

At that time the scouts of Tugai Bey brought informants,--two dragoons who just beyond Chigirin had escaped from the camp of Pototski. Hurrying on day and night, they had succeeded in getting considerably in advance of their camp. They were brought immediately to Hmelnitski.

Their account confirmed what was already known to Hmelnitski concerning the forces of young Stephen Pototski; but they brought him intelligence, besides, that the leaders of the Cossacks sailing down in the boats with the German infantry were old Barabash and Krechovski.

When he heard the last name, Hmelnitski sprang up. "Krechovski? the commander of the registered Pereyasláv Cossacks?"

"The same, serene hetman!" answered the dragoons.

Hmelnitski turned to the colonels surrounding him. "Forward!" commanded he, with thundering voice.

Less than an hour later the tabor was moving on, though the sun was already setting and the night did not promise to be clear. Certain terrible reddish clouds rolled along on the western side of the heavens, like dragons or leviathans, and approached one another as if wishing to begin battle.

The tabor turned to the left, toward the bank of the Dnieper. The host marched quietly, without songs, without noise of drums or trumpets, and as quickly as the grass permitted, which was so luxuriant in that neighborhood that the regiments buried in it were lost from view at times, and the many-colored flags seemed to sail along the steppe. The cavalry beat a road for the wagons and the infantry, which, advancing with difficulty, soon fell considerably in the rear.

Night covered the steppes. An enormous red moon rose slowly in the heavens, but, hidden repeatedly by the clouds, flamed up and was quenched like a lamp smothered by the blowing of the wind.

It was well after midnight when, to the eyes of the Cossacks and the Tartars, black gigantic masses seemed outlined clearly on the dark background of the sky. These were the walls of Kudák.

Scouts, hidden by darkness, approached the fortress as carefully and quietly as wolves or night-birds. And now perhaps a surprise for the sleeping fortress!

But suddenly a flash on the ramparts rent the darkness. A terrible report shook the rocks of the Dnieper, and a fiery ball, leaving a circle of sparks in the air, fell among the grass of the steppe. The gloomy cyclops Grodzitski gave notice that he was watching.

"The one-eyed dog!" muttered Tugai Bey to Hmelnitski; "he sees in the night."

The Cossacks avoided the fortress and marched on. They could not think of taking it at a time when the armies of the crown were marching against them. But Grodzitski fired after them from his cannon till the walls of the fortress trembled; not so much to injure them--for they passed at a good distance--as to warn the troops sailing down the Dnieper, who at that time might be not far away.

But the thunder of the guns of Kudák found echo first of all in the heart and hearing of Pan Yan. The young knight, brought by the command of Hmelnitski with the Cossack tabor, became seriously ill on the second day. In the fight at Hortitsa he had not received, it is true, a mortal wound, but he had lost so much blood that little life was left in him. His wounds, dressed in Cossack fashion by the old inspector of weights and measures, opened; fever attacked him, and that night he lay half senseless in a Cossack telega, unconscious of God's world.

The cannon of Kudák first roused him. He opened his eyes, raised himself in the wagon, and began to look around. The Cossack tabor glided along in the darkness, like a circle of dream figures, but the fortress roared and was lighted with rosy smoke; fiery balls sprang along the steppe, snapping and barking, like infuriated dogs. At this sight such sadness and sorrow seized Skshetuski that he was ready to die on the spot, if he could only go even in spirit to his friends. War! war! and he in the camp of the enemy, disarmed, sick, unable to rise from the wagon! The Commonwealth in danger, and he not flying to save it! There in Lubni the troops are surely moving. The prince, with lightning in his eyes, is flying before the ranks; and on whatever side he turns his baton, three hundred lances strike like three hundred thunderbolts. Here a number of well-known faces begin to appear before the eyes of the lieutenant. Little Volodyovski, at the head of his dragoons, with his thin sabre in hand,--the king of swordsmen; whoever crosses weapons with him is as if in the tomb. There Pan Podbipienta raises his executioner's snatch-cowl! Will he cut off the three heads, or will he not? The priest Yaskolski waves the banners, and prays with his hands lifted to heaven. But he is an old soldier; therefore, unable to restrain himself, he thunders out at times, "Strike! kill!" Mailed riders incline half-way to the horse's ear. The regiments rush on, open their ranks, and close. Battle and tumult are there!

Suddenly the vision changes. Before the lieutenant stands Helena, pale, with dishevelled hair; and she cries: "Save me, for Bogun pursues!"

Skshetuski tears himself from the wagon, till a voice--but a real one--calls to him: "Lie down, child, or I will bind you."

That was the essaul of the tabor, Zakhar, whom Hmelnitski had commanded to guard the lieutenant as the eye in his head. He puts him back in the wagon, covers him with a horse-skin, and asks: "What's the matter with you?"

Now Skshetuski has perfect presence of mind. The visions vanish. The wagons move along the very bank of the Dnieper. A cool breeze is blowing from the river, and the night is growing pale. Water-birds have begun their morning noise.

"Listen, Zakhar! have we passed Kudák already?" asked Skshetuski.

"We have," answered the Zaporojian,

"And where are you going?"

"I don't know. There will be a battle, they say; but I don't know."

At these words Skshetuski's heart beat joyfully. He had supposed that Hmelnitski would besiege Kudák, and with that the war would begin. Meanwhile the haste with which the Cossacks pushed on permitted the inference that the armies of the Crown were already near, and that Hmelnitski was passing the fortress so as not to be forced to give battle under its cannon.

"I may be free to-day," thought the lieutenant, and raised his eyes to heaven in thanks.

CHAPTER XIV.

The thunder of the guns of Kudák was heard also by the forces descending in boats under the command of old Barabash and Krechovski. These forces were composed of six thousand registered Cossacks, and one of picked German infantry led by Colonel Hans Flick.

Pan Nikolai Pototski, the hetman, hesitated long before he sent the Cossacks against Hmelnitski; but since Krechovski had an immense influence over them, and Pototski trusted Krechovski absolutely, he merely commanded the Cossacks to take the oath of allegiance, and sent them off in the name of God.

Krechovski was a soldier full of experience and of great reputation in previous wars. He was a client of the Pototskis, to whom he was indebted for everything,--his rank of colonel, his nobility, which they obtained for him in the Diet, and finally for broad lands situated near the confluence of the Dniester and Lada, which he held for life. He was connected, therefore, by so many bonds with the Commonwealth and the Pototskis, that a shadow of a suspicion could not rise in the mind of the hetman. Krechovski was, besides, a man in his best days, for he was scarcely fifty years old, and a great future was opening before him in the service of the country. Some were ready to see in him the successor of Stephen Hmeletski, who, beginning his career as a simple knight of the steppe, ended it as voevoda of Kieff and senator of the Commonwealth. It was for Krechovski to advance by the same road, along which he was impelled by bravery, a wild energy, and unbridled ambition, equally eager for wealth and distinction. Through this ambition he had struggled a short time before for the starostaship of Lita; and when at last Pan Korbut received it, Krechovski buried the disappointment deep in his heart, but almost fell ill of envy and mortification. This time fortune seemed to smile on him again; for having received from the hetman such an important military office, he could consider that his name would reach the ears of the king; and that was important, for afterward he had only to bow to receive the reward, with the words dear to the heart of a noble: "He has bowed to us and asked that we grant him; and we remembering his services, do grant, etc." In this way were wealth and distinction acquired in Russia; in this way enormous expanses of the empty steppe, which hitherto had belonged to God and the Commonwealth, passed into private hands; in this way a needy stripling grew to be a lord, and might strengthen himself with the hope that his descendants would hold their seats among senators.

Krechovski was annoyed that in the office committed to him he must divide authority with Barabash; still it was only a nominal division. In reality, the old colonel of Cherkasi, especially in the latter time, had grown so old and worn that his body alone belonged to this earth; his mind and soul were continually sunk in torpidity and lifelessness, which generally precede real death. At the beginning of the expedition he roused up and began to move about with considerable energy, as if at the sound of the trumpet the old soldier's blood had begun to course more vigorously within him, for he had been in his time a famous Cossack and a leader in the steppe; but as soon as they started the plash of the oars lulled him, the songs of the Cossacks and the soft movement of the boats put him to sleep, and he forgot the world of God. Krechovski ordered and managed everything. Barabash woke up only to eat; having eaten his fill, he inquired, as was his custom, about this and that. He was put off with some kind of answer; then he sighed and said,--

"I should be glad to die in some other war, but God's will be done!"

Connection with the army of the crown marching under Stephen Pototski was severed at once. Krechovski complained that the hussars and the dragoons marched too slowly, that they loitered too long at the crossings, that the young son of the hetman had no military experience; but with all that he gave orders to move on.

The boats moved along the shores of the Dnieper to Kudák, going farther and farther from the armies of the crown.

At last one night the thunder of cannon was heard. Barabash slept without waking. Flick, who was sailing ahead, entered the scout-boat and repaired to Krechovski.

"Colonel," said he, "those are the cannon of Kudák! What are we to do?"

"Stop your boats. We will spend the night in the reeds."

"Apparently Hmelnitski is besieging the fortress. In my opinion we ought to hurry to the relief."

"I do not ask you for opinions, but give orders. I am the commander."

"But, Colonel--"

"Halt and wait!" said Krechovski. But seeing that the energetic German was twitching his beard and not thinking of going away without a reason, he added more mildly: "The castellan may come up to-morrow morning with the cavalry, and the fortress will not be taken in one night."

"But if he does not come up?"

"Well, we will wait even two days. You don't know Kudák. They will break their teeth on the walls, and I will not go to relieve the place without the castellan, for I have not the right to do so. That is his affair."

Every reason seemed to be on Krechovski's side. Flick therefore insisted no longer, and withdrew to his Germans. After a while the boats began to approach the right bank and push into the reeds, that for a width of more than forty rods covered the river, which had spread widely in that part. Finally the plash of oars stopped; the boats were hidden entirely in the reeds, and the river appeared to be wholly deserted. Krechovski forbade the lighting of fires, singing of songs, and conversation. Hence there fell upon the place a quiet unbroken save by the distant cannon of Kudák.

Still no one in the boats except Barabash slept. Flick, a knightly man and eager for battle, wished to hurry straight to Kudák. The Cossacks asked one another in a whisper what might happen to the fortress. Would it hold out or would it not hold out? Meanwhile the noise increased every moment. All were convinced that the castle was meeting a violent assault.

"Hmelnitski isn't joking; but Grodzitski isn't joking, either," whispered the Cossacks. "What will come tomorrow?"

Krechovski was probably asking himself the very same question, as, sitting in the prow of his boat, he fell into deep thought. He knew Hmelnitski intimately and of old. Up to that time he had always considered him a man of uncommon gifts, to whom only a field was wanting to soar like an eagle; but now Krechovski doubted him. The cannon thundered unceasingly; therefore it must be that Hmelnitski was really investing Kudák.

"If that is true," thought Krechovski, "he is lost. How is it possible, having roused the Zaporojians and secured the assistance of the Khan, having assembled forces such as none of the Cossack leaders has hitherto commanded, instead of marching with all haste to the Ukraine, rousing the people and attaching to himself the town Cossacks, breaking the hetmans as quickly as possible, and gaining the whole country before new troops could come to its defence, that he, Hmelnitski, an old soldier, is storming an impregnable fortress, capable of detaining him for a whole year? And is he willing that his best forces should break themselves on the walls of Kudák, as a wave of the Dnieper is dashed on the rocks of the Cataracts? And will he wait under Kudák till the hetmans are reinforced and surround him, like Nalivaika at Solonitsa?"

"If he does, he is a lost man," repeated Krechovski once more. "His own Cossacks will give him up. The unsuccessful assault will cause discontent and disorder. The spark of rebellion will go out at its very birth, and Hmelnitski will be no more terrible than a sword broken at the hilt. He is a fool! Therefore," thought Krechovski, "to-morrow I will land my Cossacks and Germans on the bank, and the following night will fall on him unexpectedly, when he is weakened by assaults. I will cut the Zaporojians to pieces, and throw down Hmelnitski bound at the feet of the hetman. It is his own fault, for it might have been otherwise."

The unbridled ambition of Krechovski soared on the wings of a falcon. He knew well that young Pototski could not arrive on the following night by any possibility. Who, then, was to sever the head of the hydra? Krechovski! Who was to put down the rebellion which might wrap the whole Ukraine in a terrible conflagration? Krechovski! The old hetman might be angry for a while that this had taken place without the participation of his son; but he would soon get over that, and meanwhile all the rays of glory and the favors of the king would descend on the conqueror's head. No! It would be necessary, however, to divide the glory with old Barabash and with Grodzitski.

Krechovski scowled darkly; but suddenly his face grew bright. "They will bury that old block Barabash in the ground to-morrow or next day. Grodzitski, if he can only remain at Kudák to frighten the Tartars from time to time with his cannon, will ask for no more. Krechovski alone will remain. If he can only become hetman of the Ukraine!"

The stars twinkled in the sky, and it appeared to the colonel that those were the jewels in his baton; the wind sounded in the reeds, and it seemed to him the rustling of the hetman's standard. The guns of Kudák thundered unceasingly.

"Hmelnitski has given his throat to the sword," continued the colonel in thought, "but that is his own fault. It might have been otherwise. If he had gone straight to the Ukraine, it might have been otherwise. There all is seething and roaring; there lies powder, only waiting for a spark. The Commonwealth is powerless, but it has forces in the Ukraine; the king is not young, and is sickly. One battle won by the Zaporojians will bring incalculable results."

Krechovski covered his face with his hands, and sat motionless. The stars came down nearer and nearer, and settled gradually on the steppe. The quail hidden in the grass began to call. Soon the day would break.

At last the meditations of the colonel became strengthened into a fixed purpose. Next day he would strike Hmelnitski and grind him in the dust. Over his body he would go to wealth and dignities. He would be the instrument of punishment in the hands of the Commonwealth, its defender, in the future its dignitary and senator. After victory over the Zaporojians and the Tartars they would refuse him nothing.

Still, they had not given him the starostaship of Lita. When he remembered this, Krechovski clenched his fists. They had not given him this, in spite of the powerful influence of his protectors the Pototskis, in spite of his military services, simply because he was a new man and his rival drew his origin from princes. In that Commonwealth it was not enough to be a noble, it was necessary to wait till that nobility was covered with must like old wine, till it was rusty like iron.

Hmelnitski alone could introduce a new order of things, to which the king himself would become favorable; but the unfortunate man had preferred to beat out his brains against the walls of Kudák.

The colonel gradually grew calm. They had refused him the starostaship,--what of that? They would strive all the more to recompense him, especially after his victory,--after quenching the rebellion, after freeing the Ukraine from civil war, yes, the whole Commonwealth! They would refuse him nothing; then he would not need even the Pototskis.

His drowsy head inclined upon his breast, and he fell asleep, dreaming of starostaships, of dignities, of grants from the king and the Diet.

When he woke it was daybreak. In the boats all were still sleeping. In the distance the waters of the Dnieper were gleaming in a pale, fugitive light. Around them reigned absolute stillness. It was the stillness that roused him. The cannon of Kudák had ceased to roar.

"What is that?" thought Krechovski. "The first attack is repulsed, or maybe Kudák is taken?"

But that was unlikely. No; the beaten Cossacks were lying somewhere at a distance from the fortress, licking their wounds, and the one-eyed Grodzitski was looking at them through the port-hole, aiming his guns anew. To-morrow they would repeat the storm, and again break their teeth. The day had now come. Krechovski roused the men in his own boat, and sent a boat for Flick. Flick came at once.

"Colonel," said Krechovski, "if the castellan does not come before evening, and if the storm is repeated during the night, we will move to the relief of the fortress."

"My men are ready," answered Flick.

"Issue powder and balls to them."

"I have done so."

"We land during the night and go by the steppe in the greatest quiet. We will come upon them with a surprise."

"Gut! sehr gut! But mightn't we go on a little in the boats? It is twenty miles to the fortress,--rather far for infantry."

"The infantry will mount Cossack horses."

"Gut! sehr gut!"

"Let the men lie quietly in the reeds, not go on shore; make no noise, kindle no fires, for smoke would betray us. We must not be revealed."

"There is such a fog that the smoke will not be seen."

Indeed the river, the inlet overgrown with reeds, in which the boats were hidden, and the steppe were covered as far as the eye could see with a white, impenetrable fog. But it was only the beginning of day; so the fog might rise and uncover the expanse of the steppe.

Flick departed. The men in the boats woke gradually. Krechovski's commands to keep quiet and take the morning meal without tumult were made known. No person going along the shore or sailing in the middle of the river would have even imagined that in the adjoining thicket several thousand men were hidden. The horses were fed from the hand, so that they should not neigh. The boats, covered with fog, lay tied up in the reeds. Here and there only passed a small two-oared boat carrying biscuits and commands; with this exception, the silence of the grave reigned everywhere.

Suddenly in the reeds, rushes, and shore-grass all around the inlet were heard strange and very numerous voices, calling,--

"Pugú! pugú!"

Then quiet. "Pugú! pugú!"

And again silence, as if those voices, calling on the banks, waited for an answer.

But there was no answer. The calling sounded a third time, but more quickly and impatiently.

"Pugú! pugú!"

This time from the side of the boats was heard in the middle of the fog the voice of Krechovski,--

"But who is there?"

"A Cossack from the meadows."

The hearts of the Cossacks hidden in the boats beat unquietly. That mysterious call was well known to them. In that manner the Zaporojiana made themselves known to one another in their winter quarters; in that way in time of war they asked to conference their brothers, the registered and town Cossacks, among whom were many belonging in secret to the Brotherhood.

The voice of Krechovski was heard again; "What do you want?"

"Bogdan Hmelnitski, the Zaporojian hetman, announces that his cannon are turned on the Poles."

"Inform the Zaporojian hetman that ours are tamed to the shore."

"Pugú! Pugú!"

"What more do you want?"

"Bogdan Hmelnitski, the Zaporojian hetman, invites his friend Colonel Krechovski to a conference."

"Let him give hostages."

"Ten kuren atamans."

"Agreed."

That moment the shores of the inlet bloomed with Zaporojians as if with flowers; they stood up from the grass in which they had been hidden. From the steppe approached their cavalry and artillery, tens and hundreds of their banners, flags, and bunchuks. They marched with singing and beating of kettledrums. All this was rather like a joyful greeting than a collision of hostile forces.

The Cossacks on the river answered with shouts. Meanwhile boats came up bringing the kuren atamans. Krechovski entered one of the boats and went to the shore. There a horse was given him, and he was conducted immediately to Hmelnitski.

Seeing him, Hmelnitski removed his cap, and then greeted him cordially.

"Colonel," said he, "my old friend and comrade! When the hetman of the crown commanded you to seize me and bring me to the camp, you did not do it, but you warned me so that I might save myself by flight; for that act I am bound to you in thankfulness and brotherly love."

While saying this he stretched out his hand kindly; but the swarthy face of Krechovski remained cold as ice. "Now, therefore, after you have saved yourself, worthy hetman, you excite rebellion!"

"I go to ask reparation for the wrongs inflicted on myself, on you, on the whole Ukraine, with the charter of Cossack rights granted by the king in my hand, and with the hope that our merciful sovereign will not count it evil in me."

Krechovski looked quickly into the eyes of Hmelnitski, and asked with emphasis: "Have you invested Kudák?"

"I? Do you think I have lost my mind? I passed Kudák without a shot, though the old blind man celebrated it with guns. I was hurrying not to Kudák, but to the Ukraine, and to you, my old friend and benefactor."

"What do you wish, then, of me?"

"Come a little way in the steppe, and we will talk."

They spurred their horses, and rode on. They remained about an hour. On returning, the face of Krechovski was pale and terrible. He took quick farewell of Hmelnitski, who said,--

"There will be two of us in the Ukraine, and above us the king, and no man else."

Krechovski turned to the boats. Old Barabash, Flick, and the elders waited for him with impatience. "What's going on? What's going on?" he was asked on every side.

"Come out on the shore!" answered Krechovski, with a commanding voice.

Barabash raised his sleepy lids; a certain wonderful fire was gleaming in his eyes. "How is that?" asked he.

"Come to the shore; we yield!"

A wave of blood rushed to the pale and faded face of Barabash. He rose from the kettle on which he had been sitting, straightened himself up, and suddenly that bent and decrepit old man was changed into a giant full of life and power.

"Treason!" roared he.

"Treason!" repeated Flick, grasping after the hilt of his rapier.

But before he could draw it Krechovski's sabre whistled, and with one blow Flick was stretched on the ground. Then Krechovski sprang into the scout-boat standing there, in which four Zaporojians were sitting with oars in their hands, and cried: "To the boats!"

The scout-boat shot on like an arrow. Krechovski, standing in the centre of it, with his cap on his bloody sabre, his eyes like flames, cried with a mighty voice,--

"Children, we will not murder our own. Long life to Hmelnitski, the Zaporojian hetman!"

"Long life!" repeated hundreds and thousands of voices.

"Destruction to the Poles!"

"Destruction!"

The roar from the boats answered the shouts of the Zaporojians on land. But many men in the boats did not know what was going on till the news spread everywhere that Krechovski had gone over to the Zaporojians. A regular furor of joy seized the Cossacks. Six thousand caps flew into the air; six thousand muskets roared. The boats trembled under the feet of the brave fellows. A tumult and uproar set in. But that joy had to be sprinkled with blood; for old Barabash preferred to die rather than betray the flag under which he had served a lifetime. A few tens of the men of Cherkasi declared for him, and a struggle began, short but terrible,--like all struggles in which a handful of men, asking not quarter but death, defend themselves in a mass. Neither Krechovski nor any one of the Cossacks expected such resistance. The lion of other days was roused in the old colonel. The summons to lay down his arms he answered with shots; and he was seen, with baton in hand and streaming white hair, giving orders with a voice of thunder and the energy of youth. His boat was surrounded on every side. The men of those boats which could not press up jumped into the water, and by swimming or wading among the reeds, and then seizing the edge of the boat, climbed it with fury. The resistance was short. The faithful Cossacks of Barabash, stabbed, cut to pieces, torn asunder with hands, lay dead in the boat. The old man with sabre in hand defended himself yet.

Krechovski pushed forward toward him. "Yield!" shouted he.

"Traitor! destruction!" answered Barabash, raising his sabre to strike.

Krechovski drew back quickly into the crowd. "Strike!" cried he to the Cossacks.

It seemed that no one wished to raise his hand first on the old man. But unfortunately the colonel slipped in blood and fell. When lying he did not rouse that respect or that fear, and immediately a number of lances were buried in his body. The old man was able only to cry: "Jesus, Mary!"

They began to cut the prostrate body to pieces. The severed head was hurled from boat to boat, like a ball, until by an awkward throw it fell into the water.

There still remained the Germans, with whom the settlement was more difficult, for the regiment was composed of one thousand old soldiers trained in many wars. The valiant Flick had fallen, it is true, by the hand of Krechovski, but there remained at the head of the regiment Johann Werner, lieutenant-colonel, a veteran of the Thirty Years' War.

Krechovski was certain of victory, for the German boats were hemmed in on every side by the Cossacks; still he wished to preserve for Hmelnitski such a respectable reinforcement of incomparable infantry, splendidly armed, therefore he preferred to begin a parley with them.

It seemed for a time that Werner would agree, for he conversed calmly with Krechovski and listened attentively to promises of which the faithless colonel was not sparing. The pay in which the Commonwealth was in arrears was to be paid on the spot, and an additional year in advance. At the expiration of the year the soldiers might go where they pleased, even to the camp of the king.

Werner, appeared to meditate over these conditions, but meanwhile he had quietly issued a command for the boats to press up to him, so that they formed a close circle. On the edge of that circle stood a wall of infantry,--well-grown and powerful men, dressed in yellow coats and caps of the same color, in perfect battle-array, with the left foot forward and muskets at the right side ready to fire. Werner stood in the first rank with drawn sword, and meditated long; at last he raised his head.

"Colonel, we agree!"

"You will lose nothing in your new service," cried Krechovski, with joy.

"But on condition--"

"I agree to that, besides."

"If that is true, then all is settled. Our service with the Commonwealth ends in three months. At the end of three months we will go over to you."

A curse was leaving Krechovski's mouth, but he restrained the outburst. "Are you joking, worthy lieutenant?"

"No!" answered Werner, phlegmatically; "our soldierly honor commands us to keep our agreement. Our service ends in three months. We serve for money, but we are not traitors. If we were, nobody would hire us, and you yourselves would not trust us; for who could guarantee that we should not go over again to the hetmans in the first battle?"

"What do you want, then?"

"We want you to let us go."

"Why, you crazy man, that is impossible! I shall order you to be cut to pieces."

"And how many of your own will you lose?"

"A foot of you will not leave here!"

"And half of your men will not remain."

Both spoke the truth; therefore Krechovski, although the coolness of the German roused all his blood, and rage began to overpower him, did not wish to begin the battle for a while.

"Till the sun leaves the inlet," said he, "think the matter over; after that I will give the order to touch the triggers!"

And he went off hurriedly in his boat to counsel with Hmelnitski.

The silence of expectation began. The Cossack boats surrounded in a dense circle the Germans, who maintained the cool bearing possible only to old and experienced soldiers in the presence of danger. To the threats and insults which burst out on them every moment from the Cossack boats, they answered with contemptuous silence. It was in truth an imposing spectacle,--that calm in the midst of increasing outbursts of rage on the part of the Cossacks, who, shaking their lances and muskets threateningly, gnashed their teeth and, cursing, waited impatiently the signal for battle.

Meanwhile the sun, turning from the south to the west, removed gradually its golden rays from the inlet, which was slowly covered with shade. At length it was completely covered. Then the trumpet began to sound, and immediately after the voice of Krechovski was heard in the distance,--

"The sun has gone down! Have you decided yet?"

"We have!" answered Werner. And turning to the soldiers, he waved his naked sword. "Fire!" commanded he, with a quiet phlegmatic voice.

There was a roar! The plash of bodies falling into the water, the cries of rage, and rapid firing answered the voice of German muskets. Cannon drawn up on shore answered with a deep roar, and began to hurl balls on the German boats. Smoke covered the inlet completely, and only the regular salvos of the muskets amidst the shouts, roaring, whistle of Tartar arrows, and the rattle of guns and muskets, announced that the Germans were still defending themselves.

At sunset the battle was still raging, but appeared to be weaker. Hmelnitski, with his companions Krechovski, Tugai Bey, and some atamans, came to the shore to observe the struggle. The dilated nostrils of the hetman inhaled the smoke of powder, and his ears took in with pleasure the sound of the drowning and dying Germans. All three of the leaders looked on the slaughter as on a spectacle, which at the same time was a favorable omen for them.

The struggle was coming to an end. As the musketry ceased, the shouts of Cossack triumph rose louder and louder to the sky.

"Tugai Bey," said Hmelnitski, "this is our first victory."

"There are no captives!" blurted out the murza. "I want no such victories as this!"

"You will get captives in the Ukraine. You will fill all Stamboul and Galata with your prisoners!"

"I will take even you, if there is no one else!" Having said this, the wild Tugai Bey laughed ominously; then he added: "Still I should be glad to have those 'Franks.'"

The battle had ended. Tugai Bey turned his horse to the camp.

"Now for Jóltiya Vodi!" cried Hmelnitski.

CHAPTER XV.

Skshetuski, hearing the battle, waited with trembling for the conclusion of it. He thought at first that Hmelnitski was meeting all the forces of the hetmans. But toward evening old Zakhar led him out of his error. The news of the treason of the Cossacks under Krechovski and the destruction of the Germans agitated Pan Yan to the bottom of his soul; for it was prophetic of future desertions, and the lieutenant knew perfectly that no small part of the armies of the hetmans was made up of Cossacks.

The anguish of the lieutenant increased, and triumph in the Zaporojian camp added bitterness to his sorrow. Everything foreshadowed the worst. There were no tidings of Prince Yeremi, and evidently the hetmans had made a terrible mistake; for instead of moving with all their forces to Kudák or waiting for the enemy in fortified camps in the Ukraine, they had divided their forces, weakened themselves of their own accord, and opened a wide field to breach of faith and treason. It is true that mention had been made previously in the Zaporojian camp of Krechovski, and of the special despatch of troops under the leadership of Stephen Pototski; but the lieutenant had given no faith to those reports. He supposed that these troops were strong advance guards which would be withdrawn in time. But it turned out otherwise. Hmelnitski was strengthened several thousand men by the treason of Krechovski, and terrible danger hung over young Pototski. Deprived of assistance and lost in the Wilderness, Hmelnitski might easily surround and crush him completely.

In pain from his wounds, in disquiet, during sleepless nights, Skshetuski had consoled himself with the single thought of the prince. The star of Hmelnitski must pale when that of the prince rises in Lubni. And who knows whether he has not joined the hetmans already? Though the forces of Hmelnitski were considerable, though the beginning of the campaign was favorable, though Tugai Bey marched with him, and in case of failure the "Tsar of the Crimea" had promised to move with reinforcements in person, the thought never rose in the mind of Skshetuski that the disturbance could endure long, that one Cossack could shake the whole Commonwealth and break its terrible power. "That wave will be broken at the threshold of the Ukraine," thought the lieutenant. "How have all the Cossack rebellions ended? They have burst out like a flame and have been stifled at the first meeting with the hetmans." Such had been the outcome up to that time. For on one side there rose a crowd of bandits from the lower country, and on the other the power whose shores were washed by two seas. The end was easily foreseen: the storm could not be lasting; it would pass, and calm would follow. This thought strengthened Skshetuski, and perhaps kept him on his feet while he was weighted with such a burden as he had never carried in his life before. The storm, though it would pass might desolate fields, wreck houses, and inflict unspeakable harm. In this storm he had almost lost his life, had lost his strength, and had fallen into bitter captivity just at the time when freedom was worth really as much to him as life itself. What, then, must be the suffering, in this uproar, of beings without power to defend themselves? What was happening to Helena in Rozlogi?

But Helena must be in Lubni already. The lieutenant in his sleep saw her surrounded by friendly faces, petted by Princess Griselda and the prince himself, admired by the knights,-- and still grieving for her hussar, who had disappeared somewhere in the Saitch. But the time would come at last when he would return, Hmelnitski himself had promised freedom; and besides, the Cossack wave would flow on and on, to the threshold of the Commonwealth, where it would be broken; then would come the end of anxiety, affliction, and dread.

The wave flowed on, indeed. Hmelnitski moved forward without delay, and marched to meet the son of the hetman. His power was really formidable; for with the Cossacks of Krechovski and the party of Tugai Bey, he led nearly twenty-five thousand trained men eager for battle. There was no reliable information concerning Pototski's numbers. Deserters declared that he had two thousand heavy cavalry and a number of field-pieces. A battle with that proportion of forces might be doubtful; for one attack of the terrible hussars was often sufficient to destroy ten times the number of troops. Thus Pan Hodkyevich, the Lithuanian hetman, in his time, with three thousand hussars at Kirchholm, ground into the dust eighteen thousand chosen men of the Swedish infantry and cavalry; and at Klushin one armored regiment with wild fury dispersed several thousand English and Scotch mercenaries. Hmelnitski remembered this, and marched, as the Russian chronicler has it, slowly and carefully; "looking, with the many eyes of his mind, on every side, like a cunning hunter, and having sentries posted five miles and farther from his camp."

In this fashion he approached Jóltiya Vodi. Two new informants were brought in. These gave assurance of the small number of Pototski's forces, and stated that the castellan had already crossed Jóltiya Vodi.

Hearing this, Hmelnitski stopped as if pinned to the earth, and intrenched himself. His heart beat joyfully. If Pototski would venture on a storm, he must be beaten. The Cossacks were unequal to armored men in the field, but behind a rampart they fought to perfection; and with such great preponderance of power they would surely repulse an assault. Hmelnitski reckoned on the youth and inexperience of Pototski. But at the side of the young castellan was an accomplished soldier,--the starosta of Jiwets, Stephen Charnetski, colonel of hussars. He saw the danger, and persuaded Pototski to withdraw beyond Jóltiya Vodi.

Nothing was left to Hmelnitski but to follow him. Next day he crossed the swamps of Jóltiya Vodi. The armies stood face to face, but neither of the leaders wished to strike the first blow. The hostile camps began to surround themselves hurriedly with trenches. It was Saturday, the 5th of May. Rain fell all day; clouds so covered the sky that from noon darkness reigned as on a winter day. Toward evening the rain increased still more. Hmelnitski rubbed his hands with joy.

"Only let the steppe get soft," said he to Krechovski, "and I shall not hesitate to meet even the hussars on the offensive; for they will be drowned in the mud with their heavy armor."

The rain fell and fell, as if Heaven itself wished to come to the aid of the Zaporojians. The armies intrenched themselves lazily and gloomily amidst streams of water. It was impossible to kindle fires. Several thousand Tartars issued from the camp to watch lest the Polish tabor, taking advantage of the fog, the rain, and the night, might try to escape. Then profound stillness fell upon the camp. Nothing was heard but the patter of rain and the sound of wind. It was certain that no one slept on either side that night.

In the morning the trumpets sounded in the Polish camp, prolonged and plaintive, as if giving an alarm; then drums began to rattle here and there. The day rose gloomy, dark, damp; the storm had ceased, but still there was rain, fine as if strained through a sieve.

Hmelnitski ordered the firing of a cannon. After it, was heard a second, a third,--a tenth; and when the usual "correspondence" of camp with camp had begun. Pan Yan said to Zakhar, his Cossack guardian: "Take me out on the rampart, that I may see what is passing."

Zakhar was curious himself, and therefore made no opposition. They mounted a lofty bastion, whence could be seen, as if on the palm of the hand, the somewhat sunken valley in the steppe, the swamp of Jóltiya Vodi, and both armies. But Pan Yan had barely given a glance when, seizing his head, he cried,--

"As God is living! it is the advance guard,--nothing more!"

In fact, the ramparts of the Cossack camp extended almost a mile and a quarter, while the Polish intrenchment looked like a little ditch in comparison with it. The disparity of forces was so great that the victory for the Zaporojians was beyond a doubt.

Pain straitened the lieutenant's heart. The hour of fall had not come yet for pride and rebellion, and that which was coming was to be a new triumph for them. At least, so it appeared.

Skirmishing under cannon-fire had already begun. From the bastion single horsemen, or groups of them, could be seen in hand-to-hand conflict. Now the Tartars fought with Pototski's Cossacks, dressed in dark blue and yellow. The cavalry rushed on one another and retreated quickly; approached from the flanks, hit one another from pistols and bows or with lances, tried to catch one another with lariats. These actions seemed from a distance more like amusement than fighting; and only the horses, running along the field without riders, showed that it was a question of life and death.

The Tartars came out thicker and thicker. Soon the plain was black from the dense mass of them. Then, too, new regiments began to issue from the Polish camp, and arrange themselves in battle-array before the intrenchment. This was so near that Pan Yan, with his quick eye, was able to distinguish clearly the flags and ensigns, and also the cavalry captains and lieutenants, who were on horseback a little on one side of the regiments.

His heart began to leap within him. A ruddy color appeared on his pale face; and just as if he could find a favorable audience in Zakhar and the Cossacks standing to their guns on the bastion, he cried with enthusiasm as the regiments marched out of the intrenchments,--

"Those are the dragoons of Balaban; I saw them in Cherkasi! That is the Wallachian regiment; they have a cross on their banner! Oh! now the infantry comes down from the ramparts!" Then with still greater delight, opening his hands: "The hussars! Charnetski's hussars!"

In fact the hussars came out, above their heads a cloud of wings; a forest of lances embellished with golden tassels and with long green and black bannerets, stood above them in the air. They went out six abreast, and formed under the wall. At the sight of their calmness, dignity, and good order tears of joy came into Skshetuski's eyes, dimming his vision for a moment.

Though the forces were so disproportionate; though against these few regiments there was blackening a whole avalanche of Zaporojians and Tartars, which, as is usual, occupied the wings; though their ranks extended so far into the steppe that it was difficult to see the end of them,--Pan Yan believed now in the victory of the Poles. His face was smiling, his strength came back; his eyes, intent on the field, shot fire, but he was unable to stand.

"Hei, my child!" muttered old Zakhar, "the soul would like to enter paradise."

A number of detached Tartar bands rushed forward, with cries and shouts of "Allah!" They were answered from the camp with shots. But these were merely threats. The Tartars, before reaching the Polish regiments, retreated on two sides to their own people and disappeared in the host.

Now the great drum of the Saitch was sounded, and at its voice a gigantic crescent of Cossacks and Tartars rushed forward swiftly. Hmelnitski was trying, apparently, to see whether he could not with one sweep dislodge those regiments and occupy the camp. In case of disorder, that was possible. But nothing of the kind took place with the Polish regiments. They remained quietly, deployed in rather a long line, the rear of which was covered by the intrenchment, and the flanks by the cannon of the camp; so it was possible to strike them only in front. For a while it seemed as if they would receive battle on the spot; but when the crescent had passed half the field, the trumpets in the intrenchment were sounded for attack, and suddenly the fence of spears, till then pointing straight to the sky, was lowered to a line with the heads of the horses.

"The hussars are charging!" cried Pan Yan.

They had, in fact, bent forward in the saddles, and were moving on, and immediately after them the dragoon regiments and the whole line of battle.

The momentum of the hussars was terrible. At the first onset they struck three kurens,--two of Stebloff, and one of Mirgorod,--and crushed them in the twinkle of an eye. The roar reached the ears of Skshetuski. Horses and men, thrown from their feet with the gigantic weight of the iron riders, fell like grain at the breath of a storm. The resistance was so brief that it seemed to Pan Yan as though some enormous dragons had swallowed the three kurens at a gulp. And they were the best troops of the Saitch. Terrified by the noise of the wings, the horses began to spread disorder in the Zaporojian ranks. The Irkleyeff, Kalnibolok, Minsk, Shkurinsk, and Titareff regiments fell into complete disorder, and pressed by the mass of the fleeing, began to retreat in confusion. Meanwhile the dragoons came up with the hussars, and began to help them in the bloody harvest. The Vasyurinsk kuren, after a desperate resistance, turned in flight to the Cossack intrenchments. The centre of Hmelnitski's forces, shaken more and more, beaten, pushed into a disorderly mass, slashed with swords, forced back in the iron onset, was unable to get time to stop and re-form.

"Devils! not Poles!" cried old Zakhar.

Skshetuski was as if bewildered. Being ill, he could not master himself. He laughed and cried at once, and at times screamed out words of command, as if he were leading the regiments himself. Zakhar held him by the skirts, and had to call others to his aid.

The battle came so near the Cossack camp that faces could be almost distinguished. There were artillery discharges from the intrenchments; but the Cossack balls, striking their own men as well as the enemy, increased the disorder. The hussars struck upon the Pashkoff kuren, which formed the guard of the hetman, in the centre of which was Hmelnitski himself. Suddenly a fearful cry was heard through all the Cossack ranks. The great red standard had tottered and fallen.

But at that moment Krechovski, at the head of his five thousand Cossacks, rushed to the fight. Sitting on an enormous cream-colored horse, he flew on in the first rank, without a cap, a sabre above his head, gathering before him the disordered Zaporojians, who, seeing the approaching succor, though without order, returned to the attack. The battle raged again in the centre of the line.

On both flanks fortune in like manner failed Hmelnitski. The Tartars, repulsed twice by the Wallachian regiments and Pototski's Cossacks, lost all eagerness for the fight. Two horses were killed under Tugai Bey. Victory inclined continually to the side of young Pototski.

But the battle did not last long. The rain, which for some time had been increasing every moment, soon became so violent that through the rush of water nothing could be seen. Not streams, but torrents of rain fell on the ground from the open flood-gates of heaven. The steppe was turned into a lake. It grew so dark that one man could not distinguish another at a few paces' distance. The noise of the storm drowned the words of command. The wet muskets and guns grew silent. Heaven itself put an end to the slaughter.

Hmelnitski, drenched to the skin, furious, rushed into his camp. He spoke not a word to any man. A tent of camelskin was pitched, under which, hiding himself, he sat alone with his sad thoughts.

Despair seized him. He understood at last what work he had begun. See! he is beaten, repulsed, almost broken, in a battle with such a small force that it could be properly considered as a scouting party. He knew how great was the power of resistance in the armies of the Commonwealth, and he took that into account when he ventured on a war. And still he had failed in his reckoning,--so at least it seemed to him at that moment. Therefore he seized himself by his shaven head, and wished to break it against the first cannon he saw. What would the resistance be at his meeting with the hetmans and the whole Commonwealth?

His thoughts were interrupted by the entrance of Tugai Bey. The eyes of the Tartar were blazing with rage; his face was pale, and his teeth glittered from behind his lips, unhidden by mustaches.

"Where is the booty, where the prisoners, where the heads of the leaders,--where is victory?" asked he, in a hoarse voice.

Hmelnitski sprang from his place. "There!" answered he loudly, pointing to the Polish camp.

"Go there, then!" roared Tugai Bey; "and if you don't go, I will drag you by a rope to the Crimea."

"I will go," said Hmelnitski,--"I will go to-day! I will take booty and prisoners; but you shall give answer to the Khan, for you want booty and you avoid battle."

"Dog!" howled Tugai Bey, "you are destroying the army of the Khan!"

For a moment they stood snorting in front of each other. Hmelnitski regained his composure first.

"Tugai Bey," said he, "be not disturbed! Rain interrupted the battle, just as Krechovski was breaking the dragoons. I know them! They will fight with less fury to-morrow. The steppe will be mud to the bottom. The hussars will be beaten. To-morrow everything will be ours."

"That's your word!" blurted out Tugai Bey.

"And I will keep it. Tugai Bey, my friend, the Khan sent you for my assistance, not for my misfortune."

"You prophesied victory, not defeat."

"A few prisoners of the dragoons are taken; I will give them to you."

"Let me have them. I will order them to be empaled."

"Don't do that. Give them their liberty. They are men from the Ukraine, from Balaban's regiment. I will send them to bring the dragoons over to our side. It will be with them as with Krechovski."

Tugai Bey was satisfied; he glanced quickly at Hmelnitski, and muttered: "Serpent!"

"Craft is the equal of courage. If we persuade the dragoons to our side, not a man of the Poles will escape,--you understand!"

"I will have Pototski."

"I will give him to you, and Charnetski also."

"Let me have some vudka now, for it is cold."

"Agreed."

At that moment entered Krechovski. The colonel was as gloomy as night. His future starostaships, dignities, castles, and wealth were covered as if with a fog. To-morrow they may disappear altogether, and perhaps out of that fog will rise in their place a rope or a gibbet. Were it not that the colonel had burned the bridges in his rear by destroying the Germans, he would surely have begun to think how to betray Hmelnitski in his turn, and go over with his Cossacks to Pototski's camp. But that was impossible now.

The three sat down, therefore, to a decanter of vudka, and began to drink in silence. The noise of the rain ceased gradually. It was growing dark.

Skshetuski, exhausted from joy, weak and pale, lay motionless in the telega. Zakhar, who had become attached to him, ordered the Cossacks to put a little felt roof over him. The lieutenant listened to the dreary sound of the rain, but in his soul it was clear, bright, and joyful. Behold, his hussars had shown what they could do; his Commonwealth had shown a resistance worthy of its majesty; the first impetus of the Cossack storm had broken on the sharp spears of the royal army. And besides there are the hetmans, there is also Prince Yeremi, and so many lords, so many nobles, so much power, and above all these the king, *primus inter pares*. Pride expanded the breast of Skshetuski, as if at that moment it contained all that power.

In feeling this, he felt, for the first time since he had lost his freedom in the Saitch, a certain pity for the Cossacks; they were guilty, but blinded, since they tried to go to the sun on a spade. They were guilty, but unfortunate, since they allowed themselves to be carried away by one man, who is leading them to evident destruction.

Then his thoughts wandered farther. Peace would come, when every one would have the right to think of his own private happiness. Then in memory and spirit he hovers above Rozlogi. There, near the lion's den, it must be as quiet as the falling of poppy-seeds. There the rebellion will never raise its head; and though it should, Helena is already in Lubni beyond a doubt.

Suddenly the roar of cannon disturbed the golden thread of his thoughts. Hmelnitski, after drinking, led his regiments again to the attack. But it ended with the play of cannon-firing. Krechovski restrained the hetman.

The next morning was Sunday. The whole day passed quietly and without a shot. The camps lay opposite each other, like the camps of two allied armies.

Skshetuski attributed that silence to the discouragement of the Cossacks. Alas! he did not know that then Hmelnitski, "looking forward with the many eyes of his mind," was occupied in bringing Balaban's dragoons to his side.

On Monday the battle began at daybreak. Pan Yan looked on it, as on the first one, with a smiling, happy face. And again the regiments of the crown came out before the intrenchment; but this time, not rushing to the attack, they opposed the enemy where they stood. The steppe had grown soft, not on the surface only, as during the first day of the battle, but to its depths. The heavy cavalry could scarcely move; this gave a great preponderance at once to the flying regiments of the Cossacks and the Tartars. The smile vanished gradually from the lieutenant's lips. At the Polish intrenchment the avalanche of attack covered completely the narrow line of the Polish regiments. It appeared as if that chain might break at any moment, and the attack begin directly on the intrenchments. Skshetuski did not observe half of the spirit or warlike readiness with which the regiments fought on the first day. They defended themselves with stubbornness, but did not strike first, did not crush the kurens to the earth, did not sweep the field like a hurricane. The soft soil had rendered fury impossible, and in fact fastened the heavy cavalry to its place in front of the intrenchment. Impetus was the power of the cavalry, and decided victories; but this time the cavalry was forced to remain on one spot.

Hmelnitski, on the contrary, led new regiments every moment to the battle. He was present everywhere. He led each kuren personally to the attack, and withdrew only before the sabres of the enemy. His ardor was communicated gradually to the Zaporojians, who, though they fell in large numbers, rushed to the attack with shouts and cries. They struck the wall of iron breasts and sharp spears, and beaten, decimated, returned again to the attack. Under this weight the regiments began to waver, to disappear, and in places to retreat, just as an athlete caught in the iron arms of an opponent grows weak, then struggles, and strains every nerve.

Before midday nearly all the forces of the Zaporojians had been under fire and in battle. The fight raged with such stubbornness that between the two lines of combatants a new wall, as it were, was formed of the bodies of horses and men. Every little while, from the battle to the Cossack intrenchments came crowds of wounded men,--bloody, covered with mud, panting, falling from weakness,--but they came with songs on their lips. Fainting, they still cried, "To the death!" The garrison left in the camp was impatient for the fight.

Pan Yan hung his head. The Polish regiments began to retreat from the field to the intrenchment. They were unable to hold out, and a feverish haste was observable in their retreat. At the sight of this twenty thousand mouths and more gave forth a shout of joy, and redoubled the attack. The Zaporojians sprang upon the Cossacks of Pototski, who covered the retreat. But the cannon and a shower of musket-balls drove them back. The battle ceased for a moment. In the Polish camp a trumpet for parley was sounded.

Hmelnitski, however, did not wish to parley. Twelve kurens slipped from their horses to storm the breastworks on foot, with the infantry and Tartars. Krechovski, with three thousand infantry, was coming to their aid in the decisive moment. All the drums, trumpets, and kettledrums sounded at once, drowning the shouts and salvos of musketry.

Skshetuski looked with trembling upon the deep ranks of the peerless Zaporojian infantry rushing to the breastworks and surrounding them with an ever-narrowing circle. Long streaks of white smoke were blown out at it from the breastworks, as if some gigantic bosom were striving to blow away the locusts closing in upon it inexorably from every side. Cannon-balls dug furrows in it; the firing of musketry did not weaken for a moment. Swarms melted before the eye; the circle quivered in places like a wounded snake, but went on. Already they are coming! They are under the breastworks! The cannon can hurt them no longer! Skshetuski closed his eyes.

And now questions flew through his head as swift as lightning: When he opens his eyes will he see the Polish banners on the breastwork? Will he see--or will he not see? There is some unusual tumult increasing every moment. Something must have happened? The shouts come from the centre of the camp. What is it? What has happened?

"All-powerful God!"

That cry was forced from the mouth of Pan Yan when opening his eyes he saw on the battlements the crimson standard with the archangel, instead of the golden banner of the crown. The camp was captured.

In the evening he learned from Zakhar of the whole course of the storm. Not in vain had Tugai Bey called Hmelnitski a serpent; for in the moment of most desperate defence the dragoons of Balaban, talked over by the hetman, joined the Cossacks, and hurling themselves on the rear of their own regiments, aided in cutting them to pieces.

In the evening the lieutenant saw the prisoners, and was present at the death of young Pototski, who, having his throat pierced by an arrow, lived only a few hours after the battle, and died in the arms of Stephen Charnetski: "Tell my father," whispered the young castellan in his last moments,--"tell my father--that--like a knight--" He could add no more. His soul left the body and flew to heaven.

Pan Yan long after remembered that pale face and those blue eyes gazing upward in the moment of death. Charnetski made a vow over the cold body to expiate the death of his friend and the disgrace of defeat in torrents of blood, should God give him freedom. And not a tear flowed over his stern face, for he was a knight of iron, greatly famed already for deeds of daring, and known as a man whom no misfortune could bend. He kept the vow. Instead of yielding to despair, he strengthened Pan Yan, who was suffering greatly from the disgrace and defeat of the Commonwealth.

Again resounded the tramp; and this time several hundred Tartar horsemen appeared on the square. They rushed on at random. The crowd stopped the way before them. They rushed at the crowd, struck, beat, and dispersed it; they lashed their horses, urging them on to the road leading to Cherkasi.

"They run like a whirlwind," said Zakhar.

Scarcely had Skshetuski moved when a second division flew by, and after that a third. The flight seemed to be general. The guards before the houses began to grow uneasy, and also to show a wish to escape. Zakhar hurried through the porch.

"Halt!" cried he to the Mirgorod men.

Smoke, heat, disorder, the tramping of horses, sounds of alarm, the howling of the crowd in the light of the conflagration, were blended in one fearful picture on which the lieutenant gazed through the window.

"What a defeat there must be! what a defeat!" cried he to Zakhar, not considering that the latter could not share his delight.

Now a new division of fugitives rushed by like lightning. The thunder of cannon shook the houses of Korsún to their foundations. Suddenly a shrieking voice began to cry right there at the house,--

"Save yourselves! Hmelnitski is killed! Hmelnitski is killed! Tugai Bey is killed!"

On the square there was a real end of the world. People in terror rushed into the flames. The lieutenant fell upon his knees, raised his hands to heaven,--

"Oh, almighty, great, and just God, praise to thee in the highest!"

Zakhar interrupted his prayer, running into the room from the antechamber.

"Come now," said he, panting, "come and promise pardon to the Mirgorod men, for they wish to go away; and if they go, the crowd will fall upon us."

Skshetuski went out to the porch. The Mirgorod men were moving around unquietly before the house, exhibiting a firm determination to leave the place and flee by the road leading to Cherkasi. Fear had taken possession of every one in the town. Each moment new crowds came, fleeing, as if on wings, from the direction of Krutáya Balka,--peasants, Tartars, town Cossacks, Zaporojians, in the greatest disorder. And still Hmelnitski's principal forces must be fighting yet. The battle could not be entirely decided, for the cannon were thundering with redoubled force. Skshetuski turned to the Mirgorod men.

"Because you have guarded my person well," said he, loftily, "you need no flight to save yourselves, for I promise you intercession and favor with the hetman."

The Mirgorod men uncovered their heads. Pan Yan put his hands on his hips, and looked proudly on the square, which grew emptier each moment. What a change of fate! Here is the lieutenant, a short time since a captive, dragged after the Cossack camp; now he has become among insolent Cossacks as a lord among subjects, as a noble among peasants, as an armored hussar among camp-followers. He, a captive, has now promised favor, and heads are uncovered in his presence, while submissive voices cry with that prolonged tone indicating fear and obedience,--

It was not given to Skshetuski to see the battle, for he remained in Korsún with the camp. Zakhar lodged him on the square, in the house of Zabokshytski, whom the crowd had already hanged, and placed a guard from the remnants of the Mirgorod kuren; for the crowd robbed continually, and killed every man who seemed to them a Pole. Through the broken windows Skshetuski saw the multitude of drunken peasants, bloody, with rolled-up shirt-sleeves, going from house to house, from cellar to cellar, and searching all corners, garrets, lofts; from time to time a terrible noise announced that a nobleman, a Jew, a man, a woman, or a child had been found. The victim was dragged to the square and gloated over in the most fearful manner. The crowd fought with one another for the remnants of the bodies; with delight they rubbed the blood on their faces and breasts, and wound the still steaming entrails around their necks. They seized little Jews by the legs and tore them apart amid the wild laughter of the mob. They rushed upon houses surrounded by guards in which distinguished captives were confined,--left living because large ransoms were expected from them. Then the Zaporojians or the Tartars standing guard repulsed the crowd, thumping the assailants on the heads with their pikestaffs, bows, or ox-hide whips. Such was the case before the house where Skshetuski was. Zakhar gave orders to handle the crowd without mercy, and the Mirgorod men executed the order with pleasure; for the men of the lower country received the assistance of the mob willingly in time of insurrection, but had more contempt for them than they had for the nobility. It was not in vain therefore that they called themselves "nobly born Cossacks." Later Hmelnitski himself presented more than once considerable numbers of the mob to the Tartar, who drove them to the Crimea, where they were sold into Turkey and Asia Minor.

The crowd rioted on the square, and reached such wild disorder that at last they began to kill one another. The day was drawing to an end. One side of the square and the priest's house were on fire. Fortunately the wind blew the fire toward the field, and prevented the extension of the conflagration. But the gigantic flame lighted up the square as brightly as the sun's rays. The excitement became too great for restraint. From a distance came the terrible roar of cannon; it was evident that the battle at Krutaya Balka was growing fiercer and fiercer.

"It must be pretty hot for ours there," muttered old Zakhar. "The hetmans are not trifling. Ah! Pan Pototski is a real soldier." Then he pointed through the window at the crowd. "Oh!" said he, "they are revelling now; but if Hmelnitski is beaten, then there will be revelling over them."

At that moment the tramp of cavalry was heard, and a number of riders rushed to the square on foaming horses. Their faces black from powder, their clothes torn, and the heads of some of them bound in rags showed that they had hurried straightway from battle.

"People who believe in God, save yourselves! The Poles are beating ours!" they cried in loud voices.

Tumult and disorder followed. The multitude moved like a wave tossed by the wind. Suddenly wild dismay possessed all. They rushed to escape; but the streets were blocked with wagons, one part of the square was on fire, there was no place for flight. The crowd began to press and cry, to beat, choke one another, and howl for mercy, though the enemy was far away.

The lieutenant, when he heard what was taking place, grew almost wild from joy. He began to run through the room like a madman, to beat his breast with his hands with all his power, and to cry,--

"I knew that it would be so! As I am alive, I knew it! This is the meeting with the hetmans, with the whole Commonwealth! The hour of punishment has come! What is this?"

Hmelnetski, knowing this perfectly, admitted that now this dislike would cease, and Pototski would first reach out his hand in reconciliation, which would secure for him the assistance of a famous warrior and his powerful troops. With such forces united under a leader like the prince, Hmelnitski did not dare yet to measure strength, for he had not yet sufficient confidence in himself. He determined therefore to hasten, and together with the news of the defeat of Jóltiya Vodi, appear in the Ukraine, and strike the hetmans before the succor of the prince could arrive.

He gave no rest to his troops, therefore, but at daybreak after the battle hurried on. The march was as rapid as if the hetman were fleeing. It was as if an inundation were covering the steppe and rushing forward, collecting all the waters on the way. Forests, oak-groves, grave-mounds were avoided; rivers were crossed without halting. The Cossack forces increased on the road, for new crowds of peasants fleeing from the Ukraine were added to them continually.

They brought news of the hetmans, but contradictory. Some said that Prince Yeremi was yet beyond the Dnieper; others that he had joined the forces of the crown. But all declared that the Ukraine was already on fire. The peasants were not only fleeing to meet Hmelnitski in the Wilderness, but burning villages and towns, throwing themselves on their masters, and arming everywhere. The forces of the crown had been fightings for the past two weeks. Stebloff was destroyed; at Derenhovtsi a bloody battle had been fought. The town Cossacks in various places went over to the side of the people, and at all points were merely waiting for the word. Hmelnitski had reckoned on all this, and hastened the more.

At last he stood on the threshold. Chigirin opened wide her gates. The Cossack garrison went over at once to his regiments. The house of Chaplinski was wrecked; a handful of nobles, seeking refuge in the town, were cut to pieces. Joyful shouts, ringing of bells, and processions ceased not for a moment. The whole region flamed up at once. All living men, seizing scythes and pikes, joined the Zaporojians; endless crowds hastened to the camp from every side. There came also joyful, because certain, tidings that Yeremi had indeed offered his assistance to the hetmans, but had not yet joined them.

Hmelnitski felt relieved. He moved on without delay, and advanced through insurrection, slaughter, and fire. Ruin and corpses bore witness to this. He advanced like an avalanche, destroying everything in his path. The country rose before him, and was a desert behind. He went like an avenger, like a legendary dragon; his footsteps pressed out blood, his breath kindled conflagrations.

In Cherkasi he halted with his main forces, sending in advance the Tartars under Tugai Bey and the wild Krívonos, who came up with the Polish hetmans at Korsún and attacked them without delay. The Tartars were forced to pay dearly for their boldness. Repulsed, decimated, scattered, they retreated in confusion.

Hmelnitski hurried to their aid. On the way news reached him that Senyavski with some regiments had joined the hetmans, who had left Korsún, and were marching on Boguslav. This was true. Hmelnitski occupied Korsún without resistance, and leaving there his trains and provisions, in a word, his whole camp, hurried after them. He had no need to follow long, for they had not gone far. At Krutaya Balka his advance guard came upon the Polish camp.

"The Commonwealth has passed through more than one defeat," said Charnetski, "but she contains within her inexhaustible force. No power has broken her as yet, and she will not be broken by a sedition of serfs, whom God himself will punish, since by rising up against authority, they are putting themselves against his will. As to defeat, true, it is sad; but who have endured defeat?--the hetmans, the forces of the crown? No! After the defection and treason of Krechovski, the division which Pototski led could be considered only an advance guard. The uprising will spread undoubtedly through the whole Ukraine, for the serfs there are insolent and trained to fighting; but an uprising in that part is no novelty. The hetmans will quell it, with Prince Yeremi, whose power stands unshaken as yet; the more violent the outburst, when once put down, the longer will be the peace, which may last perhaps forever. He would be a man of little faith and a small heart, who could admit that some Cossack leader, in company with one Tartar murza, could really threaten a mighty people. Evil would it be with the Commonwealth, if a simple outbreak of serfs could be made a question of its fate or its existence. In truth we did set out contemptuously on this expedition," said Charnetski; "and though our division is rubbed out, I believe that the hetmans are able to put down this rebellion, not with the sword, not with armor, but with clubs."

And while he was speaking in this manner, it seemed that not a captive, not a soldier after a lost battle was speaking, but a proud hetman, certain of victory on the morrow. This greatness of soul and faith in the Commonwealth flowed like balsam over the wounds of the lieutenant. He had had a near view of the power of Hmelnitski, therefore it blinded him somewhat, especially since success had followed it to that moment. But Charnetski must be right. The forces of the hetmans were still intact, and behind them stood the power of the Commonwealth, the rights of authority, and the will of God. The lieutenant therefore went away strengthened in soul and more cheerful. When going he asked Charnetski if he did not wish to begin negotiations for his freedom with Hmelnitski at once.

"I am the captive of Tugai Bey," said Charnetski; "to him I will pay my ransom. But with that fellow Hmelnitski I will have nothing to do; I give him to the hangman."

Zakhar, who had made it easy for Skshetuski to see the prisoners, comforted him while returning to the telega.

"Not with young Pototski, but with the hetmans is the difficulty. The struggle is only begun, but what will be the end, God knows! The Cossacks and Tartars have taken Polish treasure, it is true, but it is one thing to take and another to keep. And you, my child, do not grieve, do not despair, for you will get your freedom in time. You will go to your own people, and I, old man, shall be sorry for you. It is sad for an old man alone in the world. With the hetmans it will be hard, oh, how hard!"

In truth the victory, though brilliant, did not in the least decide the struggle for Hmelnitski. It might even be unfavorable for him, because it was easy to foresee that now the Grand Hetman, to avenge his son, would press upon the Cossacks with special stubbornness, and would leave nothing undone to break them at once. The Grand Hetman, however, cherished a certain dislike for Prince Yeremi, which, though veiled with politeness, was still evident enough in various circumstances.

"Show favor to us, lord!"

"It will be as I have said," returned the lieutenant.

He was indeed sure of the efficacy of his intercession with the hetman, with whom he was acquainted, for he had often borne letters to him from Prince Yeremi, and knew how to secure his favor. He stood, therefore, with his hands on his hips; and joy was on his face, lighted up with the blaze of the conflagration.

"Behold! the war is at an end, the wave is broken at the threshold!" thought he. "Pan Charnetski was right: the forces of the Commonwealth are unexhausted, its power unbroken."

When he thought of this, pride swelled his breast,--not ignoble pride, coming from a hoped-for satisfaction of vengeance, from the conquest of an enemy; not the gaining of freedom, which now he expected every moment; nor because caps were removed before him; but he felt proud because he was a son of that victorious and mighty Commonwealth, against whose gates every malice, every attack, every blow, is broken and crushed like the powers of hell against the gates of heaven. He felt proud, as a patriotic nobleman, that he had received strength in his despondency, and was not deceived in his faith. He desired no revenge.

"She has conquered like a queen, she will forgive like a mother," thought he.

Meanwhile the roar of cannon was changed to prolonged thunder. Horses' hoofs clattered again over the empty streets. A Cossack, bareheaded and in his shirt-sleeves, dashed into the square on a barebacked horse, with the speed of a thunderbolt; his face, cut open with a sword, was streaming with blood. He reined in the horse, stretched forth his hands, and when he had taken breath, with open mouth began to cry,--

"Hmelnitski is beating the Poles! The serene great mighty lords, the hetmans and colonels, are conquered,--the knights and the cavalry!"

When he had said this, he reeled and fell to the ground. The men of Mirgorod sprang to assist him.

Flame and pallor passed over the face of Skshetuski.

"What does he say?" asked he feverishly of Zakhar. "What has happened? It cannot be. By the living God, it cannot be!"

Silence! Only the hissing of flames on the opposite side of the square, shaking out clusters of sparks, and from time to time a burnt house falls with a crash.

Now more couriers rush in. "Beaten are the Poles,--beaten!"

After them follow a detachment of Tartars. They march slowly, for they surround men on foot, evidently prisoners.

Skshetuski believes not his own eyes. He recognizes perfectly on the prisoners the uniform of the hetmans' hussars; then he drops his hands, and with a wild, strange voice repeats persistently, "It cannot be! it cannot be!"

The roar of cannon was still to be heard. The battle was not finished, but through all the unburnt streets Zaporojians and Tartars were crowding in, their faces black, their breasts heaving, but they were coming as if intoxicated, singing songs. Thus return soldiers from victory.

The lieutenant grew pale as a corpse. "It cannot be!" repeated he in a hoarser voice,--"it cannot be! The Commonwealth--"

A new object arrested his attention. Krechovski's Cossacks enter the town, bringing bundles of flags. They come to the centre of the square, and throw them down. Polish flags!

The roar of the artillery weakens, and in the distance is heard the rumble of approaching wagons. One of them is in advance,--a lofty Cossack telega, and after it a line of others, all surrounded by Cossacks of the Pashkoff kuren, in yellow caps; they pass near the house where the Mirgorod men are standing.

Skshetuski put his hand over his eyes, for the glare of the burning blinded him, and looked at the prisoners sitting in the first wagon. Suddenly he sprang back, began to beat the air with his hands, like a man struck with an arrow in the breast, and from his lips came a terrible unearthly cry: "Jesus, Mary! the hetmans!"

He dropped into the arms of Zakhar; his eyes became leaden, his face grew stiff and rigid as that of a corpse.

A few minutes later three horsemen rode into the square of Korsún, at the head of countless regiments. The middle rider, in red uniform, sat on a white horse, holding a gilded baton at his side. He looked as proud as a king. This was Hmelnitski. On one side of him rode Tugai Bey, on the other Krechovski.

The Commonwealth lay prostrate in dust and blood at the feet of a Cossack.

CHAPTER XVI.

Some days passed by. It appeared to men as if the vault of heaven had suddenly dropped on the Commonwealth. Jóltiya Vodi; Korsún; the destruction of the armies of the crown, ever victorious hitherto in struggles with the Cossacks; the capture of the hetmans; the awful conflagration in the whole Ukraine; slaughters, murders, unheard of since the beginning of the world,--all these came so suddenly that men almost refused to believe that so many misfortunes could come upon one land at a time. Many, in fact, did not believe it; some became helpless from terror, some lost their senses, some prophesied the coming of antichrist and the approach of the day of judgment. All social ties were severed; all intercourse between people and families was interrupted. Every authority ceased; distinction of persons vanished. Hell had freed from its chains all crimes, and let them out on the world to revel; therefore murder, pillage, perfidy, brutality, violence, robbery, frenzy, took the place of labor, uprightness, and conscience. It seemed as though henceforth people would live not through good, but through evil; that the hearts and intentions of men had become inverted, and that they held as sacred that which hitherto had been infamous, and that as infamous which hitherto had been sacred. The sun shone no longer upon the earth, for it was hidden by the smoke of conflagrations; in the night, instead of stars and moon, shone the light of fires. Towns, villages, churches, palaces, forests, went up in flames. People ceased to converse; they only groaned or howled like dogs. Life lost its value. Thousands perished without an echo, without remembrance. And from out all these calamities, deaths, groans, smoke, and burnings, there rose only one man. Every moment loftier and higher, every moment more terribly gigantic, he wellnigh obscured the light of day, and cast his shadow from sea to sea. That man was Bogdan Hmelnitski.

A hundred and twenty thousand men, armed and drunk with victory, stood ready at his nod. The mob had risen on all sides; the Cossacks of the towns joined him in every place. The country from the Pripet to the borders of the Wilderness was on fire. The insurrection extended in the provinces of Rus, Podolia, Volynia, Bratslav, Kieff, and Chernigoff. The power of the hetman increased each day. Never had the Commonwealth opposed to its most terrible enemy half the forces which he then commanded. The German emperor had not equal numbers in readiness. The storm surpassed every expectation. The hetman himself did not recognize at first his own power, and did not understand how he had risen so high. He shielded himself yet with justice, legality, and loyalty to the Commonwealth, for he did not know then that he might trample upon these expressions as empty phrases; but as his forces grew there rose in him that immeasurable, unconscious egotism the equal of which is not presented by history. The understanding of good and evil, of virtue and vice, of violence and justice, were confounded in the soul of Hmelnitski with the understanding of injuries done him, or with his personal profit. That man was honorable who was with him; that man was a criminal who was against him. He was ready to complain of the sun, and to count it as a personal injustice if sunshine were not given at his demand. Men, events, nay, the whole world, he measured with his own *ego*. But in spite of all the cunning, all the hypocrisy of the hetman, there was a kind of deformed good faith in this theory of his. All Hmelnitski's crimes flowed from this theory, but his good deeds as well; for if he knew no bounds in his cruelty and tyranny to an enemy, he knew how to be thankful for every even involuntary service which was rendered him.

Only when he was drunk did he forget even good deeds, and bellowing with fury, with foam on his lips, issue bloody orders, for which he grieved afterward. And in proportion as his success grew, was he oftener drunk, for unquiet took increasing possession of him. It would seem that triumph carried him to heights which he did not wish to occupy. His power amazed other men, but it amazed himself too. The gigantic hand of rebellion seized and bore him on with the swiftness of lightning and inexorably. But whither? How was all this to end? Commencing sedition in the name of his own wrongs, that Cossack diplomat might calculate that after his first successes, or even after defeats, he could begin negotiations; that forgiveness would be offered him, satisfaction and recompense for injustice and injuries. He knew the Commonwealth intimately,--its patience, inexhaustible as the sea; its compassion, knowing neither bounds nor measure, which flowed not merely from weakness, for pardon was offered Nalivaika when he was surrounded and lost. But after the victory at Jóltiya Vodi, after the destruction of the hetmans, after the kindling of civil war in all the southern provinces, affairs had gone too far. Events had surpassed all expectations, and now the struggle must be for life and death. To whose side would victory incline?

Hmelnitski inquired of soothsayers, took counsel of the stars, and strained his eyes into the future, but saw nothing ahead save darkness. At times, therefore, an awful unquiet raised the hairs on his head, and in his breast despair raged like a whirlwind. What will be?--what will be? For Hmelnitski, observing more closely than others, understood at once, better than many, that the Commonwealth knew not how to use its own forces,--was unconscious of them,--but had tremendous power. If the right man should grasp that power in his hand, who could stand against him? And who could guess whether terrible danger, the nearness of the precipice and destruction, might not put an end to broils, internal dissensions, private grievances, rivalries of magnates, wrangling, the babbling of the Diets, the license of the nobility, and the weakness of the king? Then a half-million of escutcheoned warriors alone could move to the field, and crush Hmelnitski, even if he were aided not only by the Khan of the Crimea, but by the Sultan of Turkey himself.

Of this slumbering power of the Commonwealth the late King Vladislav was aware, as well as Hmelnitski; and therefore he labored all his life to initiate a mortal struggle with the greatest potentate on earth, for only in this way could that power be called into life. In accordance with this conviction, the king did not hesitate to throw sparks on the Cossack powder. Were the Cossacks really destined to cause that inundation, in order to be overwhelmed in it at last?

Hmelnitski understood, too, that in spite of all the weakness of the Commonwealth its resistance was tremendous. Against this Commonwealth, so disorderly, ill-united, insubordinate, the Turkish waves, the most terrible of all were broken as against a cliff. Thus it was at Khotím which he saw almost with his own eyes. That Commonwealth, even in times of weakness, planted its standards on the walls of foreign capitals. What resistance will it offer, what will it not do when brought to despair, when it must either die or conquer?

In view of this, every triumph of Hmelnitski was to him a new danger, for it hastened the moment when the sleeping lion would wake, and brought negotiations nearer the impossible. In every victory lay a future defeat, and in every intoxication bitterness at the bottom. After the storm of the Cossacks would come the storm of the Commonwealth. Already it seemed to Hmelnitski that he heard its dull and distant roar. Behold, from Great Poland, Prussia, populous Mazovia, Little Poland, and Lithuania will come crowds of warriors! They need but a leader.

Hmelnitski had taken the hetmans captive, but in that good fortune there lurked also an ambush of fate. The hetmans were experienced warriors, but no one of them was the man demanded by that period of tempest, terror, and distress. The leader at that time could be but one man. That man was Prince Yeremi Vishnyevetski. Just because the hetmans had gone into captivity the choice would be likely to fall on the prince. Hmelnitski in common with all had no doubt of this.

Meanwhile news flew from beyond the Dnieper to Korsún, where the Zaporojian hetman had stopped to rest after the battle, that the terrible prince had started for Lubni; that on the road he was stamping out rebellion; that after his passage villages, hamlets, towns, farmhouses, had vanished, and the places in which they had been were bristling with bloody impaling-stakes and gibbets. Terror doubled and trebled the number of his forces; it was said that he led fifteen thousand of the choicest troops to be found in the Commonwealth.

In the Cossack camp, shortly after the battle at Krutaya Balka, the cry, "Yeremi is coming!" was heard among the Cossacks and spread a panic among the mob, who began to run away unreasoningly. This alarm astonished Hmelnitski greatly.

He had his choice then,--either to march with all his power against the prince and seek him beyond the Dnieper, or, leaving a part of his forces to capture the castles of the Ukraine, move into the heart of the Commonwealth. An expedition against the prince was not without danger, Hmelnitski, in spite of the preponderance of his forces, might suffer defeat in a general engagement, and then all would be lost at once. The mob, who composed the great majority, gave evidence that they would flee at the very name of Yeremi. Time was necessary to change this mob into an army capable of facing the regiments of the prince. Besides, Yeremi would not be likely to accept a general battle, but would be content with defence in castles and partisan war which might last entire months, if not years, and by that time the Commonwealth would surely collect new forces and move to reinforce him.

Hmelnitski therefore determined to leave Vishnyevetski beyond the Dnieper, strengthen himself in the Ukraine, organize his power, then march on the Commonwealth and force it to terms. He calculated that the suppression of the rebellion on the east of the Dnieper alone would occupy for a long time all the forces of the prince, and leave a free field to himself. He hoped therefore to foment rebellion by sending single regiments to aid the mob, and finally he thought it would be possible to deceive the prince by negotiations, and retard matters by waiting till the power of Vishnyevetski should be broken. In view of this he remembered Pan Yan.

Some days after Krutaya Balka, and on the very day of the alarm of the mob, he had Skshetuski called before him. He received him in the house of the starosta, in presence of Krechovski only, who was long known to Skshetuski; and after he had greeted him kindly, though not without a lofty air corresponding to his present position, he said,--

"Lieutenant Skshetuski, for the kindness which you have shown me I have ransomed you from Tugai Bey and promised you freedom. Now the hour has come. I give you this baton of a colonel to secure a free passage, in case any of the forces should meet you, and a guard for protection against the mob. You may return to your prince."

Skshetuski was silent; no smile of joy appeared on his face.

"But are you able to take the road, for I see that illness of some kind is looking out through your eyes?"

Pan Yan, in truth, seemed like a shadow. Wounds and recent events had weakened the young giant, who looked as though he could give no promise of surviving till the morrow. His face had grown yellow, and the black beard, long untrimmed, added to the wretchedness of his appearance. This rose from internal suffering. The knight's heart was almost broken. Dragged after the Tartar camp, he had been a witness of all that had happened since they issued from the Saitch. He had seen the defeat and disgrace of the Commonwealth, and the hetmans in captivity; he had seen the Cossack's triumph, pyramids of heads cut from fallen soldiers, noblemen hanged by the ribs, the breasts of women cut off, and maidens dishonored; he had seen the despair of daring and the baseness of fear; he had seen everything, endured everything, and suffered the more because the thought was in his bosom and brain, like the stab of a knife, that he himself was the remote cause, for he and no other had cut Hmelnitski loose from the lariat. But was a Christian knight to suppose that succor given one's neighbor could bring such fruit? His pain therefore was beyond measure.

When he asked himself what was happening to Helena, and when he thought what might happen if an evil fate should keep her in Rozlogi, he stretched his hands to heaven and cried in a voice in which quivered deep despair, almost a threat: "God! take my life, for I am punished beyond my deserts!" Then he saw that he was blaspheming, fell on his face, and prayed for salvation, for forgiveness, for mercy on his country and that innocent dove, who maybe had called in vain for God's help and his. In one word, he had suffered so much beyond his power that the freedom granted did not rejoice him; and that Zaporojian hetman, that conqueror who wished to be magnanimous by showing his favor, made no impression upon him at all. Seeing this, Hmelnitski frowned and said,--

"Hasten to take advantage of my favor, lest I change my mind; for it is my kindness and belief in a just cause which makes me so careless as to provide an enemy for myself, for I know well that you will fight against me."

To which Skshetuski answered: "If God gives me strength."

And he gazed at Hmelnitski, till he looked into the depth of his soul. The hetman, unable to endure the gaze, cast his eyes to the ground, and after a moment said,--

"Enough of this! I am too powerful to be troubled by one sick man. Tell the prince your lord what you have seen, and warn him to be less insolent; for if my patience fails I will visit him beyond the Dnieper, and I do not think my visit will be pleasant to him."

Skshetuski was silent.

"I say, and repeat once more," added Hmelnitski, "I am carrying on war, not with the Commonwealth, but with the kinglets; and the prince is in the first rank among them. He is an enemy to me and to the Russian people, an apostate from our church, and a savage tyrant. I hear that he is quelling the uprising in blood; let him see to it that he does not spill his own."

Thus speaking, he became more and more excited, till the blood began to rush to his face, and his eyes flashed fire. It was evident that one of those paroxysms of anger and rage in which he lost his memory and presence of mind altogether was seizing him.

"I will command Krívonos to bring him with a rope!" cried he. "I will trample him under foot, and mount my horse on his back!"

Skshetuski looked down on the raging Hmelnitski, and then said calmly: "Conquer him first."

"Hetman," said Krechovski, "let this insolent noble go his way, for it does not become your dignity to be affected by anger against him; and since you have promised him freedom he calculates that either you will break your word or listen to his invectives."

Hmelnitski bethought himself, panted awhile, then said,--

"Let him go then, and give him a baton, as I have said, and forty Tartars, who will take him to his own camp, so that he may know that Hmelnitski returns good for good." Then turning to Pan Yan, he added: "You know that we are even now. I liked you in spite of your insolence, but if you fall into my hands again you will not escape."

Skshetuski went out with Krechovski.

"Since the hetman has let you off with your life," said Krechovski, "and you can go where you please, I tell you, for old acquaintance' sake, to seek safety in Warsaw rather than beyond the Dnieper, for you will not leave there alive. Your time has passed. If you were wise you would come to our side, but I know that it is useless to tell you this. You would rise as high as we."

"To the gallows," muttered Skshetuski.

"They would not give me the starostaship of Lita, but now I can take, not only one, but ten such places. We will drive out the Konyetspolskis, Kalinovskis, Pototskis, Lyubomirskis, Vishnyevetskis, Zaslavskis, and all the nobility, and divide their estates; which must be according to the will of God, for he has already given us two great victories."

Pan Yan was thinking of something else, and did not hear the prating of the colonel, who continued,--

"When after the battle I saw the high mighty hetman of the crown, my lord and benefactor, bound in Tugai Bey's quarters, and he was pleased immediately to call me a Judas and unthankful, I answered him: 'Serene, great voevoda! I am not unthankful, for when I shall be in possession of your castles and property, I will make you my under-starosta if you will promise not to get drunk.' Oh, ho! Tugai Bey will get ransom for those birds that he has caught, and therefore he spares them; were it not for that, Hmelnitski and I would talk differently to them. But see! the wagon is ready for you and the Tartars are on hand. Where do you wish to go?"

"To Chigirin."

"'As thou makest thy bed, so wilt thou sleep.' The Tartars will conduct you even to Lubni, for such are their orders. See, however, that your prince does not have them impaled, as he surely would Cossacks. This is why Tartars are given to you. The hetman has ordered that your horse be given you. Farewell! Remember us with kindness. Give our hetman's respects to your prince, and if he be persuaded to come to Hmelnitski with homage, he may find favor. Farewell!"

Pan Yan seated himself in the wagon, which the Tartars surrounded at once; and they moved on. It was difficult to pass through the square, which was completely packed with Zaporojians and the mob. Both were cooking kasha for themselves, while singing songs over the victory of Jóltiya Vodi and Korsún, composed by blind minstrels, a multitude of whom came from all sides to the camp. Between the fires burning under the kasha kettles, lay here and there bodies of murdered women over whom orgies had taken place in the night, or stood pyramids of heads cut from the bodies of killed and wounded soldiers. These bodies and heads had begun to decay and give out an offensive odor, which however did not seem to be at all disagreeable to the assembled crowds. The town bore marks of devastation and the wild license of Zaporojians. Doors and windows were torn out; the shivered fragments of a thousand objects, mixed with hair and straw, covered the square. The eaves of houses were ornamented with hanged men, for the greater part Jews; and here and there the crowd amused themselves by clinging to the feet of pendent corpses and swinging on them.

On one side of the square were the black ruins of burnt buildings, among them those of the parish church; the ruins were hot, and smoke was rising from them. The odor of burning permeated the air. Beyond the burnt houses was the Tartar camp, which Skshetuski had to pass, and crowds of captives watched by Tartar guards. Men from the neighborhood of Chigirin, Cherkasi, and Korsún, who had been unable to hide, or who had not fallen under the axe of the mob, went into captivity. The prisoners were soldiers, captured in the two battles; and townspeople of the region about, who had been unable or unwilling to join the uprising; nobles living on their own lands, separately or in communes; officials of under-starostas; owners of small tracts of land; village nobles of both sexes, and children. There were no old men, for the Tartars killed them as unfit for sale. They had driven in also whole Russian villages and settlements,--an act which Hmelnitski did not dare to oppose. In many places it happened that men went to the Cossack camp, and as a reward the Tartars burned their cottages, and carried off their wives and children. But in the universal letting loose and growing wild of souls, no one inquired or thought about that. The mob who took arms gave up their native villages, their wives and children. Their wives were taken from them; but they took other and better women, for they were Polish. After they had sated themselves with the charms of these they killed them, or sold them to Tartars. Among the prisoners also were young matrons of the Ukraine, tied by threes and fours to one rope with young women of the petty nobility. Captivity and misfortune equalized condition.

The sight of these beings shocked the lieutenant to the bottom of his soul, and roused a thirst for vengeance. Tattered, half naked, exposed to the vile jeers of pagans who were loitering through curiosity in crowds on the square, pushed, struck, or kissed by disgusting lips, they lost their memory and will. Some sobbed, or resisted loudly; others, with staring eyes and bewildered faces, yielded passively to everything. Here and there was heard a shriek wrested from some captive, slaughtered without mercy for an outburst of despairing resistance. The cracking of whips, the whistling of ox-hide lashes, was heard among the crowd of men, and was mingled with screams of pain, with the whining of children, the bellowing of cattle, and the neighing of horses. The booty was not yet divided and arranged for removal; therefore the greatest disorder prevailed everywhere. Wagons, horses, horned cattle, camels, sheep, women, men, heaps of stolen clothing, vessels, arms,--all, thrust into one enormous camp, waited arrangement and order. Scouting-parties drove in from time to time new crowds of people and herds of cattle, laden barges sailed down the Kos, and from the chief camp new people arrived continually to sate their eyes with the sight of the collected wealth. Some, drunk on kumis or vudka, dressed in strange costumes,--in chasubles and surplices, in robes of Russian priests, or even in women's clothes,--began to dispute, quarrel, and scream over the possession of certain articles. The Tartar herdsmen, sitting on the ground among the cattle, amused themselves,-- some by giving piercing melodies on their pipes, others by playing dice or beating one another with clubs. Crowds of dogs which had followed their masters barked and howled plaintively.

Skshetuski at length passed this human gehenna, full of groans, tears of misery, and hellish sounds. He had expected to breathe more freely; but the moment he was beyond the camp a new and terrible sight struck his eyes. In the distance was the camp proper, from which came a continual neighing of horses, and near which thousands of Tartars swarmed in the field by the side of the road leading to Cherkasi. The youthful warriors amused themselves with shooting for exercise from bows at the weaker prisoners, or the sick who were unable to endure the long road to the Crimea. A number of bodies lay around, thrown on the road, as full of holes as a sieve; some of them still quivered convulsively. Those at whom they were shooting hung bound by the hands to trees near the roadside. Among these were also old women. Shouts accompanied laughter of approval for good arrow-shots.

"Fine fellows! The bow is in good hands!"

Around the principal camp they were dressing thousands of cattle and horses for the sustenance of the warriors. The ground was drenched with blood. The sickening odor of raw flesh stifled the breath in the breast, and among the piles of meat red Tartars hurried around with knives in their hands. The day was oppressive, the sun scorching. Skshetuski with his escort barely reached the open field after an hour's travelling; but from afar there came for a long time the tumult and bellowing of cattle from the main camp. Along the road traces of the passage of plunderers were evident. Here and there were burnt gardens, chimneys standing alone, young grain trodden under foot, trees broken, cherry-orchards near the cottages cut down for fuel. On the high-road lay thickly, in one place, the carcasses of horses; in another the bodies of men mutilated fearfully, blue, swollen, and above and over them flocks of crows and ravens, flying with tumult and noise at the approach of people. The bloody work of Hmelnitski thrust itself upon the sight everywhere, and it was difficult to understand against whom the man had raised his hands, since his own country groaned first of all under the weight of misfortune.

In Mleyeff, Skshetuski met Tartar parties urging on new crowds of prisoners. Gorodische was burned to the ground. There remained standing only the stone bell-tower of the church, and the old oak-tree in the middle of the square, covered with terrible fruit; for upon it were suspended a number of tens of little Jews, hanged there three days before. There were killed also many nobles from Konoplanka, Staroselo, Venjovka, Balaklei, Vodachevo. The town itself was empty; for the men had gone to Hmelnitski, and the women, children, and old men had fled to the woods before the expected invasion by the armies of Prince Yeremi. From Gorodische, Skshetuski went through Smila, Zabotin, and Novoselyets to Chigirin, stopping only to rest his horse. They entered the town on the second day in the afternoon. War had spared the place; only a few houses were wrecked, and among them that of Chaplinski was razed to the ground. In the town was stationed Colonel Naókolopályets, and with him a thousand Cossacks; but both he and they and the whole population lived in the greatest terror, for they all seemed convinced that the prince might come at any moment and wreak vengeance such as the world had never heard of. It was unknown who had circulated these reports, or where they had come from; fear perhaps had created them. Enough that it was repeated continually that the prince was sailing on the Sula, that he was already on the Dnieper, had burned Vasyutinets, and had cut off the people in Borysi, and that every approach of men on horseback caused boundless panic. Skshetuski caught up these reports eagerly; for he understood that though false they prevented the extension of the rebellion beyond the Dnieper, where the hand of the prince pressed directly.

Skshetuski wished to learn something more certain from Naókolopályets; but it appeared that the lieutenant-colonel, like others, knew nothing about the prince, and would have been glad himself to extract some news from Skshetuski. Since all boats, large and small, had been brought over to that bank of the river, fugitives from the other shore did not come to Chigirin.

Skshetuski, without waiting longer in Chigirin, gave orders to be ferried over, and set out for Rozlogi. The assurance that he would soon convince himself of what had happened to Helena, and the hope that perhaps she was safe, or had taken refuge with her aunt and the princes in Lubni, brought back his strength and health. He left the wagon for his horse, and urged without sparing his Tartars, who, thinking him an envoy and themselves attendants given under his command, dared not oppose him. They flew on therefore as if hunted. Behind them rose yellow clouds of dust hurled up by the hoofs of the horses. They swept past farms, gardens, and villages. The country was empty, the habitations of men depopulated; for a long time they could not find a living soul. It is likely, too, that every one hid at their approach. Here and there Skshetuski gave orders to search in orchards and bee-gardens, grain-mows and the roofs of barns, but they discovered no man.

Beyond Pogrebi one of the Tartars first espied a certain human form trying to hide among the rushes which grew on the banks of the Kagamlik. The Tartars rushed to the river, and a few minutes later brought before Skshetuski two persons entirely naked. One of them was an old man; the other a stripling, perhaps fifteen or sixteen years of age. The teeth of both were chattering with terror, and for a long time they were unable to utter a word.

"Where are you from?" asked Skshetuski.

"Nowhere, sir!" answered the old man. "We go begging with a lyre, and this dumb boy leads me."

"Where are you coming from now,--from what village? Speak boldly; nothing will happen to you."

"We, sir, travelled through all the villages, till some devil stripped us. We had good boots, he took them; we had good caps, he took them; good coats from people's charity, he took them, and did not leave the lyre."

"I ask you, you fool, from what village you come."

"I don't know, sir,--I am an old man. See, we are naked; we are freezing at night, in the daytime we ask the charity of people to cover us and feed us; we are hungry!"

"Listen, louts! Answer my question, or I will hang you!"

"I don't know, my lord. If I am this or that, or there will be anything, let me alone."

It was evident that the old man, unable to decide who his questioner was, determined not to give any answer.

"Were you in Rozlogi, where the Princes Kurtsevichi live?"

"I don't know, sir."

"Hang him!" cried Skshetuski.

"I was, sir," cried the old man, seeing there was no trifling.

"What did you see there?"

"We were there five days ago, and then in Brovarki; we heard that the knights had come there."

"What knights?"

"I don't know, sir; one said Poles, another said Cossacks."

"To horse!" shouted Skshetuski to the Tartars.

The party rushed on. The sun was setting precisely as on that day when the lieutenant, after meeting Helena and the princess on the road, rode by them at the side of Rozvan's carriage. The Kagamlik shone with purple, just as it had then; the day went to rest with more quiet, more warmth and calm. But that time Pan Yan rode on with a breast full of happiness and awakening feelings of delight; now he rushes on like a condemned man, driven by a whirlwind of trouble and evil forebodings. The voice of despair calls from his soul, "Bogun has carried her away, you will never see her again!" and a voice of hope, "She is safe!" And these voices so pulled him between them that they almost tore his heart asunder. He urged the horses to their last strength. One hour followed another. The moon rose and mounted higher and higher, grew paler and paler. The horses were covered with foam, and snorted heavily. They rushed into the forest, it was passed in a flash; they rushed into the ravine; beyond the ravine was Rozlogi. Another moment, and the fate of the knight would be settled. The wind whistles into his ears from the speed, his cap falls from his head, the horse groans under him as if ready to drop. Another moment, and the ravine opens. At last! at last!

Suddenly an unearthly shriek comes from the breast of Skshetuski. The house, granaries, stables, barns, picket-fence, and cherry-orchard had all disappeared. The pale moon shone upon the hill, and on a pile of black ruins which had ceased to smoke. No sound broke the silence.

Skshetuski stood before the trench speechless; he merely raised his hands, looked, and shook his head in bewilderment. The Tartars stopped their horses. He dismounted, sought out the remains of the burned bridge, passed the trench on the cross-pieces, and sat on the stone lying in the middle of the yard. Having sat down, he began to look around like a man who tries to recognize a place in which he finds himself for the first time. Presence of mind left him. He uttered no groan. After a while he placed his hands on his knees, dropped his head, and remained motionless; it might have been supposed that he was asleep. Indeed, if not asleep, he had become torpid; and through his brain passed dim visions instead of thoughts. He saw Helena as she looked when he parted with her before his last journey; but her face was veiled as it were by mist, therefore her features could not be distinguished. He wished to bring her out of that misty covering, but could not, and went away with heavy heart. Then there passed before him the square at Chigirin, old Zatsvilikhovski, and the impudent face of Zagloba; that face remained before his eyes with a special persistence, until at length the gloomy visage of Grodzitski took its place. After that he saw Kudák again, the Cataracts, the fight at Hortitsa, the Saitch, the whole journey, and all the events to the last day and hour. But farther there was darkness! What was happening to him at the present he saw not. He had only a sort of indefinite feeling that he was going to Helena, to Rozlogi, but his strength had failed; that he was resting on ruins. He wanted to rise and go farther, but an immeasurable weakness bound him to the place, as if a hundred-pound ball were fastened to his feet.

He sat and sat. The evening was advancing. The Tartars arranged themselves for the night, made a fire, cooked pieces of horse-flesh, and having satisfied their hunger, lay down on the ground.

But before an hour had passed they sprang to their feet again. From a distance came a noise like the sound made by a great number of cavalry when moving on a hurried march.

The Tartars fastened as quickly as possible a white cloth on a pole, and renewed the fire vigorously, so that it might be seen from a distance that they were messengers of peace.

The tramp and snorting of horses, the clatter of sabres, came nearer and nearer; and soon there appeared on the road a division of cavalry, which surrounded the Tartars at once.

A short parley followed. The Tartars pointed to a figure sitting on the rising ground,--which was perfectly visible, for the light of the moon fell on it,--and said they were escorting an envoy, but from whom he could tell best himself.

The leader of the division went with some of his companions to the rising ground, but had scarcely come up and looked into the face of the sitting man, when he opened his arms and cried,--

"Skshetuski! By the living God, it is Skshetuski!"

The lieutenant did not move.

"But, Lieutenant, don't you know me? I am Bykhovets. What is the matter with you?"

The lieutenant was silent.

"Rouse yourself, for God's sake! Here, comrade, come to your mind!"

This was really Pan Bykhovets, who was marching in the vanguard of all Vishnyevetski's forces.

Other regiments came up. News of the discovery of Pan Yan spread like lightning in the regiments, therefore all hurried to greet their favorite comrade. Little Volodyovski, the two Sleshinskis, Dzik, Orpishevski, Migurski, Yakubovich, Lents, Pan Longin Podbipienta, and a number of other officers ran as fast as they could to the eminence. But they spoke in vain to him, called him by name, pulled him by the shoulders, tried to raise him up. Skshetuski looked on them with wide-open eyes, and recognized no man; or rather, on the contrary, he seemed to recognize them, but was completely indifferent to them. Then those who knew of his love for Helena--and indeed all knew that--remembered what place they were in; looking on the black ruins and the gray ashes, they understood all.

"He has lost his mind from grief," said one.

"Despair has disturbed his mind."

"Take him to the priest; when he sees him perhaps he will come to himself."

Pan Longin wrung his hands. All surrounded the lieutenant and looked at him with sympathy. Some wiped away their tears, others sighed sadly; till suddenly a lofty figure appeared, and approaching quietly, placed his hands upon the lieutenant's head. This was the priest, Mukhovetski.

All were silent and knelt down as if waiting for a miracle; but the priest performed no miracle. Holding his hands on Pan Yan's head, he raised his eyes to the heavens, which were filled with the light of the moon, and began to pray aloud.

"'Pater noster, qui es in cœlis! sanctificetur nomen tuum, adveniat regnum tuum, fiat voluntas tua--'" Here he stopped, and after a while repeated more loudly and solemnly: "'Fiat voluntas tua!'" A deep silence reigned. "'Fiat voluntas tua!'" repeated the priest for the third time.

From the mouth of Skshetuski came a voice of measureless pain, but also of resignation: "'Sicut in cœlo, et in terra!'" Then the knight threw himself sobbing on the ground.

CHAPTER XVII.

To explain what had taken place in Rozlogi, we must return to that night when Pan Yan sent Jendzian from Kudák with a letter to the old princess. The letter contained an earnest request to take Helena and seek with all haste the protection of Prince Yeremi at Lubni, since war might begin at any moment.

Jendzian, taking his place in the boat which Pan Grodzitski sent from Kudák for powder, made his way with slow advance, for they went up the river. At Kremenchug he met the forces sailing under command of Krechovski and Barabash, despatched by the hetmans against Hmelnitski. Jendzian had a meeting with Barabash, whom he informed of the possible danger to Pan Yan on his journey to the Saitch; therefore he begged the old colonel not to fail in making urgent demand for the envoy when he met Hmelnitski. After this he moved on.

They arrived in Chigirin at daylight. They were surrounded at once by a guard of Cossacks inquiring who they were. They answered that they were going from Kudák with a letter from Grodzitski to the hetmans. Notwithstanding this, the chief of the boat and Jendzian were summoned to answer the colonel.

"What colonel?" asked the chief.

"Loboda," replied the essauls of the guard. "The Grand Hetman has ordered him to detain and examine every one coming from the Saitch to Chigirin."

They went. Jendzian walked on boldly, for he expected no harm since he was sent by authority of the hetman.

They were taken to the neighborhood of Bell-ringers' Corner, to the house of Pan Jelenski, where Colonel Loboda's quarters were. But they were informed that the colonel having set out at daybreak for Cherkasi, the lieutenant-colonel occupied his place. They waited rather long; at last the door opened, and the expected lieutenant-colonel appeared in the room. At the sight of him Jendzian's knees trembled under him. It was Bogun.

The hetman's power extended really to Chigirin; but since Loboda and Bogun had not yet gone over to Hmelnitski, but adhered publicly to the Commonwealth, the Grand Hetman had appointed them to Chigirin, and ordered them to maintain guard.

Bogun took his place at the table and began to question the newly arrived.

The chief of the boat, who brought a letter from Grodzitski, answered for himself and Jendzian. On examination of the letter, the young lieutenant-colonel began to inquire carefully what was to be heard in Kudák, and it was evident that he had a great desire to know why Grodzitski had sent men and a boat to the Grand Hetman. But the chief of the boat could not answer this, and the letter was secured with Pan Grodzitski's seal. Having finished his inquiries, Bogun was putting his hand to his purse to give the men something to buy beer, when the door opened, and Zagloba burst like a thunderbolt into the room.

"Listen, Bogun!" cried he; "that traitor Dopúla has kept his best triple mead hidden. I went with him to the cellar. I looked, I saw something in the corner; it was hay and it wasn't hay. I asked, 'What is that?' 'Dry hay,' said he. When I looked more closely, the top of a bottle was sticking up, like the head of a Tartar, out of the grass. 'Oh, you son of a such a one,' said I, 'let's divide the labor! Do you eat the hay, for you are an ox; and I will drink the mead, for I am a man.' I brought the fat bottle for an honest trial; only let us have the glasses now!"

Having said this, Zagloba put one hand on his hip, and with the other raised the bottle above his head and began to sing,--

"Hei Yagush, hei Kundush, but give us the glasses, Give a kiss, and then care for naught else."

Here Zagloba, seeing Jendzian, stopped suddenly, placed the bottle on the table, and said,--

"As God is dear to me! this is Pan Yan's young man."

"Whose?" asked Bogun, hastily.

"Pan Skshetuski's, the lieutenant who went to Kudák, and before going treated me to such mead from Lubni that I wish all would keep it behind their tavern-signs. What is your master doing? Is he well?"

"Well, and asked to be remembered to you," said Jendzian, confused.

"He is a man of mighty courage. How do you come to be in Chigirin? Why did your master send you from Kudák?"

"My master," said Jendzian, "has his affairs in Lubni, on which he directed me to return, for I had nothing to do in Kudák."

All this time Bogun was looking sharply at Jendzian, and suddenly he said: "I too know your master, I saw him in Rozlogi."

Jendzian bent his head, and turning his ear as if he had not heard, inquired: "Where?"

"In Rozlogi."

"That place belongs to the Kurtsevichi," said Zagloba.

"To whom?" asked Jendzian again.

"Oh, I see you are hard of hearing," said Bogun, curtly.

"Because I have not slept enough."

"You will sleep enough yet. You say that your master sent you to Lubni?"

"Yes."

"Doubtless he has some sweetheart there," interrupted Zagloba, "to whom he sends his love through you."

"How do I know, worthy sir? Maybe he has, maybe he has not," said Jendzian. Then he bowed to Bogun and Zagloba. "Praise be to--" said he, preparing to go out.

"Forever!" said Bogun. "But wait, my little bird; don't be in a hurry! And why did you hide from me that you are the servant of Pan Skshetuski?"

"You didn't ask me, and I thought, 'What reason have I to talk of anything?' Praise be to--"

"Wait, I say! You have some letters from your master?"

"It is his affair to write, and mine to deliver, but only to him to whom they are written; therefore permit me to bid farewell to you, gentlemen."

Bogun wrinkled his sable brows and clapped his hands. Two Cossacks entered the room.

"Search him!" cried he, pointing to Jendzian.

"As I live, violence is done me! I am a nobleman, though a servant, and, gentlemen, you will answer for this in court."

"Bogun, let him go!" said Zagloba.

But that moment one of the Cossacks found two letters in Jendzian's bosom, and gave them to the lieutenant-colonel. Bogun directed the Cossacks to withdraw at once, for not knowing how to read, he did not wish to expose himself before them; then turning to Zagloba, he said,----

"Read, and I will look after this young fellow." Zagloba shut his left eye, on which he had a cataract, and read the address:--

"To my gracious lady and benefactress, Princess Kurtsevichova in Rozlogi."

"So you, my little falcon, are going to Lubni, and you don't know where Rozlogi is?" said Bogun, surveying Jendzian with a terrible look.

"Where they send me, there I go!"

"Am I to open it? The seal of a nobleman is sacred," remarked Zagloba.

"The hetman has given me the right to examine all letters. Open and read!"

Zagloba opened and read:--

"My gracious Lady,--I inform you that I have arrived in Kudák, from which, with God's assistance, I shall go to-morrow morning to the Saitch. But now I am writing in the night, not being able to sleep from anxiety lest something may happen to you from that bandit Bogun and his scoundrels. Pan Grodzitski tells me that we are on the eve of a great war, which will rouse the mob; therefore I implore and beseech you this minute,--even before the steppes are dry, even if on horseback,--to go with the princess to Lubni; and not to neglect this, for I shall not be able to return for a time. Which request you will be pleased to grant at once, so that I may be sure of the happiness of my betrothed and rejoice after my return. And what need have you of dallying with Bogun and throwing sand in his eyes from fear, after you have given the princess to me? It is better to take refuge under the protection of my master, the prince, who will not fail to send a garrison to Rozlogi; and thus you will save your property. In the mean while I have the honor, etc."

"Ho, ho! my friend Bogun," said Zagloba, "the hussar wants in some way to put horns on you. So you have been paying compliments to the same girl! Why didn't you speak of this? But be comforted, for once upon a time it happened to me--"

But the joke that he had begun died suddenly on his lips. Bogun sat motionless at the table, but his face was pale and drawn, as if by convulsions; his eyes closed, his brows contracted. Something terrible had happened to him.

"What's the matter?" asked Zagloba.

The Cossack began to wave his hand feverishly, and from his lips issued a suppressed hoarse voice: "Read--read the other letter!"

"The other is to Princess Helena."

"Read! read!"

Zagloba began:--

"Sweetest, beloved Halshko, mistress and queen of my heart! Since in the service of the prince I had but little time to stop at Rozlogi, I write therefore to your aunt, that you and she go to Lubni, where no harm can happen to you from Bogun, and our mutual affection cannot be exposed to interruption--"

"Enough!" cried Bogun; and jumping up in madness from the table, he sprang toward Jendzian.

The unfortunate young fellow, struck straight in the breast, groaned and fell to the floor. Frenzy carried Bogun away; he threw himself on Zagloba and snatched the letters from him.

Zagloba, seizing the fat bottle of mead, sprang to the stove and cried out,--

"In the name of the Father, Son, and Holy Ghost, have you grown wild, man, or mad? Calm down! be mild! Stick your head in the water-pail! A hundred devils take you! Do you hear me?"

"Blood! blood!" howled Bogun.

"Have you lost your mind? Thrust your head in the water-pail, I tell you! You have blood already,--you have spilt innocent blood. That unfortunate youth is already breathless. The devil has snared you, or you are the devil yourself with something to boot. Come to your senses, the deuce take you, you son of a pagan!"

While crying out in this fashion, Zagloba pushed around to the other side of the table, and bending over Jendzian felt of his breast and put his hand to his mouth, from which blood was flowing freely.

Bogun seized himself by the head, and howled like a wounded wolf. Then he dropped on the bench, without ceasing to howl, for the spirit within was torn from rage and pain. Suddenly he sprang up, ran to the door, kicked it open, and hurried to the anteroom.

"I hope you will break your neck!" muttered Zagloba to himself. "Go and smash your head against the stable or the barn,--though, as a horned beast, you can knock your head without danger. But he is a fury! I have never seen anything like him in my life. He snapped his teeth like a dog going to bite. But this boy is alive yet, poor fellow! In truth, if this mead won't help him, he lied when he said he was a noble."

Thus muttering, Zagloba placed Jendzian's head on his knees and began to pour the mead through his blue lips.

"We will see if you have good blood in you. If it is Jewish, when mixed with mead or wine it will boil; if clownish, being torpid and heavy, it will sink. Only the blood of a noble becomes lively and forms excellent liquor, which gives manhood and daring to the body. The Lord gave different drinks to different people, so that each one might have his own appropriate pleasure."

Jendzian groaned faintly.

"Ah, ha! you want more. No, brother, let me have some too,--that's the style. Now, since you have given sign of life, I think I'll take you to the stable and put you somewhere in a corner, so that dragon of a Cossack may not tear you to pieces when he gets back. He is a dangerous friend, the devil take him! for I see that his hand is quicker than his wit."

Zagloba raised Jendzian from the floor with ease, showing unusual strength, carried him to the anteroom, and then to the yard, where a number of Cossacks were playing dice on a rug spread on the ground. They greeted him, and he said,--

"Boys, take this youngster for me, put him on the hay, and let some one run for a barber."

The command was obeyed immediately, for Zagloba as a friend of Bogun enjoyed consideration among the Cossacks.

"And where is the colonel?" he asked.

"He ordered his horse and went to the regimental quarters. He commanded us also to be ready and have our horses saddled."

"Is mine ready?"

"Ready."

"Then bring it; I will find the colonel at the regiment. But here he comes!"

In fact, Bogun was to be seen through the arched gateway riding from the square. After him appeared in the distance the lances of a hundred and some tens of Cossacks, apparently ready for the march.

"To horse!" cried Bogun to the Cossacks who had remained in the yard. All moved quickly. Zagloba went through the gate, and looked attentively at the young leader.

"You are going on a journey?" asked he.

"Yes."

"And whither is the devil taking you?"

"To a wedding."

Zagloba drew nearer.

"Fear God, my son! The hetman ordered you to guard the town. You are going away yourself, and taking the Cossacks with you,--disobeying orders. Here the mob is merely waiting a favorable moment to rush on the nobility. You will destroy the town and expose yourself to the wrath of the hetman!"

"To the devil with the hetman and the town!"

"It is a question of your head."

"What do I care for that?"

Zagloba saw that it was useless to talk with the Cossack. He had made up his mind, and though he were to bury himself and others, he was determined to carry his point. Zagloba guessed, too, where the expedition was going; but he did not know himself what to do,-- whether to go with Bogun or to remain. It was dangerous to go, for it was the same as to enter upon a hazardous and criminal affair in rough, warlike times. But to remain? The mob was in fact only waiting for news from the Saitch,--the moment of signal for slaughter; and maybe they would not have waited at all had it not been for Bogun's thousand Cossacks and his authority in the Ukraine.

Zagloba might have taken refuge in the camp of the hetmans; but he had his reasons for not doing that,--whether it was a sentence for having killed some one or some little defect in accounts he himself only knew; it is sufficient that he did not wish to show himself. He was sorry to leave Chigirin, it was so pleasant for him; no one inquired about anything there, and Zagloba had become so accustomed to everybody,--to the nobility, the managers of crown estates, and the Cossack elders. True, the elders had scattered in different directions, and the nobility sat in their corners fearing the storm; but Bogun was the prince of companions and drinkers. Having become acquainted at the glass, he made friends with Zagloba straightway. After that one was not seen without the other. The Cossack scattered gold for two, the noble lied, and each being of restless mind was happy with the other. But when it came to him either to remain in Chigirin and fall under the knife of the rabble or to go with Bogun, Zagloba decided for the latter.

"If you are so determined," said he; "I will go too; I may be of use or restrain you when necessary. We have become altogether accustomed to each other; but I had no thought of anything like this."

Bogun made no answer. Half an hour later two hundred Cossacks were in marching order. Bogun rode to the head of them, and with him Zagloba. They moved on. The peasants standing here and there on the square looked at them from under their brows, and whispered, discussing about where they were going, whether they would return soon or would not return.

Bogun rode on in silence, shut up in himself, mysterious and gloomy as night. The Cossacks asked not whither he was leading them. They were ready to go with him even to the end of the earth.

After crossing the Dnieper, they appeared on the highway to Lubni. The horses went at a trot, raising clouds of dust; but as the day was hot and dry, they were soon covered with foam. They slackened their pace then, and stretched out in a straggling band along the road. Bogun pushed ahead. Zagloba came up abreast of him, wishing to begin conversation.

The face of the young leader was calmer, but mortal grief was clearly depicted on it. It seemed as if the distance in which his glance was lost toward the north beyond the Kagamlik, the speed of the horse, and the breeze of the steppe were quieting the storm within him which was roused by the reading of the letters brought by Jendzian.

"The heat flies down from heaven," said Zagloba. "It is feverish even in a linen coat, for there is no breeze what ever. Bogun! look here, Bogun!"

The leader gazed with his deep, dark eyes as if roused from sleep.

"Be careful, my son," said Zagloba, "that you are not devoured by melancholy, which when it leaves the liver, its proper seat, strikes the head and may soon destroy a man's reason. I did not know that you were such a hero of romance. It must be that you were born in May, which is the month of Venus, in which there is so much sweetness in the air that even one shaving begins to feel an affection for another; therefore men who are born in that month have greater curiosity in their bones for women than other men. But he has the advantage who succeeds in curbing himself; therefore I advise you to let revenge alone. You may justly cherish hatred against the Kurtsevichi; but is she the only girl in the world?"

Bogun, as if in answer not to Zagloba but to his own grief, said in a voice more like that of revery than conversation,--

"She is the one cuckoo, the only one on earth!"

"Even if that were true, if she calls for another, she is nothing to you. It is rightly said that the heart is a volunteer; under whatever banner it wants to serve, under that it serves. Remember too that the girl is of high blood, for the Kurtsevichi I hear are of princely family. Those are lofty thresholds."

"To the devil with your thresholds, families, and parchments!" Here Bogun struck with all his force on the hilt of his sword. "This is my family, this is my right and parchment, this is my matchmaker and best man! Oh, traitors! oh, cursed blood of the enemy! A Cossack was good enough for you to be a friend and a brother with whom to go to the Crimea, get Turkish wealth, divide spoils. Oh! you fondled him and called him a son, betrothed the maiden to him. Now what? A noble came, a petted Pole. You deserted the Cossack, the son, the friend,-- plucked out his heart. She is for another; and do you gnaw the earth, Cossack, if you like!"

The voice of the leader trembled; he ground his teeth, and struck his broad breast till an echo came from it as from an underground cave.

Silence followed. Bogun breathed heavily. Pain and anger rent in succession the wild soul of the Cossack, which knew no restraint. Zagloba waited till he should become wearied and quiet.

"What do you wish to do, unhappy hero,--how will you act?"

"Like a Cossack,--in Cossack fashion."

"Oh, I see there is something ahead! But no more of this! One thing I will tell you, that the place is within Vishnyevetski's rule and Lubni is not distant. Pan Skshetuski wrote to the princess to take refuge there with the maiden,--which means that they are under the prince's protection; and the prince is a fierce lion--"

"The Khan is a lion, and I rushed up to his throat and held the light to his eyes."

"What, you crazy brain! do you wish to declare war against the prince?"

"Hmelnitski has rushed on the hetmans. What do I care for your prince?"

Pan Zagloba became still more alarmed. "Shu! to the devil with this! This smells simply of rebellion. Vis armata, raptus puellae, and rebellion,--this comes to the executioner, the rope, and the gallows. A splendid six-in-hand, you may go high in it, if not far. The Kurtsevichi will defend themselves."

"What of that? Either I must perish, or they. I would have given my life for the Kurtsevichi, since I held them as brothers, and the old princess as a mother. Into her eyes I looked as a dog looks! And when the Tartars caught Vassily, who went to the Crimea and rescued him? I! I loved them and served them as a slave, for I thought that I was earning the maiden. And for this they sold me like a slave to an evil fate and misfortune. They drove me away; but I will go now, and first I will bow down to them in return for the bread and salt that I have eaten in their house, and I will pay them in Cossack fashion. I will go, for I know my road."

"And where will you go, when you begin with the prince,--to the camp of Hmelnitski?"

"If they had given me the girl, I should have been your Polish brother, your friend, your sabre, your sworn soul, your dog. I should have taken my Cossacks, called others together in the Ukraine, then moved against Hmelnitski, and my own brothers, the Zaporojians, and torn them with hoofs. Did I wish reward for this? No! I should have taken the girl and gone beyond the Dnieper, to the steppes of God, to the wild meadows, to the quiet waters. That would have been enough for me; but now--"

"Now you have become enraged."

Bogun made no answer, struck his horse with the nogaika, and rushed on. But Zagloba began to think of the trouble into which he had got himself. There was no doubt that Bogun intended to attack the Kurtsevichi, to avenge the injustice done him, and carry off the girl by force. Zagloba would have kept him company, even in an undertaking like this. In the Ukraine such affairs happened frequently, and sometimes they went unpunished. True, when the offender was not a noble, such a deed became complicated, more dangerous; but the enforcement of justice on a Cossack was difficult, for where was he to be found and seized? After the deed he escaped to the wild steppe, beyond the reach of human hand; and how many could see him? When war broke out, and Tartars invaded the country, the offender appeared again, for at such times laws were asleep. In this way Bogun, too, might save himself from responsibility. Besides, Zagloba had no need of giving him active assistance, and taking on himself half the fault. He would not have done this in any case; for though Bogun was his friend, still it did not beseem Zagloba, a noble, to engage with a Cossack against a noble, especially as he was acquainted with Skshetuski, and had drunk with him. Zagloba was a disturber of no common order, but his turbulence had a certain limit. To frolic in the public houses of Chigirin, with Bogun and other Cossack elders, especially at their expense,--but it was well too, in view of Cossack troubles, to have such people as friends. Zagloba, though he had got a scratch here and there, was very careful of his own skin; therefore he saw at once that through this friendship he had got into a desperate muddle. For it was clear that if Bogun should carry off the maiden, the betrothed of Vishnyevetski's lieutenant and favorite, he would come into collision with the prince; then nothing would remain for him but to take refuge with Hmelnitski and join the rebellion. To this Zagloba mentally opposed his positive veto. To join the rebellion for the beautiful eyes of Bogun was altogether beyond his intention, and besides he feared Yeremi as he did fire.

"Oh, misery!" muttered he to himself; "I have caught the devil by the tail, and this time he will catch me by the head and twist my neck. May lightning strike this Bogun, with his girl face and his Tartar hand! I've gone to a wedding, indeed, a regular dog-fight, as God is dear to me! May lightning strike all the Kurtsevichi and all the women! What have I to do with them? They are not necessary to me. No matter who has the grist, they will grind it on me. And for what? Do I want to marry? Let the evil one marry, it is all the same to me; what business have I in this affair? If I go with Bogun, then Vishnyevetski will flay me; if I leave Bogun, the peasants will kill me, or he will do it without waiting for them. The worst of all is to be intimate with a bear. I am in a nice plight. I should rather be the horse on which I am sitting, than Zagloba. I've come out on Cossack folly. I've hung to a water-burner; justly, therefore, will they flay me on both sides."

While occupied with these thoughts, Zagloba sweated terribly, and fell into worse humor. The heat was great; the horse travelled with difficulty, for he had not been on the road for a long time, and Pan Zagloba was a heavy man. Merciful God! what would he have given then to be sitting in the shade at an inn, over a glass of cool beer, not to weary himself in the heat and rush on over the scorching steppe!

Though Bogun was in a hurry, he slackened his pace, for the heat was terrible. They fed the horses a little. During that time Bogun spoke to the essauls,--apparently gave them orders, for up to that time they did not know where they were going. The last word of the command reached Zagloba's ear,--

"Wait the pistol-shot!"

"Very well, father."

Bogun turned suddenly to Zagloba: "You will go in advance with me."

"I?" asked Zagloba, in evident bad humor. "I love you so much that I have already sweated out one half of my soul; why should I not sweat out the other half? We are like a coat and its lining, and I hope the devil will take us together,--which is all the same to me, for I think it cannot be hotter in hell than here."

"Forward!"

"At breakneck speed."

They moved on, and soon after them the Cossacks; but the latter rode slowly, so that in a short time they were a good distance in the rear, and finally were lost to sight.

Bogun and Zagloba rode side by side in silence, both in deep thought. Zagloba pulled his mustache, and it was evident that he was working vigorously with his brain; he was planning, perhaps, how to extricate himself from the whole affair. At times he muttered something to himself half audibly; then again he looked at Bogun, on whose face was depicted now unrestrained anger, now grief.

"It is a wonder," thought Zagloba to himself, "that though such a beauty, he was not able to bring the girl to his side. He is a Cossack, it is true, but a famous knight and a lieutenant-colonel, who sooner or later will become a noble, unless he joins the rebellion, which depends entirely on himself. Pan Skshetuski is a respectable cavalier and good-looking but he cannot compare in appearance with the Cossack, who is as beautiful as a picture. Ha! they will grapple when they meet, for both are champions of no common kind."

"Bogun, do you know Pan Skshetuski well?" asked Zagloba, suddenly.

"No," answered the Cossack, briefly.

"You will have difficult work with him. I saw him when he opened the door for himself with Chaplinski. He is a Goliath in drinking as well as fighting."

Bogun made no reply, and again they were both buried in their own thoughts and anxieties; following which, Zagloba repeated from time to time: "So there is no help!"

Some hours passed. The sun had travelled far to the west, toward Chigirin; from the east a cool breeze sprang up. Zagloba took off his lynx-skin cap, raised his hand to his sweat-moistened head, and repeated again: "So there is no help!"

Bogun roused himself, as if from sleep. "What do you say?" he inquired.

"I say that it will be dark directly. Is it far yet?"

"No."

In an hour it had grown dark in earnest, but they had already reached a woody ravine. At the end of the ravine a light was gleaming.

"That is Rozlogi," said Bogun, suddenly.

"Is it? Whew! there is something cold in that ravine."

Bogun reined in his horse. "Wait!" said he.

Zagloba looked at him. The eyes of the leader, which had the peculiarity of shining in the night, were gleaming at that moment like a pair of torches.

Both of them stood for a long time motionless at the edge of the ravine. At length the snorting of horses was heard in the distance. These were Bogun's Cossacks coming on slowly from the depth of the forest.

The essaul approached for orders, which Bogun whispered in his ear; then the Cossacks halted again.

"Forward!" said Bogun to Zagloba.

Soon the dark masses of buildings around the mansion, the storehouses and well-sweeps stood in outline before their eyes. It was quiet in the yard. The dogs did not bark. A great golden moon shone above the buildings. From the garden came the odor of the cherry and apple blossoms. Everywhere it was quiet,--a night so wonderful that in truth it lacked only the sound of a lyre somewhere under the windows of the beautiful princess. There was light yet in some parts of the house.

The two horsemen approached the gate.

"Who is there?" called the voice of the night-guard.

"Don't you know me, Maksim?"

"Oh, that is you! Glory to God!"

"For the ages of ages. Open the gate! And how is it with you?"

"All is well. You haven't been in Rozlogi for a long time."

The hinges of the gate squeaked sharply, the bridge fell over the fosse, and the two horsemen rode into the square.

"Look here, Maksim! don't shut the gate, and don't raise the bridge, for I am going out directly."

"Oh! you hurry as if you had come for fire."

"True! Tie the horse to the post!"

CHAPTER XVIII.

The Kurtsevichi were not sleeping yet. They were supping in that anteroom, filled with weapons, which extended the whole width of the house, from the garden to the square on the other side. At the sight of Bogun and Zagloba, they sprang to their feet. On the face of the princess was reflected not only astonishment, but displeasure and fright as well. Only two of the young men were present,--Simeon and Nikolai.

"Oh, Bogun!" exclaimed the princess. "But what are you here for?"

"I came to do you homage, mother. Are you not glad to see me?"

"I am glad to see yon,--glad; but I wonder that you came, for I heard that you were on guard in Chigirin. But whom has God sent to us with you?"

"This is Pan Zagloba,--a noble, my friend."

"We are glad to see you, sir," said the princess.

"We are glad," repeated Simeon and Nikolai.

"Worthy lady!" said Zagloba, "an untimely guest, it is true, is worse than a Tartar; but it is known also that whoever wishes to enter heaven must receive the traveller into his house, give meat to the hungry, and drink to the thirsty"--

"Sit down, then; eat and drink," said the old princess. "We are thankful that you have come. But, Bogun, I did not expect to see you; perhaps you have some business with us."

"Perhaps I have," answered Bogun, slowly.

"What is it?" asked the princess, disturbed.

"When the moment comes, we will talk about it. Let us rest a little. I have come straight from Chigirin."

"It is evident that you were in a hurry to see us."

"And whom should I be in a hurry to see, if not you? Is Princess Helena well?"

"Well," replied the old lady, dryly.

"I should like to gladden my eyes with her."

"Helena is sleeping."

"That is too bad, for I shall not stay long."

"Where are you going?"

"War, mother! There is no time for aught else. Any moment the hetmans may send us to the field, and it will be a pity to strike Zaporojians. Was it seldom that we went with them for Turkish booty? Isn't it true, Princes? We sailed upon the sea with them, ate bread and salt with them, drank and caroused, and now we are their enemies."

The princess looked quickly at Bogun. The thought flashed through her mind that perhaps Bogun intended to join the rebellion, and came to tamper with her sons.

"And what do you think of doing?" inquired she.

"I, mother? Well, it is hard to strike our own, but it is demanded."

"That is what we will do," said Simeon.

"Hmelnitski is a traitor!" added the young Nikolai.

"Death to traitors!" said Bogun.

"Let the hangman light their way," added Zagloba.

Bogun began to speak again: "So it is in this world. He who to-day is your friend is to-morrow a Judas. It is impossible to trust any one."

"Except good people," said the princess.

"True, you can believe good people; therefore I believe and love you; for you are good people, not traitors."

There was something so strange in the voice of the leader that in a moment deep silence reigned. Zagloba looked at the princess, and blinked with his sound eye; but the princess fixed her glance on Bogun.

He spoke on: "War does not give life to men, but death; therefore I wanted to see you once more before going to the field. And you would mourn over me, for you are my friends from the heart, are you not?"

"We are, as God is our aid. From childhood we have known you."

"You are our brother," added Simeon.

"You are princes, you are nobles, and you did not despise the Cossack; you took him to your house and promised him the maiden, your relative, for you knew that for the Cossack there was neither life nor existence without her; so you had mercy on the Cossack."

"There is nothing to talk about," said the princess, hurriedly.

"But there is, mother, something to talk about; for you are my benefactress, and I have asked of this noble, my friend, to make me his son and give me his escutcheon, so that you may not be ashamed to give your relative to a Cossack. Pan Zagloba has agreed to this, and we shall seek the permission of the Diet, and when the war is over will go to the Grand Hetman, who is kind to me. He can assist. He too acquired nobility for Krechovski."

"God give you aid!" said the princess.

"You are sincere people, and I thank you. But before the war I should like to hear once more from your lips that you give me the maiden, and that you will keep your word. The word of a noble is not smoke, and you are a princess."

Bogun spoke with a slow and solemn voice, but at the same time in his speech there vibrated, as it were, a threat declaring that there must be consent to what he demanded.

The old princess looked at her sons; they looked at her, and for a moment silence continued. Suddenly the falcon, sitting on her perch by the wall, began to make a noise, though it was long before daylight; others followed her. The great eagle woke, shook his wings, and began to scream. The pitch-pine burned low; it was growing gloomy and dark in the room.

"Nikolai, put wood on the fire!" said the old princess.

The young prince threw on more wood.

"Well, do you consent?" inquired Bogun.

"We must ask Helena."

"Let her speak for herself; you speak for yourselves. Do you promise?"

"We promise," said the mother.

"We promise," said the sons.

Bogun stood up suddenly, and turning to Zagloba, said with a clear voice,--

"My friend Zagloba, ask for the maiden too; maybe they will give her to you."

"What do you mean, Cossack? Are you drunk?" cried the princess.

Bogun, in place of an answer, took out Skshetuski's letter, and turning to Zagloba, said: "Read!"

Zagloba took the letter, and began to read it in the midst of deep silence. When he had finished, Bogun crossed his arms on his breast.

"To whom then do you give the girl?" asked he.

"Bogun!"

The voice of the Cossack became like the hiss of a serpent: "Traitors, murderers, faith-breakers, Judases!"

"Sons, to your sabres!" screamed the princess.

The princes sprang like lightning to the walls, and seized their arms.

"Quiet, gentlemen, quiet!" began Zagloba.

But before he had finished speaking, Bogun drew a pistol from his belt and fired.

"Jesus!" groaned Prince Simeon. Advancing a step, he began to beat the air with his hands, and fell heavily on the floor.

"People, to the rescue!" screamed the princess, in despair.

But that moment, in the yard and from the side of the garden, were heard other volleys. The windows and the doors flew open with a crash, and several tens of Cossacks rushed into the room.

"Destruction!" thundered wild voices.

The alarm-bell was tolled on the square. The birds in the room began to scream. Uproar, firing, and shouts took the place of the recent quiet of a drowsy house.

The old princess threw herself, howling like a wolf, on the body of Simeon, shuddering in the last convulsions; but soon two Cossacks seized her by the hair and drew her aside. Meanwhile Nikolai, driven to the corner of the room, defended himself with fury and the boldness of a lion.

"Aside!" cried Bogun suddenly, to the Cossacks around him. "Aside!" repeated he, with a thundering voice.

The Cossacks withdrew. They thought that he wished to save the life of the young man. But Bogun himself, with sabre in hand, rushed on the prince.

Now began a terrible hand-to-hand struggle, on which the princess, whose hair was grasped by four iron hands, looked with glaring eyes and open mouth. The young prince hurled himself like a storm on the Cossack, who, retreating slowly, led him out into the middle of the room. Then suddenly stooping, he parried a powerful blow, and from defence changed to attack.

The Cossacks, holding their breath, let their sabres hang, and motionless, as if fastened to the floor, followed with their eyes the course of the conflict. Only the breathing and panting of the combatants were heard in the silence, with the gnashing of teeth, and the sharp click of the swords striking each other.

For a while it appeared as if Bogun would yield to the gigantic power and obstinacy of the youth, for he began again to retreat and defend himself. His countenance was contracted as if by over-exertion. Nikolai redoubled his blows; dust rose from the floor and covered the two men with a cloud, but through the masses of it the Cossacks saw blood flowing from the face of their leader.

All at once Bogun sprang aside; the prince's sword struck the empty air. Nikolai staggered from the effort and bent forward; that instant the Cossack struck him such a blow on the neck that he dropped as if struck by lightning.

The joyful cries of the Cossacks were mingled with the unearthly shriek of the princess. It seemed as though the ceiling would break from the noise. The struggle was finished. The Cossacks rushed at the weapons hanging along the walls, and began to pull them down, tearing from one another the most costly sabres and daggers, and trampling upon the bodies of the princes and their own comrades who had fallen at the hands of Nikolai. Bogun permitted everything. He stood at the door leading to Helena's rooms, guarding the way. He breathed heavily from weariness; his face was pale and bloody, for the sword of the prince had struck his head twice. His wandering look passed from the body of Nikolai to the body of Simeon, and then fell upon the blue face of the princess, whom the Cossacks, holding by the hair, pressed to the floor with their knees, for she was tearing herself from their hands to the bodies of her children.

The tumult and confusion in the room increased every moment. The Cossacks tied the servants with ropes and tormented them without mercy. The floor was covered with blood and dead bodies, the room filled with smoke from pistol-shots; the walls were stripped, the birds killed.

All at once the door at which Bogun stood was opened wide. He turned and started back. In the door appeared the blind Vassily, and at his side Helena, dressed in a white gown, pale herself as the gown, with eyes starting out from terror, and with open mouth.

Vassily carried in both hands a cross, which he held as high as his face. In the midst of the uproar in the room, in the presence of the corpses, and the blood scattered in pools on the floor, in front the glitter of sabres and of flashing eyes, that lofty figure had an appearance of wonderful solemnity. Emaciated, with hair growing gray, and with depressions instead of eyes, you would have said that it was a spirit, or a dead body which had left its shroud and was coming for the punishment of crime.

The clamor ceased; the Cossacks drew back in a fright. Silence was broken by the calm, but painful and groaning voice of the prince,--

"In the name of the Father, the Saviour, the Spirit, and the Holy Virgin! Oh, you men who come from distant lands, do you come in the name of God?--for blessed is the wayfarer who goes announcing the word of God. And do you bring good news? Are you apostles?"

A deathlike stillness reigned after the words of Vassily; but he turned slowly with the cross to one side and then the other, and continued,--

"Woe to you, brothers, for whoso makes war for gain or vengeance will be damned forever. Let us pray, so that we obtain mercy. Woe to you, brothers, woe to me! Woe! woe! woe!"

A groan came from the breast of the prince.

"Lord, have mercy upon us!" answered the dull voices of the Cossacks, who under the influence of fear began to make the sign of the cross in terror.

Suddenly a wild piercing shriek from the princess was heard: "Vassily! Vassily!"

There was something in her voice as full of anguish as in the last voice of life passing away. But the Cossacks pressing her with their knees knew that she could not escape from their hands.

The prince shuddered, but immediately covered himself with the cross, on the side from which the voice came, and said: "Oh, lost soul, crying from the abyss, woe to thee!"

"Lord, have mercy upon us!" repeated the Cossacks.

"To me!" said Bogun to the Cossacks that moment, and he staggered.

The Cossacks sprang and supported him under the shoulders.

"You are wounded, father?"

"I am! But that is nothing; I have lost blood. Here, boys! guard this young woman as the eyes in your head. Surround the house; let no one out! Princess--"

He could say no more; his lips grew white, and his eyes were covered with a mist.

"Bear the ataman to the rooms!" cried Zagloba, who creeping out of some corner or another appeared unexpectedly at Bogun's side. "This is nothing, nothing at all," said he, feeling the wounds with his fingers. "He will be well to-morrow. I will take care of him. Mix up bread and spider-webs for me! You, boys, go off to the devil with yourselves, to frolic with the girls in the servants' quarters, for you have nothing to do here; but let two carry the ataman. Take him--that's the way! Be off now! What are you standing here for? I will take care of the house, I will look after everything."

Two Cossacks carried Bogun to the adjoining room; the rest went out of the antechamber.

Zagloba approached Helena, and rapidly blinking his one eye, said in a quick low voice,--

"I am Pan Skshetuski's friend; have no fear. Only put your prophet to bed and wait for me."

Having said this, he went to the room in which the two essauls had put Bogun on a Turkish divan. Then he sent them for bread and spider-webs; and when these were brought from the servants' quarters he set about nursing the young ataman with the dexterity which every noble possessed at that period, and which he acquired in plastering heads cut up in duels at the petty Diets.

"Tell the Cossacks," said he to the essauls, "that to-morrow the ataman will be as well as a fish, and not to trouble about him. He got a scratch, but came out splendidly, and to-morrow he can have his wedding even without a priest. If there is a wine-cellar in the house, then you may use it. See, his wounds are dressed already! Now go, that the ataman may rest."

The essauls moved toward the door.

"But don't drink the whole cellar dry," added Zagloba.

Sitting at Bogun's pillow, he looked at him attentively.

"Well, the devil won't take you on account of these wounds, though you got good ones. You won't move hand or foot for two days," muttered he to himself, looking at the pale face and closed eyes of the Cossack. "The sabre was unwilling to cheat the executioner; for you are his property and from him you will not escape. When they hang you the devil will make a doll out of you for his imps, as you are pretty-faced. No, brother, you drink well, but you will drink no longer with me. You may seek companions for yourself among crawfish-dealers, for I see that you like to kill people, but I will not fall upon noble houses with you in the night. May the hangman light your way!"

Bogun groaned slightly.

"Oh, groan and sigh! To-morrow you'll groan better. But wait, you Tartar soul, you wanted the princess? I don't wonder, for she is a beauty; but if you get her, then I'll let the dogs eat my wit. Hair will grow on the palms of my hands first."

The uproar and hum of many voices came from the square to the ears of Zagloba.

"Ah! they have got to the cellar surely," he muttered. "Drink like horseflies, so that you will sleep well. I will watch for all of you, though I don't know whether you will be glad of my watching to-morrow."

Then he rose to see if the Cossacks had really made the acquaintance of the princess's cellar, and went to the anteroom, where a terrible sight met his eyes. In the middle of the room lay the bodies of Simeon and Nikolai, already cold, and in the corner of the room the body of the princess in a sitting posture, inclined just as she had been bent by the Cossacks. Her eyes were open, her teeth exposed. The fire, burning in the chimney, filled the whole room with a faint light, trembling in pools of blood; the depth of the room was obscure in the shadow. Zagloba approached the princess to see if she was breathing, and placed his hand on her face; it was cold already. He hurried to the square, for terror seized him in that room.

The Cossacks had begun their revel on the outside. Fires had been kindled, by the light of which Zagloba saw barrels of mead, wine, and spirits with the heads broken in. The Cossacks dipped from them as from a well, and drank with all their might. Some, already warmed by drink, chased the young women from the servants' quarters; some of the young women, seized by fright, struggled and ran away, springing through the fire, others amidst bursts of laughter and shouting allowed themselves to be caught and drawn toward the barrels, or fires at which they were dancing the Cosachka. The Cossacks rushed into the dance as if mad; in front of them the girls now pushing forward, now retreating before the violent movements of their partners.

The spectators either kept time with tin cups, or sang. Cries of "U-ha!" were heard louder and louder, with the accompaniment of howling of dogs, neighing of horses, and bellowing of cattle to be slaughtered for the feast.

At the distant fires were seen peasants from around Rozlogi,--neighbors, who at the sound of shots and cries had rushed from the village in crowds to see what was going on. They did not think of defending the princess, for the Kurtsevichi were hated in the place; they only looked on the revelling of the Cossacks, elbowing one another, whispering, and approaching nearer and nearer the barrels of vudka and mead. The orgies grew more and more tumultuous, the drinking increased. The Cossacks no longer dipped from the barrels with cups, but thrust their heads in up to the neck, and sprinkled the dancing girls with vudka and mead. Their faces were inflamed, steam rose from their heads; and some were already staggering.

Zagloba, coming out on the porch, cast his eye on the drinking crowd, then looked carefully at the sky.

"Clear, but dark," he muttered; "when the moon goes down you might strike them in the face, they wouldn't see you.--Go on, my boys," he cried, "go on! Don't spare yourselves; your teeth won't grow stiff. A fool is he who won't drink to-day to the health of his ataman! Go on with the barrels! Go on with the girls! U-ha!"

"U-ha!" shouted the Cossacks, joyfully.

Zagloba looked around on every side.

"Oh, you wretches, rogues, good-for-nothings!" shouted he, all at once; "you drink yourselves like horses after a journey, but to the men on guard around the house not a drop. Hallo there! change the guards for me this minute!"

The order was executed without delay, and in a moment a number of tipsy Cossacks ran to relieve the guards, who up to that time had taken no part in the revelry. They came in at once with a haste easily understood.

"Help yourselves!" cried Zagloba, "help yourselves!" pointing to the barrels.

"We thank you!" answered the Cossacks, dipping in the cups.

"In an hour relieve these for me."

"Very well," said the essaul.

It seemed quite natural to the Cossacks that Zagloba should take the command in place of Bogun. It had happened already more than once, and they were glad of it because he always permitted them everything. The guards therefore drank with the others. Zagloba entered into conversation with the peasants of Rozlogi.

"Well, my man," asked he of an old "sub-neighbor," "is it far from here to Lubni?"

"Oh, very far, very far!"

"Could a man get there by morning?"

"Oh, no!"

"In the afternoon?"

"In the afternoon, perhaps."

"And how do you go there?"

"By the high-road."

"Is there a high-road?"

"Oh, yes; Prince Yeremi commanded that there should be a road, and there it is."

Zagloba spoke loud on purpose, so that in the shouting and noise a large number of Cossacks might hear him.

"Give them vudka too," said he to the Cossacks, pointing to the peasants; "but first give me some mead, for the night is cold."

One of the Cossacks drew mead from the barrel into a gallon pail, which he passed on his cap to Zagloba.

Zagloba took the pail carefully in both hands, so that it should not overflow, raised it to his lips, and pushing his head back, began to drink slowly, but without drawing breath. He drank and drank, till the Cossacks began to wonder.

"Look at him," said one to another, "plague take him!"

Meanwhile Zagloba's head went back slowly, till at last he took the gallon measure from his reddened face, pursed out his lips, raised his brows, and said, as if to himself,--

"Oh, it is not bad! Old mead!--evident at once that it is not bad. A pity to give such mead to your scoundrelly throats,--dregs would be good enough for you! Strong mead! I know that it has comforted me, and that I feel a little better."

Indeed, Pan Zagloba felt better; his head became clear, he grew daring; and it was evident that his blood mixed with mead formed the excellent liquor of which he had spoken himself, and from which bravery and daring went through the whole man. He beckoned to the Cossacks to drink more, and turning, passed with a leisurely step along the whole yard; he examined every corner carefully, crossed the bridge over the fosse, and went around the picket-fence to see if the guards were watching the house carefully. The first sentry was asleep; the second, the third, and the fourth also. They were weary from the journey, and besides had come to their posts drunk, and had fallen asleep straightway.

"I might steal any one of them, and make him my man," said Zagloba.

Then he turned straight to the yard, entered the ill-omened anteroom again, looked at Bogun, and seeing that he gave no sign of life, withdrew to Helena's door, and opening it quietly, entered the room, from which there came a sound as of prayer.

It was really Prince Vassily's room. Helena, however, was there with the prince, with whom she felt in greater safety. The blind Vassily was kneeling before an image of the Holy Virgin, in front of which a lamp was burning. Helena was at his side. Both of them were praying aloud. Seeing Zagloba, she turned her astonished eyes on him. He placed his finger on his lips.

"I am a friend of Pan Skshetuski," said he.

"Rescue me!" answered Helena.

"It is for that I have come; trust in me."

"What have I to do?"

"It is necessary to escape while that devil is lying unconscious."

"What must I do?"

"Put on man's clothes; and when I knock at the door, come out."

Helena hesitated; distrust shone in her eyes. "Can I trust you?"

"What better can you do?"

"True, true; but swear that you will not betray me."

"Your mind is disturbed, to ask that. But if you wish, I swear. So help me God and the holy cross! Destruction waits you here, salvation is in flight."

"That is true, that is true."

"Put on male attire as quickly as you can, and wait."

"And Vassily?"

"What Vassily?"

"My crazy cousin."

"Destruction threatens you, not him," said Zagloba. "If he is crazy, he is sacred to the Cossacks. Indeed, I noticed that they take him for a prophet."

"That is true, and he has offended Bogun in nothing."

"We must leave him; otherwise we are lost, and Pan Skshetuski with us. Hurry, my lady, hurry!"

With these words Zagloba left the room and went directly to Bogun. The chief was pale and weak, but his eyes were open.

"You are better?" asked Zagloba.

Bogun wished to speak, but could not.

"You cannot speak?"

Bogun moved his head in sign that he could not, but at the same time suffering was stamped on his face. His wounds had evidently grown painful from movement.

"And you are not able to cry?"

Bogun gave a sign only with his eyes that he could not.

"Nor move?"

The same sign.

"So much the better; for you will not speak, nor cry, nor move. Meanwhile I will go to Lubni with the princess. If I don't sweep her away from you, then I will let an old woman grind me to bran in a mill. What a scoundrel! You think that I haven't enough of your company, that I will be hail-fellow-well-met with trash? Oh, you scoundrel! you thought that for your wine, your dice, and your plebeian loves I would kill people and go into rebellion with you? No, nothing of the sort, my handsome fellow!"

As Zagloba went on, the dark eyes of the chief opened wider and wider. Was he dreaming, was he awake, or was Zagloba jesting?

But Zagloba talked on: "What do you stare so for, like a cat? Do you think that I won't do this? Perhaps you would like to send your respects to somebody in Lubni? A barber could be sent to you, for a good one can be had from the prince."

The pale visage of the chief became terrible. He understood that Zagloba was speaking in earnest. Lightning flashes of despair and rage shot from his eyes; a flame rushed into his face. With superhuman effort he raised himself and a cry broke from his lips.

"Hi! Cos--"

He had not finished when Zagloba, with the speed of lightning, threw Bogun's coat over his head, and in a moment had wound it completely around him and thrown him on his back.

"Don't cry, for it hurts you," said he quietly, panting heavily. "Your head might go to aching to-morrow; therefore as a good friend I am careful of you. In this fashion you will be warm and sleep comfortably, not scream your throat out. Lest you tear your clothes, I will bind your hands; and all this through friendship, that you may remember me with gratitude."

With the belt on the Cossack he bound his hands; then with his own belt he tied his feet. Bogun felt nothing now; he had fainted.

"A sick man should lie quietly," said Zagloba, "so that humor may not fly to his head; from this comes delirium. Well, good health to you! I might rip you with a knife, which would probably be the best use for you, but I am ashamed to kill a man in peasant fashion. Quite another affair if you choke before morning, for that has happened to more than one pig. Good health, and return my love! Maybe we shall have another meeting; but if I try to hasten it, then let some one flay me and make horse-cruppers of my skin."

When he had finished this speech Zagloba went to the anteroom, quenched the fire in the chimney, and knocked at Vassily's door. A slender figure emerged from it at once.

"Is that you?" asked Zagloba.

"It is."

"Come on! If we only reach the horses--but then the Cossacks are all drunk, the night is dark; before they wake we shall be far away. Be careful! the princes are lying here."

"In the name of the Father, Son, and Holy Ghost!" whispered Helena.

CHAPTER XIX.

Two persons rode quietly and slowly through the woody ravine which skirted the dwelling at Rozlogi. The night had become very dark, for the moon had gone down long before, and besides clouds covered the sky. In the ravine nothing could be seen three steps ahead of the horses, which stumbled over the roots of the trees sticking across the road. They went for a long time with the greatest care, till at length, when they saw the end of the ravine, and the open steppe, lighted a little by the gray reflection of the clouds, one of the riders whispered, "Spur on!"

They shot ahead, like two arrows sent from Tartar bows. Nothing followed them but the sound of hoofs. The dark steppe seemed to fly from under their beasts. Single oak-trees standing here and there by the roadside swept past like phantoms, and they fled for a long time without rest or drawing breath, till finally the horses dropped their ears and began to snort from weariness, their gait grew heavy and slow.

"There is no help for it, the horses must slacken their pace," said one of the travellers, a heavy man.

Just then dawn began to push night from the steppe. Every moment a broader expanse came out from the darkness; the thistles of the steppe were outlined indistinctly, the distant trees, the mounds; every moment more light was diffused in the air. The whitish gleams lighted up the faces of the riders too. They were Pan Zagloba and Helena.

"No help for it, we must let the horses slacken their speed," said Zagloba. "Yesterday they came from Chigirin to Rozlogi without resting. They cannot endure this kind of travelling long. I am afraid they may drop dead. How do you feel?"

Here Zagloba looked at his companion, and not waiting for her to answer, cried out,--

"Oh, let me look at you in the daylight! Oh, ho! are those your cousin's clothes? It must be said you are a splendid Cossack. I've not had in all my life such another waiting-man; but I think Pan Skshetuski will take him from me soon. But what is this? Oh, for God's sake, twist up your hair! Unless you do there will be no doubt as to your sex."

In fact, over Helena's shoulders flowed a torrent of black hair, let loose by the speed of the course and the dampness of the night.

"Where are we going?" asked she, winding up her hair with both hands, and trying to put it under her cap.

"Where our eyes take us."

"Then not to Lubni?"

Alarm was reflected on Helena's face, and in the quick glance which she threw at Zagloba reawakened distrust was evident.

"Do you see," said he, "I have my own reason; and believe me I have reckoned everything carefully, and my reckoning is based on the following wise maxim: Do not escape in the direction in which you will be pursued. If they are pursuing us at this moment, they are pursuing in the direction of Lubni; for I inquired yesterday in a loud voice about the road, and before setting out I told Bogun that we should go in that direction. Therefore we shall go to Cherkasi. If they follow us, it will not be quickly, for it will take them two days to discover that we are not on the Lubni road. By that time we shall be in Cherkasi, where the Polish regiments of Pivnitski and Rudomina are stationed; and in Korsún are all the forces of the hetmans. Do you understand now?"

"I understand, and while life lasts I shall be thankful to you! I do not know who you are or whence you came to Rozlogi; but I think God sent you to defend and save me, for I should stab myself rather than fall into the power of that robber."

"He is a dragon, terribly intent on pursuing you."

"What in my misfortune have I done to him that he should pursue me? I have known him long, and long have I hated him, long since has he roused in me nothing but fear. Am I the only woman in the world, that he should love me, and shed so much blood on my account,--that he should kill my cousins? When I remember it my blood grows cold. What shall I do? Where shall I hide from him? Do not wonder at my complaining, for I am unhappy. I am ashamed of such affection; I should prefer death a hundred times."

Helena's cheeks were flushed; tears were flowing over them, forced out by anger, contempt, and pain.

"I will not deny," said Zagloba, "that a great misfortune has come upon your house; but permit me to say that your relatives are partly to blame. They should not have promised your hand to the Cossack, and then betrayed him. When this was discovered he became so enraged that no persuasion of mine could avail. I am sorry for your two dead cousins, and especially for the younger; for he was still a mere youth, but it was evident at a glance that he would have ripened into a mighty warrior."

Helena began to cry.

"Tears are not proper to those garments which you wear; wipe them away therefore, and say to yourself that this was the will of God. God will punish the outlaw too, who is indeed already punished; for he has shed blood in vain, and has lost you, the one chief object of his desires."

Here Zagloba stopped; after a while he spoke again:--

"Oh, dear Lord, what a dressing he would give me if I should fall into his hands! He would make a lizard out of my skin. You do not know that I have already received the crown of martyrdom from the Turks; but I have had enough, I do not wish another; therefore I do not go to Lubni, but to Cherkasi. It would be pleasant to take refuge with the prince, but if they should catch us while going there! You heard, as I was untying the horse from the post, how one of Bogun's serving-men woke up. But if he had raised the alarm then? They would have been ready for the chase at once, and would have caught us in an hour; for they have the fresh horses of Rozlogi, from which I had no time to select. Oh, I tell you he is a wild beast, that Bogun! I have such a horror of him that I would rather take a look at the devil than at him."

"God save us from his hands!"

"He has ruined himself. He abandoned Chigirin, in spite of the orders of the hetman; he has come into collision with Vishnyevetski. Nothing now remains for him but to flee to Hmelnitski. But he will lose his daring if Hmelnitski is beaten, and that may happen. Jendzian met troops beyond Kremenchug, sailing down the river under Barabash and Krechovski, against Hmelnitski; and, besides, young Stephan Pototski is moving by land with his hussars; but Jendzian waited ten days in Kremenchug to repair his boat. Therefore the battle must have taken place before he reached Chigirin. We were expecting news every moment."

"Then Jendzian brought letters from Kudák, did he?" asked Helena.

"Yes, there were letters from Skshetuski to the princess and to you; but Bogun seized them, and from them learned everything. Then he struck down Jeodzian at once, and set out to take vengeance on the Kurtsevichi."

"Oh, unfortunate youth! He has shed his blood on my account."

"Do not grieve; he will recover."

"When did this happen?"

"Yesterday morning. For Bogun to fell a man is no more than for another to toss off a glass of wine. And after the reading of the letters, he roared so that all Chigirin trembled."

Conversation was interrupted for a moment. Daylight had come. The rosy dawn, streaked with opals, bright gold, and purple, was glowing in the east. The breeze was fresh; the horses, now rested, moved gladly.

"Let us go on, in God's name, and quickly! Our horses have drawn breath, and we have no time to lose," said Zagloba.

They went again at a gallop, and rushed on for two or three miles without rest. All at once a dark point appeared ahead of them, which approached with amazing rapidity.

"What can that be?" asked Zagloba. "Let us draw up a little. That's a man on horseback."

In fact, some horseman was approaching them at full speed. Bent forward in the saddle, with face hidden in the mane of the horse, he continued to urge with a nagaika the stallion, which seemed not to touch the ground.

"What kind of devil can he be, and why does he flee so? But he just flies!" said Zagloba, taking out a pistol from the holsters, to be ready in every event.

Meanwhile the courier had come within thirty yards.

"Stop!" thundered Zagloba, aiming his pistol; "who are you?"

The horseman reined in his steed, and sat erect in the saddle; but the moment he looked he cried, "Pan Zagloba!"

"Pleshnyevski, attendant of the starosta of Chigirin! But what are you doing here? Where are you fleeing to?"

"Oh, turn back with me! Misfortune! The anger of God, the judgment of God!"

"What has happened? Speak!"

"Chigirin is taken by the Zaporojians. The peasants are slaughtering the nobles."

"In the name of the Father and Son! What do you say? Has Hmelnitski come?"

"Pototski is killed, Charnetski in captivity. The Tartars are marching with the Cossacks. Tugai Bey--"

"But Barabash and Krechovski?"

"Barabash is killed, Krechovski has gone over to Hmelnitski. Krívonos moved on the hetmans last night, Hmelnitski before daybreak this morning. He has tremendous forces. The country is on fire, peasants rising everywhere; blood is flowing. Save yourself!"

Zagloba's eyes were starting out, his mouth open, and he was so astonished that he could not speak.

"Save yourself!" repeated Pleshnyevski.

"Jesus and Mary!" groaned Zagloba.

"Jesus and Mary!" repeated Helena, and burst into tears.

"Escape! There is no time to be wasted."

"Where! To what place?"

"To Lubni."

"But are you going there?"

"Yes; to the prince, the voevoda."

"Devil take it all!" cried Zagloba. "But where are the hetmans?"

"At Korsún. But Krívonos is fighting with them already."

"Krívonos or Prostonos, may the plague consume him! I have no reason to go where he is."

"You are running to your own destruction, as into a lion's mouth."

"And who sent you to Lubni? Your lord?"

"Oh! he escaped with his life; and a friend whom I have among the Zaporojians saved my head, and helped me to flee. I am going to Lubni of my own will, for I don't know where else to take refuge."

"But avoid Rozlogi, for Bogun is there. He also wishes to join the rebellion."

"Oh, for God's sake, save us! In Chigirin they said that the peasants would rise immediately beyond the Dnieper!"

"Maybe I maybe! But go your own way wherever you please, for I have enough to do to think of my own skin."

"That is what I'll do," said Pleshnyevski; and lashing his horse with the nagaika, he rushed on.

"But avoid Rozlogi!" called Zagloba after him. "Should you meet Bogun, don't tell him that you have seen me. Do you hear?"

"I hear," answered Pleshnyevski. "God be with you!" And he raced away as if hunted.

"Well, devil, here's an overcoat for you! I've got out of many a trouble, but I have never been in anything like this. Hmelnitski in front, Bogun in the rear; and since this is so, I wouldn't give a broken orta for either my front or rear, or my whole skin. I was a fool not to go to Lubni with you, but it is no time to talk of that now. Pshaw, pshaw! All my wit at the present moment isn't fit to grease a pair of boots with. What is to be done? Where am I to go? In the whole Commonwealth it appears there is not a corner where a man can leave the world with his own death, and not have death given him. I would rather be excused from such presents; let others take them."

"Most worthy sir," said Helena, "I know that my cousins Yuri and Fedor are in Zólotonosha; maybe they could save us."

"In Zólotonosha? Wait a moment! In Chigirin I knew Pan Unyejitski, who owns the estates of Krapivna and Chernobái, near Zólotonosha. But that place is far from here, farther than Cherkasi. What is to be done? If there is no other place, why, we will take refuge even there. But we must leave the highway; it is safer to go by the steppe and woods. If we hide somewhere a week, even in the woods, perhaps by that time the hetmans will finish with Hmelnitski, and it will be more peaceable in the Ukraine."

"God did not save us from the hands of Bogun to let us perish. Have courage!"

"Wait a moment! Some spirit enters me anew. I have been in many a trouble. In a leisure hour I will tell you what happened to me in Galáts, and you will see at once that I was in a terrible place that time; still I slipped out by my own wit from those dangers and escaped in safety, though as you see my beard has grown gray a little. But we must leave the highway. Turn, my lady! You ride as well as the best Cossack. The grass is high, and no eye can see us."

In fact, the grass became higher and higher as they entered the steppe, so that at last they were hidden in it entirely. But it was difficult for the horses to move through that thicket of stalks, both slender and heavy, and at times sharp and cutting. Soon they became so tired that they were completely exhausted.

"If we want these horses to serve us further, we must dismount, unsaddle them, and let them roll and eat awhile, otherwise they will not go on. I see that we shall reach the Kagamlik before long. I should like to be there now. There is no place to hide in like reeds; when you are in them the devil himself can't find you. But we must not go astray."

He dismounted and assisted Helena from the horse, then took off the saddles and produced a supply of provisions which he had prudently provided in Rozlogi.

"We must strengthen ourselves," said he, "for the road is long; and do you make some vow to Saint Raphael for our safe passage. There is an old fortress in Zólotonosha, and perhaps there is some kind of garrison there now. Pleshnyevski said that beyond the Dnieper the peasants are rising. H'm! this may be true, for the people are quick at rebellion everywhere; but the hand of the prince is on the country behind them, and it is a devil of a hand for weight! Bogun has a strong neck; but if that hand should fall on it, the neck would bend to the earth,--which God grant, amen! But eat something, Princess!"

Zagloba took a little knife-case out of his boot-leg and gave it to Helena; then he placed before her, on the saddlecloth, roast beef and bread.

"Eat!" said he. "'When there is nothing in the stomach, we have peas and cabbage for brains.' 'If you want to keep your head right, eat roast beef.' But we have made fools of ourselves once, for apparently it would have been better to flee to Lubni; but the chance is gone now. The prince will surely move with his forces to the Dnieper, to assist the hetmans. We have lived to terrible times, when there is civil war, the worst of all evils. There will not be a corner for peaceable persons. It would have been better for me if I had joined the priesthood, for which I had a vocation, being a quiet and sober man; but fortune ordained otherwise. Oh, my God, my God! I should be canon of Cracow now, chanting my prayers, for I have a very beautiful voice. But what is to be done? From my youth up, girls pleased me! You wouldn't believe what a handsome fellow I was; whenever I looked at a woman, it was as if lightning struck her. If I were twenty years younger now, Pan Skshetuski would have something on his hands. Ah, you are a splendid Cossack! No wonder young men are rushing after you, and battling to win you. Pan Skshetuski is no common warrior. I saw the punishment he gave Chaplinski. True, he had something in his head; but when he took him by the neck and--pardon me--by the trousers, and when he battered the door open with him, I tell you that every bone in Chaplinski came out of its pocket. Old Zatsvilikhovski told me too that your betrothed is a great knight, the favorite of the prince. I saw myself in a moment that he was a soldier of uncommon daring and of experience beyond his years. He acts quickly. Though your company may be dear to me, I don't know how much I should give if we were in Zólotonosha now. I see that we must stay in the grass during the day and travel at night. But I don't know whether you will be able to endure such toil."

"Oh, I am in good health. I will endure every hardship. We could start even this moment."

"You have courage beyond women! The horses have rolled; I will saddle them at once, so as to be ready in every event. I shall not feel at ease till I see the reeds and rushes of the Kagamlik. If we hadn't left the road, we should have come upon the river nearer Chigirin, but here it is about five miles to it from the road. That is my estimate, at least. We shall cross to the other bank at once. I must tell you that I have a great desire to sleep. The entire night before last I went around in Chigirin, yesterday we drove with the Cossacks at a terrible pace to Rozlogi, and last night you and I rode away from Rozlogi. I want to sleep so much that I have lost all wish to talk; and though I have not the habit of being silent,--for philosophers say that a cat should be a hunter, and a man a talker,--still I find my tongue has grown lazy. Pardon me, then, if I doze."

"Oh, there is nothing to make excuse for," said Helena.

Pan Zagloba had really no need to accuse his tongue of sloth, for it had been going unceasingly since daylight; but in truth he wished to sleep. When he sat on the horse again, he began to doze at once, and soon he was sleeping soundly. He fell asleep from weariness and from the sound of the grass bent apart by the breasts of the horses.

Meanwhile Helena gave herself up to the thoughts which were whirling in her head like a flock of birds in the air. Up to that moment events had followed one another so quickly that she was unable to render account of all that had happened to her. The attack, the frightful scenes of death, terror, unexpected rescue, and flight,--all came like a storm in the course of a single night. And besides, so many unintelligible things! Who was this who had saved her? He had told her his name, it is true, but that name explained in no way the motives of his action. Whence did he come to Rozlogi? He said that he had come with Bogun; he had evidently kept company with him, was his acquaintance and friend. But in such a case why did he save her, and expose himself to the greatest danger and the terrible revenge of the Cossack? To understand this it was necessary to know Zagloba well, with his unruly head and his kindly heart. Helena had known him only six hours. And that unknown man with his impudent face, a swaggerer, a drunkard, is her savior. If she had met him three days before, he would have roused in her aversion and distrust; but now she looks on him as a good angel, and flees with him--whither? To Zólotonosha or anywhere else,--she herself knows not yet clearly. What a change of fate! Yesterday she lay down to rest under the quiet roof where she was born; to-day she is in the steppe, on horseback, in male attire, without home, without refuge. Behind her is the terrible chief, with designs on her honor; before her conflagration, peasant rebellion, civil war with all its ambushes, alarms, and horrors. And all her hope is in that man? No! it is still in some one more powerful than violence, war, murder, and conflagration. Here she raised her eyes to heaven and said,--

"Oh, do thou save me, great and merciful God! Rescue the orphan, the unhappy, the wanderer! Let thy will be done, but let thy mercy be manifest."

Indeed the mercy had been made manifest, for she had been caught away from the most terrible hands, and saved by an incomprehensible miracle of God. Danger had not passed yet, but perhaps rescue was not distant. Who knows where he is whom she has chosen with her heart? He must have returned already from the Saitch; perhaps he is somewhere in that same steppe. He will seek her and find her, and then joy will take the place of tears, and rejoicing of grief; alarm and terror will disappear forever, peace and pleasure will come. The brave simple heart of the girl was filled with trust, and the steppe rustled sweetly around her; the breeze which moved the grass blew at the same time pleasant thoughts to her brain. She is not an orphan, then, in this world, since she has here at her side one strange, unknown guardian, and still another, known and beloved, who is caring for her. He will not desert her, he will take her for good; and he is a man of iron, stronger and mightier than those rising against her in that hour.

The steppe rustled sweetly; from the flowers came odors strong and intoxicating; the ruddy tops of the thistle spread out their purple bunches; the white pearls of the mikalief and the feathers of the steppe grass bent toward her, as if recognizing a maiden sister in that Cossack, with long tresses, milk-white face, and red lips. They bent toward her as if wishing to say: "Cry not, beautiful maiden! we too are in the care of the Lord," A calm, increasing every moment, came to her from the steppe. Pictures of death and pursuit were blotted from her mind, and straightway a sort of weakness seized her, but a sweet one; slumber began to close her eyelids; the horses went slowly, the movement lulled her. She dropped asleep.

CHAPTER XX.

Helena was wakened by the barking of dogs. Opening her eyes, she saw in the distance before her a great shady oak, an enclosure, and a well-sweep. She roused her companion at once: "Oh, wake up!"

Zagloba opened his eyes. "What is this? Where are we?"

"I don't know."

"Wait a moment! This is a Cossack wintering-place."

"So it appears to me."

"Herdsmen live here, no doubt. Not too pleasant company! And these dogs howl as if wolves had bitten them. There are horses and men at the enclosure. No help for it; we must ride up to them, lest they pursue us if we pass. You must have been asleep."

"I was."

"One, two, three, four horses saddled,--four men there at the enclosure. Well, that is no great force. True, they are herdsmen. They are doing something in a hurry. Hallo there, men, come this way!"

The four Cossacks approached immediately. They were, in fact, herders who watched horses in the steppe during the summer. Zagloba noticed at once that only one of them had a sabre and a gun. The other three were armed with horse-jaws fastened to staves, but he knew that such herdsmen were often dangerous to travellers.

When all four approached they gazed from under their brows at the new-comers; in their bronzed faces could not be found the least trace of welcome. "What do you want?" asked they, without removing their caps.

"Glory to God!" said Zagloba.

"For the ages of ages! What do you want?"

"Is it far to Syrovati?"

"We don't know of any Syrovati."

"And what is this place called?"

"Gusla."

"Give our horses water."

"We have no water; it is dried up. But where do you ride from?"

"From Krivaya Rudá."

"Where are you going?"

"To Chigirin."

The herdsmen looked at one another. One of them, black as a bug and crooked-eyed, began to gaze intently at Zagloba. At last he asked: "Why did you leave the highway?"

"It was hot there."

The crooked-eyed man put his hand on the reins of Zagloba's horse: "Come down from the horse, come down! You have nothing to go to Chigirin for."

"How so?" asked Zagloba, quietly.

"Do you see that young fellow there?" asked crooked-eye, pointing to one of the herdsmen.

"I do."

"He has come from Chigirin. They are slaughtering Poles there."

"And do you know, fellow, who is following us to Chigirin?"

"Who?"

"Prince Yeremi."

The insolent face of the herdsman dropped in a moment. All, as if by command, removed their caps.

"Do you know, you trash!" continued Zagloba, "what the Poles do to those who slaughter? They hang them. And do you know how many men Prince Yeremi has, and do you know that he is no farther than two or three miles from here? And how have you received us, you dog souls! What stuff you tell!--the well is dried up, you have no water for horses! Ah, basilisks! I'll show you!"

"Oh, don't be angry, Pan! The well is dried up. We go to the Kagamlik with our horses, and bring water for ourselves. But say the word and we will run for water."

"Oh, I can get on without you! I will go with my attendant. Where is the Kagamlik?" inquired he, sternly.

"About a mile and a quarter from here," said the crooked-eyed man, pointing to a line of reeds.

"And must I return this way, or can I go along the bank?"

"Go by the bank. The river turns to the road about a mile from here."

"Dash ahead, young man!" said Zagloba, turning to Helena.

The pretended youth turned his horse and galloped on.

"Listen!" said Zagloba, turning to the herdsman. "If the vanguard comes up, say that I went to the road along the river."

"I will."

A quarter of an hour later Zagloba was riding again by the side of Helena.

"I invented the prince for them in season," said he, blinking with his cataract-covered eye. "Now they will stay all day waiting for the vanguard. They shuddered at the mere name of the prince."

"T see you have such ready wit that you will save us from every trouble," said Helena, "and I thank God for sending me such a guardian."

These words went to the heart of the noble. He smiled, stroked his beard, and said,--

"Well, hasn't Zagloba a head on his shoulders? Cunning as Ulysses! and I must tell you, had it not been for that cunning, the crows would have eaten me long ago. Can't help it, I must save myself. They believed easily that the prince was coming, for it is probable that he will appear to-morrow or next day in this neighborhood with a fiery sword like an archangel. And if he should only strike Bogun somewhere on the road, I would make a vow to walk barefoot to Chenstokhova. Even if those herdsmen did not believe, the very mention of the power of the prince was enough to restrain them from attacks on our lives. Still I tell you that their impudence is no good sign to us, for it means that the peasants here have heard of the victories of Hmelnitski, and will become more and more insolent every moment. We must keep therefore to the waste places and visit few villages, for they are dangerous. We have got into such a snare that, as I live, it would be hard to invent a worse one."

Alarm again seized Helena. Wishing to get some word of hope from Zagloba, she said: "But you will save me and yourself this time?"

"Of course," said the old fox; "the head is given to think about the body. I have become so attached to you that I will struggle for you as for my own daughter. But, to tell the truth, the worst is that we don't know where to take refuge, for Zólotonosha is no safe asylum."

"I know surely that my cousins are there."

"They are, or they are not; they may have left there and returned to Rozlogi by a different road from the one we are travelling. I count more on the garrison, if there is only half a regiment in the castle. But here is the Kagamlik and plenty of reeds. We will cross to the other side, and instead of going with the current toward the road, we will go up stream to elude pursuit. It is true that we shall go toward Rozlogi, but not far."

"We shall approach Brovarki," said Helena, "from which there is a road to Zólotonosha."

"That is better. Stop your horse!"

They watered the horses. Zagloba, leaving Helena carefully hidden in the reeds, went to look for a ford. He found one easily, for it was only a few yards from the place to which they had come,--just where the herdsmen used to drive their horses through the river, which was shallow enough, but the bank was inconvenient because overgrown with reeds and soft. When they had crossed the river they hurried up stream and rode without resting till night. The road was bad; for the Kagamlik had many tributary streams, which spreading out toward the mouth formed swamps and soft places. Every little while it was necessary to look for fords, or to push through reeds difficult of passage for mounted travellers. The horses were tired and barely able to drag their legs along; at times they stumbled so badly that it seemed to Zagloba they could hold out no longer. At last they came out on a lofty dry bank covered with oaks. But it was night already, and very dark. Further movement was impossible, for in the darkness it was easy to stumble into deep swamps and perish. Zagloba therefore decided to wait till morning.

He unsaddled the horses, fettered and let them out to graze; then he gathered leaves for a bed, spread the saddlecloths over them, and covering both with a burka, said to Helena,--

"Lie down and sleep, for you have nothing better to do. The dew will wash your eyes, and that is good. I will put my head on the saddle too, for I don't feel a bone in my body. We will not make a fire, for the light would attract herdsmen. The night is short, and we will move on at daybreak. We doubled on our tracks like hares, not advancing much, it is true; but we have so hidden the trail that the devil who finds us will puff. Good-night!"

"Good-night!"

The slender young Cossack knelt down and prayed long with eyes raised to the stars. Zagloba took the saddle on his shoulders and carried it to some distance, where he sought out a place to sleep. The bank was well chosen for a halting-place; it was high and dry, also free from mosquitoes. The thick leaves of the oak-trees might furnish a passable protection from rain.

Helena could not sleep for a long time. The events of the past night rose at once in her memory as vividly as life. In the darkness appeared the faces of her murdered aunt and cousins. It seemed to her that she was shut up in the chamber with their bodies, and that Bogun would come in a moment. She saw his pale face and his dark sable brows contracted, with pain, and his eyes fixed upon her. Unspeakable terror seized her. But will she really see on a sudden through the darkness around her two gleaming eyes?

The moon, looking for a moment from behind the clouds, whitened with a few rays the oaks, and lent fantastic forms to the stumps and branches. Landrails called in the meadows, and quails in the steppes; at times certain strange and distant cries of birds or beasts of the night came to them. Nearer was heard the snorting of their horses, who eating the grass and jumping in their fetters went farther and farther from the sleepers. But all those sounds quieted Helena, for they dissipated the fantastic visions and brought her to reality; told her that that chamber which was continually present before her eyes, and those corpses of her friends, and that pale Bogun, with vengeance in his looks, were an illusion of the senses, a whim of fear, nothing more. A few days before, the thought of such a night under the open sky in the desert would have frightened her to death; now, to gain rest she was obliged to remember that she was really on the bank of the Kagamlik, and far from home.

The voices of the quails and landrails lulled her to sleep. The stars twinkled whenever the breeze moved the branches, the beetles sounded in the oak-leaves; she fell asleep at last. But nights in the desert have their surprises too. Day was already breaking, when from a distance terrible noises came to Helena's ears,--howling, snorting, later a squeal so full of pain and terror that the blood stopped in her veins. She sprang to her feet, covered with cold sweat, terror-stricken, and not knowing what to do. Suddenly Zagloba shot past her. He rushed without a cap, in the direction of the cry, pistol in hand. After a while his voice was heard: "U-ha! u-ha!" a pistol-shot, then all was silent. It seemed to Helena as if she had waited an age. At last she heard Zagloba below the bank.

"May the dogs devour you, may your skins be torn off, may the Jews wear you in their collars!"

Genuine despair was in the voice of Zagloba.

"What has happened?" inquired Helena.

"The wolves have eaten our horses."

"Jesus, Mary! both of them?"

"One is eaten, the other is maimed so that he cannot stand. They didn't go more than three hundred yards, and are lost."

"What shall we do now?"

"What shall we do? Whittle out sticks for ourselves and sit on them. Do I know what we shall do? Here is pure despair. I tell you, the devil has surely got after us,--which is not to be wondered at, for he must be a friend of Bogun, or his blood relation. What are we to do? May I turn into a horse if I know,--you would then at least have something to ride on. I am a scoundrel if ever I have been in such a fix."

"Let us go on foot."

"It is well for your ladyship to travel in peasant fashion, with your twenty years, but not for me with my circumference. I speak incorrectly, though, for here any clown can have a nag, only dogs travel on foot. Pure despair, as God is kind to me! Of course we shall not sit here, we shall walk on directly; but when we are to reach Zólotonosha is unknown to me. If it is not pleasant to flee on horseback, it is sorest of all on foot. Now the worst thing possible has happened to us. We must leave the saddles and carry on our own shoulders whatever we put between our lips."

"I will not allow you to carry the burden alone; I too will carry whatever is necessary."

Zagloba was pleased to see such resolution in Helena.

"I should be either a Turk or a Pagan to permit you. Those white hands and slender shoulders are not for burdens. With God's help I will manage; only I must rest frequently, for, always too abstemious in eating and drinking, I have short breath now. Let us take the saddle-cloths to sleep on and some provisions; but there will not be much of them, since we shall have to strengthen ourselves directly."

Straightway they began the strengthening, during which Pan Zagloba, abandoning his boasted abstemiousness, busied himself about long breath. Near midday they reached a ford through which men and wagons passed from time to time, for on both banks there were marks of wheels and horses' tracks.

"Maybe that is the road to Zólotonosha."

"There is no one to ask."

Zagloba had barely stopped speaking, when voices reached their ears from a distance.

"Wait!" whispered Zagloba, "we must hide."

The voices continued to approach them.

"Do you see anything?" inquired Helena.

"I do."

"Who are coming?"

"A blind old man with a lyre. A youth is leading him, Now they are taking off their boots. They will come to us through the river."

After a time the plashing of water indicated that they were really crossing. Zagloba and Helena came out of the hiding-place.

"Glory be to God!" said the noble, aloud.

"For the ages of ages!" answered the old man. "But who are you?"

"Christians. Don't be afraid, grandfather!"

"May Saint Nicholas give you health and happiness!"

"And where are you coming from, grandfather?"

"From Brovarki."

"And where does this road lead to?"

"Oh, to farmhouses and villages."

"It doesn't go to Zólotonosha?"

"Maybe it does."

"Is it long since you left Brovarki?"

"Yesterday morning."

"And were you in Rozlogi?"

"Yes. But they say that the knights came there, that there was a battle."

"Who said that?"

"Oh, they said so in Brovarki. One of the servants of the princess came, and what he told was terrible!"

"And you didn't see him?"

"I? I see no man, I am blind."

"And this youth?"

"He sees, but he is dumb. I am the only one who understands him."

"Is it far from here to Rozlogi, for we are going there?"

"Oh, it is far!"

"You say, then, that you were in Rozlogi?"

"Yes, we were."

"So!" said Zagloba; and suddenly he seized the youth by the shoulder. "Ha! scoundrels, criminals, thieves! you are going around as spies, rousing the serfs to rebellion. Here, Fedor, Oleksa, Maksim, take them, strip them naked, and hang or drown them; beat them,--they are rebels, spies,--beat, kill them!"

He began to pull the youth about and to shake him roughly, shouting louder and louder every moment. The old man threw himself on his knees, begging for mercy; the youth uttered sounds of terror peculiar to the dumb, and Helena looked with astonishment at the attack.

"What are you doing?" inquired she, not believing her own eyes.

But Zagloba shouted, cursed, moved hell, summoned all the miseries, misfortunes, and diseases, threatened with every manner of torment and death.

The princess thought that his mind had failed.

"Go away!" cried he to her; "it is not proper for you to see what is going to take place here. Go away, I tell you!"

He turned to the old man. "Take off your clothes, you clown! If you don't, I'll cut you to pieces."

When he had thrown the youth to the ground Zagloba began to strip him with his own hands. The old man, frightened, dropped his lyre, his bag, and his coat as quickly as he could.

"Throw off everything or you will be killed!" shouted Zagloba.

The old man began to take off his shirt.

Helena, seeing whither matters were tending, hurried away, and as she fled she heard the curses of Zagloba.

After she had gone some distance she stopped, not knowing what to do. Near by was the trunk of a tree thrown down by the wind; she sat on this and waited. The noises of the dumb youth, the groans of the old man, and the uproar of Zagloba came to her ears.

At last all was silent save the twittering of birds and the rustle of leaves. After a time the heavy steps of a man panting were heard. It was Zagloba. On his shoulders he carried the clothing stripped from the old man and the youth, in his hands two pair of boots and a lyre. When he came near he began to wink with his sound eye, to smile, and to puff. He was evidently in perfect humor.

"No herald in a court would have shouted as I have," said he, "until I am hoarse; but I have got what I wanted. I let them go naked as their mother bore them. If the Sultan doesn't make me a pasha, or hospodar of Wallachia, he is a thankless fellow, for I have made two Turkish saints. Oh, the scoundrels! they begged me to leave them at least their shirts. I told them they ought to be grateful that I left them their lives. And see here, young lady! Everything is new,--the coats and the boots and the shirts. There must be nice order in that Commonwealth, in which trash dress so richly. But they were at a festival in Brovarki, where they collected no small amount of money and bought everything new at the fair. Not a single noble will plough out so much in this country as a minstrel will beg. Therefore I abandon my career as a knight, and will strip grandfathers on the highway, for I see that in this manner I shall arrive at fortune more quickly."

"For what purpose did you do that?" asked Helena.

"Just wait a minute, and I will show you for what purpose."

Saying this, he took half the plundered clothing and went into the reeds which covered the bank. After a time the sounds of a lyre were heard in the rushes, and there appeared, not Pan Zagloba, but a real "grandfather" of the Ukraine, with a cataract on one eye and a gray beard. The "grandfather" approached Helena, singing with a hoarse voice,--

"Oh, bright falcon, my own brother,
High dost thou soar,
And far dost thou fly!"

The princess clapped her hands, and for the first time since her flight from Rozlogi a smile brightened her beautiful face.

"If I did not know that it was you, I should never have recognized you."

"Well," said Zagloba, "I know you have not seen a better mask at a festival. I looked into the Kagamlik myself; and if ever I have seen a better-looking grandfather, then hang me. As for songs, I have no lack of them. What do you prefer? Maybe you would like to hear of Marusia Boguslava, of Bondarivna, or the death of Sierpahova; I can give you that. I am a rogue if I can't get a crust of bread among the worst knaves that exist."

"Now I understand your action, why you stripped the clothing from those poor creatures,--because it is safer to go over the road in disguise."

"Of course," said Zagloba; "and what do you suppose? Here, east of the Dnieper, the people are worse than anywhere else; and now when they hear of the war with the Zaporojians, and the victories, of Hmelnitski, no power will keep them from rebellion. You saw those herdsmen who wanted to get our skins. If the hetmans do not put down Hmelnitski at once, the whole country will be on fire in two or three days, and how should I take you through bands of peasants in rebellion? And if you had to fall into their hands, you would better have remained in Bogun's."

"That cannot be! I prefer death," interrupted Helena.

"But I prefer life; for death is a thing from which you cannot rise by any wit. I think, however, that God sent us this old man and the youth. I frightened them with the prince and his whole army as I did the herdsmen. They will sit in the reeds naked for three days from terror, and by that time we shall reach Zólotonosha in disguise somehow. We shall find your cousins and efficient aid; if not, we will go farther to the hetmans,--and all this in safety, for grandfathers have no fear of peasants and Cossacks. We might take our heads in safety through Hmelnitski's camp. But we have to avoid the Tartars, for they would take you as a youth into captivity."

"Then must I too disguise myself?"

"Yes; throw off your Cossack clothes, and disguise yourself as a peasant youth,--though you are rather comely to be a clodhopper's child, as I am to be a grandfather; but that is nothing. The wind will tan your face, and my stomach will fall in from walking. I shall sweat away all my thickness. When the Wallachians burned out my eye, I thought that an absolutely awful thing had come upon me; but now I see it is really an advantage, for a grandfather not blind would be suspected. You will lead me by the hand, and call me Onufri, for that is my minstrel name. Now dress up as quickly as you can, since it is time for the road, which will be so long for us on foot."

Zagloba went aside, and Helena began at once to array herself as a minstrel boy. Having washed in the river, she cast aside the Cossack coat, and took the peasant's svitka, straw hat, and knapsack. Fortunately the youth stripped by Zagloba was tall, so that everything fitted Helena well.

Zagloba, returning, examined her carefully, and said,--

"God save me! more than one knight would willingly lay aside his armor if he only had such an attendant as you; and I know one hussar who would certainly. But we must do something with that hair. I saw handsome boys in Stamboul, but never one so handsome as you are."

"God grant my beauty may work no ill for me!" said Helena. But she smiled; for her woman's ear was tickled by Zagloba's praise.

"Beauty never turns out ill, and I will give you an example of this; for when the Turks in Galáts burned out one of my eyes, and wanted to burn out the other, the wife of the Pasha saved me on account of my extraordinary beauty, the remnants of which you may see even yet."

"But you said that the Wallachians burned your eye out."

"They were Wallachians, but had become Turks, and were serving the Pasha in Galáts."

"They didn't burn even one of your eyes out."

"But from the heated iron a cataract grew on it. It's all the same. What do you wish to do with your tresses?"

"What! I must cut them off?"

"You must. But how?"

"With your sabre."

"It is well to cut a head off with this sword, but hair--I don't know how."

"Well, I will sit by that log and put my hair across it, you can strike and cut it off; but don't cut my head off!"

"Oh, never fear! More than once have I shot the wick from candles when I was drunk, without cutting the candle. I will do no harm to you, although this act is the first of its kind in my life."

Helena sat near the log, and throwing her heavy dark hair across it, raised her eyes to Zagloba. "I am ready," said she; "cut!"

She smiled somewhat sadly; for she was sorry for those tresses, which near the head could hardly be clasped by two hands. Zagloba had a sort of awkward feeling. He went around the trunk to cut more conveniently, and muttered:

"Pshaw, pshaw! I would rather be a barber and cut Cossack tufts. I seem to be an executioner going to my work; for it is known to you that they cut the hair off witches, so that the devils shouldn't hide in it and weaken the power of torture. But you are not a witch; therefore this act seems disgraceful to me,--for which if Pan Skshetuski does not cut my ears, then I'll pay him. Upon my word, shivers are going along my arm. At least, close your eyes!"

"All ready!" said Helena.

Zagloba straightened up, as if rising in his stirrups for a blow. The metallic blade whistled in the air, and that moment the dark tresses slipped down along the smooth bark to the ground.

"All over!" said Zagloba, in his turn.

Helena sprang up, and immediately the short-cut hair fell in a dark circle around her face, on which blushes of shame were beating,--for at that period the cutting of a maiden's hair was considered a great disgrace; therefore it was on her part a grievous sacrifice, which she could make only in case of extreme necessity. In fact, tears came to her eyes; and Zagloba, angry at himself, made no attempt to comfort her.

"It seems to me that I have ventured on something dishonorable, and I repeat to you that Pan Skshetuski, if he is a worthy cavalier, is bound to cut my ears off. But it could not be avoided, for your sex would have been discovered at once. Now at least we can go on with confidence. I inquired of the old man too about the road, holding a dagger to his throat. According to what he said, we shall see three oaks in the steppe; near them is the Wolf's Ravine, and along the ravine lies the road through Demiánovka to Zólotonosha. He said that wagoners go by the road, and it would be possible to sit with them in the wagons. You and I are passing through a grievous time, which I shall ever remember; for now we must part with the sabre, since it befits neither the minstrel nor his boy to have marks of nobility about their persons. I will push it under this tree. God may permit me to find it here some other day. Many an expedition has this sabre seen, and it has been the cause of great victories. Believe me, I should be commander of an army now were it not for the envy and malice of men who accused me of a love for strong drinks. So is it always in the world,--no justice in anything! When I was not rushing into destruction like a fool, and knew how to unite prudence with valor like a second Cunctator, Pan Zatsvilikhovski was the first to say that I was a coward. He is a good man, but he has an evil tongue. The other day he gnawed at me because I played brother with the Cossacks; but had it not been for that you would not have escaped the power of Bogun."

While talking, Zagloba thrust the sabre under the tree, covered it with plants and grass, then threw the bag and lyre over his shoulder, took the staff pointed with flintstones, waved his hands a couple of times, and said,--

"Well, this is not bad. I can strike a light in the eyes of some dog or wolf with this staff and count his teeth. The worst of all is that we must walk; but there is no help. Come!"

They went on,--the dark-haired youth in front, the old man following. The latter grunted and cursed; for it was hot for him to travel on foot, though a breeze passed over the steppe. The breeze burned and tanned the face of the handsome boy. Soon they came to the ravine, at the bottom of which was a spring which distilled its pure waters into the Kagamlik. Around that ravine not far from the river three strong oaks were growing on a mound; to these our wayfarers turned at once. They came also upon traces of the road, which looked yellow along the steppe from flowers which were growing on droppings of cattle. The road was deserted; there were neither teamsters, nor tar-spots on the ground, nor gray oxen slowly moving. But here and there lay the bones of cattle torn to pieces by wolves and whitening in the sun. The wayfarers went on steadily, resting only under the shade of oak-groves. The dark-haired boy lay down to slumber on the green turf, and the old man watched. They passed through streams also; and when there was no ford they searched for one, walking for a distance along the shore. Sometimes, too, the old man carried the boy over in his arms, with a power that was wonderful in a man who begged his bread. But he was a sturdy minstrel! Thus they dragged on till evening, when the boy sat down by the wayside at an oak-forest and said,--

"My breath is gone, I have spent my strength; I can walk no farther, I will lie down here and die."

The old man was terribly distressed. "Oh, these cursed wastes,--not a house nor a cottage by the roadside, nor a living soul! But we cannot spend the night here. Evening is already falling, it will be dark in an hour,--and just listen!"

The old man stopped speaking, and for a while there was deep silence. But it was soon broken by a distant dismal sound which seemed to come from the bowels of the earth; it did really come from the ravine, which lay not far from the road.

"Those are wolves," said Zagloba. "Last night we had horses,--they ate them; this time they will get at our own persons. I have, it is true, a pistol under my svitka; but I don't know whether my powder would hold out for two charges, and I should not like to be the supper at a wolf's wedding. Listen! Another howl!"

The howling was heard again, and appeared to be nearer.

"Rise, my child!" said the old man; "and if you are unable to walk, I will carry you. What's to be done? I see that I have a great affection for you, which is surely because living in a wifeless condition I am unable to leave legitimate descendants of my own; and if I have illegitimate they are heathen, for I lived a long time in Turkey. With me ends the family of Zagloba, with its escutcheon 'In the Forehead.' You will take care of my old age, but now you must get up and sit on my shoulders."

"My feet have grown so heavy that I cannot move."

"You were boasting of your strength. But stop! stop! As God is dear to me, I hear the barking of dogs. That's it. Those are dogs, not wolves. Then Demiánovka, of which the old minstrel told me, must be near. Praise be to God in the highest! I had thought not to make a fire on account of the wolves; for we should have surely gone to sleep, we are so tired. Yes, they are dogs. Do you hear?"

"Let us go on," said Helena, whose strength returned suddenly.

They had barely come out of the wood when smoke from a number of cottages appeared at no great distance. They saw also three domes of a church, covered with fresh shingles, which shone yet in the dusk from the last gleams of the evening twilight. The barking of dogs seemed nearer, more distinct each moment.

"Yes, that is Demiánovka; it cannot be another place," said Zagloba. "They receive minstrels hospitably everywhere; maybe we shall find supper and lodging, and perhaps good people will take us farther. Wait a moment! this is one of the prince's villages; there must be an agent living in it. We will rest and get news. The prince must be already on the way. Rescue may come sooner than you expect. Remember that you are a mute. I began at the wrong end when I told you to call me Onufri, for since you are a mute you cannot call me anything. I shall speak for you and for myself, and, praise be to God! I can use peasants' speech as well as Latin. Move on, move on! Now the first cottage is near. My God! when will our wanderings come to an end? If we could get some warmed beer, I should praise the Lord God for even that."

Zagloba ceased, and for a time they went on in silence together; then he began to talk again.

"Remember that you are dumb. When they ask you about anything, point to me and say, 'Hum, hum, hum! niyá, niyá!' I have seen that you have much wit, and besides, it is a question of our lives. If we should chance on a regiment belonging to the hetmans or the prince, then we would tell who we are at once, especially if the officer is courteous and an acquaintance of Pan Skshetuski. It is true that you are under the guardianship of the prince, and you have nothing to fear from soldiers. Oh! what fires are those bursting out in the glen? Ah, there are blacksmiths--there is a forge! But I see there is no small number of people at it. Let us go there."

In the cleft which formed the entrance to the ravine there was a forge, from the chimney of which bundles and bunches of golden sparks were thrown out; and through the open doors and numerous chinks in the walls sparkling light burst forth, intercepted from moment to moment by dark forms moving around inside. In front of the forge were to be seen in the evening twilight a number of dark forms standing together in knots. The hammers in the forge beat in time, till the echo was heard all about; and the sound was mingled with songs in front of the forge, with the buzz of conversation and the barking of dogs. Seeing all this, Zagloba turned immediately into the ravine, touched his lyre, and began to sing,--

"Hei! on the mountain
Reapers are seen,
Under the mountain,
The mountain green,
Cossacks are marching on."

Singing thus, he approached the crowd of people standing in front of the forge. He looked around. They were peasants, for the most part drunk. Nearly all of them had sticks in their hands; on some of these sticks were scythes, double-edged and pointed. The blacksmiths in the forge were occupied specially in the making of these points and the bending of the scythes.

"Ah, grandfather! grandfather!" they began to call out in the crowd.

"Glory be to God!" said Zagloba.

"For the ages of ages!"

"Tell me, children, is this Demiánovka?"

"Yes, it is Demiánovka. But why do you ask?"

"I ask because men told me on the way," continued the grandfather, "that good people dwell here, that they will take in the old man, give him food and drink, let him spend the night, and give him some money. I am old; I have travelled a long road, and this boy here cannot go a step farther. He, poor fellow, is dumb; he leads me because I am sightless. I am a blind unfortunate. God will bless you, kind people. Saint Nicholas, the wonder-worker, will bless you. Saint Onufri will bless you. In one eye there is a little of God's light left me; in the other it is dark forever. So I travel with my lyre. I sing songs, and I live like the birds on what falls from the hands of kind people."

"And where are you from, grandfather?"

"Oh, from afar, afar! But let me rest, for I see here by the forge a bench. And sit down, poor creature!" said he, showing the bench to Helena. "We are from Ladava, good people, and left home long, long ago; but to-day we come from the festival in Brovarki."

"And have you heard anything good there?" asked an old peasant with a scythe in his hand.

"We heard, we heard, but whether it is anything good we don't know. Many people have collected there. They spoke of Hmelnitski,--that he had conquered the hetman's son and his knights. We heard, too, that the peasants are rising against the nobles on the Russian bank."

Immediately the crowd surrounded Zagloba, who, sitting by Helena, struck the strings of the lyre from time to time.

"Then you heard, father, that the people are rising?"

"I did; for wretched is our peasant lot."

"But they say there will be an end to it?"

"In Kieff they found on the altar a letter from Christ, saying there would be fearful and awful war and much blood-spilling in the whole Ukraine."

The half-circle in front of the bench on which Zagloba sat contracted still more.

"You say there was a letter?"

"There was, as I am alive. About war and the spilling of blood. But I cannot speak further, for the throat is dried up within me, poor old man!"

"Here is a measure of gorailka for you, father; and tell us what you have heard in the world. We know that minstrels go everywhere and know everything. There have been some among us already. They said that the black hour would come from Hmelnitski on the lords. We had these scythes and pikes made for us, so as not to be the last; but we don't know whether to begin now or to wait for a letter from Hmelnitski."

Zagloba emptied the measure, smacked his lips, thought awhile, and then said: "Who tells you it is time to begin?"

"We want to begin ourselves."

"Begin! begin!" said numerous voices. "If the Zaporojians have beaten the lords, then begin!"

The scythes and pikes quivered in strong hands, and gave out an ominous clatter. Then followed a moment of silence, but the hammers in the forge continued to beat. The future killers waited for what the old man would say. He thought and thought; at last he asked,--

"Whose people are you?"

"Prince Yeremi's."

"And whom will you kill?"

The peasants looked at one another.

"Him?" asked the old man.

"We couldn't manage him."

"Oh, you can't manage him, children, you can't manage him! I was in Lubni, and I saw that prince with my own eyes. He is awful! When he shouts the trees tremble in the woods, and when he stamps his foot a ravine is made. The king is afraid of him, the hetmans obey him, and all are terrified at him. He has more soldiers than the Khan or the Sultan. Oh, you can't manage him, children, you can't manage him! He is after you, not you after him. And I know what you don't know yet, that all the Poles will come to help him; and where there is a Pole, there is a sabre."

Gloomy silence seized the crowd; the old man struck his lyre again, and raising his face toward the moon, continued:

"The prince is coming, he is coming, and with him as many beautiful plumes and banners as there are stars in heaven or thistles on the steppe. The wind flies before him and groans; and do you know, my children, why the wind groans? It groans over your fate. Mother Death flies before him with a scythe, and strikes; and do you know what she strikes at? She strikes at your necks."

"O Lord, have mercy on us!" said low, terrified voices.

Again nothing was heard but the beating of hammers.

"Who is the prince's agent here?" asked the old man.

"Pan Gdeshinski."

"And where is he?"

"He ran away."

"Why did he run away?"

"He ran away, for he heard that they were making scythes and pikes for us. He got frightened and ran away."

"So much the worse, for he will tell the prince about you."

"Why do you croak, grandfather, like a raven?" asked an old peasant. "We believe that the black hour is coming on the lords; and there will be neither on the Russian nor Tartar bank lords or princes,--only Cossacks, free people; there will be neither land-rent, nor barrel-tax, nor mill-tax, nor transport-tax, nor any more Jews, for thus does it stand in the letter from Christ which you yourself spoke of. And Hmelnitski is as strong as the prince. Let them go at it!"

"God grant!" said the old man. "Oh, bitter is our peasant lot! It was different in old times."

"Who owns the land? The prince. Who owns the steppe? The prince. Who owns the woods? The prince. Who has the cattle? The prince. And in old times it was God's woods and God's steppe; whoever came first, took it, and was bound to no man. Now everything belongs to the lords and princes."

"All belongs to you, my children; but I tell you one thing you yourselves know, that you can't manage the prince here. I tell you this,--whoever wants to slay lords, let him not stay here till Hmelnitski has tried his hand on the prince, but let him be off to Hmelnitski, and right away, to-morrow, for the prince is on the road already. If Pan Gdeshinski brings him to Demiánovka, the prince won't leave one of you alive; he will kill the last man of you. Make your way to Hmelnitski. The more of you there, the easier for Hmelnitski to succeed. Oh, but he has heavy work before him! The hetmans in front of him, the armies of the king without number, and then the prince more powerful than the hetmans. Hurry on, children, to help Hmelnitski and the Zaporojians; for they, poor men, won't hold out unless you help, and they are fighting against the lords for your freedom and property. Hurry! You will save yourselves from the prince and you will help Hmelnitski."

"He speaks the truth!" cried voices in the crowd.

"He speaks well!"

"A wise grandfather!"

"Did you see the prince on the road?"

"See him I didn't, but I heard in Brovarki that he had left Lubni, that he is burning and slaying; and where he finds even one pike before him, he leaves only the sky and the earth behind."

"Lord, have mercy on us!"

"And where are we to look for Hmelnitski?"

"I came here, children, to tell you where to look for Hmelnitski. Go, my children, to Zólotonosha, then to Trakhtimiroff, and there Hmelnitski will be waiting for you. There people are collecting from all the villages, houses, and cottages; the Tartars will come there too. Go! Unless you do, the prince will not leave you to walk over the earth."

"And you will go with us, father?"

"Walk I will not, for the ground pulls down my old legs. But get ready a telega, and I will ride with you. Before we come to Zólotonosha I will go on ahead to see if there are Polish soldiers. If there are, we will pass by and go straight to Trakhtimiroff. That is a Cossack country. But now give me something to eat and drink, for I am hungry, and this lad here is hungry too. We will start off in the morning, and along the road I will sing to you of Pan Pototski and Prince Yeremi. Oh, they are terrible lions! There will be great bloodshed in the Ukraine. The sky is awfully red, and the moon just as if swimming in blood. Beg, children, for the mercy of God, for no one will walk long in God's world. I have heard also that vampires rise out of their graves and howl."

A vague terror seized the crowd of peasants; they began to look around involuntarily, make the sign of the cross and whisper among themselves. At last one cried out,--

"To Zólotonosha!"

"To Zólotonosha!" repeated all, as if there in particular were refuge and safety.

"To Trakhtimiroff!"

"Death to the Poles and lords!"

All at once a young Cossack stepped forward, shook his pike, and cried: "Fathers, if we go to Zólotonosha to-morrow, we, will go to the manager's house to-night."

"To the manager's house!" cried a number of voices at once.

"Burn it up! take the goods!"

But the minstrel, who held his head drooping on his breast, raised it and said,--

"Oh, children, do not go to the manager's house, and do not burn it, or you will suffer. The prince may be close by, he is going along with his army; he will see the fire, he will come, and there will be trouble. Better give me something to eat and show me a place to rest. And do you keep your peace!"

"He tells the truth!" said a number of voices.

"He tells the truth, and, Maksim, you are a fool!"

"Come, father, to my house for bread and salt and a cup of mead, and rest on the hay till daylight," said an old peasant, turning to the minstrel.

Zagloba rose, and pulled the sleeve of Helena's svitka. She was asleep.

"The boy is tired to death; he fell asleep under the very sound of the hammers," said Zagloba. But in his soul he thought: "Oh, sweet innocence, thou art able to sleep amidst pikes and knives! It is clear that angels of heaven are guarding thee, and me in thy company."

He roused her, and they went on toward the village, which lay at some distance. The night was calm and quiet; the echo of the striking hammers followed them. The old peasant went ahead to show the way in the darkness; and Zagloba, pretending to say his prayers, muttered in a monotone,--

"O God, have mercy on us, sinners--Do you see, Princess--O Holy Most Pure--what would have happened to us without this peasant disguise?--As it is on earth, so in heaven--We shall get something to eat, and to-morrow ride to Zólotonosha instead of going on foot--Amen, amen, amen!--Bogun may come upon our tracks, for our tracks will not deceive him; but it will be late, for we shall cross the Dnieper at Próhorovka--Amen!--May black death choke them, may the hangman light their way! Do you hear, Princess, how they are howling at the forge?--Amen!--Terrible times have come on us, but I am a fool if I don't rescue you even if we have to flee to Warsaw itself."

"What are you muttering there, brother?" asked the peasant.

"Oh, nothing! I am praying for your health. Amen, amen!"

"Here is my cottage."

"Glory be to God!"

"For the ages of ages!"

"I beg you to eat my bread and salt."

"God will reward you."

A little later the minstrel had strengthened himself powerfully with mutton and a good portion of mead. Next morning early, he moved on with his attendant lad, in a comfortable telega, toward Zólotonosha, escorted by a number of mounted peasants armed with pikes and scythes.

They went through Kovraiets, Chernobái, and Krapivna. The wayfarers saw that everything was seething; the peasants were arming at all points, the forges were working from morning till night, and only the terrible name and power of Prince Yeremi still restrained the bloody outburst. West of the Dnieper the tempest was let loose in all its fury. News of the defeat at Korsún had spread over all Russia with the speed of lightning, and every living soul was rushing forth.

CHAPTER XXI.

Next morning after the flight of Zagloba, the Cossacks found Bogun half suffocated in the coat in which Zagloba had wrapped him; but since his wounds were not serious he returned soon to consciousness. Remembering everything that had happened, he fell into a rage, roared like a wild beast, stained his hands with blood from his own wounded head, and struck at the men with his dagger, so that the Cossacks dared not come near him. At last, being unable to support himself in the saddle, he ordered them to bind a Jew cradle between two horses, and sitting in it, he hurried on as if insane in the direction of Lubni, supposing that the fugitives had gone thither. Resting on the Jew bed on down, and in his own blood, he raced over the steppe like a vampire hurrying back to its grave before daybreak; and after him speeded his trusty Cossacks, with the thought in mind that they were hurrying to evident death. They flew on in this way to Vassílyevka, where there was a garrison of one hundred Hungarian infantry belonging to Prince Yeremi. The furious leader, as if life had become loathsome to him, fell upon these without hesitation, rushing first into the fire himself, and after a struggle of some hours' duration cut the men to pieces, with the exception of a few whom he spared to gain from them a confession through torture. Learning that no noble with a maiden had escaped by that road, and not knowing himself what to do, he tore away his bandages from excess of pain.

To go farther was impossible; for everywhere toward Lubni were stationed the forces of the prince, whom the villagers that had run away during the battle at Vassílyevka must have already informed of the attack. The faithful Cossacks therefore bore away their ataman weakened from rage, and took him back to Rozlogi. On their return they found not a trace of the buildings; for the peasants of the neighborhood had plundered and burned them, together with Prince Vassily, thinking that in case the Kurtsevichi or Prince Yeremi should wish to inflict punishment, the blame could be cast easily on Bogun and his Cossacks. They had burned every out-house, cut down the cherry-orchard, and killed all the servants. The peasants had taken unsparing vengeance for the harsh rule and oppression which they had endured from the Kurtsevichi.

Just beyond Rozlogi, Pleshnyevski, who was carrying tidings of the defeat at Jóltiya Vodi from Chigirin, fell into the hands of Bogun. When asked where and for what purpose he was going, he hesitated and failed to give clear answers; he fell under suspicion, and when burned with fire, told of the victory of Hmelnitski, and also of Zagloba, whom he had met the day before. The leader rejoiced, and drew a long breath. After he had hanged Pleshnyevski, he hurried on, feeling certain that Zagloba would not escape him. The herdsmen gave some new indications, but beyond the ford all traces disappeared. The ataman did not meet the minstrel whom Zagloba had stripped of his clothing, for he had gone lower down along the Kagamlik, and besides was so frightened that he had hidden like a fox in the reeds.

A day and a night more passed; and since the pursuit toward Vassílyevka occupied two days precisely, Zagloba had much time on his side. What was to be done then? In this difficult juncture the essaul came to Bogun with advice and assistance. He was an old wolf of the steppe, accustomed from youth to track Tartars through the Wilderness.

"Father," said he, "they fled to Chigirin,--and they have done wisely, for they have gained time,--but when they heard of Hmelnitski and Jóltiya Vodi from Pleshnyevski, they changed their road. You have seen yourself, father, that they left the high-road and rushed to one side."

"To the steppe?"

"In the steppe I could find them, father; but they went toward the Dnieper, to go to the hetmans; therefore they went either through Cherkas or Zólotonosha and Próhorovka; and if they went even to Pereyasláv, though I don't believe that, still we shall find them. We should go, one to Cherkasi, another to Zólotonosha, along the wagon-road; and quickly, for as soon as they cross the Dnieper, they will hasten to the hetmans, or Hmelnitski's Tartars will pick them up."

"You hurry to Zólotonosha, and I will go to Cherkasi," said Bogun.

"All right, father."

"And keep a sharp lookout, for he is a cunning fox."

"Ai, father! I am cunning too."

Having settled the plan of pursuit in this way, the leader and the essaul turned immediately,-- one to Cherkasi; the other higher up, to Zólotonosha. In the evening of the same day the old essaul Anton reached Demiánovka.

The village was deserted; only the women were left, for all the men had gone beyond the river to Hmelnitski. Seeing armed men and not knowing who they were, the women had hidden in the thatch and in the barns. The Cossacks had to search long; but at last they found an old woman, who feared nothing, not even the Tartars.

"And where are the men, mother?" asked Anton.

"Do I know?" answered she, showing her yellow teeth.

"We are Cossacks, mother, don't be afraid; we are not from the Poles."

"The Poles? May the evil one--"

"You are glad to see us, I suppose?"

"You?" The old woman hesitated a moment. "The plague take you!"

Anton was at a loss what to do, when suddenly the door of one of the cottages squeaked, and a young, fair-looking woman came out.

"Ai! good men, I heard that you were not Poles."

"True, we are not."

"Are you from Hmelnitski?"

"Yes."

"Not from the Poles?"

"By no means."

"And why do you ask for the men?"

"I ask if they have gone already."

"They have gone."

"Glory be to God! And tell us now, did a noble go by here,--a cursed Pole with a young woman?"

"A noble? A Pole? I didn't see them."

"Was no one here?"

"There was a 'grandfather.' He persuaded the men to go to Hmelnitski through Zólotonosha, for he said that Prince Yeremi was coming here."

"Where?"

"Here. And from here would go to Zólotonosha, so the old man said."

"And the old man persuaded the men to rise?"

"He did."

"And he was alone?"

"No, With a dumb boy."

"How did he look?"

"Who?"

"The old man."

"Oh, ai! old, very old. He played on a lyre, and complained of the lords. But I did not see him."

"And he persuaded the men to rise?" asked Anton.

"He did."

"Well, good-by, young woman."

"God be with you!"

Anton stopped in deep thought. If the old man was Zagloba disguised, why did he persuade the peasants to go to Hmelnitski, and where did he get the disguise? Where did he leave the horses, for he fled on horseback? But, above all, why did he incite peasants to rebellion and warn them of the coming of the prince? A noble would not have warned them, and first of all he would have taken refuge under the protection of the prince. And if the prince is really going to Zólotonosha, in which there is nothing strange, then he will pay for Vassílyevka without fail. Here Anton shuddered; for that moment he saw a new picket in the gate, exactly like an empaling stake.

"No! That old man was only a minstrel and nothing more. There is no reason to go to Zólotonosha unless they fled that way."

But Zagloba had disappeared. What was to be done further? Wait?--but the prince might come up. Go to Próhorovka and cross the Dnieper?--that would be to fall into the hands of the hetmans.

It was growing rather narrow for the old wolf of the Wilderness in the broad steppes. He felt also that being a wolf he had come upon a fox in Pan Zagloba. Then he struck his forehead. But why did that "grandfather" take the people to Zólotonosha, beyond which is Próhorovka, and beyond that and the Dnieper the hetmans and the whole camp of the king? Anton determined that come what might, he would go to Próhorovka.

"When I am at the river, if I hear that the forces of the hetmans are on the other side, then I will not cross, I will go along the bank and join Bogun opposite Cherkasi. Besides, I shall get news of Hmelnitski along the road."

Anton already knew, from the story of Pleshnyevski, that Hmelnitski had occupied Chigirin; that he had sent Krívonos against the hetmans, and was to follow him at once with Tugai Bey. Anton was an experienced soldier, and knowing the situation of the country well, was sure that the battle must have been fought already. In such an event it was necessary to know what was to be done. If Hmelnitski had been beaten, the forces of the hetmans would spread over the whole country along the Dnieper in pursuit; in that case there would be no sense in looking for Zagloba. But if Hmelnitski had won,--which in truth Anton did not greatly believe,--it was easier to beat the son of the hetman than the hetman, a van detachment than the whole army.

"Oh," thought the old Cossack, "our ataman would do better to think of his own skin than of a young girl! Near Chigirin he might have crossed the Dnieper, and from there slipped off to the Saitch in time. Here between Prince Yeremi and the hetmans it will be difficult for him to make his way."

With these thoughts he moved on quickly with the Cossacks in the direction of the Sula, which he had to cross just beyond Demiánovka, wishing to go to Próhorovka. They went to Mogilna, situated at the river itself. Here fortune served Anton; for Mogilna, like Demiánovka, was deserted. He found, however, scows ready, and ferrymen who took over peasants fleeing to the Dnieper.

The Trans-Dnieper did not dare to rise under the hand of the prince; but to make up for this the peasants left all the hamlets, settlements, and villages, to join Hmelnitski and rally to his banners. The news of the victory of the Zaporojians at Jóltiya Vodi flew like a bird through the whole Trans-Dnieper. The wild inhabitants could not remain in quiet, though there especially they had experienced hardly any oppression; for, as has been said, the prince, merciless to rebels, was a real father to peaceful settlers. His overseers on this account feared to commit injustice on people intrusted to them. But that people, changed not long before from robbers into agriculturists, were weary of the harshness of regulations and order. They fled therefore to where the hope of wild freedom gleamed. In many villages even the women fled to Hmelnitski. In Chabanovets and Vysoki the whole population turned out, burning the houses behind them so as to have no place for return. In those villages in which a few people still remained, they were forced to arms.

Anton began to inquire at once of the ferrymen for news beyond the Dnieper. There were reports, but contradictory, confused, unintelligible. It was said that Hmelnitski was fighting with the hetmans; some said that he was beaten, others that he was victorious. A peasant fleeing toward Demiánovka said that the hetmans were taken captive. The ferrymen suspected that he was a noble in disguise, but were afraid to detain him because they had heard that the forces of the prince were at hand. A certain fear increased the number of the prince's armies everywhere, and made of them omnipresent divisions; for there was not a single village in the whole Trans-Dnieper in which it was not said that the prince was "right here, close by." Anton saw that they considered his party everywhere as belonging to Prince Yeremi.

But soon he set the ferrymen at rest, and began to inquire about the Demiánovka peasants.

"Oh yes; they passed. We took them to the other side," said a ferryman.

"And there was a minstrel with them?"

"Yes, there was."

"And a dumb boy with the old man,--a lad?"

"Yes; there was."

"What did the minstrel look like?"

"He was not old, heavy, had eyes like a fish, and on one of them a cataract."

"Oh, that is he!" muttered Anton, and inquired further: "And the boy?"

"Oh, father ataman," said the ferryman, "an angel, out and out! We have never seen such a boy."

In the mean while they were coming to the shore.

"Ah, we will bring her to the ataman!" muttered Anton to himself. Then he turned to the Cossacks: "To horse!"

They shot on like a flock of frightened bustards, though the road was difficult, for the country was broken into gorges. But they entered a broad ravine at the bottom of which was a kind of natural path formed by the flowing of a spring. The ravine extended to Kavraiets. They rushed on some miles without halting; Anton, on the best horse, ahead. The broad mouth of the ravine was already visible when Anton suddenly pulled in his horse till his hind shoes crushed the stones.

"What is this?"

The entrance was suddenly darkened with men and horses. A troop entered in pairs, and formed six abreast. There were about three hundred horsemen. Anton looked; and although he was an old soldier hardened to every danger, his heart thumped within his breast and on his face came a deathly pallor. He recognized the dragoons of Prince Yeremi.

It was too late to flee. Anton's party was separated from the dragoons by scarcely two hundred yards, and the tired horses of the Cossacks could not go far in escape. The dragoons, seeing them, rode up on a trot. In a moment the Cossacks were surrounded on every side.

"Who are you?" asked the commander, sternly.

"Bogun's men!" answered Anton, seeing that it was necessary to tell the truth. But recognizing the lieutenant whom he had seen in Pereyasláv, he cried out at once with pretended joy: "Oh, Pan Kushel! Thank God!"

"Ah! is that you, Anton?" asked the lieutenant, looking at the essaul. "What are you doing here? Where is your ataman?"

"The Grand Hetman has sent our ataman to the prince to ask for assistance; so he has gone to Lubni, and he has commanded us to go along through the villages to catch deserters."

Anton lied as if for hire; but he trusted in this,--since the dragoons were going away from the Dnieper, they could not know yet of the attack on Rozlogi, nor of the battle at Vassílyevka, nor of any of Bogun's undertakings.

Still the lieutenant added: "One might say you wanted to steal over to the rebellion."

"Oh, Lieutenant, if we wanted to go to Hmelnitski, we should not be on this side of the Dnieper."

"That," said Kushel,--"is an evident truth which I am not able to deny. But the ataman will not find the prince in Lubni."

"Where is he?"

"He was in Priluka; but it is possible that he started yesterday for Lubni."

"Too bad! The ataman has a letter from the hetman to the prince. And may I make bold to ask if you are coming from Zólotonosha?"

"No; we were stationed at Kalenki, and now we have received orders to go to Lubni, like the rest of the army. From there the prince will move, with all his forces. But where are you going?"

"To Próhorovka, for the peasants are crossing there."

"Have many of them fled?"

"Oh, many, many!"

"Well, then, go! God be with you!"

"Thank you kindly, Lieutenant. God conduct you!"

The dragoons opened their ranks, and Anton's escort rode out from among them to the mouth of the ravine.

After he had issued from the ravine, Anton stopped and listened carefully; and when the dragoons had vanished from sight, and the last echo had ceased, he turned to his Cossacks, and said,--

"Do you know, you simpletons, that were it not for me, you would soon be gasping, empaled on stakes, in Lubni? And now, forward, even if we drive the last breath out of our horses!"

They rushed on with all speed.

"We are lucky, and doubly so," thought Anton,--"first, in escaping with sound skins, and then because those dragoons were not marching from Zólotonosha, and Zagloba missed them; for if he had met them, he would have been safe from every pursuit."

In truth, fortune was very unfavorable to Zagloba in not letting him come upon Kushel and his company; for then he would have been rescued at once, and freed from every fear.

Meanwhile the news of the catastrophe at Korsún came upon Zagloba at Próhorovka like a thunderbolt. Reports had already been passing through the villages and farmhouses on the road to Zólotonosha of a great battle, even of the victory of Hmelnitski; but Zagloba did not lend them belief, for he knew from experience that every report grows and grows among the common people to unheard of dimensions, and that specially of the preponderance of the Cossacks the people willingly told wonders. But in Próhorovka it was difficult to doubt any longer. The terrible and ominous truth struck like a club on the head. Hmelnitski had triumphed, the army of the king was swept away, the hetmans were in captivity, and the whole Ukraine was on fire.

Zagloba lost his head at first, for he was in a terrible position. Fortune had not favored him on the road, for at Zólotonosha he did not find the garrison, and the old fortress was deserted. He doubted not for a moment that Bogun was pursuing him, and that sooner or later he would come upon his trail. He had doubled back, it is true, like a hunted hare; but he knew, through and through, the hound that was hunting him, and he knew that that hound would not allow himself to be turned from the trail. Zagloba had Bogun behind, and before him a sea of peasant rebellion, slaughter, conflagration, Tartar raids, and raging mobs. To flee in such a position was a task difficult of accomplishment, especially with a young woman who, though disguised as a minstrel boy, attracted attention everywhere by her extraordinary beauty. In truth, it was enough to make a man lose his head.

But Zagloba never lost it long. Amid the greatest chaos in his brain he saw perfectly one thing, or rather felt it most clearly,--that he feared Bogun a hundred times more than fire, water, rebellion, slaughter, or Hmelnitski himself. At the very thought that he might fall into the hands of the terrible leader, the skin crept on his body. "He would flay me," repeated he, continually. "But in front is a sea of rebellion!"

One method of salvation remained,--to desert Helena, and leave her to the will of God; but Zagloba did not wish to do that, and did not let the thought enter his head. What was he to do?

"Ah," thought he, "it is not the time to look for the prince. Before me is a sea; I will give a plunge into this sea. At least I shall hide myself, and with God's aid swim to the other shore." And he determined to cross to the right bank of the Dnieper.

This was no easy task at Próhorovka. Nikolai Pototski had already collected for Krechovski and his men all the scows and boats, large and small, from Pereyasláv to Chigirin. In Próhorovka there was only one leaky scow. Thousands of people, fleeing from the neighborhood of the Dnieper, were waiting for that scow. All the cottages, cow-houses, barns, sheds in the entire village were taken. Everything was enormously dear. Zagloba was in truth forced to earn a bit of bread with his lyre and his song. For twenty-four hours there was no passage. The scow was injured twice, and had to be repaired. Zagloba passed the night sitting on the bank of the river with Helena, together with crowds of drunken peasants who were sitting around fires. The night, too, was windy and cold. The princess was worn out and in pain, for the peasant boots galled her feet; she was afraid of becoming so ill as to be unable to move. Her face grew dark and pale, her marvellous eyes were quenched; every moment she feared that she should be recognized under her disguise, or that Bogun's men would come up. That same night she beheld a terrible sight. A number of nobles who had tried to take refuge in the domains of Vishnyevetski from Tartar attack were brought from the mouth of the Ros by peasants, and put to death on the bank of the river.

Besides this, in Próhorovka there were two Jews, with their families. The maddened crowd hurled them into the river; and when they did not go to the bottom at once, they were pushed down with long sticks, together with their wives and children. This was accompanied by uproar and drunkenness. Tipsy men frolicked with tipsy women. Terrible outbursts of laughter sounded ominously on the dark shores of the Dnieper. The winds scattered the fire; red brands, and sparks driven by the wind, flew along, and died on the waves. Occasionally alarm sprang up. At one time and another a drunken, hoarse voice would cry in the darkness, "Save yourselves! Yeremi is coming!" And the crowd rushed blindly to the shore, trampled on one another, and pushed one another into the water. Once they came near running over Zagloba and the princess. It was an infernal night, and seemed endless. Zagloba begged a quart of vudka, drank himself, and forced the princess to drink; otherwise she would have fainted or caught a fever. At last the waves of the Dnieper began to whiten and shine. Light had come. The day was cloudy, gloomy, pale. Zagloba wished to cross, with all haste, to the other side. Happily the scow was repaired, but the throng in front of it was enormous.

"A place for the grandfather, a place for the grandfather!" cried Zagloba, holding Helena between his outstretched arms, and defending her from the pressure. "A place for the grandfather! I am going to Hmelnitski and Krívonos. A place for the grandfather, good people! My dear fellows, may the black death choke you and your children! I cannot see well; I shall fall into the water; my boy will be drowned. Give way, children! May the paralysis shake every limb of you; may you die on the stake!"

Thus brawling, begging, pushing the crowd apart with powerful arms, he urged Helena forward to the scow, clambered on himself, and then began to brawl again,--

"There are plenty of you here already. Why do you crowd so? You will sink the scow. Why do so many of you push on here? Enough, enough! Your turn will come; and if it doesn't, small matter!"

"Enough, enough!" cried those who had got on the scow. "Push off, push off!"

The oars bent, and the scow began to move from the shore. A swift current bore it downward at once, somewhat in the direction of Domontov.

They had passed about one half the stream, when on the Próhorovka side shouts and cries were heard. A terrible disturbance rose among the people near the river. Some ran as if wild toward Domontov; others jumped into the water. Some shouted and waved their hands, or threw themselves on the ground.

"What is that? What has happened?" was asked on the scow.

"Yeremi!" cried one voice.

"Yeremi, Yeremi! Let us flee," cried others.

The oars began to beat feverishly on the water; the scow sped on through the waves like a Cossack boat. At the same moment horsemen appeared on the Próhorovka shore.

"The armies of Yeremi!" shouted some on the boat.

The horsemen rode along the shore, turned, asked the people about something. At last they began to call out to the boatmen: "Stop, stop!"

Zagloba looked, and cold sweat covered him from head to foot. He recognized Bogun's Cossacks. It was, in fact, Anton with his men.

But, as already stated, Zagloba never lost his head long. He covered his eyes like a man of poor sight, looking; he must have looked a good while. At last he began to cry, as if some one were pulling him out of his skin,--

"Oh, children, those are the Cossacks of Vishnyevetski! Oh, for the sake of God and his Holy Purest Mother, quick, to the shore! We will resign ourselves to the loss of those who are left, and break the scow; if not, death to us all!"

"Oh, hurry, hurry! break the scow!" cried others.

A shouting was raised, in which nothing could be heard of the cries from the Próhorovka side. Then the scow grated upon the gravel of the shore. The peasants began to spring out; but some of them were not able to land before others were breaking the railing and cutting the bottom with their axes. The planks and broken pieces began to fly through the air. The ill-fated boat was destroyed with frenzy, torn to pieces; terror lent strength to the raging people.

And all this time Zagloba was screaming: "Cut! slash! break! tear! burn! Save yourselves! Yeremi is coming! Yeremi is coming!"

Shouting in this fashion, he looked with his sound eye at Helena and began to mutter significantly.

Meanwhile from the other shore the shouts increased in view of the destruction of the boat, but it was so far away they could not understand what was said. The waving of hands seemed like threatening, and only increased the speed of destruction.

The scow disappeared after a while, but suddenly from every breast there came a cry of horror.

"They are springing into the water! they are swimming to us!" roared the peasants.

In fact, one horseman in advance and after him a number of others urged their horses into the water to swim to the other shore. It was a deed of almost insane daring; for increased by the spring flood, the river rushed on more powerfully than usual, forming here and there many eddies and whirlpools. Borne away by the impetus of the river, the horses could not swim straight across; the current began to bear them on with extraordinary swiftness.

"They will not swim across!" cried the peasants.

"They are drowning!"

"Glory be to God! Oh! oh! one horse has gone down already! Death to them!"

The horses had swum a third part of the river, but the water bore them down with increasing speed. Evidently they began to lose strength; gradually too they sank deeper and deeper. After a little the men on their backs were in the water to their girdles. The peasants from Shelepukhi ran to the water to see what was going on; now only the horses' heads looked out above the water, which reached the breasts of the men. But now they had swum half the river. Suddenly one horse's head and one man disappeared under the water; after that a second, a third, a fourth, a fifth,--the number of swimmers decreased each moment. On both sides of the river a deep silence reigned in the crowds, but all ran with the course of the water to see what would happen. Now two thirds of the river was crossed; the number of swimmers still decreased, but the heavy snorting of horses and the voices of the heroes urging them on was heard; it was clear that some would cross.

"Hi, children! to your muskets! Destruction to the prince's men!"

Puffs of smoke burst forth; then the rattle of muskets. A cry of despair was heard from the river, and after a while horses and men had vanished. The river was cleared; only here and there in the distance, in the whirl of the waves, looked black for an instant the belly of a horse, gleamed red for a moment the cap of a Cossack.

Zagloba looked at Helena, and muttered.

CHAPTER XXII.

Prince Vishnyevetski knew of the defeat at Korsún before Skshetuski had been found sitting on the ruins of Rozlogi, since Polyanovski, one of his hussar officers, had brought news of it to Segotin. Previous to that the prince had been in Priluka, and from there had sent Boguslav Mashkevich with a letter to the hetmans, inquiring when they would order him to march with all his forces. But as Pan Mashkevich did not return for a long time with the answer of the hetmans, the prince moved on toward Pereyasláv, sending orders on every side to the detachments that the regiments which were scattered here and there in the Trans-Dnieper should assemble as quickly as possible at Lubni.

But news came that some Cossack regiments disposed in outposts along the borders next the Tartars had dispersed or joined the insurrection. Thus the prince saw his forces suddenly decreased, and was grieved not a little; for he did not expect that those men whom he had led so often to victory could ever desert him. However, upon meeting with Pan Polyanovski and receiving news of the unexampled catastrophe, he concealed it from the army and went on toward the Dnieper, thinking to march at random into the midst of the storm and uprising, and either revenge the defeat, wipe away the disgrace of the armies, or shed his own blood. He judged that there must be some, and perhaps large, portions of the army of the Crown left after the defeat. These, if joined to his division of six thousand, might measure themselves with Hmelnitski with hope of victory.

Halting at Pereyasláv, he ordered Pan Volodyovski and Pan Kushel to send their dragoons in every direction,--to Cherkasi, Mantovo, Sekirnaya, Buchach, Staiki, Trakhtimiroff, and Rjischeff,--to collect all the boats and craft which they could find anywhere. Then the army was to cross from the left side to Rjischeff.

The messengers heard of the defeat from fugitives whom they met here and there; but at all the above-mentioned places they could not find a single boat, since, as already stated, the Grand Hetman of the Crown had taken one half of them long before for Krechovski and Barabash, and the rebellious mob on the right bank had destroyed the rest through fear of the prince. But Volodyovski crossed over with ten men to the right bank on a raft which he had fashioned in haste from tree-trunks, and seized a number of Cossacks, whom he brought to the prince, who learned from them of the enormous extent of the rebellion and the terrible fruits of the defeat at Korsún. The whole Ukraine had risen to the last man. The insurrection had spread like a deluge, which covering a level land occupies more and more space at each twinkle of an eye. The nobles defended themselves in large and small castles; but many of these castles had been already captured.

Hmelnitski was increasing in power every moment. The captured Cossacks gave the number of his army at two hundred thousand men, and in a couple of days it might be doubled. For this reason he remained in Korsún after the battle, and took immediate advantage of the peace to marshal the people into his countless hosts. He divided the mob into regiments, appointed colonels from the atamans and experienced Zaporojian essauls, and sent detachments or whole divisions to capture neighboring castles. Considering all this. Prince Yeremi saw that on account of the absence of boats the construction of which for an army of six thousand men would occupy several weeks' time, and on account of the strength of the enemy which had increased beyond measure, there was no means of crossing the Dnieper in those parts in which he then found himself. Pan Polyanovski, Colonel Baranovski, the commander of the camp, Alexander Baranovski, Volodyovski, and Vurtsel were in favor of moving to the north toward Chernigoff, which was on the other side of dense forests, thence they would march on Lubech, and cross the river to Braginoff. It was a long and perilous journey; for beyond the Chernigoff forests, in the direction of Braginoff, were enormous swamps, which were not easy of passage even for infantry, and what must they be for heavy cavalry-wagons and artillery. The proposal, however, pleased the prince; but he wished, before going on that long and as he considered unavoidable road, to show himself once more in his Trans-Dnieper domains, prevent immediate outbreak, gather the nobles under his wing, transfix the people with terror, and leave behind the memory of that terror, which in the absence of the master would be the only safeguard to the country and the guardian of all who were unable to march with the army. Besides this, Princess Griselda, the Princesses Zbaraskie, the ladies in waiting, the whole court, and some regiments,--namely, the infantry,--were still in Lubni. The prince therefore determined to go to Lubni for a last farewell.

The troops moved that very day, and at their head Pan Volodyovski with his dragoons, who, though all Russian without exception, still held by the bonds of discipline and trained as regular soldiers, almost surpassed in loyalty the other regiments. The country was quiet yet. Here and there had been formed ruffianly bands which plundered castle and cottage alike. These bands the prince destroyed in great part along the road and empaled on stakes. The common people had risen in no place. Their minds were seething, fire was in the eyes and souls of the peasants, they armed in secret and fled beyond the Dnieper; but fear was still superior to the thirst for blood and murder. It might be considered of ill-omen for the future, however, that the inhabitants of those villages from which the peasants had not gone to Hmelnitski fled at the approach of the army, as if fearing that the terrible prince would read in their faces that which was hidden in their hearts and would punish them in advance. And he did punish wherever he found the least sign of incipient rebellion; and as he had a nature unbounded both in rewarding and punishing, he punished without measure and without mercy. It might have been said at that time that two vampires were careering along both banks of the Dnieper,--one, Hmelnitski, devouring nobles; the other, Prince Yeremi, destroying the uprisen people. It was whispered among the peasants that when these two met the sun would be darkened and the water in all rivers run red. But the meeting was not at hand; for Hmelnitski, the conqueror at Jóltiya Vodi and Korsún,--that Hmelnitski who had battered into fragments the armies of the Crown, who had taken captive the hetmans, and who was then at the head of hundreds of thousands of warriors,--simply feared that lord of Lubni, who was going to look for him west of the Dnieper. The armies of the prince had passed Sleporod. The prince himself stopped to rest at Philipovo, where he was informed that envoys had come from Hmelnitski with a letter and begged for an audience. The prince gave orders to produce them at once. Then the six Zaporojians entered the house of the under-starosta where the prince was stopping. They entered boldly enough, especially the chief of them, the ataman Sukhaya Ruká, distinguished through the victory of Korsún and his new rank of colonel. But when they saw the prince such fear seized them that they fell at his feet, not daring to utter a word.

The chieftain, surrounded by his principal knights, ordered them to rise, and asked what they had brought.

"A letter from the hetman," answered Sukhaya Ruká.

The prince fixed his eyes on the Cossack, and answered quietly, but with emphasis on every word,--

"From a bandit, a ruffian, and a robber,--not from a hetman!"

The Zaporojians grew pale, or blue rather, and dropping their heads on their breasts stood in silence at the door. Then the prince ordered Pan Mashkevich to take the letter and read it.

The letter was humble, though it was after Korsún. The fox had gained the upper hand of the lion in Hmelnitski, the serpent of the eagle, for he remembered that he was writing to Vishnyevetski. He flattered in order to quiet, and then the more easily to sting. He wrote that what had happened was through the fault of Chaplinski, and that the fickleness of fortune had met the hetmans; hence it was not his fault, but their evil fate and the oppressions which the Cossacks had endured in the Ukraine. Still he asked the prince not to be offended, to pardon him, and he would ever remain his obedient and willing servant; and to win favor for his envoys and save them from anger, he declared that he had dismissed in safety Pan Skshetuski, the hussar officer taken in the Saitch.

Now followed complaints against the haughtiness of Skshetuski, who had refused to take letters from Hmelnitski to the prince, by which action he had put a great slight upon the dignity of the hetman and the whole Zaporojian army. To haughtiness and contempt like this which the Cossacks met with from the Poles at every step, did Hmelnitski attribute specially all that had happened from Jóltiya Vodi to Korsún. The letter ended with assurances of regret, and of loyalty to the Commonwealth, together with offers of service to Yeremi.

The envoys themselves were astonished when they heard this letter; for they had no previous knowledge of its contents, and supposed that it contained abase and harsh challenges rather than requests. One thing was clear to them,--Hmelnitski had no wish to risk everything with such a famous leader, and instead of moving on him with all his forces, was delaying and deceiving him with humility, and waiting apparently till the forces of the prince should be worn out on campaigns and struggles with various detachments; in one word, he seemed to fear the prince. The envoys became still more subservient, and during the reading perused the prince's face carefully to see if they could find in it the hour of their death. Though in coming they were prepared to die, still fear seized them then. The prince listened quietly, but from time to time dropped the lids of his eyes as if wishing to restrain the thunderbolts hidden within, and it was as visible as if on the palm of the hand that he was holding terrible anger in check. When the letter was finished he answered no word to the envoys, but merely ordered Volodyovski to remove and keep them under guard; then he turned to the colonels himself and said,--

"Great is the cunning of this enemy, for he wishes to lull me with that letter so as to attack me asleep; or he will move into the heart of the Commonwealth, conclude terms, and receive immunity from the yielding estates and the king, and then he will feel himself safe,--for if I wanted to war with him after that, not he, but I should act against the will of the Commonwealth, and be held as a rebel."

Vurtsel caught himself by the head. "Oh, vulpes astuta!"

"Well, gentlemen, what action do you advise?" asked the prince. "Speak boldly, and then I will indicate to you my own will."

Old Zatsvilikhovski, who had left Chigirin some time before and joined the prince, said,--

"Let it be according to the will of your Highness; but if we are permitted to speak, then I will say that you have sounded the intentions of Hmelnitski with your usual quickness, for they are what you say and no other. I should think, therefore, that there is no need of paying attention to his letter, but after securing the future safety of the princess, to cross the Dnieper and begin war before Hmelnitski settles any conditions. It would be a shame and dishonor for the Commonwealth to suffer such insults to pass unpunished. But," here he turned to the colonels, "I wait your opinions, not giving my own as infallible."

The commander of the camp, Alexander Zamoiski, struck his sabre and said,--

"Worthy colonel, age speaks through you, and wisdom also. We must tear off the head of that hydra before it grows and devours us."

"Amen!" said the priest Mukhovetski.

Other colonels, instead of speaking, followed the example of the commander, shook their sabres, breathed hard, and gritted their teeth; but Vurtsel said,--

"It is a downright insult to the name of your Highness that that ruffian should dare to write to you. A koshevoi ataman has rank confirmed and recognized by the Commonwealth, with which the kuren atamans can cloak their action. But this is a pretended hetman, who can be considered in no light but that of a robber; and Pan Skshetuski acted in a praiseworthy manner when he refused to take his letters to your Highness."

"That is just what I think," said the prince; "and since I cannot reach him, he will be punished in the persons of his envoys." Then he turned to the colonel of the Tartar regiment of his guard: "Vershul, order your Tartars to behead those Cossacks; and for their chief let a stake be trimmed, and seat him on it without delay."

Vershul inclined his head, which was red as a flame. The priest Mukhovetski, who usually restrained the prince, crossed his hands as if in prayer, and looked imploringly into his eyes, wishing to find mercy.

"I know, priest, what you want," said the prince, "but it cannot be. This is necessary on account of the cruelties which they have committed west of the Dnieper, for our own dignity, and for the good of the Commonwealth. It must be shown convincingly that there is some one yet who is not afraid of that outcast, and treats him as a bandit,--who, though he writes with submission, acts with insolence, and conducts himself in the Ukraine as if he were an independent prince, and has brought such a paroxysm on the Commonwealth as it has not gone through for many a day."

"Your Highness, as he states, he liberated Pan Skshetuski unharmed," said the priest, timidly.

"I thank you in Skshetuski's name for comparing him with butchers." Here the prince frowned. "But enough! I see," continued he, turning to the colonels, "that your voices are all for war; this too is my will. We march on Chigirin, collecting nobles by the way. We will cross at Bragin, then move to the south. Now to Lubni!"

"God be on our side!" said the colonels.

At this moment the door opened, and in it appeared Roztvorovski, lieutenant of the Wallachian regiment, sent two days before with three hundred horse on a reconnoissance.

"Your Highness," cried he, "the rebellion is spreading. Rozlogi is burned. The garrison at Vassflyevka is cut to pieces!"

"How? what? where?" was asked on every side.

But the prince motioned with his hand to be silent, and asked: "Who did it,--marauders or troops?"

"They say Bogun did it."

"Bogun?"

"Yes."

"When did it happen?"

"Three days ago."

"Did you follow the trace, catch up with them, seize informants?"

"I followed, but could not come up, for I was three days too late. I collected news along the road. They returned to Chigirin, then separated,--one half going to Cherkasi, the other to Zölotonosha and Próhorovka."

Here Pan Kushel said: "I met the detachment that was going to Próhorovka, and informed your Highness. They said they were sent by Bogun to prevent peasants from crossing the Dnieper; therefore I let them pass."

"You committed a folly, but I do not, blame you. It is difficult not to be deceived when there is treason at every step, and the ground under one's feet is burning," said the prince.

Suddenly he seized himself by the head. "Almighty God!" cried he, "I remember that Skshetuski told me Bogun was making attempts on the honor of Kurtsevichovna; I understand now why Rozlogi was burned. The girl must have been carried away. Here, Volodyovski!" said the prince, "take five hundred horse and move on again to Cherkasi; let Bykhovets take five hundred Wallachians and go through Zólotonosha to Próhorovka. Don't spare the horses; whoever rescues the girl for me will have Yeremiovka for life. On! on!" Then to the colonels: "And we will go to Lubni through Rozlogi."

Thereupon the colonels hurried out of the under-starosta's house and galloped to their regiments. Soldiers rushed to their horses. They brought to the prince the chestnut steed which he usually rode on his expeditions. And soon the regiments moved, and stretched out like a long and many-colored gleaming serpent over the Philipovo road.

Near the gate a bloody sight struck the eyes of the soldiers. On stakes of the hurdle-fence were to be seen the severed heads of the five Cossacks, which gazed on the army marching past with the dead whites of their open eyes; and some distance beyond the gate, on a green mound struggled and quivered the ataman Sukhaya Ruká, sitting upright, empaled on a stake. The point had already passed through half his body; but long hours of dying were indicated yet for the unfortunate ataman, for he might quiver there till night before death would put him to rest. At that time he was not only living, but he turned his terrible eyes on the regiments as each one of them passed by,--eyes which said: "May God punish you, and your children, and your grandchildren to the tenth generation, for the blood, for the wounds, for the torments! God grant that you perish, you and your race; that every misfortune may strike you! God grant that you be continually dying, and that you may never be able either to die or to live!" And although he was a simple Cossack,--although he died not in purple nor cloth of gold but in a common blue coat, and not in the chamber of a castle but under the naked sky on a stake,--still that torment of his, that death circling above his head, clothed him with dignity, and put such a power into his look, such an ocean of hate into his eyes, that all understood well what he wanted to say, and the regiments rode past in silence. But he in the golden gleam of the midday towered above them, shining on the freshly smoothed stake like a torch.

The prince rode by, not turning an eye; the priest Mukhovetski made the sign of the cross on the unfortunate man; and all had passed, when a youth from the hussar regiment, without asking any one for permission, urged his horse to the mound, and putting a pistol to the ear of the victim, ended his torments with a shot. All trembled at such daring infraction of military rules, and knowing the rigor of the prince, they looked on the youth as lost; but the prince said nothing. Whether he pretended not to hear or was buried in thought, it is sufficient that he rode on in silence, and only in the evening did he order the young man to be called.

The stripling stood before the face of his lord barely alive, and thought that the ground was opening under his feet. But the prince inquired,--

"What is your name?"

"Jelenski."

"You fired at the Cossack?"

"I did," groaned he, pale as a sheet.

"Why did you do it?"

"Because I could not look at the torment."

"Oh, you will see so much of their deeds that at a sight like this pity will fly from you like an angel; but because on account of your pity you risked your life, the treasurer in Lubni will pay you ten golden ducats, and I take you into my personal service."

All wondered that the affair was finished in this way; but meanwhile it was announced that a detachment from Zólotonosha had come, and attention was turned in another direction.

CHAPTER XXIII.

Late in the evening the army arrived in Rozlogi by moonlight. There they found Pan Yan sitting on his Calvary. The knight, as is known, had lost his senses altogether from pain and torment; and when the priest Mukhovetski brought him to his mind, the officers bore him away and began to greet and comfort him, especially Pan Longin Podbipienta, who for three months past had been a popular officer in Skshetuski's regiment. Pan Longin was ready also to be his companion in sighing and weeping, and for his benefit made a new vow at once, that he would fast every Tuesday of his life, if God would in any way send solace to the lieutenant.

Skshetuski was conducted straightway to Vishnyevetski at a peasant's cottage. When the prince saw his favorite he said not a word; he only opened his arms to him and waited. Skshetuski threw himself into those arms with loud weeping. Yeremi pressed him to his bosom and kissed him on the forehead, and the officers present saw the tears in his worthy eyes. After a while he began to speak,--

"I greet you as a son, for I thought I should never see you again. Bear your burden manfully, and remember that you will have thousands of comrades in misfortune who will leave wives, children, parents, and friends; and as a drop of water is lost in an ocean, so let your suffering sink in the sea of universal pain. When such terrible times have come on our dear country, whoever is a man and has a sword at his side will not yield himself to weeping over his own loss, but will hasten to the rescue of the common mother, and either find relief in his conscience or lie down in a glorious death, receive a heavenly crown, and with it eternal happiness."

"Amen!" said the priest Mukhovetski.

"Oh, I should rather see her dead!" groaned the knight.

"Weep, then, for great is your loss, and we will weep with you; for you have come not to Pagans, wild Scythians, or Tartars, but to brothers and loving comrades. Say to yourself, 'To-day I will weep over myself, but to-morrow is not mine;' for remember that to-morrow we march to battle."

"I will go with you to the end of the world; but I cannot console myself. It is so grievous for me without her that I cannot, I cannot--"

The poor fellow seized himself by the head, then put his fingers between his teeth, and gnawed them to overcome the groans, for a storm of despair was tearing him afresh.

"You have said, 'Thy will be done!'" said the priest, severely.

"Amen, amen! I yield to his will, but with pain. I cannot help it," answered the knight, with a broken voice.

They could see how he struggled and writhed, and his suffering wrung tears from them all. The most sensitive were Volodyovski and Podbipienta, who poured out whole streams. The latter clasped his hands and said pitifully:

"Brother, dear brother, contain yourself!"

"Listen!" said the prince on a sudden, "I have news that Bogun rushed off from here toward Lubni, for he cut down my men at Vassílyevka. Do not despair too soon, for perhaps he did not find her; if he did, why should he rush on toward Lubni?"

"As true as life, that may be the case," cried some of the officers. "God will console you."

Skshetuski opened his eyes as if he did not understand what they were saying. Suddenly hope gleamed in his mind, and he threw himself at the feet of the prince.

"Oh, your Highness!" cried he, "my life, my blood--"

He could speak no further. He had grown so weak that Pan Longin was obliged to raise him and place him on the bench; but it was evident from his looks that he had grasped at that hope as a drowning man at a plank, and that his pain had left him. The officers fanned that spark, saying he might find the princess in Lubni. Afterward they took him to another cottage, and then brought him mead and wine. He wished to drink, but could not, his throat was so straitened. His faithful comrades drank instead; and when they had grown gladsome they began to embrace and kiss him, and to wonder at his meagreness and the marks of sickness which he bore on his face.

"Oh, you look like one risen from the dead," said portly Pan Dzik.

"It must be they insulted you in the Saitch, and gave you neither food nor drink."

"Tell us what happened to you."

"I will tell you some time," said Skshetuski, with a weak voice. "They wounded me, and I was sick."

"They wounded him!" cried Pan Dzik.

"They wounded him, though an envoy!" added Pan Sleshinski. The officers, astounded at Cossack insolence, looked at one another, and then began to press forward to Pan Yan with great friendliness.

"And did you see Hmelnitski?"

"I did."

"Well, give him here!" said Migurski; "we will make mince-meat of him in a minute."

The night passed in such conversation. Toward morning it was announced that the second party, despatched on the more distant road to Cherkasi, had returned. It was evident the men of this party had not come up with Bogun; they had brought wonderful news, however. They brought many people whom they had found on the road, and who had seen Bogun two days before. These people said that the chief was evidently pursuing some one, for he inquired everywhere if a fat noble had not been seen fleeing with a young Cossack. Besides, he was in a terrible hurry, and flew at breakneck speed. The people also affirmed that they had not seen Bogun taking away a young woman, and they would have seen her without fail if she had been with him, for only a few Cossacks were following the chief.

New consolation, but also new anxiety, entered the heart of Pan Yan, for these stories were simply beyond his comprehension. He did not understand why Bogun, pursuing first in the direction of Lubni, threw himself on the garrison at Vassílyevka, and then returned suddenly in the direction of Cherkasi. That he had not carried off Helena appeared to be certain, for Pan Kushel had met Anton's party, and she was not with them. The people now brought from the direction of Cherkasi had not seen her with Bogun. Where could she be then? Where was she hiding? Had she escaped? If so, in what direction? Why should she not escape to Lubni, instead of Cherkasi or Zólotonosha? Still Bogun's parties were pursuing and hunting somebody around Cherkasi and Próhorovka. But why were they inquiring about a noble with a young Cossack? To all these questions the lieutenant found no answer.

"Put your heads together, talk the matter over, explain what this means," said he to the officers, "for my head is unequal to the task."

"I think she must be in Lubni," said Pan Migurski.

"Impossible!" rejoined Zatsvilikhovski; "for if she were in Lubni then Bogun would hurry to Chigirin, and would not expose himself to the hetmans, of whose defeat he could not have known at that time. If he divided his Cossacks and pursued in two directions, I tell you that he was pursuing no one but her."

"And why did he inquire for an old noble and a young Cossack?"

"No great sagacity is needed to guess that. If she fled, she was not in woman's dress, but surely in disguise, so as not to be discovered. It is my opinion, then, that that Cossack is she."

"Sure as life, sure as life!" repeated the others.

"Well, but who is the noble?"

"I don't know that," replied the old man, "but we can ask about it. The peasants must have seen who was here and what happened. Let's have the man of this cottage brought in."

The officers hurried, and brought by the shoulder a "sub-neighbor" from the cow-house.

"Well, fellow," said Zatsvilikhovski, "were you here when the Cossacks with Bogun attacked the castle?"

The peasant, as was customary, began to swear that he had not been present, that he had not seen anything, did not know anything. But Zatsvilikhovski knew with whom he had to deal; therefore he said,--

"Oh, I know, you son of a Pagan, that you were right here when they plundered the place. Lie to some one else. Here is a gold ducat for you, and there is a soldier with a sword. Take your choice. Besides, if you do not tell, we will burn the village, and harm will come to poor people through you."

Then the "sub-neighbor" began to tell of what he had seen. When the Cossacks fell to revelling on the square before the house, he went with others to see what was going on. They heard that the old princess and her sons were killed, but that Nikolai had wounded the ataman, who lay as if lifeless. What happened to the young woman they could not discover; but at daybreak next morning they heard that she had escaped with a noble who had come with Bogun.

"That's it! that's it!" said Zatsvilikhovski. "Here is your gold ducat. You see that no harm has come to you. And did you or any one in the neighborhood see that noble?"

"I saw him; but he was not from this place."

"What did he look like?"

"He was as big as a stove, with a gray beard, and swore like a minstrel; blind of one eye."

"Oh, for God's sake!" said Pan Longin, "that must be Pan Zagloba."

"Zagloba, who else!"

"Zagloba? Wait!--Zagloba?--maybe it is. He kept company with Bogun in Chigirin,--drank and played dice with him. Maybe it is he. The description fits him."

Here Zatsvilikhovski turned again to the peasant.

"And that noble fled with the young lady?"

"Yes; so we heard."

"Do you know Bogun well?"

"Oh, very well! He used to be here for months at a time."

"But maybe that noble took her away for Bogun?"

"No; how could he do that? He bound Bogun,--tied him up with his coat,--then, they say, carried off the young lady as far as the eye of people could see. The ataman howled like a werewolf, and before daylight had himself bound between horses, and rushed off toward Lubni, but did not find them; then he rushed in another direction."

"Praise be to God!" said Migurski; "she may be in Lubni. That he hurried in the direction of Cherkasi is nothing; not finding her in one place, he tried in another."

Pan Yan was already on his knees, praying fervently.

"Well, well," said the old standard-bearer, "I did not think there was such mettle in Zagloba that he would dare to attack such a hero as Bogun. True, he was very friendly to Skshetuski for the triple mead of Lubni which we drank in Chigirin, He mentioned it to me more than once, and called him a distinguished cavalier. Well, well, this cannot find a place yet in my head, for he drank up no small amount of Bogun's money. But that he should bind Bogun and carry off the lady! I did not expect such a daring deed from him, for I held him a squabbler and a coward. Cunning he is, but a tremendous exaggerator; and all the bravery of such people is generally on their lips."

"Let him be as he likes; it is enough that he has snatched the princess from the hands of robbers," said Volodyovski. "And since, as is evident, he has no lack of stratagems, he has surely fled with her in such fashion as to be safe from the enemy himself."

"His own life depended on that," said Migurski.

Then they turned to Pan Yan and said: "Comfort yourself, dear comrade; we shall all be your best men yet!"

"And drink at the wedding."

Zatsvilikhovski added: "If he fled beyond the Dnieper and heard of the defeat at Korsún, he was obliged to return to Chernigoff, and in that case we shall come up to him on the road."

"Here is to the happy conclusion of all the troubles and sufferings of our friend!" called out Sleshinski.

They began to raise their glasses to the health of Pan Yan, the princess, their future descendants, and Zagloba. Thus passed the night. At daybreak the march was sounded, and the forces moved for Lubni.

The journey was made quickly, for the troops of the prince went without a train. Pan Yan wished to gallop ahead with the Tartar regiment, but was too weak. Besides, Prince Yeremi kept him near his own person, for he wished to hear the account of his mission to the Saitch. The knight was obliged, therefore, to give an account of how he had travelled, how they attacked him at Hortitsa and dragged him into the Saitch, but was silent concerning his disputes with Hmelnitski, lest it might seem that he was praising himself. The prince was affected most by the news that old Grodzitski had no powder, and therefore could not defend himself long.

"That is an unspeakable loss," said he, "for that fortress might cause great damage and hindrance to the rebellion. Grodzitski is a famous man, really a *decus et præsidium* to the Commonwealth. Why did he not send to me for powder? I should have given it to him from the cellars of Lubni."

"He thought evidently that by virtue of his office the Grand Hetman should think of that," said Pan Yan.

"I can believe it," added the prince, and was silent.

After a while, however, he continued: "The Grand Hetman is an old and experienced soldier, but he had too much self-confidence, and thereby has ruined himself; he underestimated the whole rebellion, and when I hurried to him with assistance he did not look at me at all agreeably. He did not wish to divide the glory with any one, feared the victory would be attributed to me."

"That is my opinion too," said Skshetuski, gravely.

"He thought to pacify the Zaporojians with clubs. God has punished the insolence. This Commonwealth is perishing through that same kind of pride, which is hateful to God, and of which perhaps no one is free."

The prince was right; and in truth he was not himself without blame, for it was not so long since, in his dispute over Gadyach with Pan Alexander Konyetspolski, the prince entered Warsaw with four thousand men, whom he ordered, in case he should be pressed to take the oath in the Senate, to break into the Chamber and fall upon them all; and he did this through nothing else but insolent pride, which would not allow him to be brought to oath instead of giving his word. Maybe he remembered this affair at that moment; for he fell to thinking, and rode on in silence, his eyes wandering over the broad steppes which lay on both sides of the road. Perhaps he thought of the fate of that Commonwealth which he loved with all the power of his ardent spirit, and to which the day of wrath and calamity seemed approaching.

After midday the swelling cupolas of Lubni churches and the glittering roof and pointed towers of St. Michael appeared from the lofty bank of the Sula. The army marched without hurry, and entered before evening.

The prince went immediately to the castle, where, in accordance with orders sent in advance, everything had been made ready for the road. The regiments were disposed for the night in the town,--which was no easy matter, for there was a great concourse of people in the place. Roused by reports of the progress of civil war on the right bank and of ferment among the peasants, all the nobles east of the Dnieper had crowded to Lubni. They had come even from distant settlements, with their wives, children, servants, horses, camels, and whole herds of cattle. There had come also the prince's agents, under-starostas and all kinds of officials from among the nobles, tenants, Jews; in a word, all against whom the rebellion might turn sharp knives. You would have said that some great annual fair was going on at Lubni; for there were not wanting even merchants of Moscow and Astrakhan Tartars, who, coming to the Ukraine with goods, halted there in view of war. On the square stood thousands of wagons of the most varied forms,--some with willow-bound wheels, others having wheels without spokes, cut out of one piece of wood,--Cossack telegas, and equipages of nobles. The more distinguished guests were lodged in the castle and in inns; the unimportant and servants, in tents near the churches. In the streets fires were kindled, at which food was cooking; and everywhere was a throng, a stir, a bustle, as in a bee-hive. The most varied costumes and colors were to be seen. There were present soldiers of the prince from different regiments, haiduks and Turkish grooms, Jews in black cloaks, peasants, Armenians in violet caps, Tartars in fur coats. The air was full of the sounds of different languages, of shouts, curses, cries of children, barking of dogs, and bellowing of cattle.

The people greeted the approaching regiments joyfully, for they saw in them assurance of safety and deliverance. Some went to the castle to shout in honor of the prince and princess. The most varied reports passed through the crowd,--one that the prince would stay in Lubni; another that he was going far away to Lithuania, where it would be necessary to follow him; a third, that he had already defeated Hmelnitski. The prince, after the greeting with his wife was over, and the announcement of the journey on the following day, looked with anxiety on those crowds of wagons and people which were to follow the army, and be fetters to his feet by lessening the speed of the march. His only comfort was the thought that beyond Bragin, in a quieter country, all would disperse, take refuge in various corners, and be a burden no longer. The princess herself, with ladies in waiting and the court, were to be sent to Vishnyovets, so that the prince without care or hindrance might move into the fire with his whole force. The preparations at the castle had been made already,--wagons were filled with effects and valuables, supplies were collected, all persons of the court were ready to take their seats in the wagons and on horseback at a moment's notice. This readiness was the work of Princess Griselda, who in calamity had as great a soul as her husband, and who, in truth, was equal to him in energy and unbending temper.

The prince was pleased with what he saw, though his heart was rent at the thought that he must leave the Lubni nest in which he had known so much happiness and had won so much glory. This sorrow, too, was shared by the whole army, the servants, and the entire court; for all felt certain that when the prince would be far away in battle, the enemy would not leave Lubni in peace, but would avenge on those beloved walls all the blows which they had suffered at the hands of Yeremi. Cries and lamentations were not lacking, especially among the women, and among those whose children were born there, and those who were leaving the graves of their parents behind.

CHAPTER XXIV.

Pan Yan, who had galloped in advance of the regiments to the castle to inquire for the princess and Zagloba, did not find them. They had neither been seen nor heard of, though there was news of the attack on Rozlogi and the destruction of the troops at Vassílyevka. The knight locked himself up in his quarters at the arsenal, together with his disappointed hopes. Sorrow, fear, and affliction rushed upon him again; but he defended himself from them as a wounded soldier on the battle-field defends himself from crows and ravens flocking around to drink his warm blood and tear his flesh. He strengthened himself with the thought that Zagloba, being fertile in stratagems, might make his way to Chernigoff and hide on receiving news of the defeat of the hetmans. He remembered then that old man whom he met on the way to Rozlogi, and who, together with his boy, as he said himself, had been stripped of his clothes by some devil, and had sat three days in the reeds of the Kagamlik, fearing to come out into the world. The thought occurred to Skshetuski at once that it must be Zagloba who had stripped them in order to get a disguise for himself and Helena. "It cannot be otherwise," repeated he; and he found great consolation in this thought, since such disguise made flight much more easy. He hoped that God, who watches over innocence, would not abandon Helena; and wishing the more to obtain this favor for her, he determined to purify himself from his sins. He left the arsenal therefore; and on searching for the priest Mukhovetski, and finding him engaged in consoling some women, he begged to have his confession heard.

The priest led him to a chapel, entered the confessional at once, and began to hear him. When he had finished, the priest instructed, edified, and consoled him, strengthened his faith, and then rebuked him, saying: "A Christian is not permitted to doubt the power of God, or an individual to grieve more over his own misfortune than that of his country; but you have more tears for your personal interests--that is, for your friends--than for the nation, and grieve moreover your love than over the catastrophe that has come upon all." Then he described the defeats, the fall, the disgrace of the country, in such lofty and touching speech that he roused at once great patriotism in the heart of the knight, to whom his own misfortunes seemed so belittled that he was almost unable to see them. The priest reproved him for the animosity and hatred against the Cossacks which he had observed in him.

"The Cossacks you will crush," said he, "as enemies of the faith and the country, as allies of the Pagan; but you will forgive them for having injured you, and pardon them from your heart, without thought of vengeance. And when you manifest this, I know that God will comfort you, restore your love to you, and send you peace."

Then the priest made the sign of the cross over Pan Yan, blessed him, and went out, having enjoined as penance to lie in the form of a cross till morning before the crucified Christ.

The chapel was empty and dark; only two candles were burning before the altar, casting rosy and golden gleams on the face of Christ, cut from alabaster and full of sweetness and suffering. Hours passed away, and the lieutenant lay there motionless as if dead; but he felt with increasing certainty that bitterness, despair, hatred, pain, grief, suffering, were unwinding themselves from his heart,--crawling out of his breast, creeping away like serpents, and hiding somewhere in the darkness. He felt that he was breathing more freely, that a kind of new health and new strength were entering into him, that his mind was becoming clearer and a species of happiness was embracing him; in a word, he found before that altar and before that Christ all, whatever it might be, that a man of those ages could find,--a man of unshaken faith, without a trace or a shadow of doubt.

Next morning the lieutenant was as if reborn. Work, movement, and bustle began, for this was the day of leaving Lubni. Officers from early morning had to review the regiments to see that horses and men were in proper order, then lead them to the field, and put them in marching array. The prince heard holy Mass in the Church of St. Michael, after which he returned to the castle and received deputations from the Greek clergy and from the townspeople of Lubni and Khoról. Then he mounted the throne, in the hall painted by Helm, surrounded by his foremost knights; and here Grubi, the mayor of Lubni, gave his farewell in Russian in the name of all the places belonging to the prince's Trans-Dnieper domains. He begged him first of all not to depart, not to leave them as sheep without a shepherd; hearing which, other deputies, clasping their hands, repeated, "Do not go away! do not go away!" And when the prince answered that he must go, they fell at the feet of their good lord in regret,--or pretended regret, for it was said that many of them, notwithstanding all the kindness of the prince, were very friendly to the Cossacks and Hmelnitski. But the more wealthy of them were afraid of the disturbance which they feared would arise immediately on the departure of the prince and his forces. Vishnyevetski answered that he had tried to be a father, not a lord, to them, and implored them to remain loyal to the king and the Commonwealth,--the mother of all, under whose wings they had suffered no injustice, had lived in peace, had grown in wealth, feeling no yoke such as strangers would not fail to lay upon them. He took farewell of the Greek clergy with similar words; after that came the hour of parting. Then was heard throughout the whole castle the weeping and lamentation of servants; the young ladies and ladies in waiting fainted, and they were barely able to restore Anusia Borzobogata to her senses. The princess herself was the only woman who entered a carriage with dry eyes and uplifted head, for the proud lady was ashamed to show the world that she suffered. Crowds of people stood near the castle; all the bells in Lubni were tolling; the Russian priests blessed with their crosses the departing company; the line of carriages and equipages could scarcely squeeze through the gates of the castle.

Finally the prince mounted his horse. The regimental flags were lowered before him; cannon were fired from the walls. The sounds of weeping, the bustle and shouting of crowds were mingled with the sounds of bells and guns, with the blare of trumpets and the rattle of drums. The procession moved on.

In advance went the Tartar regiments, under Roztvorovski and Vershul; then the artillery of Pan Vurtsel, the infantry of Makhnitski; next came the princess with her ladies, then the whole court, and wagons with valuables; after them the Wallachian regiment of Pan Bykhovets; finally, the body of the army, the picked regiments of heavy artillery, the armored regiments, and hussars; the rear was brought up by the dragoons and the Cossacks.

After the army came an endless train of wagons, many-colored as a serpent, and carrying the families of all those nobles who after the departure of the prince would not remain east of the Dnieper.

The trumpets sounded throughout the regiments; but the hearts of all were straitened. Each one looking at those walls thought to himself: "Dear houses, shall I see you again in life?" It is easy to depart, but difficult to return; and each left as it were a part of his soul in those places, and a pleasant memory. Therefore all turned their eyes for the last time on the castle, on the town, on the towers of the Polish churches, on the domes of the Russian, and on the roofs of the houses. Each one knew what he was leaving behind, but did not know what was waiting there in that blue distance toward which the tabor was moving.

Sadness therefore was in the soul of each person. The town called to the departing ones with the voices of bells, as if beseeching and imploring them not to leave it exposed to uncertainty, to the evil fortune of the future; it called out as if by those sad sounds it wished to say farewell and remain in their memory.

Though the procession moved away, heads were turned toward the town, and in every face could be read the question: "Is this the last time?"

It was the last time. Of all the army and throng of thousands who in that hour were going forth with Prince Vishnyevetski, neither he himself nor any one of them was ever to look again upon that town or that country.

The trumpets sounded. The tabor moved on slowly, but steadily; and after a time Lubni began to be veiled in a blue haze, the houses and roofs were blended into one mass brightly distinct. Then the prince urged his horse ahead, and having ridden to a lofty mound stood motionless and gazed long. That town gleaming there in the sun, and all that country visible from the mound was the work of his ancestors and himself. For the Vishnyevetskis had changed that gloomy wilderness of the past into a settled country, opened it to the life of people, and it may be said, created the Trans-Dnieper. And the greater part of that work the prince had himself accomplished. He built those Polish churches whose towers stood there blue over the town; he increased the place, and joined it with roads to the Ukraine; he felled forests, drained swamps, built castles, founded villages and settlements, brought in settlers, put down robbers, defended from Tartar raids, maintained the peace necessary to husbandman and merchant, and introduced the rule of law and justice. Through him that country had lived, grown, and flourished,--he was the heart and soul of it; and now he had to leave all.

And it was not that colossal fortune, great as an entire German principality, which the prince regretted, but he had become attached to the work of his hands. He knew that when he was absent everything was absent; that the labor of years would be destroyed at once; that toil would go for nothing, ferocity would be unchained, flames would embrace villages and towns, the Tartar would water his horse in those rivers, woods would grow out of ruins; that if God granted him to return everything would have to be begun anew, and perhaps his strength would fail, time be wanting, and confidence such as he had enjoyed at first would not be given him. Here passed the years which were for him praise before men, merit before God; and now the praise and the merit are to roll away in smoke.

Two tears flowed slowly down his face. These were his last tears, after which remained in his eyes only lightning.

The prince's horse stretched out his neck and neighed, and this neighing was answered immediately by other steeds under the banners. These sounds roused the prince from his revery and filled him with hope. And so there remains to him yet six thousand faithful comrades,--six thousand sabres with which the world is open to him, and to which the prostrate Commonwealth is looking as the only salvation. The idyl beyond the Dnieper is at an end; but where cannon are thundering, where villages and towns are in flames, where by night the wail of captives, the groans of men, women, and children are mingled with the neighing of Tartar horses and Cossack tumult, there is an open field, and there he may win the glory of a savior and father of his country. Who will reach for the crown, who rescue the fatherland, disgraced, trodden under the feet of peasants, conquered, dying, if not he, the prince,--if not those forces which shine there below him in their armor and gleam in the sun?

The tabor passed by the foot of the mound; and at the sight of the prince standing with his baton in his hand on the eminence under the cross, all the soldiers gave forth one shout: "Long live the prince! long live our leader and hetman Yeremi Vishnyevetski!"

A hundred banners were lowered to his feet. The hussars sounded their horns, and the drums were beaten to accompany the shouts. Then the prince drew forth his sabre, and raising it with his eyes to heaven, said,--

"I, Yeremi Vishnyevetski, voevoda of Rus, prince in Lubni and Vishnyovets, swear to thee, O God, One in a Holy Trinity, and to thee, Most Holy Mother, that, raising this sabre against ruffianism by which our land is disgraced, I will not lay it down while strength and life remain to me, until I wash out that disgrace and bend every enemy to the feet of the Commonwealth, give peace to the Ukraine, and drown servile insurrection in blood. And as I make this oath with a sincere heart, so God give me aid. Amen!"

He stood yet awhile longer looking at the heavens, then rode down slowly from the height to the regiments. The army marched that evening to Basani, a village belonging to Pani Krynitska, who received the prince on her knees at the gate; for the peasants had laid siege to her house and she was keeping them off with the assistance of the more faithful of her servants, when the sudden arrival of the army saved her and her nineteen children, of whom fourteen were girls. When the prince had given orders to seize the aggressors, he sent a Cossack company to Kanyeff under command of Captain Ponyatovski, who brought that same night five Zaporojians of the Vasyutin kuren. These had all taken part in the battle of Korsún, and when burned with fire gave a detailed account of the battle. They stated that Hmelnitski was still in Korsún, but that Tugai Bey had gone with captives, booty, and both hetmans to Chigirin, whence he intended to return to the Crimea. They heard also that Hmelnitski had begged him earnestly not to leave the Zaporojian army, but to march against the prince. The murza, however, would not agree to this, saying that after the destruction of the armies and the hetmans, the Cossacks could go on alone; he would not wait longer, for his captives would die. They put Hmelnitski's forces at two hundred thousand, but of rather poor quality; of good men only fifty thousand,--that is, Zaporojians and Cossacks subject to lords, or town Cossacks who had joined the rebellion.

On receiving these tidings the prince grew strong in spirit, for he hoped that he too would increase considerably in strength by the accession of nobles on the west of the Dnieper, stragglers from the army of the Crown, and detachments belonging to Polish lords. Therefore he set out early next morning.

Beyond Pereyaslav the army entered immense gloomy forests extending along the course of the Trubej to Kozelets, and farther on to Chernigoff itself. It was toward the end of May, and terribly hot. In the woods, instead of being cool, it was so sultry that men and horses lacked air for breathing. Cattle, driven after the army, fell at every step, or when they caught the smell of water, rushed to it as if wild, overturning wagons and causing dismay. Horses too began to fall, especially those of the heavy cavalry. The nights were unendurable from the infinite number of insects and the overpowering odor of pitch, which the trees dropped in unusual abundance by reason of the heat.

They dragged on in this way for four days; at length on the fifth day the heat became unnatural. When night came the horses began to snort and the cattle to bellow plaintively, as if foreseeing some danger which men could not yet surmise.

"They smell blood!" was said in the tabor among the crowds of fugitive families of nobles.

"The Cossacks are pursuing us! there will be a battle!"

At these words the women raised a lament, the rumor reached the servants, panic and disturbance set in; the people tried to drive ahead of one another, or to leave the track and go at random through the woods, where they got entangled among the trees.

But men sent by the prince soon restored order. Scouts were ordered out on every side, so as to be sure whether danger was threatening or not.

Skshetuski, who had gone as a volunteer with the Wallachians, returned first toward morning and went straightway to the prince.

"What is the trouble?" asked Yeremi.

"Your Highness, the woods are on fire."

"Set on fire?"

"Yes; I seized a number of men who confessed that Hmelnitski had sent volunteers to follow you and to set fire, if the wind should be favorable."

"He wanted to roast us alive without giving battle. Bring the people here!"

In a moment three herdsmen were brought,--wild, stupid, terrified,--who immediately confessed that they were in fact commanded to set fire to the woods. They confessed also that forces were despatched after the prince, but that they were going to Chernigoff by another road, nearer the Dnieper.

Meanwhile other scouts returned. All brought the same report: "The woods are on fire."

But the prince did not allow himself to be disturbed in the least by this. "It is a villanous method," said he; "but nothing will come of it. The fire will not go beyond the rivers entering the Trubej."

In fact, into the Trubej, along which the army marched to the north, there fell so many small rivers forming here and there broad morasses, impassable for fire, that it would have been necessary to ignite the woods beyond each one of them separately. The scouts soon discovered that this was being done. Every day incendiaries were brought in; with these they ornamented the pine-trees along the road.

The fires extended vigorously along the rivers to the east and west, not to the north. In the night-time the heavens were red as far as the eye could see. The women sang sacred hymns from dusk to the dawning of the day. Terrified wild beasts from the flaming forests took refuge on the road and followed the army, running in among the cattle of the herds. The wind blew in the smoke, which covered the whole horizon. The army and the wagons pushed forward as if through a dense fog, which the eye could not penetrate. The lungs had no air; the smoke bit the eyes, and the wind kept driving it on more and more each moment. The light of the sun could not pierce the clouds, and there was more to be seen in the night-time than in the day, for flames gave light. The woods seemed to have no end.

In the midst of such burning forests and such smoke did Prince Yeremi lead his army. Meanwhile news came that the enemy was marching on the other side of the Trubej. The extent of his power was unknown, but Vershul's Tartars affirmed that he was still far away.

One night Pan Sukhodolski came to the army from Bodenki, on the other side of the Desna. He was an old attendant of the prince, who some years before had settled in a village. He was fleeing before the peasants, but brought news as yet unknown in the army.

Great consternation was caused when, asked by the prince for news, he answered: "Bad, your Highness! You know already of the defeat of the hetmans and the death of the king?"

The prince, who was sitting on a small camp-stool in front of the tent, sprang to his feet. "How?--is the king dead?"

"Our merciful lord gave up the spirit in Merech a week before the catastrophe at Korsún."

"God in his mercy did not permit him to live to such times!" said the prince; then seizing himself by the head, he continued: "Awful times have come upon the Commonwealth! Convocations and elections,--an interregnum, dissensions, and foreign intrigues,--now, when the whole people should become a single sword in a single hand. God surely has turned away his face from us, and in his anger intends to punish us for our sins. Only King Vladislav himself could extinguish these conflagrations; for there was a wonderful affection for him among the Cossacks, and besides, he was a military man."

At this time a number of officers--among them Zatsvilikhovski, Skshetuski, Baranovski, Vurtsel, Makhnitski, and Polyanovski--approached the prince, who said: "Gentlemen, the king is dead!"

Their heads were uncovered as if by command. Their faces grew serious. Such unexpected news deprived all of speech. Only after a while came an expression of universal sorrow.

"May God grant him eternal rest!" said the prince.

"And eternal light shine upon him!"

Soon after the priest Mukhovetski intoned "Dies Iræ;" and amidst those forests and that smoke an unspeakable sorrow seized their hearts and souls. It seemed to all as if some expected rescue had failed; as if they were standing alone in the world, in presence of some terrible enemy, and they had no one against him except their prince. So then all eyes turned to him, and a new bond was formed between Vishnyevetski and his men.

That evening the prince spoke to Zatsvilikhovski in a voice that was heard by all,--

"We need a warrior king, so that if God grants us to give our votes at an election, we will give them for Prince Karl, who has more of the military genius than Kazimir."

"Vivat Carolus rex!" shouted the officers.

"Vivat!" repeated the hussars, and after them the whole army.

The prince voevoda had no thought, indeed, that those shouts raised east of the Dnieper, in the gloomy forests of Chernigoff, would reach Warsaw, and wrest from his grasp the baton of Grand Hetman of the Crown.

CHAPTER XXV.

After the nine days' march of which Mashkevich was the Xenophon, and the three days' passage of the Desna, the army reached Chernigoff at last. Skshetuski entered first of all with the Wallachians. The prince ordered him to the place on purpose, so that he might inquire sooner about the princess and Zagloba. But here, as in Lubni, neither in the town nor the castle did he hear anything of them. They had vanished somewhere without a trace, like a stone in the water, and the knight himself knew not what to think. Where could they have hidden themselves? Certainly not in Moscow, nor in the Crimea, nor in the Saitch. There remained only one hypothesis, that they had crossed the Dnieper; but in such an event they would find themselves at once in the midst of the storm. On that side there were slaughter and swarms of drunken peasants, Zaporojians, and Tartars, from whom not even a disguise would protect Helena; for those wild Pagans were glad to take boys captive, for whom they found a great demand in the markets of Stamboul. A terrible suspicion entered Skshetuski's head,--that possibly Zagloba had taken her to that side on purpose to sell her to Tugai Bey, who might pay him more liberally than Bogun; and this thought drove him to the very verge of madness. But Podbipienta, who had known Zagloba longer than Skshetuski, quieted him considerably in this respect.

"My dear brother," said he, "cast that thought out of your head! That noble has done nothing of the sort. The Kurtsevichi had treasures enough, which Bogun would have been willing to give him. Had he wished to ruin the girl, he would not have exposed his life, and he would have made his fortune."

"True," said the lieutenant; "but why has he fled with her across the Dnieper, instead of going to Lubni or Chernigoff?"

"Well, quiet your mind, my dear fellow! I know that Zagloba. He drank with me and borrowed money of me. He does not care for money,--either his own or another man's. If he has his own he will spend it, and he won't repay another's if he borrows; but that he would undertake such a deed I do not believe."

"He is a frivolous man," said Pan Yan.

"Frivolous he may be, but he is a trickster who will outwit any man, and slip out of every danger himself. And as the priest with prophetic spirit said that God would give her back to you, so will it be; for it is just that every sincere affection should be rewarded. Console yourself with this hope, as I console myself."

Here Pan Longin began to sigh deeply, and after a while added: "Let us inquire once more at the castle. Maybe they passed by here."

They inquired everywhere, but to no purpose. There was not a trace even of the passage of the fugitives. The castle was full of nobles with their wives and children, who had shut themselves in against the Cossacks. The prince endeavored to persuade them to go with him, and warned them that the Cossacks were following in his tracks. They did not dare to attack the army, but it was likely they would attack the castle and the town after his departure. The nobles in the castle, however, were strangely blinded.

"We are safe behind the forests," said they to the prince. "No one will come to us here."

"But I have passed through these forests," said he.

"You have passed, but the rabble will not. These are not the forests for them."

The nobles refused to go, continuing in their blindness, for which they paid dearly later on. After the passage of the prince the Cossacks came quickly. The castle was defended manfully for three weeks, then was captured and all in it were cut to pieces. The Cossacks committed terrible cruelties, and no one took vengeance on them.

When the prince arrived at Lubech on the Dnieper he disposed his army there for rest, but went himself with the princess and court to Bragin, situated in the midst of forests and impassable swamps. A week later the army crossed over too. They marched then through Babitsa to Mozir, where, on the day of Corpus Christi, came the moment of separation; for the princess with the court had to go to Turoff to the wife of the voevoda of Vilna, her aunt, but the prince with the army into fire in the Ukraine.

At the farewell dinner the prince and princess, the ladies in waiting, and most of the distinguished officers were present. But the usual animation was not evident among the ladies and cavaliers, for more than one soldier heart was cut by the thought that he would soon have to leave the chosen one, for whom he wished to live, fight, and die; more than one pair of bright or dark maiden eyes were filled with tears of sorrow because "*he* is going to the war among bullets and swords, among Cossacks and wild Tartars,--is going and may not return."

When the prince began to speak in taking farewell of his wife and court, the young ladies fell to crying one after another as plaintively as kittens; but the knights, being of sterner stuff, rose from their places, and seizing the hilts of their swords, shouted in unison,--

"We will conquer and return!"

"God give you strength!" answered the princess.

Then there rose a shout that made the walls and windows tremble.

"Long life to the princess! Long life to our mother and benefactress! Long life to her! long life to her!"

The officers loved her for her love to them, for her greatness of soul, her liberality and kindness, for her care of their families. Prince Yeremi loved her above all things; for theirs were two natures created as it were for each other, as much alike as two goblets of gold and bronze.

Then all went up to her, and each one knelt with his goblet before her chair, and she, embracing the head of each one, spoke some word of kindness. But to Skshetuski she said,--

"It is likely that more than one knight here will receive a scapula or a ribbon at parting; and since you have not here the one from whom most of all you would wish to receive a memento, take this from me as from a mother."

While saying this, she removed a golden cross set with turquoise and hung it upon his neck. He kissed her hands with reverence.

It was evident that the prince was greatly pleased at this attention shown Skshetuski; for of late he had given him increased affection because in his mission to the Saitch he had upheld the dignity of the prince and refused to take letters from Hmelnitski. They rose from the table. The young ladies, catching on the wing the words of the princess spoken to Pan Yan and receiving them as a sign of approval and permission, began immediately to bring, one a scapula, another a scarf, a third a cross, which seeing, the knights present approached, if not his chosen, at least his favorite one. Therefore Ponyatovski came to Jitinska; Bykhovets to Bogovitinyanka, for recently he had grown pleasing to her; Roztvorovski to Jukovna; red Vershul to Skoropadska; Colonel Makhnitski, though old, to Zavyeska. Only Anusia Borzobogata Krasenska, though the most beautiful of all, stood under the window deserted and alone; her face was flushed, her eyes with drooping lids shot from their corners glances full of anger and of a prayer not to put such an affront on her. Seeing this, the traitor Volodyovski came up and said,--

"I too wished to beg Panna Anna for a memento, but I abandoned, resigned, my wish, thinking I should not be able to push my way to her through the dense throng."

Anusia's cheeks burned still more hotly, but without a moment's hesitation she answered,--

"You would like to get a keepsake from other hands than mine, but you will not get it; for if it is not too crowded for you there, it is too high."

The blow was well directed and double, for in the first place it turned the sarcasm to the low stature of the knight, and in the second to his passion for Princess Barbara Zbaraska. Pan Volodyovski fell in love first with the elder sister Anna; but when she was betrothed he recovered from his pain and in silence made an offering of his heart to Barbara, thinking that no one suspected it. When therefore he heard this from Anusia, though he was a champion of the first degree both with sword and tongue, he was so confused that he forgot his speech and muttered something wide of the mark,--

"You are aiming high too, as high indeed as the head of Pan Podbipienta."

"He is in truth higher than you in arms and in manners," said the resolute girl. "Thank you for reminding me!" Then she called to the Lithuanian: "Will you come this way? I wish to have my knight too, and I do not know that I could bind my scarf on a braver breast than yours."

Pan Podbipienta stared as if uncertain whether he heard correctly; finally he cast himself on his knees, so that the floor trembled.

"My benefactress!"

Anusia fastened the scarf, and then her little hands disappeared entirely under the blond mustaches of Pan Longin. There was heard only the sound of kissing and muttering, hearing which Volodyovski said to Lieutenant Migurski, "One would swear that a bear had broken into a bee-hive and was eating the honey." Then he went away with a certain anger, for he felt Anusia's sting, and moreover he had been in love with her in his time.

But the prince had already begun to take farewell of the princess, and an hour later the court set out for Turoff, and the army for the Pripet.

During the night at the crossing, while they were building rafts to carry over the cannon, and the hussars were doing the work, Pan Longin said to Skshetuski,--

"Look here, brother, a misfortune!"

"What has happened?" asked the lieutenant.

"Why, the news from the Ukraine!"

"What news?"

"The Zaporojians tell me that Tugai Bey has gone with the horde to the Crimea."

"Well, what of that? You will not cry over that, I suppose."

"But, my brother, you told me--and you were right, were you not?--that I could not count Cossacks' heads, and if the Tartars are gone where am I to get the three Pagan heads? Where should I look for them? and oh, how much I need them!"

Skshetuski, though suffering himself, laughed, and answered: "I understand what the matter is, for I saw how you were made a knight to-day."

"That is true. Why hide it longer? I have fallen in love, brother,--fallen in love. That is the misfortune."

"Don't torment yourself. I do not believe that Tugai Bey has gone, and besides you will meet as many Pagans as there are mosquitoes over our heads."

In fact, whole clouds of mosquitoes swept over the horses and men; for the troops went into a country of impassable morasses, swampy forests, soft meadows, rivers, creeks, and streams,-- into an empty, gloomy land, one howling wilderness, concerning the inhabitants of which it was said in those times,--

"Nobleman Nakedness (Holota   )
Gave with his daughter
Two kegs of wagon grease,
One wreath of mushrooms,
One jar of mud-fish,
And one ridge of swamp."

In this swamp, however, there grew not only mushrooms, but, in spite of the above sarcasm, great lordly fortunes. But at this time the prince's men, who, for the greater part had been reared on the lofty dry steppes of the Trans-Dnieper, could not believe their own eyes. True, there were swamps in their country and forests in places, but here the whole region seemed to be one swamp. The nights were clear and bright. As far as the eye could see by the light of the moon not two yards of dry ground were visible. Only tufts of earth looked black above the water, the trees appeared to grow out of the water, water spattered from under the feet of the horses, water sprinkled the wheels of the wagons and the cannon.

Vurtsel fell into despair: "A wonderful march!" said he; "near Chernigoff we were in danger from fire, and now water is drowning us."

Indeed the earth, in contradiction to its nature, did not give a firm support to the foot, but bent and trembled as if wishing to open and swallow those who moved upon it.

The troops were four days passing the Pripet; then they had to cross almost every day rivers and streams flowing through shaky ground. And nowhere was there a bridge. All the people crossed in boats. After a few days fog and rain began. The men did their utmost to get out of those enchanted regions at last, and the prince urged and pushed them on. The soldiers, seeing too that he did not spare himself,--he was on horseback from dawn till dark, leading the army and overseeing its advance, directing everything in person,--did not dare to murmur, though really they labored beyond their strength. To toil from morning till night and in the water was the common lot of all. The horses began to lose their hoofs; many of the artillery horses died, so that the infantry and Volodyovski's dragoons drew cannon themselves. The picked regiments, such as Skshetuski's and Zatsvilikhovski's hussars, and the armored regiments took their axes to make roads. It was a famous march, in cold and water and hunger, in which the will of the leader and the ardor of the soldiers broke through every barrier. No one hitherto had dared to lead an army through that country during the high water of spring. Happily the march was not interrupted by any accident. The people were peaceable and without thought of rebellion; though afterward roused by the Cossacks and incited by example, they did not wish to rally to the banners of sedition. They looked with sleepy eyes on the passing legions, who issued from the pine woods and swamps as if enchanted, and passed on like a dream; they furnished guides, and did quietly and obediently all that was asked of them.

In view of this the prince punished severely every military license, and the army was not followed by groans, curses, and complaints; and when after the passage of the army it was learned in some smoky village that Prince Yeremi had passed, the people shook their heads, and said quietly, "Why, he is good-natured."

At last, after twenty days of superhuman toil and effort, the forces of the prince appeared in the region of revolt. "Yarema is coming! Yarema is coming!" was heard over the whole Ukraine, to the Wilderness, to Chigirin and Yagorlik. "Yarema is coming!" was heard in the towns, villages, farms, and clearings; and at the report the scythes, forks, and knives dropped from the hands of the peasants, faces grew pale, wild bands hurried toward the south in the night, like wolves at the sound of the hunter's horn; the Tartar, wandering around for plunder, sprang from his horse and put his ear to the ground from time to time; in the castles and fortresses that were still uncaptured, bells were sounded and "Te Deum laudamus" was sung.

And that terrible lion laid himself down on the threshold of a rebellious land and rested. He was gathering his strength.

CHAPTER XXVI

Hmelnitski remained awhile at Korsún, and then pushed on to Bélaya Tserkoff, where he established his capital. The horde was disposed in camp on the other side of the river, sending out parties through the whole province of Kieff. Pan Longin Podbipienta therefore had been grieving in vain over the dearth of Tartar heads. Skshetuski foresaw correctly that the Zaporojians seized by Ponyatovski at Kanyeff gave false information. Tugai Bey not only had not departed, but had not gone even to Chigirin. What is more, new Tartar reinforcements came from every side. The petty sovereigns of Azoff and Astrakhan, who had never been in Poland before, came with four thousand warriors. Twelve thousand of the Nogai horde came, and twenty thousand of the Bélgorod and Budjak hordes,--all sworn enemies hitherto of the Zaporojians and the Cossacks, now brothers and sworn allies against Christian blood. Finally the Khan Islam Giréi himself came with twelve thousand from Perekop. The whole Ukraine suffered from these friends; not only the nobles suffered, but the Russian people, whose villages were burned, cattle driven away, and whose wives and children were hurried into captivity. In those times of murder, burning, and bloodshed there was only one rescue for the peasant, and that was to flee to Hmelnitski,--where from being a victim he became a destroyer, and ravaged his own country; but at least his life was safe. Unhappy country! When rebellion broke out in it Pan Nikolai Pototski punished and wasted it to begin with; then the Zaporojians and the Tartars, who came as if for its liberation; and now Yeremi Vishnyevetski hovered over it.

Therefore all who were able fled to Hmelnitski's camp; even nobles fled, for other means of safety were not to be found. Thanks to this, Hmelnitski increased in power; and if he remained long in Bélaya Tserkoff and did not move at once to the heart of the Commonwealth, it was above all to give order to these lawless and wild elements.

In his iron hands they changed quickly into military strength. Skeleton regiments of trained Zaporojians were at hand; the mob was divided among these. Colonels were appointed from koshevoi atamans of long standing; single parties were sent out to capture castles, and receive thereby training for battle. They were men valiant by nature, fitted beyond all others for war, used to arms, familiar with fire and the bloody front of battle, through Tartar raids.

Two colonels, Handja and Ostap, went to Nestorvar, which they captured, cutting to pieces all the Jews and nobles among its inhabitants, and beheading Prince Chetvertinski's miller on the threshold of the castle. Ostap made the princess his captive. Others went in other directions, and success attended their arms; for a terror of the heart seized the Poles,--a terror "unusual to that people," who dropped the weapons from their hands and lost their strength.

More than once it happened that the colonels importuned Hmelnitski: "Why don't you move on Warsaw? Why do you stay resting here, getting information from wizards, and filling yourself with gorailka, letting the Poles recover from their terror and assemble their men?" More than once also the drunken crowd howled in the night-time, surrounding the quarters of Hmelnitski, asking him to lead them against the Poles. The hetman had raised the rebellion and given it a terrible power, but now he began to see that this power was urging him forward to an unknown future; therefore he gazed often into that future with uncertain eye, tried to solve the riddle of it, and in the face of that future was disturbed at heart.

As has been said, among those colonels and atamans he alone knew what terrible power there was in the apparent weakness of the Commonwealth. He had raised the rebellion, gained the victory at Jóltiya Vodi, at Korsún had swept away the armies of the Crown,--but what further?

He assembled the colonels then in council, and glancing at them with bloodshot eyes before which they all trembled, proposed the very same question,--"What further? What do you want? To go to Warsaw? Then Prince Vishnyevetski will be here, and kill your wives and children with the speed of lightning. He will leave only earth and water behind, and will follow to Warsaw, marching with the whole power of the nobles who will join him. Then, caught between two fires, we shall perish; if not in battle, empaled on stakes. You cannot depend on Tartar friendship. To-day they are with us; to-morrow they may turn against us and rush off to the Crimea, or sell our heads to the Poles. Well, what more will you say? March on Vishnyevetski? He would detain our forces and those of the Tartar till armies could be enrolled in the heart of the Commonwealth and brought to his aid. Choose!"

The alarmed colonels were silent, and Hmelnitski continued:--

"Why are you silent? Why do you urge me no longer to go to Warsaw? If you know not what to do, then rely on me, and with God's help I will save my own head and yours, and win satisfaction for the Zaporojian army and all the Cossacks."

In fact, there remained one method,--negotiation. Hmelnitski knew well how much he could extort from the Commonwealth in that way. He calculated that the Diets would rather agree to liberal concessions than to taxes, levies of troops, and war, which would have to be long and difficult. Finally, he knew that in Warsaw there was a strong party, and at the head of it the king himself (news of whose death had not yet come), with the chancellor and many nobles, who would be glad to hinder the growth of the colossal fortunes of the magnates of the Ukraine, and to create a power for the hands of the king out of the Cossacks, conclude a permanent peace with them, and use those thousands of warriors for foreign wars. In these conditions Hmelnitski might acquire a distinguished position for himself, receive the baton of hetman from the king, and gain countless concessions for the Cossacks.

This was why he remained long in Bélaya Tserkoff. He armed his men, sent general orders in every direction, collected the people, created whole armies, took possession of castles, for he knew they would negotiate only with power, but he did not move into the heart of the Commonwealth. If he could conclude peace by negotiation, then either the weapon would drop from the hand of Vishnyevetski, or, if the prince would not lay it aside, then not Hmelnitski, but Vishnyevetski, would be the rebel carrying on war against the will of the king and the Diets. He would move then on Vishnyevetski, but by command of the king and the Commonwealth; and the last hour would have struck not for Vishnyevetski alone, but for all the kinglets of the Ukraine, with their fortunes and their lands.

Thus meditated the self-created Zaporojian hetman; such was the pile that he built for the future. But on the scaffolding of this edifice the dark birds, Care, Doubt, Fear, sat many a time, and ominous was their croaking. Will the peace party be strong enough in Warsaw? Will it begin negotiations with him? What will the Diet and the Senate say? Will they close their ears in the capital to the groans and cries of the Ukraine? Will they shut their eyes to the flames of conflagration? Will not negotiations be prevented by the influence of the magnates possessing those immeasurable estates, the preservation of which will be for their interest? And has the Commonwealth become so terror-stricken that it will forgive him?

On the other hand, Hmelnitski's soul was rent by the doubt. Has not the rebellion become too inflamed and too developed? Would those wild masses allow themselves to be confined within any limits? Suppose he, Hmelnitski, should conclude peace, the cut-throats may continue to murder and burn in his name, or take vengeance on his head for their deluded hopes. Then that swollen river, that sea, that storm! An awful position! If the outbreak had been weaker, they would not negotiate with him, by reason of his weakness; but because the rebellion is mighty, negotiations, by the force of things, may be defeated. Then what will happen?

When such thoughts besieged the weighty head of the hetman he shut himself up in his quarters, and drank whole days and nights. Then among the colonels and the mob the report went around: "The hetman is drinking!" and following his example, all drank. Discipline was relaxed, prisoners killed, fights sprang up, booty was stolen. The day of judgment was beginning, the reign of horror and ghastliness. Bélaya Tserkoff was turned into a real Inferno.

One day Vygovski, a noble captured at Korsún and made secretary to the hetman, came in. He began to shake the drinker without ceremony, till seizing him by the shoulders he seated him on the low bench and brought him to his senses.

"What is it? What the plague--" demanded Hmelnitski.

"Rise up, Hetman, and come to yourself!" answered Vygovski. "An embassy has come."

Hmelnitski sprang to his feet, and in a moment was sober.

"Hi, there!" he cried to the Cossack sitting at the threshold, "give me my cap and baton. Who has come? From whom?"

"The priest Patroni Lasko, from Gushchi, from the voevoda of Bratslav."

"From Pan Kisel?"

"Yes."

"Glory to the Father and Son, glory to the Holy Ghost and to the Holy Most Pure!" said Hmelnitski, making the sign of the cross. His face became clear, he regained his good humor,--negotiations had begun.

But that day there came news of a character directly opposed to the peaceful embassy of Pan Kisel. It was stated that Prince Yeremi, after he had given rest to his army, wearied with its march through the woods and swamps, had entered into the rebellious country; that he was killing, burning, beheading; that a division sent under Skshetuski had dispersed a band of two thousand Cossacks with a mob and cut them to pieces; that the prince himself had taken Pogrébische, the property of the princes Zbaraski, and had left only earth and water behind him. Awful things were related of the storm and taking of Pogrébische,--for it was a nest of the most stubborn murderers. The prince, it was said, told the soldiers: "Kill them so they will feel they are dying." The soldiers therefore allowed themselves the wildest excesses of cruelty. Out of the whole town not a single soul escaped. Seven hundred prisoners were hanged, two hundred seated on stakes. Mention is made also of boring out eyes with augers and burning on slow fires. The rebellion was put down at once in the whole neighborhood. The inhabitants either fled to Hmelnitski or received the lord of Lubni on their knees with bread and salt, howling for mercy. The smaller bands were all rubbed out, and in the woods, as stated by fugitives from Samorodka, Spichina, Pleskoff, Vakhnovka, there was not a tree on which a Cossack was not hanging. And all this was done not far from Bélaya Tserkoff and the many-legioned armies of Hmelnitski.

So when Hmelnitski heard of this he began to roar like a wounded aurochs. On one side negotiations, on the other the sword. If he marches against the prince, it will mean that he does not want the negotiations proposed through Pan Kisel, the Lord of Brusiloff. His only hope was in the Tartars. Hmelnitski jumped up and hurried to the quarters of Tugai Bey.

"Tugai Bey, my friend!" said he, after giving the usual salaams, "as you saved me at Jóltiya Vodi and Korsún, save me now! An envoy has come here from the voevoda of Bratslav, with a letter, in which the voevoda promises satisfaction, and to the Zaporojian army the restoration of its ancient freedom, on condition that I cease from war, which I must do to show my sincerity and good-will. At the same time news has come that my enemy, Prince Vishnyevetski, has razed Pogrébische and left no man living. He is cutting down my warriors, empaling them, boring out their eyes with augers. I cannot move on him. To you I come, asking that you move on your enemy and mine with your Tartars; otherwise he will soon attack our camp here."

The murza, sitting on a pile of carpets taken at Korsún or stolen from the houses of nobles, swayed backward and forward some time, contracted his eyes as if for closer thinking; at last he said,--

"Allah! I cannot do that."

"Why?" asked Hmelnitski.

"Because, as it is, I have lost for you beys and men enough at Jóltiya Vodi and Korsún, why should I lose more? Yeremi is a great warrior! I will march against him if you march, but not alone. I am not such a fool as to lose in one battle all that I have gained so far; better send out my detachments for booty and captives. I have done enough for you unbelieving dogs. I will not go myself, and I will dissuade the Khan from going. I have spoken."

"You swore to give me aid."

"I did; but I swore to make war at your side, not instead of you. Go away from here!"

"I let you take captives from my own people, gave you booty, gave you the hetmans."

"Yes, for if you had not I should have given you to them."

"I will go to the Khan."

"Be off, I tell you!"

The pointed teeth of the murza had already begun to gleam from under his mustache. Hmelnitski knew that he had nothing to get from him, and it was dangerous to stop longer; he rose therefore and went in fact to the Khan.

But he got the same answer from the Khan. The Tartars had their own minds and were looking for their own profit. Instead of venturing on a general battle against a leader who was considered invincible, they preferred to send out plundering parties and enrich themselves without bloodshed.

Hmelnitski returned in a rage to his own quarters, and from despair was going to the decanter again, when Vygovski took it away from him.

"You will not drink, worthy hetman!" said he. "There is an envoy, and you must finish with him first."

Hmelnitski was furious. "I will have you and the envoy empaled!"

"I will not give you gorailka. Are you not ashamed, when fortune has raised you so high, to fill yourself with gorailka, like a common Cossack? Pshaw! it must not be. News of the envoy's arrival has spread about the army, and the colonels want a council. It is not for you to drink now, but to forge the iron while it is hot; for now you can conclude peace and receive all you want; afterward it will be too late, and my life and yours are involved in this. You should send an envoy at once to Warsaw, and ask the king for favor."

"You are a wise head," said Hmelnitski. "Command them to ring the bell for council, and tell the colonels on the square that I shall come out directly."

Vygovski went out, and in a moment the bell was ringing for council. At the sound the Zaporojian army began to assemble immediately. The leaders and colonels sat down,--the terrible Krívonos, Hmelnitski's right hand; Krechovski, the sword of the Cossacks; the old and experienced Filon Daidyalo, colonel of Kropivnik; Fedor Loboda, of Pereyaslàv; the cruel Fedorenko, of Kalnik; the wild Pushkarenko, of Poltava, whose command was composed of herdsmen alone; Shumeiko, of Nyejin; the fiery Chernota, of Gadyach; Yakubovich, of Chigirin; besides Nosach, Gladki, Adamovich, Glukh, Pulyan, Panich. Not all the colonels were present; for some were on expeditions, and some were in the other world,--sent there by Prince Yeremi.

The Tartars were not invited this time to the council. The Brotherhood assembled on the square. The crowding multitudes were driven away with clubs and even with whirlbats, on which occasion cases of death were not wanting.

Finally Hmelnitski himself appeared, dressed in red, wearing his cap, the baton in his hand. By his side walked the priest Patroni Lasko, white as a dove; and on the other side Vygovski, carrying papers.

Hmelnitski took a place among the colonels, and sat for a time in silence; then he removed his cap as a sign that the council was open. He rose and began to speak;--

"Gentlemen, colonels, and atamans! It is known to you how we were forced to seize arms on account of the great injustices which we suffered without cause, and with the aid of the most serene Tsar of the Crimea, demand from the Polish lords our ancient rights and privileges, taken from us without the will of his Majesty the King, which undertaking God has blessed; and having sent a terror upon our faithless tyrants, altogether unusual to them, has punished their untruth and oppression, and rewarded us with signal victories, for which we should thank him with grateful hearts. Since, then, their insolence is punished, it is proper for us to think how the shedding of Christian blood may be restrained, which the God of mercy and our orthodox faith command; but not to let the sabres from our hands until our ancient rights and privileges are restored in accordance with the will of his most serene Majesty the King. The voevoda of Bratslav writes me, therefore, that this may come to pass, which I too believe, for it is not we who have left obedience to his Majesty the King and the Commonwealth, but the Pototskis, the Kalinovskis, the Vishnyevetskis, the Konyetspolskis, whom we have punished; therefore a proper concession and reward is due to us from his Majesty and the estates. I beg you therefore, gentlemen, to read the letter of the voevoda of Bratslav, sent to me through Father Patroni Lasko, a noble of the orthodox faith, and to determine wisely whether the spilling of Christian blood is to be restrained, and concessions and rewards made to us for our obedience and loyalty to the Commonwealth."

Hmelnitski did not ask whether the war was to be discontinued, but he asked for a decision to suspend the war. Immediately, therefore, murmurs of discontent were raised, which soon changed into threatening shouts, directed mainly by Chernota of Gadyach.

Hmelnitski was silent, but noted carefully where the protests came from, and fixed firmly in his memory those who opposed him.

Vygovski then rose with the letter of Kisel in his hand. Zorko had brought a copy to be read to the Brotherhood. A deep silence followed. The voevoda began the letter in these words:--

"CHIEF OF THE ZAPOROJIAN ARMY OF THE COMMONWEALTH.

"MY OLD AND DEAR FRIEND,--While there are many who understand you to be an enemy of the Commonwealth, I not only am thoroughly convinced myself of your loyalty to the Commonwealth, but I convince other senators and colleagues of mine of it. Three things are clear to me: First, that though the army of the Dnieper guards its glory and its freedom for centuries, it maintains always its faith to the king, the lords, and the Commonwealth; second, that our Russian people are so firm in their orthodox faith that every one of us prefers to lay down his life rather than to violate that faith in any regard; third, that though there be various internal blood-spillings (as now has happened, God pity us!), still we have all one country in which we were born and use our rights, and there is not indeed in the whole world another such rule and another such land as ours, with respect to rights and liberties. Therefore we are all of us in the same manner accustomed to guard the crown of our mother; and though there be various circumstances (as happens in the world), still reason commands us to consider that it is easier in a free government to make known our injuries than having lost that mother, not to find another such, either in a Christian or a pagan world."

Loboda of Pereyasláv interrupted the reading. "He tells the truth," said he.

"He tells the truth," repeated other colonels.

"Not the truth! He lies, dog-believer!" screamed Chernota.

"Be silent! You are a dog-believer yourself!"

"You are traitors. Death to you!"

"Death to you!"

"Listen; wait awhile! Read! He is one of us. Listen, listen!"

The storm was gathering in good earnest, but Vygovski began to read again. There was silence a second time.

The voevoda wrote, in continuation, that the Zaporojian army should have confidence in him, for they knew well that he, being of the same blood and faith, must wish it well. He wrote that in the unfortunate blood-spilling at Kuméiki and Starets, he had taken no part; then he called on Hmelnitski to put an end to the war, dismiss the Tartars or turn his arms against them, and remain faithful to the Commonwealth. Finally; the letter ended in the following words:--

"I promise you, since I am a son of the Church of God, and as my house comes from the ancient blood of the Russian people, that I shall myself aid in everything just. You know very well that upon me in this Commonwealth (by the mercy of God) something depends, and without me war cannot be declared, nor peace concluded, and that I first do not wish civil war," etc.

Now rose immediate tumult for and against; but on the whole the letter pleased the colonels, and even the Brotherhood. Nevertheless, in the first moment it was impossible to understand or hear anything on account of the fury with which the letter was discussed. The Brotherhood, from a distance, seemed like a great vortex, in which swarms of people were seething and boiling and roaring. The colonels shook their batons, sprang at and thrust their fists in one another's eyes. There were purple faces, inflamed eyes, and foam on the mouth; and the leader of all who called for war was Chernota, who fell into a real frenzy. Hmelnitski too, while looking at his fury, was near an outbreak, before which everything generally grew silent as before the roaring of a lion. But Krechovski, anticipating him, sprang on a bench, waved his baton, and cried with a voice of thunder,--

"Herding oxen is your work, not counselling, you outrageous slaves!"

"Silence! Krechovski wants to speak!" cried Chernota, first, who hoped that the famous colonel would speak for war.

"Silence! silence!" shouted others.

Krechovski was respected beyond measure among the Cossacks, for the important services which he had rendered, for his great military brain, and wonderful to relate, because he was a noble. They were silent at once, therefore, and all waited with curiosity for what he would say. Hmelnitski himself fixed an uneasy glance on him.

But Chernota was mistaken in supposing that the colonel would declare for war. Krechovski, with his quick mind, understood that now or never might he obtain from the Commonwealth those starostaships and dignities of which he dreamed. He understood that at the pacification of the Cossacks they would try to detach and satisfy him before many others, with which Pan Pototski, being in captivity, would not be able to interfere. On this account he spoke as follows:--

"My calling is to give battle, not advice; but as we are in council, I feel impelled to give my present opinion, since I have earned your favor as well if not better than others. Why did we kindle war? We kindled present war for the restoration of our liberties and rights, and the voevoda of Bratslav writes that this restoration will take place. Therefore, either it will, or it will not. If it will not, then war; if it will, peace! Why spill blood in vain? Let them pacify us, and we will pacify the crowd, and the war will stop. Our father Hmelnitski has arranged and thought out all this wisely,--that we are on the side of his Majesty the King, who will give us a reward for that; and if the lordlings will oppose, then he will let us have our sport with them, and we will have it. I should not advise to send the Tartars off; let them arrange themselves in camps in the Wilderness, and stay till we have one thing or another."

Hmelnitski's face brightened when he heard these words; and now the colonels in immense majority, began to call for a suspension of war and an embassy to Warsaw, to ask the Lord of Brusiloff to come in person to negotiate. Chernota still shouted and protested; but the colonel fixed threatening eyes on him and said,--

"You, Chernota, Colonel of Gadyach, call for war and bloodshed; but when the light cavalry of Dmukhovski advanced upon you at Korsún, you squealed like a little pig, 'Oh, brothers, my own brothers, save me!' and you ran away in the face of your whole regiment."

"You lie!" roared Chernota. "I am not afraid of the Poles, nor of you."

Krechovski squeezed the baton in his hand and sprang toward Chernota; others began also to belabor the Gadyach colonel with their fists. The tumult increased. On the square the Brotherhood bellowed like a herd of wild bulls.

Then Hmelnitski himself rose a second time.

"Gentlemen, colonels, friends," said he, "you have decided to send envoys to Warsaw, to mention our faithful services to his most serene Majesty the King, and to ask for a reward. But also whoever wishes war may have it,--not with the king nor the Commonwealth, for we have never carried on war with either, but with our greatest enemy, who is now red with Cossack blood, who at Starets bathed himself in it, and still does not cease to bathe himself, and continues in his hatred of the Zaporojian armies; to whom I sent a letter and envoys asking him to abandon that hatred, but who cruelly murdered my envoys, gave no answer to me, not paying respect to your chief, through which he is guilty of contempt against the whole Zaporojian army. And now, having come from the Trans-Dnieper, he has destroyed Pogrébische, punishing innocent people, for whom I have shed bitter tears. From Pogrébische, as I was informed this morning, he marched to Nyemiroff, and left no person alive there. And since the Tartars from fear and terror will not march against him, he will be seen soon on the way to destroy us here, innocent people, against the will of our affectionate king and the whole Commonwealth; for in his insolence he regards no man, and as he is now rebelling, so is he always ready to rebel against the will of his Majesty the King."

It grew very still in the assembly; Hmelnitski drew breath and spoke on:--

"God has rewarded us with a victory over the hetmans, but Yeremi is worse than the hetmans and all the kinglets,--a son of Satan, living by pure injustice. Against whom I should march myself were it not that in Warsaw he would begin to cry, through his friends, that I do not want peace, and blacken our innocence before the king. That this should not happen, it is necessary that his Majesty the King and the whole Commonwealth should know that I do not want war, that I am sitting here in quiet, and that he first comes on us with war. Therefore I am not able to move, I must remain for negotiations with the voevoda of Bratslav. That he, devil's son, should not break our power, it is necessary to make a stand against him and destroy his power as we did that of our enemies, those gentlemen, the hetmans at Jóltiya Vodi and Korsún. Therefore I ask some of you to go against him of your own will, and I will write to the king that that took place aside from me, and for our absolute defence against the hatred and attacks of Vishnyevetski."

Profound silence reigned in the assembly. Hmelnitski continued:--

"To whomsoever wishes to go on this undertaking I will give men enough, good men, and I will give cannon and artillerists, so that with God's aid he may sweep aside our enemy and gain a victory over him."

But not one of the colonels stepped forward.

"Sixty thousand chosen men I will give," said crafty Hmelnitski.

Silence. And they were all fearless warriors, whose battle-shouts had echoed more than once around the walls of Tsargrad.[12] And perhaps for this very reason each one of them feared to lose the glory he possessed, by meeting the terrible Yeremi.

Hmelnitski eyed the colonels, who under the influence of that glance looked to the ground. The face of Vygovski put on a look of satanic malice.

"I know a hero," said Hmelnitski, mournfully, "who would speak at this moment, and not avoid this work, but he is not among us."

"Bogun!" exclaimed some voices.

"Yes. He has already swept away Yeremi's garrison at Vassílyevka; but they wounded him in the engagement, and he lies now in Cherkasi struggling with Mother Death. And since he is not here, there is no one here as I see. Where is Cossack renown? Where are the Pavlyuks, the Nalivaikas, the Lobodas, and the Ostranitsas?"

A short, thick man, with a blue and gloomy face, and a mustache red as fire over a crooked mouth, and with green eyes, rose from the bench, pushed forward toward Hmelnitski, and said, "I will go." This was Maksim Krívonos.

Shouts of "Glory to him!" rose in thunder; but he stood with his baton at his side, and spoke with a hoarse and halting voice,--

"Do not think, Hetman, that I feel fear. I should have stood up at first, but I thought, 'There are better than I!' But matters being as they are, I will go. Who are you? [turning to the colonels]. You are the heads and the hands; but I have no head, only hands and a sword. Once my mother bore me! War is my mother and my sister. Vishnyevetski slaughters, I will slaughter; he hangs, and I will hang. But you, Hetman, give me good warriors; for with a mob you can do nothing with Vishnyevetski. And so I go to take castles, kill, slaughter, hang! Death to the white hands!"

Another ataman stepped forward. "I will go with you, Maksim." This was Pulyan.

"And Chernota of Gadyach, and Gladki of Mirgorod, and Nosach will go with you," said Hmelnitski.

"We will," said they, in one voice; for the example of Krívonos roused them, and courage entered them.

"Against Yeremi, against Yeremi!" thundered shouts through the assembly. "Cut! slay!" repeated the Brotherhood; and after a time the council became a carousal. The regiments assigned to Krívonos drank deeply, for they were going to death. They knew this well themselves, but there was no fear in their hearts. "Once our mother bore us!" repeated they after their leader; and on this account they spared nothing on themselves, as is usual before death. Hmelnitski permitted and encouraged this; the crowd followed their example. The legions began to sing songs in a hundred thousand voices. Horses let loose and prancing through the camp raised clouds of dust, and caused indescribable disorder. They were chased with cries and shouts and laughter. Great crowds loitered along the river, fired muskets, crowded and pushed to the quarters of the hetman himself, who finally ordered Yakubovich to drive them away. Then began fighting and confusion, till a drenching rain drove them all to the wagons and tents.

In the evening a storm burst forth in the sky. Thunder rolled from one end of the clouds, to the other; lightning flashed through the whole country, now with white and now with ruddy blaze. In the light of these flashes Krívonos marched out of camp at the head of sixty thousand men,--some from the best warriors, the rest from the mob.

CHAPTER XXVII.

Krívonos marched then from Bélaya Tserkoff through Skvira and Pogrébische to Makhnovka. Wherever he passed, traces of human habitation vanished. Whoever did not join him perished under the knife. Grain was burned standing, with forests and gardens. At the same time the prince carried annihilation in his hand. After the razing of Pogrébische, and the baptism of blood which Pan Baranovski gave to Nyemiroff, the prince's army destroyed a number of other considerable bands, and halted in camp at Raigorod, where during a month they scarcely got off their horses. They were weakened by toil, and death had decreased them notably. Rest was necessary, for the hands of these reapers in the harvest of blood had relaxed. The prince wavered, therefore, and thought whether it would not be better to go for a time to a more peaceable region to rest and recruit his forces, especially his horses, which were more like skeletons of beasts than living creatures, since they had not eaten grain for a month, subsisting only on trampled grass.

But after they had halted a week tidings were brought that reinforcements were coming. The prince went out to meet them, and really met Pan Yanush Tishkyevich, the voevoda of Kieff, who came with fifteen hundred good men, and with him Pan Krishtof Tishkyevich, under-judge of Bratslav; young Pan Aksak, quite a youth yet, but with a well-armed company of his own; and many nobles, such as the Senyuts, the Palubinskis, the Jitinskis, the Yelovitskis, the Kyerdéis, the Boguslavskis,--some with escorts, others without. The entire force formed nearly two thousand horse, besides attendants.

The prince was greatly pleased, and invited thankfully to his quarters the voevoda, who could not cease wondering at the poverty and simplicity of the place. For the prince, by so much as he lived like a king in Lubni, by that much did he permit himself no comfort in the field, wishing to give an example to the soldiers. He lived therefore in one room, which the voevoda of Kieff, squeezing through the narrow door, was hardly able to enter, by reason of his enormous thickness, till he ordered his attendant to push him from behind. In the cottage, besides the table, wooden benches, and a bed covered with horse-skin, there was nothing except a little room near the door, in which an attendant slept, always ready for service. This simplicity greatly astonished the voevoda, who lived in comfort and carried carpets with him. He entered finally, and gazed with curiosity on the prince, wondering how so great a spirit could find its place in such simplicity and poverty. He had seen Yeremi from time to time at the Diets in Warsaw, was in fact a distant relative of his, but did not know him intimately. Now, when he began to speak with him, he recognized at once that he had to do with an extraordinary man; and he, an old senator and soldier, who used to clap his senatorial colleagues on the shoulders, and say to Prince Dominik Zaslavski, "My dear," and was familiar with the king himself, could not attain familiarity like this with Vishnyevetski, though the prince received him kindly, for he was thankful for the reinforcements.

"Worthy voevoda," said he, "praise be to God that you have come with your people, for I have worked here to my last breath."

"I have noticed, by your soldiers, that they have worked, poor fellows, which disturbs me not a little, for I have come with the request that you hasten to save me."

"And is there hurry?"

"Periculum in mora, periculum in mora! Ruffians to the number of several thousand have appeared, with Krívonos at their head, who, as I have heard, was sent against you; but having received information that you had moved on Konstantinoff, he went there, and on the road has invested Makhnovka, and has wrought such desolation that no tongue can describe it."

"I have heard of Krívonos, and waited for him here; but since I find that he has missed me, I must seek him. Really the affair will not bide delay. Is there a strong garrison in Makhnovka?"

"There are two hundred Germans in the castle, very good men, who will hold out yet for some time. But the worst is, that many nobles have assembled in the town with their families, and the place is fortified only by earthworks and palisades, and cannot resist long."

"In truth, the affair suffers no delay," repeated the prince. Then turning to his attendant, he said: "Jelenksi, run for the colonels!"

The voevoda of Kieff was sitting meanwhile on a bench, and panting. He had some expectation of supper; for he was hungry, and liked good eating.

Presently the tramp of armed men was heard, and the prince's officers entered,--black, thin, bearded, with sunken eyes, with traces of indescribable labor on their faces. They bowed in silence to the prince and his guests, and waited for his words.

"Gentlemen, are the horses at their places?"

"Yes, ready as always."

"It is well. In an hour we will move on Krívonos."

"Hi!" said the voevoda of Kieff; and he looked in wonderment at Pan Kryshtof, the sub-judge of Bratslav.

The prince continued: "Ponyatovski and Vershul will march first; after them Baranovski will go with his dragoons, and in an hour we will move with the cannon of Vurtsel."

The colonels bowed and left the room, and soon the trumpets were heard sounding to horse. The voevoda of Kieff did not expect such haste, and did not indeed wish it, since he was hungry and tired. He counted on resting about a day with the prince, and then moving. Now he would have to mount his horse at once, without sleeping or eating.

"But, your Highness," said he, "are your soldiers able to reach Makhnovka? I see they are terribly tired, and the road is a long one."

"Don't let your head ache over that. They go to a battle as to a concert."

"I see that; I see they are sulphurous fellows. But my men are road-weary."

"You have just said, 'Periculum in mora.'"

"Yes; but we might rest for the night. We have come from near Hmelnik."

"Worthy voevoda, we have come from Lubni and the Trans-Dnieper."

"We were a whole day on the road."

"We a whole month."

The prince went out to arrange in person the order of march. The voevoda stared at the under-judge, struck his palms on his knees, and said,--

"Ah! I have got what I wanted, you see. As God lives, he will kill me with hunger. Here is swimming in hot water for you! I come for aid, and think that after great solicitation they will move in two or three days; but now they won't give us time to draw breath. May the devil take them! The stirrup-strap has galled my leg; my traitor of an attendant buckled it badly. My stomach is empty. The devil take them! Makhnovka is Makhnovka; but my stomach is my stomach. I am an old soldier, have fought in more wars probably than he has, but never in such helter-skelter fashion. Those are devils, not men; they don't eat, don't sleep,--just fight. As God is dear to me, they never eat anything. They look like ghosts, don't they?"

"Yes; but they have fiery courage," answered Pan Kryshtof, who was in love with soldier life. "God bless us, what disorder and tumult in other camps when it comes to marching--how much running, arranging wagons, sending for horses! But now, do you hear? the light cavalry is on the march."

"Is it possible? Why, this is terrible," said the voevoda.

But young Pan Aksak clasped his boyish hands. "Ah, that is a mighty leader!" said he in ecstasy.

"Oh, there is milk under your nose!" snapped the voevoda. "Cunctator too was a great leader! Do you understand?"

At this moment the prince came in. "Gentlemen, to horse! We march."

The voevoda did not restrain himself. "Order something for us to eat. Prince, for I am hungry," cried he, in an outburst of ill-humor.

"Oh, my worthy voevoda," said the prince, laughing and taking hold of him by the shoulder, "forgive me, forgive me! With all my heart. But in war one forgets these things."

"Well, Pan Kryshtof, haven't I told you that they don't eat?" asked the voevoda, turning to the under-judge of Bratslav.

The supper did not last long, and a couple of hours later even the infantry had left Raigorod. The army marched through Vinnitsa and Litin to Hmelnik; on the way Vershul met a Tartar party in Saverovka, which he and Volodyovski destroyed, and freed a few hundred captives,-- almost all young women. There began the ruined country; all around were traces of the hand of Krívonos. Strijavka was burned, and its population put to death in a terrible manner. Apparently the unfortunates had resisted Krívonos; therefore the savage chief had delivered them to sword and flame. On an oak-tree at the entrance to the village hung Pan Strijovski himself, whom Tishkyevich's men recognized at once. He was entirely naked, and had around his neck an enormous necklace of heads strung on a rope; they were the heads of his wife and six children. Everything in the village itself was burned to the ground. They saw on both sides of the road a long row of "Cossack candles,"--that is, people with hands raised above their heads, and tied to stakes driven into the ground, wound around with straw steeped in pitch and set on fire at the hands. The greater part of them had only their hands burned, for the rain had evidently stopped the further burning. But those bodies were terrible, with their distorted faces and black stumps of hands stretched to heaven. The odor of putrefaction spread round about. Above the stakes whirled circles of ravens and crows, which at the approach of the troops flew away with an uproar from the nearer stakes to sit on the farther ones. A number of wolves galloped off before the regiments to the thicket. The men marched on in silence through the alley, and counted the "candles." There were between three and four hundred of them.

They passed at length that unfortunate village, and breathed the fresh air of the field. But traces of destruction extended farther. It was the first half of July. The grain was almost ripe, for an early harvest was looked for. But entire fields were partly burned, partly trampled, tangled, trodden into the earth. It might have been thought that a hurricane had passed over the land. In fact, the most terrible of all hurricanes had passed,--civil war. The soldiers of the prince had seen more than once rich neighborhoods ruined by Tartar raids; but such a storm, such mad destruction, they had never seen. Forests were burned as well as grain. Where fire had not devoured the trees the bark and leaves were swept from them by a tongue of fire; they were scorched by its breath, smoked, blackened, and the tree-trunk stuck up like a skeleton. The voevoda of Kieff looked, and could not believe his eyes. Maidyanóe, Zbar,--villages, houses,--nothing but burned ruins! On one side and another the men had run off to Krívonos; the women and children had been taken captive by that part of the horde which Vershul and Volodyovski had crushed out. On the earth a wilderness; in the air flocks of ravens, crows, jackdaws, and vultures, which had flown hither, God knows whence, to the Cossack harvest. Fresher traces of the passage of troops were seen each moment. From time to time they came upon broken wagons, bodies of cattle and men not yet decayed, broken cups, brass kettles, bags of wet flour, ruins still smoking, stacks of grain recently begun and left unfinished.

The prince urged his regiments on to Hmelnik without drawing breath. The old voevoda seized himself by the head, repeating sadly,--

"My Makhnovka, my Makhnovka! I see we shall not come in time."

Meanwhile news was brought to Hmelnik that Makhnovka was besieged, not by old Krívonos himself, but by his son with several thousand men, and that it was he who had committed such inhuman devastations along the road. The place was already taken, according to accounts. The Cossacks on capturing it had cut to pieces the nobles and the Jews, and taken the women of the nobles to camp, where a fate worse than death awaited them. But the castle, under the leadership of Pan Lyeff, held out yet. The Cossacks stormed it from the Bernardine monastery, in which they had put the monks to death. Pan Lyeff, using all his strength and powder, gave no hope of holding out longer than one night.

The prince therefore left the infantry, the guns, and the main strength of the army, which he ordered to go to Bystrika, and galloped on to the relief with the voevoda, Pan Kryshtof, Pan Aksak, and two thousand soldiers. The old voevoda was for delay, for he had lost his head.

"Makhnovka is lost! We shall arrive too late! We would better leave it, defend other places, and provide them with garrisons."

But the prince would not listen to him. The under-judge of Bratslav urged the advance, and the troops rushed to the fight.

"Since we have come thus far, we will not leave without blood," said the colonels; and they went on.

About two miles and a half from Makhnovka a few riders, moving as fast as their horses could carry them, halted in front of the troops. It was Pan Lyeff and his companions. Seeing him, the voevoda of Kieff guessed at once what had happened.

"The castle is taken!" he cried.

"It is!" answered Pan Lyeff; and that moment he fainted, for he was cut with swords, was shot through, and had lost much blood. But the others began to tell what had taken place. The Germans on the wall were cut down to the last man, for they preferred to die rather than yield. Pan Lyeff had forced his way through the thick of the mob and the broken gates. In the rooms of the tower a few tens of nobles were defending themselves; to those speedy succor should be given.

The cavalry swept on with all speed. Soon the town and castle were visible on a hill, and above them a dense cloud of smoke from the fire which had already begun. The day was coming to an end. The sky was flushed with gigantic golden and purple lights, which the troops mistook at once for a conflagration. By these flashes the Zaporojian regiments could be seen, and dense masses of a mob rushing through the gates to meet the Polish troops,--the more confidently since no one in the town knew of the approach of Yeremi. It was supposed that the voevoda of Kieff alone was marching with succor. It was evident that vudka had blinded them entirely, or the recent capture of the castle had inspired them with immeasurable insolence; for they descended the hill boldly, and only when they had reached the plain did they form for battle, which they did with great readiness, thundering with their drums and trumpets. In view of this a shout of joy went up from every Polish breast, and the voevoda of Kieff had an opportunity to admire a second time the discipline of Vishnyevetski's troops. Halting in view of the Cossacks, they formed at once in battle-array, the heavy cavalry in the centre, the light horse at the wings, so that there was no necessity of manœuvres, they could begin on the spot.

"Oh, Pan Kryshtof, what men!" said the voevoda. "They fell into order at once; they could give battle without a leader."

But the prince, like a provident chief, flew, with baton in hand, between the companies, examined, and gave final orders. The evening twilight was reflected on his silver armor, and he was like a bright flame flying between the ranks, he alone glistening amid the dark armor.

Three regiments formed the centre of the foremost line. The first of these was led by the voevoda of Kieff himself, the second by young Pan Aksak, the third by Pan Kryshtof Tishkyevich; after these, in the second line, were the dragoons under Baranovski, and finally the gigantic hussars of the prince, led by Pan Yan. Vershul, Kushel, and Ponyatovski occupied the wings. There were no cannon, for Vurtsel had remained in Bystrika. The prince galloped to the voevoda, motioned with his baton, and said,--

"Do you begin, because of the injustice done you!"

The voevoda in turn waved his hand; the soldiers bent in their saddles and moved on. It was evident at once by his style of leadership that the voevoda, though heavy and dilatory,--for he was bent with age,--was an experienced and valiant soldier. To spare his troops he did not start them at the highest speed, but led them slowly, quickening the march as he approached the enemy. He went himself in the front rank, with baton in hand; his attendant merely carried his long and heavy sword, but not heavy for the hand of the old voevoda. The mob on foot hurried with scythes and flails against the cavalry, in order to restrain the first impetus and lighten the attack for the Zaporojians. When they were separated by only a few tens of yards, the people of Makhnovka recognized the voevoda by his gigantic stature and corpulence, and began to cry out,--

"Hi! serene great mighty voevoda, the harvest is near; why don't you order out your subjects? Our respects, serene lord! We will perforate that stomach of yours."

They sent a shower of bullets on the cavalry, but without harm, for the horses were going like a whirlwind and struck mightily. The clatter of flails and the sound of scythes were heard on the armor; then cries and groans. The lances opened a way in the dense mass of the mob, through which the infuriated horses rushed like a tempest, trampling, overturning, mashing. And as on the meadow when a rank of mowers advance, the rich grass disappears before them and they go on swinging the handles of their scythes, just so did the broad avalanche of the mob contract, melt, disappear, pushed by the breasts of horses. Unable to keep their places, they began to waver. Then thundered the shout, "Save yourselves!" and the whole mass, throwing down scythes, flails, forks, guns, rushed back in wild dismay on the Zaporojian regiments behind. But the Zaporojians, fearing lest the fleeing throng should disorder their ranks, placed their lances against them; the mob, seeing this resistance, rushed with a howl of despair to both sides, but were immediately hurled back by Kushel and Ponyatovski, who had just moved from the wings of the prince's division.

The voevoda, now riding over the bodies of the mob, was in the front of the Zaporojians and rushed toward them. They too rushed at him, wishing to answer momentum with momentum. They struck each other like two waves going in opposite directions, which when they meet form a foaming ridge. So horses rose before horses, the riders like a wave, the swords above the wave like foam. The voevoda discovered that he was not working with a mob now, but with stern and trained Zaporojian warriors. The two lines pressed each other mutually, bent, neither being able to break the other. Bodies fell thickly, for there man met man, and steel struck steel. The voevoda himself, putting his baton under his belt, and taking the sword from his attendant, worked in the sweat of his brow, puffing like a blacksmith's bellows. And with him the two Senyuts, the Kyerdéis, the Boguslavskis, the Yelovitskis, and the Polubinskis wriggled as if in boiling water.

But on the Cossack side the fiercest of all was Ivan Burdabut, the lieutenant-colonel of the Kalnik regiment, a Cossack of gigantic strength and stature. He was the more terrible because he had a horse which fought as well as its master. More than one man reined in his steed and drew back so as not to meet that centaur spreading death and desolation. The brothers Senyut sprang at him; but the horse caught in its teeth the face of Andrei the younger and mashed it in the twinkle of an eye. Seeing this, the elder brother, Rafal, struck the beast above the eyes; he wounded, but did not kill it, for the sabre hit the great bronze button on the forehead of the horse. At that moment Burdabut plunged a weapon under the beard of Senyut, and deprived him of life. So fell the two brothers, and lay in their gilded armor in the dust, under the hoofs of horses; but Burdabut rushed on like a flame to more distant ranks, and struck in a flash the attendant of Prince Polubinski, a sixteen-year-old stripling, whose right shoulder he cut off together with the arm. Seeing this, Pan Urbanski, wishing to avenge the death of a relative, tired at Burdabut in the very face, but missed,--only shot away his ear and dashed him with blood. Terrible then was Burdabut with his horse, both black as night, both covered with blood, both with wild eyes and distended nostrils, raging like a tempest. And Pan Urbanski did not escape death; for like an executioner, Burdabut cut off his head with a blow, and the head of old Jitinski in his eightieth year, and the heads of the two Nikchemnis, each with one stroke. Others began to draw back with terror, especially as behind the Cossack gleamed a hundred Zaporojian sabres, and a hundred lances, already moistened in blood.

The furious chief saw at last the voevoda, and giving an awful shout of joy, hurried toward him, hurling down horses and riders in his path. But the voevoda did not retreat. Trusting in his uncommon strength, puffing like a wounded wild boar, he raised the sword above his head and urging on his horse rushed to Burdabut. His end would have come without doubt,--and Fate had already caught in her shears the thread of his life, which she afterward cut in Okra-- had not Silnitski, his sword-bearer, hurled himself like lightning on the Cossack and seized him by the waist before his sword was satisfied. While Burdabut was putting him aside, the Kyerdéis shouted, summoning assistance for the voevoda; several tens of people sprang forth at once, and separated him from Burdabut. Then a stubborn fight set in. But the wearied regiments of the voevoda began to yield to greater Zaporojian strength, draw back, and break ranks, when Pan Kryshtof, under-judge of Bratslav, and Pan Aksak hurried up with fresh regiments. True, new Cossack regiments rushed in at that moment to the fight; but still below stood the prince, with the dragoons of Baranovski and the hussars of Skshetuski, who had taken no part as yet in the action.

Then the bloody conflict raged anew. Darkness had already fallen, but flames had caught the outer houses of the town. The fire lighted the field of struggle, and both lines, Polish and Cossack, were seen distinctly pounding each other at the foot of the hill; the colors of the standards could be seen, and even the faces of the men. Vershul, Ponyatovski, and Kushel had already been in fire and action; for having finished with the mob, they struck the Cossack wings, which under their pressure began to move toward the hill. The long line of combatants bent its ends toward the town, and began to extend out more and more; for when the Polish wings advanced, the centre, pressed by superior Cossack power, retreated toward the prince. Three new Cossack regiments went to break it; but at that moment the prince pushed on Baranovski's dragoons, and these raised the strength of the combatants.

The hussars alone remained with the prince. From a distance they seemed like a dark grove growing straight from the ground,--a terrible avalanche of iron men, horses, and lances. The breeze of evening stirred the banners above their heads, and they stood quietly, not fretting for battle before the issue of command; patient, for trained and experienced in many a fight they knew that their portion of blood would not miss them. The prince, in his silver armor, with gilded baton in hand, strained his eyes toward the battle; and on the left wing Skshetuski, standing a little sideways at the end,--being lieutenant, his sleeve was rolled up on his shoulder,--with arm bare to the elbow, and holding in his powerful hand a broadsword instead of a baton, waited calmly for the order.

The prince shaded with his left hand his eyes from the glare of the burning. The centre of the Polish half-circle retreated gradually toward him, overborne by superior power which was not long kept back by Pan Baranovski,--the same who had razed Nyemiroff. The prince saw, as if on his hand, the heavy work of the soldiers. The long lightning of sabres raised itself above the black line of heads, then vanished in the blows. Riderless horses dropped out of that avalanche of combatants, and neighing ran along the plain with floating mane; the flames of the burning for a background, they were like beasts of hell. The red banner floating for a time over the throng fell suddenly to rise no more; but the eye of the prince ran along the line of combat as far as the hill toward the town, where at the head of two picked regiments stood young Krívonos, waiting the moment to hurl himself on the centre and break the weakened ranks of the Poles.

At length he started, running with a terrible shout straight on the dragoons of Baranovski; but the prince was waiting for that moment too.

"Lead on!" cried he to Skshetuski.

Skshetuski raised his broadsword, and the iron host shot past.

They did not run long, for the line of battle had approached them considerably. Baranovski's dragoons opened to the right and left with lightning speed to clear a way for the hussars against the Cossacks. The hussars swept through this pass with their whole momentum against the victorious companies of Krívonos.

"Yeremi! Yeremi!" shouted the hussars.

"Yeremi!" repeated the whole army.

The terrible name contracted the hearts of the Zaporojians with a shudder of fear. In that moment they learned for the first time that it was not the voevoda of Kieff who was leading, but the prince himself. Besides, they were unable to resist the hussars, who crushed them with their weight as falling walls crush people standing beneath. The only safety for them was to open toward both sides, let the hussars through, and then strike them on the flanks; but those flanks were already guarded by the dragoons and light horse of Vershul, Kushel, and Ponyatovski, who, having dislodged the Cossack wings, pushed them to the centre. Now the form of battle changed, for the light regiments became as it were the two sides of a street, along the centre of which flew the hussars with wild impetus, driving, breaking, pushing, overturning men and horses; and before them fled bellowing and howling the Cossacks to the hill and the town. If the wing of Vershul had been able to join the wing of Ponyatovski, the Cossacks would have been surrounded and cut to pieces; but neither Vershul nor Ponyatovski could make the junction by reason of the exceeding rush of fugitives, whom they struck, however, at the flanks till their arms grew weak from cutting.

Young Krívonos, though valiant and furious, when he understood that his own inexperience had to meet such a leader as the prince, lost presence of mind and fled at the head of others to the town. Pan Kushel, who was nearsighted, standing at the flank, saw the fugitive, urged on his horse, and gave the young leader a sabre-stroke in the face. He did not kill him, for his helmet turned the sword-edge; but he sprinkled him with blood and deprived him still more of courage. He came near paying for the deed with his life, for that moment Burdabut turned on him with the remnant of the Kalnik regiment.

Twice had Burdabut tried to make head against the hussars, but, twice pushed back and beaten by a power as if supernatural, he was obliged to give way with the rest. At last, having collected his men, he determined to strike Kushel on the flank and burst through his dragoons to the open field; but before he could break them the road to the town and the hill was so packed with people that a quick retreat became impossible. The hussars, in view of this press of men, restrained their onset, and having broken their lances, began to hew with swords. Then there was a struggle, confused, disorderly, furious, merciless, seething in the press, uproar, and heat, amid the steam from men and horses. Body fell upon body, horses' hoofs sank in the quivering flesh. At points the masses were so dense that there was no room for sabre-strokes; so they fought with the hilts, with knives, with fists. Horses began to whine. Here and there voices were heard: "Mercy, Poles!" These voices grew louder, increased, outsounded the clash of swords, the bite of iron on the bones of men, the groans and the terrible death-rattle of the perishing. "Mercy, mercy!" was heard with increasing plaintiveness; but mercy shone not above that avalanche of stragglers as the sun above a storm; only the flames of the town shone above them.

But Burdabut at the head of the men of Kalnik asked for no mercy. He lacked room for battle. He opened a way with his dagger. He met the big Pan Dzik, and punching him in the stomach rolled him from his horse. Dzik, crying, "O Jesus!" raised himself no more from under the hoofs which tore out his entrails. There was room enough at once. Burdabut laid open with his sabre the head and helmet of Sokolski; then he brought down, together with their horses, Pans Priyam and Chertovich, and there was still more room. Young Zenobius Skalski slashed at his head, but the sabre turned in his hand and struck with its side. Burdabut gave Skalski a back-hand blow with his left fist in the face, and killed him on the spot. The men of Kalnik followed him, cutting and stabbing with their daggers. "A wizard! a wizard!" the hussars began to cry out. "Iron cannot harm him! he is frantic!" He had foam on his mustaches, and rage in his eyes. At last Burdabut saw Skshetuski, and recognizing an officer by the upturned sleeve, rushed upon him.

All held their breaths, and the battle stopped, looking at the struggle of the two terrible knights. Pan Yan was not frightened at the cry of "Wizard;" but anger boiled in his breast at the sight of so much destruction. He ground his teeth and pushed on the enemy with fury. The horses of both were thrown on their haunches. The whistle of steel was heard, and suddenly the sabre of the Cossack flew into pieces under the blow of the Polish sword. It seemed as if no power could save Burdabut, when he sprang and grappled with Skshetuski, so that both appeared to form one body, and a knife gleamed above the throat of the hussar.

Death stood before the eyes of Pan Yan at that moment, for he could not use his sword. But quick as lightning he dropped the sword, which hung by a strap, and seized the hand of the enemy in his own. For a while the two hands trembled convulsively in the air; but iron must have been the grip of Pan Yan, for the Cossack howled like a wolf, and before the eyes of all the knife fell from his stiffened fingers as grain is squeezed out of its husk. Skshetuski let drop the crushed hand, and grasping the Cossack by the shoulder bent his terrible forehead to the pummel of the saddle, then drawing with his left hand the baton from his own belt, he struck once, twice. Burdabut coughed, and fell from his horse.

At the sight of this the men of Kalnik groaned and hastened to take vengeance. Now the hussars sprang forward and cut them to pieces.

At the other end of the hussar avalanche the battle did not cease for a moment, for the throng was less dense. Pan Longin, girt with Anusia's scarf, raged with his broadsword. The morning after the battle the knights looked with wonder on those places, pointing out shoulders cut off with armor, heads split from the forehead to the beard, bodies cut into halves, an entire road of men and horses. They whispered to one another, "See, Podbipienta fought here!" The prince himself examined the bodies; and though that morning he was very much afflicted by various reports, he wondered, for he had never seen such blows in his life.

But meanwhile the battle seemed to approach its end. The heavy cavalry pushed on again, driving before it the Zaporojian regiments which were seeking refuge in the direction of the hill and the town. The regiments of Kushel and Ponyatovski barred return to the fugitives. Surrounded on all sides, they defended themselves to the very last; but with their death they saved others, for two hours later when Volodyovski entered the place in advance with his Tartars of the guard, he did not find a single Cossack. The enemy, taking advantage of the darkness,--for rain had put out the fire,--had seized the empty wagons of the town in a hurry, and forming a train with that quickness peculiar to Cossacks alone, left the town, passed the river, and destroyed the bridges behind them.

The few tens of nobles who had defended themselves in the castle were liberated. Then the prince commanded Vershul to punish the townspeople who had joined the Cossacks, and set out in pursuit of the enemy himself. But he could not capture the tabor without cannon and infantry. The enemy having gained time by burning the bridges, for it was necessary to go far along the river around a dam to cross, disappeared so quickly that the wearied horses of the prince's cavalry were barely able to come up with them. Still the Cossacks, though famous for fighting in tabors, did not defend themselves so bravely as usual. The terrible certainty that the prince himself was pursuing them, so deprived them of courage that they despaired of escape altogether. Their end would surely have come,--for after a whole night's firing Baranovski had seized forty wagons and two cannon,--had it not been for the voevoda of Kieff, who opposed further pursuit and withdrew his men. Between him and the prince sharp words arose, which were heard by many of the colonels.

"Why do you," asked the prince, "wish to let the enemy escape, when you showed such bravery against them in battle? The glory which you won yesterday, you have lost to-day by negligence."

"I do not know," said the voevoda, "what spirit lives in you, but I am a man of flesh and blood. After labor I need rest; so do my men. I shall always attack the enemy as I have to-day, when they present a front, but I will not pursue them when defeated and fleeing."

"Cut them to pieces!" shouted the prince.

"What will come of that work?" asked the voevoda. "If we destroy these people, the elder Krívonos will come, burn, destroy, kill, as his son has in Strijavka, and innocent people will suffer for our rage."

"Oh, I see," said the prince, with anger, "you belong with the chancellor and with those commanders of theirs, to the peace faction, which would put down rebellion through negotiations; but, by the living God, nothing will come of that as long as I have a sabre in my fist!"

To this Tishkyevich answered: "I belong not to a faction, but to God,--for I am an old man, and shall soon have to stand before him; and be not surprised if I do not wish to have too great a burden of blood, shed in civil war, weighing me down. If you are angry because the command passed you by, then I say that for bravery the command belonged to you rightly. Still perhaps it is better that they did not give it to you, for you would have drowned not the rebellion alone in blood, but with it this unhappy country."

The Jupiter brows of Yeremi contracted, his neck swelled, and his eyes began to throw out such lightning that all present were alarmed for the voevoda; but at that moment Pan Yan approached quickly, and said,--

"Your Highness, there is news of the elder Krívonos."

Immediately the thoughts of the prince were turned in another direction, and his anger against the voevoda decreased. In the mean while four men were brought in who had come with tidings. Two of them were orthodox priests, who on seeing the prince threw themselves on their knees before him.

"Save us! save us!" cried they, stretching their hands to him.

"Whence do you come?"

"We are from Polónnoe. The elder Krívonos has invested the castle and the town; if your sabre is not raised above his neck, we shall all perish."

The prince answered: "I know that a mass of people have taken refuge there in Polónnoe, but mostly Russians, as I am informed. Your merit before God is that instead of joining the rebellion you oppose it and remain with your mother the Commonwealth; still I fear some treason on your part, such as I found in Nyemiroff."

Thereupon the envoys began to swear by all the saints in heaven that they were waiting for him as a savior, as prince, and that there was not a thought of treason in them. They spoke the truth; for Krívonos, having surrounded them with fifty thousand men, vowed their destruction for this special reason,--that, being Russians, they would not join the rebellion.

The prince promised them aid; but since his main forces were in Bystrika, he was obliged to wait. The envoys went away with consolation in their hearts. The prince turned to the voevoda, and said,--

"Pardon me! I see now that we must let the young Krívonos go, so as to catch the old one. I judge therefore that you will not leave me in this undertaking."

"Of course not!" answered the voevoda.

Then the trumpets sounded the retreat to the regiments who had followed the Cossacks. It was necessary to rest and eat, and let the horses draw breath. In the evening a whole division arrived from Bystrika, and with it Pan Stakhovich, an envoy from the voevoda of Bratslav. Pan Kisel wrote the prince a letter full of homage, saying that like a second Marius he was saving the country from the last abyss; he wrote also of the joy which the arrival of the prince from the Trans-Dnieper roused in all hearts, and wished him success; but at the end of the letter appeared the reason for which it was written. Kisel stated that negotiations had been begun, that he with other commissioners was going to Bélaya Tserkoff, and had hopes of restraining and satisfying Hmelnitski. Finally he begged the prince not to press so hard on the Cossacks before negotiations, and to desist from military action as far as possible.

If the prince had been told that all his Trans-Dnieper possessions were destroyed, and all the towns levelled to the earth, he would not have been pained so acutely as he was over that letter. Skshetuski, Baranovski, Zatsvilikhovski, the two Tishkyevichi, and the Kyerdéis were present. The prince covered his eyes with his hands, and pushed back his head as if an arrow had struck him in the heart.

"Disgrace! disgrace! God grant me to die rather than behold such things!"

Deep silence reigned among those present, and the prince continued,--

"I do not wish to live in this Commonwealth, for to-day I must be ashamed of it. The Cossack and the peasant mob have poured blood on the country, and joined pagandom against their own mother. The hetmans are beaten, the armies swept away. The fame of the nation is trampled upon, its majesty insulted, churches are burned, priests and nobles cut down, women dishonored, and what answer does the Commonwealth give to all these defeats and this shame, at the very remembrance of which our ancestors would have died? Here it is! She begins negotiations with the traitor, the disgracer, the ally of the Pagan, and offers him satisfaction. Oh, God grant me death! I repeat it, since there is no life in the world for us who feel the dishonor of our country and bring our heads as a sacrifice for it."

The voevoda of Kieff was silent, and the under-judge of Bratslav answered after a while,--

"Pan Kisel does not compose the Commonwealth."

"Do not speak to me of Pan Kisel," said the prince; "for I know well that he has a whole party behind him. He has struck the mind of the primate, the chancellor, and Prince Dominik, and many lords who to-day in the interregnum bear rule in the Commonwealth and represent its majesty, but rather disgrace it by weakness unworthy of a great people; for this conflagration is to be quenched by blood, and not by negotiations, since it is better for a knightly nation to perish than to become low-lived and rouse the contempt of the whole world for themselves."

The prince again covered his eyes with his hands. The sight of that pain and sorrow was so sad that the colonels knew not what to do by reason of the tears that came into their eyes.

"Your Highness," Zatsvilikhovski made bold to say, "let them use their tongues; we will continue to use our swords."

"True," answered the prince; "and my heart is rent with the thought of what we shall do farther on. When we heard of the defeat of our country we came through burning forests and impassable swamps, neither sleeping nor eating, using the last power we had to save our mother from destruction and disgrace. Our hands drop down from toil, hunger is gnawing our entrails, wounds are torturing us, but we regard no toil if we can only stop the enemy. They say that I am angry because command has not come to me. Let the whole world judge if those are more fitted for it who got it; but I, gentlemen, take God and you to witness that I as well as you do not bring my blood in sacrifice for rewards and dignities, but out of pure love for the country. But when we are giving the last breath in our bodies, what do they tell us? Well, that the gentlemen in Warsaw, and Pan Kisel in Gushchi are thinking of satisfaction for our enemy. Infamy, infamy!"

"Kisel is a traitor!" cried Baranovski.

Thereupon Pan Stakhovich, a man of dignity and courage, rose, and turning to Baranovski, said,--

"Being a friend of the voevoda of Bratslav, and an envoy from him, I permit no man to call him a traitor. His beard too has grown gray from trouble, and he serves his country according to his understanding,--it may be mistakenly, but honorably!"

The prince did not hear this answer, for he was plunged in meditation and in pain. Baranovski did not dare to pick a quarrel in his presence; he only fastened his eyes steadily on Pan Stakhovich, as if wishing to say, "I shall find you," and put his hand on his sword-hilt.

Meanwhile Yeremi recovered from his revery, and said gloomily: "There is no other choice but to fail in upholding obedience (for during the interregnum they are the government) or the honor of our country for which we are laboring to devote--"

"From disobedience flows all the evil in the Commonwealth," said the voevoda of Kieff, with seriousness.

"Are we therefore to permit the disgrace of our country? And if to-morrow we are commanded to go with ropes around our necks to Tugai Bey and Hmelnitski, are we to do that for obedience' sake?"

"Veto!" called Pan Kryshtof.

"Veto!" repeated Kyerdéi.

The prince turned to the colonels. "Speak, veterans!" said he.

Pan Zatsvilikhovski began: "Your Highness, I am seventy years old. I am an orthodox Russian, I was a Cossack commissioner, and Hmelnitski himself called me father, and ought rather to speak for negotiations; but if I have to speak for *disgrace* or *war*, then till I go to the grave I shall say war!"

"War!" said Skshetuski.

"War, war!" repeated several voices, in fact those of all present. "War, war!"

"Let it be according to your words," said the prince, seriously; and he struck the open letter of Kisel with his baton.

CHAPTER XXVIII.

A day later, when the army halted in Ryltsoff, the prince summoned Pan Yan and said,--

"Our forces are weak and worn out, but Krívonos has sixty thousand, and his army is increasing every day, for the mob is coming to him. Besides, I cannot, depend on the voevoda of Kieff, for he belongs at heart to the peace party. He marches with me, it is true, but unwillingly. We must have reinforcements from some source. I learned a little while ago that not far from Konstantinoff there are two colonels,--Osinski with the royal guard, and Koritski. Take one hundred Cossacks of my guard, for safety, and go to these colonels with a letter from me, asking them to come here without delay, for in a couple of days I shall fall upon Krívonos. No one has acquitted himself of important missions better than you, therefore I send you; and this is an important mission."

Skshetuski bowed, and set out that evening for Konstantinoff, going at night so as to pass unnoticed; for here and there the scouts of Krívonos or squads of peasants were circling about. These formed robber bands in the forests and on the roads; but the prince gave orders to avoid battles, so that there should be no delay. Marching quietly therefore, he reached Visovati at daylight, where he found both colonels, and was greatly rejoiced at the sight of them. Osinski had a picked regiment of dragoons of the guard, trained in foreign fashion, and Germans. Koritski had a regiment of German infantry, composed almost entirely of veterans of the Thirty Years' War. These were soldiers so terrible and skilful that in the hands of the colonel they acted like one swordsman. Both regiments were well armed and equipped. When they heard of joining the prince, they raised shouts of joy at once, as they were yearning for battles, and knew too that under no other leader could they have so many. Unfortunately both colonels gave a negative answer; for both belonged to the command of Prince Dominik Zaslavski, and had strict orders not to join Vishnyevetski. In vain did Skshetuski tell them of the glory they might win under such a leader, and what great service they could render the country. They would not listen, declaring that obedience was the first law and obligation for military men. They said they could join the prince only in case the safety of their regiments demanded it.

Pan Yan went away deeply grieved, for he knew how painful this fresh disappointment would be to the prince, and how greatly his forces were wearied and worn by campaigning, by continual struggling with the enemy, scattering isolated detachments, and finally by continual wakefulness, hunger, and bad weather. To measure himself in these conditions with an enemy tenfold superior in number would be impossible. Skshetuski saw clearly, therefore, that there must be delay in acting against Krívonos; for it was necessary to give a longer rest to the army and to wait for a new accession of nobles to the camp.

Occupied with these thoughts, Skshetuski went back to the prince at the head of his Cossacks. He was obliged to go cautiously and at night, so as to escape the scouts of Krívonos and the numerous independent bands, made up of Cossacks and peasants,--sometimes very strong,--which raged in that neighborhood, burning dwellings, cutting down nobles, and hunting fugitives along the highroads. He passed Baklai and entered the forests of Mshyna,--dense, full of treacherous ravines and valleys. Happily he was favored on the road by good weather after the recent rains. It was a glorious night in July, moonless, but crowded with stars. The Cossacks went along in a narrow trail, guided by the foresters of Mshyna,--very trusty men, knowing the forests perfectly. Deep silence reigned among the trees, broken only by the cracking of dry twigs under the horses' hoofs,--when suddenly there came to the ears of Pan Yan and the Cossacks a kind of distant murmur, like singing interrupted by cries.

"Listen!" said the lieutenant, in a low voice; and he stopped the line of Cossacks. "What is that?"

The old forester bent forward to him. "Those are crazy people who go through the woods now and scream. Their heads are turned from cruelty. Yesterday we met a noblewoman who was going around looking at the pines and crying, 'Children! children!' It is evident that the peasants had killed her children. She stared at us and whined so that our legs trembled under us. They say that in all the forests there are many such."

Though Pan Yan was a fearless man, a shudder passed over him from head to foot. "Maybe it is the howling of wolves. It is difficult to distinguish."

"What wolves? There are no wolves in the woods now; they have all gone to the villages, where there are plenty of dead men."

"Awful times!" answered the knight, "when wolves live in the villages, and people go howling through the woods! Oh, God, God!"

After a while silence came again. There was nothing to be heard but the sounds usual among the tops of the pine-trees. Soon, however, those distant sounds rose and became more distinct.

"Oh!" said one of the foresters, suddenly, "it seems as though some large body of men were over there. You stay here; move on slowly. I will go with my companions to see who they are."

"Go!" said Skshetuski. "We will wait here."

The foresters disappeared. They did not return for about an hour. Skshetuski was beginning to be impatient, and indeed to think of treason, when suddenly some one sprang out of the darkness.

"They are there!" said he, approaching the lieutenant.

"Who?"

"A peasant band."

"Many of them?"

"About two hundred. It is not clear what is best to do, for they are in a pass through which our road lies. They have a fire, though the light is not to be seen, for it is below. They have no guards, and can be approached within arrow-shot."

"All right!" said Skshetuski; and turning to the Cossacks, he began to give orders to the two principal ones.

The party moved on briskly, but so quietly that only the cracking of twigs could betray their march. Stirrup did not touch stirrup; there was no clattering of sabres. The horses, accustomed to surprises and attacks, went with a wolfs gait, without snorting or neighing. Arriving at the place where the road made a sudden turn, the Cossacks saw at once, from a distance, fires and the indefinite outlines of people. Here Skshetuski divided his men into three parties,--one remained on the spot; the second went by the edge along the ravine, so as to close the opposite exit; the third dismounted, and crawling along on hands and feet, placed themselves on the very edge of the precipice above the heads of the peasants.

Skshetuski, who was in the second party, looking down, saw as if on the palm of his hand a whole camp, two or three hundred yards distant. There were ten fires, but burning not very brightly; over these hung kettles with food. The odor of smoke and of boiling meat came distinctly to the nostrils of Skshetuski and the Cossacks. Around the kettles peasants were standing or lying, drinking and talking. Some had bottles of vudka in their hands; others were leaning on pikes, on the ends of which were empaled as trophies the heads of men, women, and children. The gleam of the fire was reflected in their lifeless eyes and grinning teeth; the same gleam lighted up the faces of the peasants, wild and cruel. There, under the wall of the ravine, a number of them slept, snoring audibly; some talked; some stirred the fire, which then shot up clusters of golden sparks. At the largest fire sat, with his back to the ravine and to Skshetuski, a broad-shouldered old minstrel, who was thrumming on his lyre; in front of him was a half-circle of peasants. To the ears of Skshetuski came the following words:

"Ai! grandfather,--sing about the Cossack Holota!"

"No," cried the others; "sing of Marusia Boguslavka!"

"To the devil with Marusia! About the lord of Potok! About the lord of Potok!" shouted the greatest number of voices.

The "grandfather" struck his lyre with more force, coughed, and began to sing,--

"Halt! look around! stand in amaze, thou who art master of many! Since thou wilt be equal to him who is owner of nothing on earth; For he who moves all things is manager now, the mighty, the merciful God! And he puts on his scales all our woes, and he weighs them to know. Halt! look around! stand in amaze, thou who dost soar, With thy mind seeing wisdom down deep and afar!"

The minstrel was silent, and sighed; and after him the peasants sighed. Every moment more of them collected around him. But Skshetuski, though he knew that all his men must be ready now, did not give the signal for attack. The calm night, the blazing fires, the wild figures, and the song about Nikolai Pototski, still unfinished, roused in the knight certain wonderful thoughts, certain feelings and yearnings of which he could not himself give account. The uncured wounds of his heart opened; deep sorrow for the near past, for lost happiness, for those hours of quiet and peace, pressed his heart. He fell to thinking, and was sad. Then the "grandfather" sang on,--

"Halt!   look   around!   stand   in   amaze,   thou   who   mak'st   war
With   arrows,   bows,   powder,   and   ball,   with   the   sharp-cutting   sword!
For   knights,   too,   and   horsemen,   before   thee   were   many,
Who   fought   with   such   weapons   and   fell   by   the   sword.
Halt!   look   around!   stand   in   amaze,   forget   thou   thy   pride!
Thou   who   from   Potok   to   Slavuta   farest,   turn   then   this   way.
Innocent   men   thou   tak'st   by   the   ears   and   stripp'st   them   of   will;
Thou   heedest   no   king,   thou   knowest   no   Diet,   art   thy   own   single   law;
Hei!   be   amazed,   grow   not   enraged!   thou   in   thy   power,
With thy baton alone, as thou lustest, thou turnest the whole Polish land."

The "grandfather" stopped again, and at that time a pebble slipped from under the arm of one of the Cossacks, which had been resting on it, and began to roll down, rattling as it fell. A number of peasants shaded their eyes with their hands, and looked up quickly into the tree; then Skshetuski saw that the time had come, and fired his pistol into the middle of the crowd.

"Kill! slash!" cried he. Thirty Cossacks fired as it were straight into the faces of the crowd, and after the firing slipped like lightning down the steep walls of the ravine, among the terrified and confused peasants.

"Kill! slay!" was thundered at one end of the ravine.

"Kill! slay!" was repeated by furious voices at the other end.

"Yeremi! Yeremi!"

The attack was so unexpected, the terror so great, that the peasants, though armed, offered no resistance. It had been related in the camp of the rebellious mob that Yeremi, by the aid of the evil spirit, was able to be present and to fight at the same time in a number of places. This time, his name falling upon men who expected nothing and felt safe--really like the name of an evil spirit--snatched the weapons from their hands. Besides, the pikes and scythes could not be used in the narrow place; so that, driven like a flock of sheep to the opposite wall of the ravine, hewn down with sabres through the foreheads and faces, beaten, cut up, trampled under foot, in the madness of fear they stretched out their hands, and seizing the merciless steel, perished. The still forest was filled with the ominous uproar of the fight. Some tried to escape over the steep wall of the ravine, and wounding their hands with climbing, fell back on the sabre's edge. Some died calmly, others cried for mercy; some covered their faces with their hands, not wishing to see the moment of death; others threw themselves on the ground, face downward; but above the whistling of sabres, the groans of the dying, rose the shout of the assailants, "Yeremi! Yeremi!"--a shout which made the hair stand erect on the heads of the peasants, and death seem more terrible.

The minstrel gave a blow on the forehead to one of the Cossacks, and knocked him down; seized another by the hand, to stop the blow of the sabre, and bellowed from fear like a buffalo. Others, seeing him, ran up to cut him to pieces; but Skshetuski interfered.

"Take him alive!" shouted he.

"Stop!" roared the minstrel. "I am a noble. Loquor latine! I am no minstrel. Stop, I tell you! Robbers, bullock-drivers, sons of--"

But the minstrel had not yet finished his litany when Pan Yan looked into his face, and cried, till the walls of the ravine gave back the echo, "Zagloba!" And suddenly rushing upon him like a wild beast, he drove his fingers into the shoulders and thrust his face up to the face of the man, and shaking him as he would a pear-tree, roared: "Where is the princess? where is the princess?"

"Alive, well, safe!" roared back the minstrel; "unhand me! The devil take you, you are shaking the soul out of me!"

Then that knight, whom neither captivity nor wounds nor grief nor the terrible Burdabut could bring down, was brought down by happiness. His hands dropped at his side, great drops of sweat came out on his forehead; he fell on his knees, covered his face with his hands, and leaning his head against the wall of the ravine, remained in silence, evidently thanking God.

Meanwhile the unfortunate peasants had been slaughtered, and were lying dead on the ground, except a few who were bound for the executioner in the camp so as to torture a confession from them. The struggle was over, the uproar at an end. The Cossacks gathered around their leader, and seeing him kneeling under the rock, looked at him with concern, not knowing but he was wounded. He rose, however, with a face as bright as though the light of morning were shining in his soul.

"Where is she?" asked he of Zagloba.

"In Bar."

"Safe?"

"The castle is a strong one; no attack is feared. She is under the care of Pani Slavoshevska and with the nuns."

"Praise be to God in the highest!" said the knight; and in his voice there trembled deep emotion. "Give me your hand; I thank you from my very soul."

Suddenly he turned to the Cossacks. "Are there many prisoners?"

"Seventeen."

"A great joy has met me, and mercy is in me," said Pan Yan. "Let them be free!"

The Cossacks could not believe their ears. There was no such custom as that in the armies of Vishnyevetski.

The lieutenant frowned slightly. "Let them go free!" he repeated.

The Cossacks went away; but after a while the first essaul returned and said: "They do not believe as; they do not dare to go."

"Are their bonds loose?"

"Yes."

"Then leave them here, and to horse yourselves!"

Half an hour later the party was moving on again along the quiet, narrow road. The moon had risen, and sent long white streaks to the centre of the forest and lighted its dark depths. Zagloba and Skshetuski, riding ahead, conversed together.

"But tell me everything about her that you know," said the knight. "Then you rescued her from the hands of Bogun?"

"Of course; and besides, when going away, I bound up his face so that he could not scream."

"Well, you acted splendidly, as God is dear to me! But how did you get to Bar?"

"That IS a long story, better at another time; for I am terribly tired, and my throat is dried up from singing to those rapscallions. Haven't you anything to drink?"

"I have a little flask of gorailka; here it is."

Zagloba seized the flask and raised it to his mouth. A protracted gurgling was heard; and Pan Yan, impatient, without waiting the end, inquired further: "Did you say well?"

"What a question!" answered Zagloba; "everything is well in a dry throat."

"But I was inquiring about the princess."

"Oh, the princess! She is as well as a deer."

"Praise be to God on high! And she is comfortable in Bar?"

"As comfortable as in heaven,--couldn't be more so. Every one cleaves to her for her beauty. Pani Slavoshevska loves her as her own daughter. And how many men are in love with her! You couldn't count them on a rosary. But she, in constant love for you, thinks as much of them as I do now of this empty flask of yours."

"May God give health to her, the dearest!" said Skshetuski, joyfully. "Then she remembers me with pleasure?"

"Remembers you? I tell you that I myself couldn't understand where she got breath for so many sighs; these sighs made every one pity her, and most of all the little nuns, for she brought them to her side through her sweetness. Then she sent me too into these dangers, in which I have almost lost my life, to find you without fail and see if you were alive and well. She tried several times to send messengers, but no one would go. At last I took pity on her, and set out for your camp. If it hadn't been for the disguise, I should have laid down my head surely. But the peasants took me for a minstrel everywhere, as I sing very beautifully."

Skshetuski became silent from joy. A thousand thoughts and reminiscences thronged into his head. Helena stood as if living before him, as he had seen her the last time in Rozlogi, just before leaving for the Saitch,--charming, beautiful, graceful, and with those eyes black as velvet, full of unspeakable allurement. It seemed to him that he saw her, felt the warmth beating from her cheeks, heard her sweet voice. He recalled that walk in the cherry-garden and the cuckoo, and those questions which he gave the bird, and the bashfulness of Helena. Indeed the soul went out of him; his heart grew weak from love and joy, in presence of which all his past sufferings were like a drop in the sea. He did not know himself what was happening to him. He wanted to shout, fall on his knees and thank God again, then inquire without end. At last he began to repeat:--

"She is alive, well?"

"Alive, well," answered Zagloba, like an echo.

"And she sent you out?"

"Yes."

"And you have got a letter?"

"I have."

"Give it to me."

"It is sewed into my clothes; besides, it is night now. Restrain yourself."

"I cannot. You see yourself."

"I see."

Zagloba's answers became more and more laconic; at last he nodded a couple of times and fell asleep.

Skshetuski saw there was no help; therefore he gave himself up again to meditation, which was interrupted after a while by the tramp of a considerable body of cavalry approaching quickly. It was Ponyatovski with Cossacks of the guard, whom the prince had sent out to meet Skshetuski, fearing lest some harm might have met him.

CHAPTER XXIX.

It is easy to understand how the prince received the statement which Skshetuski made of the refusal of Osinski and Koritski. Everything had so combined that it needed such a great soul as that iron prince possessed, not to bend, not to waver, or let his hands drop. In vain was he to spend a colossal fortune on the maintenance of armies; in vain was he to struggle like a lion in a net; in vain was he to tear off one head of the rebellion after another, showing wonders of bravery all for nothing. A time was coming in which he must feel his own impotence, withdraw somewhere to a distance, to a quiet place, and remain a silent spectator of what was being done in the Ukraine. And what was it that rendered him powerless? Not the swords of the Cossacks, but the ill-will of his own people. Was it not reasonable for him to hope when he marched from the Trans-Dnieper in May that when like an eagle from the sky he should strike rebellion, when in the general dismay and confusion he should first raise his sword over his head, the whole Commonwealth would come to his aid, and put its power and its punishing sword in his hand? But what did happen? The king was dead, and after his death the command was put into other hands, and he, the prince, was passed by ostentatiously. That was the first concession to Hmelnitski. The soul of the prince did not suffer for the office he had lost; but it suffered at the thought that the insulted Commonwealth had fallen so low that it did not seek a death-struggle, but drew back before one Cossack, and preferred to restrain his insolent right hand by negotiations.

From the time of the victory at Makhnovka worse and worse tidings were brought to the camp,--first news of negotiations sent through Pan Kisel; then news that Volynian Polesia was covered with the waves of insurrection; then the refusal of the colonels, showing clearly how far the commander-in-chief, Prince Dominik Zaslavski-Ostrogski, was hostile. During Skshetuski's absence Pan Korsh Zenkovich came to camp with information that all Ovruch was on fire. The people had been quiet, and not anxious for rebellion; but the Cossacks, coming under Krechovski and Polksenjits, forced the mob to enter their ranks. Castles and villages were burned; the nobles who did not escape were cut to pieces, and among others old Pan Yelets, a former servant and friend of the Vishnyevetskis. In view of this, the prince had decided after a juncture with Osinski and Koritski to overwhelm Krívonos, and then move north toward Ovruch, and after an agreement with the hetman of Lithuania, to seize the rebels between two fires. But all these plans had fallen through now on account of the refusal of both colonels caused by Prince Dominik. For Yeremi, after all the marches, battles, and labors, was not strong enough to meet Krívonos, especially when not sure of the voevoda of Kieff, who belonged heart and soul to the peace party. Pan Yanush yielded before the importance and power of Yeremi, and had to go with him; but the more he saw his authority broken the more inclined was he to oppose the warlike wishes of the prince, as was shown at once.

Skshetuski gave his account, and the prince listened to it in silence. All the officers were present; their faces were gloomy at the news of the refusal. All eyes turned to the prince when he said,--

"Prince Dominik, of course, sent them the order."

"Yes, they showed it to me in writing."

Yeremi rested his arms on the table and covered his face with his hands; after a while he said,--

"This indeed is more than a man can bear. Am I to labor alone, and instead of assistance meet only obstructions? Could I not have gone to my estates in Sandomir and lived quietly? And what prevented me from doing so, except love of country? This is my reward for toil, for loss of fortune and blood."

The prince spoke quietly, but such bitterness and pain trembled in his voice that all present were straitened with sorrow. Old colonels--veterans from Putívl, Starets, Kuméiki,--and young men victorious in the last conflicts, looked at him with unspeakable sorrow in their eyes; for they knew what a heavy struggle that iron man was having with himself, how terribly his pride must suffer from the humiliation put upon him. He, a prince, "by the grace of God;" he, a voevoda in Russia, senator of the Commonwealth,--must yield to some Hmelnitski or Krívonos. He, almost a monarch, who recently had received ambassadors from foreign rulers, must withdraw from the field of glory, and confine himself in some little castle, waiting for the outcome of a war directed by others or for humiliating negotiations. He, predestined for great things, conscious of ability to direct them, had to confess that he was without power.

This suffering, together with his labors, was marked on his figure. He had become greatly emaciated; his eyes had sunk; his hair, black as the wing of a raven, had begun to grow gray. But a certain grand tragic calm was spread over his countenance, for pride guarded him from betraying his suffering.

"Well, let it be so," said he; "we will show this unthankful country that we are able not only to fight, but to die for it. Indeed I should prefer a more glorious death,--to fall in some other war than in a domestic squabble with serfs--"

"Do not speak of death," interrupted the voevoda of Kieff; "for though it is unknown what God has predestined to any man, still death may be far away. I do homage to your military genius and your knightly spirit; but I cannot take it ill, either of the viceroy, the chancellor, or the commanders, if they try to stem civil war by negotiations, for in it the blood of brothers is flowing, and who, unless a foreign enemy, can reap advantage from the stubbornness of both sides?"

The prince looked long into the eyes of the voevoda, and said emphatically,--

"Show favor to the conquered, and they will accept it with thanks and will remember it, but you will be only despised by conquerors. Would that no one had ever done injustice to these people! But when once insurrection has flamed up, we must quench it with blood, not negotiations; if we do not, disgrace and destruction to us!"

"Speedy ruin will come if we wage war each on his own account," answered the voevoda.

"Does that mean that you will not go on with me?"

"I call God to witness that this is out of no ill-will to you; but my conscience tells me not to expose my men to evident destruction, for their blood is precious, and will be of value to the Commonwealth yet."

The prince was silent awhile; then turning to his colonels, he said,--

"You, my old comrades, will not leave me now!"

At these words the colonels, as if impelled by one power and one will, rushed to the prince. Some kissed his garments; some embraced his knees; others, raising their hands to heaven, cried,--

"We are with you to the last breath, to the last drop of blood! Lead us, lead us! we will serve without pay."

"And let me die with you," cried young Pan Aksak, blushing like a girl.

At sight of this the voevoda of Kieff was moved; but the prince went from one to another, pressed the head of each one, and thanked him. A mighty enthusiasm seized on young and old. From the eyes of the warriors sparks flashed; they grasped their sabres from moment to moment.

"I will live with you, die with you!" said the prince.

"We will conquer!" cried the officers. "Against Krívonos! On Polónnoe! Whoever wishes to leave us, let him leave. We will do without aid. We wish to share neither glory nor death."

"It is my will," said the prince, "that before moving on Krívonos we take even a short rest to restore our strength. It is now the third month that we are on horseback, scarcely ever dismounting. The flesh is leaving our bones from excessive toil and change of climate. We have no horses; the infantry are barefoot. Let us go then to Zbaraj; there we will recruit and rest. Perhaps too some soldiers will join us, and we will move into the fire with new forces."

"When do you wish to start?" asked old Zatsvilikhovski.

"Without delay, old soldier, without delay!" Here the prince turned to the voevoda: "And where do you wish to go?"

"To Gliniani, for I hear that forces are collecting there."

"Then we will conduct you to a safe place, so that no harm may happen to you."

The voevoda said nothing, for he felt rather ill at ease. He was leaving, and the prince still showed care for him and intended to conduct him. Was there irony in the words of the prince? The voevoda did not know. Still the voevoda did not abandon his design; for the colonels of the prince looked on him more inimically every moment, and it was clear that in any other less disciplined army there would have been an outbreak against him.

He bowed and went out; and the colonels went, each to his own regiment to make ready for the march. Skshetuski alone remained with the prince.

"What kind of soldiers are in those regiments?" asked the prince.

"So good that you cannot find better. Dragoons drilled in German fashion, and with infantry of the guard, veterans of the Thirty Years' War. When I saw them I thought they were Roman legionaries."

"Many of them?"

"Two regiments with the dragoons,--just three thousand men."

"Oh, it is a pity, it is a pity! Great things might be done with their assistance."

Suffering was already depicted on the face of the prince. After a while he said as if to himself,--

"It is unfortunate that such commanders were chosen in times of defeat! Ostrorog would be the right man if war could be put down with eloquence and Latin; Konyetspolski is my brother-in-law and a warrior by nature; but he is young, without experience. Zaslavski is worst of all. I know him of old. He is a man of small heart and narrow mind. His business is to slumber over the cup, not to manage an army. I do not speak of this in public, lest it might be thought that malice moves me, but I foresee terrible disaster, especially now, at this time, when such people have the helm in their hands! Oh, God, God, remove this cup from me! What will happen to this country? When I think of it I would prefer death, for I am greatly wearied, and I tell you that I shall not last long. My spirit is rushing to the war, but my body lacks strength."

"You should care more for your health, in which the whole country is deeply concerned, and which is already greatly injured by toil."

"The country thinks differently, it is evident, when it avoids me and drags the sabre out of my hand."

"God grant when Prince Karl changes his cap for a crown, he will see whom to elevate and whom to punish; but you are powerful enough to care for no one at present."

"I will go my own way."

The prince did not notice perhaps that, like the other "kinglets," he was carrying on a policy of his own; but if he had noticed it, he would not have abandoned it, for he felt clearly that that was the only one that could save the honor of the Commonwealth.

Again followed a moment of silence, soon broken by the neighing of horses and the sound of trumpets. The regiments were mustering for the march. These sounds roused the prince from meditation. He shook his head as if wishing to shake off suffering and evil thoughts; then he said,--

"You had a quiet journey?"

"I met, in the forest, a large body of peasants, a couple of hundred men whom I destroyed."

"Well done! And you took prisoners, for that is an important thing now?"

"I did, but--"

"But you have commanded them to be executed already? Is that true?"

"No, I set them free."

Yeremi looked with wonderment at Skshetuski; then his brows contracted suddenly. "What was that for? Do you too belong to the peace party?"

"Your Highness, I brought an informant; for among the peasants was a disguised noble who remained alive. I freed the others, for God showed mercy to me and comfort. I will bear the punishment. That noble was Pan Zagloba, who brought me tidings of the princess."

The prince approached Pan Yan quickly. "She is alive and well?"

"Praise be to God on high, she is."

"And where is she?"

"In Bar."

"That is a strong fortress, my boy!" Here the prince raised his hands, and taking Skshetuski's head, kissed him a number of times on the forehead. "I rejoice in your gladness, for I love you as a son."

Pan Yan kissed the prince's hand with emotion, and though for many a day he would have willingly shed his blood for him, he felt again that at his command he would spring into rolling flames. To such a degree did that terrible and cruel Yeremi know how to win the hearts of the knights.

"Well, I do not wonder that you let those men go free. You will go unpunished. But he's a sharp fellow, that noble! Then he took her from the Trans-Dnieper to Bar, praise be to God! In these grievous times this is a real delight to me also. He must be a fox of no common kind. But let's have a look at this Zagloba."

Skshetuski moved quickly toward the door; but at that moment it was opened suddenly, and there appeared in it the flaming head of Vershul, who had been on a distant expedition with the Tartars of the guard.

"Your Highness," cried he, panting, "Krívonos has taken Polónnoe, cut down ten thousand people, among them women and children."

The colonels began to assemble again, and crowd around Vershul. The voevoda of Kieff hurried up also. The prince was astonished, for he had not expected such news.

"But Russians were shut up in there! It cannot be!"

"Not a living soul escaped."

"Do you hear?" said the prince, turning to the voevoda. "Negotiate with an enemy like that, who does not spare even his own!"

The voevoda snorted and said: "Oh, the curs! If that is the case, then may the devils take it all! I will go with you."

"Then you are a brother to me," said the prince.

"Long live the voevoda of Kieff!" said Zatsvilikhovski.

"Success to concord!"

The prince turned again to Vershul. "Where did they go after Polónnoe? Unknown?"

"To Konstantinoff, probably."

"Oh, God save us! Then the regiments of Osinski and Koritski are lost, for they cannot escape with infantry. We must forget our wrongs and hurry to their aid. To horse! to horse!"

The face of the prince brightened with joy, and a glow enlivened his emaciated cheeks, for the path of glory was open before him again.

CHAPTER XXX.

The army passed Konstantinoff and halted at Rosolovtsi; for the prince calculated that when Koritski and Osinski would receive news of the taking of Polónnoe, they would retreat to Rosolovtsi, and if the enemy should pursue them he would fall in among all the forces of the prince as into a trap, and thus meet with sure defeat. That forecast was justified in great part. The troops occupied their positions, and remained in silent readiness for the fight. Smaller and larger scouting-parties were sent in every direction from the camp. The prince, with a number of regiments, took his position in the village and waited. Toward evening Vershul's Tartars brought news that infantry was approaching from the direction of Konstantinoff. Hearing this, the prince went out before the door of his quarters, surrounded by officers, and with them a number of the principal attendants, to look upon the arrival. Meanwhile the regiments, announcing themselves by sound of trumpet, halted before the village; and two colonels hastened, panting and with all speed, to the prince to offer him their service. These were Osinski and Koritski. When they saw Vishnyevetski with a magnificent suite of knights, they were greatly confused, uncertain of their reception, and bowing profoundly, they waited in silence for what he would say.

"The wheel of fortune turns and brings down the haughty," said the prince. "You did not wish to come at our request, but now you come at your own desire."

"Your Highness," said Osinski, with firmness, "we wished with all our souls to serve with you, but the order was definite. Let him who issued it answer for it. We beg pardon; though we are innocent, for as soldiers we were obliged to obey and be silent."

"Then Prince Dominik has withdrawn the order?" asked the prince.

"The order is not withdrawn," said Osinski, "but it is no longer binding, since the only salvation and refuge for our forces is with you, under whose command we wish henceforth to live and serve and die."

These words, full of manly power, and the form of Osinski produced the very best impression on the prince and the officers; for he was a famous soldier, and though still young, not more than forty years of age, was full of warlike experience which he had acquired in foreign armies. Every military eye rested on him with pleasure. Tall, straight as a reed, with yellow mustaches brushed upward and a Swedish beard, he recalled completely by his uniform and stature the colonels of the Thirty Years' War. Koritski, a Tartar by origin, resembled him in nothing. Low in stature and dumpy, he had a gloomy look, and his appearance was strange in a foreign uniform, not befitting his Oriental features. He led a picked German regiment, and had a reputation for bravery as well as moroseness, and the iron rigor with which he held his soldiers.

"We wait the commands of your Highness," said Osinski.

"I thank you for your decision, and I accept your services. I know that a soldier must obey; and if I sent for you, it was because I was unaware of the order. Not only shall we pass henceforth good and evil times together, but I hope that you will be pleased with your new service."

"If you are pleased with us and with our officers."

"Very good!" said the prince. "Is the enemy far behind you?"

"Scouting-parties are near, but the main force may arrive here to-morrow."

"Very well, we have time then. Order your regiments to march across the square; let me look at them, so I may know what kind of soldiers you bring me, and if much can be done with them."

The colonels returned to their regiments, and soon after were marching at the head of them into the camp. Soldiers of the picked regiments of the prince hurried out like ants to look at their new comrades. The royal dragoons, under Captain Giza, marched in front with heavy Swedish helmets and lofty crests. They rode Podolian horses, but matched and well fed. These men, fresh and rested, with bright and glittering uniforms, had a splendid appearance in comparison with the emaciated regiments of the prince, in tattered uniforms, faded from rain and sun. After these followed Osinski with his regiment, and in the rear Koritski. A murmur of applause was heard among the prince's cavalry at the sight of the deep German ranks. Their collars red, on their shoulders shining muskets, they marched thirty in a rank, with the step of a single man, strong and thundering. Tall, sturdy fellows all of them,--old soldiers who had been in more than one country and in more than one battle, for the most part veterans of the Thirty Years' War, skilled, disciplined, and experienced.

When they marched up to the prince, Osinski cried, "Halt!" and the regiment stood as if foot-bound to the earth; the officers raised their staffs, the standard-bearer raised his standard, and waving it three times, lowered it before the prince. "Vorwärts!" commanded Osinski, "Vorwärts!" repeated the officers, and the regiments advanced again. In the same way but in almost better form, did Koritski present his troops. At the sight of all this the soldiers' hearts were rejoiced; and Yeremi, judge beyond judges, put his hands on his hips with delight, looked, and smiled,--for infantry was just what he wanted, and he was sure that it would be difficult for him to find better in the whole world. He felt increased in power, and hoped to accomplish great things in war. The suite began to speak of different military topics and of the various kinds of soldiers to be seen in the world.

"The Zaporojian infantry is good, especially behind intrenchments," said Sleshinski; "but these are better, for they are better drilled."

"Of course a great deal better!" said Migurski.

"But they are heavy men," said Vershul. "If I had to do it, I should undertake to tire them out with my Tartars in two days, so that on the third I could slaughter them like sheep."

"What are you talking about? The Germans are good soldiers."

To this Pan Longin Podbipienta answered in his singing Lithuanian voice: "How God in his mercy has endowed different nations with different virtues! As I hear, there is no cavalry in the world better than ours, and again neither our infantry nor the Hungarian can be compared with the German."

"Because God is just," remarked Zagloba. "For instance, he gave you a great fortune, a big sword, and a heavy hand, but small wit."

"Zagloba has fastened on him like a horse-leech," said Pan Yan, smiling.

But Podbipienta contracted his eyes and spoke with the mildness usual to him: "An outrage to hear! And he gave you too long a tongue."

"If you maintain that God did ill in giving me what I have, then you will go to hell with your virtue, for you wish to oppose his will."

"Oh, who can out-talk you? You talk and talk."

"Do you know how a man is different from an animal?"

"How?"

"By reason and speech."

"Oh, he has given it to him, he has given it to him!" said Mokrski.

"If you don't understand why in Poland there is better cavalry and among the Germans better infantry, I will explain it to you."

"Why is it? why is it?" asked several voices.

"This is why: When the Lord God created the horse he brought him before men, so that they should praise his works. And on the bank stood a German, for the Germans are always pushing themselves everywhere. The Lord God showed the horse to the German, and asked: 'What is this?' 'Pferd!' answered the German. 'What!' exclaimed the Creator; 'do you say "Pfe!" to my work? But you will never ride on this creature, you lubber!--or if you do, you will ride like a fool.' Having said this, the Lord made a present of the horse to the Pole, This is why the Polish cavalry is the best. Then the Germans began to hurry after the Lord on foot and to beg forgiveness of him, and that is why the Germans have become the best infantry."

"You have calculated everything very cleverly," said Podbipienta.

Further conversation was interrupted by new guests, who hurried up with the tidings that approaching the camp were forces which could not be Cossacks, for they were not from Konstantinoff, but from an entirely different direction,--from the river Zbruch. Two hours later those troops came on with such a thundering of trumpets and drums that the prince became angry and sent an order to them to be quiet, for the enemy was in the neighborhood. It turned out that they were followers of Samuel Lashch, commander of the royal vanguard, an officer of the king, for the rest a celebrated adventurer, wrongdoer, turbulent, quarrelsome, but a great soldier. He led eight hundred men of the same stamp as himself,--part nobles, part Cossacks, all of whom deserved hanging according to sound justice. But Yeremi was not afraid of the insubordination of these warriors, trusting that in his hands they would turn into obedient lambs, and make up in bravery and daring for their other defects.

It was a lucky evening. On the previous day the prince, weighed down by the expected departure of the voevoda of Kieff, had determined to defer the war till the arrival of reinforcements, and to retreat to some quiet place for a time. To-day he was again at the head of nearly twelve thousand men; and although Krívonos had five times that number, still since the greater part of the rebel forces was formed of the rabble, the two armies might be considered of equal strength. Now the prince had no thought of rest. Shutting himself up with Lashch, the voevoda of Kieff, Zatsvilikhovski, Makhnitski, and Osinski, he held a council on the conduct of the war. It was determined to give Krívonos battle on the morrow, and if he did not appear himself, to go in search of him.

It was already dark night; but since the recent rains, so annoying to the soldiers at Makhnovka, the weather had continued to be splendid. On the dark vault of the heavens glittered swarms of golden stars. The moon appeared on high and whitened all the roofs of Rosolovtsi. No one in the camp thought of sleeping. All were conjecturing about to-morrow's battle, and preparing for it; chatting in ordinary fashion, singing, and promising themselves great pleasure. The officers and the most distinguished attendants, all in excellent humor, gathered around a great fire, and passed the time with their cups.

"Tell us further," said they to Zagloba; "when you were crossing the Dnieper, what did you do, and how did you reach Bar?"

Zagloba emptied a quart cup of mead, and said,--

"'Sed jam nox humida cœlo præcipitat Suadentque sidera cadentia somnos, Sed si tantus amor casus cognoscere nostros, Incipiam ...'

Gentlemen, if I should begin to tell all in detail, ten nights would not suffice, and surely mead would be required; for an old throat, like an old wagon, needs lubrication. It is enough if I tell you that I went to Korsún, to the camp of Hmelnitski himself with the princess, and took her out of that hell in safety."

"Jesus, Mary! Did you enchant them?" cried Zatsvilikhovski.

"It is true that I enchanted them," said Zagloba, "for I learned that hellish art when I was still in youthful years from a witch in Asia, who, having fallen in love with me, divulged all the secret tricks of her black art. But I could not enchant much, for it was trick against trick. Around Hmelnitski are swarms of soothsayers and wizards, who have brought so many devils into his service that he uses them to work as he would peasants. When he goes to sleep, a devil has to pull his boots off; when his clothes are dusty, a devil beats them with his tail; when he is drunk, Hmelnitski gives this or that devil a box on the snout, saying, 'You don't do your work well.'"

The pious Pan Longin crossed himself, and said: "With them the power of hell; with us the power of heaven."

"T was afraid the black fellows would betray me to Hmelnitski,--tell who I was, and whom I was conducting; but I conjured them into silence with certain words. I was afraid too that Hmelnitski would know me, for I had met him in Chigirin a year before, twice at Dopula's. There were also other colonels whom I knew; but my stomach had fallen in, my beard had grown to my waist, my hair to my shoulders, my disguise had changed the rest, no one recognized me."

"Then you saw Hmelnitski himself, and spoke with him?"

"Did I see Hmelnitski? Just as I see you. More than that; he sent me as a spy into Podolia to distribute his manifestoes among the peasants on the road. He gave me a baton as a safeguard against the Tartars, so that from Korsún I went everywhere in safety. Peasants or men from below met me. I put the staff under their noses, and said, 'Smell this, children, and go to the devil!' Then I ordered them everywhere to give me plenty to eat and drink, and they did; and wagons, too, for which I was glad; and I was always looking after my poor princess, lest she might give out after such great fatigues and terror. I tell you, gentlemen, that before we arrived at Bar she had recovered to such a degree that there were few people in Bar who didn't gaze at her. There are many pretty girls in that place, for the nobles have assembled there from distant regions, but in comparison with her they are as owls to a jay. The people admire her, and you would if you could see her."

"It must be they couldn't help it," said little Pan Volodyovski.

"But why did you go to Bar?" asked Migurski.

"Because I said to myself, I will not stop till I come to a safe place. I had no confidence in small castles, thinking that the rebellion might reach them. But if it should go to Bar, it would break its teeth there. Pan Andrei Pototski has built up strong walls, and cares as much for Hmelnitski as I do for an empty glass. Do you think that I did badly in going so far from the conflagration? If I had not, that Bogun would surely have pursued; and if he had caught up, I tell you he would have made tidbits of me for the dogs. You don't know him, but I do. May the devil fly away with him! I shall have no peace till they hang the man. God grant him that happy end--amen! And surely there is no one with whom he has such an account as with me. Brrr! When I think of it a chill passes over me; so that now I am forced to use stimulants, though by nature I am opposed to drink."

"What do you say?" interrupted Podbipienta. "Why, my dear brother, you take up liquid like a well-sweep."

"Don't look into the well, my dear man, for you will see nothing wise at the bottom. But a truce to this! Travelling then with the baton and manifestoes of Hmelnitski, I met no great hindrances. When I came to Vinnitsa, I found there the troops of Pan Aksak, now present in this camp; but I had not put off my minstrel skin yet, for I feared the peasantry. But I got rid of the manifestoes. There is a saddler there called Suhak, a Zaporojian spy, who was sending intelligence to Hmelnitski. Through this fellow I sent off the manifestoes; but I wrote such sentences on the backs of them that Hmelnitski will surely order the saddler to be flayed when he reads them. But right under the very walls of Bar such a thing happened to me that I came very near being lost at the shore of refuge."

"How was that? How?"

"I met some drunken soldiers, wild fellows, who heard how I called the princess, 'Your Ladyship,' for I was not so careful then, being near our own people. And they began: 'What sort of minstrel is that? What sort of a lad is it whom he calls "Your Ladyship"?' Then they looked at the princess, and saw she was as beautiful as a picture. 'Bring her nearer to us,' said they. I pushed her behind me into the corner, and to the sabre--"

"That is a wonder," said Volodyovski,--"that you, dressed as a minstrel, had a sabre at your side."

"That I had a sabre? And who told you that I had a sabre? I had not; but I grabbed a soldier's sabre that lay on the table,--for it was in a public house at Shipintsi, I stretched out two of my assailants in the twinkle of an eye. The others rushed on me. I cried, 'Stop, you dogs, for I am a noble!' Next moment they called out, 'Stop! stop! Scouts are coming!' It appeared that they were not scouts, but Pani Slavoshevska with an escort, whom her son was conducting, with fifty horsemen,--young fellows. These stopped my enemies. I went to the lady with my story, and roused her feelings so that she opened the floodgates of her eyes. She took the princess into her carriage, and we entered Bar. But do you think this is the end? No!"

Suddenly Sleshinski interrupted the narrative. "But, look! is that the dawn? What is it?"

"Oh, it cannot be the dawn," said Skshetuski. "Too early."

"It is toward Konstantinoff."

"Yes. Don't you see it is brighter?"

"As I live, a fire!"

At these words the faces of all became serious. They forgot the narrative and sprang to their feet.

"Fire! Fire!" repeated several voices.

"That is Krívonos who has come from Polónnoe."

"Krívonos with all his forces."

"The advance guard must have set fire to the town or the neighboring villages."

Meanwhile the trumpets sounded the alarm in low notes. Just then old Zatsvilikhovski appeared suddenly among the knights. "Gentlemen," said he, "scouts have come with news. The enemy is in sight! We move at once. To your posts! to your posts!"

The officers hurried with all speed to their regiments. The attendants put out the fires, and in a few moments darkness reigned in the camp. But in the distance from the direction of Konstantinoff the heavens reddened each moment more intensely and over a broader space. In this gleam the stars grew paler and paler. Again the trumpets sounded low. "To horse!" was heard through the mouthpiece. Indistinct masses of men and horses began to move. Amid the silence were heard the tramp of horses, the measured step of infantry, and finally the dull thump of Vurtsel's cannon; from moment to moment the clatter of muskets or the voices of command were heard. There was something threatening and ominous in that night march, in those voices, murmurs, clatter of steel, the gleam of armor and swords. The regiments descended to the Konstantinoff road, and moved over it toward the conflagration like a great dragon or serpent making its way through the darkness. But the luxuriant July night was drawing to a close. In Rosolovtsi the cocks began to crow, answering one another through the whole town. Five miles of road divided Rosolovtsi from Konstantinoff, so that before the army on its slow march had passed half the interval dawn rose behind the brightness of the conflagration, pale as if frightened, and filled the air more and more with light, winning from the darkness forests, woods, groves, the whole line of the highway and the troops marching upon it. It was possible to distinguish clearly the people, the horses, and the close ranks of infantry. The cool morning breeze rose and quivered among the flags above the heads of the knights.

Vershul's Tartars marched in front, behind them Ponyatovski's Cossacks, then the dragoons, Vurtsel's artillery, the infantry and hussars last. Zagloba rode near Skshetuski; but he was somewhat uneasy in the saddle, and it was apparent that alarm was seizing him, in view of the approaching battle.

"Listen a moment!" said he to Skshetuski, in a low whisper as if he feared some one might overhear him.

"What do you say?"

"Will the hussars strike first?"

"You say that you are an old soldier, and you don't know that hussars are reserved to decide the battle at the moment when the enemy is straining his utmost power?"

"I know that, I know that, but I wanted to be sure."

A moment of silence ensued. Then Zagloba lowered his voice still more, and inquired further: "Is this Krívonos with all his forces?"

"Yes."

"How many men is he leading?"

"Sixty thousand, counting the mob."

"Oh, the devil take him!" said Zagloba.

Pan Yan smiled under his mustache.

"Don't think that I am afraid," whispered Zagloba. "But I have short breath, and don't like a crowd, for it is hot, and as soon as it is hot I can do nothing. I like to take care of myself in single combat. Not the head, but the hands win in this place. Here I am a fool in comparison with Podbipienta. I have on my stomach here those two hundred ducats which the prince gave me; but believe me I would rather have my stomach somewhere else. Tfu! tfu! I don't like these great battles. May the plague bruise!"

"Nothing will happen to you. Take courage!"

"Courage? That is all I am afraid of. I fear that bravery will overcome prudence in me. I am too excitable. Besides, I have had a bad omen: when we sat by the fire two stars fell. Who knows, maybe one of them is mine."

"For your good deeds God will reward you and keep you in health."

"Well, if only he doesn't reward me too soon."

"Why didn't you stay in the camp?"

"I thought it would be safer with the army."

"It is. You will see that there is no great trouble. We are accustomed to this fighting, and custom is second nature. But here is the Sluch and Vishovati Stav already."

In fact the waters of Vishovati Stav, divided from the Sluch by a long dam, glittered in the distance. The army halted at once along the whole line.

"Is this the place so soon?" asked Zagloba.

"The prince will put the army in line," said Skshetuski.

"I don't like a throng; I tell you, I don't like a throng."

"Hussars on the right wing!" was the command which came from the prince to Pan Yan.

It was broad daylight. The fire had grown pale in the light of the rising sun, whose golden rays were reflected on the points of the lances, and it appeared as though above the hussars a thousand lights were gleaming. After its lines were arranged, the army concealed itself no longer, and began to sing in one voice, "Hail, O ye gates of salvation!" The mighty song resounded over the dewy grass, struck the pine grove, and sent back by the echo, rose to the sky. Then the shore on the other side of the dam grew black with crowds of Cossacks. As far as the eye could reach regiment followed regiment,--mounted Zaporojians armed with long lances, infantry with muskets, and waves of peasants armed with scythes, flails, and forks. Behind them was to be seen, as if in fog, an immense camp or movable town. The creaking of thousands of wagons and the neighing of horses reached the ears of the prince's soldiers. But the Cossacks marched without their usual tumult, without howling, and halted on the other side of the dam. The two opposing forces looked at each other for some time in silence.

Zagloba, keeping all the time close to Skshetuski, looked on that sea of people and muttered,--

"Lord, why hast thou created so many ruffians? Hmelnitski must be there with his mob and their vermin. Isn't that an outbreak, tell me? They will cover us with their caps. Ah! in the old time it was so pleasant in the Ukraine! They are rolling on, rolling on! God grant that the devils may roll you in hell, and all that is coming on us! May the glanders devour you!"

"Don't swear. To-day is Sunday."

"True, it is Sunday. Better think of God. 'Pater noster, qui es in cœlis'--No respect to be looked for from these scoundrels--'Sanctificetur nomen tuum'--What is going to be done on that dam?--'Adveniat regnum tuum'--The breath is already stopped in my body--'Fiat voluntas tua'--God choke you, you Hamans! But look! what is that?"

A division formed of a few hundred men separated from the dark mass and pushed forward without order toward the dam.

"That is a skirmishing-party," said Skshetuski. "Our men will go out to them directly."

"Has the battle begun, then, already?"

"As God is in heaven!"

"May the devil take them!" Here the ill-humor of Zagloba was beyond measure. "And you are looking at it as a theatre in carnival time!" cried he, in disgust at Skshetuski; "just as if your own skin were not in peril."

"I told you that we are used to it."

"And you will go to the skirmish too, of course?"

"It is not very becoming for knights of picked regiments to fight duels with such enemies. No one does that who stands on dignity; but in these times no one thinks of dignity."

"Our men are marching already!" cried Zagloba, seeing the red line of Volodyovski's dragoons moving at a trot toward the dam.

They were followed by a number of volunteers from each regiment. Among others went the red Vershul, Kushel, Ponyatovski, the two Karvichi, and Pan Longin Podbipienta from the hussars. The distance between the two divisions began to diminish rapidly.

"You will see something," said Skshetuski to Zagloba, "Look especially at Volodyovski and Podbipienta. They are splendid fighters. Do you see them?"

"Yes."

"Well, look at them! You will have something to enjoy."

CHAPTER XXXI.

When the warriors drew near each other, they reined in their horses and opened in mutual abuse.

"Come on! come on! We will feed the dogs with your carrion right away!" cried the prince's soldiers.

"Your carrion is not fit even for dogs!" answered the Cossacks.

"You will rot here on the dam, you infamous robbers!"

"For whom it is fated, that one will rot; but the fish will pick your bones soon."

"To the dung-heaps with your forks, you trash! Dung-forks are fitter for you than sabres."

"If we are trash, our sons will be nobles, for they will be born of your girls."

Some Cossack, evidently from the Trans-Dnieper, pushed forward, and placing his palms around his mouth, cried with a loud voice: "The prince has two nieces; tell him to send them to Krívonos."

It grew dim in Volodyovski's eyes when he heard this blasphemy, and he spurred his horse on to the Zaporojian.

Skshetuski, on the right wing with his hussars, recognized him from a distance, and cried to Zagloba: "Volodyovski is rushing on! Volodyovski! Look there! there!"

"I see!" said Zagloba. "He has already reached him. They are fighting! One, two! I see perfectly. It is all over. He is a swordsman, plague take him!"

At the second blow the Cossack fell to the ground as if struck by lightning, and fell with his head to his comrades, as an evil omen to them.

Then a second sprang forward, in a scarlet kontush stripped from some noble. He fell upon Volodyovski a little from the flank, but his horse stumbled at the very moment of the blow. Volodyovski turned, and then could be seen the master; for he only moved his hand, making a light, soft motion,--invisible, so to speak,--but still the sabre of the Zaporojian sprang up, flew into the air. Volodyovski seized him by the shoulder, and pulled him with his horse toward the Polish side.

"Save me, brothers!" cried the prisoner.

He offered no resistance, knowing that in case he did he would be thrust through that moment. He even struck his horse with his heels to urge him on; and so Volodyovski led him as a wolf leads a kid.

In view of this, a couple of tens of warriors rushed out from both sides of the river, for no more could find place on the dam. They fought in single combat, man with man, horse with horse, sabre with sabre; and it was a wonderful sight, that series of duels, on which both armies looked with the greatest interest, drawing auguries from them of the future success. The morning sun shone upon the combatants, and the air was so transparent that even the faces might be seen from both sides. Any one looking from a distance would have thought that it was a tournament or games. But at one moment a riderless horse would spring from the tumult; at another, a body would tumble from the dam into the clear mirror of the water, which splashed up in golden sparks and then moved forward in a circling wavelet farther and farther from shore.

The courage of the soldiers in both armies grew as they beheld the bravery of their own men and their eagerness for the fight. Each sent good wishes to its own. Suddenly Skshetuski clasped his hands and cried,--

"Vershul is lost; he fell with his horse. Look! he was sitting on the white one."

But Vershul was not lost, though he had indeed fallen with his horse; for they had both been thrown by Pulyan, a former Cossack of Prince Yeremi, then next in command to Krívonos. He was a famous skirmisher, and had never left off that game. He was so strong that he could easily break two horseshoes at once. He had the reputation of being invincible in single combat. When he had thrown Vershul he attacked a gallant officer, Koroshlyakhtsits, and cut him terribly,--almost to the saddle. Others drew back in fear. Seeing this, Pan Longin turned his Livonian mare against him.

"You are lost!" cried Pulyan, when he saw the foolhardy man.

"It can't be helped," answered Podbipienta, raising his sabre for the blow.

He had not, however, his Zervikaptur, that being reserved for ends too important to permit its use in desultory combat. He had left it in the hands of his faithful armor-bearer in the ranks, and had merely a light blade of blue steel engraved with gold. Pulyan endured its first blow, though he saw in a moment that he had to do with no common enemy, for his sword quivered to the palm of his hand. He endured the second and the third blow; then, either he recognized the greater skill of his opponent in fencing, or perhaps he wished to exhibit his tremendous strength in view of both armies, or, pushed to the edge of the dam, he feared to be thrown into the water by Pan Longings enormous beast. It is enough that after he had received the last blow he brought the horses side by side, and seized the Lithuanian by the waist in his powerful arms.

They grasped each other like two bears when they are fighting for a female. They wound themselves around each other like two pines which, having grown from a single stump, intertwine till they form but one tree. All held breath and gazed in silence on the struggle of the combatants, each one of whom was considered the strongest among his own. You would have said that both had become one body, for they remained a long time motionless. But their faces grew red; and only from the veins which swelled on their foreheads, and from their backs bent like bows, could you suspect under that terrible quiet the superhuman tension of the arms which crushed them.

At length both began to quiver; but by degrees the face of Pan Longin grew redder and redder and the face of the Cossack bluer and bluer. Still a moment passed. The disquiet of the spectators increased.

Suddenly the silence was broken by a hollow, smothered voice: "Let me go--"

"No, my darling!" Something gave a sudden and terrible rattle, a groan was heard as if from under the ground, a wave of black blood burst from Pulyan's mouth, and his head dropped on his shoulder.

Pan Longin lifted the Cossack from his seat, and before the spectators had time to think what had happened, threw him on his own saddle and started on a trot toward Skshetuski's regiment.

"Vivat!" cried the Vishnyevetski men.

"Destruction!" answered the Zaporojians.

Instead of being confused by the defeat of their leader, they attacked the enemy the more stubbornly. A crowded struggle followed, which the narrowness of the place made the more venomous; and the Cossacks in spite of their bravery would certainly have yielded to the greater skill of their opponents, had it not been that suddenly the trumpets from the camp of Krívonos sounded a retreat.

They withdrew at once; and their opponents, after they had stopped awhile to show that they had kept the field, withdrew also. The dam was deserted; there remained on it only bodies of men and horses, as if in testimony of that which would be,--and that road of death lay black between the two armies,--but a light breath of wind wrinkled the smooth surface of the water and sounded plaintively through the leaves of the willows standing here and there above the banks of the pond.

Meanwhile the regiments of Krívonos moved like countless flocks of starlings and plover. The mob went in advance, then the regular Zaporojian infantry, companies of cavalry, Tartar volunteers, and Cossack artillery, and all without much order. They hurried before the others, wishing to force the dam by countless numbers, and then inundate and cover the army of the prince. The savage Krívonos believed in the fist and the sabre, not in military art. Therefore he urged his whole power to the attack, and ordered the regiments marching from behind to push on those in front, so that they must go even if against their will. Cannon-balls began to plunge into the water like wild swans and divers, causing no damage however to the prince's troops, by reason of the distance. The torrent of people covered the dam and advanced without hindrance. A part of that wave on reaching the river sought a passage, and not finding it turned back to the embankment, and marched in such a dense throng that, as Osinski said afterward, one might have ridden on horseback over their heads, and so covered the embankment that not a span of free earth remained.

Yeremi looked on this from the high shore, his brows wrinkled, and from his eyes flashed malicious lightning toward those crowds. Seeing the disorder and rush of the regiments of Krívonos, he said to Makhnitski,--

"The enemy begin with us in peasant fashion, and disregarding military art, come on like beaters at a hunt, but they will not reach this place."

Meanwhile, as if challenging his words, the Cossacks had come to the middle of the embankment. There they paused, astonished and disquieted by the silence of the prince's forces. But just at that moment there was a movement among these forces, and they retreated, leaving between themselves and the embankment a broad half-circle, which was to be the field of battle.

Then the infantry of Koritski opened, disclosing the throats of Vurtsel's cannon, turned toward the embankment, and in the corner formed by the slough and the embankment shone among the thickets along the bank the muskets of Osinski's Germans.

It was clear in a moment to military men on whose side the victory must be. Only a mad leader like Krívonos could rush to battle on conditions according to which he could not even pass the river in case Vishnyevetski wished to prevent him.

But the prince permitted part of his enemy's army to cross the embankment so as to surround and destroy it. The great leader took advantage of the blunders of his opponents, who did not even consider that it was impossible to reinforce his men on the other bank, except through a narrow passage over which no considerable number of men could be sent at one time; practised soldiers therefore looked with wonder at the action of Krívonos, who was not forced by anything to such a mad undertaking.

He was forced by ambition alone and a thirst for blood. He had learned that Hmelnitski, in spite of the preponderance of power under Krívonos, fearing the result of a battle with Yeremi, was marching with all his forces to his aid. Orders came not to deliver battle; but for that very reason Krívonos determined to deliver it.

Having taken Polónnoe, he got the taste of blood, and did not like to divide it with any one; therefore he hastened. He would lose half of his men,--well, what of that! With the rest he would overwhelm the slender forces of the prince and cut them to pieces. He would bring the head of Vishnyevetski as a present to Hmelnitski.

The billows of the mob had reached the end of the embankment, passed it, and spread over the half-circle abandoned by Yeremi's army. But at this moment the concealed infantry of Osinski opened upon them in the flank, and from the cannon of Vurtsel there bloomed out long wreaths of smoke, the earth trembled from the roar, and the battle began along the whole line.

Clouds of smoke concealed the shores of the Sula, the pond, the embankment, and even the field itself, so that all was hidden, save at times the scarlet, glittering uniforms of the dragoons, and the crests gleaming over the flying helmets, as everything seethed in that terrible cloud. The bells of the town were ringing, and mingled their sad groans with the deep bellowing of the guns. From the Cossack camp regiment after regiment rolled on to the embankment.

Those who crossed and reached the other side of the river extended in the twinkle of an eye into a long line and rushed with rage on the prince's regiments. The battle extended from one end of the pond to the bend in the river and the swampy meadows, which were flooded that rainy summer.

The mob and the men of the lower country had to conquer or perish, having behind them water, toward which they were pushed by the infantry and cavalry of the prince.

When the hussars moved forward, Zagloba, though he had short breath and did not like a throng, galloped with the others, because in fact he could not do otherwise without danger of being trampled to death. He flew on therefore, closing his eyes, and through his head there flew with lightning speed the thought, "Stratagem is nothing, stratagem is nothing; the stupid win, the wise perish!" Then he was seized with spite against the war, against the Cossacks, the hussars, and every one else in the world. He began to curse, to pray. The wind whistled in his ears, the breath was hemmed in his breast. Suddenly his horse struck against something; he felt resistance. Then he opened his eyes, and what did he see? Scythes, sabres, flails, a crowd of inflamed faces, eyes, mustaches,--and all indefinite, unknown, all trembling, galloping, furious. Then he was transported with rage against those enemies, because they are not going to the devil, because they are rushing up to his face and forcing him to fight. "You wanted it, now you have it," thought he, and he began to slash blindly on every side. Sometimes he cut the air, and sometimes he felt that his blade had sunk into something soft. At the same time he felt that he was still living, and this gave him extraordinary hope. "Slay! kill!" he roared like a buffalo. At last those frenzied faces vanished from his eyes, and in their places he saw a multitude of visages, tops of caps, and the shouts almost split his ears. "Are they fleeing?" shot through his head. "Yes!" Then daring sprang up in him beyond measure. "Scoundrels!" he shouted, "is that the way you meet a noble?" He sprang among the fleeing enemy, passed many, and entangled in the crowd began to labor with greater presence of mind now.

Meanwhile his comrades pressed the Cossacks to the bank of the Sula, covered pretty thickly with trees, and drove them along the shore to the embankment, taking no prisoners, for there was no time.

Suddenly Zagloba felt that his horse began to spread out under him; at the same time something heavy fell on him and covered his whole head, so that he was completely enveloped in darkness.

"Oh, save me!" he cried, beating the horse with his heels.

The steed, however, apparently wearied with the weight of the rider, only groaned and stood in one place.

Zagloba heard the screams and shouts of the horsemen rushing around him; then that whole hurricane swept by and all was in apparent quiet.

Again thoughts began to rush through his head with the swiftness of Tartar arrows: "What is this? What has happened? Jesus and Mary, I am in captivity!"

On his forehead drops of cold sweat came out. Evidently his head was bound just as he had once bound Bogun. That weight which he feels on his shoulder is the hand of a Cossack. But why don't they hang him or kill him? Why is he standing in one place?

"Let me go, you scoundrel!" cried he at last, with a muffled voice.

Silence.

"Let me go! I'll spare your life. Let me go, I say!"

No answer.

Zagloba struck into the sides of his horse again with his heels, but again without result; the prodded beast only stretched out wider and remained in the same place.

Finally rage seized the unfortunate captive, and drawing a knife from the sheath that hung at his belt, he gave a terrible stab behind. But the knife only cut the air.

Then Zagloba pulled with both hands at the covering which bound his head, and tore it in a moment. What is this?

No Cossack. Deserted all around. Only in the distance was to be seen in the smoke the red dragoons of Volodyovski flying past, and farther on the glittering armor of the hussars pursuing the remnant of the defeated, who were retreating from the field toward the water. At Zagloba's feet lay a Cossack regimental banner. Evidently the fleeing Cossack had dropped it so that the staff hit Zagloba's shoulder, and the cloth covered his head.

Seeing all this, and understanding it perfectly, that hero regained his presence of mind completely.

"Oh, ho!" said he, "I have captured a banner. How is this? Didn't I capture it? If justice is not defeated in this battle, then I am sure of a reward. Oh, you scoundrels! it is your luck that my horse gave out! I did not know myself when I thought I was greater in strategy than in bravery. I can be of some higher use in the army than eating cakes. Oh, God save us! some other crowd is rushing on. Don't come here, dog-brothers; don't come this way! May the wolves eat this horse! Kill! slay!"

Indeed, a new band of Cossacks were rushing toward Zagloba, raising unearthly voices, closely pursued by the armored men of Polyanovski. And perhaps Zagloba would have found his death under the hoofs of their horses, had it not been that the hussars of Skshetuski, having finished those whom they had been pursuing, turned to take between two fires those onrushing parties. Seeing this, the Zaporojians ran toward the water, only to find death in the swamps and deep places after escaping the sword. Those who fell on their knees begging for quarter died under the steel. The defeat was terrible and complete, but most terrible on the embankment. All who passed that, were swept away in the half-circle left by the forces of the prince. Those who did not pass, fell under the continual fire of Vurtsel's cannon and the guns of the German infantry. They could neither go forward nor backward; for Krívonos urged on still new regiments, which, pushing forward, closed the only road to escape. It seemed as though Krívonos had sworn to destroy his own men, who stifled, trampled, and fought one another, fell, sprang into the water on both sides, and were drowned. On one side were black masses of fugitives, and on the other masses advancing; in the middle, piles and mountains and rows of dead bodies; groans, screams, men deprived of speech; the madness of terror, disorder, chaos. The whole pond was full of men and horses; the water overflowed the banks.

At times the artillery was silent. Then the embankment, like the mouth of a cannon, threw forth crowds of Zaporojians and the mob, who rushed over the half-circle and went under the swords of the cavalry waiting for them. Then Vurtsel began to play again with his rain of iron and lead; the Cossack reinforcement barred the embankment. Whole hours were spent in these bloody struggles.

Krívonos, furious, foaming at the mouth, did not give up the battle yet, and hurried thousands of men to the jaws of death.

Yeremi, on the other side, in silver armor, sat on his horse, on a lofty mound called at that time the Kruja Mogila, and looked on. His face was calm; his eye took in the whole embankment, pond, banks of the Sluch, and extended to the place in which the enormous tabor of Krívonos stood wrapped in the bluish haze of the distance. The eyes of the prince never left that collection of wagons. At last he turned to the massive voevoda of Kieff, and said,--

"We shall not capture the tabor to-day."

"How? You wished to--"

"Time is flying quickly. It is too late. See! it is almost evening."

In fact, from the time the skirmishers went out, the battle, kept up by the stubbornness of Krívonos, had lasted already so long that the sun had but an hour left of its whole daily half-circle, and inclined to its setting. The light, lofty, small clouds, announcing fair weather and scattered over the sky like white-fleeced lambs, began to grow red and disappear in groups from the field of heaven. The flow of Cossacks to the embankment stopped gradually, and those regiments that had already come upon it retreated in dismay and disorder.

The battle was ended, and ended because the enraged crowd fell upon Krívonos at last, shouting with despair and madness,--

"Traitor! you are destroying us. You bloody dog! We will bind you ourselves, and give you up to Yeremi, and thus secure our lives. Death to you, not to us!"

"To-morrow I will give you the prince and all his army, or perish myself," answered Krívonos.

But the hoped for to-morrow had yet to come, and the present to-day was a day of defeat and disorder. Several thousand of the best warriors of the lower country, not counting the mob, lay on the field of battle, or were drowned in the pond and river. Nearly two thousand were taken prisoners; fourteen colonels were killed, not counting sotniks, essauls, and other elders. Pulyan, next in command to Krívonos, had fallen into the hands of the enemy alive, but with broken ribs.

"To-morrow we will cut them all up," said Krívonos. "I will neither eat nor drink till it is done."

In the opposite camp the captured banners were thrown down at the feet of the terrible prince. Each of the captors brought his own, so that they formed a considerable crowd,--altogether forty. When Zagloba passed by, he threw his down with such force that the staff split. Seeing this, the prince detained him, and asked,--

"And you captured that banner with your own hands?"

"At your service, your Highness."

"I see that you are not only a Ulysses, but an Achilles."

"I am a simple soldier, but I serve under Alexander of Macedon."

"Since you receive no wages, the treasurer will pay you, in addition to what you have had, two hundred ducats for this honorable exploit."

Zagloba seized the prince by the knees, and said, "Your favor is greater than my bravery, which would gladly hide itself behind its own modesty."

A scarcely visible smile wandered over the dark face of Skshetuski; but the knight was silent, and even later on he never said anything to the prince, or any one else, of the fears of Zagloba before the battle; but Zagloba himself walked away with such threatening mien that, seeing him, the soldiers of the other regiments pointed at him, saying,--

"He is the man who did most to-day."

Night came. On both sides of the river and the pond thousands of fires were burning, and smoke rose to the sky in columns. The wearied soldiers strengthened themselves with food and gorailka, or gave themselves courage for tomorrow's battle by relating the exploits of the present day. But loudest of all spoke Zagloba, boasting of what he had done, and what he could have done if his horse had not failed.

"I can tell you," said he, turning to the officers of the prince, and the nobles of Tishkyevich's command, "that great battles are no novelty for me. I was in many of them in Moldavia and Turkey; but when I was on the field I was afraid--not of the enemy, for who is afraid of such trash!--but of my own impulsiveness, for I thought immediately that it would carry me too far."

"And did it?"

"It did. Ask Skshetuski. The moment I saw Vershul falling with his horse, I wanted to gallop to his aid without asking a question. My comrades could scarcely hold me back."

"True," said Skshetuski, "we had to hold you in."

"But," interrupted Karvich, "where is Vershul?"

"He has already gone on a scouting expedition, he knows no rest."

"See then, gentlemen," said Zagloba, displeased at the interruption, "how I captured the banner."

"Then Vershul is not wounded?" inquired Karvich again.

"This is not the first one that I have captured in my life, but none cost me such trouble."

"He is not wounded, only bruised," answered Azulevich, a Tartar, "and has gulped water, for he fell head first into the pond."

"Then I wonder the fish didn't die," said Zagloba, with anger, "for the water must have boiled from such a flaming head."

"But he is a great warrior."

"Not so great, since a half John[13] was enough for him. Tfu! it is impossible to talk with you. You might learn from me how to capture banners from the enemy."

Further conversation was interrupted by the youthful Pan Aksak, who approached the fire at that moment.

"I bring you news, gentlemen," said he, with a clear half-childish voice.

"The nurse hasn't washed his bib, the cat has drunk his milk, and his cup is broken," muttered Zagloba.

But Pan Aksak paid no attention to this fling at his youth, and said: "They are burning Pulyan."

"The dogs will have toast," said Zagloba.

"And he is making a confession. The negotiations are broken. Kisel is nearly wild. Hmel (hops) is coming with all his forces to help Krívonos."

"Hops? What hops? Who is making anything of hops? If hops are on the road, there will be beer then. We don't care for hops," said Zagloba, looking at the same time with fierce, haughty eyes at those around.

"Hmel is coming; but Krívonos didn't wait, therefore he lost--"

"Yes, he played and lost."

"Six thousand Cossacks are already in Makhnovka. Two thousand Bogun is leading."

"Who? who?" asked Zagloba instantly, in a changed voice.

"Bogun."

"Impossible!"

"That is the confession of Pulyan."

"Ah, here is a cake for you, grandmother!" cried Zagloba, piteously. "Can they get here soon?"

"In three days. But on the way to battle they will not hurry too much, so as not to tire their horses."

"But I will hurry!" muttered Zagloba. "Oh, angels of God, save me from that ruffian! I would gladly give my captured banner if that water-burner would only break his neck on the way to this place. I hope too that we shall not wait here long. We have shown Krívonos what we can do, and now it is time to rest. I hate that Bogun so much that I cannot call to mind his devilish name without abomination. I did make a choice! I couldn't stay in Bar? Bad luck brought me here."

"Don't worry yourself," whispered Skshetuski, "for it is a shame! Between you and me nothing threatens you here."

"Nothing threatens me? You don't know him! Why, he might creep up to us now among the fires here." Zagloba looked around disquieted. "And he is as enraged at you as at me."

"God grant me to meet him!" said Pan Yan.

"If that is a favor, then I have no wish to receive it. In my character of Christian I forgive him all his offences willingly, but on condition that he be hanged two days before. I am not alarmed, but you have no idea what surpassing disgust seizes me. I like to know with whom I have to deal,--if with a noble, then a noble; if with a peasant, then a peasant,--but he is a sort of incarnate devil, with whom you don't know what course to take. I ventured many a thing with him; but such eyes as he made when I bound his head, I cannot describe to you,--to the hour of my death I shall remember them. I don't wish to rouse the devil while he sleeps. Once is enough for a trick. I will say to you also that you are ungrateful, have no thought of that unhappy woman."

"How so?"

"Because," said Zagloba, drawing the knight away from the fire, "you stay here and gratify your military caprice and fancy by fighting day after day, while she is drowning herself in tears, waiting in vain for an answer. Another man with real love in his heart and pity for her grief wouldn't do this, but would have sent me off long ago."

"Do you think then of returning to Bar?"

"Even to-day, for I have pity on her."

Pan Yan raised his eyes yearningly to the stars and said,--

"Do not speak to me of insincerity, for God is my witness that I never raise a bit of bread to my mouth or take a moment of sleep without thinking of her first, and nothing can be stronger in my heart than the thought of her. I have not sent you with an answer hitherto because I wished to go myself to be with her at once. And there are no wings in the world and no speed which I would not use could they serve me in going to her."

"Then why don't you fly?"

"Because I cannot before battle. I am a soldier and a noble, therefore I must think of honor."

"But to-day we are after the battle; therefore we can start, even this minute."

Pan Yan sighed.

"To-morrow we attack Krívonos."

"I don't understand your ways. You beat young Krívonos; old Krívonos came, and you beat old Krívonos. Now what's-his-name (not to mention him in an evil hour), Bogun, will come, you will beat him. Hmelnitski will come. Oh, what the devil! And as it will go on this way it would be better for you to enter into partnership with Podbipienta at once, then there would be a fool with continence plus his mightiness Skshetuski, total two fools and one continence. Let's have peace, for, as God lives, I will be the first to persuade the princess to put horns on you; and at Bar lives Andrei Pototski, and when he looks at her fire flashes out of his eyes. Tfu! if this should be said by some young fellow who had not seen a battle and wanted to make a reputation, then I could understand; but not you, who have drunk blood like a wolf, and at Makhnovka, I am told, killed a kind of infernal dragon of a man-eater. I swear, by that moon in heaven, that you are up to something here, or that you have got such a taste of blood that you like it better than your bride."

Skshetuski looked involuntarily at the moon, which was sailing in the high starry heavens like a ship above the camp.

"You are mistaken," said he, after a while. "I do not want blood, nor am I working for reputation, but it would not be proper to leave my comrades in a difficult struggle in which the whole regiment must engage, *nemine excepto*. In this is involved knightly honor, a sacred thing. As to the war it will undoubtedly drag on, for the rabble has grown too great; but if Hmelnitski comes to the aid of Krívonos, there will be an intermission. To-morrow Krívonos will either fight or he will not. If he does, with God's aid he will receive dire punishment, and we must go to a quiet place to draw breath. During these two months we neither sleep nor eat, we only fight and fight; day and night we have nothing over our heads, exposed to all the attacks of the elements. The prince is a great leader, but prudent. He does not rush on Hmelnitski with a few thousand men against legions. I know also that he will go to Zbaraj, recruit there, get new soldiers,--nobles from the whole Commonwealth will hurry to him,--and then we shall move to a general campaign. To-morrow will be the last day of work, and after to-morrow I shall be able to accompany you to Bar with a clean heart. And I will add, to pacify you, that Bogun can in no wise come here to-morrow and take part in the battle; and even if he should I hope that his peasant star will pale, not only before that of the prince, but before my own."

"He is an incarnate Beelzebub. I have told you that I dislike a throng; but he is worse than a throng, though I repeat it is not so much from fear as from an unconquerable aversion I have for the man. But no more of this. Tomorrow comes the tanning of the peasants' backs, and then to Bar. Oh, those beautiful eyes will laugh at the sight of you, and that face will blush! I tell you, even I feel lonely without her, for I love her as a father. And no wonder. I have no legitimate children; my fortune is far away, for it is in Turkey, where my scoundrelly agents steal it all; and I live as an orphan in the world, and in my old age I shall have to go and live with Podbipienta at Myshekishki."

"Oh, no; don't let your head ache over that! You have done something for us; we cannot be too thankful to you."

Further conversation was interrupted by some officer who passing along inquired: "Who stands there?"

"Vershul!" exclaimed Skshetuski, recognizing him by his voice. "Are you from the scouting-party?"

"Yes; and now from the prince."

"What news?"

"Battle to-morrow. The enemy are widening the embankment, building bridges over the Stira and Sluch, and on the morrow wish to come to us without fail."

"What did the prince say to that?"

"The prince said: 'All right!'"

"Nothing more?"

"Nothing. He gave no order to hinder them, and axes are chopping; they will work till morning."

"Did you get informants?"

"I captured seven. All confessed that they have heard of Hmelnitski,--that he is coming, but probably far away yet. What a night!"

"Yes, you can see as in the day. And how do you feel after the fall?"

"My bones are sore. I am going to thank our Hercules and then sleep, for I am tired. If I could doze a couple of hours--good-night!"

"Good-night!"

"Go you to sleep also," said Skshetuski to Zagloba; "for it is late, and there will be work to-morrow."

"And the next day a journey," said Zagloba.

They turned, said their prayers, and then lay down near the fire.

Soon the fires began to go out one after another. Silence embraced the camp; but the moon cast on the men silver rays, with which it illumined every little while new groups of sleepers. The silence was broken only by the universal, mighty snoring, and the call of the sentinels watching the camp.

But sleep did not close the heavy lids of the soldiers long. Scarcely had the first dawn whitened the shadows of night when the trumpets in every corner of the camp thundered the *reveille*.

An hour later the prince, to the great astonishment of the knights, drew back along the whole line.

CHAPTER XXXII.

But it was the retreat of a lion needing room for a spring.

The prince purposely allowed Krívonos to cross so as to inflict on him the greater defeat. In the very beginning of the battle he had the cavalry turned and urged on as if in flight, seeing which the men of the lower country and the mob broke their ranks to overtake and surround him. Then Yeremi turned suddenly, and with his whole cavalry struck them at once so terribly that they were unable to resist. The prince's troops pursued them five miles to the crossing, then over the bridges, the embankment, and two miles and a half to the camp, cutting and killing them without mercy. The hero of the day was the sixteen-year-old Pan Aksak, who gave the first blow and produced the first disorder. Only with such an army, old and trained, could the prince use such stratagems, and feign flight which in any other ranks might become real. This being the case, the second day ended still more disastrously for Krívonos than the first. All his field-pieces were taken, and a number of flags,--among them several royal flags captured by the Cossacks at Korsún. If the infantry of Koritski and Osinski with the cannon of Vurtsel could have followed the cavalry, the camp would have been taken at a blow. But before they came up it was night, and the enemy had already retreated a considerable distance, so that it was impossible to reach them. But Zatsvilikhovski captured half the camp, and with it enormous supplies of arms and provisions. The crowd seized Krívonos twice, wishing to give him up to the prince; and the promise of an immediate return to Hmelnitski barely sufficed to save him. He fled therefore with the remaining half of his tabor, with a decimated army, beaten and in despair, and did not halt till he reached Makhnovka, where when Hmelnitski came up, in the moment of his first anger, he ordered him to be chained by the neck to a cannon.

But when his first anger had passed the Zaporojian hetman remembered that the unfortunate Krívonos had covered Volynia with blood, captured Polónnoe, and sent thousands of nobles to the other world, left their bodies without burial, and had been victorious everywhere till he met Yeremi. For these services the Zaporojian hetman took pity on him, and not only ordered him to be freed immediately from the cannon, but restored him to command, and sent him to Podolia to new conquests and slaughters.

The prince now announced to his army the rest so much desired. In the last battle it had suffered considerable losses, especially at the storming of the tabor by the cavalry, behind which the Cossacks defended themselves with equal stubbornness and adroitness. Five hundred soldiers were killed; Colonel Mokrski, severely wounded, died soon after; Pan Kushel, Ponyatovski, and young Aksak were shot, but not dangerously; and Zagloba, becoming accustomed to the throng, took his place manfully with the others, struck twice with a flail, he fell on his back, and being unable to move, lay as dead in Skshetuski's wagon.

Fate hindered the plan of going to Bar; for they could not start immediately, especially since the prince had sent Pan Yan, at the head of a number of troops, as far as Zaslav, to exterminate the bands of peasants assembled there. The knight went without mentioning Bar to the prince, and during five days burned and slaughtered till he cleared the neighborhood.

At last, even the soldiers became wearied beyond measure by the uninterrupted fighting, distant expeditions, ambuscades, and watching; he decided therefore to return to the prince, who, as he was informed, had gone to Tarnopol.

On the eve of his return he stopped at Sukhojintsi, on the Khomor. He disposed his soldiers in the village, took his lodgings for the night in a peasant's cottage, and because he was greatly wearied from labor and want of rest, fell asleep at once, and slept like a stone all night.

About morning, when half asleep, half awake, he began to doze and dream. Wonderful images were in movement before his eyes. It seemed to him that he was in Lubni, that he had never left the place, that he was sleeping in his room in the armory, and that Jendzian, as was his wont in the morning, was bustling around with clothes and preparing for his master's rising. Gradually, however, consciousness began to scatter the phantoms. He remembered that he was in Sukhojintsi, not in Lubni. Still the form of his servant did not dissolve in mist, and Pan Yan saw him continually sitting under the window, occupied in oiling armor-straps, which had shrunk considerably from the heat. But he still thought that it was a vision of sleep, and closed his eyes again. After a while he opened them. Jendzian was sitting under the window.

"Jendzian," called Skshetuski, "is that you, or is it your ghost?"

The young fellow, frightened by the sudden call, dropped the breastplate on the floor with a clatter, spread his arms, and said: "Oh, for God's sake! why do you scream, my master, that I am like a ghost? I am alive and well!"

"And you have come back?"

"But have you sent me off?"

"Come here to me; let me embrace you."

The faithful youth fell upon the floor, and caught Skshetuski by the knees. Skshetuski kissed him on the forehead with joy, and repeated: "You are alive, you are alive!"

"Oh, my master, I cannot speak from joy that I see you again in health! You shouted so that I let the breastplate fall. The straps have shrunk up,--it is clear that you have had no one. Praise be to thee, O God! Oh, my dear master!"

"When did you come back?"

"Last night."

"Why didn't you wake me up?"

"Why should I wake you up? I came early to take your clothes."

"Where did you come from?"

"From Gushchi."

"What were you doing there? What has happened to you? Tell me."

"Well, you see the Cossacks came to Gushchi, which belongs to the voevoda of Bratslav, to plunder and burn, and I was there earlier, for I went there with Father Patroni Lasko, who took me to Hmelnitski from Gushchi; for the voevoda sent him to Hmelnitski with letters. I went back with him, therefore, and at that time the Cossacks were burning Gushchi; and they killed Father Patroni for his love to us, and no doubt they would have killed the voevoda too, if he had been there, though he belongs to their church and is their great benefactor--"

"But speak clearly and don't confuse things, for I cannot understand. You have been with the Cossacks, then, and spent some time with Hmelnitski. Is that true?"

"Yes, with the Cossacks; for when they took me in Chigirin they thought I was one of their men. Now put on your clothes, my master! Dress--Oh, Lord bless me, everything you have is worn out, so there is nothing to lay hands on. But don't be angry with me because I did not deliver in Rozlogi the letter which you wrote in Kudák. That rascal, Bogun, took it from me, and had it not been for that fat noble I should have lost my life."

"I know, I know. It is not your fault. That fat noble is in the camp. He has told me everything just as it was. He has also stolen from Bogun the lady, who is in good health and living at Bar."

"Praise be to God for that! I knew too that Bogun didn't get her. Then of course the wedding is not far away?"

"It is not. From here we shall go by orders to Tarnopol, and from there to Bar."

"Thanks be to God on high! He will surely hang himself, that Bogun; but a witch has already foretold him that he will never get her of whom he is thinking, and that a Pole will have her. That Pole is surely you."

"How do you know this?"

"I heard it. I must tell you everything in order, and do you dress, my master, for they are cooking breakfast for you. When I was going in the boat from Kudák we were a long time sailing, for it was against the current, and besides the boat got injured, and we had to repair it. We were going on then, going on, my master, going on--"

"Go on! go on!" interrupted Skshetuski, impatiently.

"And we came to Chigirin; and what happened to me there you know already."

"I do."

"I was lying there in the stable without a sight of God's world. And then Hmelnitski came immediately after the departure of Bogun, with a tremendous Zaporojian force. And as the Grand Hetman had previously punished a great many Chigirin people for their love to the Zaporojians, many of them were killed and wounded. Therefore the Cossacks thought that I was from Chigirin. They didn't kill me, but gave me necessary provisions and care, and didn't let the Tartars take me, though they let them do everything else. When I came to myself I began to think what I was to do. Those rascals by this time had gone to Korsún and defeated the hetmans. Oh, my master, what my eyes saw is not to be described. They concealed nothing from me, knew no shame, because they took me for one of themselves. I was thinking whether to flee or not, but I saw it would be safer to remain until a better opportunity should offer itself. When they began to bring in from the battlefield at Korsún cloths, silver, plate, precious stones, oh, my master, my heart nearly burst, and my eyes almost came out of my head. Such robbers!--they sold six silver spoons for a thaler, and later for a quart of vudka; a golden button or brooch or a hat cockade you might buy with a pint. Then I thought to myself: 'Why should I sit idle? Let me make something. With God's help I will return some time to the Jendzians at Podlesia, where my parents are living. I will give this to them, for they have a lawsuit with the Yavorskis, which has been going on now for fifty years, and they have nothing to continue it with.' I bought then so much stuff of every kind that it took two horses to carry it. This was the consolation of my sorrows, for I was terribly grieved on your account."

"Oh, Jendzian, you are always the same; you must have profit out of everything."

"What is the harm, if God has blessed me? I do not steal; and if you gave me a purse for the road to Rozlogi, here it is. I ought to return it, for I didn't go to Rozlogi."

Saying this, the young fellow unbuckled his belt, took out the purse, and placed it before the knight. Skshetuski smiled and said,--

"Since you had such good luck, you are surely richer than I; but keep the purse."

"I thank you very humbly. I have collected a little, with God's favor. My father and mother will be glad, and my grandfather, who is now ninety years old. But they will continue their lawsuit with the Yavorskis till the last penny, and send them out with packs on their backs. You will also be the gainer, for I shall not mention that belt you promised me in Kudák, though it suited me well."

"Yes, for you have already reminded me! Oh, such a son of a----! A regular insatiable wolf! I don't know where that belt is; but if I promised, I will give you, if not that one, another."

"I thank you, my master," said he, embracing Skshetuski's knees.

"No need of that! Go on; tell what happened!"

"The Lord then sent me some profit among the robbers. But I was tormented from not knowing what had happened to you, and lest Bogun had carried off the lady; till they brought me word that he was lying in Cherkasi barely alive, wounded by the prince's men. I went to Cherkasi, since, as you are aware, I know how to make plasters and dress wounds. The Cossacks knew that I could do this. Well, Donyéts, a colonel, sent me to Cherkasi, and went with me himself to nurse that robber. There a burden fell from my heart, for I heard that our young lady had escaped with that noble. I went then to Bogun. I was thinking, 'Will he know me or not?' But he was lying in a fever, and at first didn't know me. Later on he knew me, and said, 'You were going with a letter to Rozlogi?' 'Yes,' I answered. Then he said again, 'I struck you in Chigirin?' 'Yes.' 'Then you serve Pan Skshetuski?' 'I am serving no one now,' I replied. 'I had more evil than good in that service, therefore I chose to go to the Cossacks for freedom; and I am nursing you now for ten days, and am restoring you to health.' He believed me, and became very confidential. I learned from him that Rozlogi was burned, that he had killed the two princes. The other Kurtsevichi wished at first to go to our prince, but could not, and escaped to the Lithuanian army. But the worst was when he remembered that fat noble. Then, my master, he gnashed his teeth like a man cracking nuts."

"Was he long sick?"

"Long, long. His wounds healed quickly; then they opened again, for he didn't take care of them at first. I sat many a night with him,--may he be cut up!--as with some good man. And you must know, my master, that I swore by my salvation to take vengeance on him; and I will keep my oath, though I have to follow him all my life; for he maltreated me, an innocent person, and pounded me like a dog. And I am no trash, either! He must perish at my hand unless somebody else kills him first. I tell you that about a hundred times I had a chance, for often there was no one near him but me. I thought to myself, 'Shall I stab him or not?' But I was ashamed to kill him in his bed."

"It was praiseworthy of you not to kill him while sick and weak. That would be the deed of a peasant, not of a noble."

"And you know, my master, I had the same thought. I recollected too that when my parents sent me from home my grandfather blessed me, and said, 'Remember, you dunce, that you are a noble. Have ambition, serve faithfully; but don't let any man trample on you.' He said also that when a noble acts in peasant fashion the Lord Jesus weeps. I recalled that phrase and I restrained myself. I had to let the chance pass. And now he was more confidential. More than once he asked, 'How shall I reward you?' And I said, 'Any way you wish,' And I cannot complain. He supplied me bountifully, and I took all he gave me; for I thought to myself, 'Why should I leave it in the hands of a robber?' On his account others gave me presents; for I tell you, my master, that there is no one so beloved as he, both by the men from below and the mob, though there is not a noble in the Commonwealth who has such contempt for the mob as he."

Here Jendzian began to twist his head as if he remembered and wondered at something; and after a while he said,--

"He is a strange man, and it must be confessed that he is altogether of noble nature. And that young lady,--but he loves her! Oh, mighty God, but he loves her! As soon as he was a little restored, Dontsovna came to him to soothsay; but she told him nothing good. She is a brazen-faced giantess who is in friendship with devils, but she is a good-looking woman. When she laughs you would swear that a mare was neighing in the meadow. She has white teeth so strong that she might chew up a breastplate. When she walks the ground trembles. And, by the evident visitation of God, my good looks attracted her. Then she wouldn't pass without catching me by the head or the sleeve and jerking me. More than once she said, 'Come!' But I was afraid that the devil might break my neck if I went, and then I should lose all I had gathered; so I answered, 'Haven't you enough of others?' She said, 'You please me; though you are a stripling, you please me.' 'Be off, bass-viol!' I said. Then said she again, 'I like you, I like you!'"

"But you saw the soothsaying?"

"I did; and I heard it. There was a sort of smudge, a seething and squeaking, and shadows, so that I was frightened. She was standing in the middle of the room, looking stern, with sullen black brows, and repeated: 'The Pole is near her! the Pole is near her! Chili! huk! chili! the Pole is near her!' Then she poured wheat into a sieve, and looked. The grains went around like insects, and she repeated: 'Chili! huk! chili! the Pole is near her!' Oh, my master, if he were not such a robber it would be sad to look at his despair! After every answer she gave he used to grow white as a shirt, fall on his back, clasp his hands over his head, twist and whine, and beg forgiveness of the princess that he came with violence to Rozlogi and killed her cousins. 'Where art thou, cuckoo, the loved one, the only one? I would have borne you in my arms, and now I cannot live without you! I will not approach you. I will be your slave if my eyes can only see you!' Then he remembered Zagloba again, ground his teeth, bit the bed, till sleep overpowered him; and in sleep he groaned and sighed."

"But did she never prophesy favorably for him?"

"I don't know, my master, for he recovered, and besides I left him. The priest Lasko came, so Bogun arranged that I should go with him to Gushchi. The robbers there found out that I had property of different kinds, and I too made no secret of the fact that I was going to help my parents."

"And they didn't rob you?"

"Perhaps they would have done so, but fortunately there were no Tartars there then, and the Cossacks did not dare to rob me from fear of Bogun. Besides they took me for one of their own. Even Hmelnitski himself ordered me to keep my ears open and report what would be said at the voevoda's, if there should be a meeting there. May the hangman light his way! I went then to Gushchi. Krívonos's detachments came and killed Father Lasko. I buried half my treasure, and escaped with the rest when I heard that you were near Zaslav. Praise be to God on high that you are in good health, and that you are preparing for your wedding. Then the end of every evil will come. I told those scoundrels who went against the prince our lord, that they wouldn't come back. They have caught it. Now maybe the war is over."

"How over? It is only beginning now with Hmelnitski."

"And you will fight after the wedding?"

"But did you think that cowardice would seize me at the wedding?"

"I didn't think that. I know that whomsoever it seizes, it won't seize you. I just ask; for when I take to my parents what I have collected I should like to go with you. Maybe God will help me to avenge my wrong on Bogun; for since it is not proper to take an unfair advantage, where shall I find him, if not in the field? He will not hide himself."

"What a determined fellow you are!"

"Let every one have his own. And as I promised to follow him to Turkey, it cannot be otherwise. And now I will go with you to Tarnopol, and then to the wedding. But why do you go to Bar by Tarnopol? It is not on the road in any way."

"I must take home my regiment."

"I understand."

"Now give me something to eat," said Pan Yan.

"I've been looking out for that. The stomach is the main thing."

"After we have eaten we will start at once."

"Praise be to God for that, though my poor nag is worn to death."

"I will order them to give you a pack-horse; you can ride on it."

"Thank you humbly," said Jendzian, smiling with delight at the thought that including the purse and the belt a third present had come to him now.

CHAPTER XXXIII.

Pan Yan rode at the head of the prince's squadrons, but to Zbaraj instead of Tarnopol, for a new order had come to march to the latter place; and on the road he told his faithful attendant his own adventures,--how he had been taken in captivity at the Saitch, how long he had remained there, and how much he had suffered before Hmelnitski had liberated him. They advanced slowly; for though they had no trains or baggage, their road lay through a country which was so ruined that the greatest exertions were necessary to obtain provisions for men and horses. In places they met crowds of famished people, especially women and children, who implored God for death or Tartar captivity; for then, though in bonds, they would be fed. And still it was harvest time in that rich land flowing with milk and honey; but the parties of Krívonos had destroyed everything that could be destroyed, and the remnant of the inhabitants fed themselves on the bark of the trees. Near Yampol they first entered a country which was not so much injured by war, and having had more rest and provisions in plenty, they went with hurried march to Zbaraj, where they arrived in five days after leaving Sukhojintsi.

There was a great concourse in Zbaraj. Prince Yeremi was there with his whole army, and besides him no small number of soldiers and nobles had come. War hung in the air, nothing else was mentioned; the town and neighborhood were swarming with armed men. The peace party in Warsaw, maintained in its hopes by Pan Kisel, the voevoda of Bratslav, had not given up, it is true, negotiations, and continued to believe that it would be possible to allay the storm with them; still they understood that negotiations could have results only when there was a powerful army to support them. The Diet of convocation was held therefore amidst the threatenings and thunderings of war such as usually precede an outbreak. The general militia was called out, and enlisted soldiers were concentrated; and though the chancellor and commanders still believed in peace, the war feeling was predominant in the minds of the nobles. The victories won by Prince Yeremi fired the imagination. The minds of men were burning with a desire for vengeance on the peasants, and a desire to pay back for Jóltiya Vodi and Korsún, for the blood of so many thousands who had died martyrs' deaths, for the disgrace and humiliation. The name of the terrible prince was bright with the sunlight of glory,--it was on every lip, in every heart; and together with that name was heard, from the shores of the Baltic to the Wilderness, the ominous word "War!"

War! War! Signs in the heavens announced it also, the excited faces of the populace, the glittering of swords, the nightly howling of dogs before the cottages, and the neighing of horses, catching the odor of blood. War! Escutcheoned men through all the lands and districts and houses and villages drew out their old armor and swords from the storehouses. The youths sang songs about Yeremi; the women prayed before altars; and armored men were marching to the field in Prussia and Livonia as well as in Great Poland and populous Mazovia, and away to God's own Carpathian peaks, and the dark pine forests of Beskid.

War lay in the nature of things. The plundering movement of the Zaporojie and the popular uprising of the Ukraine mob demanded some higher watchwords than slaughter and robbery, than a struggle against serfdom and the land-grabbing of magnates. Hmelnitski knew this well, and taking advantage of the slumbering irritation from mutual abuses and oppressions, of which there was never a lack in those harsh times, he changed a social into a religious struggle, kindled popular fanaticism, and dug in the very beginning between the two camps an abyss which could be filled neither with parchments nor negotiations, but only with blood.

Wishing for negotiations from his soul, he wished them only to secure his own power; but afterward--what was to be afterward the Zaporojian hetman did not think; he did not look into the future and had no care for it. He did not know, however, that that abyss which he had created was so great that no negotiations could fill it, at least in such a time as he, Hmelnitski, could demand. The quick politician did not guess that he would not be able to enjoy in peace the bloody fruits of his life; and still it was easy to understand that when the armed legions should stand before each other, the parchment for the inscription of treaties would be the field, and the pens, swords and lances.

Events tended, by the force of things, toward war; and even ordinary people, led by instinct alone, felt that it could not be otherwise; and throughout the whole Commonwealth the eyes of men were turned more and more to Yeremi, who from the beginning had proclaimed a war of life and death. In the shadow of his gigantic figure the chancellor, the voevoda of Bratslav, and the commanders were more and more effaced, and among them the powerful Prince Dominik, formal commander-in-chief. Their importance drooped, and obedience to their government decreased. The army and the nobles were ordered to march to Lvoff and then to Gliniani, which they did accordingly in larger and larger divisions. The regular troops assembled, and after them men of the nearest provinces; but immediately fresh events began to threaten the authority of the Commonwealth. Now not only the less disciplined squadrons of the militia, not only the private troops, but the regular soldiers when at the place of muster refused obedience to the commanders, and in defiance of orders marched to Zbaraj to place themselves under the command of Yeremi. This was done first by the nobles of Kieff and Bratslav, who had previously served in large part under Yeremi. They were followed by the nobles of Rus and Lubelsk, and these by the troops of the Crown, and it was not difficult to understand that all would follow in their steps.

Yeremi, who had been slighted, neglected by design, was becoming, by the force of things, the hetman and supreme leader of all the power of the Commonwealth. The nobles and the army, devoted to him soul and body, waited only for his nod. Authority, war, peace, the future of the Commonwealth, rested in his hands. Each day he grew, for each day new squadrons marched to him, and he was becoming so gigantic that his shadow began to fall not only on the chancellor and the commanders, but on the Senate, on Warsaw, and the whole Commonwealth.

In circles hostile to him, those of the chancellor at Warsaw and in the camp of the commander-in-chief, in the suite of Prince Dominik, and around the voevoda of Bratslav, they began to mutter against his measureless ambition and pride; the affair of Gadyach was mentioned, when the insolent prince came with four thousand men to Warsaw, and entering the Senate, was ready to hew down all, not excepting the king himself.

"What might not be expected from such a man, and what must he be now after that Xenophontine return from the Trans-Dnieper, after all those military advantages and victories which had given him such an immense reputation? To what unendurable haughtiness must that favor of the soldiers and the nobles raise him? Who will stand against him to-day? What will become of the Commonwealth in which one citizen rises to such power that he can trample upon the will of the Senate, and snatch away their authority from the leaders appointed by the Commonwealth? Does he intend really to decorate Prince Karl with the crown? He is Marius, it is true; but God grant that he become not a Coriolanus or a Catiline, for he is equal to both in ambition and pride."

Thus did they speak in Warsaw and in military circles, especially in the suite of Prince Dominik, the rivalry between whom and Yeremi had caused no little damage to the Commonwealth. But that Marius was sitting that moment at Zbaraj, gloomy, unconsulted. Recent victories gave no light to his countenance. Whenever some new squadron of regulars or district militia appeared at Zbaraj he went out to see it, determined its value at a glance, and immediately fell into musing. Soldiers gathered around him with shouts, fell on their knees before him, crying: "Hail, invincible chief, Slavonic Hercules! We will stand by thee to the death." But he answered: "My respects to you, gentlemen! We are all soldiers of Christ, and I am too insignificant in rank to be the steward of your blood;" and he returned to his quarters, fled from men, struggled in solitude with his thoughts. In this way whole days passed.

Meanwhile the town was in a tumult with swarm after swarm of new troops. The militia drank from morning till night; walking along the streets, they raised quarrels and disputes with officers of foreign levy. The regular soldiers, feeling also the reins of discipline relaxed, indulged in eating, drinking, and play. Every day there were new guests; consequently new feasts and amusements with the young women of Zbaraj. The troops crammed every street, were stationed too in the neighboring villages; and what a variety of horses, arms, uniforms, plumes, chain armor, and steel caps,--uniforms of various provinces! It seemed like a general carnival to which half the Commonwealth had come. At one moment dashes in a carriage of some magnate, gilt or purple, drawn by six or eight plumed horses; ahead of it outriders in Hungarian or German liveries; attending it household janissaries, Cossacks or Tartars. At another some legionaries appear glittering in velvet or satin without armor, and thrust apart the crowds with their Anatolian or Persian steeds. The plumes of their caps and brooches at their necks are glittering with brilliants and rubies, but all make way for them in sign of respect. Here before a balcony stands an officer of the country infantry, with fresh, bright collar, a long staff in his hand, pride in his face, a village heart in his breast; farther on glitter the rising helmets of the dragoons, the caps of the German infantry, lynx-skin caps of the militia; servants on errands squirm about as if in hot water. Here and there the streets are packed with wagons; in one place the wagons enter, squeaking mercilessly; every place is full of shouts, and cries of "Out of the road!"--curses of servants, disputes, fights, neighing of horses. The narrower streets are packed to such a degree with hay and straw that it is impossible to squeeze through.

Amidst this multitude of bright uniforms glittering with all the colors of the rainbow, amidst velvet and cloths and shining satin glittering with brilliants, how strangely appear the regiments of the prince, haggard, tattered, emaciated, with rusty armor, faded and torn uniforms! Soldiers of the best regiments looked like wandering minstrels, worse than the attendants from other commands; but all bow before these rags, before this rust and shabbiness, for they are the banners of heroes. War is a cruel mother; like Saturn, she devours her own children, and whom she does not devour, she gnaws as a dog gnaws bones. Those faded uniforms signify stormy nights, marches amidst the rage of the elements or the burning of the sun; that rust on the steel means the unwiped blood of the man himself, of the enemy, or both together. So the Vishnyevetski men had the first place everywhere. They were the story-tellers in the taverns and the quarters, and others were listeners. Sometimes a spasm would seize one of the listeners, and striking his hands on his hips, he would say, "May the bullets strike you, for you are devils, not men!" But they would answer, "Not ours the merit, but the leader's, whose like the round of the earth has not shown to this day." All feasts therefore ended in shouts: "Vivat Yeremi! Vivat the prince voevoda, the leader of leaders, the hetman of hetmans!"

The nobles, after they had drunk awhile, would rush out on the streets and fire guns and muskets. The prince's men warned them that their freedom was but for a time,--that a moment would come when the prince would take them in hand and enforce discipline such as they had never heard of. They took advantage of the opportunity all the more. "Let us rejoice while we are free," they cried. "When the time for obedience comes we will listen, for we have some one to obey who is not *baby* nor *Latin* nor *feather-bed*." And the unfortunate Prince Dominik always came out worst, for the soldiers' tongues ground him to bran. They said that he prayed whole days, and in the evening hung to the handle of a mug, spat on his stomach, and with one eye open inquired, "What is that?" They said also that he took "jalap" at night, and that he saw as many battles as there were depicted on his carpet by Dutch art. No one defended him any longer, and no one pitied him; and those who were in open opposition to military discipline attacked him most savagely.

But all were surpassed by Zagloba, with his satire and ridicule. He had already recovered from the pain in his back, and was now in his element. How much he ate and drank it is vain to describe, for the thing passes human belief. Crowds of nobles followed and surrounded him continually, and he related, talked, and bantered with those who entertained him; he looked down, as an old soldier, on those who were going to war, and said to them, with all the pride of experience,--

"Gentlemen, you know as much about the hardships of war as a nun does of marriage. You have fresh clothes, and perfumed, the odor of which, though pleasant, I shall try in the first battle to keep on the lee side of me. The man who has not snuffed military garlic does not know how it draws tears. No one will bring you, gentlemen, your mug of hot beer of a morning, or your wine punch. The stomach will fall away from you, and you will shrink up like a pancake in the sun. Believe me, experience is the foundation of everything. I have been in many straits, and have captured more than one flag; but I must tell you, gentlemen, that none came to me with such difficulty as that at Konstantinoff. The devil take those Zaporojians! Seven sweats, I tell you, gentlemen, came out of me before I seized the flag-staff. You may ask Pan Yan, who killed Burdabut; he saw it with his own eyes, and admired the deed. But now all you have to do is to shout in the ear of any Cossack 'Zagloba!' and you will see what he will tell you. But why do I talk to you, who only know how to kill flies on the walls with the palms of your hands?"

"But how was it,--how?" asked a crowd of young men.

"Well, gentlemen, do you want my tongue to get red-hot with turning in my mouth, like an axle in a wagon?"

"Then you must pour wine around it," said the nobles.

"We might do that," answered Zagloba; and glad to find grateful listeners, he told them all, from the journey to Galáts and the flight from Rozlogi, to the capture of the banner at Konstantinoff. They listened with open mouths. Sometimes they murmured when, glorifying his own bravery, he presumed too much on their lack of experience; but he was invited and entertained each day in a new place.

The time was passed, then, in pleasure and tumult at Zbaraj, till old Zatsvilikhovski and others of a more serious turn wondered that the prince suffered these feasts so long. But Yeremi remained in his own quarters. It was evident that he gave rein to the soldiers, so that all might taste every enjoyment before new conflicts. Skshetuski arrived now, and dropped as it were at once into a whirlpool of boiling water. He wanted rest in the circle of his companions; but still more did he wish to visit Bar,--to go to his loved one, and forget all his past troubles, all his fears and sufferings, in her embrace. He appeared before the prince therefore without delay, to report on his expedition to Zaslav and obtain leave of absence.

He found the prince changed beyond recognition, so that he was astonished at his appearance, and asked in his mind: "Is this the chief whom I saw at Makhnovka and Konstantinoff?" For there stood before him a man bent with the burden of care, with sunken eyes and shrivelled lips, as if suffering from a grievous internal disease. When asked for his health he answered briefly and dryly that he was well, so the knight did not dare inquire further. Having made his report, he began immediately to ask for two months' absence from the squadron, that he might marry and take his wife to Skshetushevo.

On hearing this the prince woke as it were from sleep. The expression of kindness habitual to him reappeared on his gloomy face, and embracing Pan Yan, he said,--

"This is the end of your suffering. Go, go! May God bless you! I should like to be at your wedding myself, for I owe that to Kurtsevichovna, as the daughter of Vassily, and to you as a friend; but at this time it is impossible for me to move. When do you wish to start?"

"To-day, if I could, your Highness."

"Then set out to-morrow. You cannot go alone. I will give you three hundred of Vershul's Tartars to bring her home in safety. You will go quickest with them, and you will need them, for bands of ruffians are wandering about. I will give you a letter to Andrei Pototski; but before I write to him, before the Tartars come, and before you are ready, it will be to-morrow evening."

"As your Highness commands. I make bold to request further that Volodyovski and Podbipienta go with me."

"Very well. Come again to-morrow morning for my farewell and a blessing. I should like also to send your princess a present. She is of a noted family. You will both be happy, because you are worthy of each other."

The knight knelt and embraced the knees of his beloved chief, who repeated several times,--

"God make you happy! God make you happy! But come again to-morrow morning."

Still the knight did not go; he lingered as if wishing to ask for something else. At last he broke out: "Your Highness!"

"And what more do you say?" asked the prince, mildly.

"Pardon my boldness, but--my heart is cut, and from sorrow comes great boldness. What affects your Highness? Does trouble weigh you down, or is it disease?"

The prince put his hand on Skshetuski's head. "You cannot know this," said he, with sweetness in his voice. "Come to-morrow morning."

Skshetuski rose and went out with a straitened heart.

In the evening old Zatsvilikhovski came to Skshetuski's quarters, and with him little Volodyovski, Pan Longin, and Zagloba. They took their seats at the table, and Jendzian came into the room bearing a keg and glasses.

"In the name of Father and Son!" cried Zagloba. "I see that your man has risen from the dead."

Jendzian approached, and embraced Zagloba's knees. "I have not risen from the dead, for I did not die, thanks to you for saving me."

Then Skshetuski added: "And afterward he was in Bogun's service."

"Oh, that fellow would find promotion in hell," said Zagloba. Then, turning to Jendzian, he said: "You couldn't have found much joy in that service; here is a thaler for pleasure."

"Thank you humbly," said Jendzian.

"He," cried Pan Yan, "is a perfect rogue. He bought plunder of the Cossacks. You and I couldn't purchase what he has now, even if you were to sell all your estates in Turkey."

"Is that true?" asked Zagloba. "Keep my thaler for yourself, and grow up, precious sapling; for if you'll not serve for a crucifix, you will serve at least for a gallows-tree. The fellow has a good eye." Here Zagloba caught Jendzian by the ear, and pulling it, continued: "I like rogues, and I prophesy that you will come out a man, if you don't remain a beast. And how does your master Bogun speak of you, hi?"

Jendzian smiled, for the words and caress flattered him, and answered; "Oh, my master, when he speaks of you, he strikes fire with his teeth."

"Oh, go to the devil!" cried Zagloba, in sudden anger. "What are you raving about?"

Jendzian went out. They began to discuss the journey of the morrow, and the great happiness which was awaiting Pan Yan. Mead soon improved Zagloba's humor; he began to talk to Skshetuski, and hint of christenings, and again of the passion of Pan Andrei Pototski for the princess. Pan Longin sighed. They drank, and were glad with their whole souls. Finally the conversation touched upon military events and the prince. Skshetuski, who had not been in the camp for many days, asked,--

"Tell me, gentlemen, what has happened to our prince? He is somehow another man; I cannot understand it. God has given him victory after victory. They passed him by in the command. What of that? The whole army is rushing to him now, so that he will be hetman without any one's favor, and will destroy Hmelnitski; but it is evident that he suffers, and suffers from something--"

"Perhaps the gout is taking hold of him," said Zagloba, "Sometimes when it gets a pull at me in the great toe, I am despondent for three days at a time."

"I tell you, brothers," said Podbipienta, nodding his head, "I haven't heard this myself from the priest Mukhovetski, but I heard that he told some one why the prince is so tormented--I do not say this myself; he is a kindly man, good, and a great warrior,--why should I judge him? But since the priest says so--but do I know that it is so?"

"Just look, gentlemen, at this Lithuanian!" cried Zagloba. "Am I not right in making fun of him, since he doesn't know human speech? What did you wish to say? You circle round and round, like a rabbit about her nest, but cannot come to a point."

"What did you really hear?" asked Skshetuski.

"Well, since for that--they say that the prince has shed too much blood. He is a great leader, but knows no measure in punishment, and now sees, it seems, everything red,--red in the daytime, red at night, as if a red cloud were surrounding him--"

"Don't talk nonsense!" shouted Zatsvilikhovski, with rage. "Those are old wives' tales. There was no better master for the rabble in time of peace; and as to his knowing no mercy for rebels,--well, what of that? That is a merit, not an offence. What torments, what punishments, would be too great for those who have deluged the country in blood, who have given their own people captive to Tartars, who know neither God, king, country, nor authorities? Where will you show me such monsters as they, where such cruelties as they have perpetrated on women and little children? Where can you find such criminal wretches? For them the empaling stake and the gallows are too much. Tfu, tfu! You have an iron hand, but a woman's heart. I saw how you whined, when they were burning Pulyan, that you would rather have killed him on the spot. But the prince is no old woman; he knows how to reward and how to punish. What is the use of telling me such nonsense?"

"But I have said, father, that I don't know," explained Pan Longin.

The old man puffed for a long time yet, and smoothing his milk-white hair, muttered: "Red, h'm! red,--that's news. In the head of him who invented that it is green, and not red!"

A moment of silence followed, but through the windows came the uproar of the revelling nobles. Little Volodyovski broke the silence reigning in the room.

"Well, father, what do you think can be the matter with our prince?"

"H'm!" said the old man, "I am not his confidant, therefore I do not know. He is thinking of something, he is struggling with himself,--a hot battle of some kind,--it cannot be otherwise; and the greater the soul, the fiercer the torture."

The old knight was not mistaken; for in that same hour the prince, the leader, the conqueror, lay in the dust in his own quarters, before the crucifix, and was fighting one of the most desperate battles of his life.

The guards at the castle of Zbaraj called out midnight, but Yeremi was still conversing with God and with his own lofty soul. Reason, conscience, love of country, pride, perception of his own power and great destiny, were turned into combatants within his breast, and fought a stubborn battle with one another, from which his breast was bursting, his head was bursting, and pain contorted all his limbs. Now, in spite of the primate, the chancellor, the senate, the generals, against the will of the government, the regular soldiers, the nobles, the foreign troops in private service, were going over to that conqueror,--in one word, the whole Commonwealth was placing itself in his hands, taking refuge under his wings, committing its fortune to his genius, and in the person of its choicest sons was crying: "Save, for you alone can save!" In one month or in two there will be at Zbaraj one hundred thousand warriors, ready for a struggle to the death with the serpent of civil war. Here pictures of a future surrounded with light immeasurable, of glory and power, began to pass before the eyes of the prince. Those who wished to pass him by and subdue him are trembling, and he takes those iron legions and leads them into the steppes of the Ukraine, to victories and triumphs such as history has not yet known. The prince feels in himself corresponding power, and from his shoulders wings shoot forth like the wings of the archangel Michael. And at that moment he turns into such a giant that the whole castle, all Zbaraj, all Russia, cannot contain him. As God lives, he will rub out Hmelnitski, he will trample the rebellion, he will bring back peace to the fatherland! He sees extended plains, legions of troops; he hears the roar of artillery. A battle! a battle! Victory unheard of, unparalleled! Legions of bodies, hundreds of banners, cover the blood-stained steppe, and he tramples on the body of Hmelnitski, and the trumpets sound victory, and that sound flies from sea to sea. The prince rises, rushes up, extends his hands to Christ, around whose head is a mild purple light. "Oh, Christ, Christ!" he cries, "thou knowest, thou seest that I can; tell me that I should do this."

But Christ hung his head on his breast, and was as silent, as sorrowful as if he had been crucified the moment before.

"To thee be the praise!" cried the prince. "Non mihi, non mihi, sed nomini tuo da gloriam! To the glory of the faith of the Church and of all Christianity! Oh, Christ, Christ!" And a new image opened before the eyes of the hero. That career was not ended by the victory over Hmelnitski. The prince, having destroyed the rebellion, grows strong on its body. He becomes gigantic in power. Legions of Cossacks are joined to legions of Poles, and he goes farther,-- strikes the Crimea, reaches the terrible dragon in his den; he erects the cross where hitherto bells had never called the faithful to prayer. He will go also to those lands which the princes Vishnyevetski have already trampled with the hoofs of their horses, and will extend the boundaries of the Commonwealth, and with them the Church, to the remotest corners of the earth. Where then is the limit to this impetus, where the bounds to this glory, power, and strength? There are none whatever.

The pale light of the moon falls into the chamber of the castle, but the clock beats a late hour, and the cocks are crowing. It will soon be day; but will it be a day in which with the sun in heaven a new sun will shine upon earth?

Yes, it will. The prince would be a child and not a man if he did not do this, if for any reasons whatever he drew back before the voice of these destinies. Now he feels a certain calm, which the merciful Christ had evidently poured on him,--praise to him for that! His mind has become more sober; he takes in more easily too with the eyes of his soul the condition of the country and all its affairs. The policy of the chancellor and those magnates in Warsaw, as well as of the voevoda of Bratslav, is evil, and destructive for the country. To trample the Zaporojie first, and squeeze an ocean of blood out of it, break it, annihilate it, bend, and conquer, and then only acknowledge that everything is finished; to restrain all oppression; to introduce order, peace; being able to kill, to restore to life,--that was the only path worthy of that great, that lordly Commonwealth. It might have been possible perhaps to choose another path long before, but not now. What in truth could negotiations lead to then? Armed legionaries stand against one another in thousands; and even if negotiations were concluded, what power could they have! No, no! those are dream visions, shadows, a war extended over whole ages, a sea of tears and blood for the future. Let them take the only course which is great, noble, full of power, and he will wish and ask for nothing more. He will settle again in Lubni, and will wait quietly till the terrible trumpets call him to action again.

Let them take it? But who? The Senate? The stormy Diet? The chancellor, the primate, or the commanders? Who, besides him, understands this great idea, and who can carry it out? If such a man can be found, it is well. But where is he? Who has the power? He alone,--no one else. To him the nobles come; to him the armies gather; in his hand is the sword of the Commonwealth,--but the Commonwealth when the king is on the throne. But now when there is no king the will of the people rules. It is the supreme law, expressed not only in the Diets, not only through deputies, the Senate, and chancellors, not only through written laws and manifestoes; but still more powerfully, more emphatically, more definitely, by action. And who rules in action? The knightly estate; and this knightly estate is assembling at Zbaraj, and says to him, "You are the leader." The whole Commonwealth without voting gives him authority by the power of events, and repeats, "You are the leader." And should he draw back? What appointment does he wish besides? From whom is he to expect it? Is it from those who are endeavoring to ruin the Commonwealth and to conquer him? Why should he, why should he? Is it because when panic seized upon all, when the hetmans went into captivity, and the armies were lost, magnates hid themselves in their castles, and the Cossack put the foot on the breast of the Commonwealth, he alone pushed away that foot and raised from the dust the fainting head of that mother; sacrificed for her everything,--life, fortune; saved her from shame, from death,--he the conqueror!

Let him who has rendered more service, take the power. Let it rest in the hands of the man to whom it belongs more of right. He will resign that burden willingly, and say to God and the Commonwealth, "Let thy servant depart in peace;" for he is wearied, greatly weakened, and besides he is sure that neither the memory of him nor his grave will disappear.

But if there is no such person, he would be doubly and trebly a child and not a man if he should resign that power, that bright path, that brilliant, immense future, in which lies the salvation of the Commonwealth, its power, glory, and happiness. And why should he?

The prince raised his head again proudly, and his flaming glance fell on Christ; but Christ hung his head on his breast, and remained in silence as painful as if they had crucified him the moment before.

Why should he? The hero pressed his heated temples with his hands. Maybe there is an answer. What is the meaning of those voices which amidst the golden rainbow visions of glory, amidst the thunder of coming victories, amidst the forebodings of grandeur, of power, call out so mercilessly to his soul, "Oh, halt, unfortunate one!" What means that unrest which goes through his breast like the shudder of alarm? What means it that when he shows himself most clearly and convincingly that he ought to take the power, something there in the depths of his conscience whispers, "You deceive yourself; pride misleads you; Satan promises you the glories of the kingdom"?

And again a fearful struggle began in the soul of the prince; again he was carried away by a whirlwind of alarms, uncertainty, and doubts.

What are the nobles doing who join him instead of the commanders? Trampling on law. What is the army doing? Violating discipline. And is he, a citizen, is he, a soldier, to stand at the head of lawlessness? Is he to cover it with his own dignity? Is he to give an example of insubordination, arbitrariness, disregard of law, and all merely to receive power two months earlier; for if Prince Karl shall be elected to the throne, power will not pass him by? Is he to give such a fearful example to succeeding ages? For what will happen? To-day Prince Yeremi acts in this way; to-morrow, Konyetspolski, Pototski Firlei, Zamoyski, or Lyubomirski. And if each one, without reference to law and discipline, acts according to his own ambition; if the children follow the example of their fathers and grandfathers,--what future is before that unhappy country? The worms of arbitrariness, disorder, self-seeking have so gnawed the trunk of that Commonwealth, that under the axe of civil war the rotten wood is scattered, the dry limbs fall from the tree. What will happen when those whose duty it is to guard and save it as the apple of the eye put fire under it? What will happen then? Ob, Jesus, Jesus! Hmelnitski too shields himself with the public good, and does nothing else; still he rises up against law and authority.

A shudder passed through the prince from his feet to his head. He wrung his hands. "Am I to be another Hmelnitski, O Christ?"

But Christ hung his head on his breast, and was as painfully silent as if crucified the moment before.

The prince struggled on. If he should assume power, and the chancellor, the Senate, and the commanders should proclaim him a rebel, then what would happen? Another civil war? And then the question. Is Hmelnitski the greatest and most terrible enemy of the Commonwealth? More than once she has been invaded by still greater powers. When two hundred thousand armored Germans marched at Grünwald on the regiments of Yagello, and when at Khotím half Asia appeared in the fight, destruction seemed still nearer. And what had become of these hostile powers? No; the Commonwealth is not in danger from wars, and wars will not be her destruction. But why, in view of such victories, of such reserved power, of such glory, is she, who crushed the knights of the cross and the Turks, so weak and incompetent that she is on her knees before one Cossack, that her neighbors are seizing her boundaries, that nations are ridiculing her, that no one listens to her voice, or regards her anger, and that all are looking forward to her destruction?

Ah! it is specifically the pride and ambition of magnates, each one acting by himself; self-will is the cause of it. The worst enemy is not Hmelnitski, but internal disorder, waywardness of the nobles, weakness and insubordination of the army, uproar of the Diets, brawls, disputes, confusion, weakness, self-seeking, and insubordination,--insubordination, above all. The tree is rotting and weakening from the heart. Soon will men see how the first storm will throw it; but he is a parricide who puts his hand to such work. Cursed be he and his children to the tenth generation!

Go then, O conqueror of Nyemiroff, Pogrébische, Makhnovka, Konstantinoff,--go, prince voevoda,--go, snatch command from leaders, trample upon law and authority, give an example to posterity how to rend the entrails of the mother!

Terror, despair, and fright were reflected in the face of the prince. He screamed terribly, and seizing himself by the hair, fell in the dust before the crucifix. The prince repented, and beat his worthy head on the stone pavement, and from his breast struggled forth the dull voice,--

"O God, be merciful to me a sinner! O God, be merciful to me a sinner! God, be merciful to me a sinner!"

The rosy dawn was already in the sky, and then came the golden sun and lighted the hall. In the cornices the chattering of sparrows and swallows began. The prince rose and went to rouse his attendant Jelenski, who was sleeping on the other side of the door.

"Run," said he, "to the orderlies, and tell them to summon to me from the castle and the town the colonels of the regular army and of the militia."

Two hours later the hall began to be filled with the mustached and bearded forms of warriors. Of the prince's people there came old Zatsvilikhovski, Polyanovski, Pan Yan with Zagloba, Vurtsel, Maknitski, Volodyovski, Vershul, Ponyatovski, almost all the officers to the ensigns, except Kushel, who was in Podolia on a reconnoissance. From the regular army came Osinski and Koritski. Many of the more distinguished nobles were unable to rise from their feather-beds so early; but no small number, even of these, were assembled,--among them personages of various provinces, from castellans to sub-chamberlains. Murmurs and conversation resounded, and there was a noise as in a hive; but all eyes were turned to the door through which the prince was to come.

All grew silent as the prince entered. His face was calm and pleasant; only his eyes reddened by sleeplessness, and his pinched features testified of the recent struggle. But through that calm and even sweetness appeared dignity and unbending will.

"Gentlemen," said he, "last night I communed with God and my own conscience as to what I should do. I announce therefore to you, and do you announce to all the knightly order, that for the sake of the country and that harmony needful in time of defeat, I put myself under the commanders."

A dull silence reigned in the assembly.

In the afternoon of that day, in the court of the castle three hundred of Vershul's Tartars stood ready to journey with Pan Yan; and in the castle the prince was giving to the officers of the army a dinner which at the same time was a farewell feast to our knight. He was seated therefore by the prince as "the bridegroom;" and next to him sat Zagloba, for it was known that his daring and management had saved "the bride" from mortal peril. The prince was in good spirits, for he had cast the burden from his heart. He raised the goblet to the success of the future couple. The walls and windows trembled from the shouts of those present. In the anteroom was a bustle of servants, among whom Jendzian had the lead.

"Gentlemen," said the prince, "let this third goblet be for posterity. It's a splendid stock. God grant that the apples may not fall far from the tree! From this falcon may noble falconets spring!"

"Success to them! success to them!"

"In thanks!" cried Pan Yan, emptying an enormous goblet of Malmoisie.

"Success to them! success to them!"

"Crescite et multiplicamini!"

"You ought to furnish half a squadron," said old Zatsvilikhovski, laughing.

"Oh, he will fill the army entirely! I know him," said Zagloba.

The nobles roared with laughter. Wine rose to their heads. Everywhere were to be seen flushed faces, moving mustaches; and the good feeling was increasing every moment.

Just then at the threshold of the hall appeared a gloomy figure, covered with dust; and in view of the table, the feast, and the gleaming faces, it stopped at the door as if hesitating to enter. The prince saw it first, wrinkled his brows, shaded his eyes, and said,--

"But who is there? Ah, that is Kushel! From the expedition. What news do you bring?"

"Very bad, your Highness!" said the young officer, with a strange voice.

Suddenly silence reigned in the assembly, as if some one had put it under a spell. The goblets raised to the lips remained half-way; all eyes were turned to Kushel, on whose wearied face pain was depicted.

"It would have been better had you not spoken, since I am joyful at the cup," said the prince; "but since you have begun, speak to the end."

"Your Highness, I too should prefer not to be an owl, for these tidings halt on my lips."

"What has happened? Speak!"

"Bar is taken!"

CHAPTER XXXIV.

Ok a certain calm night a band of horsemen, about twenty in number, moved along the right bank of the Valadinka in the direction of the Dniester. They went very slowly, the horses almost dragging one foot after the other. A short distance in front of the others rode two, as it were an advance guard; but evidently there was no cause for guarding or being on the watch, since for a whole hour they had been talking together instead of looking at the country about them. Reining in their horses every little while, they looked at the party behind, and one of them called out at this moment: "Slowly there! slowly!" And the others went still more slowly, scarcely moving.

At last the party, pushing out from behind the eminence which had covered them with its shadow, entered the open country, which was filled with moonlight, and then it was possible to understand the reason of their careful gait. In the centre of the caravan two horses abreast carried a swing tied to their saddles, and in this swing lay the form of some person. The silver rays lighted its pale face and closed eyes.

Behind the swing rode ten armed men. From their lances without bannerets, it was evident that they were Cossacks. Some led pack-horses, others rode by themselves; but while the two riders in front seemed to pay not the least attention to the country about them, those behind glanced around on every side with unquiet and alarm. And still the region seemed to be a perfect desert.

Silence was unbroken save by the noise of the horses' hoofs and the calling of one of the riders in front, who from time to time repeated his warning: "Slowly! carefully!"

At length he turned to his companion. "Horpyna, is it far yet?" he inquired.

The companion called Horpyna, who in reality was a gigantic young woman disguised as a Cossack, looked at the starry heavens and replied,--

"Not far. We shall be there before midnight. We shall pass the Enemy's Mound, the Tartar Valley, and right there is the Devil's Glen. Oh, it would be terrible to pass that place between midnight and cockcrow! It's possible for me, but for you it would be terrible, terrible!"

The first rider shrugged his shoulders and said: "I know the devil is a brother to you, but there are weapons against the devil."

"Devil or not, there are no weapons," answered Horpyna. "If you, my falcon, had looked for a hiding-place through the whole world for your princess, you could not have found a better. No one will pass here after midnight unless with me, and in the glen no living man has yet put foot. If any one wants soothsaying, he waits in front of the glen till I come out. Never fear! Neither Pole nor Tartar will get there, nor any one, any one. The Devil's Glen is terrible, you will see for yourself."

"Let it be terrible, but I say that I shall come as often as I like."

"If you come in the daytime."

"Whenever I please. And if the devil stands in my road, I'll seize him by the horns."

"Oh, Bogun, Bogun!"

"Oh, Dontsovna, Dontsovna, don't trouble yourself about me! Whether the devil takes me or not is no concern of yours; but I tell you this,--take council with your devils when you please, if only no harm comes to the princess; but if anything happens to her, then neither devils nor vampires will tear you from my grasp."

"Oh, they tried to drown me once when I lived with my brother on the Don, another time the executioner was going to cut my head off in Yampol,--I didn't care for that. But this is another thing. I will guard her out of friendship for you, so that no spirit will make a hair of her head fall, and in my hands she is safe from men. She won't escape you."

"And, you owl, if you talk this way, why do you prophesy evil? Why do you hoot in my ear, 'Pole at her side! Pole at her side!'"

"It was not I that spoke, but the spirits. But now perhaps there is a change. I will prophesy for you to-morrow on the water of the mill-wheel. On the water everything is clearly visible, but it is necessary to look a long time, you will see yourself. But you are a furious dog; if the truth is told, you are angry and wish to kill one."

Conversation was interrupted, and only the striking of the horses' feet against the stones was heard, and certain sounds from the direction of the river, like the chirping of crickets.

Bogun paid not the least attention to these sounds, though they might astonish one in the night. He raised his face to the moon and fell into deep thought.

"Horpyna!" said he, after a while.

"What?"

"You are a witch; you must know whether or not it is true that there is an herb of some kind that whoever drinks of it must fall in love,--lubystka, is it?"

"Yes, lubystka. But unfortunately for you, lubystka will not help. If the princess hadn't fallen in love with some one else, then you might give it to her; but if she is in love, do you know what will happen?"

"What?"

"She will love the other man still more."

"Oh, perish with your lubystka! You know how to prophesy evil, but you don't know how to help."

"Listen to me! I know other herbs which grow from the earth; whoever drinks them will be like a stump two days and two nights, knowing nothing of the world. I will give her those herbs, and then--"

The Cossack shuddered in his saddle, and fixed on the witch his eyes gleaming in the darkness. "What are you croaking about?" he asked.

"Then you can--" said the witch, and burst into loud laughter like the neighing of a mare. This laughter resounded with ill-omened echo through the windings of the glen.

"Wretch!" said Bogun.

Then the light of his eyes went out gradually; he dropped again into meditation, and at length began to speak as if to himself,--

"No, no! When we captured Bar, I rushed first to the monastery, so as to defend her from the drunken crowd and smash the head of any man who should come near her; but she stabbed herself with a knife, and now has no consciousness of God's world. If I lay a finger on her, she will stab herself again, or jump into the river if you are not careful,--ill-fated that I am!"

"You are at heart a Pole, not a Cossack, if you will not constrain the girl in Cossack fashion--"

"That I were a Pole, that I were a Pole!" cried Bogun, grasping the cap on his head with both hands, for pain had seized him.

"The Polish woman must have bewitched you," muttered Horpyna.

"Ai! if she has not," answered he, sadly, "may the first bullet not pass me; may I finish my wretched life on the empaling stake! I love one in the world, and that one does not love me!"

"Fool!" cried Horpyna, with anger; "but you have got her!"

"Hold your tongue!" cried he, with rage. "If she lays hands on herself, then what? I'll tear you apart and then myself. I'll break my head against a rock, I'll gnaw people like a dog. I would have given my soul for her, Cossack fame. I would have fled beyond the Yagorlik from the regiments to the end of the earth, to live with her, to die at her side. That's what I would have done. But she stabbed herself with a knife, and through whom? Through me! She stabbed herself with a knife! Do you hear?"

"That's nothing. She will not die."

"If she dies, I will nail you to the door."

"You have no power over her."

"I have none, I have none. Would she had stabbed me,--it would have been better had she killed me!"

"Silly little Pole! She should have been kind to you. Where will she find your superior?"

"Arrange this, and I will give you a pot of ducats and another of pearls. In Bar we took booty not a little, and before that we took booty too."

"You are as rich as Prince Yeremi, and full of fame. They say Krívonos himself is afraid of you."

The Cossack waved his hand. "What is that to me if my heart is sore--"

And silence came again. The bank of the river grew wider and more desolate. The pale light of the moon lent fantastic forms to the trees and the rocks. At last Horpyna said,--

"This is the Enemy's Mound. We must ride together."

"Why?"

"It is a bad place."

They reined in their horses, and after a while the party coming on behind joined them. Bogun rose in the stirrups and looked into the cradle.

"Is she asleep?" he asked.

"She is sleeping as sweetly as an infant," answered an old Cossack.

"I gave her a sleeping dose," said the witch.

"Slowly, carefully!" said Bogun, fixing his eyes on the sleeper; "don't wake her! The moon is looking straight into her face, my dear one!"

"It shines quietly, it will not wake her," whispered one of the Cossacks.

The party moved on. Soon they arrived at the Enemy's Mound. It was a low hill lying close to the river and sloping like a round shield on the earth. The moon covered the place entirely with its beams, lighting up the white stones scattered over the whole extent of it. In some spots they lay singly; in others they formed heaps, as it were fragments of buildings, ruined castles, and churches. Here and there stone slabs stuck up, planted endwise in the earth like gravestones in a cemetery. The whole mound was like a great ruin, and perhaps in other ages, long before the days of the Yagellons, human life flourished upon it; now not only the mound but the whole neighborhood as far as Rashkoff was an empty waste, in which wild beasts alone found refuge, and in the night evil spirits held their dances.

The party had scarcely reached half the height of the mound, when the light breeze which had been blowing hitherto changed into a regular whirlwind, which began to encircle the mound with a certain gloomy, ominous whistling; and then it appeared to the Cossacks that among those ruins were heard heavy sighs, issuing as it were from straitened breasts, sad groans, laughter, wailing, and puling of infants. The whole mound began to be alive, to call with various voices. From behind the stones lofty dark figures seemed to look, shadows of strange forms glided along quietly among the slabs. Far off in the darkness gleamed lights like the eyes of wolves. Finally, from the other end of the mound, from among the thickest heaps and piles, was heard a low guttural howling, to which other howling responded at once.

"Vampires!" whispered a young Cossack, turning to the old essaul.

"No, werewolves," answered the old essaul, in a still lower voice.

"O Lord, have mercy on us!" said others in terror, removing their caps and crossing themselves devoutly.

The horses began to point their ears forward and snort. Horpyna, riding at the head of the party, muttered unintelligible words, as it were a sort of Satanic Pater-noster. When they had arrived at the other end of the mound, she turned and said,--

"Well, it is over. We are safe now. I had to keep them back with a charm, for they were very hungry."

A sigh of relief came from every breast. Bogun and Horpyna rode ahead again; but the Cossacks, who a little while before had held their breaths, began to whisper and talk. Each one remembered what had happened to him when he met ghosts or werewolves.

"We couldn't have passed without Horpyna," said one.

"She is a powerful witch."

"And our ataman does not fear even the werewolf. He didn't look, didn't listen, only turned toward his princess."

"If what happened to me happened to him, he wouldn't have been so free from danger," said the old essaul.

"And what happened to you, Father Ovsivuyu?"

"Once, while riding from Reimentarovka to Gulaipolye, I passed near some mounds at night, and I saw something jump from a grave behind me on the saddle. I looked; it was a little child, blue and pale! Evidently the Tartars had taken it captive with its mother and it had died without baptism. Its eyes were burning like candles, and it wailed and wailed. It jumped from the saddle to my neck, and I felt it biting me behind the ear. O Lord, save us! it is a vampire! I had served long in Wallachia, where there are more vampires than people, but where there are weapons against them. I sprang from the horse and thrust my dagger into the ground. 'A vaunt! disappear!' and it groaned, seized the hilt of the dagger, and slipped down along the edge under the grass. I cut the ground in the form of a cross and rode off."

"Are there so many vampires in Wallachia, father?"

"Every other Wallachian after death becomes a vampire, and the Wallachian vampires are the worst of all. They call them brukolaki."

"And who is stronger, father,--the werewolf or the vampire?"

"The werewolf is stronger, but the vampire is more stubborn. If you are able to get the upper hand of the werewolf, he will serve you, but vampires are good for nothing except to follow blood. The werewolf is always ataman over the vampires."

"And Horpyna commands the werewolves?"

"Yes, surely. As long as she lives she will command them. If she had not power over them, then the ataman would not give her his cuckoo, for werewolves thirst for maiden's blood above all."

"But I have heard that they have no approach to an innocent soul."

"To a soul they have not, but to a body they have."

"Oh, it would be a pity! She is a beauty. Blood and milk! our father knew what to take in Bar."

Ovsivuyu smacked his tongue. "There is no denying it; she is a golden Pole."

"But I am sorry for her," said a young Cossack. "When we were putting her in the swing she clasped her white hands and begged, saying, 'Kill me; do not ruin me, unfortunate one!'"

"No harm will come to her."

Further conversation was interrupted by the approach of Horpyna.

"Hei! young men," said the witch, "this is Tartar Valley, but don't fear; it is terrible here only one night in the year. Right after it is the Devil's Glen, and then my place."

In fact, the howling of dogs was soon heard. The party entered the mouth of the glen, running at right angles to the river, and so narrow that four horses could hardly enter it abreast. At the bottom of this chasm flowed a rivulet, changing color in the light of the moon like a snake, and running quickly to the river. But as the party pushed on, the precipitous and jagged walls receded from each other, leaving a rather roomy, slightly ascending valley, enclosed at each side with cliffs. The place was covered here and there with lofty trees. No wind was blowing. Long, dark shadows of the trees lay on the ground, and in the spaces flooded with the light of the moon certain white, round, or prolonged objects gleamed sharply, in which the Cossacks recognized with terror the skulls and leg-bones of men. They looked around therefore with distrust, marking their foreheads from time to time with the cross. Soon a light glimmered in the distance between the trees, and at that same time two terrible dogs ran up, enormous, black, with gleaming eyes, barking and howling at the sight of the men and horses. At the voice of Horpyna they stopped, however, and began to run around the riders, sneezing and panting.

"They are not what they seem," whispered the Cossacks.

"They are not dogs," said old Ovsivuyu, in a voice betraying deep conviction.

Just then a cottage became visible behind the trees; back of it a stable; farther and higher up another dark building. The cottage appeared strong and well-built, and in its windows a light was shining.

"This is my dwelling," said Horpyna to Bogun, "and up there is the mill which grinds grain for us; and I tell fortunes from the water on the wheel. I will tell yours. Your princess will live in the best chamber; but if you wish to ornament the walls, we can remove her to the other side immediately. Stop and dismount!"

The party halted, and Horpyna began to cry: "Cheremís, I say! Cheremís!"

A figure holding a bunch of burning pitch-pine came out in front of the cottage, and raising the torch, began to look in silence at those present. It was an old man, an ugly creature, small, quite a dwarf, with a flat, square face, and slanting eyes, like cracks.

"What sort of devil are you?" asked Bogun.

"Don't ask him," said the giantess; "his tongue is cut out. Come nearer and listen!" continued the witch; "it is better, perhaps, to carry the princess to the mill. The Cossacks will fit up her chamber, and drive nails that would wake her up."

The Cossacks, having dismounted, began to untie the swing carefully. Bogun watched over everything with the greatest care, and carried the head of the swing himself when it was taken to the mill. The dwarf lighted the way in advance with the torch. The princess, put to sleep by Horpyna with a decoction of somniferous herbs, did not wake; her eyelids merely trembled a little from the light of the torch. Her face appeared alive from those red gleams. Perhaps, also, wonderful dreams soothed the girl, for she smiled sweetly during the journey, which was like a funeral. Bogun looked at her, and it appeared to him that his heart would break the ribs in his breast. "My darling, my cuckoo!" whispered he quietly; and the terrible though beautiful face of the chief became mild, and flamed with the great light of love, which had seized him, and was seizing him every moment the more, as fire, forgotten by the traveller, seizes the wild steppe.

Horpyna, walking at his side, said: "When she wakes from this sleep she will be well. Her wound will heal, and she will be well."

"Glory be to God! glory be to God!" answered the chief.

The Cossacks began to loosen from six horses great packs in front of the cottage, and to take out the booty,--rich stuffs, carpets, and other valuables taken at Bar. A good fire was kindled in the room; and when some brought in new tapestry, others put it up to the wooden walls of the room. Bogun not only thought of a safe cage for his bird, but he determined so to furnish it that captivity should not seem unendurable. He came soon from the mill and directed the work himself. The night was passing away, and the moon had already removed its pale light from the summits of the cliffs. In the cottage were still heard the muffled blows of hammers. The simple room had become more like a chamber, when the walls were covered with drapery and the floor carpeted. The sleeping princess was brought back and placed on soft cushions.

Then all grew silent, except that in the stable for some time yet bursts of laughter were heard in the stillness like the neighing of a horse: the young witch was wrestling with the Cossacks, giving them fisticuffs and kisses.

CHAPTER XXXV.

The sun was high when the princess opened her eyes from sleep on the following day. Her glance rested first on the ceiling, and remained there long; then it took in the whole room. In her breast returning consciousness struggled still with the remnants of sleep and visions. On her face were depicted wonder and disquiet. Where is she, whence did she come, and in whose power is she? Is she dreaming yet, or is she awake? What means the splendor with which she is surrounded? What has happened to her?

At that moment the awful scenes of the taking of Bar rose before her as if in life. She remembered everything,--the slaughter of thousands of nobles, townspeople, priests, nuns, and children; the faces of the mob smeared in blood, their necks and heads wound around with the still steaming entrails, the drunken uproar, that day of judgment for the ruined town; finally the appearance of Bogun and her seizure. She remembered also how in a moment of despair she had fallen upon a knife held by her own hand, and the cold sweat stood on her temples. It was evident that the knife slipped along her shoulder, for she suffers only a little pain; but immediately she feels that she is alive, that strength and health are returning to her, and finally she remembers that she has been borne a long time somewhere in a swing. But where is she now? In some castle, is she saved, rescued, out of danger? And again her eyes wandered around the room. The windows in it were small, square, as in a peasant's cottage, and the world outside could not be seen through them; for instead of panes o£ glass, they were fitted with pieces of white membrane. Was it really a peasant's cottage? No, for the unbounded luxury within bears witness against that. Instead of a ceiling over her head was an enormous piece of purple silk on which were embroidered golden stars and a moon; the walls were entirely hung in brocade; on the floor lay a many-colored carpet, covered as with living flowers. In front of the fireplace was a Persian rug; golden fringes, silks, velvets, everywhere, from the walls of the ceiling to the pillows on which her head is reposing. The bright light of day, penetrating the window membranes, lighted up the interior, but was lost in the purple, dark violet, and sapphire colors of the velvet, forming a kind of enchanted rainbow darkness. The princess marvelled, did not believe her eyes. Was this some witchery, or had not the troops of Yeremi rescued her from the hands of Cossacks and put her away in one of the prince's castles?

She clasped her hands. "Oh, Holy Most Pure! grant that the first face to appear at the door shall be the face of my guardian and friend!"

Then through the heavy fringed bed-curtain came to her the flowing sound of a distant lute, and at the same time a voice began to accompany with the familiar song,--

"Oh, this loving
Is worse than sickness!
Sickness I can live through,
And grow well again;
But my faithful loving
I cannot part with while I live."

The princess raised herself, and the longer she listened the wider stared her eyes from terror. At last she screamed and fell as if dead on the cushions. She recognized the voice of Bogun.

Her scream passed evidently through the walls of the chamber; for after a while the heavy curtain rustled, and the chief himself appeared on the threshold.

Kurtsevichovna covered her eyes with her hands, and her whitened and quivering lips repeated, as if in a fever: "Jesus, Mary! Jesus, Mary!"

And yet the sight which so terrified her would have rejoiced the eyes of more maidens than one, for there was a blaze from the apparel and the countenance of the young hero. The diamond buttons of his uniform glittered like stars in heaven, his dagger and sabre were covered with precious stones, his coat of silver cloth and his scarlet kontush doubled the beauty of his brunette face; and he stood before her, lithe, dark-browed, magnificent,--the beauty of all the Ukraine heroes. But his eyes were in mist, like stars curtained by haze, and he looked on her with obedience; and seeing that fear did not leave her face, he began to speak in a low, sad voice,--

"Have no fear, Princess!"

"Where am I? where am I?" asked she, looking at him through her fingers.

"In a safe place, far from war. Fear not, my dear soul! I brought you here from Bar, so that no harm might come to you from man or war. The Cossacks spared no one in Bar; you alone came out alive."

"What are you doing here? Why do you pursue me?"

"I pursue you! Oh, merciful God!" And the chief extended his arms as a man who is confronted by a great injustice.

"I fear you terribly," she said.

"And why do you fear? If you say so, I shall not move from the door. I am your slave; I will sit here at the door and look into your eyes. Evil I do not wish you. Why do you hate me? Oh, merciful God! you thrust a knife into your body at the sight of me, though you have known me long, and knew that I was going to defend you. You know I am not a stranger to you, but a heartfelt friend; and you stabbed yourself with a knife."

The pale cheeks of the princess were suddenly suffused with blood. "I preferred death to disgrace; and I swear, if you do not respect me, I will kill myself, even if I were to lose my soul!"

The eyes of the maiden flashed fire, and the chief knew that there was no trifling with the princely blood of the Kurtsevichi; for in her frenzy she would carry out her threat, and a second time would point the knife with more success. He made no answer, therefore, merely advanced a couple of steps toward the window, and sitting on bench covered with gold brocade, hung his head.

Silence lasted for a time.

"Be at rest," said he. "While my head is clear, while Mother Gorailka does not heat my brain, you are for me like an image in the church. But since I found you in Bar I have ceased to drink. Before that I drank and drank, drowning my sorrow with Mother Gorailka. What could I do? But now I take to my mouth neither sweet wine nor spirits."

The princess was silent.

"I will look on you," he continued, "comfort my eyes with your face, then go."

"Give me back my liberty!" said she.

"But are you in captivity? You are mistress here. And where do you want to go? The Kurtsevichi have perished, fire has devoured villages and towns; the prince is not in Lubni, he is marching against Hmelnitski and Hmelnitski against him; war is everywhere, blood is flowing; every place is filled with Cossacks and Tartars and soldiers. Who will have sympathy and respect for you? Who will defend you, if not I?"

The princess raised her eyes, for she remembered that there was another in the world who would give her protection, sympathy, and defence; but she would not speak his name, so as not to rouse the fierce lion. Deep sorrow therefore pressed her heart. Was he for whom her soul was yearning still alive? While in Bar she knew that he was, for immediately after the departure of Zagloba she heard Skshetuski's name coupled with the victories of the terrible prince. But from that time how many days and nights had passed, how many battles might have been fought, how many perils have reached him. News of him could come to her then only through Bogun, of whom she neither wished nor dared to inquire.

Her head then dropped on the cushions. "Am I to remain a prisoner here?" asked she, with a groan. "What have I done to you, that you follow me like misfortune?"

The Cossack raised his head, and began to speak so quietly that scarcely could he be heard.

"What have you done to me? I know not; but this I do know, that if I am misfortune to you, you too are misfortune to me. If I had not loved you, I should have been free as the wind in the field, free in heart and in soul, and full of glory as was Konashevich Sahaidachny himself. Your face is my misfortune, your eyes are my misfortune; neither freedom is dear to me, nor Cossack glory! What were beauties to me, till from being a child you had grown to be a woman? Once I captured a galley with maidens the most beautiful, for they were on the way to the Sultan; and no one of them touched my heart. The Cossack brothers played with them; then I ordered a stone to the neck of each, and into the water they went. I feared no man, I minded nothing. I went with war against the Pagan. I took booty, and like a prince in his castle was I in the steppe. And to-day what am I? I sit here; I am a slave. I crave a kind word from you and cannot receive it; I have never heard it, even when your aunt and your cousins gave you to me. Oh, if you, girl, had been different to me, then what has come to pass would not have been! I should not have stricken down your cousins, I should not have joined fraternal hands with rebellion and peasants; but through you I have lost my mind. If you had wished to lead me anywhere, you could have led me where you liked, and I should have given you my blood, my soul. Now I am steeped in blood of nobles; but in old times I killed only Tartars, and brought you booty, that you might be clothed in gold and jewels like cherubim of the Lord. Why did you not love me, then? Oh, it is heavy and sad at my heart! I cannot live with you nor without you, nor far away nor near you, neither on the mountain nor in the valley, my dove, my precious heart! But forgive me that I came for you to Rozlogi in Cossack style, with sabre and fire; but I was drunk with anger at the princes, and I drank gorailka on the way,-- unhappy outlaw! But afterward, when you escaped me, I howled like a dog, and my wounds tortured me, and I could not eat. I begged death to take me; and you want me to yield you now, to lose you a second time, my dove, my heart!"

The chief stopped, for his voice broke in his throat, and he began to groan. Helena's face grew red and pale by turns. The more of measureless love there was in Bogun's words, the greater the gulf which opened before her, bottomless, and without hope of rescue.

The Cossack rested awhile, regained self-command, and continued,--

"Ask what you like. See how the room is decorated! This is mine; this is booty from Bar, which I brought for you on six horses. Ask what you wish,--yellow gold, shining garments, bright jewels, willing slaves. I am rich, I have enough of my own; and Hmelnitski will not spare treasures on me, and Krívonos will not spare them. You will be like Princess Vishnyevetski. I will win castles for you, give you half the Ukraine; for though I am a Cossack, not a noble, I am a bunchuk ataman. Under me are ten thousand men,--more than Prince Yeremi commands. Ask what you like, only not to flee from me,--only stay with me and love me, O my dove!"

The princess raised herself on the cushions. She was very pale, but her sweet and marvellous face expressed such unbroken will, pride, and power that the dove was most like an eagle at that moment.

"If you are waiting for my answer," said she, "then know that if I had even a lifetime to groan out in captivity with you, never, never should I love you, God be my aid!"

Bogun struggled with himself a moment. "Do not tell me such things," said he, with a hoarse voice.

"Do not speak to me of your love; it brings me shame and offence. I am not for you."

The chief rose. "And for whom, then, are you, Princess Kurtsevichovna? And whose would you have been in Bar but for me?"

"Whoso saves my life to give me shame and captivity is my enemy, not my friend."

"And do you suppose that the peasants would have killed you? The thought is terrible."

"The knife would have killed me, but you wrenched it from me."

"And I will not give it up, for you must be mine," burst out the Cossack.

"Never! I prefer death."

"You must and will be."

"Never!"

"Well, if you were not wounded, after what you have told me, I should send my Cossacks to Rashkoff to-day and have a monk brought here, and to-morrow I should be your husband. Then what? It is a sin not to love your husband and fondle him. Ai! you high mighty lady, the love of a Cossack is an offence, an anger to you. And who are you that I am for you a peasant? Where are your castles and boyars and troops? At what are you angry,--at what are you offended? I took you in war; you are a captive. If I were a peasant, I should teach you reason on the white shoulders with the whip, and without a priest would have enough of your beauty,--if I were a peasant, not a knight!"

"Angels of heaven, save me!" whispered the princess.

But in the mean while greater and greater fury rose to the face of Bogun, and anger seized him by the hair.

"I know," said he, "why you're offended, why you resist me. You preserve for another your maiden modesty. But in vain, as I live, as I am a Cossack! Nakedness [115] the noble! The insincere, miserable Pole barely saw you, merely turned with you in the dance,--death to him!--and took you captive altogether. Then let the Cossack suffer, break his head. But I will reach this Pole, and I will order him torn out of his skin, will nail him up. Do you know that Hmelnitski is marching on the Poles, and I go with him; and I will find your dove even under the ground, and when I return I will throw his head at your feet as a present."

Helena did not hear the last words of the ataman. Pain, anger, wounds, emotion, terror, took her strength; an immeasurable weakness came upon all her limbs, her eyes and her thoughts grew dark, and she fell into a swoon.

The chief stood some time, pale from anger, with foam on his lips. Then he saw the lifeless head hanging back powerless, and from his lips went out a roar almost unearthly. "It is all over with her! Horpyna! Horpyna!" And he threw himself on the floor.

The giantess rushed into the room with all speed. "What is the matter?"

"Help! help!" cried Bogun. "I have killed her, my soul, my light!"

"What! Did you scold her?"

"I have killed her, I have killed her!" groaned he; and he wrung his hands over his head.

But Horpyna, approaching the princess, soon discovered that it was not death, but a deep faint, and putting Bogun outside the door, began to assist her. The princess opened her eyes after a time.

"My dear, there is nothing the matter with you," said the enchantress. "You were frightened at him, I see, and darkness settled on you; but the darkness will pass and health will come. You are like a nut, my girl; you have long to live in the world and enjoy happiness."

"Who are you?" asked the princess, with a weak voice.

"I? Your servant, for he so ordered it."

"Where am I?"

"In the Devil's Glen. A pure wilderness here; you will see no one but him."

"Do you live here?"

"My farm is here. I am Dontsovna. My brother is a colonel under Bogun; he leads young heroes, and I stay here, and will care for you in this golden chamber. From a cottage it has become a bower, so that light gleams from it. He has brought all this for you."

Helena looked at the lively face of the young woman, and it seemed to her full of sincerity.

"But will you be good to me?"

The white teeth of the young witch gleamed in a smile. "I shall; why shouldn't I? But do you be good also to the ataman. He is a falcon, he is a glorious hero, he will--"

Here the witch bent to the ear of Helena, whispered something, then burst into laughter.

"Be off!" screamed the princess.

CHAPTER XXXVI.

Two days later in the morning Horpyna sat with Bogun under the willow near the mill-wheel, and looked at the water foaming on it.

"You will be careful of her, you will guard her, you will not let your eye off her, so that she shall never leave the glen."

"The glen has a narrow neck near the river, but there is space enough here. Order the neck to be filled with stones, and we shall be as if in the bottom of a jug. When I need to go out I shall find a way."

"How do you live here?"

"Cheremís plants corn under the cliffs, cultivates grapes, and snares wild fowl. With what you have brought she will want nothing unless bird's milk. Have no fear! She will not leave the glen, and no one will know of her unless your men say she is here."

"I have made them swear silence. They are faithful fellows; they will say nothing, even if straps were torn from their skin. But you said yourself that people came here to you as to a soothsayer."

"Sometimes they come from Rashkoff, and sometimes when they hear of me they come from God knows what places. But they stay at the river; no one enters the glen, for they are afraid. You saw the bones. These were people who wished to enter; their bones are lying around."

"Did you kill them?"

"Whoever killed them, killed them! Those in search of soothsaying wait at the opening of the glen and I go to the wheel. What I see in the water, I tell them. I shall examine for you directly, but I don't know whether anything will be seen, for it does not always appear."

"If only you see nothing bad!"

"If I see something bad, you will not go; and in that case it would be better not to go."

"I must. Hmelnitski sent me a letter to Bar to return, and Krívonos ordered me. The Poles are marching on us now with great forces, so we must concentrate."

"When will you come back?"

"I know not. There will be a great battle such as has not been yet. Either death to us or to the Poles. If they beat us, I will hide here; if we are victorious, I will come for my cuckoo and take her to Kieff."

"And if you perish?"

"Being a witch, it is for you to tell."

"But if you perish?"

"Once my mother bore me."

"Oh, pshaw! But what shall I do with the girl,--twist her neck, or how?"

"But touch her with your hand and I will have you drawn on a stake with oxen." The chief fell into gloomy thought. "If I perish, tell her to forgive me."

"Ah, she is a thankless Pole that for such love she does not love. If I were wooed in that way, I should not resist you." Saying this, Horpyna nudged the chief in the side twice, showing all her teeth in laughter.

"Go to the devil!" said the Cossack.

"Oh, be quiet! I know that you are not for me."

Bogun looked into the foaming water on the wheel as if he wished himself to soothsay.

"Horpyna!" said he after a while.

"Well, what is it?"

"When I have gone will she be sorry for me?"

"If you are not willing to constrain her in Cossack fashion, then perhaps it is better for you to go."

"I will not, I cannot, I dare not. I know that she would die."

"Then maybe it is better for you to go. While she sees you she will not wish to know you, but when she has been a couple of months with me and Cheremís, you will be dearer to her."

"If she were well, I know what I should do. I should bring a priest from Rashkoff and have a marriage celebrated; but now I am afraid, for if she were frightened, she would die. You have seen yourself."

"Leave us in peace. What do you want of a priest and a marriage? You are not a real Cossack. I want neither Pole nor Russian priest here. There are Dobrudja Tartars in Rashkoff, you want to get them on our shoulders too; and if you should bring them, how much of the princess would you see? What has got into your head? Go your way and come back."

"But look in the water and tell me what you see. Tell the truth and don't lie, even if you should see me dead."

Dontsovna approached the mill-stream and raised a gate holding back the water at the fall. All at once the swift current rushed with redoubled force, the wheel began to turn more swiftly, until at last it was covered with liquid dust; the foam, beaten fine, rolled under the wheel like boiling water.

The witch bent her eyes into the boiling mass and seizing the tresses near her ears, began to cry,--

"I call! I call! Appear! In the oaken wheel, in the white foam, in the clear mist, whether evil, whether good, appear!"

Bogun approached and sat at her side. His face denoted fear and feverish curiosity.

"I see!" screamed the witch.

"What do you see?"

"The death of my brother. Two bullocks are drawing him on a stake."

"To the devil with your brother!" muttered Bogun, who wished to know something else.

For a time was heard only the thunder of the wheel whirling around in fury.

"Blue is my brother's head, how blue! The ravens are tearing it," said the witch.

"What else do you see?"

"Nothing. Oh, how blue! I call! I call! In the oaken wheel, in the white foam, in the clear mist, appear! I see--"

"What?"

"A battle! The Poles are fleeing before the Cossacks."

"And I am pursuing?"

"I see you too. You encounter a little knight. Hur! hur! hur! Be on your guard against the little knight."

"And the princess?"

"She is not there. I see you again, and with you some one who is betraying you,--your false friend."

Bogun was devouring with his eyes at one instant the foam, at another Horpyna; and at the same time he worked with his brain to aid the soothsaying.

"What friend?"

"I don't see. I don't know whether old or young."

"Old, he must be old!"

"Maybe he is old!"

"I know who he is. He has betrayed me once already. An old noble with a blue beard and a white eye. Death to him! But he is not a friend of mine."

"He is lying in wait for you, I see again--Stop! the princess is here too; she is in a crown, a white dress, above her a hawk."

"That is I."

"Maybe it is. A hawk--or a falcon? A hawk!"

"That is I."

"Wait! All has vanished. In the oaken wheel, in the white foam-- Oh! oh! many soldiers, many Cossacks, oh, many, like trees in the forest or thistles in the steppes; and you are above all,-- they are bearing three bunchuk standards before you."

"And the princess is with me?"

"She is not; you are in the camp."

The wheel roared till the whole mill trembled.

"Oh, how much blood, how much blood! how many corpses,--wolves above them, ravens above them, plague above them! Corpses and corpses,--far away nothing but corpses, nothing to be seen but blood!"

Suddenly a breath of wind whirled the mist from the wheel; and at the same time higher up above the mill appeared the deformed Cheremís with a bundle of wood on his shoulders.

"Cheremís, let down the sluice!" cried the girl.

When she had said this she went to wash her hands and face in the stream, and the dwarf stopped the water at once.

Bogun sat in thought. He was roused first by the coming of Horpyna.

"You saw nothing more?" he asked.

"What appeared, appeared; I shall see nothing more."

"And you are not lying?"

"By my brother's head, I spoke the truth. They were empaling him, drawing him on with oxen. I grieve for him. But death is written not for him alone. Oh, what bodies appeared! Never have I seen so many; there will be a great war in the world."

"And you saw her with a hawk above her head?"

"Yes."

"And was she in a wreath?"

"In a wreath and a white robe."

"And how do you know that that hawk was I? I spoke to you of that young Polish noble,--maybe it was he?"

The girl wrinkled her brows and grew thoughtful. "No," said she after a while, shaking her head; "if it had been the Pole, it would have been an eagle."

"Glory to God, glory to God! I will go now to the Cossacks to prepare the horses for the road. We go to-night."

"So you are going surely?"

"Hmelnitski has ordered, and Krívonos too. You know well that there will be a great war, for I read the same in Bar in a letter from Hmelnitski."

Bogun in reality could not read, but he was ashamed of it; he did not wish to pass for illiterate.

"Then go!" said the witch. "You are lucky,--you will be hetman. I saw three bunchuks above you as I see these fingers."

"And I shall be hetman and marry the princess,--I cannot take a peasant."

"You would talk differently with a peasant girl, but you are afraid of her. You should be a Pole."

"I am no worse."

Bogun now went to the stable to the Cossacks, and Horpyna set about preparing dinner.

In the evening the horses were ready for the road, but the chief was in no hurry to depart. He sat on a roll of carpets in the chamber, with lute in hand, and looked on his princess, who had risen from the couch, but had thrust herself into the other corner of the room, and was repeating in silence the rosary without paying any heed to the chief, just as if he had not been in the room. He, on the contrary, followed with his eyes every movement of hers, caught with his ears every sigh, and knew not what to do with himself. From time to time he opened his mouth to begin conversation, but the words would not leave his throat. The face pale, silent, and with an expression of decisive sternness in the brows and mouth, deprived him of courage. Bogun had not seen this expression on the princess before, and involuntarily he remembered similar evenings at Rozlogi, which appeared before him as if real,--how they sat, he and the Kurtsevichi around an oaken table, the old princess husking sunflower seeds, the princes throwing dice from a cup, he looking on the beautiful princess just as he was looking now. But in the old time he was happy, for then he told of his expeditions with the Zaporojians, she listened, and at times her dark eyes rested on his face, and her open red lips showed with what interest she listened; now she would not even look. Then when he played on the lute she would listen and look, till the heart melted within him. And, wonder of wonders, he is now master of her,--he has taken her with armed hand; she is his captive, his prisoner; he can command her. But nevertheless in the old time he felt himself nearer, more her equal in rank. The Kurtsevichi were her cousins, she was as a sister; she was not only his cuckoo, falcon, dearest, dark-browed, but also a relative. Now she sits before him a proud lady, gloomy, silent, merciless. Ah, but anger is boiling within him! He would like to show her what it means to slight a Cossack; but he loves this merciless woman, he would shed his blood for her. But how many times had anger seized his breast! when suddenly an unseen hand, as it were, grasps him by the hair, and a voice shouts in his ear, "Stop!" He belches forth something like a flame, beats his forehead on the earth, and stops. The Cossack squirms now, for he feels that he is oppressive to her in that room. Let her but smile and give a kind word, he would fall at her feet and go to the devil, to drown in Polish blood all his grief and anger together with the insult put upon him. But in that room he is like a captive before that princess. If he had not known her of old, if she were a Pole taken from the first noble castle, he would have more daring; but she is Princess Helena, for whom he had asked the Kurtsevichi, and for whom he was willing to give up Rozlogi and all he had. And the more ashamed he is of being a slave before her, the less bold is he.

An hour passed. From before the cottage came the murmur of the talk of the Cossacks, who were surely in their saddles and waiting for the ataman; but the ataman was in torture. The bright light of the torch falls on his face, on the rich kontush, and on the lute. And she--if she would even look! The ataman felt bitter, angry, sad, and awkward. He would like to bid farewell with tenderness, and he fears the parting,--fears that it will not be such as from his soul he desires,--fears to go away in bitterness, anger, and pain.

Oh, if she were not that Princess Helena,--the Princess Helena stabbed with a knife, threatening death with her own hand; but dear, dear, and the more cruel and proud, the dearer is she!

Then a horse neighed near the window. The chief mustered courage.

"Princess," said he, "it is already my hour for the road."

She was silent.

"And you will not say to me, 'With God'?"

"Go, with God!" said she, with dignity.

The Cossack's heart was pressed. She said the words he wanted, but not in the way he wanted.

"Well I know," said he, "that you are angry with me, that you hate me; but I tell you that another would have been worse to you than I. I brought you here, for I could not do otherwise; but what harm have I done you? Have not I treated you well, like a queen? Tell me yourself. Am I such an outlaw that you will not give me a kind word? And, moreover, you are in my power."

"I am in the power of God," said she, with the same dignity as before; "but because you restrain yourself in my presence, I thank you for that."

"Then I go with even such a word. Maybe you will regret me; maybe you will be sorry."

Helena was silent.

"I am sorry to leave you here alone," said Bogun, "sorry to go away; but I must. It would be easier for me if you were to smile, if you were to give a crucifix with a sincere heart. What can I do to appease you?"

"Give me back my freedom, and God will forgive you all, and I will forgive and bless you."

"Maybe you will forgive me yet; maybe you will be sorry yet that you have been so harsh to me."

Bogun wished to buy a word of farewell, even for half a promise which he did not think of keeping, and got what he wanted, for a light of hope gleamed in Helena's eyes and the harshness vanished from her face. She crossed her arms on her breast and fixed a clear glance on him.

"If you would only--"

"Well, I don't know," said the Cossack, in a low voice, for shame and pity seized him at the same time by the throat. "I cannot now, I cannot. The Tartars are in the Wilderness, their parties are going everywhere. The Dobrudja Tartars are moving from Rashkoff. I cannot, for it is terrible; but when I come back--I am a child in your presence, you can do what you like with me--I don't know, I don't know--"

"May God inspire you! May the Holy Most Pure inspire you! God go with you!" And she stretched out her hand to him.

Bogun sprang forward and fastened his lips on it. Suddenly he raised his head, met her look of dignity, and dropped her hand. Then retreating toward the door, he bowed to his girdle in Cossack fashion, bowed again at the door, and disappeared behind the curtain.

Soon there came through the window animated conversation, a clatter of arms, and later the words of a song in several voices:--

"Glorious   fame   will   rise
Among   the   Cossacks,
Among   the   heroes,
For   many   a   year,
Till the end of time."

The voices and clatter retreated, and grew fainter each moment.

CHAPTER XXXVII.

"The Lord has wrought an evident miracle in her favor already," said Zagloba to Volodyovski and Podbipienta, while sitting in Skshetuski's quarters,--"an evident miracle, I say, in permitting me to wrest her from the grasp of those dogs and to guard her the whole way. Let us hope that he will be merciful to her and to us once more. If she is only living! Something whispers to me that Bogun has carried her away; for just think, the informants tell us that after Pulyan he has become the second in command,--may the devils command him!--therefore he must have been present at the taking of Bar."

"He might not have found her in that crowd of unfortunates, for twelve thousand people were cut to pieces there," said Volodyovski.

"Oh, you don't know him! I would swear that he knew she was in Bar. It cannot be but he has saved her from slaughter and taken her somewhere."

"You do not give us much consolation; for in Skshetuski's place, I should rather have her perish than fall into his scoundrelly hands."

"The other is no consolation; for if she has perished, she was disgraced."

"Desperation!" exclaimed Volodyovski.

"Desperation!" repeated Pan Longin.

Zagloba pulled his beard; at last he burst out: "May the mange devour the whole race of curs! May the Pagans twist bow-strings out of their entrails! God created all nations, but the devil created these sons of Sodom. May barrenness strike the trash!"

"I did not know that sweet lady," said Volodyovski, gloomily, "but I would that misfortune met me rather than her."

"Once in my life I saw her," said Pan Longin; "but when I think of her, life is a burden of regret."

"You describe your own feelings," said Zagloba; "but what do you think of me, who loved her like a father, and rescued her from that misery,--what do you think of me?"

"And what do you think of Pan Yan?" asked Volodyovski.

The knights were in despair and sank into silence. Zagloba came to himself first.

"Is there no help?" he asked.

"If there is no help, it is our duty to take vengeance," said Volodyovski.

"Oh, if God would only give a general battle!" sighed Pan Longin. "It is said that the Tartars have already crossed the river, and formed a camp in the steppe."

"We cannot leave her," said Zagloba, "the poor thing, without undertaking something for her rescue. I have battered my old bones around the world enough already; it would be better for me now to lie somewhere in a baker's shop quietly, for warmth's sake! But for her I would go again even to Stamboul; I would put on a peasant's coat again and take a lute, on which I cannot look without disgust."

"You are fertile in stratagems; think of something," said Podbipienta.

"A great many plans have gone through my head already. If Prince Dominik had half as many, Hmelnitski would be disembowelled and hanging by the legs on a gibbet. I have already spoken of this to Skshetuski, but you can say nothing to him at present. Sorrow has seared him, and drags him down more than sickness. You see to it that his reason is not disturbed. It often happens that from great grief the mind, like wine, changes until it is completely soured."

"Yes, yes!" answered Pan Longin.

Volodyovski started up impatiently, and asked: "What are your plans then?"

"My plans? Well, first we must find out whether she--poor dear, may the angels guard her from every evil!--is alive yet; and this we can do in two ways,--either we shall find among the Prince's Cossacks trusty and sure men, who will undertake to escape to the Cossacks, mingle among Bogun's men, and find out something from them--"

"I have Russian dragoons," interrupted Volodyovski, "I will find such men."

"Wait a moment!--or catch an informant from those scoundrels who took Bar; maybe they know something. They all look at Bogun as at a rainbow, because his devilish daring pleases them; they sing songs about him,--may their throats rot!--and one talks to another about what he did and what he didn't do. If he has carried off our unfortunate lady, then it is not hidden from them."

"Well, we can send men to inquire, and to catch an informant also," remarked Podbipienta.

"You have struck the point. If we discover that she is alive, that is the chief thing. Now, since you wish sincerely to help Pan Yan, put yourself under my orders, for I have most experience. We will disguise ourselves as peasants, and try to find out where he has concealed her, and once we know that, my head for it, we shall get her. I and Pan Yan risk most, for Bogun knows us, and if he should catch us, our own mothers wouldn't recognize us afterward, but he hasn't seen either of you."

"He has seen me," said Podbipienta, "but that is nothing."

"Maybe too the Lord will give him into our hands," said Volodyovski.

"Well, I don't want to look at him," said Zagloba; "may the hangman look at him! We must begin carefully, so as not to spoil the whole undertaking. It cannot be that he alone knows of her concealment, and I assure you, gentlemen, that it is safer to inquire of some one else."

"Maybe too the men whom we send out will discover. If the prince only permits, I will select trusty men, and send them even to-morrow."

"The prince will permit it; but that they will discover anything, I doubt. Listen, gentlemen! another method occurs to me,--instead of sending out people or seizing informants, to disguise ourselves as peasants and start without delay."

"Oh, that is impossible!" cried Volodyovski.

"Why impossible?"

"Don't you know military service? When a body of troops is mustered *nemine excepto*, it is sacred. Even if his father and mother were dying, a soldier would not ask leave of absence, for before battle this would be the greatest deed of disgrace which a soldier could commit. After a general engagement, when the enemy is defeated it is permissible, but not before. And consider, Skshetuski at first wanted to rush off, fly away, and rescue her, but he did nothing of the kind. He has a reputation, the prince is fond of him; and he made no request, for he knows his duty. Ours is public duty, and this is a private matter. I do not know how it is in some other land, though I think it is the same everywhere; but with the prince our voevoda it is an unheard of thing to ask leave before a battle, especially for officers! Though Skshetuski's soul were rent, he would not go with such a proposition to the prince."

"He is a Roman and a rigorist, I know," said Zagloba; "but if some one should give the prince a hint, maybe he would grant permission of his own instance, to Skshetuski and to you."

"That would not enter his mind. The prince has the whole Commonwealth on his mind. Do you think that now, when there is a rush of the most important affairs, affecting the whole nation, he would take up any private question? And even if he should give a permission unasked, which is unlikely, as God is in heaven, no one of us would leave the camp at present; for we too owe our first service to our unhappy country, not to ourselves."

"I am aware of that. I am acquainted with service from of old; therefore I told you that this method passed through my head, but I did not say that it stayed there. Besides, to tell the truth, while the power of the rabble stands untouched we could not do much; but when they are defeated and hunted down,--when their only thought will be to save their own throats,--we can go among them boldly and get information more easily. Oh, if the rest of the army would only come up at once! If it does not, we shall surely die of weariness at this Cholganski Kamen. If our prince had the command, we should be moving now; but Prince Dominik, it is evident, stops often for refreshments, since he is not here yet."

"He is expected in three days."

"God grant as soon as possible! But Konyetspolski will be here to-day?"

"Yes."

At that moment the door opened, and Skshetuski entered. His features seemed as if chiselled out of stone by pain, such calm and cold came from them. It was strange to look on that young face, as severe and dignified as though a smile had never appeared on it; and it would have been easy to imagine that if death were to strike it there would be little change. Skshetuski's beard had grown half-way to his breast, in which beard, among hairs black as the raven's wing, here and there were winding silver threads. His comrades and trusty friends guessed at his suffering, for he did not exhibit it. He was self-possessed, apparently calm, and almost more diligent, in his military service than usual, and entirely occupied with the impending war.

"We have been speaking of your misfortune, which is at the same time our own," said Zagloba; "for God is our witness that we can console ourselves with nothing. This, however, would be a barren sentiment if we were to aid you only in shedding tears; therefore we have determined to shed blood also,--to rescue the unfortunate lady, if she still walks upon the earth."

"God reward you!" said Skshetuski.

"We will go with you even to Hmelnitski's camp," said Volodyovski.

"God reward you!" repeated Skshetuski.

"We know that you have sworn to seek her, living or dead; therefore we are ready, even to-day."

Skshetuski, having seated himself on a bench, fixed his eyes on the ground and made no answer. At last anger got control of Zagloba. "Does he intend to give her up?" thought he. "If he does, God be with him! I see there is neither gratitude nor memory in the world. But men will be found yet to rescue her, or I shall have to yield my last breath."

Silence reigned in the room, interrupted only by the sighs of Pan Longin. Meanwhile little Volodyovski approached Skshetuski and shook him by the shoulder.

"Where are you from now?" asked he.

"From the prince."

"What news?"

"I am going out on a reconnoissance to-night."

"Far?"

"To Yarmolintsi, if the road is clear."

Volodyovski looked at Zagloba, and they understood each other at once.

"That is toward Bar," muttered Zagloba.

"We will go with you."

"You must go for permission, and ask if the prince has not appointed other work for you."

"We will go together. I have also something else to ask."

They rose and went. The quarters of the prince were some distance away, at the other end of the camp. In the antechamber they found a crowd of officers from different squadrons; for forces were marching from every direction to Cholganski Kamen. All were hurrying to offer their services to the prince. Volodyovski had to wait some time before he and Podbipienta were permitted to stand before the face of their chief; but to make up for this, the prince gave them permission at once to go, and to send out some Russian dragoons, who, feigning desertion from the camp, should escape to Bogun's Cossacks and inquire about the princess. To Volodyovski he said,--

"I will find various duties for Skshetuski myself, for I see that suffering has settled in him and is eating him up. I am unspeakably sorry for him. Has he said nothing to you about her?"

"But little. At first he wanted to go at random among the Cossacks, but he remembered that the squadron is mustered in full,--that we are at the service of the country, which must be saved before aught else; therefore he did not appear before you at all. God alone knows what is taking place within him."

"And is trying him severely. Watch over him; for I see that you are a trusty friend of his."

Volodyovski bowed low and went out; for at that moment the voevoda of Kieff entered with the starosta of Stobnik and Pan Denhoff, and a number of other military dignitaries.

"Well, what is the result?" asked Pan Yan.

"I go with you; but first I must go to my squadron, for I have a number of men to send out."

"Let us go together."

They went; and with them Podbipienta, Zagloba, and old Zatsvilikhovski, who was on the way to his squadron. Not far from the tents of Volodyovski's dragoons they met Pan Lashch, walking, or rather staggering, at the head of a number of nobles, for he and his comrades were completely drunk. At the sight of this Zagloba sighed. The two men had fallen in love with each other at Konstantinoff, because, from a certain point of view, they had natures as much alike as two drops of water. For Pan Lashch, though a formidable knight, and terrible against Pagans as few men were terrible, was also a notorious drinker and feaster, who loved, above all things, to pass the time free from battle, prayers, attacks, and quarrels, in the circle of men like Zagloba, to drink with might and main, and listen to jokes. He was a roysterer on a grand scale, who himself alone had caused so much disturbance, had so many times risen up against the law, that in any other State he would have lost his life long before. More sentences than one were hanging over him, but even in time of peace he troubled himself little about those; and now, in time of war, everything passed into forgetfulness all the more. He joined the prince at Rosolovtsi, and had rendered no small service at Konstantinoff; but since they had halted at Zbaraj he had become quite unendurable, through the tumults which he raised. No one had given regular count or calculation to the wine that Zagloba had drunk at his quarters, or the stories he had told, to the great delight of the host, who urged him to come every day.

But since the news of the taking of Bar, Zagloba had become gloomy, lost his humor and vivacity, and no longer visited Pan Lashch. Pan Lashch, indeed, thought that the jovial nobleman had gone somewhere from the army, when suddenly he saw him. He extended his hand, and said,--

"My greetings to you. Why don't you come to see me? What are you doing?"

"I am attending Skshetuski," answered Zagloba, gloomily.

The colonel did not like Skshetuski on account of his dignity, and nicknamed him "The Grave." He knew of his misfortune perfectly well, for he was present at the banquet in Zbaraj when news of the capture of Bar came in. But being of unrestrained nature, and drunk at the moment, he did not respect human suffering, and seizing the lieutenant by the button, inquired,--

"So, then, you are crying for a girl? And was she pretty, hei?"

"Let me go, please," said Skshetuski.

"Wait!"

"On my way to service you cannot command me. I am free of you."

"Wait!" said Lashch, with the stubbornness of a drunken man. "You have service, but I have none. There is no one to command me here." Then lowering his voice, he repeated the question, "But she was pretty, hei?"

The lieutenant frowned, "I tell you, sir, better not touch a sore spot."

"Not touch? Never fear! If she was pretty, she is alive."

Skshetuski's face was covered with a deathly pallor, but he restrained himself, and said: "I hope I shall not forget with whom I am talking--"

Lashch stuck out his eyes. "What! Are you threatening me, threatening me,--for one little wench?"

"Go your way!" shouted old Zatsvilikhovski, trembling with anger.

"Ah, sneaks, rabble, lackeys!" roared the commander. "Gentlemen, to your sabres!"

Drawing his own, he sprang at Skshetuski; but that moment the steel whistled in Skshetuski's hand, and the sabre of the commander hopped like a bird through the air, and staggered by the blow, he fell his whole length on the ground.

Skshetuski did not strike again. He became pale as a corpse, as if stunned, and that moment a tumult arose. From one side rushed in the soldiers of the commander; from the other Volodyovski's dragoons hurried like bees from a hive. Many hastened up, not knowing what the matter was; sabres began to rattle; any moment the tumult might have changed into a general battle. Happily Lashch's comrades, seeing that Vishnyevetski's men were arriving every moment, made sober from fear, seized the commander and started off with him.

In truth, if Lashch had had to do with other and less disciplined forces, they would have cut him into small pieces with their swords; but old Zatsvilikhovski, recollecting himself, merely cried, "Stop!" and the sabres were sheathed. Nevertheless there was excitement throughout the whole camp, and the echo of the tumult reached the ears of the prince just as Pan Kushel, who was on duty, rushed into the room in which the prince was holding counsel with the voevoda of Kieff, the starosta of Stobnik, and Pan Denhoff, and shouted,--

"Your Highness, the soldiers are fighting with sabres!"

At that moment Lashch, pale and beside himself with rage, but sober, shot in like a bomb.

"Your Highness, justice! It is in this camp as with Hmelnitski,--no respect for blood or rank. Dignitaries of the Crown are slashed with sabres! If your Highness will not mete out justice, will not punish with death, then I myself will mete it out."

The prince sprang up from the table. "What has happened? Who has attacked you?"

"Thy officer, Skshetuski."

Genuine astonishment was reflected on the face of the prince. "Skshetuski?"

Suddenly the doors were opened, and in walked Zatsvilikhovski. "Your Highness, I was a witness," said he.

"I have not come here to give reasons, but to demand punishment," cried Lashch.

The prince turned and fastened his eyes upon him. "Stop! stop!" said he, quietly and with emphasis.

There was something so terrible in his eyes and in his hushed voice that Lashch, though notorious for insolence, became silent at once, as if he had lost his speech, and the spectators grew pale.

"Speak!" said the prince to Zatsvilikhovski.

Zatsvilikhovski described the whole affair,--how the commander, led by an ignoble sentiment, unworthy not only of a dignitary but of a noble, began to blaspheme against the suffering of Pan Skshetuski, and then rushed upon him with a sabre; with moderation, in truth unusual to his age, the lieutenant had used his weapon only to ward off the aggressor. Finally the old man ended his story thus,--

"And since, as your Highness knows, up to my seventieth year lying has not stained my lips, nor will it while I live, I could not under oath change one word in my story."

The prince knew that Zatsvilikhovski's words were equal to gold, and besides he knew Lashch too well. He gave no answer then; he merely took a pen and began to write. When he had finished he looked at the commander. "Justice will be meted out to you," said he.

The commander opened his mouth and wished to speak, but somehow the words did not come to him; he merely put his hand on his hip, bowed, and went out proudly from the room.

"Jelenski," said the prince, "you will give this letter to Pan Skshetuski."

Volodyovski, who had not left the lieutenant, was astonished somewhat at seeing the messenger come in, for he was sure that they would have to appear at once before the prince. The messenger left the letter and went out in silence. When he had read it Skshetuski handed the letter to his friend. "Read!" said he.

Volodyovski glanced at it, and shouted: "Promotion to the head of the regiment!" And seizing Skshetuski by the neck, he kissed him on both cheeks.

A full lieutenant in the hussar regiment was almost a military dignitary. The captain of that one in which Skshetuski served was the prince himself, and the titular lieutenant was Pan Sufchinski, of Senchi, a man already old and out of service. Skshetuski had long performed the active duties of both offices,--a condition of service often found in regiments like his, in which the first two places were not infrequently merely titular offices. Captain in the royal regiment was the king himself; in that of the primate, the primate. The lieutenant and captain in both were high dignitaries of the court. They were actually commanded by deputies, who on this account were called in ordinary speech colonels and lieutenants. Such an actual lieutenant or colonel was Skshetuski. But between the actual filling of the office, between the dignity accorded in current speech and the real one, there was still a great difference. In the present instance, by virtue of his appointment, Skshetuski became one of the first officers of the prince.

But while his friends were overflowing with joy, congratulating him on his new honor, his face did not change for a moment, but remained just the same, severe and stone-like; for there were not offices nor dignities in the world that could brighten it. He rose, however, and went to thank the prince.

Meanwhile little Volodyovski walked up and down in his quarters rubbing his hands. "Well, well," he said, "appointed lieutenant in the hussar squadron in youthful years. I think this has happened to no one before."

"If God would only return his happiness!" said Zagloba.

"That is it, that is it. Did you see that he did not quiver?"

"He would prefer resigning," said Pan Longin.

"Gentlemen," sighed Zagloba, "what wonder! I would give these five fingers of mine for her, though I captured a banner with them."

"Sure enough."

"But Pan Sufchinski must be dead," remarked Volodyovski.

"He is surely dead."

"Who will take the lieutenancy then? The banneret is a stripling, and performs the duties only since the battle at Konstantinoff."

This question remained unanswered; but the colonel himself, Skshetuski, brought the answer to it when he returned.

"My dear sir," said he to Pan Podbipienta, "the prince has appointed you lieutenant."

"Oh, my God, my God!" groaned Pan Longin, placing his hands together as if in prayer.

"He might as well have appointed his Livonian mare," muttered Zagloba.

"Well, and the scouting-party?" asked Volodyovski,

"We shall go without delay," answered Skshetuski.

"Has the prince given orders to take many troops?"

"One Cossack and one Wallachian squadron, five hundred men altogether."

"Hallo! that is an expedition, not a party. If that is the case, it is time for us to take the road."

"To the road, to the road!" repeated Zagloba. "Maybe God will help us to get some tidings."

Two hours later, precisely at sunset, the four friends rode out from Cholganski Kamen toward the south. About the same time Lashch left the camp with his men. A multitude of knights from different regiments witnessed his departure, not sparing shouts and sneers. The officers crowded around Pan Kushel, who told the reason why the commander was dismissed, and how it happened.

"I delivered the order of the prince," said Kushel; "and you may believe it was a perilous mission, gentlemen, for when he read it he began to bellow like a bullock when branded with iron. He was rushing at me with a sword,--a wonder he didn't hit me; but it appears that he saw Pan Koritski's Germans surrounding his quarters, and my dragoons with spears in their hands. Then he began to shout: 'All right! all right! I'll go away, since they drive me off. I'll go to Prince Dominik, who will receive me thankfully. I will not,' said he, 'serve with minstrels; but as I am Lashch, I will have vengeance, as I am Lashch; and from that sneak,' said he, 'I must have satisfaction!' I thought he would stifle from venom; he slashed the table from rage time after time. And I tell you, gentlemen, that I am not sure some evil will not come on Skshetuski, for there is no trifling with the commander. He is a stubborn and proud man, who has never yet allowed an offence to pass. He is daring, and a dignitary besides."

"What can touch Skshetuski under the protection of the prince?" asked one of the officers. "The commander, though ready for everything, will be wary of such a hand."

Meanwhile the lieutenant, knowing nothing of the vows which the commander had made against him, withdrew at the head of his party farther and farther from the camp, turning his way toward Ojigovtsi to the Bug and Medvedovka. Though September had withered the leaves on the trees, the night was calm and warm as in July; for such, indeed, was that whole year, in which there was scarcely any winter, and in spring everything was in bloom at a time when in former years deep snow was still lying on the steppes. After a rather moist summer, the first months of autumn were dry and mild, with clear days and bright moonlight nights. They travelled along the easy road, not taking special care, for they were still too near the camp to be threatened by any attack. They rode briskly; Skshetuski ahead with a few horsemen, and behind him Volodyovski, Zagloba, and Podbipienta.

"Look, gentlemen, how the light of the moon shines on that hill!" whispered Zagloba. "You might swear that it is day. It is said that only in time of war are there such nights, so that spirits may leave their bodies without knocking their heads against trees in the dark, like sparrows against the cross-pieces in a barn, and more easily find the way. Today is Friday, the day of the Saviour, in which poisonous vapors do not issue from the ground, and evil powers have no approach to men. I feel somehow easier, and hope takes possession of me."

"That is because we are now on the way and will undertake some rescue."

"The worst thing, in grief, is to sit in one place. When you get on horseback, all your despair flies down from the shaking, till you shake it off completely and entirely."

"I do not believe," whispered Volodyovski, "that you can shake off everything in that way,-- for example, love, which clings to the heart like a wood-tick."

"If love is genuine," said Pan Longin, "then even if you should wrestle with it as with a bear, it would throw you."

Having said this, Podbipienta relieved his swollen breast with a sigh which was like the puff of a blacksmith's bellows; but little Volodyovski raised his eyes to heaven, as if seeking among the stars that one which was shining on Princess Barbara.

The horses began to snort in the whole company, and the soldiers answered, "Health, health!" Then all was silent till some melancholy voice began to sing in the rear ranks:

"You   are   going   to   the   war,   my   boy,
You   are   going   to   the   war!
Your   nights   will   be   cold,
And your days will be hot--"

"Old soldiers say that horses always snort as a good omen, as my deceased father used to tell me," said Volodyovski.

"Something whispers, as it were, in my ear, that we are not going for nothing," answered Zagloba.

"God grant that some consolation enter the heart of the lieutenant!" sighed Pan Longin.

Zagloba began to nod and turn his head like a man who is unable to conquer some idea, and at last said,--

"Something altogether different is in my head, and I must get rid of the thought, for I cannot endure it. Have you noticed that for some time Skshetuski--I am not sure, maybe he dissembles--but still he, as it were, thinks less than any of us of saving that unfortunate lady."

"Nonsense!" said Volodyovski. "It is his disposition never to confess anything to any one. He has never been different."

"Yes, that so far as it goes; but just remember, when we gave him hope, he said, 'God reward you,' both to me and to you, as coldly as if it had been some common affair. And God is witness, on his part that was black ingratitude; for what that poor woman has wept and grieved for him could not be inscribed on an ox-hide. I have seen it with my own eyes."

Volodyovski shook his head. "It cannot be that he has given her up, though it is true that the first time when that devil seized her from him in Rozlogi, he despaired so that we feared he would lose his mind; but now he shows more reflection. If God has poured peace into his soul, it is better. As true friends, it is our duty to be comforted by this."

Volodyovski then spurred his horse and sped on toward Pan Yan, but Zagloba rode for some time in silence by the side of Podbipienta.

"Are you not of my opinion, that if there were no love affairs a power of evil would cease in the world?"

"Whatever God has destined to any one, will not avoid him," answered the Lithuanian.

"But you never answer to the point. That is one affair, and this is another. Who caused the destruction of Troy, hei? And isn't this war about fair locks? Hmelnitski wanted Chaplinski's woman, or Chaplinski wanted Hmelnitski's; and we are breaking our necks on account of their sinful desires."

"Those are dishonorable loves; but there are honorable ones, through which the glory of God is increased."

"Now you have hit the point better. But are you going soon to work in that vineyard yourself? I hear that a scarf is bound to you for the war."

"Ah, brother! brother!"

"But three heads are in the way, are they?"

"Ah, that's the truth!"

"Well, I tell you: give a good blow, and cut them off at once from Hmelnitski, the Khan, and Bogun."

"Oh, if they would only stand in a row!" said Pan Longin, in a voice full of emotion, raising his eyes to heaven.

Meanwhile Volodyovski rode by Skshetuski, and looked from under his helmet in silence at his pallid face, till at last their stirrups touched.

"Yan," said he, "it is bad for you to forget yourself."

"I am not forgetting myself, I am praying," answered Skshetuski.

"That is a holy and praiseworthy thing; but you are not a monk, to be occupied in prayer alone."

Pan Yan turned his suffering face slowly to Volodyovski, and inquired with a dull voice, full of deathly resignation: "Tell me, Michael, what is left to me now but a monk's habit?"

"It remains to you to rescue her," answered Volodyovski.

"I will do that, if it takes my last breath. But even if I should find her alive, will it not be too late? Preserve me, O God, for I can think of everything, only not of that, God save my reason! I desire nothing more than to rescue her from those infamous hands and let her find an asylum, such as I myself shall seek. Evidently it was not the will of God. Let me pray, Michael, and don't touch my bleeding wound."

Volodyovski's heart was pressed. He wished still to console his friend, to speak of hope; but the words would not pass his lips, and they rode on in dull silence. Only the lips of Skshetuski moved rapidly in prayer, with which he wished evidently to drive away terrible thoughts. But the little knight was afraid when he looked at that face in the moonlight; for it seemed to him altogether like the face of a monk, stern, emaciated by fasting and mortification. And then that voice began again to sing, in the rear,--

"You will find when the war is over, poor fellow,
You will find when the war is over,
Everything empty at home,
And your skin full of wounds."

CHAPTER XXXVIII.

Skshetuski so marched with his detachment that he rested during the day in forests and ravines, throwing out pickets carefully, and pushed forward only in the night. Whenever he approached a village he usually surrounded it so that not a man went out, took provisions, feed for his horses, but above all collected information concerning the enemy; then he marched away without inflicting harm on the people. But when out of sight he changed his road abruptly, so that the enemy in the village might not know in what direction he had gone. The object of his expedition was to discover whether Krívonos with his forty thousand men was still besieging Kamenyets, or having given up the fruitless siege, was marching to assist Hmelnitski so as to join him for a general engagement; and further what the Dobrudja Tartars were doing,--whether they had crossed the Dnieper already and joined Krívonos, or were still on the other bank. These were important items for the Polish army, which the commanders should have tried to obtain; but being men without experience, it did not enter their heads to do so. Yeremi therefore took that burden on himself. If it should appear that Krívonos, with the hordes of Bélgorod and Dobrudja, had abandoned the siege of the impregnable Kamenyets and was marching to Hmelnitski, then it behooved them to attack the latter as quickly as possible before he had grown to his highest power.

Meanwhile the commander-in-chief. Prince Dominik Zaslavski Ostrogski, was not hastening, and at the time of Skshetuski's departure he was expected at the camp in two or three days. Evidently he was feasting along the road, according to his custom, and felt well; but the most favorable moment for breaking the power of Hmelnitski was passing, and Prince Yeremi was in despair at the thought that if the war should be carried on further in this fashion, not only Krívonos and the forces beyond the Dniester would come to Hmelnitski in season, but also the Khan himself at the head of all the forces from Perekop, Nogai, and Azoff.

There were tidings in camp that the Khan had already crossed the Dnieper, and was moving westward day and night with two hundred thousand horse; but day after day passed, and Prince Dominik did not arrive. It became more and more likely that the troops at Cholganski Kamen would have to meet forces five times more numerous, and in case of defeat nothing would prevent the enemy from breaking into the heart of the Commonwealth at Cracow and Warsaw.

Krívonos was the more dangerous in this, that in case the commanders wished to push into the heart of the Ukraine, he, by going from Kamenyets directly northward to Konstantinoff, could bar their retreat, and in every case they would be taken then between two fires. Skshetuski determined therefore not only to gain information concerning Krívonos, but to check him. Penetrated with the importance of this task, on the accomplishment of which the fate of the whole army was in part dependent, he risked willingly his own life and the lives of his soldiers, though that undertaking might have been considered insane or mad if the young knight had had the intention of checking with five hundred men in an offensive battle the forty thousand men of Krívonos reinforced by the hordes of Bélgorod and Dobrudja. But Skshetuski was too experienced a soldier to rush into insane undertakings, and he knew perfectly well that in case of battle the torrent would sweep over the bodies of himself and his men in an hour. He seized upon other means. He gave out among his own soldiers that they were merely the advance guard of a whole division of the terrible prince, and this report he spread everywhere in all the farms, villages, and towns through which it came to him to pass. And in truth it spread like a flash of lightning along Zbruch, Smotrich, Studenitsa, Ushka, Kalusik, and from them it reached the Dniester and flew on farther as if driven by the wind from Kamenyets to Yagorlik. It was repeated by Turkish pashas in Khotím, the Zaporojians in Yampol, and the Tartars in Rashkoff. And again was heard that famous cry, "Yarema is coming!" from which the hearts of the rebellious people sank, and from which they trembled, knowing neither the day nor the hour.

And no one doubted the truth of the report. The commanders would fall upon Hmelnitski, and Yeremi on Krívonos,--that lay in the order of things. Krívonos himself believed in it, and his hands dropped. What was he to do? Move on the prince? At Konstantinoff there was another spirit in his men and he had more troops; still they were beaten, decimated, barely escaped with their lives. Krívonos was sure that his Cossacks would fight madly against all other armies of the Commonwealth, and against every other leader, but with the approach of Yeremi they would speed away like a flock of swans before an eagle, or like the thistle-down of the steppes before the wind.

To wait for the prince at Kamenyets was still worse. Krívonos determined to hurry eastward as far as Bratslav, to avoid his evil spirit and move toward Hmelnitski. He knew, it is true, that circling around in this way he would not arrive in time; but at least he would hear of the results in season, and plan for his own safety.

A new report came with the wind, that Hmelnitski was already defeated. Skshetuski had spread it purposely, as he had the previous report. This time the unfortunate Krívonos knew not what to do.

Later he determined all the more to march to the east and push on as far as possible into the steppes; maybe he would meet the Tartars and find shelter among them. But first of all he wished to be sure; therefore he looked carefully among his colonels to find a man trusty and prepared for everything, so as to send him with a party to get information. But the choice was difficult; there was a lack of volunteers, and it was absolutely necessary to find a man who in case he should fall into the hands of the enemy would not disclose the plans of retreat, even if burned with fire, empaled on a stake, or broken on a wheel. At last Krívonos found the man. One night he gave the order to call Bogun, and said to him,--

"Do you hear, Yurku, my friend Yarema is marching on us with a great force; we shall all perish, unfortunates!"

"I have heard that he is coming,--you have already spoken of that, father. But why should we perish?"

"We cannot withstand him. We could another, but not Yeremi. The Cossacks are afraid of him."

"But I am not afraid of him. I cut to pieces a regiment of his at Vassílyevka beyond the Dnieper."

"I know that you are not afraid of him; your fame of a Cossack and a hero is equal to his as a prince. But I cannot give him battle, for my Cossacks are unwilling. Remember what they said at the council,--how they rushed on me with sabres because I wanted to lead them to slaughter."

"Then we will go to Hmelnitski; there we shall find blood and booty."

"They say that Hmelnitski is already defeated."

"I do not believe that, Father Maksim. Hmelnitski is a fox; he will not strike the Poles without the Tartars."

"I think so too, but we must find out. Then we could go around this devil of a Yeremi and join Hmel; but we must have information. Now, if some one who has no fear of Yeremi were to go with a party and take prisoners, I should fill his cap with ruddy sequins."

"I'll go, Father Maksim,--not for sequins, but for Cossack, for heroic glory."

"You are the next ataman to me, and since you are willing to go, you will become first ataman yet over the Cossacks, good hero, for you are not afraid of Yeremi. Go, my falcon, and hereafter you have but to ask for what you want. Well, I tell you, if you were not going I should go myself; but it is not for me to go."

"No; for if you were to go, father, the Cossacks would say that you were saving your head and would scatter over the world, but when I go their courage will increase."

"Shall I give you many men?"

"I will not take many; it is easier to hide and approach with a small force. But give me about five hundred good warriors, and my head for it, I will bring you informants,--not soldiers, but officers from whom you will learn everything."

"Go at once! They are firing cannon from Kamenyets with joy,--salvation to the Poles and destruction to us innocents."

Bogun went out, and began to prepare at once for the road. His heroes, as was the fixed practice on such occasions, drank to the verge of destruction, "before Mother Death should clasp them to her breast." He too drank with them till he was snorting from gorailka.

He frolicked and revelled, then had a barrel filled with tar, and just as he was, in brocade and serge, sprang into it, sank a couple of times, once over his head, and shouted,--

"I am black as Mother Night. Polish eyes won't see me now!"

He rolled himself on Persian carpets, sprang on his horse and rode away. After him clattered, amid the darkness of night, his trusty heroes, followed by shouts: "Glory! Luck!"

Skshetuski had already pushed on to Yarmolintsi, where, meeting opposition, he baptized the townspeople in blood, and having told them that Prince Yeremi would arrive next day, gave rest to his wearied horses and men. Then assembling his officers in council, he said to them,--

"So far God has given us success. I see also, by the terror which seizes the peasants, that they take us for the advance guard of the prince, and believe that his whole force is following. We must look out, however, that they do not bethink themselves when they see that one company is going everywhere."

"And shall we go about in this way long?" asked Zagloba.

"Till we find out what Krívonos has determined."

"Then we may not come in time for the battle at the camp?"

"Maybe not."

"Well, I am not glad of that," said Zagloba. "My hand has become a little exercised on the ruffians at Konstantinoff. I captured something from them there; but that is a trifle. My fingers are itching now."

"Perhaps you will get more fighting than you expect," answered Pan Yan, seriously.

"How is that?" asked Zagloba, rather alarmed.

"Why, any day we may come upon the enemy, and though we are not here to bar the road with arms, we shall have to defend ourselves. But to return to the subject. We must occupy more country, so they may know of us in several places at once; cut down the obstinate here and there, so as to spread terror; and everywhere circulate reports. Therefore I think we must separate."

"So I think," said Volodyovski. "We shall increase in their eyes, and those who escape to Krívonos will talk about legions."

"Well, Lieutenant, you are leader here, give the orders," said Podbipienta.

"I will go through Zinkoff to Solodkovets, and farther if I can," said Skshetuski. "You, Podbipienta, will go straight down to Tatarjiski; and you, Michael, go to Kupin; and Zagloba will press on to Zbruch, near Satanoff."

"I!" exclaimed Zagloba.

"Yes. You are a man of thought and full of stratagems. I supposed you would undertake the enterprise willingly; but if not, Sergeant Kosmach will lead the fourth party."

"I will take it under my command," cried Zagloba, who was suddenly dazzled by the thought that he would be the leader of a separate party. "If I asked, it was because I am sorry to part with you."

"But have you experience in military matters?" asked Volodyovski.

"Have I experience? It hadn't yet come into the head of any stork to make a present of you to your father and mother when I was commanding larger bodies of men than this. I served all my life in the army, and should have served to this moment had it not been for the mouldy biscuit that stuck in my stomach and stayed there three years. I had to go for a bezoar to Galáts, the details of which journey I will tell in proper time, but now I am in a hurry for the road."

"Go on, then, and spread the reports that Hmelnitski is beaten, and that the prince has passed Ploskiroff," said Skshetuski. "Don't take the first informant that comes along; but when you meet scouting-parties from Kamenyets, try to get people who are able to give information about Krívonos, for those whom we have now tell contradictory stories."

"I hope I may meet Krívonos himself. I hope he will want to go on a scouting expedition. I should give him pepper and ginger. Don't be afraid! I will teach the ruffians to sing, and dance for that matter."

"In three days we shall meet again at Yarmolintsi, and now each one to his journey," said Skshetuski. "And I beg of you to spare your men."

"In three days at Yarmolintsi," repeated Volodyovski, Zagloba, and Podbipienta.

CHAPTER XXXIX.

When Zagloba found himself alone at the head of his party, he felt uncomfortable somehow and terribly alarmed, and would have given much to have at his side Skshetuski, Volodyovski, or Pan Longin, whom in his soul he admired with all his might, and near whom he felt completely safe, so blindly did he believe in their resources and bravery. At first, therefore, he rode rather gloomily at the head of his party, and looking around suspiciously on every side, measured in his mind the dangers which he might meet, and muttered,--

"It would always be livelier if some one of them were here. To whatever God predestined a man, for that he created him; and those three ought to have been born horseflies, for they love to sit in blood. They are in war just as other men are at the cup, or like fish in water. War is their play. They have light stomachs, but heavy hands. I have seen Skshetuski at work, and I know what skill he has. He hurries through men as monks through their prayers. That's his favorite work. That Lithuanian, who has no head of his own, is looking for three strange heads, and he has nothing to risk. I know that little fellow least of all, but he must be a wasp of no common kind, judging from what I saw at Konstantinoff, and what Skshetuski tells me about him,--he must be a wasp! Happily he is marching not far from me, and I think that I shall do better to join him, for if I know where to go may the ducks trample me!"

Zagloba felt so lonely in the world that he took pity upon his own loneliness.

"Indeed!" muttered he. "Every man has some one to look to; but how is it with me? I have neither comrade nor father nor mother. I am an orphan, and that is the end of it!"

At that moment the sergeant, Kosmach, approached him. "Commander, where are we marching to?" asked he.

"Where are we marching to?" repeated Zagloba. "What?" Suddenly he straightened himself in the saddle and twisted his mustache. "To Kamenyets, if such should be my will! Do you understand?"

The sergeant bowed and withdrew in silence to the ranks, unable to explain to himself what the commander was angry at. But Zagloba cast threatening glances at the neighborhood, then grew quiet and muttered further,--

"If I go to Kamenyets, I'll let a hundred blows of a stick be given on the soles of my feet, Turkish fashion. Tfu! tfu! If I only had one of those fellows with me, then I should feel more courage. What shall I begin to do with these people? I would rather be alone, for when alone a man trusts to stratagem. But now there are too many of us for stratagems and too few for defence. A very unfortunate idea of Skshetuski's to divide the detachment! And where shall I go? I know what is behind me, but who shall tell me what is in front, and who shall assure me that the devils there haven't set some snare? Krívonos and Bogun, a nice pair,--may the devils flay them! God defend me at least from Bogun! Skshetuski wants to meet him; may the Lord listen to him!--I wish him the same as I wish myself, for I am his friend,--amen! I'll work on to Zbruch, return to Yarmolintsi, and bring them more informants than they want themselves. That is not difficult."

Kosmach now approached. "Commander, some horsemen are visible behind the hill."

"Let them go to the devil! Where are they,--where?"

"There, on the other side of the hill, I saw flags."

"Troops?"

"They appear to be troops."

"May the dogs bite them! Are there many of them?"

"You can't tell, for they are far away. We might hide here behind these rocks and fall on them unawares, for their road lies this way. If their numbers are too great, Pan Volodyovski is not far off; he will hear the shots and hasten to our aid."

Daring rose suddenly to Zagloba's head like wine. It may be that despair gave him such an impulse to action; possibly hope that Volodyovski was still near. Enough that he waved his naked sabre, rolled his eyes terribly, and cried,--

"Hide behind the rocks! We will show those ruffians--" The trained soldiers of the prince turned behind the rocks, and in the twinkle of an eye placed themselves in battle-array, ready for a sudden attack.

An hour passed. At last the noise of approaching people was heard. An echo bore the sounds of joyful songs; and a moment later the sounds of fiddles, bagpipes, and a drum reached the ears of the men lurking in ambush. The sergeant came to Zagloba again, and said,--

"They are not troops, Commander, nor Cossacks. It is a wedding."

"A wedding? I'll play a tune for them; let them wait a bit."

Saying this, he rode out, and after him the soldiers, and formed in line on the road. "After me!" cried Zagloba, threateningly.

The line moved on a trot, then a gallop, and passing around the cliff, stood suddenly in front of the crowd of people, frightened and confused by the unexpected sight.

"Stop! stop!" was the cry from both sides.

It was really a peasant wedding. In front rode the piper, the flute-player, the fiddler, and two drummers, already somewhat intoxicated, and playing dance-music out of tune. Behind them was the bride, a brisk young woman in a dark jacket, with hair flowing over her shoulders. She was surrounded by her bridesmaids, singing songs and carrying wreaths in their hands. All the girls were sitting on horseback, man-fashion, adorned with wild-flowers. They looked at a distance like a party of handsome Cossacks. In another line rode the bridegroom on a sturdy horse, with his groomsmen, having wreaths on long poles, like pikes. The rear of the party was brought up by the parents of the newly married and guests, all on horseback. In light wagons strewn with straw were drawn a number of kegs of gorailka, mead, and beer, which belched out a pleasant odor along the rough, stony road.

"Halt! halt!" was shouted from both sides. The wedding-party was confused. The young girls raised a cry of fear, and drew back to the rear. The young men and elder groomsmen rushed forward to protect the young women from the unexpected attack.

Zagloba sprang before them, and brandishing his sabre, which gleamed in the eyes of the terror-stricken peasants, began to shout,--

"Ha, you bullock-drivers, dog-tails, rebels! You wanted to join the insurrection! You are on the side of Hmelnitski, you scoundrels! You are going to spy out something; you are blocking the road to troops,--raising your hand against nobles! Oh, I'll give it to you, you foul spirits of curs! I'll order you to be fettered, to be empaled, O rascals, Pagans! Now you will pay for all your crimes."

A groomsman, old, and white as a dove, jumped from his horse, approached the noble, and holding his stirrup humbly, began to bow to his girdle and implore,--

"Have mercy, serene knight! Do not ruin poor people! God is our witness that we are innocent. We are not going to a rebellion. We are going from the church at Gusiatyn. We crowned our relative Dmitry, the blacksmith, with Ksenia, the cooper's daughter. We have come with a wedding and with a dance."

"These are innocent people," whispered the sergeant.

"Out of my sight! They are scoundrels; they have come from Krívonos's to a wedding!" roared Zagloba.

"May the plague kill him!" cried the old man. "We have never looked on him with our eyes; we are poor people. Have mercy on us, serene lord, and let us pass; we are doing harm to no man, and we know our duty."

"You will go to Yarmolintsi in fetters!"

"We will go wherever you command. Our lord, it is for you to command, for us to obey. But you will do us a kindness, serene knight! Order your soldiers to do us no harm, and you yourself pardon us simple people. We now beat to you humbly with the forehead, to drink with us to the happiness of the newly married. Drink, your mercy, to the joy of simple people, as God and the holy Gospels command."

"But don't suppose that I forgive you if I drink," said Zagloba, sharply.

"No, no, my lord," exclaimed with joy the old man; "we don't dream of it. Hei, musicians!" cried he, "strike up for the serene knight, because the serene knight is kind; and you, young men, hurry for mead,--sweet mead for the knight; he will not harm poor people. Hurry, boys, hurry! We thank you, our lord."

The young men ran with the speed of wind to the kegs; and immediately the drums sounded, the fiddles squeaked sharply, the piper puffed out his cheeks and began to press the wind-bag under his arm. The groomsmen shook the wreaths on the poles, in view of which the soldiers began to press forward, twirl their mustaches, laugh, and look at the bride over the shoulders of the young fellows. The song resounded again. Terror had passed away, and here and there too was heard the joyful "U-ha! u-ha!"

Zagloba did not become serene-browed in a moment. Even when a quart of mead was brought to him, he still muttered to himself: "Oh, the scoundrels, the ruffians!" Even when he had sunk his mustaches in the dark surface of the mead, his brows did not unwrinkle. He raised his head, winked his eyes, and smacking his lips, began to taste the liquid; then astonishment, but also indignation, was seen on his face.

"What times we live in!" muttered he. "Trash are drinking such mead. O Lord, thou seest this, and dost not hurl thy bolts!" Then he raised the cup and emptied it to the bottom.

Meanwhile the emboldened wedding-guests came with their whole company to beg him to do them no harm and let them pass; and among them came the bride Ksenia, timid, trembling, with tears in her eyes, blushing and beautiful as the dawn. When she drew near she joined her hands. "Be merciful, our lord!" and she kissed the yellow boot of Zagloba. The heart of the noble became soft as wax in a moment. He loosened his leather girdle, began to fumble in it, and finding the last gold sequin of those which Prince Yeremi had given him, he said to Ksenia,--

"Here! may God bless thee, as he does every innocence!"

Emotion did not permit further speech, for that shapely dark-browed Ksenia reminded him of the princess whom Zagloba loved in his own fashion. "Where is she now, poor girl, and are the angels of heaven guarding her?" thought he, completely overpowered, ready to embrace every one and become a brother to all.

The wedding-guests, seeing this lordly act, began to shout from joy, to sing, and crowding up to him to kiss his clothes. "He is kind," was repeated in the crowd. "He is a golden Pole! he gives away sequins, he does no harm, he is a kind lord. Glory to him, luck to him!" The fiddler quivered, he worked so hard; the hands of the drummers grew weary. The old cooper, evidently a coward to his innermost lining, had held himself in the rear till that moment. Now he pushed forward, together with his wife, the cooperess, and the ancient blacksmithess, the mother of the bridegroom; and now they began such a bowing to the girdle and insistent invitation to the house for the wedding, because it was a glory to have such a guest, and a happy augury for the young couple; if not, harm would come to them. After them bowed the bridegroom and the dark-browed Ksenia, who, though a simple girl, saw in a twinkle that her request was more effective than any other. The best men shouted that the farm was near, not out of the knight's road; that the old cooper was rich, and would set out mead far better than this. Zagloba gazed at the soldiers; all were moving their mustaches as rabbits do their whiskers, foreseeing for themselves various delights in the dance and the drinks. Therefore, though they did not ask to go, Zagloba took pity on them, and after a while the groomsmen, the young women, and the soldiers were making for the farm in most perfect harmony.

In fact the farm was near, and the old cooper rich. The wedding therefore was noisy; all drank heavily, and Zagloba so let himself out that he was the first in everything. Soon strange ceremonies were begun. Old women took Ksenia to a chamber, and shutting themselves in with her, remained a long time; then they came forth and declared that the young woman was as a dove, as a lily. Thereupon joy reigned in the assembly; there rose a shout, "Glory! happiness!" The women began to clap their hands, the young fellows stamped with their feet; each one danced by himself, with a quart cup in his hand, which he emptied to "fame and happiness" before the door of the chamber. Zagloba danced also, distinguishing the importance of his birth by this only, that he drank before the door, not a quart, but half a gallon. Then the friends of the cooper and the blacksmith's wife conducted young Dmitry to the door; but since young Dmitry had no father, they bowed down to Zagloba to take his place. Zagloba consented, and passed in with the others. During this time all became quiet in the house; but the soldiers drinking in the yard before the cottage shouted, crying "Allah!" from joy, in Tartar fashion, and fired from pistols.

The greatest rejoicing and uproar began when the parents appeared again in the main room. The old cooper embraced the blacksmith's wife with delight, the young men came to the cooper's wife and raised her from her feet, and the women glorified her because she had guarded her daughter as the eye in her head, kept her as a dove and a lily. Then Zagloba opened the dance with her. They began to stamp in front of each other; and he, keeping time with his hands, dropped into the prisyadka, sprang so high, and beat the floor with his metal-shod heels in such fashion that bits flew from the planks, and sweat poured from his forehead in abundance. They were followed by others,--those who had space dancing in the room, and those who had not in the yard,--the maidens with the young men and soldiers. From time to time the cooper had new kegs brought out. Finally the whole wedding-feast was transferred from the house to the yard; piles of dry thistles and pitch-pine were set on fire, for a dark night had settled down, and the rejoicing had changed to drinking with might and main. The soldiers fired from their pistols and muskets as in time of battle.

Zagloba, purple, steaming in perspiration, tottering on his feet, forgot what was happening to him, where he was; through the steam which came from his hair he saw the faces of his entertainers, but if he were to be empaled on a stake he couldn't tell what sort of entertainers they were. He remembered that he was at a wedding, but whose wedding was it? Ha! it must be the wedding of Pan Yan and the princess. This idea seemed to him the most probable, and finally stuck in his head like a nail, and filled him with such joy that he began to shout like a madman: "Long life! let us love each other, brothers!" and every little while he filled new half-gallons. "To your success, brothers! To the health of the prince! Prosperity to us! May this paroxysm of our country pass!" Then he covered himself with tears, and stumbled going to the keg, and stumbled more and more; for on the ground, as on a field of battle, lay many a motionless body. "O God," cried Zagloba, "thou hast no longer any manhood left in this Commonwealth! There are but two men who can drink,--one Pan Lashch, and the other Zagloba. As for the rest, my God, my God!" And he raised his eyes in sorrow to the sky. Then he saw that the heavenly bodies were no longer fastened quietly in the firmament like golden nails, but some were trembling as if they wished to spring from their settings; others were whirling in a round dance; a third party of them were dancing the kazachka face to face with each other. Then Zagloba fell into terribly deep thought, and said to his musing soul,--

"Is it possible that I alone in the universe am not drunk?" But suddenly the earth itself quivered, like the stars, in a mad whirl, and Zagloba fell his whole length on the ground.

Soon awful dreams came to him. It seemed as if nightmares were sitting on his breast, pressing him, squeezing him to the ground, binding him hand and foot. At the same time tumult and as it were the sound of shots struck his ears; a glaring light passed his closed lids, and struck his eyes with an unendurable flash. He wished to rouse himself, to open his eyes, and he could not. He felt that something unusual was happening to him,--that his head was dropping back as if he were being carried by hands and feet. Then fear seized him; he felt badly, very badly, very heavy. Consciousness returned in part, but strangely, for in company with such weakness as he had never felt in his life. Again he tried to move; but when he could not, he woke up more and opened his eyelids.

Then his gaze met a pair of eyes which were fastened on him eagerly; their pupils were black as coal, and so ill-omened that Zagloba, now thoroughly awake, thought at the first moment that the devil was looking at him. Again he closed his eyes, and again he opened them quickly. Those eyes looked at him continually, stubbornly. The countenance seemed to him familiar. All at once he shivered to the marrow of his bones, cold sweat covered him, and down his spine to his feet passed thousands of ants. He recognized the face of Bogun!

CHAPTER XL.

Zagloba lay bound hand and foot to his own sabre, which was passed across behind his knees, in that same room in which the wedding was celebrated. The terrible chief sat at some distance on a bench, and feasted his eyes on the terror of the prisoner.

"Good-evening!" said he, seeing the open lids of his victim.

Zagloba made no answer, but in one twinkle of an eye came to his senses as if he had never put a drop of wine to his mouth; the ants which had gone down to his heels returned to his head, and the marrow in his bones grew cold as ice. They say that a drowning man in the last moment sees clearly all his past,--that he remembers everything, and gives himself an account of that which is happening to him. Such clearness of vision and memory Zagloba possessed in that hour; and the last expression of that clearness was a silent cry, unspoken by the lips,--

"He will give me a flaying now."

And the leader repeated, with a quiet voice: "Good-evening!"

"Brr!" thought Zagloba, "I would rather go to the furies."

"Don't you know me, lord noble?"

"With the forehead, with the forehead! How is your health?"

"Not bad; but as to yours, I'll occupy myself with that."

"I have not asked God for such a doctor, and I doubt if I could digest your medicine; but the will of God be done."

"Well, you cured me; now I'll return thanks. We are old friends. You remember how you bound my head in Rozlogi, do you not?"

Bogun's eyes began to glitter like two carbuncles, and the line of his mustaches extended in a terrible smile.

"I remember," said Zagloba, "that I might have stabbed you, and I did not."

"But have I stabbed you, or do I think to stab you? No! For me you are a darling, a dear; and I will guard you as the eye in my head."

"I have always said that you are an honorable cavalier," said Zagloba, pretending to take Bogun's words in earnest. At the same time through his mind flew the thought: "It is evident that he is meditating some special delicacy for me. I shall not die in simple style."

"You speak well," continued Bogun. "You too are an honorable cavalier; so we have sought and found each other."

"What is true is that I have not sought you; but I thank you for the good word."

"You will thank me still more before long; and I will thank you for this, that you took the young woman from Rozlogi to Bar. There I found her; and I would ask you to the wedding, but it will not be to-day nor to-morrow,--there is war at present,--and you are an old man, perhaps you will not live to see it."

Zagloba, notwithstanding the terrible position in which he found himself, pricked up his ears. "To the wedding!" he muttered.

"But what did you think?" asked Bogun. "That I was a peasant, to constrain her without a priest, or not to insist on being married in Kieff. You brought her to Bar not for a peasant, but for an ataman and a hetman."

"Very good!" thought Zagloba. Then he turned his head to Bogun. "Give the order to unbind me," said he.

"Oh, lie awhile, lie awhile! You will go on a journey. You are an old man, and you need rest before the road."

"Where do you wish to take me?"

"You are my friend, so I will take you to my other friend, Krivonos. Then we shall both think how to make it pleasant for you."

"It will be hot for me," muttered Zagloba; and again the ants were walking over his back. At last he began to speak:--

"I know that you are enraged at me; but unjustly, God knows. We lived together, and in Chigirin we drank more than one bottle. I had for you the love of a father for your knightly daring; a better love you did not find in the whole Ukraine. Isn't that true? In what way have I crossed your path? If I had not gone with you to Rozlogi, we should have lived to this day in kind friendship; and why did I go if not out of friendship for you? And if you had not become enraged, if you had not killed those unhappy people,--God is looking at me,--I should not have crossed your path. Why should I mix in other men's affairs? I would have preferred to see the girl yours; but through your Tartar courtship my conscience was moved, and besides it was a noble's house. You yourself would not have acted otherwise. I might, moreover, have swept you out of the world with the greatest gain to myself. And why did I not do it? Because I am a noble. Be ashamed of yourself too, for I know you wish to take vengeance on me. As it is, you have the girl in your hands. What do you want of me? Have not I guarded as the eye in my head this your property? Since you have respected her it is to be seen that you have knightly honor and conscience; but how will you extend to her the hand which you steep in my innocent blood? How will you say to her, 'The man who led you through the mob and the Tartars I delivered to torment'? Have shame, and let me go from these bonds and from this captivity into which you have seized me by treachery. You are young, and know not what may meet you, and for my death God will punish you in that which is dearest to you."

Bogun rose from the bench, pale with rage, and approaching Zagloba, began to speak in a voice stifled with fury,--

"Unclean swine! I will have straps torn from you, I'll burn you on a slow fire, I'll drive spikes into you, I'll tear you into rags."

In an access of fury he grasped at the knife hanging from his belt, and for a moment pressed it convulsively in his hand. The edge was already gleaming in Zagloba's eyes, when the chief restrained himself, thrust the knife back into the scabbard, and cried: "Boys!"

Six Zaporojians came into the room.

"Take that Polish carrion, throw it into the stable, and guard it as the eye in your head!"

The Cossacks took Zagloba,--two by his hands and feet, one behind by the hair,--and carrying him out of the house bore him through the yard, and threw him on a dung-heap in the stable standing at one side. Then they closed the door. Complete darkness surrounded the prisoner, but in the cracks between the wall-planks and through holes in the thatch the dim light of night penetrated here and there. After a while Zagloba's eyes grew accustomed to the darkness. He looked around, and saw there were no pigs in the stable, nor Cossacks. The conversation of the latter, however, reached him clearly through all the four walls. Evidently the whole building was surrounded closely; but in spite of these guards Zagloba drew a long breath.

First of all, he was alive. When Bogun flashed his knife above him he was convinced that his last moment had come, and he recommended his soul to God,--it is true with the greatest fear. But evidently Bogun decided to save him for a death incomparably more complicated. He desired not only to take revenge, but to glut himself with vengeance on the man who had stolen from him the beauty, belittled his Cossack glory, and covered him with ridicule, swaddling him like a baby. It was therefore a gloomy prospect for Pan Zagloba; but he was comforted by the thought that he was still living, that likely they would take him to Krívonos and begin to torture him there, and consequently he had a few, perhaps a number of days before him. In the mean while he lay in the stable alone, and could in the midst of the quiet night think of stratagems.

That was the one good side of the affair; but when he thought of the bad ones the ants began to travel over his spine in thousands.

"Stratagems! If a pig lay here in this stable, he would have more stratagems than I, for they would not tie him crosswise to a sabre. If Solomon had been bound in this way, he would have been no wiser than his trousers or my boot-heel. Oh, my God, my God, for what dost thou punish me? Of all people in the world I wanted most to avoid this scoundrel, and such is my luck that he is just the man I have not avoided. I shall have my skin dressed like sviboda cloth. If another had taken me, I might promise to join the rebellion and then run away. But another would not have believed me, and this one least of all. I feel my heart dying within me. The devils have brought me to this place. Oh, my God! my God!"

But after a while Zagloba thought that if he had his hands and feet free, he might more easily use some stratagem. Well, let him try! If he could only push the sword from under his knees, the rest would go on more easily. But how was he to push it out? He turned on his side, he could do nothing; then he fell into deep thought.

Next he began to rock himself on his back with increasing rapidity, each moment pushing himself half the length of his body ahead. He got heated; his forehead was in greater perspiration than during the dance. At times he stopped and rested; at times he interrupted the work, for it appeared some one of the Cossacks was coming to the door; then he began with renewed ardor. At last he pushed himself forward to the wall.

After that he began to sway in another direction, not from head to foot, but from side to side, so that every time he struck lightly against the wall with the sabre, which was pushed in this way from under his knees, moving more and more toward the middle of the stable from the side of the hilt. Zagloba's heart began to beat like a hammer, for he saw that this method might be effectual.

He worked on, trying to strike with the least noise, and only when the conversation of the Cossacks was louder than the light blow. At last the moment came when the end of the sheath was on a line with his wrist and his knee, and further striking against the wall could not push it out. But hanging from the other side was a considerable and much heavier part of the sabre, taking into consideration the hilt with the cross usually on sabres. Zagloba counted on that cross.

He began to rock himself for the third time, but now the great object of his efforts was to turn himself with his feet toward the wall. Attaining this, he began to push himself up with his feet. The sabre still clung under his knees and his hands, but the hilt became more and more involved in the uneven surface of the ground. At length the cross caught rather firmly. Zagloba pushed the last time. For a moment joy nailed him to the spot; the sabre had dropped out.

He removed his hands then from his knees, and though they were still bound he caught the sabre with them. He held the scabbard with his feet and drew out the blade. To cut the bonds on his feet was the work of a moment. It was more difficult in the case of his hands. He was obliged to put his sabre on the ground with the edge up, and draw the cords along the edge until he had cut them. When he had done this he was not only free from bonds, but armed. He drew a long breath, then made a sign of the cross and began to thank God.

But it was very far yet from the cutting of the bonds to the rescuing of himself from the hands of Bogun.

"What further?" asked Zagloba of himself.

He found no answer. The stable was surrounded by Cossacks; there were about a hundred. A mouse could not have passed through unobserved, and what could a man as bulky as Zagloba do?

"I see that I am beginning to come to the end of my resources," said he to himself. "My wit is only good to grease boots with, and you could buy better grease than it from the Hungarians at the fair. If God does not send me some idea, then I shall become roast meat for the crows; but if he does send me an idea, then I promise to remain in continence like Pan Longin."

The louder conversation of the Cossacks behind the wall interrupted his thoughts. He sprang up and put his ear to a crack between the timbers. The dry pine gave back the voices like the sounding-board of a lute.

"And where shall we go from here, Father Ovsivuyu?" asked one voice.

"To Kamenyets, of course," said another.

"Nonsense! The horses can barely drag their legs; they will not get there."

"That's why we stop here; they will have rest by morning."

A moment of silence followed; then the first voice was heard lower than before. "And it seems to me, father, that the ataman is going from Kamenyets to Yampol."

Zagloba held his breath.

"Be silent if your young head is dear to you!" was the answer.

Another moment of silence, but from behind the other walls came whispering.

"They are all around, on the watch everywhere," muttered Zagloba; and he went to the opposite wall. Meanwhile were heard the noise of chewing oats and the snorting of horses evidently standing right there; among these horses the Cossacks were lying on the ground and talking, for their voices came from below.

"Ah!" said one, "we have come here without sleeping, eating, or feeding our horses, so as to go on the stake in the camp of Yeremi."

"The people who have fled from Yarmolintsi saw him as I see you. What they tell is a terror. He is as big as a pine-tree; in his forehead are two firebrands, and he has a dragon under him for a horse."

"Lord, have mercy on us!"

"We ought to take that Pole with the soldiers and be off."

"How be off, when as it is the horses are just dying?"

"A bad fix, brother! If I were the ataman, I would cut off the heads of those Poles, and go back to Kamenyets, even on foot."

"We will take him with us to Kamenyets, and there our ataman will play with him."

"The devils will play with you first!" muttered Zagloba.

And, indeed, in spite of all his fear of Bogun, and maybe especially because of that, he had sworn that he would not yield himself alive. He was free from bonds, and he had a sabre in his hands,--he would defend himself. If they cut him to pieces, all right; but they wouldn't take him alive.

The snorting and groaning of horses excessively road-weary drowned the sound of further conversation, and immediately gave a certain idea to Zagloba.

"If I could get through the wall," thought he, "and jump on horseback suddenly--it is night, and before they could see what happened I should be out of sight. It is hard enough to chase through the ravines and valleys by sunlight, but what must it be in the dark? God grant me an opportunity!"

But an opportunity was not to be obtained easily. It was necessary either to throw down the wall--and to do that he would have to be Pan Podbipienta--or to burrow under it like a fox; and then they would surely hear, discover, and seize the fugitive by the neck before he could touch the stirrup with his foot. A thousand stratagems crowded into Zagloba's head; but for the very reason that they were a thousand no one of them presented itself clearly.

"It cannot be otherwise; only with my life can I pay," thought he.

Then he went toward the third wall. All at once he struck his head against something hard. He felt; it was a ladder. The stable was not for pigs, but for buffaloes, and half the length it had a loft for straw and hay. Zagloba without a moment's hesitation climbed up. Then he sat down, drew breath, and began slowly to pull up the ladder after him.

"Well, now I am in a fortress!" he muttered. "Even if they should find another ladder, they couldn't bring it here very quickly; and if I don't split the forehead of the man who comes here, then I'll give myself to be smoked into bacon. Oh, devil take it!" he burst out after a while, "in truth they cannot only smoke me, but fry and melt me into tallow. But let them burn the stable if they wish,--all right! They won't get me alive; and it is all the same whether the crows eat me raw or roasted. If I only escape those robber hands, I don't care for the rest; and I have hope that something will happen yet."

Zagloba passed easily, it is evident, from the lowest despair to hope,--in fact, such hope entered him as if he were already in the camp of Prince Yeremi. But still his position had not improved much. He was sitting on the loft, and he had a sabre in his hand; he might ward off an attack for some time, but that was all. From the loft to freedom was a road like jumping from the stove on your forehead,--with this difference, that below the sabres and pikes of the Cossacks watching around the walls were waiting for him.

"Something will happen!" muttered Zagloba; and approaching the roof he began to separate quietly and remove the thatch, so as to gain for himself an outlook into the world. This was easily done, for the Cossacks talked continually under the walls, wishing to kill the tedium of watching; and besides there sprang up a rather strong breeze, which deadened with its movement among the neighboring trees the noise which was made in removing the bundles. After a time the aperture was ready. Zagloba stuck his head through it and began to look around.

The night had already begun to wane, and on the eastern horizon appeared the first glimmer of day. By the pale light Zagloba saw the whole yard filled with horses; in front of the cottage rows of sleeping Cossacks, stretched out like long indefinite lines; farther on the well-sweep and the trough, in which water was glistening; and near it again a rank of sleeping men and a number of Cossacks with drawn sabres in their hands walking along that line.

"There are my men, bound with ropes," muttered Zagloba. "Bah!" he added after a while, "if they were mine! But they are the prince's. I was a good leader to them; there is nothing to be said on that point. I led them into the mouth of the dog. It will be a shame to show my eyes if God returns me freedom. And through what was all this? Through love-making and drinking. What was it to me that trash were marrying? I had as much business at this wedding as at a dog's wedding. I will renounce this traitorous mead, which crawls into the legs, not the head. All the evil in the world is from drinking; for if they had fallen upon us while sober, I should have gained the victory in a trice and shut Bogun up in this stable."

Zagloba's gaze fell again on the cottage in which the chief was sleeping, and rested at its door.

"Sleep on, you scoundrel!" he muttered, "sleep! And may you dream that the devils are skinning you,--a thing which will not miss you in any case! You wanted to make a sieve out of my skin; try to crawl up to me here, and we shall see if I do not cut yours so that it wouldn't do to make boots for a dog. If I could only get myself out of this place,--if I could only get out! But how?"

Indeed the problem was not to be solved. The whole yard was so packed with men and horses that even if Zagloba had got out of the stable, even if he had pushed through the thatch and sprung on one of the horses that stood right there, he could in no wise have pushed to the gate; and then how was he to get beyond the gate? Still, it seemed to him that he had solved more than half the problem. He was free, armed, and he sat in the loft as in a fortress.

"What the devil good is there," thought he, "in getting out of the rope if you are to be hanged with it afterward?" And again stratagems began to bustle in his head; but there were so many of them that he could not choose.

Meanwhile the light increased, the places around the cottage began to emerge from the shadow; the thatch of the cottage was covered as if by silver. Zagloba could distinguish accurately particular groups; he could see the red uniforms of his men, who were lying around the well, and the sheepskin coats under which the Cossacks were sleeping near the cottage.

Then suddenly some figure rose from the rank of the sleepers and began to pass with slow step through the yard, halting here and there near men and horses, speaking for a moment with the Cossacks who were guarding the prisoners, and at last approached the stable. Zagloba supposed at first that it was Bogun, for he saw that the guards spoke to that figure as subordinates to a superior.

"Eh!" he muttered, "if I had a musket now, I would show you how to cover yourself with your feet."

At this moment the figure raised its head, and on its face fell the gray light of the morning. It was not Bogun, but the sotnik Golody, whom Zagloba recognized at once, for he knew Golody well from the time of his own intimacy with Bogun in Chigirin.

"Well, boys, you are not asleep?" said Golody.

"No, father, though we should like to sleep. It is about time to change guard."

"It will be changed immediately. And that devil's imp has not got away?"

"No, no!--unless the soul has gone out of him, father, for he hasn't moved."

"Ah! he is an old fox. But look, see what he is doing, for he would go through the ground."

"This minute!" answered a number of Cossacks, going to the door of the stable.

"Throw out hay from the mow! Rub the horses! We will start at sunrise."

"All right, father!"

Zagloba, leaving at once his lookout in the opening of the thatch, crawled to the hole in the floor. At the same moment he heard the creak of the wooden hinges and the rustling of the straw under the feet of the Cossacks. His heart beat like a hammer in his breast, and he pressed the hilt of the sabre in his hand, renewing in his soul the oath that he would resign himself to be burned with the stable or be cut to pieces rather than be taken alive. He expected every moment that the Cossacks would raise a fearful uproar, but he was deceived. For a time he heard them walking more and more quickly through the whole stable. At last one said,--

"What the devil is the matter? I can't find him. We threw him in here."

"He isn't a werewolf, is he? Strike a light, Vassily; it is as dark here as in a forest."

A moment of silence followed. Evidently Vassily was looking for flint and tinder, while the other Cossacks began to call in a low voice: "Where are you?"

"Kiss the dog's ear!" muttered Zagloba.

Steel struck flint, a cluster of sparks flashed forth and lighted the dark interior of the stable and the heads of the Cossacks in their caps, then deeper darkness came down again.

"He is not here! he is not here!" cried excited voices.

That moment one sprang to the door. "Father Golody! Father Golody!"

"What's the matter?" cried the sotnik, approaching the door.

"There is no Pole."

"How, no Pole?"

"He has gone into the ground; he isn't anywhere. O God, have mercy on us! We struck fire; he is not here."

"Impossible! Oh, you will catch it from the ataman! Has he escaped, or how is it? You have been asleep."

"No, father, we have not slept. He didn't get out of the stable on our side."

"Be quiet! don't wake the ataman. If he hasn't gone out, then he must be here. Have you looked everywhere?"

"Everywhere."

"On the loft too?"

"How could he crawl on the loft when he was bound?"

"You fool! If he hadn't unbound himself, he would be here. Look on the loft! Strike a light!"

Sparks flashed again. The news flew in a moment among all the guards. They began to crowd to the stable with the haste usual on sudden occasions; hurried steps were heard, hurried questions and still more hurried answers. Advices crossed one another like swords in battle.

"To the loft! to the loft!"

"But watch outside!"

"Don't wake the ataman; if you do, there will be terror."

"The ladder is gone!"

"Bring another!"

"There is none anywhere."

"Run to the cottage; see if there is one there."

"Oh, curse the Pole!"

"Go up the corners to the thatch; get in through the thatch."

"Impossible; for the roof projects and is fastened with planks."

"Bring the lances; we will go up on the lances. Ah, the dog! he has hauled up the ladder."

"Bring the lances!" roared Golody.

Some ran for the lances, while others stretched their heads up toward the loft. Already scattered light penetrated through the open door into the stable; and with its uncertain gleam was to be seen the square opening in the loft, black and silent. From below were heard single voices.

"Now, sir noble, let down the ladder and come. You won't get away, anyhow; why put people to trouble? Come down, oh, come down!"

Silence.

"You are a wise man. If it would do you any good, you might stay up there; but since it won't help you, come down of your own accord, be a good fellow."

Silence.

"Come down! If you don't, we will skin your head and throw you head-first into the dung-heap."

Zagloba was as deaf to threats as to coaxing, sitting in the dark like a badger in his hole, preparing for a stubborn defence. He only grasped his sabre tighter, panted a little, and whispered his prayers.

Lances were now brought, three of them tied together, and placed with their points to the opening. The thought flashed through Zagloba's mind to grasp and draw them up; but he thought that the roof might be too low, and he couldn't draw them up entirely. Besides, others would be brought at once. Meanwhile the stable became crowded with Cossacks. Some held torches, others brought from wagons all kinds of ladders and poles, every one of which turned out to be too short; these they lashed together hurriedly with straps, for it was really difficult to climb on the lances. Still they found volunteers.

"I'll go," called a number of voices.

"Wait for the ladder!" said Golody.

"And what harm is it, father, to try on the lances?"

"Vassily will climb; he goes like a cat."

"Let him try."

But others began to joke immediately. "Be careful! he has a sabre; he will cut your head off. Look out! he will grab you by the head, drag you in, and treat you as a bear would."

But Vassily didn't allow himself to be frightened. "He knows," said Vassily, "that if he should lay a finger on me the ataman would give him the devil to eat; and you, brothers."

This was a warning to Zagloba, who sat quietly, and did not even mutter.

But the Cossacks, as is usual among soldiers, got into good humor, for the whole affair began to amuse them; so they kept on teasing Vassily.

"There will be one blockhead less in the white world."

"He won't think how we shall pay him for your head. He is a bold hero."

"Ho, ho! He is a werewolf. The devil knows into what form he has turned already. He is a wizard! Can't tell, Vassily, whom you will find there behind the opening."

Vassily, who had already spat on his palms and was just grasping the lances by the stem, stopped suddenly. "I'll go against a Pole," said he, "but not against the devil."

But now the ladders were lashed together and placed at the opening. It was difficult to climb them, too, for they bent immediately where they were tied, and the slender round cracked under the feet, which were placed on the lowest one to try. But Golody himself began to ascend; while going, he said,--

"My dear noble, you see that there is no joking here. If you have made up your mind to stay up there, stay; but don't fight, for we will get you anyhow, even if we have to pull the stable to pieces. Have sense!"

At last his head reached the opening and went through it slowly. All at once the whiz of a sabre was heard. The Cossack screamed fearfully, tottered, and fell, with his head cut in two.

"Cut! slash!" roared the Cossacks.

A fearful tumult began in the stable. Shouts and cries were raised, which were overborne by the thundering voice of Zagloba,--

"Oh, you scoundrels, you man-eaters, you basilisks! I'll cut you to pieces, you mangy ruffians! You'll know a knightly hand. Attacking honest people by night, shutting a noble in a stable! Scoundrels! Come to me by ones or by twos, only come! Come along; but you'll leave your heads on the dung-heap, for I'll hew them off, as I live."

"Cut! cut!" shouted the Cossacks.

"We will burn the stable."

"I'll burn it myself, you ox-tails, and you with it."

"Several,--several at a time!" shouted an old Cossack. "Support the ladder, prop it with lances, take bundles of hay on your heads and go on! We must get him."

Then he mounted, and with him two comrades. The rounds began to break, the ladders bent still more; but more than twelve strong hands seized them by the sides propped by the lances, others thrust the points of lances through the opening to ward off the blows of the sabre.

A few moments later three bodies fell on the heads of those standing below. Zagloba, heated by his triumph, bellowed like a buffalo, and poured out such curses as the world had never heard, and from which the souls of the Cossacks would have died within them, if fury had not begun to possess them. Some thrust their lances into the loft; others hurried on the ladders, though sure death waited them in the opening. Suddenly a shout was heard at the door, and into the stable rushed Bogun himself. He was without a cap, in trousers and shirt; in his hand was a drawn sabre, and in his eyes fire.

"Through the thatch!" he shouted. "Tear the thatch apart and take him alive!"

But Zagloba, seeing him, roared: "Ruffian, just come up here! I'll cut off your nose and ears. I won't touch your neck, for that belongs to the hangman. Well, are you afraid, my urchin?" Then Zagloba said to the Cossacks: "Tie that scoundrel for me, and you will all be pardoned. Well, gallows-bird! well, Jews' picture! I am alone here; only show your head on this loft! Come, come! I shall be glad to see you, I'll give you such a reception that you'll remember it with your father the devil, and your mother a harlot."

The poles of the roof now began to crack. It was evident the Cossacks were up there and tearing through the thatch.

Zagloba heard, but fear didn't deprive him of power; he was as if drunk with the battle and with blood. "I'll spring to the corner and perish there," thought he.

But that instant gun-shots were heard in the yard. A number of Cossacks rushed to the stable. "Father! father!" they shouted. "This way!"

Zagloba at the first moment did not understand what had happened, and was astonished. He looked down through the opening; there was no one there. The rafters were not cracking.

"What is it? what has happened?" he cried aloud. "Ah! I understand. They want to burn the stable, and fire from pistols at the roof."

Then was heard the uproar of people, more terrible every moment, and the tramp of horses. Shouts mixed with howls and the clatter of steel.

"My God, that must be a battle!" thought Zagloba, springing to the opening in the thatch. He looked, and his legs bent under him with delight.

In the yard a battle was raging, and soon Zagloba beheld the terrible defeat of Bogun's Cossacks. Attacked on a sudden, struck with fire from pistols placed at their heads and breasts, pushed to the fences, to the cottage and out-houses, cut with swords, thrown down by the rush of horses, trampled with their hoofs, the Cossacks perished almost without resistance. The ranks of red-uniformed soldiers, cutting furiously and pressing on the fugitives, did not allow them to form, to use their sabres, to draw breath, or to reach their horses. Only detached groups defended themselves. Some, favored by the disturbance, uproar, and smoke, succeeded in reaching their loosened saddle-girths, and perished before they touched the stirrups with a foot; others, throwing away lances and sabres, disappeared under the fences, got stuck between the posts, or jumped over the top, shouting and crying with unearthly voices. It seemed to the unfortunates that Prince Yeremi himself had fallen upon them unexpectedly, and was shivering them with his whole power. They had no time to come to their minds to look around. The shouts of the victors, the whistle of sabres, and the rattle of shots chased them like a storm. The hot breath of horses was on their necks. "Save yourselves, men!" was heard on every side. "Slay! kill!" was the response of the assailants.

At last Zagloba saw little Volodyovski as, standing near the gate at the head of a number of soldiers, he gave directions with his baton and voice, and sometimes rushed on his gray horse into the whirl, and then the moment he turned or struck, a man fell without uttering a sound. Oh, but he was a master beyond masters, little Volodyovski, and a soldier, blood and bone! He did not lose sight of the battle, but making a correction here and there, returned again, looked and corrected, like the director of an orchestra, who at times plays himself, at times stops, watching carefully over all, so that each man may fill his part.

When he saw this, Zagloba stamped on the floor of the loft till the dust rose. He clapped his hands and shouted,--

"Slay the dog-brothers! Kill them! Flay them! Cut, slash, hew, kill! On to them, on! Sabre them to a man!"

Thus he shouted and jumped till his eyes were inflamed from exertion, and he lost vision for a moment; but when he regained his eyesight he saw a still more beautiful spectacle. There, at the head of a number of Cossacks, was Bogun, rushing away on horseback like lightning, without a cap, in his shirt and trousers, and after him, at the head of his soldiers, little Volodyovski. "Slay!" shouted Zagloba; "that's Bogun." But his voice did not reach them. That moment Bogun with his heroes was over the fence, Volodyovski over the fence. Some remained behind; horses fell under others in the leap. Zagloba looked. Bogun is on the plain, Volodyovski is on the plain. Then the Cossacks scatter in their flight, and soldiers in their pursuit; individual pursuit begins. Zagloba's breath died within his breast, his eyes were almost bursting through his lids; for what does he see? Volodyovski is almost on the neck of Bogun, like a hound on a wild boar. The chief turns his head, raises his sabre; they fight. Zagloba shouts. Still another moment, and Bogun falls with his horse; and Volodyovski, leaving him, hurries after the others.

But Bogun is alive; he rises from the ground and runs to a pile of rocks surrounded with bushes.

"Hold him! hold him!" roared Zagloba. "That's Bogun!"

Then a new band of Cossacks hurry on, who till that moment had been hiding on the other side of the rocks, but now discovered, seek a new way of escape, pushed by soldiers who are about half a furlong behind. This party comes up to Bogun, bears him away, disappears from sight in the turns of the ravine, and after it disappear the soldiers.

In the yard it was silent and empty; for the soldiers of Zagloba, rescued by Volodyovski, chased after the Cossacks and pursued with the others the scattered enemy.

Zagloba let down the ladder, slipped from the loft, and coming out of the stable into the yard, said, "I am free!" Then he began to look around. In the yard lay a number of Zaporojian bodies and some Poles. He walked slowly among them, and examined each carefully. At length he knelt over one of them. Soon he rose with a canteen in his hand. "It is full!" he muttered; and placing it to his mouth he raised his head. "Not bad!" Again he looked round, and again he repeated, but with a much clearer voice, "I am free!"

He went to the cottage. On the threshold he came upon the body of the old cooper, whom the Cossacks had killed there. He disappeared inside. When he came out, around his hips, over a coat soiled with manure, glittered Bogun's belt, thickly embroidered with gold; at the belt a knife with a great ruby in the hilt.

"God has rewarded bravery," he muttered, "for the belt is pretty full. Ah, you wretched robber, I have hope that you will not escape! That little hop-of-my-thumb--may the bullets strike him!--is a lively piece, just like a wasp. I knew he was a good soldier; but to drive Bogun as he would a white-faced mare, I did not expect that of him. That there should be such strength and courage in such a little body! Bogun might carry him on a string at his belt. May the bullets strike Volodyovski!--but better, may God give him luck. He couldn't have known Bogun, or he would have finished him. Phu! how it smells of powder here, enough to pierce the nose! But if I didn't get out of a scrape this time such as I have never been in before! Praise to God! Well, well, but so to drive Bogun! I must examine this Volodyovski again, for it must be there is a devil sitting inside of him."

Zagloba sat on the threshold of the stable in meditation, and waited. Presently there appeared at a distance on the plain soldiers returning from the victory, and at their head rode Volodyovski. When he saw Zagloba, Volodyovski galloped up, and springing from his horse, came to him.

"Do I see you once more?" called he, at a distance.

"Me, in my own person," said Zagloba. "God reward you for coming with reinforcements in time!"

"Thanks be to God that I came in time!" said the little knight, pressing the palm of Zagloba with joy.

"But where did you hear of the straits in which I was?"

"The peasants of this place gave information."

"Oh, and I thought they betrayed me."

"Why should they? They are honest. The newly married barely got off with their lives, and what happened to the others they know not."

"If they are not traitors, then they are killed by the Cossacks. The master of the house lies near the door. But what of that? Tell me, is Bogun alive, did he escape,--he without a cap, in the shirt and trousers, whom you threw with his horse?"

"I hit him on the head; but it is too bad that I didn't know him. But tell me, my good Zagloba, what is the best you have done."

"What have I done?" repeated Zagloba. "Come, Pan Michael, and see." He took him by the hand and led him into the stable. "Look at that!"

Volodyovski saw nothing for a while, for he had come in from the light; but when his eyes had become used to the darkness he saw bodies lying motionless on the dung-heap. "And who cut down these men?" asked he, in astonishment.

"I!" said Zagloba. "You have asked what I did. Here it is before you!"

"But," said the young officer, "how did you do it?"

"I defended myself up there. They stormed me from below and through the roof. I don't know how long it was, for in battle a man doesn't reckon time. It was Bogun, with a strong force and chosen men. He will remember you; he will remember me too. At another time I will tell you how I fell into captivity, what I passed through, and how I settled Bogun; for I had an encounter of tongues with him. But now I am so wearied that I can scarcely stand."

"Well," repeated Volodyovski, "it is not to be denied you defended yourself manfully; but I will say this, you are a better swordsman than general."

"Pan Michael," said the noble, "it is no time for discussion. Better thank God, who has sent down to us to-day so mighty a victory, the memory of which will not soon vanish from among men."

Volodyovski looked with astonishment at Zagloba, since it had appeared to him hitherto that he alone had gained that victory which Zagloba evidently wished to share with him. But he only looked, shook his head, and said, "Let it be so."

An hour later the two friends, at the head of their united parties, moved on to Yarmolintsi.

Almost no one was missing from Zagloba's men; for sprung upon in their sleep, they offered no resistance. Bogun, being sent specially for informants, had given orders not to kill, but to take prisoners.

CHAPTER XLI.

Bogun, though a brave, clear-sighted leader, had no luck in this expedition against the supposed division of Prince Yeremi. He was merely confirmed in the belief that the prince had really moved his whole force against Krívonos; for this was the information given by the captives from among Zagloba's men, who believed most sacredly that the prince was marching after them. Nothing remained then for the unfortunate ataman but to withdraw with all speed to Krívonos; but the task was not easy. Scarcely on the third day was a party of two hundred and a few tens of Cossacks collected around him; the others had either fallen in the fight, were lying wounded on the field of struggle, or were wandering yet among the ravines and reeds, not knowing what to do, how to turn, or where to go. Besides, the party left to Bogun was not good for much; for it was beaten, inclined to flee at every alarm, demoralized, frightened. And it was made up too of chosen men; better soldiers it would be difficult to find in the whole Saitch. But the heroes didn't know with what a small force Pan Volodyovski had struck them, and that, thanks only to the unexpected attack on sleeping and unprepared men, could he inflict such a defeat. They believed most sacredly that they had been fighting, if not with the prince himself, at least with a strong detachment several times more numerous than it was. Bogun raged like fire; cut in the hand, run over, sick, beaten, he had let his inveterate enemy out of his hands, and belittled his own fame. For now those Cossacks who on the eve of the defeat would have followed him blindly to the Crimea, to hell, and against the prince himself, had lost faith and courage, and were thinking only how to carry their lives out of the defeat. Still Bogun had done everything that a leader was bound to do; he had neglected nothing, he had established pickets at a distance from the house, and rested only because the horses which had come from Kamenyets almost at one course were altogether unfit for the road. But Volodyovski, whose youth had been passed in surprising and hunting Tartars, approached the pickets like a fox in the night, seized them before they could shout or fire, and fell upon them in such fashion that Bogun could escape only in his shirt and trousers. When the chief thought of this the light grew dark in his eyes, his head swam, and despair gnawed his soul like a mad dog. He who on the Black Sea had rushed upon Turkish galleys, and galloped on the necks of Tartars to Perekop, and lighted up the eyes of the Khan with the blaze of his villages, and under the hand of the prince near Lubni itself had cut a garrison to pieces at Vassílyevka, had to flee in his shirt, bareheaded and without a sabre,--for he had lost that too in his meeting with the little knight. So at the stopping-places where the horses were fed, when no man was looking, the chief seized himself by the head and cried: "Where is my Cossack glory, where my sabre friend?" When he cried in this way a wild raving carried him away, and then he drank as if he were not a creature of God, and wanted to march against the prince, attack all his forces,--perish and disappear for the ages.

He wished it, but the Cossacks did not. "Though you kill us, father, we will not go!" was their gloomy answer to his outbursts; and vainly in accesses of fury he cut at them with his sabre and singed their faces with his pistol,--they would not, they did not go.

You would have said that the ground was slipping away from the ataman's feet, for this was not the end of his misfortune. Fearing on account of probable pursuit to go straight to the south, and thinking that perhaps Krívonos had already given up the siege, he rushed straight to the east, and came upon the party of Pan Podbipienta. Pan Longin, wakeful as a stork, did not permit an attack, but falling first on Bogun, defeated him the more easily because his Cossacks were unwilling to fight; when he had defeated him he turned him over to Skshetuski, who beat him worst of all; so that Bogun, after long wanderings in the steppes with a few horses only, without glory, without Cossacks, without booty, without informants, made his way back at last to Krívonos.

But the wild Krívonos, usually so terrible to subordinates whom fortune did not favor, was not angry this time. He knew from his own experience what an affair with Yeremi meant; therefore he even petted Bogun, comforted him, quieted him, pacified him, and when he fell into a violent fever, gave orders to nurse and cure him with all care.

The four officers of the prince, having filled the country with terror and dismay, returned safely to Yarmolintsi, where they remained several days to give rest to the men and horses. There, when they came into the same quarters, they gave to Skshetuski, each in turn, an account of what had happened to them and what they had accomplished; then they sat down by the bottle to relieve their hearts in friendly converse and satisfy their mutual curiosity.

But Zagloba gave little chance to any man to speak. He had no desire to listen, but wished only that others should listen to him,--in truth it came out that he had the most to tell.

"Gentlemen," said he, "I fell into captivity, it is true; but fortune turns around. Bogun has been all his life victorious, but we beat him this time. That is how it is usually in war. To-day you tan people, to-morrow they tan you. But God punished Bogun because he fell upon us, sleeping sweetly the sleep of the just, and roused us in such a dishonorable way. Ho, ho! he thought to terrify me with his filthy tongue; but I tell you here, gentlemen, that I cornered him so that he lost his boldness, became confused, and said what he didn't want to say. What's the use of talking long? If I hadn't got into captivity. Pan Michael and I would not have defeated him. I say both of us, because in this affair magna pars fui, and I shall not cease to insist on it to my death. So God give me health! Hear my reasons further: If I and Volodyovski had not beaten him, then Podbipienta would not have beaten him, and further Skshetuski would not have beaten him; and finally if we hadn't beaten him he would have beaten us, and who was the cause that this didn't take place?"

"Ah! it is with you as with a fox," said Pan Longin; "you wave your tail here, slink away there, and always get out."

"It's a foolish hound that runs after his own tail, for he will not catch it and will not smell anything honorable, and besides will lose his wind. How many men have you lost?"

"Twelve in all, and some wounded; they didn't strike us very hard."

"And you, Pan Michael?"

"About thirty, for I fell upon them unawares."

"And you, Lieutenant?"

"As many as Pan Longin."

"And I lost two. See yourselves who is the best leader! That's the question. Why did we come here? On the service of the prince, to get news of Krívonos. Well, I tell you, gentlemen, that I first got news of him, and from the best source, because I got it from Bogun; and I know that he is at Kamenyets, but he thinks of raising the siege, for he is afraid. I know this openly; but I know something else which will put joy into your heart, and of which I have not spoken because I wanted that we should counsel about it together. I was sick till now, for weariness overpowered me, and my bowels rose up against that villanous binding on a stick. I thought my blood would boil over."

"Tell us, for God's sake!" cried Volodyovski, "have you heard anything of our unfortunate lady?"

"Yes, God bless her," said Zagloba.

Skshetuski rose to his full height and then sat down. There followed such a silence that the buzzing of the mosquitoes was heard on the windows till Zagloba began again,--

"She lives, I know that certainly; she is in Bogun's hands. Gentlemen, it is a terrible thing; however, God has not permitted harm or disgrace to meet her. Bogun himself told me this,--he who would rather boast of something else."

"How can that be? how can that be?" asked Skshetuski, feverishly.

"If I lie, may a thunderbolt strike me!" said Zagloba, with importance, "for this is a sacred thing. Listen to what Bogun said when he wished to jeer at me before I settled him at last. 'Did you think,' said he, 'that you brought her to Bar for a peasant; that I was a peasant to constrain her by force; that I was not to be married in Kieff in the church, and monks sing for me, and three hundred candles burn for me,--me, an ataman, a hetman!' And he stamped his feet and threatened me with his knife, for he thought he was frightening me; but I told him to frighten the dogs!"

Skshetuski had now recovered himself. His monk's face lighted up; gladness and uncertainty played on it again. "Where is she now, where is she?" he asked hurriedly. "If you have found that out, then you have come from heaven."

"He did not tell me that, but two words are enough for a wise head. Remember, gentlemen, he jeered me all the while till I planted him, and then he went in. 'First I'll take you,' said he, 'to Krívonos, and then I would invite you to the wedding; but now there is war, so it will not come off soon.' Think of it, gentlemen,--'not come off soon;' therefore we have plenty of time. Secondly, think,--'first to Krívonos, then to the wedding;' therefore in no way is she at the camp of Krívonos, but somewhere farther, where the war has not reached."

"You are a man of gold," said Volodyovski.

"I thought at first," said the delightfully flattered Zagloba, "that maybe he had sent her to Kieff; but no, for he said he would go for the wedding to Kieff with her. If they will go, it means that she is not there; and he is too shrewd to take her there now, for if Hmelnitski should push into Red Russia, Kieff could be taken easily by the Lithuanian forces."

"Surely, surely!" cried Pan Longin. "Now, as God is just to me, no man could change minds with you."

"But I shouldn't change with every one, lest I might get soup instead of reason,--a thing which might easily happen among the Lithuanians."

"Oh, he is beginning again!" said Pan Longin.

"Well, since she is not with Krívonos nor in Kieff, where is she?"

"There's the difficulty."

"If you have worked it out, then tell me quickly, for fire is burning me," said Skshetuski.

"Beyond Yampol," said Zagloba, and rolled his one sound eye triumphantly.

"How do you know?" inquired Volodyovski.

"How do I know? Here is how: I was sitting in the stable,--for that brigand had me shut up in the stable, may the wild boars rip him!--and the Cossacks were talking among themselves all around. I put my ear to the wall then, and what did I hear? 'Now maybe the ataman will go beyond Yampol,' said one; and then the other answered, 'Be silent, if your young head is dear to you!' I'll give my neck that she is beyond Yampol."

"Oh, as sure as God is in heaven!" cried Volodyovski.

"He did not take her to the Wilderness; therefore, according to my head, he must have hidden her somewhere between Yampol and Yagorlik. I was once in that region when the judges of the king and the Khan met; for in Yagorlik, as you know, cattle questions of the boundary are tried, of which cases there is never a lack. Along the whole Dniester there are ravines, hidden places, and reeds in which living by themselves are people who know no authority, dwell in the wilderness, and see no neighbors. He has hidden her surely among such wild solitaries, for he would be surest of her there."

"But how can we go there now, when Krívonos bars the way?" asked Pan Longin. "Yampol too, I hear, is a nest of robbers."

To this Skshetuski replied: "Though I had to risk my life ten times, I should try to save her. I will go disguised and look for her. God will help me, I shall find her."

"I will go with you, Yan," said Volodyovski.

"And I as a minstrel with my lute. Believe me, gentlemen, that I have more experience than any of you; but since the lute has disgusted me to the last degree, I'll take bagpipes."

"I too shall be good for something," said Podbipienta.

"Of course," added Zagloba. "Whenever we need to cross the Dnieper you will carry us over, like Saint Christopher."

"I thank you from my soul, gentlemen," said Pan Yan; "and I accept your readiness with a willing heart. There is nothing to be compared with trusty friends, of whom as I see Providence has not deprived me. May the great God grant me to repay you with my health and property!"

"We are all as one man!" shouted Zagloba. "God is pleased with concord, and you will find that we shall soon see the fruit of our labors."

"Then nothing else remains to me," said Skshetuski, after a moment's silence, "but to deliver up the squadron to the prince, and start at once. We will go by the Dniester, along through Yampol to Yagorlik, and look everywhere. But if, as I hope, Hmelnitski is already crushed or will be before we reach the prince, then public service will not be in the way. Certain regiments will go to the Ukraine, to finish the remnant of the rebellion, but they will get on without us."

"Wait!" said Volodyovski; "doubtless after Hmelnitski, Krívonos's turn will come; maybe we shall go together with the regiments to Yampol."

"No, we must go there before," answered Zagloba. "But first of all give up the squadron, so as to have free hand. I hope, too, that the prince will be satisfied with us."

"Especially with you."

"That's true, for I shall bring him the best news. Believe me, I expect a reward."

"When shall we take the road?"

"We must rest till morning," said Volodyovski. "Let Skshetuski command, however, for he is chief here; but I forewarn you, if we start to-day my horses will all give out."

"I know that it is impossible to start to-day," said Skshetuski; "but I think after good oats we can go to-morrow."

They started on the following day. According to the orders of the prince, they were to return to Zbaraj and wait further orders. They went consequently through Kuzmin, aside from Felstin, to Volochisk, from which the old highway led through Hlebanovka to Zbaraj. The roads were bad; for rain was falling, though quietly. Pan Longin, going ahead with one hundred horses, broke up a few disorderly bands that had gathered around the rear of the forces of the commander-in-chief. At Volochisk they stopped for the night.

But they had barely begun a pleasant sleep after the long road, when they were roused by an alarm, and the guards informed them that cavalry detachments were approaching. Immediately came the news that it was Vershul's Tartar squadron, therefore their own men. Zagloba, Pan Longin, and Volodyovski met at once in Skshetuski's room; and right after them rushed in, like a storm, an officer of the light cavalry, breathless and covered with mud. When he had looked at him, Skshetuski cried out: "Vershul!"

"Yes, it is I," said the newly arrived, unable to catch his breath.

"From the prince?"

"Yes. Oh for breath, breath!"

"What news? All over with Hmelnitski?"

"All--over with--the Commonwealth!"

"By the wounds of Christ, what do you say? Defeat!"

"Defeat, disgrace, shame!--without a battle--a panic--oh! oh!"

Skshetuski could not believe his ears. "But speak! speak, in the name of the living God! The commanders--"

"Ran away."

"Where is our prince?"

"Retreating--without an army--I am here from the prince--the order to Lvoff--at once--they are pursuing us--"

"Who? Vershul, Vershul, come to your senses, man! Who is pursuing?"

"Hmelnitski and the Tartars."

"In the name of the Father, Son, and Holy Ghost!" cried Zagloba. "The earth is opening."

But Skshetuski understood already what the matter was. "Questions later on; now to horse!"

"To horse! to horse!"

The hoofs of the horses under Vershul's Tartars were clattering by the windows. The townspeople, roused by the arrival of troops, burst from their houses with lanterns and torches in their hands. The news flew through the town like lightning. The alarm was sounded. The town, silent a moment before, was filled with yells, tramping of horses, shouting of orders, and wailing of Jews. The inhabitants wishing to leave with the troops got ready wagons, in which they put their wives and children, with featherbeds. The mayor, at the head of a number of citizens, came to beg Skshetuski not to depart at once, but to convoy the inhabitants even to Tarnopol. Skshetuski would not listen; for the order received was explicit, to go to Lvoff as fast as his breath would let him. They hurried away therefore; and on the road Vershul, recovering breath, told what had happened, and how.

"Since the Commonwealth has been a commonwealth," said he, "never has it borne such a defeat. Tsetsora, Jóltiya Vodi, Korsún, are nothing in comparison."

Skshetuski, Volodyovski, and Pan Longin bent down to the necks of their horses, now grasping their own heads, now raising their hands to heaven. "The thing passes human belief," said they. "But where was the prince?"

"Deserted by all, thrust aside on purpose; he did not command, in fact, his own division."

"Who had command?"

"No man, and all men. I have been long in service, I have eaten my teeth in war, and yet up to this day I have not seen such armies and such leaders."

Zagloba, who had no great love for Vershul and knew him but little, began to shake his head and smack his lips; at last he said,--

"My dear sir, either your vision is confused, or you have taken some partial defeat for a general one; for what you relate passes imagination completely."

"That it passes imagination, I confess; and I'll say more to you,--that I should gladly give my head to be severed if by some miracle it should appear that I am mistaken."

"But how did you get to Volochisk first after the defeat? For I don't wish to admit that you were the first to run away. Where, then, are the forces in flight? In what direction are they fleeing? What has happened to them? Why didn't the fugitives get ahead of you? To all these questions I seek an answer in vain."

Vershul at any other time would not have permitted such questions, but at that moment he could think of nothing but the defeat; therefore he merely answered,--

"I came first to Volochisk, for the others are retreating to Ojigovtsi, and the prince hurried me off on purpose toward the place in which he thought you were, so the avalanche might not catch you through hearing the news too late; and secondly, because the five hundred horse which you have are no small comfort to him, for the greater part of his division is killed or in flight."

"Wonderful things!" said Zagloba.

"It's a terror to think of! Desperation seizes one, the heart is cut, tears flow," said Volodyovski, wringing his hands. "The country destroyed; disgrace after death,--such forces dispersed, lost. It cannot be that there is anything but the end of the world and the approach of the last judgment."

"Don't interrupt him," said Skshetuski; "let him tell all."

Vershul was silent for a time, as if collecting his strength; nothing was heard but the plashing of hoofs in the mud, for rain was falling. It was still the depth of night, and very dark, because cloudy; and in that darkness and rain the words of Vershul, who began thus to speak, had a wonderful sound of ill-omen,--

"If I had not expected to fall in battle, I should have lost my reason. You speak of the last judgment,--and I think it will come soon, for everything is going to pieces; wickedness rises above virtue, and antichrist is walking through the world. You have not seen what took place; but if you are not able to bear even the story of it, how is it with me, who saw with my own eyes the defeat and measureless disgrace? God gave us a happy beginning in this war. Our prince, after getting satisfaction at Cholganski Kamen from Pan Lashch, gave the rest to oblivion, and made peace with Prince Dominik. We were all pleased with this concord,--really a blessing of God. The prince gained a second victory at Konstantinoff, and took the place; for the enemy left it after the first storm. Then we marched to Pilavtsi, though the prince did not advise going there. But immediately on the road various machinations were manifest against him,--ill-will, envy, and evident intrigue. He was not listened to in councils, no attention was paid to his words, and above all, efforts were made to separate our division, so that the prince should not have it all in hand. If he should oppose, the blame of defeat would be thrown on him. He was silent, therefore, suffered and endured. By order of the commander-in-chief the light cavalry, together with Vurtsel and the cannon. Colonel Makhnitski, Osinski, and Koritski, were detached, so that there remained with the prince only the hussars and Zatsvilikhovski, two regiments of dragoons, and I, with a part of my squadron,--altogether not more than two thousand men. And they paid no attention to the prince; he was despised; and I heard how the clients of Prince Dominik said: 'They won't say now, after the victory, that it came through Vishnyevetski.' And they said openly that if such immeasurable glory covered Yeremi, his candidate, Prince Karl, could carry the election, and they want Kazimir. The whole army was infected with factions, so that harangues were held in circles, as if they were sending delegates to the Diets; they were thinking of everything but battle, just as if the enemy had been beaten already. But if I were to tell you of the feasting and the applauding, you would not believe me. The legions of Pyrrhus were nothing in comparison with those armies, all in gold, jewels, and ostrich feathers, with two hundred thousand camp followers. Legions of wagons followed us, horses dropped dead under the weight of gold-tipped and silken tents; wagons were breaking under provision chests. You would have thought we were going to the conquest of the world. Nobles of the general militia shook their sticks, saying, 'This is how we will pacify the trash, and not kill them with swords.' We old soldiers, accustomed to fighting without talking, had a foreboding of evil at the sight of this unheard of pride. Then began tumults against Kisel,--that he was a traitor; and tumults for him,--that he was a worthy senator. They cut one another with sabres when they were drunk; there were no commanders of camps, no one looked after order; there was no general. Each one did what he liked, went where it pleased him best, stopped, took his place where it suited him; and the camp followers raised such an uproar! Oh, merciful God! that was a carnival, not a campaign,--a carnival at which the salvation of the Commonwealth was danced away, drunk away, ridden away, and chaffered away, to the last bit."

"But we are still alive," said Volodyovski.

"And God is in heaven," added Skshetuski.

A moment of silence followed; then Vershul said,--

"We shall perish totally, unless God performs a miracle and ceases to chastise us for our sins and shows us unmerited mercy. At times I do not believe myself what I saw with my own eyes, and it seems to me that a nightmare was choking me in my sleep."

"Tell further," said Zagloba; "you came to Pilavtsi, and then what?"

"We stopped. What the commanders counselled I know not. At the last judgment they will answer for that; if they had struck Hmelnitski at once he would have been shattered and swept away, as God is in heaven, in spite of disorder, insubordination, tumult, and want of a leader. On their side was panic among the rabble; they were already taking counsel how to give up Hmelnitski and the elders, and he himself was meditating flight. Our prince rode from tent to tent, begged, implored, threatened. 'Let us strike,' said he, 'before the Tartar comes!' He tore the hair from his head. Men looked at one another, but did nothing and nothing. They drank, they had meetings. Reports came that the Tartars were marching,--the Khan with two hundred thousand horsemen. The commanders counselled and counselled. The prince shut himself up in his tent, for they had set him aside altogether. In the army they began to say that the chancellor had forbidden Prince Dominik to give battle; that negotiations were going on. Still greater disorder appeared. At last the Tartars came, but God gave us luck the first day. The prince and Pan Osinski fought, and Pan Lashch did very well. They drove the Tartar horde from the field, cut them up considerably; but afterward--" Here Vershul's voice died in his breast.

"But afterward?" asked Zagloba.

"--came the terrible, inexplicable night which I remember. I was on guard with my men by the river, when on a sudden I heard firing of cannon in the Cossack camp as if in applause, and I heard shouts. Then it occurred to me that yesterday it was said in the camp that the whole Tartar force had not arrived yet,--only Tugai Bey with a part. I thought then: 'If they are making such uproarious applause, the Khan must have come in his own person.' Then in our camp rose a tumult. I hurried thither with a few men. 'What's the matter?' They shout to me: 'The commanders have gone!' I hasten to Prince Dominik's quarters,--he is not to be found; to Ostrorog,--he is gone; to Konyetspolski,--he is not there! Jesus of Nazareth! Soldiers are flying over the square; there are shouts, tumult, yells, blazing torches. 'Where are the commanders? where are the commanders?' cry some. 'To horse! to horse!' cry others. Still others: 'Save yourselves, brothers! Treason! treason!' Hands are raised to heaven, faces are pale, eyes wild. They rush, trample, suffocate one another, mount their horses, flee weaponless at random. Others leave helmets, breastplates, arms, tents. The prince rides up at the head of the hussars in his silver armor, with six torches around him. He stands in the stirrups and cries: 'I am here, gentlemen! Rally around me!' What can he do? They don't hear him, don't see him; they rush on his hussars, break their ranks, overturn horses and men. We were barely able to save the prince himself. Then over the trampled-out fires, in darkness, like a dammed-up torrent, like a river, the whole army in wild panic rush from the camp, flee, scatter, disappear. No more an army, no more leaders, no more a Commonwealth,--nothing but unwashed disgrace and the foot of the Cossack on your neck!"

Here Vershul began to groan and to pull at his horse, for the madness of despair had caught him. This madness he communicated to the others, and they rode on in that rain and night as if bewildered. They rode a long time. Zagloba broke silence first,--

"Without battle. Oh, the rascals! Oh, such sons of-- You remember what lordly figures they cut at Zbaraj,--how they promised to eat Hmelnitski without pepper and salt. Oh, the scoundrels!"

"How could they?" shouted Vershul. "They ran away after the first battle gained over the Tartars and the mob,--after a battle in which the general militia fought like lions."

"The finger of God is in this," said Skshetuski; "but there is some secret too, which must be explained."

"If the army had fled, why that sort of thing happens in the world," said Volodyovski; "but here the leaders left the camp first, as if on purpose to lighten the victory for the enemy and give the army to slaughter."

"True, true!" said Vershul. "It is said even that they did this on purpose."

"On purpose? By the wounds of Christ, that cannot be!"

"It is said they did so on purpose; but why? Who can discover, who can guess?"

"May their graves crush them, may their race perish, and only a memory of infamy remain behind them!" said Zagloba.

"Amen!" said Skshetuski.

"Amen!" said Volodyovski.

"Amen!" repeated Pan Longin.

"There is one man who can save the fatherland yet, if they give him the baton and the remaining power of the Commonwealth. There is only one, for neither the army nor the nobles will hear of another."

"The prince!" said Skshetuski.

"Yes."

"We will rally to him; we will perish with him. Long live Yeremi Vishnyevetski!" cried Zagloba.

"Long life!" repeated a few uncertain voices. But the cry died away immediately; for when the earth was opening under their feet and the heavens seemed falling on their heads, there was no time for shouts.

Day began to break, and in the distance appeared the walls of Tarnopol.

CHAPTER XLII.

The first wrecks from Pilavtsi reached Lvoff at daybreak, September 26; and with the opening of the gates the news spread like lightning through the city, rousing incredulity in some, panic in others, and in still others a desperate desire for defence. Skshetuski with his party arrived two days later, when the whole city was packed with fugitive soldiers, nobles, and armed citizens. They were thinking of defence, for the Tartars were expected any moment; but it was not known yet who would stand at the head of the defence or how it would begin. For this reason disorder and panic prevailed everywhere. Some fled from the place, taking their families and their property with them; dwellers in the region round about sought refuge in the city. Those departing and arriving crowded the streets, fought for passage; every place was filled with wagons, packs, bags, horses, soldiers from the greatest variety of regiments; on every face was seen either uncertainty, feverish expectation, despair, or resignation. Every little while terror broke out like a sudden whirlwind, and the cries were heard: "They are coming! they are coming!" and the crowd swept like a wave, sometimes running straight ahead infected with the madness of alarm, until it appeared that another one of the fragments of the wreck was coming,--fragments which increased more and more.

But how sad was the sight of these soldiers who a short time before had marched in gold and plumes, with song on their lips and pride in their eyes, to that campaign against peasants! To-day, torn, starved, emaciated, covered with mud, on wasted horses, with shame in their faces, more like beggars than knights, they could only rouse pity, if there was time for pity in that place against the walls of which the whole power of the enemy might soon hurl itself. And each one of those disgraced knights comforted himself in this alone, that he had so many thousands of companions in shame. All concealed themselves in the first hour, so that afterward when they had recovered they might spread complaints, blame, scatter curses with threats, drag along through the streets, drink in the shops, and only increase disorder and alarm. For each one repeated: "The Tartars are here, right here!" Some saw conflagrations in the rear; others swore by all the saints that they had been forced to defend themselves against scouting-parties. The crowds surrounding the soldiers listened with strained attention. The roofs and steeples of the churches were covered with thousands of curious people; the bells tolled alarm, and crowds of women and children suffocated one another in churches in which amid flaming tapers shone the most holy sacrament.

Skshetuski pushed slowly from the Galitian gate with his party through dense masses of horses, wagons, soldiers, city guilds standing under their banners, and through people who looked with wonder at that squadron entering the town, not in disorder, but in battle-array. Men shouted that succor was coming; and again joy justified by nothing took possession of the throng, which swayed forward in order to seize Skshetuski's stirrups. Soldiers too ran up, crying: "These are Vishnyevetski men! Long live Yeremi!" The pressure became so great that the squadron was barely able to push forward step by step.

At length a party of dragoons appeared opposite, with an officer at the head. The soldiers pushed aside the throng, and the officer cried: "Out of the road! out of the road!" and struck with the side of his sword those who failed to clear the way quickly. Skshetuski recognized Kushel.

The young officer greeted his acquaintance heartily. "What times! what times!" said he.

"Where is the prince?" asked Pan Yan.

"You would have killed him with anxiety if you had delayed. He is looking for you and your men intently. He is now at the Church of the Bernardines. I am sent out to keep order in the city; but the grozwayer has just taken it in hand, and I will go with you to the church. There is a council there at this moment."

"In the church?"

"Yes. They will offer the command to the prince, for the soldiers declare that they will not defend the town under another leader."

"Let us go; I have urgent business also with the prince."

The united parties moved on. Along the road Skshetuski inquired about everything that was passing in Lvoff, and if defence was already determined on.

"That is just the question under consideration," said Kushel. "The citizens want to defend themselves. What times! People of insignificant position show more courage than nobles and soldiers."

"But the commanders, what has happened to them? Are they not here, and will there not be opposition to the prince?"

"No, unless he makes it himself. There was a fitter time to give him the command; it is late now. The commanders dare not show their faces. Prince Dominik merely took refreshments in the archbishop's palace, and went away immediately. He did well, for you cannot believe what hatred there is for him among the soldiers. He is gone already, and still they cry: 'Give him up! We will cut him to pieces!' It is sure he would not have escaped such a fate. The royal cup-bearer, Ostrorog, arrived here first, and he began to talk against the prince; but now he sits in silence, for a tumult rose against him. They laid all the blame on him to his face, and he only gulps his tears. In general it is awful, what is going on; such times have come. I say to you, thank God that you were not at Pilavtsi, that you did not flee from the place; for it is a real miracle to us who were there that we did not lose our senses altogether."

"And our division?"

"Exists no longer,--scarcely anything is left; Vurtsel gone, Makhnitski gone, Zatsvilikhovski gone. Vurtsel and Makhnitski were not at Pilavtsi, for they remained in Konstantinoff. That Beelzebub, Prince Dominik, left them there so as to weaken the power of our prince. Old Zatsvilikhovski has vanished like a stone in water. God grant he has not perished!"

"And of all the soldiers have many come here?"

"In number sufficient, but what of that? The prince alone could use them, if he would take the command; they will obey no one else. The prince was terribly alarmed about you and the soldiers. This is the only sound squadron. We were already mourning for you."

"At present he is the happy man for whom people are mourning!"

They rode in silence for a time, looking at the crowd and listening to the shouts and yells: "The Tartars! the Tartars!" In one place they beheld the terrible sight of a man torn to pieces by the mob on suspicion of being a spy. The bells were tolling incessantly.

"Will the horde be here soon?" asked Zagloba.

"The devil knows,--maybe to-day. This city will not defend itself long, for it cannot hold out. Hmelnitski is coming with two hundred thousand, besides Tartars."

"Caput!" answered Zagloba. "It would have been better for us to have gone on at breakneck speed. What have we gained so many victories for?"

"Over whom?"

"Over Krívonos, over Bogun,--devil knows whom else."

"But," said Kushel, in a low voice, turning to Skshetuski, "Yan, has God not comforted you in any way? Have you not found the one whom you were seeking? Have you not at least learned something?"

"No time to think of that," said Skshetuski. "What do I and my affairs signify in view of what has happened? All is vanity, vanity, and death at the end."

"It seems to me that the whole world will perish before long," said Kushel.

Meanwhile they reached the Bernardine Church, which was blazing with light. Immense crowds stood before the door; but they could not enter, for a line of men with halberds closed the passage, admitting only the most important officers of the army.

Skshetuski ordered his men to form a second line.

"Come," said Kushel; "half the Commonwealth is in this church."

They entered. Kushel had not exaggerated greatly. All who were best known in the army and city had assembled for council, including the voevoda, the castellans, the colonels, the captains, officers of foreign regiments, the clergy, as many nobles as the church could hold, a multitude of military of the lower grades, and a number of the town councillors with the grozwayer at their head, who was the leader of the citizens. The prince too was present, the royal cup-bearer, and one of the commanders, the voevoda of Kieff, the starosta of Stobnik, Vessel, Artsishevski, and Osinski. They sat in front of the great altar, so that the public might see them. The council was held hastily and excitedly, as is usual on such occasions. Speakers stood on benches and implored the elders not to yield the city to the hands of the enemy without defending it. "Even if we have to perish, the city will detain the enemy, the Commonwealth will recover. What is needed for defence? There are walls, there are troops, there is determination,--only a leader is wanted." And after speeches of this kind, through the crowd flew murmurs which passed into loud shouts; excitement seized the assembly. "We will perish, we will perish willingly!" they cry. "We will wipe out the disgrace of Pilavtsi, we will shield the fatherland!" And they began to shake their sabres, and the naked edges glittered in the blaze of the candles. Others cried: "Be quiet! Let the deliberations be orderly! Shall we defend or not defend?" "Defend! defend!" roared the assembly till the echo thrown back from the arches repeated, "Defend!" Who is to be the leader? Who should be the leader? "Prince Yeremi,--he is a leader, he is a hero! Let him defend the city; let the Commonwealth give him the baton. Long life to him!"

Then such a thundering roar burst forth from a thousand lungs that the walls trembled and the glass rattled in the windows of the church.

"Prince Yeremi! Prince Yeremi! Long life to Prince Yeremi! Long life, victory to him!"

A thousand sabres flashed; all eyes were turned to the prince. He rose calmly with wrinkled brow. There was silence at once, as if only poppy-seeds were falling.

"Gentlemen," said the prince, with a resonant voice, which in that silence reached every ear, "when the Cymbri and the Teutons fell upon the Commonwealth of Rome no one would accept the consulate till Marius took it. But Marius had a right to take it, for there were no leaders appointed by the senate. And I in the present straits would not avoid power, since I wish to serve my dear country with my life; but I cannot accept the command since I should offend the country, the senate, and the authorities, and a self-elected chief I will not be. Among us is the man to whom the Commonwealth has given the baton of command,--the cup-bearer of the Crown."

Here the prince could speak no further; for hardly had he mentioned the cup-bearer when there rose a terrible din and the clattering of sabres. The crowd swayed and there was a burst as of powder on which a spark has fallen. "Away with him! Destruction to him! Pereat!" was heard in the throng. "Pereat! pereat!" was roared louder and louder. The cup-bearer sprang from his seat, pale, with drops of cold sweat on his forehead; and then threatening figures approached the stalls, near the altar, and ominous words were heard: "Give him here!"

The prince, seeing whither this was tending, rose and stretched out his right hand. The crowds restrained themselves, thinking that he wished to speak. There was silence in the twinkle of an eye. But the prince wished merely to allay the storm and tumult, not to permit the shedding of blood in the church. When he saw that the most threatening moment had passed, he took his seat again.

On the second chair from the voevoda of Kieff sat the unfortunate cup-bearer; his gray hair had dropped upon his breast, his hands were hanging, and from his mouth came words interrupted by sobs: "O Lord, for my sins I accept the cross with resignation."

The old man might rouse pity in the hardest heart; but a crowd is generally pitiless. Again therefore the tumult began when the voevoda of Kieff rose and gave a sign with his hand that he wanted to speak. He was a partner in the victories of Yeremi, therefore they listened to him willingly. He turned to the prince then, and in the most feeling words adjured him not to reject the baton of command and not to hesitate to save the country. "When the Commonwealth is perishing, let laws slumber; let not the appointed chief save it, but him who has the most power to save. Take the command, then, invincible leader, take it and rescue, not this city alone, but the whole Commonwealth. Behold I, an old man, with the lips of the Commonwealth implore you, and with me all ranks of people,--all men, women, and children,--Save us! save us!"

Here followed an incident which moved all hearts. A woman in mourning approached the altar, and casting at the feet of the prince her golden ornaments and jewels, knelt before him, and sobbing loudly, cried out: "We bring you our goods; we give our lives into your hands. Save us, save us; for we perish!"

At the sight of this senators, soldiers, and then the whole throng roared with a mighty cry, and there was one voice in that church: "Save us!"

The prince covered his face with his hands; and when he raised his head tears were glittering in his eyes. Still he hesitated. What would become of the dignity of the Commonwealth if he should accept the command?

Then rose the cup-bearer of the Crown. "I am old," said he, "unfortunate, and crushed. I have a right to resign the charge which is beyond my powers, and to place it on younger shoulders. Here in the presence of this crucified God and of all the knighthood, I deliver the baton to you,--take it." And he extended the insignia to Vishnyevetski.

A moment of such silence followed that flies on the wing could be heard. At last the solemn voice of Yeremi was heard: "For my sins--I accept it."

Then a frenzy of enthusiasm ruled the assembly. The crowds broke the benches, fell at the feet of Vishnyevetski, cast down their money and treasures before him. The news spread like lightning through the whole city. The soldiers were losing their senses from joy, and shouted that they wished to go against Hmelnitski, the Tartars, the Sultan; the citizens thought no longer of surrender, but of defence to the last drop of blood; the Armenians brought money of their own accord to the city hall, before anything was said of a levy; the Jews in the synagogue raised an uproar of thanksgiving; the guns on the walls thundered forth the glad tidings; along the streets was firing of muskets, pistols, and guns. Shouts of "Long life!" continued all night. Any one not knowing the state they were in might suppose that the city was celebrating a triumph or some solemn festival. And still three hundred thousand enemies--an army greater than any which the German Emperor or the King of France could place in the field, an army wilder than the legions of Tamerlane--might at any moment invest the walls of that city.

CHAPTER XLIII.

A week later, on the morning of the 6th of October, news as unexpected as terrible burst upon Lvoff. Prince Yeremi, with the greater part of the army, had left the city secretly and had gone it was unknown whither.

Crowds gathered before the archbishop's palace; they would not believe the report at first. The soldiers insisted that if the prince had gone, he had gone without doubt at the head of a powerful division on a reconnoissance of the surrounding country. It appeared, they said, that lying spies had spread reports announcing Hmelnitski and the Tartars at any moment; for since September 26 ten days had passed, and the enemy was not yet in sight. The prince wished undoubtedly to convince himself of the danger by actual inspection, and after obtaining intelligence would return without fail. Besides, he had left a number of regiments, and everything was ready for defence.

The last was true. Every disposition had been made, the places marked out, the cannon planted on the walls. In the evening Captain Tsikhotski arrived at the head of fifty dragoons. He was surrounded immediately by the curious, but would not speak with the crowd, and went directly to General Artsishevski. Both called the grozwayer, and after consultation they went to the city hall. There Tsikhotski informed the astonished councillors that the prince had gone, not to return.

At the first moment the hands of all dropped at their sides, and some insolent lips uttered the word, "Traitor!" But that moment Artsishevski, an old leader famed for achievements in the Dutch service, rose and began to speak as follows to the military and the councillors:--

"I have heard the injurious word, which I wish no one had spoken, for even despair cannot justify it. The prince has gone and will not return. But what right have you to force a leader on whose shoulders the salvation of a whole country rests to defend your city only? What would have happened if the enemy had surrounded in this place the remaining forces of the Commonwealth? There are neither supplies of food nor of arms for so many troops here. I tell you this,--and you may trust in my experience,--that the greater the force shut up here, the shorter the defence would be; for hunger would overpower you sooner than the enemy. Hmelnitski cares more for the person of the prince than for your city; therefore, when he discovers that Vishnyevetski is not here, that he is collecting new troops and may come with relief, he will let you off more easily, and agree to terms. You are murmuring today; but I tell you that the prince, by leaving this city and threatening Hmelnitski from outside, has saved you and your children. Bear up, and defend yourselves! If you can detain the enemy some time, you may save your city, and you will render a memorable service to the Commonwealth; for during that time the prince will collect forces, arm other fortresses, rouse the torpid Commonwealth, and hasten to your rescue. He has chosen the only road of salvation; for if he had fallen here, with his army overcome by hunger, then nothing could stop the enemy, who might march on Cracow, on Warsaw, and flood the whole country, finding resistance in no place. Therefore, instead of murmuring, hurry to the walls, defend yourselves and your children, your city and the whole Commonwealth!"

"To the walls! to the walls!" repeated many of the more daring.

The grozwayer, an energetic and bold man, answered: "Your determination pleases me; and you know that the prince did not go away without planning defence. Every one here knows what he has to do, and that has happened which should have happened. I have the defence in hand, and I will defend to the last."

Hope returned again to timid hearts. Seeing this, Tsikhotski said in conclusion,--

"His Highness informs you also that the enemy is at hand. Lieutenant Skshetuski struck on a party of two thousand Tartars whom he defeated. The prisoners say that a great power is marching behind them."

This news made a deep impression. A moment of silence followed; all hearts beat more quickly.

"To the walls!" said the grozwayer.

"To the walls! to the walls!" repeated the officers and citizens present.

Meanwhile a tumult was raised outside the windows; the uproar of a thousand voices, which mingled in one undistinguishable roar like the sound of the waves of the sea. Suddenly the doors of the hall were thrown open with a crash, and a number of citizens burst into the room; and before the councillors had time to inquire what had happened, shouts were raised: "Flames in the sky! flames in the sky!"

"The word has become flesh," said the grozwayer. "To the walls!"

The hall was deserted. Soon the thunder of cannon shook the walls, announcing to the inhabitants of the city, the suburbs and villages beyond, that the enemy was coming. In the east the heavens were red as far as the eye could see. One would have said that a sea of fire was approaching the city.

The prince meanwhile had thrown himself on Zamost, and having dispersed on the road the party which Tsikhotski had mentioned to the citizens, occupied himself with repairing and arming that fortress, naturally strong, which he made impregnable in a short time. Skshetuski, with Pan Longin and a part of the squadron, remained in the fortress with Pan Weyher, the starosta of Volets. The prince went to Warsaw to obtain from the Diet means to assemble new forces, and also to take part in the election which was near. The fortunes of Vishnyevetski and the whole Commonwealth hung upon that election; for if Prince Karl were chosen the war party would win, and the prince would receive chief command of all the forces of the Commonwealth, and it would perforce come to a general struggle for life and death with Hmelnitski. Prince Kazimir, though famous for his bravery and altogether a military man, was justly considered an adherent of the policy of Ossolinski, the chancellor, therefore of the policy of negotiations with the Cossacks, and considerable concessions to them. Neither brother was sparing of promises, and each struggled to gain partisans for himself; considering therefore the equal power of both parties, no one could foresee the result of the election. The partisans of the chancellor feared that Vishnyevetski, thanks to his increasing fame and the favor which he possessed among the knighthood and the nobles, would carry the balance of minds to the side of Prince Karl; Yeremi, for these reasons, desired to support his candidate in person. Therefore he hastened to Warsaw, sure that Zamost would be able to hold in check for a long time the whole power of Hmelnitski and the Crimea. Lvoff, according to every probability, might be considered safe; for Hmelnitski could in no wise spend much time in capturing that city, since he had before him the more powerful Zamost, which barred his way to the heart of the Commonwealth.

These thoughts strengthened the resolution of the prince, and poured consolation into his heart, torn by so many terrible defeats of the country. Hope possessed him that even if Kazimir were elected, war would be unavoidable, and the terrible rebellion would have to be drowned in a sea of blood. He hoped that the Commonwealth would again put forth a powerful army, for negotiations were only possible in so far as a powerful army sustained them.

Flattered by these thoughts, the prince went under the protection of a few squadrons, having with him Zagloba and Pan Volodyovski, the first of whom swore by everything that he would carry the election of Prince Karl, for he knew how to talk to the brother nobles and how to manage them; the second commanded the escort of the prince.

At Sennitsa, not far from Minsk, a delightful though unexpected interview awaited the prince; for he met Princess Griselda, who was going from Brest-Litovsk to Warsaw for safety, with the reasonable hope that the prince would go there too. They greeted each other with emotion after a long separation. The princess, though she had an iron soul, rushed with such weeping into the embrace of her husband that she could not compose herself for several hours; for, oh! how many were the moments in which she had no hope of seeing him again, and still God granted him to return more famous than ever, covered with praise, such as had never yet beamed upon one of his house, the greatest of leaders, the one hope of the Commonwealth. The princess, tearing herself time after time from his breast, glanced through her tears at that face emaciated and embrowned, at that lofty forehead on which cares and toils had ploughed deep furrows, at those eyes inflamed with sleepless nights; and again she shed plentiful tears, and all her ladies wept too from the depths of their excited hearts.

When after a time she and the prince had become calm, they went to the house of the priest, and there inquiries were made for friends, attendants, and knights, who as it were belonged to the family, and with whom the memory of Lubni was bound up. The prince quieted the princess concerning Skshetuski, first of all explaining that he had remained in Zamost only because he did not wish to lose himself in the noise of the capital on account of the suffering which God had sent him, and preferred to heal the wounds of his heart in military service. Then he presented Zagloba and told of his deeds. "Vir incomparabilis," said he, "who not only saved Kurtsevichovna from Bogun, but took her through the camps of Hmelnitski and the Tartars; later he was with us to his great glory, and fought admirably at Konstantinoff." Hearing this, the princess did not spare praise on Zagloba, giving him her hand to kiss repeatedly, and promising a still better reward at a proper time; and the "vir incomparabilis" bowed, veiling his heroism with his modesty. Then, he strutted and looked at the ladies in waiting; for though he was old and did not promise himself much from the fair sex, still it was pleasant to him that the ladies had heard so much of his bravery and his deeds. But mourning was not absent from this otherwise glad greeting; for mentioning the grievous times of the Commonwealth, how often did the prince reply to the questions of the princess about various knights: "Killed, killed, lost." Then young women were saddened, for more than one name was mentioned among the dead that was dear.

So gladness was mingled with grief, tears with smiles. But the most afflicted of all was Volodyovski; for in vain did he look around and cast his eyes on every side,--Princess Barbara was not there. It is true that amid the toils of war and continual battles, skirmishes, and campaigns, that cavalier had forgotten her somewhat, for he was by nature as prone to love as he was inconstant; but now, when he saw the young ladies of the princess once more, when before his eyes the life at Lubni stood as if actual, he thought to himself that it would be pleasant for him too if the moment of rest should come to sigh and occupy his heart again. Since this did not happen, however, but sentiment, as if through malice, sprang up in him anew, Volodyovski suffered grievously, and looked as if he had been drenched in a pouring rain. He hung his head upon his breast; his slender mustaches, which usually curled upward like those of a May-bug till they reached his nose, were hanging too; his upturned nose had grown long; the usual serenity had vanished from his face, and he stood silent, did not even move when the prince gave unusual praise to his bravery and superiority,--for what mattered all praises to him when she could not hear them?

Finally Anusia Borzobogata took pity on him, and though they had had quarrels, she determined to comfort him. With this object, keeping her eyes on the princess, she pushed unobserved toward the knight, and at last was by his side.

"Good-day," said she; "we have not seen each other for a long time."

"Oh, Panna Anna," answered Pan Michael, in sadness, "much water has flowed past since then. We meet again in unpleasant times, and not all of us."

"True, not all! So many knights have fallen." Here Anusia sighed; then continued, after a time: "And we are not the same in number; for Panna Senyntovna has married, and Princess Barbara has remained with the wife of the voevoda of Vilna."

"And she is going to marry, of course."

"No, she is not thinking much of that. But why do you ask?"

Having said this, Anusia closed her dark eyes till two thin lines were left, and looked sideways from under her lashes at the knight.

"Oh, through good-will for the family," answered Pan Michael.

"Oh, that is proper," answered Anusia, "for Pan Michael has a great friend in Princess Barbara. More than once she inquired; 'Where is that knight who in the tournament at Lubni took off most Turkish heads, for which I gave him a reward? What is he doing? Is he still alive, and does he remember us?'"

Pan Michael raised his eyes in thankfulness to Anusia; first he was comforted, and then he observed that Anusia had improved beyond measure.

"Did Princess Barbara really say that?"

"As true as life; and she remembered, too, how you were riding over the ditch for her when you fell into the water."

"And where is the wife of the voevoda of Vilna now?"

"She was with us in Brest, and a week ago went to Belsk; from there she will go to Warsaw."

Pan Volodyovski looked at Anusia a second time, and could not restrain himself: "But Panna Anusia has attained such beauty that one's eyes ache in looking at her."

The girl smiled thankfully. "Pan Michael only says this to capture me."

"I wanted to do so in my time," said he, shrugging his shoulders. "God knows I tried to, but failed; and now I wish well to Pan Podbipienta, for he was more fortunate."

"And where is Pan Podbipienta?" inquired Anusia, dropping her eyes.

"In Zamost, with Skshetuski. He has become lieutenant in the squadron, and must attend to service; but if he knew whom he could see here, as God is in heaven he would have taken leave and come with long steps. He is a great knight, and deserving of every love."

"And in war--he met no accident?"

"It seems to me that you wish to ask, not about that, but about the three heads that he wanted to cut off."

"I do not believe that he really wanted to do that."

"But you would better, for without that there will be nothing. And he is not slow in looking for a chance, either. At Makhnovka, when we went to examine the places where he had struggled in the throng of battle, the prince himself went with us; and I tell you I have seen many a fight, but such execution I shall not see again while I live. When he puts on your scarf for battle, he does awful things. He will find his three heads: be at rest on that point."

"May each find what he seeks!" said Anusia, with a sigh.

Then Volodyovski sighed, raised his eyes, and looked suddenly toward one corner of the room. From that corner peered a visage, angry, excited, and entirely unknown to him, armed with a gigantic nose, and mustaches great as two bushes on a tavern-sign, which moved quickly, as if from pent-up passion. One might be terrified at that nose, those eyes and mustaches; but little Volodyovski was by no means timid; therefore he only wondered, and turning to Anusia asked,--

"What sort of figure is that over there in the corner, which looks at me as if it wished to swallow me whole, and moves its mustaches just like an old tom-cat at prayers?"

"What?" said Anusia, showing her white teeth; "that's Pan Kharlamp."

"What sort of Pagan is he?"

"He is no Pagan at all, but a light-horse captain in the squadron of the voevoda of Vilna, who is escorting us to Warsaw, and has to wait for the voevoda there. Let Pan Michael not come in his way, for he is a dreadful man-eater."

"I see that, I see that. But if he is a man-eater, there are others fatter than I. Why should he whet his teeth at me instead of them?"

"Because--" said Anusia; and she laughed quietly.

"Because?"

"Because he is in love with me, and has told me that he will cut to pieces every man who approaches me; and now, believe me, it is only out of regard for the prince and princess that he restrains himself. Were it not for them, he would pick a quarrel with you at once."

"Here you've got it," said Volodyovski, merrily. "That's how it is, Panna Anna. It was not for nothing, I see, that we sang, 'Tartars carry captive prisoners, you seize captive hearts.' You remember, I suppose? You cannot move, you know, without making some one fall in love with you."

"Such is my misfortune," answered Anusia, dropping her eyes.

"Ah, Panna Anna is a Pharisee; and what will Pan Longin say to this?"

"How am I to blame if this Pan Kharlamp pursues me? I can't endure him, and I don't want to look at him."

"But see to it that blood is not shed on your account. Podbipienta is so mild that you could heal a wound with him, but in love affairs it is dangerous to joke with him."

"If he cuts Kharlamp's ears off, I shall be glad."

When she had said this, Anusia whizzed off like a top, and tripped to the other side of the room to Carboni, the physician of the princess, to whom she began to whisper something with animation, and then converse; but the Italian fastened his eyes on the ceiling, as if carried away by ecstasy.

Meanwhile Zagloba approached Volodyovski, and began in merry mood to wink his one sound eye. "Pan Michael," he asked, "what sort of crested lark is that?"

"That is Panna Anusia Borzobogata, lady-in-waiting to the princess. Ah, she is a pretty little rogue,--eyes like plates, a pug as if painted, and a neck--uf!"

"Oh, she'll pass, she'll pass! My congratulations to you!"

"Oh, give us peace! She is betrothed to Podbipienta, or the same as betrothed."

"To Podbipienta! My dear sir, have fear of the Lord's wounds! Why, he has made vows of celibacy. And besides, the disproportion between them! He could carry her at his collar; she might sit on his mustaches, like a fly."

"Ah! she will manage him yet. Hercules was stronger, but a woman trapped him."

"Yes, if she only doesn't give him horns; though I should be the first to help that about, as I am Zagloba."

"There will be more than you of that sort, though in truth the girl is of good stock and honest. This is too bad, for she is young and pretty."

"You are an honorable cavalier, and that is why you praise her; but she is a lark."

"Beauty attracts people. For example, that captain over there is desperately in love with her."

"Pshaw! But look at that raven with whom she is talking now! What sort of devil is he?"

"That is an Italian,--Carboni, the physician of the princess."

"Look, Pan Michael, how his lanterns are lighted up, and his eyeballs roll as if in delirium. Oh, it is bad for Pan Longin! I know something of this business, for I had more than one experience in my youth. Another time I'll tell you of all the scrapes in which I have been, or if you wish you can listen this minute."

Zagloba began to whisper in the ear of the little knight, and to wink with more vigor than usual. But the end of the visit came. The prince seated himself by the princess in the carriage, that they might talk all they wished after the long absence; the ladies occupied carriages, the knights mounted their horses, and all moved on. The court went in advance, and the troops at some distance in the rear; for those parts were peaceable, and the squadrons were needed for ostentation alone, not safety. They went from Sennitsa to Minsk, and thence to Warsaw, stopping frequently for plentiful refreshments, according to the custom of the time.

The road was so thronged that it was barely possible to move at a walk. All were going to the election, from near neighborhoods and from distant Lithuania; so that here and there were met lordly households, whole trains of gilded carriages, surrounded by haiduks, gigantic Turkish grooms dressed in Turkish costumes; after which marched household troops,--now Hungarian, now German, now janissaries, now Cossack detachments, and finally squadrons of the matchless heavy cavalry of the Poles. Each one of the more important personages tried to appear in the most showy manner and with the greatest retinues. Among the numerous cavalcades belonging to magnates, came also the smaller local and district dignitaries. Every little while single wagons of nobles appeared from out the dust, covered with black leather and drawn by two or four horses, and in each sat a noble with a crucifix or an image of the Most Holy Lady hung on a silk ribbon around his neck. All were armed,--a musket on one side of the seat, a sabre on the other. Former or actual officers of squadrons also had lances sticking out two yards behind the seat. Under the wagons were dogs,--either setters or hounds,--not for use (for they were not going to the chase), but for the amusement of the owner. Behind were stable-boys leading horses covered with cloth to protect rich saddles from dust or rain. Farther on were drawn squeaking wagons with willow-bound wheels, in which were tents and supplies of provisions for servants and masters. When at times the wind blew the dust from the highway into the fields, the whole road was uncovered and changed like a hundred-colored serpent, or a ribbon artistically woven from gold and brocade. Here and there on the road were heard orchestras of Italians or janissaries, especially before the squadrons of royal or Lithuanian escort, of which there was no lack in this throng, for they had to go in the company of the dignitaries; and every place was full of shouts, calls, questions, disputes, since precedence was not yielded willingly by one to another.

From time to time mounted servants and soldiers galloped up to the retinue of the prince, demanding the road for such or such a dignitary, or to ask who was travelling. But when the answer came to their ears, "The voevoda of Rus!" immediately they informed their masters, who left the road free, or if they were in advance, turned aside to see the passing retinue. At places of refreshment the nobles gathered in crowds to feast their eyes with a sight of the greatest warrior of the Commonwealth. Cheers also were not lacking, to which the prince answered with thanks, first by reason of his innate politeness, and secondly wishing with that affability to win adherents for Prince Karl, of which he gained not a few by his appearance alone.

With equal curiosity did they look on the squadrons of the prince,--"those Russians," as they were called. They were not so tattered and haggard as after the battle at Konstantinoff, for the prince had given them new uniforms at Zamost; but they were always gazed at as wonders from beyond the sea, since in the opinion of those dwelling in the neighborhood of the capital they came from the end of the earth. Marvels were related of those mysterious steppes and pine-groves in which such a knighthood was born. They wondered at their sunburnt complexions, embrowned from the winds of the Black Sea; at their haughtiness of look, and a certain freedom of bearing acquired from their wild neighbors.

But after the prince, most eyes were turned on Zagloba, who, noticing that he was the centre of admiration, looked with such haughtiness and pride, and turned his eyes so threateningly that it was whispered at once in the crowd: "This must be the foremost knight of them all!" And others said: "He must have let a power of souls out of their bodies; he is as fierce as a dragon!" When words like these came to the ears of Zagloba, his only thought was to conceal his inward delight by still greater fierceness. Sometimes he answered the crowd, sometimes he joked with them, but especially with squadrons of the Lithuanian escort, in which the men of the heavy cavalry wore golden, and of the light, silver loops on their shoulders. At sight of this Zagloba would call out, "Pan Loop, there is a hook on you!" More than one officer frowned, gritted his teeth, and grasped his sabre; but remembering that that was a warrior from the squadron of the voevoda of Rus who took such liberty, he spat at last, and let the matter drop.

Nearer Warsaw the throng became so dense that it was only possible to push forward at a walk. The election promised to be more crowded than usual; for nobles from remote Russian and Lithuanian districts, who by reason of the distance could not have come for the election itself, assembled now at Warsaw for safety. The day of election was still distant, for the first sessions of the Diet had barely begun; but they had assembled a month or two in advance, so as to locate themselves in the city, renew acquaintance with this one and that, seek for promotion here and there, eat and drink at the houses of great lords, and enjoy luxury in the harvest of the capital.

The prince looked with sadness through the windows of his carriage on those crowds of knights, soldiers, and nobles, on that wealth and luxury of costume, thinking what forces could be formed of them, what armies could be put in the field. "Why is this Commonwealth, so powerful, populous, and rich, filled with valiant knights, so weak that it is not able to settle with one Hmelnitski and the Tartar savagery? Why is this? The legions of Hmelnitski could be answered with other legions if those nobles, those soldiers, that wealth and substance, those regiments and squadrons were willing to serve public as well as private interests. Virtue is perishing in the Commonwealth," thought the prince, "and the great body is beginning to decay. Manhood has long since begun to disappear in pleasant leisure; it is not warlike toil that the army and the nobles love!" The prince was right so far; but of the shortcomings of the Commonwealth he thought only as a warrior and a chieftain who wanted to turn all men into soldiers and lead them against the enemy. Bravery could be found, and was found, when wars a hundred times greater threatened soon after. It lacked still something more, which the soldier-prince at that moment saw not, but which his enemy, the chancellor of the Crown, an abler statesman than Yeremi, did see.

But behold in the gray and azure distance appeared indistinctly the pointed towers of Warsaw. Further meditations of the prince ceased. He issued orders, which the officer on duty bore immediately to Volodyovski. In consequence of these orders Pan Michael galloped from the carriage of Anusia, around which he had been hovering hitherto, to bring up the squadrons which had lagged considerably in the rear, to strengthen the line and lead it on in order. He had ridden barely a few paces when he heard some one rushing after him. It was Pan Kharlamp, captain of the light cavalry of the voevoda of Vilna, Anusia's worshipper.

Volodyovski held in his horse; for he understood at once that it would surely come to some quarrel, and Pan Michael loved such things from his soul. Kharlamp came up with him, and at first said nothing; he only puffed, and moved his mustaches threateningly, as if looking for words.

"With the forehead, with the forehead, Pan Dragoon!"

"With the forehead, Pan Escort!"

"How do you dare to call me Escort," demanded Kharlamp, grinding his teeth,--"me an officer and a captain, hei?"

Volodyovski began to throw up a hatchet which he held in his hand, turning his whole attention as it were to catching it by the handle after every turn, and answered as if unwillingly. "For I am not able to recognize rank by the loop."

"You offend a whole body of officers with whom you are not equal."

"How is that?" asked with pretended simplicity the rogue Volodyovski?

"For you serve in the foreign levy."

"Put yourself to rest," said Pan Michael. "Though I serve in the dragoons, I belong to that body of officers not of the light, but of the heavy cavalry of the voevoda. You can talk with me therefore as with an equal or as with a superior."

Kharlamp reined himself in a little, seeing that he had not to do with so insignificant a person as he had thought; but he did not cease to grit his teeth, for the coolness of Pan Michael brought him to still greater rage.

"Why do you get in my way?"

"I see that you are seeking a quarrel."

"Maybe I am; and I will tell you this [here Kharlamp bent to the ear of Volodyovski and finished in a lower voice], that I'll trim your ears if you come in my way before Panna Anna."

Volodyovski began again to throw up the hatchet very diligently, as if that were the special time for such amusement, and answered in a tone of persuasiveness: "Oh, my benefactor, permit me to live a little yet; let me go!"

"Oh, no! Nothing will come of that; you won't escape me!" said Kharlamp, seizing the little knight by the sleeve.

"I will not get away from you," said Pan Michael, with a mild voice; "but now I am on service, and am going with the order of the prince my master. Let go my sleeve, let go, I beg you; for otherwise what shall I, poor devil! do unless I go at you with this hatchet and tumble you from the horse?"

Here the voice of Volodyovski, submissive at first, hissed with such venom that Kharlamp looked at him with involuntary astonishment and dropped his sleeve. "Oh, it is all one!" said he. "You will give me a chance in Warsaw, I'll look after you!"

"I won't hide; but how can we fight in Warsaw, be so kind as to instruct me. I have never been there yet in my life; I am a simple soldier, but I have heard of court-martials which execute a man for drawing his sabre in the presence of the king or during an interregnum."

"It is evident that you have never been in Warsaw, and that you are an ignorant clown, since you are afraid of court-martials and don't know that in the interregnum a chapter is in session with which the question is easier, and you may be sure they won't take my head for your ears."

"Thank you for the information, and I will ask you for information frequently; for I see that you are a man of no ordinary experience, and I, since I practise only the lowest of the rudiments, am barely able to make an adjective agree with a noun, and if I wanted to call (which God forbid) your Honor a fool, then I know that I should say 'stultus,' and not 'stulta' or 'stultum.'"

Here Volodyovski began again to throw up the hatchet, and Kharlamp was astonished again. The blood rushed to his face, and he pulled his sabre out of the scabbard; but in the twinkle of an eye the little knight, putting his hatchet under his knee, drew his own. For a moment they looked at each other, like two stags, with distended nostrils, and with fire in their eyes; but Kharlamp considered that he would have an affair with the voevoda himself if he fell upon his officer going with an order, therefore he sheathed his sabre.

"Oh, I'll find you, you son of a such a one!" said he.

"You'll find me, you'll find me, you fish-broth!" said the little knight.

And they parted,--one going to the cavalcade, the other to the squadrons, which had approached considerably during this time, so that through the clouds of dust was heard the clatter of the hoofs on the hard road. Volodyovski straightened the cavalry and the infantry to the proper line, and moved to the head. After a while Zagloba trotted up to him.

"What did that scarecrow of the sea want of you?" asked he of Volodyovski.

"Oh, nothing!--he called me out to a duel."

"Here is trouble for you; he will punch a hole through you with his nose. Look out, Pan Michael, that you don't cut off the biggest nose in the Commonwealth, for you will have to raise a separate mound over it. Happy is the voevoda of Vilna! Others must send scouting-parties out to look for the enemy, but this one could scent them for miles. But why did he challenge you?"

"Because I rode by the carriage of Anusia Borzobogata."

"You ought to have told him to go to Pan Longin at Zamost. He would have dressed him with pepper and ginger. That fish-broth fellow has struck badly; it is evident that he has less luck than his nose."

"I said nothing to him about Pan Podbipienta," said Volodyovski, "for he might have dropped me. I'll pay court now to Anusia with redoubled fervor out of spite. I want to have my sport too; what better employment can we have in Warsaw?"

"We'll find it, Pan Michael, we'll find it," said Zagloba, winking. "When in my younger years I was a deputy from the squadron in which I served, I travelled through the whole country, but such life as I found in Warsaw I found nowhere else."

"You say it is different from what we have in the Trans-Dnieper?"

"Of course it is!"

"I am very curious," said Pan Michael. After a while he added: "Still, I'll trim the mustaches of that fish-broth, for they are too long."

CHAPTER XLIV.

A number of weeks passed. The nobles assembled in greater and greater numbers for the election. The population of the city increased tenfold; for with the crowds of nobles poured in thousands of merchants and shopkeepers of the whole world, from distant Persia to England beyond the sea. On the field of Vola a booth was built for the senate, and around it whitened already thousands of tents, with which the spacious meadows were entirely covered. No one could tell yet which of the two candidates--Prince Kazimir, the cardinal, or Karl Ferdinand, the bishop of Plotsk--would be elected. On both sides great were the efforts and exertions made. Thousands of pamphlets were given to the world, relating the merits and defects of the candidates. Both had numerous and powerful adherents. On the side of Karl stood, as is known, Prince Yeremi, who was the more terrible for his opponents, as it was always likely that he would draw after him the inferior nobles, who were enamoured of him; and with the inferior nobles lay the ultimate decision. But neither did Kazimir lack power. Seniority was in his favor. On his side was the influence of the chancellor; the primate appeared to incline to him. On his side stood the majority of the magnates, each of whom had numerous clients; and among the magnates also was Prince Dominik Zaslavski Ostrogski, voevoda of Sandomir, with greatly injured reputation after Pilavtsi and even threatened with prosecution, but always the greatest lord in the Commonwealth, nay, even in all Europe, and able at any moment to throw the immense weight of his wealth into the scale of his candidate.

Still the adherents of Kazimir more than once had bitter hours of doubt; for as has been said, everything depended on the inferior nobles, who, beginning from the 4th of October, had camped in crowds around Warsaw and were coming still in thousands from every side of the Commonwealth, and who in an incalculable majority declared for Prince Karl, attracted by the magic of Vishnyevetski's name and the liberality of the prince in public objects. Karl was a good manager and wealthy; he did not hesitate at that moment to devote considerable sums to the formation of new regiments which were to be placed under command of Yeremi. Kazimir would have followed his example willingly; it was certainly not greed that held him back, but just the opposite,--excessive liberality, the immediate result of which was an insufficiency, and continual lack of money in his treasury.

Meanwhile both sides were canvassing. Every day messengers were flying between Nyeporente and Yablonna. Kazimir in the name of his own seniority and brotherly affection adjured Karl to resign; but the bishop held back, answering that it would not become him to contemn, the fortune which might meet him, since that fortune was in the free gift of the Commonwealth, and was his to whom the Lord had designed it. Time passed; the term of six weeks was approaching, and together with it the Cossack storm. News had come that Hmelnitski, having raised the siege of Lvoff, which had ransomed itself after a number of assaults, had invested Zamost, and night and day was storming that last rampart of the Commonwealth.

It was said too that besides the delegates whom Hmelnitski had sent to Warsaw with a letter and declaration that as a noble of Poland he would give his vote to Kazimir, there were nobles hidden among the crowd, and that the city itself was full of disguised Cossack elders whom no one could detect, for they had come like regular and wealthy nobles, differing in nothing, even in speech, from other electors, especially those from the Russian provinces. Some, as was said, had crept in through simple curiosity to look at the election and Warsaw; others to spy, to obtain news, to hear talk about the war,--how many troops the Commonwealth thought of putting in the field, and what grants it proposed for the levies. Perhaps there was much truth in the reports concerning these guests; for among the Zaporojian elders were many nobles who had become Cossacks, who had picked up some Latin and therefore were not to be recognized in any way. Besides, in the distant steppes Latin did not flourish as a rule, and such princes as the Kurtsevichi did not know it any better than Bogun and other atamans.

But reports like these with which the election field as well as the city were filled, together with news of the movements of Hmelnitski and the Cossack-Tartar expeditions,--which had reached, it was said, the Vistula,--filled people's minds with alarm, and more than once became causes of tumult. In the crowd of nobles to cast on a man the suspicion of being a Zaporojian in disguise was enough to insure his being sabred into small pieces before he could show who he was. In this way innocent men might perish and the dignity of deliberations be destroyed, especially since with the custom of the time sobriety was not too much observed. The chapter "propter securitatem loci" (concerning public peace) was inadequate to stop the endless quarrels in which people were cut down for the slightest cause. But if those tumults, sabre-slashings, and drinking-bouts alarmed orderly people, penetrated with a love of good and peace, through the danger with which they threatened the country, on the other hand the reckless, the disorderly, the gamblers and disturbers felt as it were in their element; they considered this as their own special season, their day of harvest, and the more boldly permitted themselves various misdeeds.

It is needless to add that among these Zagloba was first. His primacy was secured by his great fame as a knight, his unquenchable thirst upheld by a supply of drink, a tongue so tanned that it had no equal, and by a self-confidence which nothing could shake. But he had at times his attacks of "melancholy;" then he shut himself up in a room or a tent, and did not go out, or if he did go he was in angry humor, inclined to quarrels and genuine fighting. It happened, in fact, that in such a humor he hacked up Pan Dunchevski badly, only because he had knocked against his sabre in passing. At such times he endured only the presence of Pan Michael, to whom he complained that a longing for Skshetuski and the "poor young lady" was devouring him. "We have deserted her, Pan Michael," he used to say; "we have betrayed her like Judas into godless hands. Don't excuse yourself to me with your *nemine excepto*. What is happening to her, Pan Michael, tell me that?"

In vain Pan Michael explained that had it not been for Pilavtsi, they would have been searching for "the poor young lady," but that now when the whole power of Hmelnitski separated them from her it was an impossible thing. Zagloba did not yield himself to consolation, but fell into still greater passion, cursing by what the world stands on,--"Feather-bed," "Baby," and "Latin."[16]

But these periods of gloom were of short duration. When they were over Zagloba, as if wishing to reward himself for lost time, generally revelled and drank more than ever. He spent his time in taverns in company with the mightiest drinkers or with women of the capital, in which occupation Pan Michael held him trusty companionship.

Pan Michael, a soldier and a splendid officer, possessed not, however, a farthing's worth of that seriousness which misfortune and suffering had developed, for instance, in Skshetuski. Volodyovski understood his duty to the Commonwealth in this way: he killed whomsoever he was ordered to kill,--cared for naught else. He knew nothing of public questions; he was always ready to bewail a military defeat, but it never entered his head that quarrels and tumults were as harmful to public affairs as defeats; in one word, he was a thoughtless young man who, having entered the bustle of the capital, sank in it to his ears, and stuck like a thistle to Zagloba, for he was his master in license. He went therefore with him among the nobles, to whom Zagloba at his cups related things uncreated, winning at the same time adherents for Prince Karl; he drank with him, protected him when necessary; they both circled around in the field of election and the city like flies in a pot, and there was no corner into which they did not crawl. They were at Nyeporente and in Yablonna; they were at all the feasts and dinners given by magnates; they were at taverns,--they were everywhere, and took part in everything. Pan Michael's youthful hand was restive; he wanted to exhibit himself, and to prove at the same time that the nobility of the Ukraine was better than any other and that the soldiers of the prince were higher than all. They went therefore to seek adventures on purpose among the Poles of the kingdom, as the most skilled with the sword, and specially among the partisans of Prince Dominik Zaslavski, for whom both felt a particular hatred. They engaged only with the most celebrated champions, men of undoubted and settled fame, and plotted the quarrels beforehand. "You pick the quarrel," said Pan Michael, "and then I will step in." Zagloba, very skilful in fence and by no means timid in duelling with a brother noble, did not always agree to have a substitute, especially in affairs with adherents of Zaslavski; but when it was a question with some famous swordsman, he halted in the dispute; if the noble was eager for the sword and challenged, Zagloba said: "My good sir, I should be without conscience if I were to expose you to evident death by fighting with you myself; better try my little son and pupil here, and I am not sure that you will be able to manage him." After such words Volodyovski appeared on the scene with his little upturned mustaches, nose in the air, and gaping face. Whether accepted or not, he opened the fight, and being in truth a master above masters, he generally stretched out his antagonist after a few blows. In this fashion the two found sport from which their fame increased among restless spirits and the nobles, but especially the fame of Pan Zagloba, for it was said: "If the pupil is such a man, what must the master be!" Pan Kharlamp was the one person that Volodyovski could not find for a long time. He thought: "Perhaps they have sent him back to Lithuania on business of some sort."

In this way nearly six weeks had gone, during which time public affairs had advanced notably. The protracted battle of the candidate brothers, the efforts of their adherents, the fever and storm of passion among partisans had passed, leaving scarcely trace or memory. It was now known to all that Yan Kazimir would be chosen; for Prince Karl had yielded to his brother, and resigned the candidature of his own good-will. It is a wonderful thing that the voice of Hmelnitski had great weight; for it was hoped on every side that he would yield to the authority of the king, especially when chosen according to his wish. These previsions were justified in great part. But for Vishnyevetski--who, like Cato of old, ceased not one moment from repeating that the Zaporojian Carthage must be destroyed--this turn of affairs was a fresh blow. Negotiations must be the order of the day. The prince knew, it is true, that these negotiations would either result in nothing from the start or would be broken off soon from the nature of the case, and saw war in the future; but disquiet seized him at the thought: "What will be the issue of that war? After negotiations the justified Hmelnitski will be still stronger, and the Commonwealth still weaker. And who will lead its forces against a chief so famous as Hmelnitski? Will not there be new defeats and new catastrophes which will exhaust its forces to the last?" For the prince did not deceive himself, and knew that to him, the most eager adherent of Karl, the command would not be given. Kazimir had promised, it is true, to favor his brother's adherents as much as his own. Kazimir was high-souled, but he was a partisan of the chancellor's policy. Some one else will receive the command, not the prince; and woe to the Commonwealth if he be not a leader superior to Hmelnitski! At this thought a twofold pain straitened the soul of Yeremi,--fear for the future of the country, and the unendurable feeling of a man who sees that his services are passed over, that justice will not be done him, and that others will raise their heads above his. He would not have been Yeremi Vishnyevetski if he had not been proud. He felt within himself the power to wield the baton, and he had earned the baton; therefore he suffered doubly.

It was reported among officers that the prince would not wait for the close of the election, and would leave Warsaw; but that was not true. The prince not only did not leave, but he visited, in Nyeporente, Prince Kazimir, who received him with unbounded favor; then he returned to the city for a prolonged stay, caused by military affairs. It was a question of finding support for the army, which the prince urged diligently. Besides, new regiments of dragoons and infantry were equipped at Karl's expense. Some had been sent to Russia already; others were to be drilled. For this purpose the prince sent out on every side officers expert in organizing troops. Kushel and Vershul had been sent, and finally the turn came for Volodyovski. One day he was summoned to the prince, who gave him the following order:--

"You will go by way of Babitse and Lipki to Zaborovo, where horses for the regiment are waiting; you will inspect them, reject those unfit, and pay Pan Tshaskovski for those accepted; then you will bring them for the soldiers. The money you will receive here in Warsaw from the paymaster on this my order."

Volodyovski set about the work briskly. He took the money, and on the same day he and Zagloba with eight others set out with a wagon bearing the money. They moved slowly, for that side of Warsaw was swarming with nobles, attendants, and horses; the villages as far as Babitse were so packed that in every cottage there were guests. It was easy to meet adventures in a press of people of various humors; and in spite of their greatest efforts and modest bearing, our two friends did not escape them.

On reaching Babitse they saw before the public house a number of nobles who were just mounting to continue their journey. The two parties, after saluting each other, were about to pass, when suddenly one of the riders looked at Volodyovski, and without saying a word rode up to him on a trot.

"Ah, you are here, my little fellow!" cried he. "You have been skulking, but I have found you. You won't escape me this time! Eh, gentlemen!" shouted he to his comrades, "just wait a bit. I have something to say to this little stub of an officer, and I should like to have you as witnesses of my words."

Volodyovski smiled with pleasure, for he recognized Pan Kharlamp. "God is my witness that I was not hiding," said he; "more than that, I was looking for you myself to ask if you still cherished rancor against me, but somehow we couldn't meet."

"Pan Michael," whispered Zagloba, "you are on duty."

"I remember," muttered Volodyovski.

"Come to business!" roared Kharlamp. "Gentlemen, I have promised this milksop, this bald mustache, to clip his ears for him, and I'll clip them as true as I am Kharlamp. Be witnesses, gentlemen, and you, youngster, come up here!"

"I cannot, as God is dear to me, I cannot," said Volodyovski; "let me off even for a couple of days."

"Why can you not? You are frightened, I suppose. If you do not meet me at once, I will slap you so with my sword that you'll think of your grandfather and grandmother. Oh, you dodger, you venomous gadfly, you know how to get in the way, you know how to buzz, you know how to bite, but when it comes to the sabre you are not there."

Here Zagloba interfered. "It seems to me that you are pressing matters rather far," said he to Kharlamp, "and look out that this fly does not sting; if he does, no plaster will help you. Tfu! the devil take it, don't you see that this officer is on duty? Look at that wagon with money which we are taking to the regiment, and understand that his person is not at his own disposal and he cannot meet you. Whoever can't understand that is a dunce and not a soldier. We serve under the voevoda of Rus, and we have fought men different from you; but to-day it is impossible, and what is deferred will not escape."

"It is certain," said one of Kharlamp's comrades, "that they are transporting money; he cannot meet you."

"What is their money to me?" screamed the irrepressible Kharlamp; "let him stand before me or I'll slap him with my sword."

"I will not meet you to-day, but I give you the word of a soldier to meet you in three or four days, wherever you please, the moment I have carried out my orders. And if this does not satisfy you, gentlemen, I shall give order to touch the triggers, for I shall believe that I have to do not with soldiers, but with brigands. Take yourselves off then to all the devils, for I have no time to loiter."

On hearing this, the dragoons of the escort turned the muzzles of their guns on the aggressors. That movement, as well as the decisive words of Pan Michael, produced an evident impression on the comrades of Kharlamp. "Oh, let him off!" said they. "You are a soldier yourself, you know what service is; it is certain that you will receive satisfaction. He is a bold piece, like all men of the Russian squadron; restrain yourself, since we ask you."

Pan Kharlamp blustered awhile longer, but saw at last that he would either make his companions angry or expose them to an uncertain struggle with the dragoons. He turned therefore to Volodyovski, and said: "Give me your word that you will meet me."

"I will seek you myself, were it only because you have asked twice about such a thing. To-day is Wednesday, and let it be Saturday at two o'clock in the afternoon. Select your ground."

"Here in Babitse there is a crowd of travellers," said Kharlamp; "something might interfere. Let it be over there at Lipki; it is quieter, and not far for me, because our quarters are in Babitse."

"Will there be as large a company of you as to-day?" asked the prudent Zagloba.

"Oh, it's not necessary," said Kharlamp; "I shall come only with the Selitskis, my relatives. You will be without your dragoons, I trust."

"Perhaps they fight duels with the aid of soldiers among you," replied Pan Michael; "but it is not the custom with us."

"In four days then, on Saturday," said Kharlamp. "We shall be in front of the public house at Lipki; and now with God!"

"With God!" said Volodyovski and Zagloba.

The opponents parted quietly. Pan Michael was made happy by the coming amusement, and promised himself to make a present to Pan Longin of mustaches shorn from the light-horseman. He went therefore in good spirits to Zaborovo, where he found Prince Kazimir, who had come to hunt. But Pan Michael saw his future lord only at a distance, for he was in a hurry. In two or three days he carried out his orders, inspected the horses, paid Pan Tshaskovski, returned to Warsaw, and at the appointed time, yes, an hour earlier, he was at Lipki with Zagloba and Pan Kushel, whom he had asked to be his other second.

On arriving in front of the inn kept by a Jew, they entered to moisten their throats a little with mead and amuse themselves with conversation at the glass.

"Here, scald-head! is your master at the castle?" asked Zagloba of the innkeeper.

"He is away in the town."

"Are there many nobles stopping in Lipki?"

"My house is empty. Only one has stopped with me, and he is sitting in the next room,--a rich man, with servants and horses."

"And why did he not go to the castle?"

"Because it is evident he does not know our master. Besides, the place has been closed for a month past."

"Maybe it is Kharlamp," said Zagloba.

"No," said Volodyovski.

"Well, Pan Michael, it seems to me that it is he. I'll go and see who it is. Jew, has this gentleman been long here?"

"He came to-day, not two hours ago."

"And don't you know where he came from?"

"I do not; but it must be from a distance, for his horses are used up; his men said, from beyond the Vistula."

"Why did he come here then to Lipki?"

"Who knows?"

"I'll go and see," repeated Zagloba; "perhaps it is some acquaintance." Approaching the closed door of the room, he knocked with his sword-hilt and said: "Worthy sir, may I enter?"

"Who is there?" answered a voice within.

"A friend," said Zagloba, opening the door. "Ah, begging your pardon, maybe I'm not in season," he added, pushing his head into the room. He drew back suddenly, and slammed the door as if he had looked on death. On his face was depicted terror coupled with the greatest astonishment. His mouth was open, and he looked with vacant stare on Volodyovski and Kushel.

"What is the matter?" asked Volodyovski.

"By the wounds of Christ, be quiet!" said Zagloba. "Bogun is there!"

"Who? What's happened to you?"

"There--Bogun!"

Both officers rose to their feet.

"Have you lost your reason? Compose yourself! Who is it?"

"Bogun! Bogun!"

"Impossible!"

"As I live! As I stand before you here, I swear to you by God and all the saints."

"Why are you so disturbed?" asked Volodyovski. "If he is there, then God has given him into our hands. Compose yourself! Are you sure that it is he?"

"As sure as that I am speaking to you, I saw him; he was changing his clothes."

"And did he see you?"

"I don't know; I think not."

Volodyovski's eyes gleamed like coals. "Jew," whispered he, beckoning hurriedly with his hand. "This way! Are there doors from the room?"

"No, only through this room."

"Kushel, you go under the window!" whispered Pan Michael. "Oh, he will not escape us this time!"

Kushel, without speaking a word, ran out of the room.

"Come to your senses," said Volodyovski. "Not over you, but over his neck hangs destruction. What can he do to you? Nothing!"

"Nothing; but from astonishment I am unable to catch my breath." And he thought to himself: "True, I have nothing to fear. Pan Michael is with me. Let Bogun be afraid!" And putting on a terribly savage look, he grasped the hilt of his sabre. "Pan Michael, he must not escape us."

"But is it he?--for still I can't believe. What should he be doing here?"

"Hmelnitski has sent him as a spy; that is most certain. Wait! Pan Michael, we will seize him and lay down the condition that unless he gives up the princess, we will deliver him to justice. If he gives up the princess, then let the devil take him."

"But are there not too few of us,--two, and Kushel? He will defend himself like a madman, and he has attendants also."

"Kharlamp will come with two; there will be six of us. That's enough; be quiet!"

At that moment the door opened, and Bogun entered the room. He could not have seen Zagloba looking into his room, for at the sight of him he quivered suddenly, a flush as it were went over his face, and his hand as quick as lightning rested on the hilt of his sabre; but all this lasted only the twinkle of an eye. The flush went from his face, which grew slightly pale.

Zagloba looked at him, and said nothing. The ataman also remained silent, and in the room a fly on the wing could be heard. Those two persons whose fates had crossed in such a wonderful manner pretended at the moment not to know each other. The interval was rather long; it appeared to Pan Michael that whole ages were passing.

"Jew," said Bogun, all at once, "is it far from here to Zaborovo?"

"Not far," answered the Jew. "Are you going now?"

"Yes," said Bogun, and turned toward the door leading to the anteroom.

"With your permission," sounded the voice of Zagloba.

The chief halted at once as if he had grown to the floor, and turning to Zagloba, fastened his dark and terrible eyes on him. "What do you wish?" asked he, curtly.

"It seems to me that we made acquaintance somewhere,--at a wedding on a farm in Russia, was it not?"

"Yes," said the chief haughtily, putting his hand again on the hilt.

"How does your health serve you?" asked Zagloba. "For you rode off in such haste that I had no time to bid you farewell."

"And were you sorry for that?"

"Of course I was sorry. We should have had a dance, and the company would have been larger." Here Zagloba pointed to Volodyovski. "This is the cavalier who came in, and he would have been glad of a nearer acquaintance with you."

"Enough of this!" shouted Pan Michael, rising suddenly. "I arrest you, traitor!"

"With what authority?" asked the ataman, raising his head haughtily.

"You are a rebel, an enemy of the Commonwealth, and have come here as a spy."

"And who are you?"

"Oh, I will not explain that to you; but you won't escape me!"

"We shall see," said Bogun. "I should not explain to you who I am if you had challenged me to sabres like a soldier; but since you threaten with arrest, then I will explain. Here is a letter which I carry from the Zaporojian hetman to Prince Kazimir, and not finding him in Nyeporente, I am going with it to Zaborovo. How will you arrest me now?"

Bogun looked haughtily and sneeringly at Volodyovski. Pan Michael was greatly confused, like a hound which feels that the game is escaping him; and not knowing what to do, he turned an inquiring look at Zagloba. A painful moment of silence followed.

"It is difficult indeed," said Zagloba. "Since you are an envoy, we cannot arrest you; and you will not meet this cavalier with a sabre, for you have already fled before him till the earth groaned."

Bogun's face grew purple, for that moment he recognized Volodyovski. Shame and wounded pride sprang into play in the fearless chief. The remembrance of that flight scorched him like fire. It was the single stain on the fame of his heroism,--the fame which he loved beyond life, beyond all.

The inexorable Zagloba continued in cold blood: "You had almost lost your trousers, when pity penetrated this cavalier. Tfu! young hero, you have a woman's face, and a woman's heart too. You were brave with the old princess and the lad her son, but with a knight you are a wind-bag. Carry letters, steal young ladies,--that's your work, not war! As God is dear to me, I saw with my own eyes how your trousers were flying around. Tfu, tfu! Now you talk of the sabre, for you are carrying a letter. How are we to meet you when you shield yourself with that letter? All dust in the eyes, young hero! Hmelnitski is a good soldier, Krívonos a good one; but among the Cossacks there is many a cowardly sneak."

Bogun pushed up suddenly to Zagloba, and Zagloba drew back with equal swiftness behind Volodyovski, so that the two young knights stood before each other, eye to eye.

"Not from fear did I retreat before you, but to save my men," said Bogun.

"I know not your reasons for fleeing, but I know that you fled," said Volodyovski.

"I will meet you anywhere, even here, this minute."

"Will you challenge me?" asked Volodyovski, half closing his eyes.

"You have touched my fame, tried to cast shame on me, I need your blood."

"No dispute on those points," said Volodyovski.

"No harm to the consenting party," added Zagloba. "But who will deliver the letter to the prince?"

"Give yourself no headache over that; it is my affair."

"Fight, then, if it cannot be otherwise," said Zagloba. "But if fortune favors you against this cavalier, remember that you will have to meet me. And now, Pan Michael, come out to the front of the house; I have something important to say."

The two friends went out and called Kushel from under the window of the room.

"Gentlemen, our affair is a bad one. He has really a letter to the prince; if we kill him, it is a capital crime. Remember that the chapter 'propter securitatem loci' has jurisdiction ten miles from the field of election, and he is the same as an envoy. A weighty question! We must either hide somewhere afterward, or perhaps the prince will protect us; otherwise it may go hard with us. And to let him go free again is still worse. This is the only way to liberate our poor young lady. For when he is no longer in the world we shall find her more easily. The Lord himself evidently wishes to aid her and Skshetuski; that's clear. Let us help."

"Will you invent some stratagem?" asked Kushel.

"With my stratagem I have already brought him to challenge us. But seconds are necessary,-- strangers. My idea is to wait for Kharlamp. I will undertake to make him yield his first place, and in case of need, to testify how we were challenged and obliged to defend ourselves. We must also find out more accurately from Bogun where he hid the young lady. If he has to die, she is nothing to him; perhaps he will tell if we press him. And if he won't tell, then it is better that he should not live. It is necessary to do everything with foresight and discretion. My head is bursting, gentlemen."

"Who will fight with him?" asked Kushel.

"Pan Michael first, I second," said Zagloba.

"And I third."

"Impossible!" interrupted Volodyovski. "I will fight with him alone, and that will be the end. If he brings me down, it is his fortune. Let him go in peace."

"I've told him already," said Zagloba; "but if it is your wish, I yield."

"If it is his wish, he may fight with you, but with no one else."

"Let us go to him then."

"Let us go."

They found Bogun in the main room, drinking mead. He was perfectly calm.

"Listen," said Zagloba, "for these are important questions which we want to discuss with you. You have challenged this cavalier. Very well. But you must know that since you are an envoy you are protected by law, for you come among civilized men, not among wild beasts; and therefore we cannot meet you unless you state before witnesses that you have challenged us of your own free will. A number of nobles with whom we had to fight a duel will come here, and you will make this statement before them. We will give you our knightly word that if fortune favors you against Pan Volodyovski you will go away at liberty, and no one will hinder you, unless you wish to make a trial with me."

"Agreed," said Bogun. "I will make that statement before those nobles, and I will tell my men to deliver the letter and to inform Hmelnitski, if I perish, that I made the challenge. And if God favors me to vindicate my Cossack fame against this knight, I will ask you to sabres."

When he had spoken he looked into Zagloba's eyes, Zagloba was rather confused, coughed, spat, and said,--

"Agreed! When you have made a trial of my pupil, you will know what sort of work you will have with me. But enough of this! There is another and more important point in which we appeal to your conscience; for though a Cossack, we wish to treat you as a knight. You carried off Princess Helena Kurtsevichovna, the betrothed of our comrade and friend, and you hold her secreted. Know that if we had accused you of this it would not have helped you that Hmelnitski made you his envoy, for this is 'raptus puellae,' a capital offence, which would be judged here immediately. But since you are going to combat, and may perish, bethink yourself what will happen to that unfortunate lady if you die. Do you, who love her, wish evil and destruction to her? Will you deprive her of protection and give her to shame and misfortune? Do you wish to be her executioner, even when you are dead?"

Here the voice of Zagloba sounded with unusual solemnity for him. Bogun grew pale and asked: "What do you want of me?"

"Tell us where she is hidden, so that we may find her if you die, and give her to her betrothed. If you do this, God will have mercy on your soul."

The chief rested his head on his hands, and thought deeply. The three comrades watched carefully the changes in that mobile face, which was suddenly covered with such touching grief as if neither anger, rage, nor any fierce feeling had ever played upon it, and as if that man had been created only for love and yearning. A long time this silence lasted, till finally it was broken by the voice of Zagloba, which trembled while uttering the following words,--

"If you have already put her to shame, may God condemn you and let her find shelter in a cloister."

Bogun raised his sad, moistened eyes, and said: "If I have shamed her? I know not how you Poles love, knights and cavaliers, but I am a Cossack. I protected her in Bar from death and disgrace, and afterward took her to the desert, and there guarded her as the eye in my head; did no injury to her, fell at her feet and bowed to her as before an image. If she told me to go, I went, and have not seen her since, for war detained me."

"God will remember that for you at the judgment," said Zagloba, sighing deeply, "But is she safe? Krívonos and the Tartars are there."

"Krívonos is at Kamenyets, and sent me to ask Hmelnitski whether he was to march on Kudák. He has surely gone there, and where she is there are neither Cossacks nor Poles nor Tartars. She is safe."

"Where is she, then?"

"Listen to me, Poles! Let it be as you wish. I will tell you where she is, and I will give the order to render her up; but you must give me your knightly word that if God favors me, you will not look for her. You promise for yourselves and for Pan Skshetuski, and I will tell you."

The three friends looked at one another.

"We cannot do that," said Zagloba.

"Oh, as true as life we cannot!" cried Kushel and Volodyovski.

"Is it possible?" asked Bogun. His brows were frowning and his eyes flashed. "Well, why can you not?"

"Because Pan Skshetuski is not present; and besides, you may be sure that none of us would cease to seek for her, even if you have hidden her under ground."

"So you would make this bargain with me: 'Cossack, give up your soul, and then we will sabre you!' Oh, don't wait for it! And do you think my Cossack sabre is not made of steel, that you are croaking over me like ravens over a dead carcass? And why am I to die, and not you? You want my blood, but I want yours! We shall see who gets whose."

"Then you will not tell?"

"Why talk to me? Death to you all!"

"Death to you! You deserve to be cut to pieces with sabres!"

"Try it!" said the chief, rising quickly.

Kushel and Volodyovski sprang at the same moment from the bench. Threatening looks were exchanged, breasts overflowing with anger breathed more violently, and it is unknown what might have happened, had not Zagloba, who had looked through the window, cried: "Kharlamp has come with his seconds!"

The light-horse captain with his two companions, the Selitskis, entered the room. After the first greeting, Zagloba took them aside to explain the affair. He spoke so eloquently that he soon convinced them, especially when he declared that Volodyovski asked only for a short delay, and immediately after his struggle with the Cossack would be ready to meet Kharlamp. Here Zagloba related how old and terrible was the hatred of all the soldiers of the prince for Bogun; how he was an enemy of the whole Commonwealth, and was one of the most desperate rebels; and finally, how he had carried off the princess, a lady of a noble house, the betrothed of a noble who was the mirror of every knightly virtue. "And if you are a noble and have some feeling of brotherhood, you know that the wrong inflicted on one is inflicted on the whole order. Can you let it go then unavenged?"

Kharlamp raised difficulties at first, and said that since matters were in that state, Bogun should be cut to pieces on the spot. "But let Pan Volodyovski meet me according to agreement."

Zagloba had to explain to him again why this could not be, and that it would not be knightly to attack one man from behind in this fashion. Happily the Selitskis helped him, both men of judgment and prudence, so that the stubborn Lithuanian let himself be convinced at last, and agreed to a delay.

Meanwhile Bogun went to his men, and returned with the essaul Eliasenko, to whom he told how he had challenged two nobles, and then repeated the same thing aloud, in presence of Kharlamp and the Selitskis.

"We on our part declare," said Volodyovski, "that if you come out victorious in the struggle with me, it will depend on your will whether you are to fight with Pan Zagloba, and in no case will any one else call you out, and this company will not attack you; you will go where you please. For this I give my knightly word, and I beg you, gentlemen who have just come, to add the same on your part."

"We do," said Kharlamp and the two Selitskis, solemnly. Then Bogun delivered to Eliasenko Hmelnitski's letter to the prince; and said: "You will give this letter to the prince; and if I die you will tell him and Hmelnitski that the fault was mine, and that I was not killed through treachery."

Zagloba, who had a watchful eye on everything, saw not the least disquiet on the sullen visage of Eliasenko. It was evident that he was too sure of his ataman.

Bogun then turned haughtily to the nobles: "Well, to one death, to another life," said he. "We may begin."

"Time, time!" said all, tucking back the skirts of their coats under their belts, and taking their sabres under their arms.

They went in front of the inn, and turned down to a creek which flowed among a growth of hawthorns, wild roses, and plum-trees. November had stripped, it is true, the leaves from the bushes, but the thicket was so close that it looked black as a mourning-ribbon along through the empty fields to the forest. The day was pale, but pleasant with that melancholy mildness of autumn full of sweetness. The sun embroidered softly with gold the naked branches of the trees, and lighted up the yellow, sandy banks extending some distance along the right side of the creek. The combatants and their seconds went straight to these banks.

"We will stop here," said Zagloba.

"Agreed," answered all.

Zagloba grew more and more unquiet; at last he approached Volodyovski, and whispered: "Pan Michael--"

"Well?"

"For the love of God, Pan Michael, exert yourself! In your hands now is the fate of Skshetuski, the freedom of the princess, your own life and mine. God keep you from accident! I could do nothing with this robber."

"Why did you challenge him then?"

"The word came out of itself. I trusted in you, Pan Michael. I am old, and my breath is short. I choke, and this beauty can jump like a goat. He is a fleet hound, Pan Michael."

"I'll do my best," said the little knight.

"God give you aid! Don't lose courage!"

"Why should I?"

At that moment one of the Selitskis came up to them. "He is a trim fellow, your Cossack," he whispered; "he acts with us as if he were an equal, if not a superior. What a bearing! It must be that his mother looked on some noble."

"It is more likely," said Zagloba, "that some noble looked on her."

"And so it appears to me," said Volodyovski.

"To our places!" called Bogun, suddenly.

"To our places, to our places!"

They took their places,--the nobles in a half-circle, Volodyovski and Bogun opposite each other.

Volodyovski, as a man experienced in such affairs though he was young, tested the ground first with his feet to see if it was firm; then he cast his eye about, wishing to know all the unevenness of the place. And it was apparent that he did not underestimate the affair. He had to meet with a knight the most celebrated in the whole Ukraine, of whom the people sang songs, and whose name was known through the breadth of Russia to the Crimea. Pan Michael, a simple lieutenant of the dragoons, promised himself much from that struggle, for it was either a glorious death or an equally glorious victory; therefore he neglected nothing to show himself worthy of such an opponent. He had an unusual seriousness in his face, seeing which Zagloba was frightened. "He is losing courage," thought he; "it is over with him, and then it is over with me!"

Meanwhile Volodyovski, having examined the ground carefully, began to unbutton his vest. Bogun followed his example, and both threw off their upper garments, so that they were in trousers and shirts; then they rolled up the sleeves on their right arms.

But how insignificant appeared little Pan Michael before the large and powerful ataman! He was almost invisible. The seconds looked uneasily on the broad breast of the Cossack, on the great muscles visible from under the rolled-up sleeve, like knots and cords. It seemed as though a little cock had stood up to fight with a powerful falcon of the steppes. The nostrils of Bogun were distended as if snuffing blood in advance; his face was so contracted that his dark foretop seemed to touch his brow, and the sabre quivered in his hand; he fixed his eyes rapaciously on his opponent and waited the word.

Volodyovski looked once more through the light at the edge of his sword, moved his little yellow mustache, and stood in position.

"There will be straight cuts here," muttered Kushel to Selitski.

Meanwhile the voice of Zagloba, slightly trembling, said: "In the name of God, begin!"

CHAPTER XLV.

The sabres whistled; edge clashed against edge. The place of conflict was shifted at once; for Bogun pressed on with such fury that Volodyovski sprang back a number of steps, and the seconds had to retreat too. The lightning zigzags of Bogun's sword were so swift that the astonished eyes of those present could not follow them. It seemed to them that Volodyovski was altogether surrounded and covered, and that God alone could snatch him from beneath that storm of thunderbolts. The blows were mingled in one uninterrupted whistle; the rush of the moving air struck all faces. The fury of the Cossack increased; the wild rage of conflict seized him, and like a hurricane he pushed Volodyovski before him. The little knight retreated continually, and merely defended himself. His extended right arm scarcely moved; only his hand described, without stopping, circles narrow but swift as thought, and caught the raging blows of Bogun. He put edge under edge, warded off and again defended and still retreated, fixed his eyes on the eyes of the Cossack, and in the midst of serpentine lightnings appeared calm; but on his cheeks purple spots were coming out. Zagloba closed his eyes, and heard nothing but blow after blow, bite after bite.

"He defends himself yet," thought he.

"He defends himself yet," said the Selitskis and Kushel.

"He is already pushed to the sand-bank," added Kushel, quietly.

Zagloba opened his eyes again and looked. True, Volodyovski was pushed to the bank; but evidently he was not wounded yet. The flush on his face had become deeper, and drops of sweat were on his forehead.

Zagloba's heart began to beat with hope. "Pan Michael is a master beyond masters," thought he, "and this fellow will become tired at last."

In fact Bogun's face had grown pale, sweat stood in drops on his forehead; but resistance only roused his rage, foam shone from under his mustache, and from his breast came the hoarseness of fury.

Volodyovski did not let him out of sight, and defended himself continually. Suddenly, feeling the sand-bank behind, he collected himself. It seemed to the spectators that he had fallen; meanwhile he bent, shrunk up, half squatted, and hurled his whole body as if it were a stone against the breast of the Cossack.

"He is attacking!" shouted Zagloba.

"He is attacking!" repeated the others.

So he was, in fact. The Cossack retreated now; and the little knight, having discovered the whole power of his opponent, pushed on him so briskly that the breath stopped in the breasts of the seconds. Evidently he began to warm up; his little eyes shot sparks; he squatted, he sprang, he changed position in a moment, he described circles around the Cossack, and forced him to turn where he stood.

"Oh, masterly, masterly!" said Zagloba.

"You will perish!" said Bogun, all at once.

"You will perish!" answered, like an echo, Volodyovski.

At that moment the Cossack threw, his sabre from his right to his left hand,--a feat possible only to the ablest fencers,--and gave with his left hand such a terrible blow that Volodyovski fell to the ground as if struck by lightning.

"Jesus, Mary!" screamed Zagloba.

But Volodyovski had fallen on purpose, so that the sabre of Bogun might meet only air. Then the little knight sprang up like a wildcat, and with almost the whole length of his blade cut terribly into the open breast of the Cossack.

Bogun tottered, advanced a step, and with a last effort gave the last thrust. Volodyovski warded it off with ease, and struck still twice on the inclined head. The sabre dropped from the powerless hands of Bogun, and he fell with his face on the sand, which immediately reddened under him in a broad pool of blood.

Eliasenko, present at the duel, rushed to the body of the ataman. The seconds were unable to utter a word for some time. Pan Michael too was silent; he rested both hands on his sabre and panted heavily.

Zagloba first broke the silence. "Pan Michael, come to my embrace!" said he, with emotion.

Then they surrounded him in a circle.

"You are a swordsman of the first water. May the bullets strike you!" said the Selitskis.

"You are a deceitful rogue, I see," said Kharlamp; "but I'll meet you, lest it be said that I am afraid. But though you were to slash me in such fashion as this, still I congratulate you."

"And you should put yourself at rest, for in fact you have nothing to fight about," said Zagloba.

"Impossible!" answered the light-horseman, "for it is a question here of my reputation, for which I am glad to give my life."

"I have no claim on your life. It is better to drop the matter; for to tell you the truth, I have not come in your way as you imagine. Some other man better than I will stand in your way, but not I."

"Is that true?"

"My knightly word for it."

"Then make peace with each other," cried the Selitskis and Kushel.

"Let it be so," said Kharlamp, opening his arms.

Volodyovski fell into them, and the two men kissed each other till the echoes resounded along the bank.

Kushel said: "I did not think that you could beat such a giant; and he knew too how to use a sabre."

"I had no idea that he was such a swordsman. Where could he have learned?"

Here the attention of all was directed again to the prostrate chief, whom at that time Eliasenko had turned on his back and was looking with tears for signs of life in him. It was impossible to recognize the features of Bogun, for they were covered with streaks of blood which flowed out of the wounds in his head and which immediately grew stiff in the chill air. The shirt on his breast was all in blood, but he still gave signs of life. Seemingly he was in his last agonies; his feet quivered, and his fingers hooked convulsively like claws in the sand.

Zagloba looked and waved his hand. "He has had his fill; he is parting with the world."

"Ah," said one of the Selitskis, looking at the body, "that's a corpse already!"

"Yes, for he is almost cut into bits."

"He was no common knight," muttered Volodyovski, nodding his head.

"I know something of that," added Zagloba.

Meanwhile Eliasenko tried to raise up and carry away the unfortunate ataman; but being rather a slender man and not young, and since Bogun belonged almost to the giants, he could not. It was some distance to the inn, and Bogun might die at any moment. The essaul, seeing this, turned to the nobles.

"Gentlemen," said he, clasping his hands, "for the sake of the Saviour and the Holy Most Pure, help me! Do not let him die here like a dog! I am old, not strong enough, and the men are far away."

The nobles looked at one another. Animosity against Bogun had vanished from every heart.

"True, it is hard to leave him here like a dog," muttered Zagloba. "Since we met him in a duel, he is no longer a peasant for us, but a soldier, to whom such assistance is due. Who will carry him with me, gentlemen?"

"I," said Volodyovski.

"Then carry him on my burka," added Kharlamp.

In a moment Bogun was lying on the mantle, the ends of which Zagloba, Volodyovski, Kushel, and Eliasenko held; and the whole party, in company with Kharlamp and the Selitskis, moved with slow steps toward the inn.

"He has a firm life," said Zagloba; "he is moving yet. My God, if any man had told me that I should become his nurse and carry him in this fashion, I should have thought that he was trifling with me. I have too feeling a heart, I know that myself; but life is cruel. I'll dress his wounds too. I hope we shall meet no more in this world; let him remember me kindly in the next."

"Then you think that he will not recover by any means?" asked Kharlamp.

"He! I wouldn't give a wisp of old straw for his life. Such was his fate, and he could not escape it; for even if he had succeeded with Pan Volodyovski, he wouldn't have escaped my hands. But I prefer that it has happened as it has, for already there is an outcry against me as a merciless slaughterer. And what am I to do when a man crawls into my way? I had to pay Pan Dunchevski five hundred sequins' fine, and you know, gentlemen, that estates in Russia give no income now."

"True, for they have plundered you there to the last," said Kharlamp.

"Oh, this Cossack is heavy!" said Zagloba; "I've lost my breath.--Plundered us, yes, plundered; but I hope the Diet will make some provision, otherwise we are reduced to death. But he is heavy, he is heavy! See, the blood is beginning to run again! Hurry, Pan Kharlamp, to the inn; let the Jew mix some dough with spider-web. It won't help the dead man much, but care is a Christian act, and it will be easier for him to die. Hurry, Pan Kharlamp!"

Kharlamp pushed ahead; and when at last they carried the chief into the room, Zagloba betook himself, with great knowledge of the art and expertness, to dressing him. He stopped the blood, closed the wounds, then turned to Eliasenko and said,--

"You, grandfather, are not needed here. Ride with all speed to Zaborovo, ask to be placed before the prince, deliver the letter, and tell what you saw, everything as it was. If you lie, I shall know, for I am a confidant of his Highness the Prince, and I shall command your head to be cut off. Give my respects to Hmelnitski, for he knows and loves me. We will give a fitting funeral to your ataman. You do your own work; do not loiter in corners, or some one will settle you before you can tell who you are. Be in good health, and be off!"

"Let me stay, gentlemen, even till he gets cold."

"Be off, I tell you!" said Zagloba, threateningly; "if not, I'll order the peasants to take you to Zaborovo. And my respects to Hmelnitski."

Eliasenko bowed to the girdle and went out. Zagloba said again to Kharlamp and the Selitskis,--

"I've got that Cossack off; for what has he to do here, and if some one should kill him, which might easily happen, then the blame would be laid on us. The partisans of Zaslavski and the curs of the chancellor would be first to roar with all their might that in spite of God's law Vishnyevetski's men murdered the whole Cossack embassy. But a wise head has a remedy for everything. We won't let ourselves be eaten in kasha by these fops, these parasites; and when necessary you, gentlemen, will bear witness how it all happened, and that he challenged us himself. I must order the bailiff of this place to bury him somehow. They don't know here who he was; they will think that he was a noble, and bury him decently. It's time for us too to be on the road, Pan Michael, for we have a report to make to the prince yet."

The hoarse breathing of Bogun interrupted these words.

"Oh, the soul is seeking a way for itself," said Zagloba. "It is getting dark, and the spirit will go groping to the other world. But since he put no shame on our young lady, may God give him eternal rest,--amen! Let us go, Pan Michael. From my heart I forgive him all his sins, though to tell the truth, I put myself more in his way than he put himself in mine. But the end has come. Gentlemen, I wish you good health. It was a delight to make the acquaintance of such honorable men, but remember to testify in case of need."

CHAPTER XLVI.

Prince Yeremi heard of the slaying of Bogun with notable indifference, especially when he learned that there were men outside his regiments who were ready at any moment to testify that Volodyovski had been challenged. If the affair had not happened just before the announcement of Yan Kazimir's election, if the struggle of the candidates had been still going on, the opponents of Yeremi and at their head the chancellor would certainly not have failed to forge weapons against him out of this event, in spite of all witnesses and testimony. But after Prince Karl's withdrawal, men's minds were occupied with other things, and it was easy to foresee that the whole affair would be drowned in oblivion. Hmelnitski, it is true, might raise it to show what new injuries he was enduring every day; but Yeremi justly hoped that Prince Kazimir in sending his answer would order it to be stated from himself how the envoy had perished, and Hmelnitski would not dare to doubt the truth of the prince's words.

Yeremi was anxious only that no political disturbance should rise through his soldiers. On the other hand he was glad, on Skshetuski's account, of what had happened, for the finding of Kurtsevichovna was really much more likely now. It was possible to find her, to rescue or ransom her; and the prince would surely not spare the outlay, no matter how great, if only he could save his favorite knight from suffering and restore his happiness.

Volodyovski went to the prince in great apprehension; for though in general he had little timidity, still he feared as he did fire every frown of the voevoda's brow. What was his astonishment then and joy when the prince, after he had heard the report and meditated awhile on what had happened, took a costly ring from his finger and said,--

"I praise your moderation for not attacking him first, for a great and harmful uproar might have arisen at the Diet from that. But if the princess shall be found, Skshetuski will be indebted to you for life. Reports reach me, Volodyovski, that as others are unable to keep their tongues behind their lips, you are unable to keep your sabre in its scabbard, for which punishment is due you. But since you took the part of a friend and sustained the reputation of our regiments with such a famous hero, take this ring, so as to have some memento of this day. I knew that you were a good soldier and famous at the sword, but this is like a master of masters."

"He!" said Zagloba. "He would cut the devil's horns off at the third round. If your Highness should ever have my head cut off, then I ask that no one else cut it but him, for at least I should go to the other world straightway. He cut Bogun in two in the breast, and then passed twice through his wits."

The prince was fond of knightly affairs and good soldiers; he smiled therefore with pleasure and asked: "Have you ever found your match at the sabre?"

"Skshetuski hacked me a little once, but I paid him back the time your Highness put us both behind the bars. Among others Pan Podbipienta might meet me, for he has power beyond human; and Kushel almost, if he had better eyes."

"Don't believe him, your Highness! no man can stand before him."

"And Bogun fought long?"

"I had grievous work. He knew how to throw the sabre from the right to the left hand."

"Bogun told me himself," interrupted Zagloba, "that he fought with the Kurtsevichi whole days for practice, and I saw myself how he did the same with others in Chigirin."

"Do you know what you would better do, Volodyovski?" said the prince, with pretended seriousness; "go to Zamost, challenge Hmelnitski, and with one blow free the Commonwealth from all its defeats and anxieties."

"I will go at your Highness's order, if Hmelnitski wishes to meet me," answered Volodyovski.

To which the prince answered: "We are joking, and the world is perishing! But you, gentlemen, must really go to Zamost. I have news from the Cossack camp that the moment Prince Kazimir's election is declared, Hmelnitski will raise the siege and withdraw to Russia, which he will do from real or simulated affection for the king, or because his power might more easily be broken at Zamost. Therefore you must go and tell Skshetuski what has happened, so that he may set out to look for the princess. Tell him to choose from my squadrons with the starosta of Valets as many soldiers as may be necessary for the expedition. Besides, I shall send him permission by you and give him a letter, for his happiness is very near my heart."

"Your Highness, you are a father to us all; therefore we desire to remain in faithful service to you while we live."

"I am not sure that my service will not soon be a hungry one," said the prince, "if all my fortune beyond the Dnieper is lost; but while it lasts, what is mine is yours."

"Oh," cried Volodyovski, "our poor fortunes will always be at the disposal of your Highness."

"And mine with the rest," added Zagloba.

"That is not necessary yet," answered the prince, kindly. "I still entertain the hope that if I lose everything the Commonwealth will at least remember my children."

Speaking thus, the prince seemed to have a moment of second sight. The Commonwealth in fact a few years later gave to his only son the best it had,--that is, the crown; but at that time the gigantic fortune of Yeremi was really shattered.

"Well, we got out of it," said Zagloba, when both had left the prince. "Pan Michael, you may be sure of promotion. But let us see the ring. Upon my word, it is worth about one hundred ducats, for the stone is very beautiful. Ask any Armenian in the bazaar to-morrow. For such an amount we might swim in eating and drinking and other delights. What do you think, Pan Michael? The soldier's maxim is: 'To-day I live, to-morrow decay;' and the sense of it is this,-- that it isn't worth while to think of to-morrow. Short is the life of man, Pan Michael. The great thing is this, that henceforth the prince will carry you in his heart. He would give ten times as much to make a present of Bogun to Skshetuski, and you have done it. You may expect great favors, believe me! Are the villages few that the prince has given to knights for life, or made presents of outright? What is such a ring as this? Surely some income will fall to you, and to wind up, the prince will give you one of his relatives in marriage."

Pan Michael jumped up. "How do you know that--"

"That what?"

"I wanted to say, what have you got in your head? How could such a thing take place?"

"But does it not take place? Are you not a noble, or are not all nobles equal? Are the distant relatives, male and female, of every magnate among the nobles few in number? These relatives he gives in marriage to his most important men. Very likely Sufchinski of Senchy married some distant relative of the Vishnyevetskis. Though some of us serve, we are all brothers, Pan Michael,--all brothers, since we are all descended in common from Japhet, and the whole difference is in fortune and offices to which each may arrive. There are likely enough in some other countries considerable differences between nobles, but they are mangy nobles. I understand differences between dogs; there are, for instance, pointers, and there are hounds of various kinds. But consider, Pan Michael, it cannot be so among nobles; for then we should be dog-brothers, not nobles,--which disgrace to such an honorable order Thou wilt not permit, O Lord!"

"You speak truly," said Volodyovski; "but then the Vishnyevetskis are kingly stock, almost."

"Ah, Pan Michael, just as if you are not eligible to the throne! I, first of all, would vote for you, if I should make up my mind like Pan Sigismond Skarshevski, who swears that he will vote for himself unless he is ruined at dice. Everything, thank God, with us is obtained by free vote; our poverty, not our birth, stands in the way."

"That's the case precisely," sighed Pan Michael.

"What's to be done? We are plundered to the last, and we shall be lost if the Commonwealth doesn't provide some income for us," said Zagloba, "and we shall perish miserably. What wonder is it if a man, though by nature abstemious, should like to get drunk under such oppressions? Let us go, Pan Michael, and drink a glass of small beer; we shall comfort ourselves even a little."

Thus conversing, they reached the old town and entered a wine-shop, before which a number of attendants were holding the shubas and burkas of nobles who were drinking inside. Having seated themselves before a table, they ordered a decanter and began to take counsel as to what they should do now, after the killing of Bogun.

"If Hmelnitski should leave Zamost and peace follow, then the princess is ours," said Zagloba.

"We must go to Skshetuski at once, and not let him off till he finds the girl."

"True, we will go at once; but now there is no way of getting to Zamost."

"That's all the same, if only God will favor us later."

Zagloba raised his glass. "He will, he will," said he. "Do you know, Pan Michael, what I'll tell you?"

"What is it?"

"Bogun is killed."

Volodyovski looked at him with astonishment. "Yes; who should know that better than I?"

"May your hands be holy! you know and I know. I saw how you fought; you are now before my eyes, and still I must repeat it to myself continually, for at times it seems as though I had only some kind of a dream. What a care has been removed! what a knot your sabre cut! May the bullets strike you! for God knows, this is too great to be told. No, I cannot restrain myself; let me press you once again, Pan Michael. If you will believe, when I made your acquaintance I thought to myself: 'There is a little whipper-snapper.' A nice whipper-snapper, to slash Bogun in this fashion! Bogun is gone; no trace, no ashes of him,--slain to death for the ages of ages; amen!"

Here Zagloba began to hug and kiss Volodyovski, and Pan Michael was moved to tears as if sorry for Bogun. At last, however, he freed himself from Zagloba's embraces and said: "We were not present at his death, and he is hard to kill. Suppose he recovers?"

"Oh, in God's name, what are you talking about?" said Zagloba. "I should be ready to go to-morrow to Lipki and arrange the nicest funeral for him, just after his death."

"Why should you go? You wouldn't finish a wounded man. After the sabre, whoever does not yield his breath at once is likely to pull through. A sabre is not a bullet."

"He cannot recover. He was already in the death-agony when we left. No chance of recovery! I examined his wounds myself. Let him rest, for you cut him open like a hare. We must go to Skshetuski at once and comfort him, or he may die of gnawing grief."

"Or he will become a monk; he told me so himself."

"What wonder? I should do the same in his place. I do not know a more honorable knight, and a more unhappy one I do not know. The Lord visits him grievously."

"Leave off," said Volodyovski, a little drunk, "for I am not able to stop my tears."

"Neither am I," added Zagloba; "such an honorable knight, and such a soldier! But the princess--you do not know her; such a darling!"

Here Zagloba began to howl in a low bass, for he really loved the princess; and Pan Michael accompanied him in a higher key, and they drank wine mixed with tears. Then, dropping their heads on their breasts, they sat for a time gloomily, till Zagloba struck his fist on the table.

"Pan Michael, why do we weep? Bogun is killed!"

"True," said Volodyovski.

"We ought rather to rejoice. We are fools now if we don't find her."

"Let us go," said Volodyovski, rising.

"Let us drink," corrected Zagloba. "God grant us to hold their children at the christening, and all because we slew Bogun."

"Served him right!" finished Volodyovski, not noticing that Zagloba was already sharing with him the merit of killing Bogun.

CHAPTER XLVII.

At last "Te Deum laudamus" was heard in the cathedral of Warsaw, and the king was enthroned; cannon thundered, bells were tolled, and confidence began to enter all hearts. The interregnum had passed,--a time of storms and unrest the more terrible for the Commonwealth that it happened in a period of universal disaster. Those who had been trembling at the thought of threatening dangers, now that the election had passed with unusual harmony, drew a deep breath. It seemed to many that the unparalleled civil war was over forever, and that the newly chosen king had but to pronounce sentence on the guilty. Indeed, this hope was supported by the bearing of Hmelnitski himself. The Cossacks at Zamost, while storming the castle wildly, nevertheless spoke loudly in favor of Yan Kazimir. Hmelnitski sent through the priest Huntsel Mokrski letters full of loyalty, and through other envoys obedient requests for favor to himself and the Zaporojian army. It was known also that the king, in accord with the policy of the chancellor, desired to make considerable concessions to the Cossacks. As before the catastrophe of Pilavtsi war was in every mouth, so was peace now. It was hoped that after so many disasters the Commonwealth would recover, and under the new reign would be healed from all its wounds. At last Snyarovski went with a letter of the king to Hmelnitski; and soon the joyful news was circulated that the Cossacks would withdraw from Zamost to the Ukraine, where they would wait quietly the commands of the king and the commission which was to be occupied with examining the wrongs inflicted on them. It seemed that after the storm a seven-colored rainbow hung over the land, heralding calm and fair weather.

There were not lacking, it is true, unfavorable prophecies and prognostications, but in view of the favoring reality no weight was attached to them. The king went to Chenstokhova to thank first of all the Divine Protectress for the election and to give himself to her further care, and then to Cracow to the coronation. The dignitaries followed him: Warsaw was deserted; only those exiles from Russia remained who did not dare yet to return to their ruined fortunes, or who had nothing with which to return.

Prince Yeremi, as senator of the Commonwealth, had to go with the king; but Volodyovski and Zagloba, at the head of one squadron of dragoons, went with hurried marches to Zamost to give Skshetuski the happy tidings of what had happened to Bogun, and then to go with him in search of the princess.

Zagloba left Warsaw not without a certain sadness; for in that immeasurable concourse of nobles, in the uproar of election, in the endless revelry and the brawls raised in company with Volodyovski, he was as happy as a fish in the sea. But he consoled himself with the thought that he was returning to active life, to the search for adventures, and stratagems of which he promised not to spare himself; and besides he had his own opinion about the dangers of the capital, which he laid bare to Volodyovski in the following manner:--

"It is true, Pan Michael," said he, "that we did great things in Warsaw; but God keep us from a longer visit! For I tell you we should become effeminate, like that famous Carthaginian whom the sweetness of the air of Capua weakened to the core. But worst of all are women; they bring every man to destruction. Just think, there is nothing more traitorous than woman! A man grows old, but still she attracts him."

"But you might give us peace," said Volodyovski.

"I repeat this to myself often, it being time for me to grow sedate; but I am too hot-blooded yet. You are more phlegmatic; in me, however, is passion itself. But a truce to this; we will begin another life now. More than once have I grieved for war of late. We have an excellent squadron; and around Zamost there are bands of marauders with whom we will amuse ourselves while going after the princess. We shall see Skshetuski too, and that giant, that Lithuanian stork, that hop-pole, Pan Longin, and we have not seen him for many a day."

"You are longing for him, and when you see him you give him no peace."

"Because when he talks it is as if your horse were moving his tail, and he stretches every word as a shoemaker does leather; with him everything went into strength instead of brains. When he takes any one by the shoulders he pushes the ribs through the skin; still there is not a child in the Commonwealth who could not outwit him. How is it possible that a man with such a fortune should be so dull?"

"Has he in truth such a fortune?"

"He? When I made his acquaintance he had a belt so stuffed that he could not gird himself with it, and he carried it around like a smoked sausage. You could flourish it like a staff and it would not bend. He told me himself how many villages he has,--Myshekishki, Psikishki, Pigvishki, Sirutsiani, Tsiaputsiani, Kapustsiani (or rather, Kapustsiana,[17] but adding *glowa*), Baltupye-- Who could remember all these heathen names? About half the district belongs to him! It's a great family, the Podbipienta--among soup-eaters."

"Haven't you exaggerated a little about these estates?"

"I do not exaggerate, for I repeat what I heard from him, and during his life he has never told a lie,--he is in fact too stupid for that."

"Well, then, Anusia will be a lady with a full mouth. But as to your dictum that he is stupid, I cannot agree to that in any way. He is a solid man, and so clear-headed that no one can give better counsel. But that he is not a rogue,--that is not difficult. The Lord God did not give every one such a nimble tongue as yours. There is no denying that he is a great knight and a man of the utmost honor. As proof of this you love him and are glad to see him."

"Oh, the punishment of God on him!" muttered Zagloba; "I am glad only because I can tease him with Anusia."

"I don't advise you to do that, for it is a dangerous thing. You might plaster a wound with him, but in the case of Anusia he would surely lose patience."

"Let him lose it. I'll clip his ears for him as I did for Pan Dunchevski."

"Oh, spare us! I should not like to have you try him as an enemy."

"Well, well, let me only see him."

This wish of Zagloba was fulfilled sooner than he expected. When they arrived at Konskovoli, Volodyovski determined to stay for the night, as the horses were terribly road-weary. Who can describe the astonishment of the two friends when on entering the dark anteroom of the inn they recognized Pan Podbipienta in the first noble they met!

"Oh! how are you? How long, how long!" cried Zagloba; "and the Cossacks did not cut you up in Zamost?"

Pan Podbipienta took them one after the other by the shoulders, and kissed them on the cheeks. "And have we met?" he repeated with joy.

"Where are you going?" asked Volodyovski.

"To Warsaw,--to the prince."

"The prince is not in Warsaw; he went to Cracow with the king, before whom he has to carry the globe at the coronation."

"But Pan Weyher sent me to Warsaw with a letter inquiring where the prince's regiments are to go, for God be thanked they are required no longer in Zamost."

"Then you need go no farther, for we are carrying the orders."

Pan Longin frowned; for from his soul he wished to get to the prince, to see the court, and especially one little person at that court. Zagloba began to mutter significantly to Volodyovski.

"Then I'll go to Cracow," said the Lithuanian, after a moment's thought. "I was ordered to deliver the letter, and I will deliver it."

"Let's go and order them to warm up some beer," said Zagloba.

"And where are you going?" asked Pan Longin.

"To Zamost, to Skshetuski."

"He is not in Zamost."

"Now, old woman, you've got a cake. Where is he?"

"Somewhere around Khoroschina; he is breaking up disorderly bands. Hmelnitski retreated; but his colonels are burning, robbing, and slaying along the road. The starosta of Valets has ordered Pan Jakob Rogovski to disperse them."

"And is Skshetuski with him too?"

"Yes, but they act separately; for there is great rivalry between them, of which I will tell you later on."

Meanwhile they entered the room. Zagloba ordered three gallons of warmed beer; then approaching the table at which Volodyovski had already sat down with Pan Longin, he said,--

"You do not know, Pan Podbipienta, the greatest and the happiest news,--that I and Pan Michael have slain Bogun."

The Lithuanian rose from the bench. "My own brothers, can this be?"

"As you see us here alive."

"And both of you killed him?"

"We did."

"That is news. O God, God!" said the Lithuanian, clapping his hands. "And you say that both of you--how both?"

"For I, to begin with, by stratagem brought him to this, that he challenged us,--do you understand me? Then Pan Michael met him first, and cut him up, I tell you, like a sucking pig at Easter,--opened him like a roast capon; do you understand?"

"Then you were not the second combatant?"

"But look here!" said Zagloba. "I see that you must have lost blood, and that your mind totters from weakness. Did you understand that I would fight a duel with a corpse, or that I would kill a prostrate man?"

"But you said that you had slain him together."

Zagloba shrugged his shoulders. "Holy patience with such a man! Pan Michael didn't Bogun challenge both of us?"

"He did."

"Do you understand now?"

"Well, let it be so," answered Pan Longin. "Skshetuski was looking for Bogun around Zamost; but he was no longer there."

"How was that,--Skshetuski was looking for him?"

"I must, I see, tell you everything from the beginning exactly as it happened," said Pan Longin. "We remained, as you know, in Zamost, and you went to Warsaw. We did not wait for the Cossacks very long. They came in impenetrable clouds from Lvoff, so that you could not take them all in with the eye. But our prince had supplied Zamost, so that they might have stood two years in front of it. We thought that they wouldn't storm it at all, and great was the grief among us on that account; for each had promised himself delight from their defeats, and since there were Tartars among them I too hoped that God would give me my three heads--"

"Beg of him one, but a good one," interrupted Zagloba.

"You are always the same; it is disgusting to hear you," said the Lithuanian. "We thought they wouldn't storm; they, however, as if mad in their stubbornness, went at once to building machines, and then for the storming! It transpired later that Hmelnitski himself was unwilling; but Chernota, their camp commander, began to assail him, and to say that he was afraid and wanted to fraternize with the Poles. Hmelnitski therefore permitted it, and sent Chernota first. What followed, brothers, I will not tell you. The light could not be seen from smoke and fire. They went on boldly at first, filled the ditch, mounted the walls; but we warmed them up so that they ran away from the walls and their own machines; then we rushed out after them in three squadrons, and cut them up like cattle."

Volodyovski rubbed his hands. "Oh, sorry am I not to have been at that feast!" cried he, in ecstasy.

"And I should have been of service there," said Zagloba, with calm confidence.

"There Skshetuski and Rogovski distinguished themselves most," continued the Lithuanian. "Both are grand knights; both are altogether hostile to each other. Rogovski was specially angry with Skshetuski, and beyond doubt would have sought a quarrel if Pan Weyher had not forbidden duels on pain of death. We didn't understand at first what the trouble was with Rogovski till it came out at last that he was a relative of Pan Lashch, whom the prince, as you remember, excluded from the camp for Skshetuski's sake; hence the malice in Rogovski against the prince, against us all, and especially against Skshetuski; hence the rivalry between them which covered both in the siege with great glory, for each tried to surpass the other. Both were first on the walls and in the sallies, till at last Hmelnitski got tired of storming, and began a regular siege, not neglecting meanwhile stratagems which might enable him to capture the place."

"He confides as much or more in cunning," said Zagloba.

"He is a madman and ignorant besides," continued Podbipienta. "Thinking Pan Weyher a German,--it is evident he hadn't heard of the voevodas of Pomorye of that name,--he wrote a letter wishing to persuade the starosta to treason as a foreigner and a mercenary. Then Pan Weyher wrote to him, explaining how everything was and how vainly he had approached him with his attempt. The better to show his importance, the starosta wished to send this letter through some person more important than a trumpeter; and as no officers volunteered, since it was like going to destruction to venture among such wild beasts, and some had scruples about their rank, therefore I undertook it. And now listen, for the most interesting part begins here."

"We are listening attentively," said the two friends.

"I went then, and found the hetman drunk. He received me angrily. Especially after he had read the letter, he threatened with his baton; and I, commending my soul humbly to God, thought thus to myself: 'If he touches me, I'll smash his head with my fist.' What was to be done, dear brothers,--what?"

"It was honorable on your part to have those thoughts," said Zagloba, with emotion.

"But the colonels pacified him and barred the road to me against him," said Pan Longin; "and more than all a young man, so bold that he took him by the waist and drew him away, saying, 'Don't go, father, you have been drinking.' I looked to see who was defending me, and wondered at his boldness and intimacy with Hmelnitski, till I saw that he was Bogun."

"Bogun!" cried Volodyovski and Zagloba.

"Yes, I knew him, for I made his acquaintance in Rozlogi. I listened. 'That is an acquaintance of mine,' said he to Hmelnitski. And Hmelnitski, since decision with drinking men is sudden, answered, 'If he is thy acquaintance, son, then give him fifty thalers, and I will give him an answer.' He gave me the answer; and as to the thalers, not to anger the beast, I told him to put them away for the haiduks, for it was not the custom among officers to take presents. He conducted me politely enough to the door; but I had scarcely come out when Bogun followed me. 'We met in Rozlogi,' said he. 'Yes,' I answer, 'but I did not expect, brother, to see you in this camp.' 'Not my own will, but misfortune, drove me here,' said he. In the conversation I told him that it was we who had defeated him beyond Yarmolintsi. 'I did not know with whom I had to do,' he answered; 'I was cut in the hand, and my men were good for nothing, for they thought that Prince Yeremi himself was beating them.' 'And we did not know,' said I; 'for if Pan Skshetuski had known that you were there, then one of you would not be living now.'"

"That is very certain; but what did he say then?" asked Volodyovski.

"He changed greatly, and turned the conversation. He told me how Krívonos had sent him with letters to Hmelnitski at Lvoff in order to get a little rest, and Hmelnitski wouldn't send him back, for he thought to employ him in other missions, since he was a man of presence. At last he asked, 'Where is Pan Skshetuski?' and when I answered, 'He is in Zamost,' he said, 'Zamost? Then we may meet;' and with that I bade him farewell."

"I think now that Hmelnitski sent him immediately afterward to Warsaw," said Zagloba.

"True, but wait! I returned then to the fortress, and made a report of my mission to Weyher. It was already late at night. Next day a new storm, more furious than the first. I had no time to see Skshetuski till the third day. I told him that I had seen Bogun and spoken to him. There were many officers present, and with them Rogovski. Hearing this, he said with a taunt: 'I know it is a question of a woman; but if you are such a knight as report says, now you have Bogun, call him out, and you may be sure that that fighter will not refuse you. We shall have a splendid view from the walls. But there is more talk of you Vishnyevetski men than you deserve.' Skshetuski looked at Rogovski as if he would cut him off his feet. 'Is that your advice?' asked he. 'Very good! But I don't know whether you who criticise our value would have the daring to go among the mob and challenge Bogun for me.' 'The daring I have, but I am neither groomsman nor brother to you, and I will not go.' Then others, with laughter against Rogovski, said: 'Oh, you are small now; but when it was a question of another man's skin you were big!' Then Rogovski as an ambitious fellow got his blood up. Next day he went with a challenge, but couldn't find Bogun. We didn't believe his story at first, but now after what you have told me I see that it was true. Hmelnitski must have sent Bogun away really, and you killed him."

"That was it," said Volodyovski.

"Tell us now," said Zagloba, "where to find Skshetuski, for we must find him so as to go for the princess immediately."

"You will find him easily beyond Zamost, for he is heard of there. He and Rogovski, tossing from one to the other the forces of Kalina, the Cossack colonel, destroyed them. Later Skshetuski alone broke up Tartar parties, twice defeated Burlai, and dispersed a number of bands."

"Does Hmelnitski permit that?"

"Hmelnitski disavows them, and says that they plunder in spite of his orders; if he didn't do this, no one would believe in his loyalty and obedience to the king."

"The beer is very bad in this Konskovoli," remarked Zagloba.

"Beyond Lublin you will pass through a ravaged country," continued the Lithuanian; "for the advanced parties reached that place, and the Tartars took captives everywhere, and God only knows how many they seized around Zamost and Grubeshovo. Skshetuski has already sent several thousand rescued prisoners to the fortress. He is working with all his might, regardless of health."

Here Pan Longin sighed, bowed his head in thought, and after a while continued: "And I thought: 'God in his supreme mercy will undoubtedly comfort Skshetuski, and give him that in which he sees his happiness; for great are that man's services.' In these times of corruption and covetousness, when every one is thinking of self alone, he has forgotten himself. He might have obtained permission long ago from the prince, and gone to seek the princess; but instead of that, since this paroxysm has come on the country he has not left his duty for a moment, continuing his unceasing labor with torment in his heart."

"He has a Roman soul; this cannot be denied," said Zagloba.

"We should take example from him."

"Especially you, Pan Longin, who have gone to the war, not to serve your country, but to find three heads."

"God is looking into my soul," said Podbipienta, raising his eyes to heaven.

"God has rewarded Skshetuski with the death of Bogun," said Zagloba, "and with this, that he has given a moment of peace to the Commonwealth; for now the time has come for him to seek what he lost."

"You will go with him?" asked the Lithuanian.

"And you?"

"I should be glad to go; but what will happen to the letters I am taking,--one from the starosta of Valets to the king, another to the prince, and a third from Skshetuski to the prince, with a request for leave?"

"We are taking leave to him."

"Yes, but how can I avoid delivering the letters?"

"You must go to Cracow, it cannot be otherwise; however, I tell you sincerely I should be glad, in this quest after the princess, to have such fists as yours behind my shoulders; but for any other purpose you are useless. There dissimulation will be necessary, and complete disguise in Cossack dress, to appear as peasants; but you are so remarkable with your stature that every one would ask, 'Who is that tall booby? Where did such a Cossack as that come from?' Besides, you don't know their language well. No, no! you go to Cracow, and we will help ourselves somehow."

"That is what I think too," said Volodyovski.

"Surely it must be so," answered Podbipienta. "May the merciful God bless and aid you! And do you know where she is hidden?"

"Bogun would not tell. We know only what I overheard when Bogun confined me in the stable, but that is enough."

"But how will you find her?"

"My head, my head!" said Zagloba. "I was in more difficult places than this. Now the question is only to find Skshetuski as quickly as possible."

"Inquire in Zamost. Pan Weyher must know, for he corresponds with him, and Skshetuski sends him captives. May God bless you!"

"And you too," said Zagloba. "When you are in Cracow, at the prince's, give our respects to Pan Kharlamp."

"Who is he?"

"A Lithuanian of extraordinary beauty, for whom all the maidens and ladies-in-waiting of the princess have lost their heads."

Pan Longin trembled. "My good friend, is this joking?"

"Farewell! Terribly bad beer in this Konskovoli!" concluded Zagloba, muttering at Volodyovski.

CHAPTER XLVIII.

So Pan Longin went to Cracow, his heart pierced with an arrow, and the cruel Zagloba with Volodyovski to Zamost, where they remained only one day; for the commandant informed them that he had received no news for a long time from Skshetuski, and thought the regiments which had set out under Skshetuski would go to Zbaraj to protect those regions from disorderly bands. This was the more likely since Zbaraj, being the property of the Vishnyevetskis, was specially exposed to the attacks of the mortal enemies of the prince. There lay therefore before Volodyovski and Zagloba a road long and difficult enough; but since they were going after the princess, they were obliged to pass it; therefore it was all one to them whether they should enter on it earlier or later, and they moved without delay, halting only to rest, or disperse robber bands wandering here and there.

They went through a country so ruined that frequently for whole days they did not meet a living soul. Hamlets lay in ashes, villages were burned and empty, the people either killed or gathered into captivity. They saw only corpses along the road, the skeletons of houses, of Polish and Russian churches, the unburnt remnants of villages and cottages, dogs howling on burnt ruins. Whoever had survived the Tartar-Cossack passage hid in the depth of the forest, and was freezing from cold or dying of hunger, not daring yet to leave the forest, not believing that misfortune could have passed so soon. Volodyovski was obliged to feed the horses of his squadron with the bark of trees or with half-burnt grain taken from the ruins of former granaries. But they advanced quickly, supporting themselves mainly by supplies taken from bands of robbers. It was already the end of November; and inasmuch as the preceding winter had passed, to the greatest wonder of people, without snow, frost, and ice, so that the whole order of Nature seemed reversed by it, by so much did the present one promise to be of more than usual rigor. The ground had stiffened, snow was on the fields, river-banks were bordered each morning with a transparent, glassy shell. The weather was dry; the pale sunbeams warmed the world but feebly in the midday hours. Red twilight of morning and evening flamed in the sky,--an infallible herald of an early and stern winter.

After war and hunger a third enemy of wretched humanity had to appear,--frost; and still people looked for it with desire because more surely than all negotiations was it a restrainer of war. Volodyovski, as a man of experience and knowing the Ukraine through and through, was full of hope that the expedition for the princess would take place without fail; for the chief obstacle, war, would not soon hinder it.

"I do not believe in the sincerity of Hmelnitski, that out of love for the king he withdrew to the Ukraine; for he is a cunning fox! He knows that when the Cossacks cannot intrench themselves they are useless; for in the open field, though five times the number, they cannot stand against our squadrons. They will go to winter quarters now, and send their flocks to the snow-fields; the Tartars also need to take home their captives, and if the winter is severe there will be peace till next grass."

"Perhaps longer, for still they respect the king. But we do not need so much time. With God's help we shall celebrate Skshetuski's wedding at the carnival."

"If we don't miss him this time, for that would be a new vexation."

"There are three squadrons with him, therefore it is not like hunting for a kernel of grain in a pile of chaff. Perhaps we shall come up with him yet at Zbaraj, if he is occupied in the neighborhood of robber bands."

"We cannot come up with him, but we ought to find some news of him along the road," answered Volodyovski.

Still it was difficult to get news. The peasants had seen passing squadrons here and there; they had heard of their battles with robbers, but did not know whose squadrons they were,--they might be Rogovski's as well as Skshetuski's; therefore the two friends learned nothing certain. But other news flew to their ears of great disasters to the Cossacks from the Lithuanian armies. It circled around in the form of rumors on the eve of Volodyovski's departure from Warsaw, but it was doubted then; now it flew through the whole country with great detail as an undoubted truth. The defeats inflicted by Hmelnitski on the armies of the Crown the Lithuanian armies had avenged with defeat. Polksenjits, an old leader and experienced, had yielded his head, and the wild Nebaba; and more powerful than both, Krechovski, who raised himself not to starostaships and voevodaships, nor to dignities and offices, but to the empaling stake in the ranks of insurgents. It seemed as if some marvellous Nemesis had wished to take vengeance on him for the German blood spilled on the Dnieper,--the blood of Flick and Werner, since he fell into the hands of a German regiment of Radzivil, and though shot and severely wounded was immediately empaled on a stake, on which the unfortunate quivered a whole day before he breathed out his gloomy soul. Such was the end of him who by his bravery and military skill might have become a second Stephan Hmeletski, but whom an overweening desire of wealth and dignities pushed upon the road of treason, perjury, and awful murders worthy of Krívonos himself.

With him, with Polksenjits and Nebaba, nearly twenty thousand Cossacks laid down their heads on the field of battle, or were drowned in the morasses of the Pripet; terror then flew like a whirlwind over the rich Ukraine, for it appeared to all that after the great triumphs--after Jóltiya Vodi, Korsún, Pilavtsi--the hour was coming for such defeats as the former rebellions had experienced at Solonitsa and Kuméiki. Hmelnitski himself, though at the summit of glory, though stronger than ever before, was frightened when he heard of the death of his "friend" Krechovski, and again he began to inquire of wizards about the future. They gave various prophecies,--they foretold great wars, victories, and defeats,--but they could not tell the hetman what would happen to himself.

The defeat of Krechovski and with it the winter made a prolonged peace more certain. The country began to heal, devastated villages to be populous, and hope entered slowly, gradually, into all weakened and terrified hearts. With that same hope our two friends after a long and difficult journey arrived safely at Zbaraj, and announcing themselves at the castle, went straightway to the commandant, in whom with no small astonishment they beheld Vershul.

"And where is Skshetuski?" asked Zagloba, after the first greetings.

"He is not here," answered Vershul.

"Then you have command over the garrison?"

"Yes. Skshetuski had, but he went out and gave me the garrison till his return."

"When did he promise to return?"

"He said nothing, for he didn't know himself, but he said at parting: 'If any one comes to me, tell him to wait for me here.'"

Zagloba and Volodyovski looked at each other.

"How long since he went away?" asked Volodyovski.

"Ten days."

"Pan Michael," said Zagloba, "let Pan Vershul give us supper, for men give poor counsel on an empty stomach. At supper we can talk."

"I serve you with my heart, for I was just about to sit down myself. Besides, Pan Volodyovski, as senior officer, takes command. I am with him, not he with me."

"Remain in command, Pan Kryshtof," said Volodyovski, "for you are older in years; besides I shall have to go on without doubt."

After a while supper was served. They took their places and ate. When Zagloba had quieted somewhat his first hunger with two plates of broth, he said to Vershul,--

"Can you imagine where Skshetuski has gone?"

Vershul ordered the attendant serving at the table to go out, and after a moment's reflection began,--

"I can imagine that for Skshetuski secrecy is important, therefore I did not speak before the servant. Pan Yan has taken advantage of a favorable time, for we are sure of peace till spring, and according to my calculation he has gone to seek the princess, who is in Bogun's hands."

"Bogun is no longer in the world," said Zagloba.

Zagloba related now for the third or fourth time everything as it was, for he told it always with delight. Vershul, like Pan Longin, could not wonder sufficiently at the event; at last he said,--

"Then it will be easier for Pan Yan."

"The question is, Will he find her? Did he take any men?"

"No, he went alone, with one Russian, a servant, and three horses."

"He acted wisely, for in that region the only help is in stratagem. To Kamenyets he might go with a small squadron perhaps; but in Ushitsi and Mogileff Cossacks are surely stationed, for there are good winter quarters in those places, and in Yampol, where their nest is, it is necessary to go either with a division or alone."

"And how do you know that he went specially in that direction?" asked Volodyovski.

"Because she is secreted beyond Yampol, and he knows it; but there are ravines, hollows, and reeds there so numerous that even for one knowing the place well, it is difficult to find the way, and what would it be for one not knowing? I used to go for horses to Yagorlik, and to lawsuits. I know all about the place. If we were together, perhaps we could succeed; but for him alone--I have doubts. I have doubts, unless some chance indicates the road to him, for he will not be able to make inquiries."

"Then did you wish to go with him?"

"Yes. But what shall we do now, Pan Michael? Follow him or not?"

"I rely on your prudence."

"H'm! He went ten days ago--we cannot come up with him; and besides he asked us to wait here. God knows too what road he took. Maybe through Ploskiroff and Bar along the old highway, and maybe through Kamenyets Podolsk. It is a hard question."

"Remember, besides," said Vershul, "that these are only suppositions. You are not sure that he went after the princess."

"That's it, that's it!" said Zagloba. "Perhaps he went merely to get informants somewhere, and then return to Zbaraj; for he knows that we were to go with him, and that he might expect us at this time, since it is the most favorable. This is a difficult question to settle."

"I should advise you to wait about ten days," said Vershul.

"Ten days are nothing; we should either wait or not wait at all."

"I think we should not wait; for what shall we lose if we move at once? If Skshetuski does not find the princess, God may favor us," said Volodyovski.

"You see, Pan Michael, we must not overlook anything in this case. You are still young and want adventures," said Zagloba; "but here is this danger: if he is looking for her by himself, and we look for her by ourselves, some suspicion will be easily roused in the people there. The Cossacks are cunning, and afraid that some one may find out their plans. They may have a secret understanding with the Pasha of the boundary near Khotím, or with the Tartars beyond the Dniester about a future war,--who knows? They will be watchful of strangers, particularly of strangers inquiring the way. I know them. It is easy to betray yourself, and then what?"

"The greater the reason to go. Skshetuski may fall into some difficulty where help would be required."

"That is true too."

Zagloba fell into such deep thought that his temples quivered; at last he roused himself, and said: "Taking everything into consideration, it will be necessary to go."

Volodyovski drew a deep breath with satisfaction. "And when?"

"When we have rested about three days, so that body and soul may be fresh."

Next day the two friends began to make preparations for the road, when unexpectedly on the eve of their journey Tsiga, a young Cossack, Skshetuski's attendant, arrived with news and letters for Vershul. Hearing of this, Zagloba and Volodyovski hurried to the quarters of the commandant, and read the following:--

"I am in Kamenyets, to which the road through Satanoff is safe. I am going to Yampol with Armenian merchants whom Pan Bukovski found for me. They have Tartar and Cossack passes for a free journey to Akerman. We shall go through Ushitsi, Mogileff, and Yampol with silk stuffs, stopping at all places along the road wherever there are living people. God may aid me in finding what I seek. Tell my comrades, Volodyovski and Zagloba, to wait for me in Zbaraj if they have nothing else to do; for by this road which I travel it would be impossible to go in a larger company by reason of deep distrust in the minds of Cossacks who winter in Yampol on the Dniester as far as Yagorlik, where they keep their horses in the snow. What I cannot do alone we three could not do, and I can pass more readily for an Armenian. Thank them, Pan Kryshtof, from the heart's soul for their resolution, which I shall not forget while I live; but I was not able to wait, since every day was a torment to me, and I could not know whether they would come, and it is the best time now to go when all the merchants are travelling with goods. I send back my trusty attendant whom you will care for, as I have no need of him; but I am afraid of his youth, lest he might say something somewhere. Pan Bukovski vouches for these merchants; says they are honest, and I think they are, believing as I do that everything is in the hands of the high God, who if he wishes will show his mercy to us, and shorten our sufferings."

Zagloba finished the letter, and looked at his comrades; but they were silent, till at length Vershul said,--

"I knew he went there."

"And what are we to do?" asked Volodyovski.

"What?" said Zagloba, opening his arms, "We have nothing to go for. It is well that he is with merchants, for he can look in everywhere, and no one will wonder. In every country-house there is something to be bought, for half the Commonwealth has been plundered. It would be difficult for us, Pan Michael, to go beyond Yampol. Skshetuski is as black as a Wallachian, and can pass easily for an Armenian, but they would know you at once by your little oat-colored mustaches. In peasant disguise it would be equally difficult. There is no use for us there, I must confess, though I am sorry that we shall not put our hands to freeing that poor young lady. But we did a great service to Skshetuski when we killed Bogun; for if he were alive, then I would not guarantee the health of Pan Yan."

Volodyovski was very much dissatisfied. He had promised himself a journey full of adventures, and now there was left to him a long and tedious stay at Zbaraj. "We might go as far as Kamenyets."

"What should we do there, and on what should we live?" asked Zagloba. "It's all one to what walls we fasten like mushrooms. We must wait and wait, for such a journey may occupy Skshetuski long. While a man moves he is young [here Zagloba dropped his head in melancholy on his breast]; he grows old in inaction, but it is hard. Let him get on without us. To-morrow we will offer a solemn prayer for his success. We killed Bogun; that is the main thing. Give orders to have your horses unpacked, Pan Michael! We must wait."

In fact, on the morrow began for the two friends long and dreary days of waiting, to which neither drinking nor dice could lend variety, and they dragged on without end. Meanwhile a severe winter had begun. Snow covered the ramparts of Zbaraj, and the whole land, in a shroud three feet thick. Beasts and wild birds approached the dwellings of men. Day after day came the cawing of crows and ravens, in flocks without number. All December passed; then January and February. Of Skshetuski there was not a sound.

Volodyovski went to Tarnopol to seek adventures. Zagloba was gloomy, and insisted that he was growing old.

CHAPTER XLIX.

The commissioners sent by the Commonwealth to negotiate with Hmelnitski forced their way through the greatest difficulties to Novoselki, and there halted, waiting an answer from the victorious hetman, who was stopping at that time in Chigirin. They were gloomy and depressed; for death had threatened them continually during the whole journey, and difficulties increased at every step. Day and night they were surrounded by crowds of the populace, made wild to the last degree by slaughter and war, and who were howling for the death of the commissioners. From time to time they met bands, commanded by no one, formed of robbers or wild herdsmen, without the least idea of the laws of nations, but hungry for blood and plunder. The commissioners had, it is true, a hundred horse as attendants, led by Pan Bryshovski; besides this, Hmelnitski himself, foreseeing what might meet them, sent Colonel Donyéts, with four hundred Cossacks; but that escort might easily prove inadequate, for the throngs of wild men were increasing in number each hour, and assuming a more threatening attitude. If one of the convoy or the attendants separated, even for a moment, from the company, he perished without a trace. They were like a handful of travellers surrounded by a pack of hungry wolves; and thus passed for them whole days, weeks, till at the stopping-place in Novoselki it appeared to all that their last hour had come. The convoy of dragoons and the escort of Donyéts, from evening on, fought a regular battle for the life of the commissioners, who, repeating the prayers for the dying, committed their souls to God. The Carmelite Lentovski gave them absolution, one after another, while outside the window with the blowing of the wind came terrible shouts, the report of shots, hellish laughter, the clatter of scythes, and shouts of "Death to them!" and demands for the head of the voevoda Kisel, who was the main object of their rage.

It was an awful night, and long, for it was a winter night. Kisel rested his head on his hands, and sat motionless for many hours. It was not death that he feared; for since he left Gushchi he was so exhausted, tortured, deprived of sleep, that he would have extended his hands with gladness to death; but endless despair was covering his soul. He as a Russian in blood and bone first took upon himself the rôle of pacifier in that unexampled war; he came forth everywhere, in the Senate and in the Diet, as the most ardent partisan of negotiations; he supported the policy of the chancellor and the primate; he condemned most powerfully Yeremi, and he did this in good faith, for the sake of the Cossacks and the Commonwealth; and he believed, with all his ardent spirit, that negotiations and compromises would smooth everything, would pacify, would unite; and just then, in that moment when he was bringing the baton to Hmelnitski and concessions to the Cossacks, he doubted all. He saw with his own eyes the vanity of his efforts; he saw beneath his feet a vacuum and a precipice.

"Do they want nothing but blood, do they care for no other freedom than the freedom of plunder and burning?" thought the voevoda in despair, and he stifled the groans which were tearing asunder his noble breast.

"The head of Kisel, the head of Kisel! Death to him!" was the answer of the crowds.

And the voevoda would have offered them as a willing gift that white and battered head, were it not for the remnant of his belief that it was necessary to give them and all the Cossacks something more,--rescue was immediately necessary for them and the Commonwealth. Let the future teach them to ask for the something more. And when he thought thus, a certain ray of hope and consolation lighted up for a moment that darkness which despair created in his mind, and the unfortunate old man said to himself that that mob was not the whole body of Cossacks,--not Hmelnitski and his colonels,--with whom negotiations would begin.

But can these negotiations be lasting while half a million of peasants stand under arms? Will they not melt at the first breath of spring, like the snows which at that moment covered the steppes? Here again came to the voevoda the words of Yeremi: "Kindness may be shown to the conquered alone." Here again his thoughts fell into darkness, and the precipice yawned beneath his feet.

Meantime midnight was passing. The shouting and shots had decreased in some degree; the whistle of the wind rose in their place, the yard was filled with a snowdrift; the wearied crowds had evidently begun to disperse to their houses; hope entered the hearts of the commissioners.

Voitsekh Miaskovski, a chamberlain from Lvoff, rose from the bench, listened at the window to the drifting of the snow, and said,--

"It seems to me that with God's favor we shall live till morning."

"Perhaps too Hmelnitski will send more assistance, for we shall not reach our journey's end with what we have now," said Pan Smyarovski.

Pan Zelenski, the cup-bearer from Bratslav, smiled bitterly: "Who would say that we are peace commissioners?"

"I have been an envoy more than once to the Tartars," said the ensign of Novgrodek, "but such a mission as this I have not seen in my life. The Commonwealth endures more contempt in our persons than at Korsún and Pilavtsi. I say, gentlemen, let us return, for there is no use in thinking of negotiations."

"Let us return," repeated as an echo Pan Bjozovski, the castellan of Kieff; "there can be no peace; let there be war!"

Kisel raised his lids and fixed his glassy eyes on the castellan. "Jóltiya Vodi, Korsún, Pilavtsi!" said he, in hollow tones.

He was silent, and after him all were silent. But Pan Kulchinski, the treasurer of Kieff, began to repeat the rosary in an audible voice; and Pan Kjetovski, master of the chase, seized his head with both hands, and repeated,--

"What times, what times! God have mercy upon us!"

The door opened, and Bryshovski, captain of the dragoons of the bishop of Poznania, commander of the convoy, entered the room.

"Serene voevoda," said he, "some Cossack wants to see the commissioners."

"Very well," answered Kisel; "has the crowd dispersed?"

"The people have gone away; they promised to return to-morrow."

"Did they press on much?"

"Terribly, but Donyéts' Cossacks killed a number of them. To-morrow they promise to burn us."

"Very well, let that Cossack enter."

After a while the door was opened, and a certain tall, black-bearded figure appeared at the threshold of the room.

"Who are you?" asked Kisel.

"Yan Skshetuski, colonel of hussars of Prince Vishnyevetski, voevoda of Rus."

The castellan Bjozovski, Pan Kulchinski, and the master of the chase Pan Kjetovski sprang from their seats. All of them had served the past year under the prince at Makhnovka and Konstantinoff, and knew Skshetuski perfectly. Kjetovski was even related to him.

"Is it true, is it true? Is this Pan Skshetuski?" repeated they.

"What are you doing here, and how did you reach us?" asked Kjetovski, taking him by the shoulder.

"In peasant's disguise, as you see," said Skshetuski.

"This," cried Bjozovski to Kisel, "is the foremost knight in the army of the voevoda of Rus; he is famous throughout the whole army."

"I greet him with thankful heart," said Kisel, "and I see that he must be a man of great resolution, since he has forced his way to us." Then to Skshetuski he said: "What do you wish of us?"

"That you permit me to go with you."

"You are crawling into the jaws of the dragon, but if such is your wish we cannot oppose it."

Skshetuski bowed in silence.

Kisel looked at him with astonishment. The severe face of the young knight, with its expression of dignity and suffering, struck him. "Tell me," said he, "what causes drive you to this hell, to which no one comes of his own accord?"

"Misfortune, serene voevoda."

"I have made a needless inquiry," said Kisel. "You must have lost some of your relatives for whom you are looking?"

"I have."

"Was it long since?"

"Last spring."

"How is that, and you start only now on the search? Why, it is nearly a year! What were you doing in the mean while?"

"I was fighting under the voevoda of Rus."

"Would not such a true man as he give you leave of absence?"

"I did not wish it myself."

Kisel looked again at the young knight, and then followed a silence, interrupted by the castellan of Kieff.

"The misfortunes of this knight are known to all of us who served with the prince. We shed more than one tear over them, and it is the more praiseworthy on his part that he preferred to serve his country while the war lasted instead of seeking his own good. This is a rare example in these times of corruption."

"If it shall appear that my word has any weight with Hmelnitski, then believe me I shall not spare it in your cause," said Kisel.

Skshetuski bowed a second time.

"Go now and sleep," said the voevoda, kindly; "for you must be wearied in no small degree, like all of us who have not had a moment's rest."

"I will take him to my quarters, for he is my relative," said Kjetovski.

"Let us all go to rest; who knows whether we shall sleep to-morrow night?" said Bjozovski.

"Maybe an eternal sleep," concluded the voevoda. Then he went to the small room, at the door of which his attendant was waiting, and afterward the others separated.

Kjetovski took Skshetuski to his quarters, which were some houses distant. His attendant preceded them with a lantern.

"What a dark night, and it howls louder every moment," said Kjetovski. "Oh, Pan Yan, what a day we have passed! I thought the last judgment had come. The mob almost put the knife to our throats. Bjozovski's arms grew weak, and we had already begun prayers for the dying."

"I was in the crowd," said Skshetuski. "To-morrow evening they expect a new band of robbers to whom they sent word about you. We must leave here absolutely. But are you going to Kieff?"

"That depends on the answer of Hmelnitski, to whom Prince Chetvertinski has gone. Here are my quarters; come in, I pray you, Pan Yan! I have ordered some wine to be heated, and we will strengthen ourselves before sleep."

They entered the room, in which a big fire was burning in the chimney. Steaming wine was on the table already. Skshetuski seized a glass eagerly.

"I've had nothing between my lips since yesterday," said he.

"You are terribly emaciated. It is clear that sorrow and toil have been gnawing you. But tell me about yourself, for I know of your affair. You think then of seeking the princess there among them?"

"Either her or death," answered the knight.

"You will more easily find death. How do you know that she may be there?"

"Because I have looked for her elsewhere."

"Where?"

"Along the Dniester as far as Yagorlik. I went with Armenian merchants, for there were indications that she was secreted there; I went everywhere, and now I am going to Kieff, since Bogun was to take her there."

Scarcely had the colonel mentioned the name of Bogun when the master of the chase seized himself by the head. "As God lives!" he cried, "I have not told you the most important of all. I heard that Bogun is killed."

Skshetuski grew pale. "How is that? Who told you?"

"That noble who saved the princess once, and who showed such bravery at Konstantinoff, told me. I met him when I was going to Zamost. We were passing on the road. I merely inquired for the news, and he answered me that Bogun was killed. I asked: 'Who killed him?' 'I,' said he. Then we parted."

The flame which had flashed in the face of Skshetuski was suddenly quenched. "That noble!" said he; "it is impossible to believe him. No, no, he couldn't be in a condition to kill Bogun."

"And didn't you see him, Pan Yan, for I remember too that he told me he was going to you at Zamost?"

"I did not wait for him at Zamost. He must be now at Zbaraj. I was in a hurry to overtake the commission. I did not return from Kamenyets to Zbaraj, and I did not see him. God alone knows whether even that is true which he told me about her, which he as it were overheard while captive with Bogun,--that Bogun had hidden her beyond Yampol, and then intended to take her to Kieff for marriage. Perhaps this too is untrue, like everything Zagloba said."

"Why do you go then to Kieff?"

Skshetuski was silent; for a moment nothing was heard but the whistling and howling of the wind.

"For," said Kjetovski, placing his finger on his forehead, "if Bogun is not killed, you may fall into his hands with ease."

"I go to find him," answered Skshetuski, in a hollow voice.

"Why?"

"Let God's judgment be passed between us."

"But he will not fight with you; he will simply bind you, take your life, or sell you to the Tartars."

"I am with the commissioners, in their suite."

"God grant that we bring our own lives out of this! What is the use of talking of the suite?"

"To whom life is heavy, the earth will be light."

"But have the fear of God before you, Yan! It is not a question here of death, for that avoids no man, but they can sell you to the Turkish galleys."

"Do you think that would be worse for me than the present?"

"I see that you are desperate, and trust not in the mercy of God."

"You are mistaken! I say that it is evil for me in the world, because it is; but long ago I was reconciled to the will of God. I do not beg, I do not groan, I do not curse. I do not beat my head against the wall; I merely desire to accomplish that which pertains to me while strength and life remain."

"But grief is devouring you like poison."

"God gave grief to devour, and he will send the cure when he wishes."

"I have no answer to such an argument," said Kjetovski. "In God is the only salvation; in him hope for us and the whole Commonwealth. The king went to Chenstokhova. He may obtain something from the Most Holy Lady; otherwise we shall all perish."

Silence followed, and from outside the window came only the constant "Who's there?" of the dragoons.

"True, true," said Kjetovski. "We all belong more to the dead than the living. People have forgotten to smile in this Commonwealth; they only groan like that wind in the chimney. I too have believed that happier times would come, till I went on this journey with others; but now I see that that was a barren hope. Ruin, war, hunger, murder, and nothing more,--nothing more."

Skshetuski was silent; the blaze of the fire lighted his stern, emaciated face. Finally he raised his head and said with a voice of dignity,--

"That is all temporal, which passes away, vanishes, and leaves nothing behind."

"You speak like a monk," said Kjetovski.

Skshetuski made no answer; the wind only groaned each moment move sadly in the chimney.

CHAPTER L.

Next morning early the commissioners left Novoselki, and with them Skshetuski; but that was a tearful journey, in which at every stopping-place, in every village, they were threatened with death, and met with contempt, which was worse than death,--worse specially in this, that the commissioners bore in their own persons the dignity and majesty of the Commonwealth. Pan Kisel grew ill, so that at every lodging-place he was borne from the sleigh to the house. The chamberlain of Lvoff wept over his own disgrace and that of the country. Captain Bryshovski fell ill also from sleeplessness and toil. Pan Yan therefore took his place, and led on farther that hapless suite amidst the pressure of crowds, insults, threats, skirmishes, and battles.

At Bélgorod it seemed to the commissioners again that their last hour had come. The crowd had beaten the sick Bryshovski, were killing Pan Gnyazdovski; and only the arrival of the metropolitan for an interview with the voevoda put a stop to the intended slaughter. They did not wish to admit the commissioners into Kieff at all. Prince Chetvertinski returned, February 11, from Hmelnitski without an answer. The commissioners did not know what further to do or where to go. Their return was prevented by immense parties waiting only for the breaking of negotiations to kill the envoys. The mob became more and more insolent; the bridles of the dragoons' horses were seized, and the road stopped; stones, pieces of ice, and frozen lumps of snow were thrown into the sleigh of the voevoda. At Gvozdova, Skshetuski and Donyéts had to fight a bloody battle in which they dispersed several hundred of the mob. The ensign of Novgrodek and Pan Smyarovski went with a new argument to persuade Hmelnitski to come to meet the commissioners at Kieff, but the voevoda had little hope that they would live to reach him. Meanwhile the commissioners in Khvastovo were forced to look with folded arms on the crowds killing prisoners of both sexes and of every age. Some were drowned through holes in the ice, some were drenched with water poured over them in the frost, others stabbed with forks or whittled to death with knives. Eighteen of such days passed before at last the answer came from Hmelnitski that he would not go to Kieff, but was waiting in Pereyasláv for the voevoda and the commissioners.

When they had crossed the Dnieper at Trypole and reached Voronkovo in the night, from which place it was only thirty miles to Pereyasláv, the unfortunate commissioners drew a breath of relief, thinking that their torment was over. Hmelnitski went out two miles and a half to meet them, wishing to show honor to the royal embassy, but how changed from those days in which he put himself forward as an injured man,--"quantum mutatus ab illo!" as Kisel justly wrote of him. He rode forth with a suite of horsemen, with his colonels and essauls, with martial music, under the standard, bunchuk, and crimson banner, like a sovereign prince.

The commissioners with their retinue halted at once; and Hmelnitski, riding up to the front sleigh, in which sat the voevoda, looked for a while at his venerable face, then raised his cap slightly and said,--

"With the forehead to you, Commissioners of the king, and to you, Voevoda. It had been better to commence treating with me long ago, when I was less and did not know my own power; but because the king has sent you to me, I receive you with thankful heart in my own land."

"Greetings to you, Hetman!" answered Kisel. "His Majesty the King has sent us to present his favor and mete out justice."

"I am thankful for the favor; but justice I have already meted out with this [and here he struck upon his sabre] on your necks, and I will mete out more of it if you do not give me satisfaction."

"You do not greet us very affably, Pan Hetman of the Zaporojians,--us, the envoys of the king."

"I will not speak in the cold; there will be a better time for that," replied Hmelnitski, dryly. "Let me into your sleigh, Kisel, for I wish to show you honor and ride with you."

Then he dismounted and approached the sleigh. Kisel pushed himself to the right, leaving the left side vacant. Seeing this, Hmelnitski frowned and exclaimed: "Give me the right side!"

"I am a senator of the Commonwealth," replied Kisel.

"And what is a senator to me? Pan Pototski is the first senator and hetman of the Crown; I have him in fetters with others, and can empale him to-morrow, if I wish."

A blush appeared on the pale face of Kisel. "I represent the person of the king here!" said he.

Hmelnitski frowned still more, but restrained himself and sat on the left side, muttering: "Granted; he is king in Warsaw, but I am in Russia. I see that I have not trodden enough on your necks."

Kisel gave no answer, but raised his eyes to heaven. He had already a foretaste of that which waited him, and he thought justly at that time that if the road to Hmelnitski was a Calvary, to be envoy to him was a passion indeed.

The horses moved to the town, in which twenty cannon were thundering and all the bells tolling. Hmelnitski, as if fearing that the commissioners should consider these sounds as given out exclusively in their honor, said to the voevoda,--

"I receive in this manner not only you but other ambassadors who are sent to me."

And Hmelnitski spoke the truth, for in fact embassies were sent to him as to a reigning prince. Returning from Zamost under the influence of the election and the defeats inflicted by the Lithuanian forces, the hetman had not one half of this pride in his heart; but when Kieff went forth to meet him with torches and banners, when the academy greeted him "tamquam Moijsem, servatorem, salvatorem, liberatorem, populi de servitute lechica et bono omine Bogdan,--God-given;" when finally he was called "illustrissimus princeps,"--then, according to the words of a contemporary, "the beast was elated." He had a real sense of his power, and felt the ground under his feet, which had been wanting to him hitherto.

Foreign embassies were a silent recognition as well of his power as of his separateness; the uninterrupted friendship of the Tartars, purchased by the greater part of the booty gained, and by the ill-fated captives whom that leader of the people permitted to be taken from the people, promised support against every enemy; therefore Hmelnitski, who recognized at Zamost the suzerainty and will of the king, was at that time so settled in pride, convinced of his own power, of the disorder of the Commonwealth, the incompetence of its leaders, that he was ready to raise his hand against the king himself, dreaming in his gloomy soul, not of Cossack freedom nor the restoration of the former privileges of the Zaporojians, not of justice for himself, but of a separate lordship, of a princely crown and sceptre.

And he felt himself master of the Ukraine. The Zaporojians clung to him, for never under any man's command had they so wallowed in blood and booty. A people wild by nature rallied to him; for while the peasant of Mazovia or of Great Poland bore without a murmur that burden of power and oppression which in all Europe weighed upon the "descendants of Ham," the man of the Ukraine drew into himself with the air of the steppes a love of freedom as unbounded, wild, and vigorous as the steppes themselves. Could he wish to walk after the plough of a master when his gaze was lost in the fields of God, and not of a master; when beyond the Cataracts the Saitch called to him, "Leave your lord, and come to freedom!" when the stern Tartar taught him war, accustomed his eyes to conflagration and slaughter and his hands to weapons? Was it not pleasanter for him to frolic with Hmelnitski and "slay the lords" than to bend his proud back before a land steward?

Besides this, the people rallied to Hmelnitski, for whoever did not went into captivity. In Stamboul a prisoner was exchanged for ten arrows, and three for a bow seasoned by the fire,-- such was the number of them! The multitude indeed had no choice; and one song, wonderful for that time, has remained, which long afterward succeeding generations sang of that leader called a Moses,--"Oh, that the first bullet might not miss that Hmelnitski!"

Villages, towns, and hamlets disappeared; the country was turned into a desert and a ruin,--a wound which ages were not able to heal. But that leader and hetman did not see this, or did not wish to see it; for he never saw anything by reason of himself, and he grew and fattened on blood and fire. In his own monstrous self-love he was destroying his own people and his own country; and now he brings in those commissioners to Pereyasláv with the thunder of cannon and the tolling of bells, as a separate ruler, as a hospodar, as a prince!

The commissioners went into the den of the lion hanging their heads, and the remnant of hope was quenched in them. Meanwhile Skshetuski, riding behind the second rank of sleighs, examined carefully the faces of the colonels who had come with Hmelnitski, to find among them Bogun. After fruitless search on the Dniester to a point beyond Yagorlik, the plan had long since matured in the soul of Pan Yan, as the last and only method, to find Bogun and challenge him to a death-struggle. The unfortunate knight knew, it is true, that in such a venture Bogun might destroy him without a struggle or give him up to the Tartars; but he thought better of Bogun. He was aware of his courage and mad daring, and was almost sure that, having the choice, he would fight for the princess. Therefore he formed the plan to bind Bogun by an oath that in case of his death he would let Helena go. Of himself Skshetuski did not care; and supposing that Bogun would say, "If I die, she is neither for me nor for you," he was ready to agree to this and bind himself by oath, if he could only save her from the hands of the enemy. Let her seek peace in the cloister for the rest of her life. He would seek that peace first in war, and then if death did not come to him, would seek it under the habit, as did all suffering souls in that age. The way seemed to Skshetuski straight and clear; and since at Zamost the idea of a struggle with Bogun had been given, now that his search along the reeds of the Dniester was fruitless, that way seemed the only one. With this purpose he hurried from the Dniester in one journey, resting nowhere, hoping to find Bogun without fail either near Hmelnitski or in Kieff, especially since, according to what Zagloba had said in Yarmolintsi, the chief was to be married in Kieff with three hundred tapers.

But Skshetuski sought him in vain among the colonels. He found instead many old acquaintances of peace times,--such as Daidyalo, whom he had seen in Chigirin; Yashevski, who had been an envoy from the Saitch to the Prince; Yarosha, a former sotnik of the prince; Naókolopályets, Grusha, and many others. He determined then to ask them.

"We are old acquaintances," said Skshetuski, approaching Yashevski.

"I knew you in Lubni; you are one of Prince Yeremi's knights. We drank and frolicked together in Lubni. And what is your prince doing?"

"He is well."

"In spring he will not be well. He hasn't met Hmelnitski yet; but he will meet him, and will have to go to destruction alone."

"As God judges."

"God is good to our father Hmelnitski. Your prince will never return to his Tartar bank on the east of the Dnieper. Hmelnitski has many a Cossack, and what has your prince? He is a good soldier. And are you not in his service now?"

"I attend the commissioners."

"Well, I am glad; you are an old acquaintance."

"If you are glad, then do me a service, and I shall be thankful."

"What service?"

"Tell me where is Bogun, that famous ataman, formerly of the Pereyaslāv regiment, who must have a high office among you now."

"Silence!" answered Yashevski, threateningly. "It is your luck that we are old acquaintances and that I drank with you, otherwise I should stretch you on the snow with this whirlbat."

Skshetuski was astonished; but being a man of ready courage, he squeezed his baton and asked: "Are you mad?"

"I am not mad, nor do I wish to threaten you; but there is an order from Hmelnitski that if any of you, even one of the commissioners, should ask a question, to kill him on the spot. If I do not do this, another will; therefore I warn you out of good feeling."

"But I ask in my own private affair."

"Well, it is all one. Hmelnitski told us, the colonels, and commanded us to tell others: * 'If any one asks, even about wood for the stove, or ashes, kill him.' You tell this to your people."

"I thank you for good advice," said Skshetuski.

"You are the only one; I have warned you alone. I should be the first to stretch another Pole on the ground."

They were silent. The party had already reached the gates of the town. Both sides of the road and the street were swarming with the crowd and armed Cossacks, who out of regard for the presence of Hmelnitski did not dare to scatter curses and lumps of snow at the sleighs, but who looked frowningly at the commissioners, clinching their fists or grasping the hilts of their sabres.

Skshetuski, having formed his dragoons four deep, raised his head and rode haughtily and calmly through the broad street, not paying the least attention to the threatening looks of the multitude; in his soul he only thought how much cool blood, self-reliance, and Christian patience would be necessary for him to carry through what he had planned, and not sink at the first step in that sea of hatred.

CHAPTER LI.

On the following day the commissioners had long consultations among themselves, whether to deliver the gifts of the king to Hmelnitski immediately or to wait till he should show greater obedience and a certain compunction. They decided to win him by kindness and the favor of the king. The delivery of the gifts was decided upon therefore, and on the following day that solemn act was accomplished. From early morning bells were tolled and cannon fired. Hmelnitski waited for them before his residence, in the midst of his colonels, all the officers, and countless throngs of Cossacks and people; for he wished that all should see with what honor the king surrounded him. He took his seat upon a raised place under the standard and bunchuk, wearing a mantle of purple brocade lined with sable, having at his side ambassadors from neighboring peoples. With his hand on his side, and feet resting on a velvet cushion trimmed with gold, he waited for the commissioners.

In the throng of the assembled mob from moment to moment there escaped murmurs of gladness and flattery at the sight of that leader in whom this throng, valuing power above all things, saw the embodiment of that power. For only thus the imagination of the people could represent to itself its unconquerable champion,--the crusher of hetmans, dukes, nobles, and Poles in general, who up to his time had been clothed with the charm of invincibility. During that year of battle Hmelnitski had grown old somewhat, but had not bent; his gigantic shoulders always indicated power sufficient to overcome kingdoms or to found new ones; his enormous face, red from the abuse of drink, expressed unbending will, unrestrained pride, and an insolent confidence which gave him victories. Storm and anger were slumbering in the wrinkles of that face, and you could easily know that when they were roused men bent before their terrible breath like woods before a tempest. From his eyes, surrounded by a red border, impatience was shooting that the commissioners did not come quickly enough with the presents, and from his nostrils issued two rows of steam, like two pillars of smoke from the nostrils of Lucifer; and in that mist from his own lungs he sat, purple, gloomy, and proud, flanked by envoys, in the midst of his colonels, having around them a sea of the unclean mob.

At last the commissioners' party appeared. In front marched drummers beating their drums, and trumpeters with trumpets at their mouths and swollen cheeks, beating and blowing from the brass long sad sounds, as if at the funeral of the dignity and glory of the Commonwealth. After this orchestra Kjetovski bore the baton on a satin cushion; Kulchinski, treasurer of Kieff, a crimson banner with an eagle and an inscription; and next walked Kisel alone, tall, slender, with a white beard flowing over his breast, with pain on his aristocratic face and unfathomable suffering in his soul. A few steps behind the voevoda the rest of the commissioners dropped in, and the rear was brought up by Bryshovski's dragoons, under command of Pan Yan.

Kisel walked slowly; for at that moment he saw clearly that behind the torn tatters of negotiations, from under the pretext of offering the favor and forgiveness of the king, another naked, disgusting truth peered forth, which even the blind could see and the deaf could hear, for it shouted: "Thou, Kisel, art going not to offer favor; thou art going to beg for it, thou art going to buy it with that baton and banner; and thou goest on foot to the feet of that peasant leader, in the name of the whole Commonwealth,--thou a senator, a voevoda!" For this reason the soul was rent in the lord of Brusiloff, and he felt as mean as a worm, as lowly as dust; and in his ears the words of Yeremi were roaring: "Better for us not to live, than to live in captivity under peasants and trash." And what was he, Kisel, in comparison with that prince of Lubni, who never showed himself to rebellion, except like Jupiter with frowning brow, in the smell of sulphur, the flame of war, and the smoke of powder,--what was he? Under the weight of these thoughts the heart of the voevoda was breaking, the smile had left his face, and joy his heart forever, and he felt that he would rather a hundred times die than take another step; but he went on, for his whole past pushed him forward,--all his labors, all his efforts, all the inexorable logic of his previous acts.

Hmelnitski waited for him with hand on his side, with pouting lips and frowning brow.

The party approached at last. Kisel, moving to the front, made a few steps in advance toward the elevation. The drummers stopped drumming, the trumpeters blowing, and deep silence followed in the multitude. Only the frosty wind waved the crimson banner borne by Pan Kulchinski.

Suddenly the silence was broken by a certain curt, emphatic, and commanding voice, which sounded with the unspeakable power of desperation resembling nothing and no man: "Dragoons to the rear! follow me!" That was the voice of Pan Yan.

All heads were turned toward him. Hmelnitski himself rose somewhat in his seat to see what was taking place. The blood of the commissioners rushed to their faces. Skshetuski stood in his stirrups; erect, pale, with flashing eyes, naked sabre in his hand, half turned to the dragoons, he repeated again the thundering command: "Follow me!"

Amidst the silence the hoofs of the horses clattered along the smooth surface of the street. The disciplined dragoons turned their horses on the spot; the colonel placed himself at their head, gave the sign with his sword; the whole party moved slowly back to the residence of the commissioners.

Astonishment and uncertainty were depicted on all faces, not excepting that of Hmelnitski; for in the voice and motions of the colonel there was something unusual. Still no one knew clearly whether that sudden disappearance of the escort did not belong to the ceremonial of the occasion.

Kisel alone understood that the treaty and the lives of the commissioners together with the escort hung on a thread at that moment; therefore he stood on the elevation, and before Hmelnitski had time to take in what had happened, began to speak. First he offered the favor of the king to Hmelnitski and the whole Zaporojie. But suddenly his speech was interrupted by a new occurrence, which had only this good side, that it turned attention entirely from the previous one. Daidyalo, an old colonel, standing near Hmelnitski, began to shake his baton before the voevoda, to gesticulate and cry,--

"What do you say there, Kisel? The king is king, but you kinglets, princes, nobles, have involved everything. And you, Kisel, bone of our bone, you have gone away from us, and stand with the Poles. We have enough of your talk, for we will get what we want with the sabre."

The voevoda looked with offended feeling into the eyes of Hmelnitski. "Is this the discipline in which you keep your colonels?"

"Be silent, Daidyalo!" cried the hetman.

"Be silent, be silent! You are drunk, though it is early," repeated the other colonels. "Go away, or we will pull you out by the head!"

Daidyalo wanted to clamor more, but they took him by the shoulders and put him outside the circle.

The voevoda continued with smooth and chosen words, showing Hmelnitski how great were the gifts which he was receiving; for he had the sign of lawful power, which hitherto he had exercised only as a usurper. The king, being able to chastise, had preferred to forgive him, which he did on account of the obedience which he had shown at Zamost, and because his previous acts were committed not during his reign. It was proper therefore that he, Hmelnitski, having offended so much before, should prove thankful now for favor and clemency,--should stop the shedding of blood, pacify the peasants, and proceed to a treaty with the commissioners.

Hmelnitski received the baton in silence, and the banner, which he ordered to be unfurled above his head. The mob, at sight of this, began to howl with joyous voices, so that for a time nothing could be heard. Certain satisfaction was reflected on the face of the hetman, who, after he had waited awhile, said,--

"For such great favor shown me by his Majesty the King through you in sending me command over the forces, and overlooking my previous acts, I give humble thanks. I have always said that the king was with me against you faithless dukes and kinglets; and the best proof is that he sends me satisfaction because I have cut your necks, and will further cut them if you will not obey me and the king in everything."

Hmelnitski spoke the last words in a loud voice, in a railing tone, and wrinkled his brows as if anger had begun to rise in him. The commissioners grew rigid at such an unexpected turn in his answer; but Kisel said,--

"The king, mighty hetman, commands you to stop the shedding of blood, and to begin a treaty with us."

"Blood is not shed by me, but by the Lithuanian forces," answered the hetman, harshly; "for I have intelligence that Radzivil has destroyed my Mozir and Turoff. Should this prove true, then I have enough of your prisoners,--distinguished prisoners,--and I will have their heads cut off at once. I will not proceed to a treaty now. It is difficult to begin at present, for the army is not assembled; there is only a handful of colonels here, the rest being in winter quarters. I cannot begin without them. Besides, what's the use of talking long in the frost? What you had to give me you have given, and all men now see that I am hetman from the hand of the king; and now come to me for a glass of gorailka and dinner, for I am hungry."

Having said this, Hmelnitski moved toward his residence, and after him the commissioners and colonels. In the great central room stood a table ready, bending under plundered silver, among which the voevoda, Kisel, might have found some of his own, taken the past year in Gushchi. On the table were piled up mountains of pork, beef, and Tartar pilav; throughout the whole room was an odor of millet vudka, served in silver goblets. Hmelnitski took his place, with Kisel at his right and Bjozovski at his left, and with his hand to the gorailka, said,--

"They say in Warsaw that I drink Polish blood, but I prefer gorailka, leaving the other to the dogs."

The colonels burst into laughter, from which the walls of the room trembled. Such an "appetizer" did the hetman give the commissioners before their dinner; and the commissioners gulped it without a word, in order, as the chamberlain of Lvoff wrote, "not to anger the beast." But perspiration in heavy drops covered the pale forehead of Kisel.

The entertainment commenced. The colonels took pieces of meat from the platters with their hands, the hetman himself placed pieces on the plates of Kisel and Bjozovski; and the first of the dinner passed in silence, for every one was satisfying his hunger. In the silence could be heard only the crunching of bones under the teeth of the company or the gurgling of the drinkers. At times some one threw out a word which remained without echo till Hmelnitski, who had first satisfied himself somewhat, and emptied a number of glasses of millet vudka, turned suddenly to the voevoda, and asked,--

"Who was the leader of your company?"

Disquiet was reflected on Kisel's face. "Skshetuski, an honorable knight."

"I know him," said Hmelnitski; "and why did he not wish to be present when you delivered the gifts to me?"

"He was not associated with us for assistance, but for safety, and he had an order to that effect."

"And who gave him that order?"

"I," answered the voevoda; "for I did not think that it was proper, at the delivery of the gifts, that dragoons should be standing over the necks of you and me."

"I had another opinion, for I know that soldier is stubborn."

Here Yashevski mixed in the conversation. "We don't care for the dragoons," said he. "We used to think Poles powerful through them; but we discovered at Pilavtsi that they are not the Poles of other days, who beat the Turks, Tartars, and Germans."

"Not Zamoiskis, Jolkyevskis, Khodkyevichi, Hmelyetskis, and Konyetspolskis," interrupted Hmelnitski, "but Chorzovskis and Zaiontchkovskis,--big fellows, wrapped in iron; and they were dying of terror as soon as they saw us, and ran off, though there were only three thousand Tartars in the place."

The commissioners were silent, but the eating and drinking seemed to them more and more bitter each moment.

"I beg you humbly to drink and eat," said Hmelnitski, "or I shall think that our simple Cossack fare cannot pass your lordly throats."

"Oh, if they are too narrow we can slit them open a little," said Daidyalo.

The Cossacks, feeling encouraged, burst into laughter; but Hmelnitski looked threateningly at them, and they grew silent again.

Kisel, who had been ill several days, was pale as a sheet. Bjozovski was so red that it seemed as though the blood would burst through his face. At last he could restrain himself no longer, and shouted,--

"Have we come here to dine or to be insulted?"

To this Hmelnitski answered: "You have come for a treaty; but meanwhile the Lithuanian forces are burning and slaughtering. I hear they have destroyed Mozir and Turoff; should this prove true, I shall order four hundred captives to be beheaded in your presence."

Bjozovski restrained his blood, boiling the moment before. It was true! The lives of the captives depended on the humor of the hetman,--on one twinkle of his eye; therefore it was necessary to endure everything, and besides to calm his outbursts, to bring him "ad mitiorem et saniorem mentem."

In this spirit the Carmelite Lentovski, by nature mild and timid, said in a quiet voice,--

"May the God of mercy grant that the news from Lithuania about Mozir and Turoff may be changed!"

But scarcely had he finished when Fedor Veshnyak, the colonel of Cherkasi, bent toward him and struck with his baton, wishing to hit the Carmelite on the neck. Fortunately he did not reach him, since there were four men between them; but immediately he cried out,--

"Wordy priest! it is not your affair to give the lie to me. But come outdoors, and I will show you how to respect Zaporojian colonels!"

Others, however, hurried to quiet him; but not succeeding, they put him out of the room.

"When, mighty hetman, do you wish that the commissioners should meet?" asked Kisel, wishing to give another turn to the conversation.

Unfortunately Hmelnitski was no longer sober, therefore he gave a quick and biting answer,--

"To-morrow will be business and discussion, for now I am in drink. Why do you talk now of commissions; you do not give me time to eat and drink. I have enough of this already! Now there must be war!" And he thumped the table till the dishes and cups jumped. "In those four weeks I'll turn you all feet upward and trample you, and sell the remnant to the Turkish Tsar. The king will be king, so as to execute nobles, dukes, princes. If a prince offends, cut off his head; if a Cossack offends, cut off his head! You threaten me with the Swedes, but they cannot stand before me. Tugai Bey is near me, my brother, my soul; the only falcon in the world, he is ready at once to do everything that I wish."

Here Hmelnitski, with the rapidity peculiar to drunken men, passed from anger to tenderness, till his voice trembled from emotion.

"You wish me to raise my sabre against the Turks and Tartars, but in vain. I'll go against you with my good friends. I have sent my regiments around so as to provender the horses and to be ready for the road, without wagons, without cannon. I shall find all those among the Poles. I will order any Cossack to be beheaded who takes a wagon, and I will take no carriage myself, nothing but packs and bags; in this fashion I will go to the Vistula and say: 'Poles, sit still and be quiet!' And if you say anything beyond the Vistula, then I'll find you there. We have had enough of your lordship and your dragoons, you cursed reptiles living by injustice itself!"

Here he sprang from his seat, pulled his hair, stamped with his feet, crying that there must be war, for he had already received absolution and a blessing for it; he had nothing to do with commissions and commissioners, he would not allow a suspension of arms.

Seeing at length the terror of the commissioners, and recollecting that if they went away at once, war would begin in the winter, consequently at a time when the Cossacks, not being able to entrench themselves, fought badly in the open field, he calmed down a little and again sat on the bench, dropped his head on his breast, rested his hands on his knees, and breathed hoarsely. Finally he took a glass of vudka.

"To the health of the king!" cried he.

"To his glory and health!" repeated the colonels.

"Now, Kisel, don't be gloomy," said the hetman, "and don't take to heart what I say, for I've been drinking. Fortune-tellers inform me that there must be war, but I'll wait till next grass. Let there be a commission then; I will free the captives at that time. They tell me that you are ill, so let this be to your health!"

Again Hmelnitski dropped into momentary tenderness, and resting his hand on the shoulder of the voevoda brought his enormous red face to the pale, emaciated cheeks of Kisel.

After him came other colonels, and approaching the commissioners with familiarity shook their hands, clapped them on the shoulders, repeated after the hetman: "Till next grass." The commissioners were in torment. The peasant breaths, filled with the odor of gorailka, came upon the faces of those nobles of high birth, for whom the pressure of those sweating hands was as unendurable as an affront. Threatenings also were not lacking among the expressions of vulgar cordiality. Some cried to the voevoda: "We want to kill Poles, but you are our man!" Others said: "Well, in times past, you killed our people, now you ask favors! Destruction to you!" "You white hands!" cried Ataman Vovk, formerly miller in Nestervar, "I slew my landlord. Prince Chertvertinski." "Give us Yeremi," said Yashevski, rolling along, "and we will let you off!"

It became stifling in the room and hot beyond endurance. The table covered with remnants of meat, fragments of bread, stained with vudka and mead, was disgusting. At last the fortune-tellers came in,--conjurers with whom the hetman usually drank till late at night, listening to their predictions,--strange forms, old, bent, yellow, or in the vigor of youth, soothsaying from wax, grains of wheat, fire, water, foam, from the bottom of a flask or from human fat. Among the colonels and the youngest of them there was frolicking and laughing. Kisel came near fainting.

"We thank you, Hetman, for the feast, and we bid you good-by," said he, with a weak voice.

"Kisel, I will come to you to-morrow to dine," answered Hmelnitski, "and now return home. Donyéts with his men will attend you, so that nothing may happen to you from the crowd."

The commissioners bowed and went out. Donyéts with the Cossacks was waiting at the door.

"O God! O God! O God!" whispered Kisel, quietly, raising his hands to his face.

The party moved in silence to the quarters of the commissioners. But it appeared that they were not to stop near one another. Hmelnitski had assigned them purposely quarters in different parts of the town, so that they could not meet and counsel easily.

Kisel, suffering, exhausted, barely able to stand, went to bed immediately, and permitted no one to see him till the following day; then before noon he ordered Pan Yan to be called.

"Have you acted wisely?" asked he. "What have you done? You might have exposed our lives and your own to destruction."

"Serene voevoda, mea culpa! but delirium carried me away, and I preferred to perish a hundred times rather than behold such things."

"Hmelnitski saw the slight put on him, and I was barely able to pacify the wild beast and explain your act. He will be with me to-day, and will undoubtedly ask for you. Then tell him that you had an order from me to lead away the soldiers."

"From to-day forth Bjozovski takes the command, for he is well."

"That is better; you are too stubborn for these times. It is difficult to blame you for anything in this act except lack of caution; but it is evident that you are young and cannot bear the pain that is in your breast."

"I am accustomed to pain, serene voevoda, but I cannot endure disgrace."

Kisel groaned quietly, just like an invalid when touched on the sore spot. Then he smiled with a gloomy resignation, and said,--

"Such words are daily bread for me, which for a long time I eat moistened with bitter tears; but now the tears have failed me."

Pity rose in Skshetuski's heart at the sight of this old man with his martyr's face, who was passing the last days of his life in double suffering, for it was a suffering both of the mind and the body.

"Serene voevoda," said he, "God is my witness that I was thinking only of these fearful times when senators and dignitaries of the Crown are obliged to bow down before the rabble, for whom the empaling stake should be the only return for their deeds."

"God bless you, for you are young and honest. I know that you have no evil intention. But that which you say your prince says, and with him the army, the nobles, the Diets, half the Commonwealth; and all that burden of scorn and hatred falls upon me."

"Each serves the country as he understands, and let God judge intentions. As to Prince Yeremi, he serves the country with his health and his property."

"Applause surrounds him, and he walks in it as in the sunlight," answered the voevoda. "And what comes to me? Oh, you have spoken justly! Let God judge intentions, and may he give even a quiet grave to those who in life suffer beyond measure."

Skshetuski was silent, and Kisel raised his eyes in mute prayer. After a while he began to speak,--

"I am a Russian, blood and bone. The tomb of the Princes Sviatoldovichi lies in this land; therefore I have loved it and that people of God whom it nourishes at its breast. I have witnessed injuries committed by both sides; I have seen the license of the wild Zaporojians, but also the unendurable insolence of those who tried to enslave that warlike people. What was I to do,--I, a Russian, and at the same time a true son and senator of this Commonwealth? I joined myself to those who said 'Pax vobiscum!' because my blood and my heart so enjoined; and among the men whom I joined were our father, the late king, the chancellor, the primate, and many others. I saw that for both sides dissension was destruction; I desired all my life to my last breath to labor for concord; and when blood was already shed I thought to myself, 'I will be an angel of union.' I continued to labor, and I labor still, though in pain, torment, and disgrace, and in doubt almost more terrible than all. As God is dear to me, I know not now whether your prince came too early with his sword or I too late with the olive branch; but this I see, that my work is breaking, that strength is wanting, that in vain I knock my gray head against the wall, and going down to the grave I see only darkness before me, and destruction,--O God! destruction on every side."

"God will send salvation."

"May he send a ray of it before my death, that I die not in despair!--this in return for all my sufferings. I will thank him for the cross which I carry during life,--thank him because the mob cry for my head, because they call me a traitor at the Diets, because my property is plundered, and for the disgrace in which I live,--for all the bitter reward which I have received from both sides."

When he had finished speaking, the voevoda extended his dry hands toward heaven; and two great tears, perhaps the very last in his life, flowed out of his eyes.

Pan Yan could restrain himself no longer, but falling on his knees before the voevoda, seized his hand, and said in a voice broken by great emotion,--

"I am a soldier, and move on another path; but I give honor to merit and suffering." And the noble and knight from the regiment of Yeremi pressed to his lips the hand of that Russian who some months before he with others had called a traitor.

Kisel placed both hands on Skshetuski's head. "My son," said he in a low voice, "may God comfort, guide, and bless you, as I bless you."

The vicious circle of negotiations began from that very day. Hmelnitski came rather late to the voevoda's dinner, and in the worst temper. He declared immediately that what he had said yesterday about suspension of arms, a commission at Whitsuntide, and the liberation of prisoners he said while drunk, and that he now saw an intention to deceive him. Kisel calmed him again, pacified him, gave reasons; but these speeches were, according to the words of the chamberlain of Lvoff, "surdo tyranno fabula dicta." The hetman began then with such rudeness that the commissioners were sorry not to have the Hmelnitski of yesterday. He struck Pan Pozovski with his baton, only because he had appeared before him out of season, in spite of the fact that Pozovski was nearly dead already from serious illness.

Neither courtesy and good-will nor the persuasions of the voevoda were of use. When he had become somewhat excited by gorailka and the choice mead of Gushchi, he fell into better humor, but then he would not on any account let himself speak of public affairs, saying, "If we are to drink, let us drink,--to-morrow business and discussion,--if not, I'll be off with myself." About three o'clock in the morning he insisted on going to the sleeping-room of the voevoda, which the latter opposed under various pretexts; for he had shut in Skshetuski there on purpose, fearing that at the meeting of this stubborn soldier with Hmelnitski something disagreeable might happen which would be the destruction of the colonel. But Hmelnitski insisted and went, followed by Kisel. What was the astonishment of the voevoda when the hetman, seeing the knight, nodded to him, and cried,--

"Skshetuski, why were you not drinking with us?" And he stretched out his hand to him in a friendly manner.

"Because I am sick," replied the colonel, bowing.

"You went away yesterday. The pleasure was nothing to me without you."

"Such was the order he had," put in Kisel.

"Don't tell me that, Voevoda. I know him, and I know that he did not want to see you giving me honor. Oh, he is a bird! But what would not be forgiven another is forgiven him, for I like him, and he is my dear friend."

Kisel opened wide his eyes in astonishment. The hetman turned to Pan Yan. "Do you know why I like you?"

Skshetuski shook his head.

"You think it is because you cut the lariat at Omelnik when I was a man of small note and they hunted me like a wild beast. No, it is not that. I gave you a ring then with dust from the grave of Christ. Horned soul! you did not show me that ring when you were in my hands; but I set you at liberty anyhow, and we were even. That's not why I like you now. You rendered me another service, for which you are my dear friend, and for which I owe you thanks."

Pan Yan looked with astonishment at Hmelnitski.

"See how he wonders!" said the hetman, as if speaking to some fourth person. "Well, I will bring to your mind what they told me in Chigirin when I came there from Bazaluk with Tugai Bey. I inquired everywhere for my enemy, Chaplinski, whom I did not find; but they told me what you did to him after our first meeting,--that you grabbed him by the hair and trousers, beat the door open with him, drew blood from him as from a dog."

"I did in fact do that," said Skshetuski.

"You did splendidly, you acted well. But I'll reach him yet, or treaties and commissions are in vain,--I'll reach him yet, and play with him in my own fashion; but you gave him pepper."

The hetman now turned to Kisel, and began to tell how it was: "He caught him by the hair and trousers, lifted him like a fox, opened the door with him, and hurled him into the street." Here he laughed till the echo resounded in the side-room and reached the drawing-room. "Voevoda, give orders to bring mead, for I must drink to the health of this knight, my friend."

Kisel opened the door, and called to the attendant, who immediately brought three goblets of the mead of Gushchi.

Hmelnitski touched goblets with the voevoda and Pan Yan, and drank so that his head was warmed, his face smiled, great pleasure entered his heart, and turning to the colonel he said: "Ask of me what you like."

A flush came on the pale face of Skshetuski; a moment of silence followed.

"Don't fear!" said Hmelnitski; "a word is not smoke. Ask for what you like, provided you ask for nothing belonging to Kisel."

The hetman even drunk was always himself.

"If I may use the affection which you have for me, then I ask justice from you. One of your colonels has done me an injury."

"Off with his head!" said Hmelnitski, with an outburst.

"It is not a question of that; only order him to fight a duel with me."

"Off with his head!" cried the hetman. "Who is he?"

"Bogun."

Hmelnitski began to blink; then he struck his forehead with his palm. "Bogun? Bogun is killed. The king wrote me that he was slain in a duel."

Pan Yan was astonished. Zagloba had told the truth.

"What did Bogun do to you?" asked Hmelnitski.

A still deeper flush came on the colonel's face. He feared to mention the princess before the half-drunk hetman, lest he might hear some unpardonable word.

Kisel rescued him. "It is an important affair," said he, "of which Bjozovski the castellan has told me. Bogun carried off the betrothed of this cavalier and secreted her, it is unknown where."

"But have you looked for her?" asked Hmelnitski.

"I have looked for her on the Dniester, for he secreted her there, but did not find her. I heard, however, that he intended to take her to Kieff, where he wished to come himself to marry her. Give me, O Hetman, the right to go to Kieff and search for her there. I ask for nothing more."

"You are my friend; you battered Chaplinski. I'll give you not only the right to go and seek her wherever you like, but I will issue an order that whoever has her in keeping shall deliver her to you; and I'll give you a baton as a pass, and a letter to the metropolitan to look for her among the nuns. My word is not smoke!"

He opened the door and called to Vygovski to come and write an order and a letter. Chernota was obliged, though it was after three o'clock, to go for the seal. Daidyalo brought the baton, and Donyéts received the order to conduct Skshetuski with two hundred horse to Kieff, and farther to the first Polish outposts.

Next day Skshetuski left Pereyasláv.

CHAPTER LII.

If Zagloba was bored at Zbaraj, no less bored was Volodyovski, who was longing especially for war and its adventures. They went out, it is true, from time to time with the squadron in pursuit of plundering parties who were burning and slaying on the Zbruch; but that was a small war, principally work for scouts, difficult because of the cold winter and frosts, yielding much toil and little glory. For these reasons Pan Michael urged Zagloba every day to go to the assistance of Skshetuski, from whom they had had no tidings for a long time.

"He must have fallen into some fatal trap and may have lost his life," said Volodyovski. "We must surely go, even if we have to perish with him."

Zagloba did not offer much opposition, for he thought they had stayed too long in Zbaraj, and wondered why mushrooms were not growing on them already. But he delayed, hoping that news might come from Skshetuski any moment.

"He is brave and prudent," answered he to the importunities of Volodyovski. "We will wait a couple of days yet; perhaps a letter will come and render our whole expedition useless."

Volodyovski recognized the justice of the argument and armed himself with patience, though time dragged on more and more slowly. At the end of December frost had stopped even robbery, and there was peace in the neighborhood. The only entertainment was in public news, which came thick and fast to the gray walls of Zbaraj.

They spoke about the coronation and the Diet, and about the question whether Prince Yeremi would receive the baton which belonged to him before all other warriors. They were terribly excited against those who affirmed that in view of the turn in favor of a treaty with Hmelnitski, Kisel alone could gain advancement. Volodyovski had several duels on this point, and Zagloba several drinking-bouts; and there was danger of the latter's becoming a confirmed drunkard, for not only did he keep company with officers and nobles, but he was not ashamed to go even among townspeople to christenings and weddings, praising especially their mead, for which Zbaraj was famous.

Volodyovski reproved him for this, saying that familiarity with people of low degree was not befitting a noble, since regard for a whole order would be diminished thereby; but Zagloba answered that the laws were to blame for that, because they permit townspeople to grow up in luxury and to come to wealth, which should be the portion of nobles alone; he prophesied that no good could come of such great privileges for insignificant people. It was difficult indeed to blame him in a period of gloomy winter days amidst uncertainty, weariness, and waiting.

Gradually Vishnyevetski's regiments began to assemble in greater and greater numbers at Zbaraj, from which fact war in the spring was prophesied. Meanwhile people became more lively. Among others came the hussar squadron of Pan Yan, with Podbipienta. He brought tidings of the disfavor in which the prince was at court, and of the death of Pan Yanush Tishkyevich, the voevoda of Kieff, whom, according to general report, Kisel was to succeed, and finally of the serious illness with which Pan Lashch was stricken down in Cracow. As to war, Podbipienta heard from the prince himself that only by force of events and necessity would it come, for the commissioners had gone with instructions to make every concession possible to the Cossacks. This account of Podbipienta's was received by the prince's knights with rage; and Zagloba proposed to make a protest and form a confederation, for he said he did not wish his labor at Konstantinoff to go for nothing.

All February passed with these tidings and uncertainties, and the middle of March was approaching; but from Skshetuski there was no word. Volodyovski began to insist all the more on their expedition.

"We have to seek now not for the princess," said he, "but for Pan Yan."

It was soon shown that Zagloba was right in delaying the expedition from day to day, for at the end of March the Cossack Zakhar came with a letter from Kieff addressed to Volodyovski. Pan Michael summoned Zagloba at once, and when they had closeted themselves with the messenger in a room apart, he broke the seal and read the following:--

I discovered no trace on the Dniester as far as Yagorlik. Supposing that she must be hidden in Kieff, I joined the commissioners, with whom I went to Pereyaslàv. Obtaining there the hoped for consent from Hmelnitski, I arrived at Kieff, and am making a search for her everywhere, in which the metropolitan assists me. Many of our people are hidden in private houses and in monasteries, but fearing the mob, they do not declare themselves; therefore search is difficult. God not only guided and protected me, but inspired Hmelnitski with an affection for me; wherefore I hope that He will assist me and have mercy on me for the future. I beg the priest Mukhovetski for a solemn Mass, at which you will pray for my intention.

Skshetuski.

"Praise be to God the Eternal!" cried Volodyovski.

"There is a postscript yet," said Zagloba.

"True!" answered the little knight; and he read further:--

"The bearer of this letter, the essaul of the Mirgorod kuren, had me in his honest care when I was at the Saitch and in captivity, and now he has aided me in Kieff and has undertaken to deliver this letter with risk to his life. Have him in your care, Michael, so that nothing may be wanting to him."

"'You are an honest Cossack; there is at least one such!" said Zagloba, giving his hand to Zakhar.

The old man pressed it with dignity.

"You may be sure of reward," interjected the little knight.

"He is a falcon," said the Cossack; "I like him. I did not come here for money."

"I see you are not lacking in a spirit which no noble would be ashamed of," said Zagloba. "They are not all beasts among you,--not all beasts. But no more of this! Then Pan Skshetuski is in Kieff?"

"He is."

"And in safety, for I hear that the mob is revelling?"

"He stops with Colonel Donyéts. They will do nothing to him, for our father Hmelnitski ordered Donyéts to guard him at the peril of his life as the eye in his head."

"Real wonders take place! How did Hmelnitski get such a liking for Pan Yan?"

"Oh, he has liked him a long time!"

"Did Pan Skshetuski tell you what he was looking for in Kieff?"

"Why shouldn't he tell me when he knows that I am his friend? I searched with him and searched by myself; so he had to tell me what he was looking for."

"But so far you haven't found her?"

"We have not. Whatever Poles are there yet are hiding, one does not know of the other, so that it is not easy to find any one. You heard that the mob kill people, but I have seen it; they kill not only Poles, but those who hide them, even monks and nuns. In the monastery of Nikolai the Good there were twelve Polish women with the nuns; they suffocated them in the cells together with the nuns. Every couple of days a shout is raised on the street, and people are hunted and dragged to the Dnieper. Oh, how many have been drowned already!"

"Perhaps they have killed the princess too?"

"Perhaps they have."

"No," interrupted Volodyovski; "if Bogun took her there, he must have made it safe for her."

"Where is it safer than in a monastery? But for all that they kill people there."

"Uf!" said Zagloba. "So you think, Zakhar, that she might have perished?"

"I don't know."

"It is evident that Skshetuski is in good heart," said Zagloba. "God has visited him, but he comforts him. And is it long since you left Kieff, Zakhar?"

"Oh, long! I left Kieff when the commissioners were passing there on their return. Many Poles wished to escape with them, and did escape, the unfortunates! As each one was able, over the snow, over pathless tracts, through forests, they hurried to Belogrodki; but the Cossacks pursued and beat them. Many fled, many were killed, and some Pan Kisel ransomed with what money he had."

"Oh, the dog-souls! And so you came out with the commissioners?"

"With the commissioners to Gushchi, and from there to Ostrog; farther I came alone."

"Then you are an old acquaintance of Pan Skshetuski?"

"I made his acquaintance in the Saitch, nursed him when he was wounded, and then I learned to like him as if he were my own child. I am old, and have nobody to love."

Zagloba called to the servant, gave orders to bring in mead and meat, and they sat down to supper. Zakhar ate heartily, for he was road-weary and hungry; then he sank his gray mustaches eagerly in the dark liquid, drank, smacked his lips, and said: "Splendid mead!"

"Better than the blood which you folks drink," said Zagloba. "But I think that you are an honest man, and loving Pan Skshetuski, will not go any more to the rebellion, but remain with us. It will be good for you here."

Zakhar raised his head. "I delivered the letter, now I'll go back. I am a Cossack. It is for me to be a brother with the Cossacks, not with the Poles."

"And will you beat us?"

"I will. I am a Cossack of the Saitch. We elected Hmelnitski hetman, and now the king has sent him the baton and the banner."

"There it is for you, Pan Michael! Have not I advised a protest? And from what kuren are you?"

"From the Mirgorod; but it is no longer in existence."

"What has happened to it?"

"The hussars of Pan Charnetski at Jóltiya Vodi cut it to pieces. I am under Donyéts now, with those who survived. Pan Charnetski is a real soldier; he is with us in captivity, and the commissioners have interceded for him."

"We have your prisoners too."

"That must be so. In Kieff they say that our best hero is a captive with the Poles, though some say he is dead."

"Who is that?"

"Oh, the famous ataman, Bogun."

"Bogun was killed in a duel."

"But who killed him?"

"That knight there," said Zagloba, pointing proudly to Volodyovski.

The eyes of Zakhar, who at that moment had raised the second quart of mead, stared, his face grew purple, and at last he snorted the liquid through his nostrils as he laughed. "That knight killed Bogun?" he asked, coughing violently from laughter.

"What's the matter with the old devil?" asked Volodyovski, frowning. "This messenger takes too much liberty on himself."

"Be not angry, Pan Michael!" interrupted Zagloba. "He is clearly an honest man, and if a stranger to politeness it is because he is a Cossack. On the other hand, it is the greater praise for you that though you are so paltry in appearance you have wrought such mighty deeds in your time. Your body is insignificant, but your soul is great. I myself, as you remember, when looking at you after the duel, though I saw the struggle with my own eyes, could not believe that such a whipper-snapper--"

"Oh, let us have peace!" blurted out Volodyovski.

"I am not your father, so don't be angry with me. But I tell you this; I should like to have a son like you, and if you wish, I will adopt you and convey all my property to you; for it is no shame to be great in a small body. The prince is not much larger than you, and Alexander the Great would not deserve to be his armor-bearer."

"What makes me angry," said Volodyovski, somewhat mollified, "is specially this, that nothing favorable to Skshetuski is evident from this letter. He did not lay down his head on the Dniester, God be thanked for that; but he has not found the princess yet, and what surety is there that he will find her?"

"True. But if God through us has freed him from Bogun, and has conducted him through so many dangers, through so many snares, if he has inspired even the stony heart of Hmelnitski with a wonderful affection for him, you have no reason to dry up from torment and sorrow into smoked bacon. If you do not see in all this the hand of Providence, it is clear that your wit is duller than your sabre,--a reasonable arrangement enough, since no man can have all gifts at once."

"I see one thing," answered Volodyovski, moving his mustaches,--"that we have nothing to do here, and still we must stay here till we wither up altogether."

"I shall wither up sooner than you, for I am older, and you know that turnips wither and salt meat grows bitter from age. Let us rather thank God for promising a happy end to all our troubles. Not a little have I grieved for the princess,--more indeed than you have, and little less than Skshetuski,--for she is my dear daughter, and it is true that I might not love my own so much. They say indeed that she is as much like me as one cup is like another; but I love her besides that, and you would not see me either happy or at peace if I did not hope that her trouble would soon come to an end. To-morrow I shall write a wedding-hymn; for I write very beautiful verses, though in recent times I have neglected Apollo somewhat for Mars."

"What is the use in thinking of Mars now! May the hangman take that Kisel and all the commissioners and their treaties! They will make peace in the spring as true as two and two are four. Pan Podbipienta, who saw the prince, says so too."

"Podbipienta knows as much of public affairs as a goat does of pepper. While at the court his mind was more on that tufted lark than anything else, and he pushed up to her as a dog to a partridge. God grant that some one else may get her from him! But enough of this! I do not deny that Kisel is a traitor,--all the Commonwealth knows that; but as to treaties,--well, grandmother talks both ways."

Here Zagloba turned to the Cossack. "And what, Zakhar, do they say among your folks? Will there be peace or war?"

"There will be peace till next grass, and after that there will be destruction either to us or to the Poles."

"Comfort yourself, Pan Michael. I have heard too that the mob are arming everywhere."

"There will be such a war as has not been," said Zakhar. "Our people say that the Sultan of Turkey will come and the Khan of all the hordes. Our friend Tugai Bey is near, hasn't returned home at all."

"Console yourself, Pan Michael," repeated Zagloba. "There is a prophecy too about the new king, that his whole reign will be passed under arms. It is most likely that the sabre will not be sheathed for a long time to come. Man will tremble from continual war, like a broom from shaking; but that is our soldier lot. When you have to fight, Pan Michael, keep close to me and you will see beautiful things,--you will learn how we used to fight in past and better times. Oh, my God! not such people as at present were those in years gone by. You are not like them either, Pan Michael, though you are a fierce soldier and killed Bogun."

"You speak truly, Pan," said Zakhar; "not such are people now as they used to be." Then he began to gaze at Volodyovski and shake his head. "But that this knight killed Bogun,--never, never!"

CHAPTER LIII.

Old Zakhar went back to Kieff after a few days' rest, and then came tidings that the commissioners had no great hopes of peace, or in fact almost despaired of it. They were able to obtain merely an armistice till the Russian Whitsuntide, in accordance with which a new commission was to begin, with plenary powers. But the demands and conditions put forth by Hmelnitski were so exorbitant that no one believed that the Commonwealth could agree to them. Vigorous arming was commenced therefore on both sides. Hmelnitski sent envoy after envoy to the Khan to hasten at the head of all his forces; he sent also to Stamboul, where Pan Bechinski, on behalf of the king, had resided for a considerable time. In the Commonwealth writs for the national militia were expected every moment. News came of the appointment of fresh leaders,--the cup-bearer, Ostrorog, Lantskoronski, and Firlei,--and the complete removal from military affairs of Yeremi Vishnyevetski, who was able to shield the country only at the head of his own forces. Not merely the soldiers of the prince, not merely the nobles of Russia, but also the partisans of the former commanders were indignant at such a selection and such disfavor, declaring justly that if there had been political reasons for sacrificing Yeremi while there was hope of concluding a treaty, his removal in presence of war was a great, an unpardonable blunder; for he alone was able to meet Hmelnitski, and conquer that famous leader of rebellion. Finally the prince himself came to Zbaraj for the purpose of assembling as many forces as possible, to stand in readiness on the borderland of the conflict.

An armistice had been concluded, but at every moment it proved of no avail. Hmelnitski ordered, it is true, the execution of some colonels stationed here and there in camps, who in spite of the armistice had permitted themselves to attack castles, and squadrons encamped in various places; but he was unable to restrain the masses of the people, and the numerous independent bands, who either had not heard of the armistice, or who knew not even the meaning of the word. They attacked therefore continually the boundaries secured by the agreement, thus breaking every engagement made by the hetman. On the other hand, the troops of private persons and of the king in pursuing robbers frequently passed the Pripet and the Goryn in the province of Kieff, continued into the depth of the province of Bratslav, and there, attacked by the Cossacks, fought regular battles, not infrequently bloody and stubborn. Hence continual complaints from the Cossacks and Poles of the violation of the armistice, which it was indeed beyond the power of man to observe. The armistice existed therefore so far as Hmelnitski on one side, and the king and hetmans on the other, had not moved into the field; but the war was raging, in fact, before the main forces had rushed to the combat, and the first warm rays of spring shone again upon burning villages, towns, cities, and castles, giving light to slaughter and human misfortune.

Parties from the neighborhood of Bar, Hmelnik, and Makhnovka appeared around Zbaraj, slaying, robbing, burning. Yeremi dispersed these with the hands of his colonels; but he took no part in this small warfare himself, as he intended to move with his whole division when the hetmans should be already in the field.

He sent out therefore detachments with orders to pay for blood with blood, for robbery and murder with the stake. Podbipienta went with others and gained a victory at Cherni Ostroff; but he was a knight terrible only in battle,--to prisoners taken with arms in their hands he was too indulgent; therefore he was not sent a second time. But in expeditions of this kind Volodyovski distinguished himself; as a partisan he had no rival save Vershul alone, for no one accomplished such lightning marches. No one knew how to approach the enemy so unexpectedly, break them up with such wild onset, scatter to the four winds, and exterminate by hunting down, hanging, and slaughtering; soon he was invested with terror and the favor of the prince. From the end of March to the middle of April Volodyovski dispersed seven independent parties, each one of which was three times stronger than his own; and he did not grow weary in his work, but showed a continually increasing eagerness, as if gaining it from the blood he was shedding.

The little knight, or rather the little devil, teased Zagloba to accompany him in these expeditions, for he loved his company above all things; but the worthy noble opposed every suggestion, and thus explained his inactivity:--

"My stomach is too big, Pan Michael, for these struggles and encounters; and besides, each man has his special power. To strike with hussars in the thick of the enemy in the open day, break through a camp, capture standards,--that's my forte, the Lord God created and fitted me for that; but to hunt a rabble in the night through the brush,--I leave that to you, who are as slender as a needle, and can easily push through everywhere. I am a knight of ancient date, and I prefer to tear through as the lion does, rather than creep along like a bloodhound on trails. Besides, after the evening milking I must to bed, for that is my best time."

Volodyovski therefore went alone, and alone conquered, till a certain time when, going out toward the end of April, he returned in the middle of May, as woe-begone and gloomy as if he had met a defeat and wasted his men. Thus it appeared to all; but in that long and difficult expedition Volodyovski had gone beyond Ostrog to the neighborhood of Golovna, and had defeated there, not a common band made up of the rabble, but several hundred Zaporojians, half of whom he killed and the other half captured. The more astonishing, therefore, was the profound gloom which as a fog covered his face, joyous by nature. But Pan Volodyovski said not a word to any man; scarcely had he dismounted when he went for a long conversation with the prince, taking two unknown knights, and then, in company with them, went to Zagloba without stopping, though those eager for news seized him by the sleeve along the way.

Zagloba looked with a certain astonishment on the two gigantic men, whom he had never seen before, and whose uniform, with gilt shoulder-knots, showed that they served in the Lithuanian army. Volodyovski said,--

"Shut the door, and give orders to admit no one, for we have to speak on affairs of importance."

Zagloba gave the order to the servant; then he began to look unquietly on the strangers, noting from their faces that they had nothing good to tell.

"These are," said Volodyovski, pointing to the young man, "the Princes Bulygi Kurtsevichi, Yuri and Andrei."

"The cousins of Helena!" cried Zagloba.

The princes bowed and said both at once: "Cousins of the deceased Helena."

The ruddy face of Zagloba became pale blue in a moment. He began to beat the air with his hands as if he had been struck with a bullet. He opened his lips, unable to catch breath, rolled his eyes, and said or rather groaned: "How?"

"There is news," answered Volodyovski, gloomily, "that the princess was murdered in the monastery of Nikolai the Good."

"The mob suffocated with smoke in a cell twelve young ladies and some nuns, among whom was our cousin," added Prince Yuri.

This time Zagloba's countenance, formerly blue, became so red that those present were afraid of apoplexy. Slowly his lids dropped over his eyes; he covered them with his hands, and from his mouth came a fresh groan: "Oh, world! world! world!" Then he was silent.

But the princes and Volodyovski began to complain.

"Oh, good lady, we your friends and relatives gathered together,--we who wished to go to save you," said the young knight, sighing time after time; "but it is evident that we were late with our aid. Our willingness was in vain, in vain our sabres and our courage; for you are in another and better than this bad world, waiting upon the Queen of Heaven."

"Oh, cousin," cried the gigantic Yuri, who in grief seized his hair anew, "forgive us our faults, and for every drop of your blood we will pour out three gallons."

"So help us God!" responded Andrei.

The two men stretched their hands to heaven. Zagloba rose from his seat, advanced a few steps toward the bed, tottered like one drunk, and fell on his knees before the image.

After a moment the bells in the castle sounded for midday,--sounded as gloomily as if they were death-bells.

"She is no more!" said Volodyovski again. "The angels have taken her to heaven, leaving us tears and sighs."

Sobbing shook the heavy body of Zagloba, and it trembled; but they complained without ceasing, and the bells were tolling.

At last Zagloba calmed himself; they had thought indeed that perhaps wearied by pain he had fallen asleep on his knees. After a time, however, he rose, stood up, sat on the bed; but he had become as it were another man. His eyes were red, bloodshot; his head drooping; his lower lip hung upon his beard; imbecility had settled on his face, and a certain unexampled decrepitude, so that it might in truth appear that the former Zagloba, lively, jovial, full of fancy, had died, and there remained only an old man weighted and wearied with years.

Meanwhile, in spite of the protests of the servant at the door, Podbipienta entered; and again began complaints and regrets. The Lithuanian called to mind Rozlogi, and the first meeting with the princess,--her sweetness, youth, beauty. At length he remembered that there was some one more unhappy than any of them,--her betrothed, Pan Skshetuski,--and he began to ask the little knight about him.

"Skshetuski is with Prince Koretski, at Korets, to which place he came from Kieff; and he lies there in illness, unconscious of God's world," said Volodyovski.

"Should not we go to him?" asked the Lithuanian.

"There is no reason to go," replied Volodyovski. "The prince's physician answers for his health. Pan Sukhodolski--one of Prince Dominik's colonels, but a great friend of Skshetuski-- is there, and our old Zatsvilikhovski; they both have him in care and watchfulness. He lacks for nothing, and that delirium does not leave him is the better for him."

"Oh, God of power!" said the Lithuanian, "have you seen Skshetuski with your own eyes?"

"I saw him; but if they had not told me that that was he, I should not have known him, pain and sickness have so devoured him."

"Did he recognize you?"

"He knew me undoubtedly, though he said nothing, for he smiled and nodded his head. Such pity possessed me that I could stay no longer. Prince Koretski wishes to come here with his squadron. Zatsvilikhovski will come with him, and Pan Sukhodolski swears that he will come too, even if he has an order to the contrary from Prince Dominik. They will bring Pan Yan unless disease gets the better of him."

"And whence have you tidings of the princess's death?" asked Pan Longin. "Have these young men brought it?" added he, pointing to the princes.

"No. These knights learned all by chance in Korets, where they had come with messages from the voevoda of Vilna, and came here with me, for they had letters from the voevoda to our prince. War is certain, and nothing will come of the commission."

"We know that already ourselves, but tell us who informed you of the death of the princess?"

"Zatsvilikhovski told me, and he knows it from Skshetuski. Hmelnitski gave Skshetuski permission to search for her in Kieff, and the metropolitan himself had to assist. They searched mainly in the monasteries, for those of our people who remained in Kieff are secreted in them. And they thought surely that Bogun had placed the princess in some monastery. They sought and sought and were of good heart, though they knew that the mob had suffocated twelve young ladies with smoke at Nikolai the Good. The metropolitan contended that they would not have attacked the betrothed of Bogun, but it has turned out otherwise."

"Then she was at the convent of Nikolai the Good?"

"She was. Skshetuski met Pan Yoakhim Yerlich, who was hiding in a monastery; and as he had asked every one about the princess, he asked him too. Pan Yerlich said that there were certain young ladies whom the Cossacks had taken, but at Nikolai the Good twelve remained, whom afterward they suffocated with smoke,--among them Kurtsevichovna. Skshetuski, since Yerlich is a hypochondriac and only half-witted from continual terror, did not believe him, and hurried off immediately a second time to Nikolai the Good to inquire. Unfortunately the nuns, three of whom were suffocated in the same cell, did not know the names, but hearing the description which Skshetuski gave, they said that she was the one. Then Skshetuski went away from Kieff and straightway fell ill."

"The only wonder is that he is still alive."

"He would have died undoubtedly but for that old Cossack who nursed him during captivity in the Saitch, and then came here with letters from him, and when he had returned, helped him again in his search. He took him to Korets and gave him into the hands of Zatsvilikhovski."

"May God protect him, for he has never yet consoled him!" said Podbipienta.

Volodyovski ceased, and a silence of the grave reigned over all. The princes resting upon their elbows sat motionless with frowning brows; Podbipienta raised his eyes to heaven, and Zagloba fixed his glassy gaze on the opposite wall as if sunk in the deepest thought.

"Rouse yourself!" said Volodyovski, shaking him by the shoulder. "Of what are you thinking so? You will not think out anything, and all your stratagems will be useless."

"I know that," answered Zagloba, with a broken voice. "I am thinking that I am old, that I have nothing to do in this world."

CHAPTER LIV.

"Picture to yourself," said Volodyovski to Pan Longin a few days later, "that that man has changed in one hour as if he had grown ten years older. So joyous was he, so talkative, so full of tricks, that he surpassed Ulysses himself. Now he does not let two words out of his lips, but dozes away whole days, complains of old age, and speaks as in a dream. I knew that he loved her, but I did not think that he loved her to this degree."

"What is there wonderful in that?" answered the Lithuanian, sighing. "He was the more attached to her that he snatched her from the hands of Bogun, and went through so many dangers and adventures in the flight. While there was hope his wit was exerted in inventions, and he kept on foot; but now he has really nothing to do in the world, being alone and without heart for anything."

"I tried to drink with him, hoping that drink would restore his former vigor, but in vain. He drinks, but does not think as before, does not talk about his exploits; only becomes sensitive, and then hangs his head on his breast and goes to sleep. I do not know if even Pan Yan is in greater despair than he."

"It is an unspeakable loss, for withal he was a great knight. Let us go to him, Pan Michael. He had the habit of scoffing at me and teasing me on every occasion; perhaps the desire will take him now. My God, how people change! He was such a gladsome man."

"Let us go," said Volodyovski. "It is already late; but it is most grievous for him in the evening,--for dozing all day, he is unable to sleep at night."

Thus conversing, they betook themselves to the quarters of Zagloba, whom they found sitting under the open window with his head resting on his hand. It was late; every movement in the castle had ceased; only the sentinels answered in prolonged tones, and in the thickets separating the castle from the town the nightingales brought out their passionate trills, whistling, smacking, and clapping as quickly as fall the drops in a spring shower. Through the open window came in the warm breeze of May and the clear rays of the moon, which lighted the downcast face of Zagloba and the bald crown bent toward his breast.

"Good-evening!" said the two knights.

"Good-evening!" answered Zagloba.

"Why have you forgotten yourself before the window instead of going to bed?" asked Volodyovski.

Zagloba sighed. "It is not a question of sleep with me," said he, with a drawling voice. "A year ago I was fleeing with her on the Kagamlik from Bogun, and in this same way those birds were twittering; and where is she now?"

"God has so ordained," said Volodyovski.

"Ordained to tears and sorrow, Pan Michael. There is no more consolation for me."

They were silent; but through the open window came, with power increasing each moment, the trill of the nightingales, with which all that clear night seemed filled.

"Oh, God, God!" sighed Zagloba, "exactly as it was on the Kagamlik."

Pan Longin shook a tear from his great mustaches, and the little knight said after a while,--

"Sorrow is sorrow; but drink some mead with us, for there is nothing better against sorrow. At the glass we will talk of better times."

"Let us drink," said Zagloba, with resignation.

Volodyovski ordered the servant to bring a light and decanter, and afterward, when they had sat down, knowing that reminiscences enlivened Zagloba more than anything else, he inquired: "It is just a year, is it not, since you fled with her before Bogun from Rozlogi?"

"It was in May, in May," answered Zagloba. "We passed through the Kagamlik to flee to Zólotonosha. Oh, it is hard in this world!"

"And she was disguised?"

"As a Cossack. I had to cut off her hair with my sabre, poor thing! so that she shouldn't be discovered. I know the place under the tree where I hid the hair, together with the sabre."

"Oh, she was a sweet lady!" added Longin, with a sigh.

"I tell you, gentlemen, from the first day I fell in love with her as if I had paid homage to her from youthful years. And she would clasp her hands before me and thank me for her rescue and my care. I wish they had killed me before I had lived to this day! Would that I had not lived to it!"

Then came silence again, and the three knights drank mead mixed with tears. After that Zagloba began to speak again.

"I thought to pass a calm old age with them, but now"--here his hands hung down powerless--"nowhere solace, nowhere solace, but in the grave--"

Before Zagloba had finished speaking a disturbance rose in the anteroom; some one wished to enter, and the servant would not let him in. A wordy struggle followed, in which it seemed to Volodyovski that he recognized some known voice; therefore he called to the servant not to forbid entrance further.

The door opened, and in it appeared the plump, ruddy face of Jendzian, who, passing his eyes over those present, bowed and said: "May Jesus Christ be praised!"

"For the ages of ages," said Volodyovski. "This is Jendzian?"

"I am he," said the young man, "and I bow to your knees. And where is my master?"

"Your master is in Korets, and ill."

"Oh, for God's sake, what do you tell me? And is he seriously ill, which God forbid?"

"He was, but he is better now. The doctor says he will recover."

"For I have come with news about the lady to my master."

The little knight began to nod his head in melancholy fashion. "You need not hasten, for Pan Skshetuski already knows of her death, and we here are shedding tears of mourning for her."

Jendzian's eyes were bursting from his head. "By violence! What do I hear? Is she dead?"

"Not dead, but murdered in Kieff by robbers."

"What are you talking about? In what Kieff?"

"Don't you know Kieff?"

"For God's sake, are you fooling with me? What had she to do in Kieff when she is hidden in the ravine at Valadinka, not far from Rashkoff, and the witch was commanded not to move a step till Bogun should come? As God is dear to me, must I run mad?"

"What witch are you speaking of?"

"Why, Horpyna! I know that bass-viol well."

Zagloba stood up suddenly from the bench, and began to strike out with his hands like a man who has fallen into deep water and is trying to save himself from drowning.

"By the living God, be quiet!" said he to Volodyovski. "By God's wounds, let me ask him!"

The company trembled, so pale was Zagloba, and the perspiration came out on his bald head. He sprang over the bench to Jendzian, and seizing the young fellow by the shoulders, asked in a hoarse voice,--

"Who told you that she is near Rashkoff, secreted?"

"Who should tell me? Bogun!"

"Are you mad, fellow?" roared Zagloba, shaking him like a pear-tree. "What Bogun?"

"Oh, for God's sake," called Jendzian, "why do you shake me so? Let me go, let me collect my wits, for I am losing my senses. You have turned everything over in my head. What Bogun should there be,--or don't you know him?"

"Speak, or I'll stab you!" shouted Zagloba. "Where did you see Bogun?"

"In Vlodava! What do you want of me?" cried the frightened young man. "Am I a robber?"

Zagloba lost the thread of his thought, breath failed him, and he fell on the bench panting heavily. Volodyovski came to his aid.

"When did you see Bogun?" asked Volodyovski.

"Three weeks ago."

"Then he is alive?"

"Why shouldn't he be? He told me himself how you split him up, but he has recovered."

"And he told you that the young lady is at Rashkoff?"

"Who else should tell me?"

"Listen, Jendzian! it is a question here of the life of your master and the young lady. Did Bogun himself tell you that she was not in Kieff?"

"My master, how could she be in Kieff when he secreted her at Rashkoff, and told Horpyna on peril of her life not to let her escape? But now he has given me a baton and his ring to go to her; for his wounds opened, and he had to lie down himself, it is unknown for how long."

Further words from Jendzian were interrupted by Zagloba, who sprang from the bench again, and seizing the remnant of his hair with both hands, began to shout like a madman: "My daughter is living,--by God's wounds, she is living! They didn't kill her in Kieff; she is alive, she is alive, my dearest!"

And the old man stamped with his feet, laughed and sobbed. Finally, he seized Jendzian by the head, pressed him to his bosom and began to kiss him, so that the young fellow lost his head altogether.

"Let me go, my master, for I am stifled! Of course she is alive--God grant us to go together for her, my master--But, my master!"

"Let him go, let him tell his story, for we don't understand anything yet," said Volodyovski.

"Speak, speak!" cried Zagloba.

"Begin at the beginning, brother," said Pan Longin, on whose mustaches, too, thick dew had settled down.

"Permit me, gentlemen, to draw breath," said Jendzian; "and I will close the window, for those wretches of nightingales are tearing away in the bushes at such a rate that it is impossible to speak."

"Mead!" cried Volodyovski to the servant.

Jendzian closed the window with his usual deliberation, then turned to the company and said; "You will let me sit down, for I am tired."

"Sit down!" said Volodyovski, pouring to him from the decanter borne in by the servant. "Drink with us, for you deserve it for the news which you bring. If you will only speak as soon as possible!"

"Good mead!" said he, raising the glass toward the light.

"May you be split! will you talk?" shouted Zagloba.

"You are angry at once, my master! I will talk if you wish; it is for you to command and me to obey, that's why I am a servant. But I see that I must start from the beginning and tell everything in detail."

"Speak from the beginning!"

"You remember, gentlemen, how the news of the taking of Bar came; how we thought then that the young lady was lost? So I returned to the Jendzians,--to my parents and my grandfather, who is now ninety years old--I speak correctly--no! ninety-and-one."

"May he be nine hundred!" burst out Zagloba.

"May God give him as many years as possible! I thank you, my master, for the kind word. So I returned home to visit my parents, as I by the assistance of God had passed the robbers; for as you know, the Cossacks took me up in Chigirin last year, and considered me one of themselves because I nursed Bogun when wounded, and arrived at great intimacy with him; and at the same time I collected some little from those criminals,--some silver and precious stones."

"We know, we know!" said Volodyovski.

"Well, I reached my parents, who were glad to see me, and couldn't believe their eyes when I showed them all I had collected. I had to swear to my grandfather that I had come by it honestly. Then they were glad; for you must know that they have a lawsuit with the Yavorskis about a pear-tree which stands on the line between them,--half its branches are on the land of the Yavorskis, and half on ours. Now the Yavorskis shake the tree and our pears fall, and many of them go to them. They stick to it that those in the middle are theirs, and we--"

"Don't bring me to anger, fellow!" interrupted Zagloba, "and don't speak of that which does not belong to the story!"

"First, with your pardon, my master, I am no fellow, but a noble, though a poor one, and with an escutcheon as well as you, as Pan Volodyovski and Podbipienta, friends of Pan Skshetuski, will tell you; and I repeat that this lawsuit has lasted fifty years."

"Dear little fish!" said Podbipienta, sweetly; "but tell us about Bogun, not about pear-trees."

"Of Bogun?" said Jendzian. "Well, let it be about Bogun. That Bogun thinks, my master, that he has not a more faithful friend and servant than me, though he struck me in Chigirin; for it is true I nursed him, took care of him, when the Kurtsevichi had wounded him. I lied then when I said I did not like my master's service and preferred to be with the Cossacks, for there was more profit among them; and he believed me. Why shouldn't he believe me when I brought him to health? Therefore he took a wonderful fancy to me, and what is true, rewarded me most liberally, not knowing that I had sworn to have vengeance on him for the wrong he had done me in Chigirin; and if I did not stab him at once, it was only because it is not proper for a noble to stab an enemy lying in bed, as he would stick a pig."

"Well, well," said Volodyovski, "we know that too, but how did you find him this time?"

"It was this way: When we had pushed the Yavorskis to the wall (they will have to go out with packs on their backs, it cannot be otherwise), I thought: 'Well, it is time for me to look for Bogun and pay him for the wrong he did me.' I left my parents in secret, and my grandfather; and he (there is good metal in him) said: 'If you have taken an oath, then go; if not, you will be a fool.' I went, for I thought to myself besides: 'When I find Bogun maybe I shall learn something about the lady, if she is alive; and afterward when I shoot him and go to my master with the news, that too will not be without a reward.'"

"Certainly it will not; and we will reward you also," said Volodyovski.

"And from me, brother, you will have a horse with trappings," added Podbipienta.

"I thank you most kindly," said the delighted young man; "a present is a fitting return for good news, and I won't drink away what I get from anybody--"

"Oh, the devil take me!" muttered Zagloba.

"You went away from your home and friends then?" suggested Volodyovski.

"I did; and on the way I thought: 'Where shall I go unless to Zbaraj, for it is not far from Bogun, and I can hear more readily of my master.' I go through Beloe to Vlodava, and in Vlodava I find my little horse terribly used up,--I halt for refreshment. There was a fair in the place; all the inns were full of nobles. I go to townspeople; nobles there too! Then a Jew says to me: 'I have a room, but a wounded noble has taken it. Then I say: 'This has happened well, for I know how to nurse, and your barber, as it is fair-time, cannot get through his work.' The Jew said then that the noble took care of himself, did not wish to see any man; still he went afterward to inquire. It is evident the noble was worse, for he gave orders to admit me. I enter, and I look to see who lies in the bed. Bogun! I bless myself in the name of the Father, Son, and Holy Ghost! I was frightened; but he recognized me at once, was very glad (for he takes me as his friend), and says he: 'God sent you to me! I'll not die this time.' And I say: 'What are you doing here, my master?' But he put his finger on his lips, and only afterward did he tell me of what had happened to him,--how Hmelnitski sent him to the king, who at that time was a prince,--sent him from before Zamost, and how Pan Volodyovski cut him up at Lipki."

"Did he remember me pleasantly?" asked Volodyovski.

"I cannot say, my master, otherwise than pleasantly enough. 'I thought,' says he, 'that he was some little cur; but it turns out that he is a hero of the first water, who almost cut me in two.' But when he thinks of Pan Zagloba, then he grits his teeth in great anger, because he urged you on to this fight--"

"May the hangman light him!" said Zagloba, "I am not afraid of him."

"We returned then to our former familiarity, yes, even to greater. He told me all,--how near he had been to death; how they removed him to the mansion at Lipki, taking him for a noble, and he gave himself out as Pan Hulevich from Podolia; how they cured him and treated him with great kindness, for which he swore gratitude to them till death."

"And what was he doing in Vlodava?"

"He was going to Volynia; but in Parcheva his wounds opened, for the wagon turned over with him, and he had to stop, though in great fear, for they might easily cut him to pieces there. He told me this himself. 'I was,' said he, 'sent with letters; but now I have no papers, nothing but a baton; and if they should discover who I am, not only the nobles would cut me to pieces, but the first commandant would hang me without asking permission of any man.' I remember that when he told me that, I said to him: 'It is well to know that the first commandant would hang you.' 'And how is that?' asked he. 'So as to be cautious and say nothing to any man, in which I also will serve you.' Then he began to thank me and to assure me of gratitude, and that reward would not miss me. Then he said: 'I have no money, but what jewels I have I will give you, and later I will cover you with gold; only render me one more service.'"

"And now we are coming to the princess?" said Volodyovski.

"Yes, my master, I must tell everything in detail. When he said that he had no money, I lost all heart for him, and thought to myself: 'Wait! I'll render you a service.' He said: 'I am sick, I have not strength for the journey, but a long and dangerous road awaits me. If I go to Volynia,--and it is not far from here,--then I shall be among my own; but to the Dniester I cannot go, for my strength is insufficient, and it is necessary to pass through an enemy's country, near castles and troops. Do you go for me!' 'To what place?' I ask. 'To Rashkoff, for she is hidden there with a sister of Donyéts, Horpyna.' I ask, 'Is it the princess?' 'Yes,' says he, 'I hid her there where the eye of man cannot see her; it is pleasant for her there, and she sleeps like the Princess Vishnyevetska, on golden cushions.'"

"Tell me quickly, in God's name!" shouted Zagloba.

"What is done quickly is done in the devil's fashion," answered Jendzian. "When I heard that, my master, how I rejoiced! But I did not show it, and I say: 'Is she surely there, for it must be a long time since you took her to the place?' He began to swear that Horpyna was devoted to him, would keep her ten years till his return, and that the princess was there as God is in heaven; for neither Poles nor Tartars nor Cossacks could come, and Horpyna would not disobey his order."

While Jendzian was telling the story, Zagloba trembled as in a fever, the little knight nodded his head joyfully, Podbipienta raised his eyes to heaven.

"That she is there is certain," continued the youth, "for the best proof is that he sent me to her. But I put it off at first so as to betray nothing, and I ask: 'Why should I go?' 'Because I am not able to go. If,' says he, 'I go from Vlodava to Volynia alive, I will have her taken to Kieff, for our Cossacks have the upper hand there everywhere. And you,' says he, 'go to Horpyna, and give her the order to take the princess to the monastery of the Holy Virgin in Kieff.'"

"Well, it was not to Nikolai the Good then," burst out Zagloba. "I saw at first that Yerlich was a hypochondriac, or that he lied."

"To the Holy Virgin," said Jendzian. "'I'll give you my ring,' says he, 'and baton and knife, and Horpyna will know what they mean, for we have agreed about them; and God has sent you,' says he, 'all the more because she knows you,--knows that you are my best friend. Go at once; don't fear the Cossacks, but look out for the Tartars, if there are any, and avoid them, for they will not respect the baton. Money, ducats, are buried in the ravine; take them out at once. Along the road you need only say, "Bogun's wife is travelling," and you will want for nothing. Besides,' says he, 'the witch is able to help herself. Only go, for my sake! Whom besides can I--unfortunate man!--send, whom can I trust, in this strange country, among enemies?' He begged, my master, till he almost shed tears. Finally the beast asked me to take an oath that I would go; and I took the oath, but in my mind I added: 'With my master!' Then he rejoiced, and gave me the baton, the ring, and the knife at once, and whatever jewels he had; and I took them too, for I thought, better that they be with me than with a robber. At parting he told me what ravine is above the Valadinka, how to go and how to turn so exactly, that I could get there with my eyes bound; which you will see yourselves if you go with me, as I think you will."

"Immediately! to-morrow!" said Volodyovski.

"What! to-morrow? We will order the horses to be saddled at daylight to-day."

Joy seized the hearts of all. At one moment could be heard cries of gratitude to heaven, at another the joyful rubbing of hands; then new questions put to Jendzian, to which he answered with his usual deliberation.

"May the bullets strike you!" cried Zagloba; "what a servant Skshetuski has in you!"

"Well, what of it?" asked Jendzian.

"He will cover you with gold."

"I think too that I shall not be without a reward, though I serve my master out of faithfulness."

"What did you do with Bogun?" asked Volodyovski.

"This, my master, was for me the greatest torment, that he lay sick again, and I could not put a knife into him, for my master would blame me for that. Such was my luck! What had I to do? He had told me all he had to tell, had given me all he had to give, so to my head for wit. 'Why,' say I to myself, 'should such a villain walk through the world? He imprisons a lady, and struck me in Chigirin. Better that he should not be, and let the hangman light his way. For,' I thought to myself, 'if he gets well, he will be after us with his Cossacks.' Not thinking long then, I went to Pan Rogovski, the commandant, who is in Vlodava with his squadron, and I told him that it was Bogun, the worst of the rebels. They must have hanged him before this time."

Having said this, Jendzian laughed stupidly enough, and looked on the audience as if waiting for applause; but how astonished was he when answered by silence! After some time Zagloba muttered, "No more of this!" but on the contrary Volodyovski kept silent, and Pan Longin began to click with his tongue, shake his head, and at last he said,--

"You have acted ignobly,--what is called ignobly!"

"How so, my master?" asked the astonished Jendzian; "should I have stabbed him?"

"And that would have been ugly, and this ugly. I know not which is better, to be a murderer or a Judas."

"What do you say, my master? Is it to be a Judas to give up a rebel who is an enemy of the king and the whole Commonwealth?"

"True, but still the deed is ignoble. What did you say the name of that commandant is?"

"Pan Rogovski. They said his name was Jakob."

"Ah, that's the same man!" muttered the Lithuanian. "A relative of Pan Lashch, and an enemy of Skshetuski."

But this remark was not heard, for Zagloba began,--

"Gentlemen, there is no reason for delay. God has so arranged through this youth, and has so directed, that we shall seek her under better conditions than hitherto. Praise be to God! We must leave in the morning. The prince has gone away already, but we must start without his permission, for there is no time to wait. Volodyovski will go; I with him, and Jendzian; but you, Pan Longin, would better stay, for your stature and your simplicity of soul might betray us."

"No, brother; I'll go too," said the Lithuanian.

"For her safety you must stay at home. Whoever has seen you will not forget you for a lifetime. We have the baton, it is true, but they would not believe you, even with the baton. You suffocated Pulyan in sight of Krívonos's whole rabble; and since such a pillar has stood before them, they would recognize it. You cannot go with us. You wouldn't find three heads there, and the one you have wouldn't help us much; you would ruin the undertaking."

"Sad," said the Lithuanian.

"Sad or not sad, you must stay. When we go to lift birds' nests out of the trees we will take you, but not this time."

"Disgusting to hear you!"

"Let me kiss you, for joy is in my heart. But stay! one thing more, gentlemen. This affair is of the greatest importance,--a secret. Let it not be known among the soldiers, and go from them to the peasants. Not a word to any man!"

"Not to the prince?"

"The prince is not here."

"But to Skshetuski, if he comes?"

"To him especially not a word, for he would race after us at once. He will have time enough to be glad; and God guard us from a new disappointment!--then he would lose his mind. Word of honor, gentlemen!"

"Word of honor," said Podbipienta.

"Word, word!"

"And now let us thank God."

Having said this, Zagloba knelt first, after him the others, and they prayed long and fervently.

CHAPTER LV.

The prince had really set out for Zamost a few days before for the purpose of making new levies of troops, and it was not expected that he would return soon. Volodyovski, Zagloba, and Jendzian therefore started on their journey unknown to any one and in the greatest secrecy,--to which only one person in Zbaraj was admitted, Pan Longin; but he, bound by his word, was as silent as if enchanted.

Vershul and other officers who knew of the princess's death did not suppose that the departure of the little knight with Zagloba had any connection with the betrothed of the unfortunate Skshetuski, and thought most likely that the two friends had gone to him the more since they had taken Jendzian, who was known to be a servant of Skshetuski.

They travelled straight to Hlebanovka, and there made preparations for the journey. Zagloba bought first of all, with money borrowed from Pan Longin, five Podolian horses, capable of long journeys. Horses of this breed were used by the Polish cavalry and the Cossacks; they could chase a whole day after a Tartar pony, surpassed in speed even the Turkish horses, and endured better every change of weather and cold, and rainy nights. Five such coursers did Zagloba purchase; besides he got sufficient Cossack clothing for himself and his comrades, as well as for the princess. Jendzian busied himself with the packs; and when all was provided and ready they started on the road, putting their undertaking under the guardianship of God and Saint Nikolai, the patron of young ladies.

So disguised, it was easy to take them for Cossack atamans, and frequently it happened that soldiers from Polish garrisons fastened on them, and guards scattered as far as Kamenyets; but Zagloba explained himself to them easily. They went for a long time through a safe country; for it was occupied by the squadrons of the commander Lantskoronski, which approached slowly toward Bar, in order to keep an eye on the Cossack bands gathering there. It was known universally that nothing would come of the negotiations. War hung over the country, therefore, though the main forces had not moved yet. The Pereyasláv armistice ended at Whitsuntide; partisan warfare, it is true, had not ended at any time. Now it increased, and both sides were only waiting the word.

At that time spring was rejoicing over the steppe. The earth which had been trampled by the hoofs of horses was now covered with a brocade of grass and flowers which had grown up from the bodies of the slain. Above battle-fields the lark pierced the azure of the heavens; various birds coursed through the air with their cries; the overflowed waters rippled in pools under the warm breath of the wind, and in the evenings the frogs swimming in the tepid water carried on joyous converse till late at night.

It seemed that Nature herself was eager to heal the wounds and cure the pains, to hide the graves beneath flowers. It was bright in the heavens, and on the earth fresh, breezy, gladsome; and the whole steppe, as if painted, glittered like an asphodel meadow, changed like the rainbow or like a Polish girdle on which the skilled needlewoman has joined all colors with exquisite taste. The steppe was full of the play of birds, and the broad breeze passed over it, drying the water and embrowning the faces of men.

At such a time every heart rejoices, and is filled with measureless hope. Our knights therefore were full of just such hope. Volodyovski sang continually. Zagloba straightened himself on the horse, put his shoulders with delight to the sun, and as soon as he was well warmed, said to the little knight,--

"I feel well; for, to tell the truth, next to mead and Hungarian wine there is nothing like the sun for old bones."

"It is good for everything," answered Volodyovski. "Just see how animals love to warm themselves in the sun!"

"It is lucky that we are going for the princess at such a time, for in the frosts of winter it would have been difficult to escape with the girl."

"Let us only get her into our hands, and I am a rascal if any man gets her away from us. I tell you, Pan Michael, I have only one fear, and that is in case of war the Tartars might move in those regions and snap us up; for we can get on with the Cossacks. We will give no account whatever to the peasants, for you have noticed that they take us for starshini; the Zaporojians respect the batons, and the name of Bogun will be a shield to us."

"I am acquainted with the Tartars, for while in the Lubni domains life passed in endless disputes with them. Vershul and I never had rest," answered Pan Michael.

"And I know them," said Zagloba. "I have told you how I passed several years in their company and might have risen to great dignities among them, but since I didn't wish to become a mussulman I had to leave all. Besides, they wanted to inflict a martyr's death on me because I was persuading their principal mulla to the true faith."

"But you said some other time that that was in Galáts."

"Galáts in its own way, and the Crimea in its own. But if you think the world ends in Galáts, then surely you don't know where pepper grows. There are more sons of Belial than Christians in this world."

Here Jendzian broke into the conversation. "Not only may we receive harm from Tartars," said he, "but I have not informed you that Bogun told me that unclean powers are guarding that ravine. The giantess herself who guards the princess is a powerful witch, intimate with devils who may warn her against us. I have, it is true, a bullet, which I moulded on consecrated wheat, for a common one would not take her; but besides there are probably whole regiments of vampires who guard the entrance. It is for your heads to see that no harm comes to me; if it should, my reward would be lost."

"Oh, you drone!" said Zagloba. "We have nothing to think of but your safety. The devil won't twist your neck; and even if he should it is all one, for you will go to hell anyhow for your covetousness. I'm too old a sparrow to be caught with chaff; and beat into yourself that if she is a powerful witch I am a more powerful wizard, for I learned the black art in Persia. She serves the devils, and they serve me, and I could plough with them as with oxen; but I don't want to do so, keeping in mind, as I do, the salvation of my own soul."

"That is well, my master; but for this time use your power, for it is always better to be on the safe side."

"But I have more confidence in our just cause and the protection of God," said Volodyovski. "Let the devils be the guard of Horpyna and Bogun, but with us are the angels of heaven, whom the best brigade in hell cannot withstand. On our behalf I make an offering of seven white wax candles to Saint Michael the Archangel."

"Then I will add one more," said Jendzian, "so that Pan Zagloba shouldn't frighten me with damnation."

"I will be the first to pack you off to hell," said the noble, "if it should appear that you don't know the places well."

"Why shouldn't I know? If we only reach Valadinka, I can find the place with my eyes bound. We will go along the shore toward the Dniester, and on the right hand will be the ravine, which we shall recognize by this, that the entrance to it is closed with a rock. At the first glance it will seem altogether impossible of entrance, but in the rock is an opening through which two horses can pass abreast. Once inside, no one can escape us, for that is the only entrance and exit. All around, the sides are so high that a bird can barely fly over them. The witch kills people who enter without permission, and there are many bones of men inside. Bogun gave orders not to notice these, but to ride on and shout: 'Bogun! Bogun!' Then she will come out to us with friendship. Besides Horpyna, there is Cheremís, who is a good marksman. We must kill them both."

"I say nothing about Cheremís, but it will be enough to tie the woman."

"How could you tie her? She is so strong that she tears armor to pieces like a shirt, and a horseshoe crumbles in her hand. Pan Podbipienta might possibly overpower her, but not we. But leave the matter; I have a consecrated bullet. Let the black hour come on that she-devil; otherwise she would fly after us like a wolf, and would howl to the Cossacks, and we should fail to bring back not only the young lady, but our own heads."

In such conversation and counsels their time passed on the road. They travelled hurriedly, passing villages, hamlets, farms, and grave-mounds. They went through Yarmolintsi to Bar, from where they were to advance in the direction of Yampol and the Dniester. They went through the neighborhood in which Volodyovski had defeated Bogun and freed Zagloba from his hands; they even came to the same farm and stopped there over night. Sometimes they slept under the open sky in the steppes, and Zagloba enlivened these halting-places by narratives of his previous adventures, some of which had happened and some of which had never taken place. But the conversations were mostly about the princess and her coming liberation from captivity with the witch.

Issuing at length from the regions held in curb by the garrisons and squadrons of Lantskoronski, they entered the Cossack country, in which nothing remained of the Poles, for those who had not fled were exterminated by fire and sword. May had departed, followed by a sultry June, while they had barely finished a third of the journey, for the road was long and difficult. Happily no danger threatened them from the side of the Cossacks. They gave no account of themselves to the peasant parties, who usually took them for Zaporojian starshini. Still, they were asked from time to time who they were. Zagloba, if the inquirer was from the lower country, showed Bogun's baton; if a common murderer from the mob, then, without getting from the horse, he struck the man with his foot in the breast and knocked him to the ground. The bystanders, seeing this, opened a way for them, thinking that they were not only their own, but also very distinguished, since they struck people,--"perhaps Krívonos, Burlai, or Father Hmelnitski himself."

Zagloba complained greatly of the fame of Bogun, for the Zaporojians annoyed him too much with inquiries about the chief, through which delays on the road were not infrequent. And generally there was no end to the questions,--whether he was well, or alive, for the report of his death had spread as far as Yagorlik and the Cataracts. But when the travellers declared that he was well and free, and that they were his messengers, they were kissed and honored; all hearts were open to them, and even purses, of which the cunning servant of Skshetuski did not omit to take advantage.

In Yampol they were received by Burlai who with Zaporojian troops and the rabble was waiting for the Tartars of Budjak. This was an old and distinguished colonel. Years before he had taught Bogun his military craft. He went on expeditions over the Black Sea with him, and in one of these expeditions the two had plundered Sinope in company. He loved him therefore as a son, and received his messengers with gladness, not exhibiting the least distrust, especially since he had seen Jendzian with Bogun the previous year. But when he learned that Bogun was alive and going to Volynia, from joy he gave a feast to the messengers and drank with them himself.

Zagloba was afraid that Jendzian, when he had drunk wine, might say something dangerous; but it turned out that the youth, cunning as a fox, knew how to manage, so that speaking the truth only when practicable, he did not imperil their affair, but won still greater confidence. It was strange, however, for our knights to hear those conversations carried on with such terrible sincerity in which their own names were repeated so often.

"We heard," said Burlai, "that Bogun was slain in a duel. And don't you know who cut him?"

"Volodyovski, an officer of Prince Yeremi," answered Jendzian, calmly.

"If I could get my hands on Volodyovski, I would pay him for our falcon. I'd pull him out of his skin."

Volodyovski at this moved his oat-colored mustaches, and looked at Burlai with such a look as a hound gives a wolf which he is not permitted to seize by the throat; and Jendzian said,--

"That's why I give you his name, Colonel."

"The devil will have real fun with that fellow Jendzian," thought Zagloba.

"But," continued Jendzian, "he is not so much to blame himself, for Bogun challenged him without knowing what a sabre he was summoning. There was another noble there, the greatest enemy of Bogun, who had once snatched the princess from his hands."

"And who is he?"

"Oh, he is an old sot who used to hang around our ataman in Chigirin and pretend to be his best friend."

"He'll hang yet!" shouted Burlai.

"I'm a fool if I don't cut the ears off that puppy!" muttered Zagloba.

"They so cut him up," continued Jendzian, "that another in his place would have been eaten by the crows long ago; but there is a horned soul in our ataman, and he recovered, though he barely dragged himself to Vlodava; and there he would have failed surely but for us. We helped him off to Volynia, where our people have the upper hand, and he sent us here for the princess."

"These women will be the death of him," muttered Burlai. "I told him that long ago. Would it not have been better for him to take a girl in Cossack fashion, and then a stone around her neck and into the water, as we did in the Black Sea?"

Here Volodyovski scarcely restrained himself, so wounded was he in his feeling for the sex; but Zagloba laughed, and said: "Surely it would have been better."

"But you were old friends," said Burlai, "you did not desert him in need; and you, boy [here lie turned to Jendzian], you are the best of them all, for I saw in Chigirin how you nursed and cared for our falcon. I am your friend for that. Tell me what you want,--men or horses? I'll give them to you, so that no harm may meet you on the return."

"We do not need men," said Zagloba, "for we shall go through our own country and among our own people, and God keep us from evil adventure! It is worse with a large party than with a small one; but some of the swiftest horses would be of service."

"I'll give you such that the ponies of the Khan would not overtake them."

Jendzian now spoke up, not to lose an opportunity: "And give us a little money, Ataman, for we have none, and beyond Bratslav a measure of oats is a thaler."

"Then come with me to the storeroom," said Burlai.

Jendzian didn't let this be said twice, and disappeared through the door with the old colonel; and when after a while he returned joy was beaming from his round face, and his blue coat was bulging out over his stomach.

"Well, go with God," said the old Cossack; "and when you get the girl stop in to see me, so that I may look at Bogun's cuckoo."

"Impossible, Colonel," said the youth, boldly; "for that Pole is terribly afraid, and once stabbed herself with a knife. We are afraid that something evil may happen to her. Better let the ataman manage her himself."

"He will manage her; she won't be afraid of him. The Pole is white-handed, doesn't like the Cossacks," muttered Burlai. "Go! God be with you! You haven't far now."

From Yampol to Valadinka it was not so very far; but the road was difficult, or rather a continual absence of roads stretched before the knights; for at that time those regions were still a desert, with rarely a house or a dwelling. They went then from Yampol somewhat to the west, withdrawing from the Dniester, to go afterward with the course of the Valadinka toward Kashkoff; for only thus could they strike the ravine. Light was growing in the heavens; for the feast at Burlai's had lasted till late at night, and Zagloba calculated that they would not find the ravine before sundown; but that was exactly what he wanted, for he wished after freeing Helena, to leave the night behind him. While they were travelling they spoke of how fortune had favored them so far in everything along the whole road; and Zagloba, mentioning the feast with Burlai, said,--

"See how those Cossacks who live in brotherhood uphold one another in every trouble! I do not speak of the mob,--whom they despise, and for whom, if the devil helps them to throw off our dominion, they will be still worse masters than the Poles; but in the Brotherhood one is ready to jump into the fire for another, not like our nobles."

"Not at all, my master," said Jendzian. "I was among them a long time, and I saw how they tear one another like wolves; and if Hmelnitski were gone, who sometimes by power, sometimes by policy, keeps them in check, they would devour one another. But this Burlai is a great warrior among them, and Hmelnitski himself respects him."

"But you feel contempt for the man, of course, since he let you rob him. Oh, Jendzian, you will not die your own death!"

"What is written for each man, my master, that he'll have; but to deceive an enemy is praiseworthy, and pleasing to God."

"I do not blame you for that, but for greed, which is the feeling of a peasant, unworthy of a noble; for this you will be damned without fail."

"I will not spare money for candles in the church when I succeed in gaining anything, so that God too should have some profit from me and bless me; and it is no sin to help my parents."

"What a rascal, what a finished scoundrel!" cried Zagloba to Volodyovski. "I thought my tricks would go with me to the grave; but I see that this is a still greater rogue. So through the cunning of this youth we shall free our princess from Bogun's captivity, with Bogun's permission, and on Burlai's horses! Has any man ever seen such a thing? And to look at him you wouldn't give three copper coins for the fellow!"

Jendzian laughed with satisfaction, and said: "Will that be bad for us, my master?"

"You please me, and were it not for your greed I should take you into my service; but since you have tricked Bogun in such style, I forgive you for having called me a sot."

"It was not I who called you that, but Bogun."

"Well, God has punished him."

In such conversation the morning passed; but when the sun had rolled up high on the vault of heaven they became serious, for in a few hours they were to see Valadinka. After a long journey they were near their object at last; and disquiet, natural in such cases, crept into their hearts. Was Helena still alive? And if alive, would they find her? Horpyna might have taken her out, or might at the last moment have hidden her somewhere else among the secret places of the ravine, or have killed her. Obstacles were not all overcome yet, dangers were not all passed. They had, it is true, all the tokens by which Horpyna was to recognize them as Bogun's messengers, carrying out his will; but would the devils or the spirits forewarn her? Jendzian feared this most; and even Zagloba, though pretending to be an expert in the black art, did not think of this without alarm. In such a case they would find the ravine empty or (what was worse) Cossacks from Rashkoff ambushed in it. Their hearts beat more strongly; and when finally, after some hours yet of travelling, they saw from the lofty rim of the ravine the glittering ribbon of water, the plump face of Jendzian paled a little.

"That is the Valadinka," said he, in a suppressed voice.

"Already?" inquired Zagloba, in an equally low voice. "Are we so near as that?"

"May God guard us!" replied Jendzian. "Oh, my master, begin your exorcisms, for I am awfully afraid."

"Exorcisms are folly. Let us bless the river and the secret places,--that will help more."

Volodyovski was the calmest of all, but he kept silent, examining however his pistols carefully, and added new powder; then he felt to see if his sabre would come out of the scabbard easily.

"I have a consecrated bullet too in this pistol here," said Jendzian. "In the name of the Father, Son, and Holy Ghost! Let us move on!"

"Move on! move on!" said Volodyovski.

After a time they found themselves on the bank of the little river, and turned their horses in the direction of its course. Here Volodyovski stopped them, and said,--

"Let Jendzian take the baton, for the witch knows him, and let him be the first to talk with her, so that she may not get frightened at us and run off with the princess into some hiding-place."

"I will not go first, no matter what you do," said Jendzian.

"Then go last, you drone!"

Having said this, Volodyovski went first, after him Zagloba, and in the rear with the pack-horses clattered Jendzian, looking around with apprehension on every side. The hoofs of the horses rattled over the stones, around about reigned the dull silence of the desert; but grasshoppers and crickets hidden in the cliff chirped, for it was a sultry day, though the sun had passed the meridian considerably. Night had come at last to the eminence, rounded like an upturned shield, on which rocks fallen apart and burnt from the sun presented forms like ruins, tumble-down houses, and church-steeples; you might have thought it a castle or a place stormed by an enemy.

Jendzian looked at Zagloba and said: "This is the Devil's Mound; I know it from what Bogun told me. No living thing passes here by night."

"If it does not, it can," answered Zagloba. "Tfu! what a cursed land! But at least we are on the right road."

"The place is not far," said Jendzian.

"Praise be to God!" answered Zagloba; and his mind was turned to the princess.

He had wonderful thoughts, and seeing those wild banks of the Valadinka, that desert and silent wilderness, he scarcely believed that the princess could be so near,--she for whose sake he had passed through so many adventures and dangers, and loved so that when the news of her death came he knew not what to do with his life and his old age. But on the other hand a man becomes intimate, even with misfortune. Zagloba, who had grown familiar with the thought that she had been taken away and was far off in Bogun's power, did not dare to say now to himself: "The end of grief and search has come, the hour of success and peace has arrived." Besides other thoughts crowded to his brain: "What will she say when she sees him? Will she not dissolve into tears when like a thunderbolt comes to her that rescue, after such long and painful captivity? God has his wonderful ways," thought Zagloba, "and so succeeds in correcting everything that from this come the triumph of virtue and the shame of injustice. It was God who first gave Jendzian into the hands of Bogun, and then made friends of them. God arranged that War, the stern mother, called away the wild ataman from the fastnesses to which like a wolf he had carried his plunder. God afterward delivered him into the hands of Volodyovski, and again brought him into contact with Jendzian. All is so arranged that now, when Helena may have lost her last hope and when she expects aid from no side, aid is at hand! Oh, cease your weeping, my daughter! Soon will joy come to you without measure! Oh, she will be grateful, clasp her hands, and return thanks!" Then she stood before the eyes of Zagloba as if living, and he was filled with emotion and lost altogether in thinking of what would happen in an hour.

Jendzian pulled him by the sleeve from behind. "My master!"

"Well!" said Zagloba, displeased that the course of his thoughts was interrupted.

"Did you not see a wolf spring across before us?"

"What of that?"

"But was it only a wolf?"

"Kiss him on the snout."

At this moment Volodyovski reined in his horse. "Have we lost the road," he asked, "for it should be here?"

"No, we have not," answered Jendzian; "we are going as Bogun directed. I wish to God it were all over."

"It will not be long, if we ride well."

"I want to tell you another thing. When I am talking to the witch keep an eye on Cheremís; he must be a terribly nasty fellow, but shoots fearfully with his musket."

"Oh, cavalry, don't be afraid!"

They had barely gone some yards when the horses pricked up their ears and snorted. Jendzian's skin began to creep at once; for he expected that at any moment the howling of vampires might be heard from the cliffs in the rocks, or some unknown and repulsive form would creep out. But it appeared that the horses snorted only because they were passing near the retreat of that wolf who had so disturbed the youth a little while before. Round about was silence; even the grasshoppers had ceased chirping, for the sun had already inclined to the other side of the sky. Jendzian made the sign of the cross and calmed himself.

Volodyovski held in his horse suddenly. "I see the ravine," said he, "in the throat of which a rock is thrust, and in the rock there is a breach."

"In the name of the Father, Son, and Holy Ghost!" muttered Jendzian.

"After me!" commanded Pan Michael, turning his horse. Soon they were at the breach, and passed through as under a stone arch. Before them opened a deep ravine, thickly overgrown with bushes at the sides, widening in the distance to a broad half-circle,--a small plain, enclosed as it were by gigantic walls.

Jendzian began to shout as loud as the power in his breast permitted: "Bogun! Bogun! Witch, come out! Bogun! Bogun!"

They halted and remained for some time in silence; then the youth began to shout again: "Bogun! Bogun!"

From a distance came the barking of dogs.

"Bogun! Bogun!"

On the left rim of the ravine on which the ruddy and golden rays of the sun were falling the thick branches of the plum and wild-cherry trees began to rustle; and after a while there appeared, almost at the very source of the spring, a human form, which bending forward and covering its eyes with its hand looked carefully at the travellers.

"That's Horpyna," said Jendzian; and putting his palms around his mouth, he began to shout a third time: "Bogun! Bogun!"

Horpyna began to descend, bending back to keep her balance. She came on quickly, and after her rolled along a sort of dumpy little man with a long Turkish gun in his hand. Twigs broke under the weighty step of the witch; stones rolled from under them and rattled to the bottom of the ravine. Bent in that fashion, in the ruddy glare she seemed really some gigantic superhuman creature.

"Who are you?" called she in a loud voice, when she had reached the bottom.

"How are you, bass-viol!" said Jendzian, to whom his usual deliberation returned at the sight of human beings instead of spirits.

"You are Bogun's servant? I know you, you fellow; but who are these?"

"Friends of Bogun."

"Ah, she is a handsome witch," muttered Pan Michael, under his mustaches.

"And what have you come for?"

"Here is the baton, the knife, and the ring for you,--you know what they mean?"

The giantess took them in her hands and began to examine them carefully; then she said,--

"They are the same! You have come for the princess?"

"Yes! Is she well?"

"She is. Why didn't Bogun himself come?"

"Bogun is wounded."

"Wounded? I saw that in the mill."

"If you saw it, why do you ask? You lie, you bugle-horn!" said Jendzian, confidently.

The witch showed in a smile teeth white as the teeth of a wolf, and doubling her hand nudged Jendzian in the side: "You are a boy, you are a fellow, you are."

"Be off!"

"You won't give a kiss, will you? And when will you take the princess?"

"Right away; we will only rest the horses."

"Well, take her! I will go with you."

"What do you want to go for?"

"Death is fated for my brother; the Poles will empale him on a stake. I will go with you."

Jendzian bent toward the saddle as if for easier conversation with the giantess, and his hand rested unobserved on the butt of a pistol.

"Cheremís! Cheremís!" said he, wishing to turn the attention of his comrades on the dwarf.

"Why do you call him? His tongue is cut out."

"I am not calling him, I'm only admiring his beauty. You will not leave him,--he is your husband."

"He is my dog!"

"And there are only two of you in the ravine?"

"Two,--the princess is the third."

"That's well. You will not leave him?"

"I will go with you," said she.

"But I tell you that you will remain."

There was something in the voice of the youth of such a character that the giantess turned on the spot with an alarmed face, for suspicion suddenly entered her mind.

"What do you mean?" asked she.

"This is what I mean!" answered Jendzian; and he thundered at her from the pistol so near that the smoke covered her completely for a moment.

Horpyna pushed back with open arms; her eyes protruded, a kind of unearthly yell rose out of her throat; she tottered and fell on her back, full length.

At the same moment Zagloba cut Cheremís through the head with a sabre so that the bone gritted under its edge. The deformed dwarf uttered no groan; he merely wound himself in a lump like a worm, and began to quiver. But the fingers of his hand opened and closed in succession like the claws of a dying wild-cat.

Zagloba wiped the steaming sabre with the skirt of his coat. Jendzian, springing from the horse and taking up a stone, threw it on the broad breast of Horpyna; then he began to look for something in his bosom.

The enormous body of the witch dug the ground yet with its feet, convulsions twisted her face terribly, on her grinning teeth came out a bloody foam, and dull rattles issued from her throat.

Meanwhile the youth got from his bosom a piece of consecrated chalk, drew a cross with it on the stone, and said: "Now she will not rise!" Then he sprang into the saddle.

"To horse!" commanded Volodyovski.

They rushed like a whirlwind along the brook running through the middle of the ravine; they passed the oaks scattered thinly along the road, and a cottage appeared before their eyes. Farther on was the lofty mill, the moist wheel of which glittered like a ruddy star in the rays of the sun. Under the cottage two enormous black dogs, tied with ropes at the corner, sprang at the men, barking with rage and howling.

Volodyovski, riding in advance, arrived first, sprang from his horse, ran to the entrance, kicked in the door, and rushed to the anteroom with clattering sabre.

In the anteroom on the right through an open door was seen a wide room, with shavings scattered about and a smoking fireplace; on the left the door was closed. "She must be there!" thought Volodyovski; and he sprang toward the door. He pushed; it opened. He stepped on the threshold and stood there as if fastened.

In the depth of the room, with head resting on the edge of a couch, was Helena Kurtsevichovna, pale, with hair falling on her neck and shoulders. With frightened eyes fixed on Volodyovski, she asked: "Who are you? What do you want?" for she had never seen the little knight before.

He was astonished at the sight of that beauty and that room covered with silk and brocade. At last he came to his speech, and said hurriedly: "Have no fear, we are the friends of Skshetuski."

That moment the princess threw herself on her knees: "Save me!" she cried, clasping her hands.

Just then Zagloba, trembling, purple, and out of breath, rushed in. "It is we!" cried he,--"it is we with succor!"

Hearing these words and seeing the familiar face, the princess bent over like a cut flower, her hands dropped, her eyes were covered with their bordered curtains. She had fainted.

CHAPTER LVI.

The horses were given barely time to rest, and the return was begun with such speed that when the moon had risen on the steppe the party was already in the neighborhood of Studenka, beyond the Valadinka. Volodyovski rode in front, looking carefully on every side. Next came Zagloba at the side of Helena; and Jendzian closed the procession, driving the pack animals and two saddle-horses, which he had not failed to take from Horpyna's stable. Zagloba's mouth was not closed; and in truth he had something to tell the princess, who shut up in the wild ravine knew nothing of what was passing in the world. He told her how they had looked for her at first; how Skshetuski, without knowing of the duel, had sought Bogun as far as Pereyasláv; how finally Jendzian gained the secret of her concealment from the ataman and brought it to Zbaraj.

"Merciful God!" said Helena, raising her beautiful pale face to the moon; "then Pan Skshetuski went beyond the Dnieper for me?"

"To Pereyasláv, as I tell you. And surely he would have come with us now, but we had no time to send for him as we wished to hurry to your aid at once. He knows nothing as yet of your safety, and offers prayers for your soul every day; but have no sorrow for him now. Let him suffer a while longer since such a reward is awaiting him."

"And I thought that all had forgotten me, and I was only imploring the Lord for death."

"Not only did we not forget you, but all the time our single thought was how to come to your aid. Wonders we planned. I was drying my brain, and so was Skshetuski; but that was to be expected. This knight too who is riding in front of us spared neither toil nor sword."

"May God reward him!"

"It is clear that you both have that which makes people cleave to you; but in truth you owe Volodyovski gratitude, for as I said we cut up Bogun like a pike."

"In Rozlogi, Pan Skshetuski spoke much of Volodyovski as of his best friend."

"And justly. He has a great soul in a little body. This moment he is somehow dull. It is evident that your beauty has stunned him; but wait, let him only grow used to it and he will come to himself. Oh! he and I worked wonders at the election."

"Then there is a new king?"

"Poor girl! In this cursed wilderness you don't know that Yan Kazimir was elected last autumn and has been reigning eight months. There will be a great war this time with the rabble. God grant us good fortune, for Yeremi has been set aside and others appointed who are altogether unfitted."

"And will Pan Skshetuski go to the war?"

"He is a true soldier, and I don't think you can stop him. He and I are alike! When powder entices, nothing can restrain us. Oh, we gave it to the ruffians in grand fashion last year! The whole night would be short were I to tell you all as it happened. We shall be sure to go, but with a light heart now. The main thing is that we have found you, poor girl, without whom life was a burden to us."

The princess inclined her sweet face to Zagloba. "I know not why you love me, but it is sure that you do not love me more than I do you."

Zagloba began to puff with satisfaction. "Then you love me?"

"As I live, I do."

"God reward you, for my old age will be lighter. Women pursue me yet, as was the case in Warsaw more than once during the election. Volodyovski is witness of that. But I don't care for love, and in spite of my hot blood, I am content with the feeling of a father."

Silence followed; but the horses began to snort violently, one after another,--a favorable omen.

"Good health, good health!" said the travellers.

The night was clear; the moon rose higher and higher in the sky, which was filled with twinkling stars, that became weaker and paler. The tired horses lessened their speed, and weariness seized the travellers. Volodyovski reined in his horse first.

"The dawn is not distant," said he; "it is time to rest."

"It is," said Zagloba. "I am so sleepy that my horse seems to have two heads."

But before resting, Jendzian prepared supper. He made a fire, removed the saddle-bags from a horse, and took out provisions which he had obtained from Burlai in Yampol, such as corn bread, cold meat, and Wallachian wine. At the sight of these two leather bags, well filled out with liquid which gave forth a pleasant sound, Zagloba forgot his sleep; the others also fell to eating and drinking with a good will. There was abundance for all; and when they were satisfied, Zagloba wiped his mouth and said,--

"Till death I shall not cease to repeat, 'Wondrous are the judgments of God!' Now, my young lady, you are free; and here we sit comforted under the sky, drinking Burlai's wine. I will not say that Hungarian would not be better, for this smells of the skin, but on the road it will pass."

"There is one thing at which I cannot wonder sufficiently," said Helena,--"that Horpyna consented so easily to give me up to you."

Zagloba looked at Volodyovski, then at Jendzian, and blinked rapidly.

"She consented, for she had to. There is nothing to hide, for it is no shame that we rubbed out both Cheremís and the witch."

"How?" asked the princess, with fright.

"Didn't you hear the shots?"

"I heard them, but thought Cheremís was firing."

"It was not Cheremís, but this young fellow here, who shot the witch through and through. The devil sits in him, we don't dispute that. But he could not act otherwise; for the witch-- whether it was because she knew something, or was stubborn--insisted on going with us. It was difficult to permit that, for she would have seen at once that we were not going to Kieff. He shot her, and I killed Cheremís,--a real African monster,--and I think that God will not count it ill of me. There must be a universal disgust of him in even the regions below. Just before leaving the ravine I went ahead and pulled the bodies aside a little, so that you might not be frightened at them or take it as a bad omen."

"In these terrible times I have seen too many dead persons who were kindred of mine to be frightened at the sight of slain bodies," said the princess; "still I should prefer not to have blood shed, so that God might not punish us for it."

"It was not a knightly deed," said Volodyovski, harshly. "I would not put my hand to it."

"What is the use of thinking over it," said Jendzian, "when it could not be avoided? If we had destroyed some good person I should not speak; but an enemy of God may be killed; and I myself saw how that witch entered into fellowship with devils. It is not for her that I am sorry."

"And why is Pan Jendzian sorry?" asked the princess.

"Because money is buried there, of which Bogun told me; but you gentlemen were so urgent that I had no time to dig it up, though I know well where it is, near the mill. My heart was cut also at having to leave so much property of every kind in that room where you, my lady, lived."

"Just see what a servant you are going to have!" said Zagloba to the princess. "With the exception of his master, there is no one, not the devil himself, from whom he would not strip skin to make a coat-collar for himself."

"With God's help, Jendzian will not complain of my ingratitude," answered Helena.

"I thank you humbly," said he, kissing her hand.

During this time Volodyovski sat with a sullen look, drinking wine quietly from the skin, till his unusual silence attracted Zagloba's attention.

"Ah, Pan Michael," said he, "you have given us scarcely a word." Here the old man turned to Helena. "I have not told you that your beauty has deprived him of reason and speech."

"You would better take a nap before daylight," was the little knight's reply; and he began to move his mustaches like a rabbit trying to gain courage.

But the old noble was right. The beauty of the princess had kept the little knight in a sort of continual ecstasy. He looked at her, looked again, and in his mind he asked: "Can it be that such a woman moves upon the earth?"

He had seen much beauty in his day. Beautiful were the Princesses Anna and Barbara Zbaraska, and Anusia Borzobogata, charming beyond expression. Panna Jukovkna, to whom Roztvorovski was paying court, had many a charm, and so had Vershulovna and Skoropadska and Bohovitnianka; but none of these could compare with that marvellous flower of the steppe. In presence of the others Volodyovski was vivacious, full of speech; but now, when he looked on those velvet eyes, sweet and languishing, on the silken lashes, the shade of which fell on the pupils, on the arrowy form, on the bosom lightly moved by the breath, on the bloom of the lips,--when Volodyovski looked at all this, he simply forgot the tongue in his mouth; and what was worse, he seemed awkward, stupid, and above all diminutive,--so small as to be ridiculous. "She is a princess, and I am a little boy," thought he, in bitterness; and he would have rejoiced could some giant have issued from the darkness by chance, for then poor Pan Michael would have shown that he was not so small as he seemed. He was irritated also because Zagloba, evidently glad that his daughter was so attractive, coughed every little while, quizzed, and winked fearfully. And each instant she was more beautiful, as calm and sweet she sat before the fire, shone on by the rosy flame and the white moon.

"Confess, Pan Michael," said Zagloba, early next day, when they found themselves alone for a moment, "that there is not such another girl in the Commonwealth. If you show me another such, I will let you call me idiot and give me a drubbing."

"I do not deny," said the little knight, "that she is dainty and rare, such as I have not seen till this hour; for even those forms of goddesses cut from marble which seem alive, and which we saw in the Kazanovski palace, are not to be compared with her. I do not wonder that the best men are risking their lives for her, for she is worth it."

"Well, well," said Zagloba, "as God lives, you cannot tell when she is better, morning or evening, for she always moves in beauty, like a rose. I have told you that I was once of extraordinary beauty myself, but I should have been forced to yield to her, though some say she resembles me as one cup does another."

"Go to the devil!" cried the little knight.

"Don't be angry, Pan Michael, for you are bad enough to the eye already. You gaze on her as a goat on a head of cabbage. One might swear that longing has seized you; but the sausage is not for the dog."

"Tfu!" cried Volodyovski. "Are you not ashamed, being an old man, to talk such nonsense?"

"And why are you frowning?"

"Because you think we have passed all danger, like a bird in the air, and are entirely safe; but now careful deliberation is needed, so that when we have escaped one evil we may avoid another. There is a terrible road before us yet, and God knows what may happen, for these regions to which we are going must be already on fire."

"When I stole her from Bogun out of Rozlogi it was worse, for there was pursuit in the rear and rebellion in front; still I passed through the whole Ukraine as through a flame, and went to Bar. And why is the head on my shoulders? At the worst, it is not far to Kamenyets."

"True; but it is not far for the Turks and Tartars, either."

"Oh, what stuff do you tell me?"

"I tell you the truth, and say that it is worth thinking over. It is better to avoid Kamenyets and move on towards Bar; for the Cossacks will respect the baton. With the rabble we can get on; but if the Tartars see us, all is lost. I know them of old, and I could flee before a Tartar party with the birds and the wolves; but if we were to meet them I could be of no service."

"Then let us go through Bar or around Bar; let the plague take the limes and cherries of Kamenyets. You don't know that Jendzian took a baton from Burlai. We can go everywhere among the Cossacks singing. We have passed the worst of the Wilderness; we shall enter a settled country. We must think of stopping here and there at a farm about the time of evening milking, for such a place is more proper and comfortable for the princess. But it seems to me, Pan Michael, that you look at things in too sombre a light. Just think that three men like us-- without flattery to you or me--should not be able to make our way in the steppe! We'll join our stratagems to your sabre; and now for it! Nothing better can be done. Jendzian has Burlai's baton; and that is the main thing, for Burlai commands all Podolia at present, and if we are once beyond Bar, Lantskoronski is there, with the squadrons of the Crown. On, Pan Michael, let us lose no time!"

And in fact they lost no time, but tore on through the steppes toward the north and the west as fast as their horses could go. On the heights of Mogileff they entered a more settled land, so that in the evening it was not difficult anywhere to find farms or villages in which to spend the night; but the ruddy dawn always found them on horseback and on the road. Fortunately the summer was dry,--warm days, with dewy nights, and in the early morning the whole steppe was silvered as with frost. The wind dried the waters, the rivers decreased, and they crossed without difficulty.

Going for some time along and above Lozova, they stopped for a somewhat longer rest than usual in Shargorod, where there was a Cossack regiment not belonging to Burlai's command. There they found messengers from Burlai, and among them Kuna, a sotnik (captain), whom they had seen in Yampol at the feast with Burlai. He was somewhat surprised that they were not going through Bratslav, Raigorod, and Skvira to Kieff; but no suspicion remained in his mind, especially when Zagloba explained to him that they had not taken that road from fear of the Tartars, who were about to march from the direction of the Dnieper. Kuna told them then that Burlai had sent him to proclaim the campaign, and that he himself was ready to come at any moment, with all the forces at Yampol and the Budjak-Tartars to Shargorod, whence they would advance immediately.

Couriers had come from Hmelnitski to Burlai with news that war had begun, and with orders to lead all the regiments to Volynia. Burlai had long wished to move on Bar, and was merely awaiting the Tartar reinforcements, for somehow it had begun to go badly at Bar for the rebellion. Lantskoronski, the Polish commander, had cut up considerable bands there, captured the place, and put a garrison in the castle. Several thousand Cossacks had been killed. Burlai wished to avenge these and recapture the castle; but Kuna said that the final orders of Hmelnitski to march on Volynia prevented these plans, and Bar would not be besieged unless the Tartars should insist on it.

"Well, Pan Michael," said Zagloba the next day, "Bar is before us and we might hide the princess there a second time; but the devil take it, I have no more trust in Bar, or any other fortress, since these ruffians have more cannon than the armies of the Crown. This, however, troubles me somewhat, that clouds are gathering around."

"Not only are clouds gathering," answered the knight, "but a storm is rolling up behind, namely the Tartars; and if Burlai should come up with us he would be greatly astonished that we are not going to Kieff, but in the opposite direction."

"He would be ready to show us another road. May the devil show him first the straightest road to his own kingdom! Let us make an agreement, Pan Michael. I will explain everything to the Cossacks, but let your wit work against the Tartars."

"It is easier for you to manage the ruffians who take us for their own," answered Volodyovski. "Against the Tartars there is but one help,--to flee with all swiftness, to slip out of the snare while there is time. We must buy good horses on the road wherever we can, so as to have fresh ones at any moment."

"Pan Longin's purse will suffice for that, and if it does not we will take Burlai's money from Jendzian. But now forward!"

And they pushed on still more hurriedly, till foam covered the sides of the ponies and fell like snow-flakes on the green steppe. After they had passed Derla and Ladava, Volodyovski bought new horses in Barek, without leaving the old ones; for those which they had as a gift from Burlai were of rare breed, and they kept them attached by the bridle, and drove on, making shorter stops and night-rests. Every one was in good health, and Helena in excellent spirits. Though wearied with the road, she felt that every day gave her new strength. In the ravine she had passed a secluded life and scarcely left her gilded room, not wishing to meet the shameless Horpyna and listen to her talk and persuasion; now the fresh breeze of the steppe brought back her health. The roses bloomed on her face, the sun darkened her complexion, but her eyes gained brightness; and when at times the wind blew the hair over her forehead, you would have said she was some gypsy, the most wonderful soothsayer, or that a gypsy queen was travelling in the wide steppe,--flowers springing up before her, knights following behind.

Volodyovski grew accustomed to her beauty by degrees, as the journey brought them together, so that finally he became used to her; then he regained his speech and cheerfulness, and often while riding at her side told of Lubni, and especially of his friendship for Pan Yan, thinking she heard this with gladness; at times he even teased her, saying: "I am Bogun's friend and am taking you to him."

Then she would fold her hands as if in great dread, and say in a sweet voice: "Oh, cruel knight, better kill me at once than do that!"

"Impossible, I must take you!" answered the stern knight.

"Strike!" said she, closing her eyes and stretching her neck to him.

Then the ants began to travel along the back of the little knight. "That girl goes to the head like wine!" thought he; "but I cannot drink this wine, for it is another's." The honest Pan Michael then shook himself and urged his horse forward. When he plunged into the grass like a sea-mew into water, the ants fell from him; he turned all his attention to the journey. Was it safe, were they going well, or was any adventure approaching them from any side? He straightened himself in the stirrups, raised his yellow mustaches over the waving grass, looked, sniffed, listened like a Tartar when he is prowling in the wild fields through the grass of the steppe.

Zagloba too was in the best of spirits. "It is easier for us to escape now," said he, "than when on the Kagamlik we had to sneak off on foot like dogs, with our tongues hanging out. My tongue at that time was so dried up in my mouth that I could have planed a tree with it, but now, thanks be to God, I have something to sleep on in the evening, and something to wet my throat with from time to time."

"Do you remember how you carried me over the water?"

"God grant us to wait! you'll have something to carry in your arms; I'll bet Skshetuski's head on that."

"Ho! ho!" laughed Jendzian.

"Desist, I beg you," whispered the princess, blushing and dropping her eyes.

Thus they conversed over the steppe, to shorten the time. Finally, beyond Barek and Yeltushkoff they entered a country recently gnawed by the teeth of war. There bands of armed ruffians raged; there also, not long before, Lantskoronski burned and slew, for it was only a few days since he had withdrawn to Zbaraj. Our travellers learned also from the people of the town that Hmelnitski and the Khan had set out with all their forces against the Poles, or rather against the commanders whose forces were in mutiny and refused to serve except under the command of Prince Yeremi. In this connection it was generally prophesied that destruction or the end of either the Poles or the Cossacks would surely come, for Father Hmelnitski and Yeremi were to meet. The whole country was as if on fire. All were rushing to arms and marching to the north to join Hmelnitski. From the lower Dniester, Burlai was advancing with his entire force; and along the road every regiment was in motion from garrisons, quarters, and pastures, for the order had come to all. They marched then in hundreds, in squadrons, in thousands; and at their flank rolled on like a river the mob, armed with flails, forks, knives, and pikes. Horseboys and herdsmen left their herds, settlers their lands, bee-keepers their bees, wild fishermen their reeds by the Dnieper, hunters the woods. Hamlets, villages, and towns were deserted. In three provinces there remained at home but old women and children, for even the young women had gone with the men against the Poles. Simultaneously from the east approached with his entire main army Hmelnitski, like an ominous storm, crushing by the way with his mighty hand castles, great and small, and killing all who were left from the previous defeats.

Having passed Bar, full of gloomy reminiscences for the princess, our travellers took the high-road leading through Latichi and Ploskiri to Tarnopol, and farther to Lvoff. Now, they met more frequently, at one time regular tabors of wagons, at another detachments of Cossack infantry and cavalry; now parties of peasants; now countless herds of cattle surrounded with clouds of dust, and driven on as food for the Cossack and the Tartar armies. The road became dangerous, for they were asked continually what they wanted, whence they came, and where they were going. Zagloba showed the Cossack companies Burlai's baton, and said,--

"We are sent from Burlai; we are taking Bogun's wife."

At sight of the baton of the terrible colonel, the Cossacks generally opened the way the more readily, since every one understood that if Bogun was alive he must be near the forces of the commanders in the neighborhood of Zbaraj or Konstantinoff. But it was far more difficult for the travellers to pass the mob with its wild parties of herdsmen, ignorant, drunk, and having almost no idea of the ensigns given by colonels for a safe conduct. Had it not been for Helena, these half-savage people would have taken Zagloba, Volodyovski, and Jendzian for their own,--in fact they did so even as it was; but Helena attracted universal attention by her sex and unusual beauty, hence the dangers had to be overcome with the greatest care.

At one time Zagloba showed the baton, at another Volodyovski his teeth, and more than one corpse fell behind them. A number of times the unapproachable steeds of Burlai alone saved them from too grievous adventure, and the journey so favorable at the beginning grew more difficult each day. Helena, although brave by nature, began to fail in health from continual alarm and sleeplessness, and looked in truth like a captive dragged against her will into the tent of an enemy. Zagloba exerted himself savagely, and was continually inventing new stratagems which the little knight put into practice at once; both of them consoled the princess as best they could.

"We have only to pass the swarm which is now in front," said Volodyovski, "and reach Zbaraj, before Hmelnitski with the Tartars fills the region about."

They learned on the road that the commanders had concentrated at Zbaraj, and intended to defend themselves there. They went to that place, expecting justly that Prince Yeremi would come to the commanders with his division, since a part of his forces (and that a considerable one) had its permanent post at Zbaraj. The swarms grew thinner on the road, for the country occupied by the squadrons of the Crown began only fifty miles beyond. The Cossack parties did not dare therefore to push on farther; they preferred to wait, at a safe distance, the arrival of Burlai from one and Hmelnitski from the other side.

"Only fifty miles now! only fifty miles!" repeated Zagloba, rubbing his hands. "If we could but reach the first Polish squadrons, we might go to Zbaraj in safety."

But Volodyovski determined to supply himself with fresh horses at Ploskiri, for those which he had bought at Barek were already useless, and it was necessary to spare Burlai's steeds for a black hour. This precaution became imperative, since news came that Hmelnitski was already at Konstantinoff, and the Khan with all his hordes was moving from Pilavtsi.

"Jendzian and I will remain here with the princess near the town, for it is better not to show ourselves on the market-place," said the little knight to Zagloba, when they came to a deserted house about two furlongs from the town, "and you go and inquire if there are horses for sale or exchange. It is evening now, but we will travel all night."

"I'll return soon," said Zagloba.

He went to the town. Volodyovski told Jendzian to let out the saddle-girths a little, so that the horses might rest; then he conducted Helena into the house, begging her to strengthen herself with some wine and with sleep.

"I should like to pass those fifty miles before daybreak to-morrow," said he; "then we shall all rest."

But he had scarcely brought the wine-skin and food when there was a clatter in front of the house. The little knight looked out through the window.

"Zagloba has already returned," said he; "it is evident that he has found no horses."

The door opened that moment, and Zagloba appeared in it, pale, blue, sweating, puffing. "To horse!" he cried.

Volodyovski was too experienced a soldier to lose time on inquiries. He didn't lose it even in saving the skin of wine,--which Zagloba carried off nevertheless,--but he seized the princess with all haste, took her out, put her on the saddle, gave a last look to see if the girths were drawn, and cried, "Forward!"

The hoofs clattered, and soon horses and riders had vanished in the darkness like a party in a dream. They flew on a long time without rest, till at last nearly five miles of road separated them from Ploskiri. Before the rising of the moon darkness became so dense that every pursuit was impossible. Volodyovski drew near Zagloba, and asked,--

"What was the matter?"

"Wait, Pan Michael, wait! I am terribly blown. I came near losing the use of my legs. Uf!"

"But what was the matter?"

"The devil in his own person,--the devil or a dragon! If you cut one head off him, another will grow."

"But speak plainly!"

"I saw Bogun on the market-square."

"Are you mad?"

"I saw him on the square, as I live, and with him five or six men, for I nearly lost the use of my legs. They held torches for him, and I thought, 'Some devil is standing in our road.' I lost all hope of a successful end to our undertaking. Can this imp of hell be immortal, or what? Don't speak of him to Helena. Oh, for God's sake, you slew him; Jendzian gave him up! That wasn't enough; he is alive now, free, and stands in the way. Oh, my God, my God! I tell you, Pan Michael, that I would rather see a ghost in a graveyard than him. And what devilish luck that I am the first to meet him everywhere! It's luck to cram down a dog's throat. Are there no other people in the world? Let others meet him. No! always I, and I."

"But did he see you?"

"If he had seen me, Pan Michael, you wouldn't be looking at me now. That alone was wanting."

"It would be important to know whether he is chasing after us, or is going to Valadinka to Horpyna with the intention of seizing us on the road."

"It seems to me that he is going to Valadinka."

"It must be so. Then we shall go on in one direction and he in the opposite; now there are five miles and more between us, and soon there will be twenty-five. Before he hears about us on the road, and returns, we shall be not only in Zbaraj, but in Jolkvi."

"Your speech, Pan Michael, thank God! is like a plaster to me. But tell me how it can be that he is free, when Jendzian gave him into the hands of the commandant of Vlodava?"

"Oh, he simply ran away!"

"The head of a commandant like that should be struck off. Jendzian! Jendzian!"

"What do you wish, my master?" asked the youth, reining in his horse.

"To whom did you deliver Bogun?"

"To Pan Rogovski."

"And who is this Pan Rogovski?"

"He is a great knight, a colonel of an armored regiment of the king."

"There it is for you!" said Volodyovski, snapping his fingers. "Don't you remember what Pan Longin told about Skshetuski's enmity with Rogovski? He is a relative of Pan Lashch, on account of whose disgrace he has a hatred for Skshetuski."

"I understand, I understand!" shouted Zagloba. "He is the one who must have let Bogun out through spite. But that is a capital offence, and smells of death. I'll be the first to report it."

"If God lets me meet him," muttered Volodyovski, "we shall be sure not to go to a tribunal."

Jendzian did not know yet what the trouble was, for after his answer he pushed forward again to the princess.

They were riding slowly. The moon had risen; the mists, which since evening had settled upon the land, fell away, and the night became clear. Volodyovski was sunk in meditation. Zagloba was digesting for some time yet the remnants of his astonishment; at last he said,--

"Bogun would have given it to Jendzian now if he had caught him."

"Tell him the news; let him be afraid too, and I'll go immediately to the princess," answered the little knight.

"Here, Jendzian!"

"Well, what is it?" asked the youth, reining in his horse again.

Zagloba came up with him. He was silent for a while, waiting for Volodyovski and the princess to ride far enough away. At last he asked: "Do you know what has happened?"

"No."

"Pan Rogovski set Bogun at liberty. I saw him in Ploskiri."

"In Ploskiri? To-day?" asked Jendzian.

"Yes. Why don't you drop from the saddle?"

The rays of the moon fell straight on the round face of the youth, and Zagloba saw on it not terror, but, to his utmost astonishment, that expression of stern, almost brutal stubbornness which Jendzian had when he killed Horpyna.

"Well, are you not afraid of Bogun?"

"My master," answered the youth, "if Pan Rogovski has let him go, then I must seek revenge on him again myself for the wrong done me and the insult. I do not forgive him, for I took an oath; and if we were not conducting the lady, I should turn back on the road at once. Let what belongs to me be mine."

"I am glad not to have offended this young fellow."

They spurred their horses, and soon came up with the princess and Volodyovski. In an hour they turned through the Medvédovka and entered a forest extending from the very bank of the river in two black walls along the road.

"I know the neighborhood well," said Zagloba. "There will soon be an end to this forest; after it is about a mile and a quarter of level land, and then another forest still larger extending to Matchin. God grant us to find Polish squadrons there!"

"It is high time that rescue came," muttered Volodyovski.

They rode awhile in silence over a road clearly lighted by the rays of the moon.

"Two wolves have run across," said Helena, suddenly.

"Yes," said Volodyovski, "and here is a third."

The gray shadow shot across a little more than a hundred rods in front of the horses.

"There is a fourth," said the princess.

"No, that is a deer. Look,--two, three!"

"What the devil!" cried Zagloba. "Deer chasing wolves! The world, I see, is overturned."

"Let us go a little faster," cried Volodyovski, with a voice of alarm. "Jendzian, come this way and go ahead with the lady!"

They shot on; but Zagloba bent forward as they rode to Volodyovski's ear, and inquired: "Pan Michael, what tidings?"

"Evil!" answered the little knight. "You have seen wild beasts rushing from their lairs and escaping in the night."

"But what does that mean?"

"It means that they are frightened."

"Who frightens them?"

"Troops, Cossack or Tartar, are coming toward us from the right hand."

"But it may be our squadrons?"

"Impossible, for the beasts are fleeing from the east, from Pilavtsi. Doubtless, then, the Tartars are marching in a wide body."

"Let us flee, Pan Michael, in God's name!"

"There is no help. Oh, if the princess were not here, we could go quite near them; but with her the passage will be very difficult if they set eyes on us."

"Have the fear of God, Pan Michael. Shall we turn to the woods and run after the wolves, or what?"

"Impossible; for though the enemy would not reach us at once, they would deluge the country in front of us, and then how should we escape?"

"May brimstone thunderbolts shake them! This alone was wanting to us. Oh, Pan Michael, are you not mistaken? You know wolves follow an army; they do not run before it."

"Those at the flanks follow the army and gather in from every side, but those in front get frightened. Look! on the right, between the trees, there is a fire."

"Jesus of Nazareth, King of the Jews!"

"Silence! Is there much more of this forest?"

"We shall be at the end in a moment."

"And then a field?"

"Yes, O Jesus!"

"No noise! Beyond the field there is another forest?"

"Extending to Matchin."

"We shall be all right if they don't overtake us in this field. If we reach the second forest in safety, we are at home. Let us go together then. Luckily the princess and Jendzian are on Burlai's horses."

They put spurs to the horses, and joined the princess and Jendzian.

"What fire is that on the right?" asked the princess.

"There is no use in hiding it from you; that may be Tartars."

"Jesus, Mary!"

"Have no fear. My neck for it, we shall escape them, and our squadrons are in Matchin."

"For God's sake, let us be off!" said Jendzian.

They were silent, and sped on like ghosts. The trees began to grow thinner; they were reaching the end of the forest, and the fire was somewhat dimmer too. Suddenly Helena turned to Volodyovski.

"Swear to me, gentlemen," said she, "that I shall not go alive into their hands."

"You will not," said Volodyovski, "while I am alive."

They had barely passed the end and come into an open field about a mile in width, and on the other side of it another line of forest stood dark. That bald space of earth open on every side was all silvered over from the rays of the moon. All things were as visible on it as in the daytime.

"This is the worst piece of road," whispered Volodyovski to Zagloba; "for if they are in Chorni Ostroff, they will pass between these forests."

Zagloba gave no answer; he only pressed the horse with his heels.

They had run to the middle of the field, the opposite forest was growing nearer each moment and more distinct, when suddenly the little knight stretched out his hand to the east. "Look!" said he to Zagloba; "do you see?"

"Some kind of branches and thicket in the distance."

"Those branches are moving. Now on, on, push on! for they see us beyond a doubt."

The wind whistled past the ears of the fleeing; the forest of salvation drew nearer each instant.

All at once out of that dark mass approaching from the right side of the field flew on as it were the roar of sea waves, and the next moment one great shout rent the air.

"They see us!" bellowed Zagloba. "Dogs, ruffians, devils, wolves, scoundrels!"

The forest was so near that the fugitives almost felt its cold, austere breath; but also the cloud of Tartars became each moment more clearly outlined, and from the dark body of it long arms began to push out like the horns of some gigantic monster, and approached the fugitives with inconceivable rapidity. The trained ear of Volodyotski already distinguished clearly: "Allah! Allah!"

"My horse has stumbled!" shouted Zagloba.

"That is nothing!" cried Volodyovski

But through his head that moment there flew like thunderbolts the questions: "What will happen if the horses do not hold out? What will happen if one of them falls?" They were valiant Tartar steeds of iron endurance, but they had come already from Ploskiri, resting but little on that wild flight from the town to the first forest. They might, it is true, take the led horses, but they too were tired. "What is to be done?" thought Volodyovski; and his heart throbbed with alarm,--perhaps for the first time in his life,--not for himself, but for Helena, whom during that long journey he had come to love as his own sister. And he knew too that the Tartars when they had once begun pursuit would not relinquish it very soon. "Let them keep on, they will not catch her," said he, setting his teeth.

"My horse has stumbled!" cried Zagloba a second time.

"That is nothing!" answered Volodyovski again.

They were now in the forest, darkness around them; but single Tartar horsemen were not farther than a few hundred yards behind. But the little knight knew now what to do.

"Jendzian," cried he, "turn with the lady to the first path leading out of the highway."

"Good, my master!"

The little knight turned to Zagloba. "Pistol in hand!" At the same time, seizing the bridle of Zagloba's horse, he began to restrain his course.

"What are you doing?" cried the noble.

"Nothing! Hold in your horse!"

The distance between them and Jendzian, who had escaped with Helena, increased every moment. At last he came with her to a point where the highway turned rather sharply toward Zbaraj, and straight ahead lay a narrow forest-trail half hidden by branches. Jendzian rushed into it, and in a twinkle the two had disappeared in the thicket and the gloom.

Meanwhile Volodyovski had stopped his own horse and Zagloba's.

"In the name of God's mercy, what are you doing?" roared Zagloba.

"We delay the pursuit. There is no other salvation for the princess."

"We shall perish!"

"Let us perish. Stop here right by the side of the road,--right here!"

Both stood close under the trees in the darkness; presently the mighty thumping of Tartar horses approached and roared like a storm till the whole forest was filled with it.

"It has come!" said Zagloba, raising the skin of wine to his mouth. He drank and drank, then shook himself. "In the name of the Father, Son, and Holy Ghost," coughed he. "I am ready for death."

"This minute! this minute!" cried Volodyovski. "Three of them are riding in advance; that is what I wanted."

In fact three horsemen appeared on the clear road, mounted evidently on the best horses,--"wolf-hunters," so called in the Ukraine, for they came up with wolves in the chase,-- and two or three hundred yards behind them a few hundred others, and still farther a whole dense throng of the horde.

When the first three came in front of the ambush two shots were discharged; then Volodyovski sprang like a panther into the middle of the road, and before Zagloba had time to think what was done the third Tartar was on the ground.

"Forward!" shouted the little knight.

Zagloba did not let the order be repeated, and they rushed over the road like a pair of wolves hunted by a pack of angry dogs. That moment the other Tartars hastened to the corpses, and seeing that those hunted wolves could bite to death they curbed their horses a little, waiting for their comrades.

"As you see, I knew that I should stop them," said Volodyovski.

But although the fugitives gained a few hundred steps, the interruption in the chase did not last long. Only the Tartars pressed on in a larger crowd, not pushing forward singly.

The horses of the fugitives were wearied by the long road, and their speed slackened, especially that of Zagloba's horse, which bearing such a considerable burden stumbled once and twice. What there was left of the old man's hair stood on end at the thought that he should fall.

"Pan Michael, dearest Pan Michael, do not abandon me!" cried he, in despair.

"Oh, be of good heart!" answered the little knight.

"May the wolves tear this hor--"

He had not finished this sentence when the first arrow hissed near his ear, and after it others began to hiss and whistle and sing as if they were horseflies and bees. One passed so near that its head almost grazed Zagloba's ear.

Volodyovski turned and again fired twice from his pistol at the pursuers.

Zagloba's horse stumbled now so heavily that his nostrils were almost buried in the earth.

"By the living God, my horse is dying!" shouted he, in a heart-rending voice.

"From the saddle to the woods!" thundered Volodyovski.

Having given this order, he stopped his own horse, sprang off, and a moment later he and Zagloba vanished in the darkness. But this movement did not escape the slanting eyes of the Tartars, and several tens of them springing from their horses also gave chase. The branches tore the cap from Zagloba's head, beat him on the face and caught his coat, but putting his feet behind his belt he made off as if he were thirty years of age. Sometimes he fell, but he was up again and off quicker than ever, puffing like a bellows. At last he fell into a deep hole, and felt that he could not crawl out again, for his strength had failed him completely.

"Where are you?" called Volodyovski, in a low voice.

"Down here! It's all over with me,--save me, Pan Michael."

Volodyovski sprang without hesitation to the hole and clapped his hand on Zagloba's mouth: "Be silent! perhaps they will pass us! We will defend ourselves anyhow."

By that time the Tartars came up. Some of them did in fact pass the hole, thinking that the fugitives had gone farther; others went slowly, examining the trees and looking around on every side. The knights held the breath in their breasts.

"Let some one fall in here," thought Zagloba, in despair; "I'll fall on him."

Just then sparks scattered on every side; the Tartars began to strike fire. By the flash their wild faces could be seen, with their puffed cheeks and lips sticking out, blowing the lighted tinder. For a time they kept going around a few tens of steps from the hole like ill-omened forest phantoms, drawing nearer and nearer.

But at the last moment wonderful sounds of some sort, murmurs, and confused cries began to come from the highway and to rouse the slumbering depths. The Tartars stopped striking fire, and stood as if rooted to the earth. Volodyovski's hand was biting into the shoulder of Zagloba.

The cries increased, and suddenly red lights burst forth, and with them was heard a salvo of musketry,--once, twice, three times,--followed by shouts of "Allah!" the clatter of sabres, the neighing of horses, tramping, and confused uproar. A battle was raging on the road.

"Ours, ours!" shouted Volodyovski.

"Slay! kill! strike! cut! slaughter!" bellowed Zagloba.

A second later a number of Tartars rushed past the hole in the wildest disorder, and vanished in the direction of their party. Volodyovski did not restrain himself; he sprang after them, and pressed on in the thicket and darkness.

Zagloba remained at the bottom of the hole. He tried to crawl up, but could not. All his bones were aching, and he was barely able to stand on his feet.

"Ah, scoundrels!" said he, looking around on every side, "you have fled; it is a pity some one of you did not stay,-- I should have company in this hole, and I would show him where pepper grows! Oh, pagan trash, they are cutting you up like beasts this minute! Oh, for God's sake, the uproar is increasing every moment! I wish that Yeremi himself were here; he would warm you. You are shouting, 'Allah! Allah!' The wolves will shout 'Allah!' over your carrion pretty soon. But that Pan Michael should leave me here alone! Well, nothing wonderful; he is eager, for he is young. After this last adventure I would follow him anywhere, for he is not a friend to leave one in distress. He is a wasp! In one minute he stung three! If at least I had that wine-skin with me! But those devils have surely taken it, or the horses have trampled it. Besides insects are devouring me in this ditch! What's that?"

The shouts and discharges of musketry began to recede in the direction of the field and the first forest.

"Ah, ah!" thought Zagloba, "they are on their necks. Oh, dog-brothers, you could not hold out! Praise be to God in the highest!"

The shouts receded farther and farther.

"They ride lustily," muttered he. "But I see that I shall have to sit in this ditch. It only remains now for the wolves to eat me. Bogun to begin with, then the Tartars, and wolves at the end! God grant a stake to Bogun and madness to the wolves! Our men will take care of the Tartars not in the worst fashion. Pan Michael! Pan Michael!"

Silence gave answer to Zagloba; only the pines murmured, and from afar came the sounds fainter and fainter.

"Shall I lie down to sleep here, or what? May the devil take it! Pan Michael!"

But Zagloba's patience had a long trial yet, for dawn was in the sky when the clatter of hoofs was heard again on the road and lights shone in the forest.

"Pan Michael, I am here!"

"Crawl out."

"But I cannot."

Volodyovski with a torch in his hand stood over the hole, and giving his hand to Zagloba, said: "Well, the Tartars are gone; we drove them to the other forest."

"But who came up?"

"Kushel and Roztvorovski, with two thousand horse. My dragoons are with them too."

"Were there many of the Pagans?"

"A couple of thousand."

"Praise be to God! Give me something to drink, for I am faint."

Two hours later Zagloba, having eaten and drunk what he needed; was sitting on a comfortable saddle in the midst of Volodyovski's dragoons, and at his side rode the little knight, who said,--

"Do not worry; for though we shall not come to Zbaraj in company with the princess, it would have been worse if she had fallen into the hands of the heathen."

"But perhaps Jendzian will come back yet to Zbaraj."

"He will not. The highway will be occupied; the party which we drove back will return soon and follow us. Besides Burlai may appear at any moment before Jendzian could come in. Hmelnitski and the Khan are marching on the other side from Konstantinoff."

"Oh, for God's sake! Then he will fall into a trap with the princess."

"Jendzian has wit enough to spring through between Zbaraj and Konstantinoff in time, and not let the regiments of Hmelnitski nor the parties of the Khan catch him. You see I have great confidence in his success."

"God grant it!"

"He is a cunning lad, just like a fox. You have no lack of stratagem, but he is more cunning. We split our heads a great deal over plans to rescue the girl, but in the end our hands dropped, and through him the whole has been directed. He'll slip out this time like a snake, for it is a question of his own life. Have confidence,--for God, who saved her so many times, is over her now; and remember that in Zbaraj you bade me have confidence when Zakhar came."

Zagloba was strengthened somewhat by these words of Pan Michael, and then fell into deep thought.

"Pan Michael," he said after a time, "have you asked Kushel what Skshetuski is doing?"

"He is in Zbaraj, and well; he came from Prince Koretski's with Zatsvilikhovski."

"But what shall we tell him?"

"Ah, there is the rub!"

"Does he think yet that the girl was killed in Kieff?"

"He does."

"Have you told Kushel or any one else where we are coming from?"

"I have not, for I thought it better to take counsel first."

"I should prefer to say nothing of the whole affair. If the girl should fall again into Cossack or Tartar hands (which God forbid!), it would be a new torture, just as if some one were to tear open all his wounds."

"I'll give my head that Jendzian takes her through."

"I should gladly give my own to have him do so; but misfortune rages now in the world like a pestilence. Better be silent, and leave everything to the will of God."

"So let it be. But will not Podbipienta give the secret to Skshetuski?"

"Don't you know him? He gave his word of honor, which for that Lithuanian is sacred."

Here Kushel joined them. They rode on together, talking, by the first rays of the rising sun, of public affairs, of the arrival at Zbaraj of the commanders in consequence of Yeremi's wishes, of the impending arrival of the prince himself, and the inevitable and awful struggle with the whole power of Hmelnitski.

CHAPTER LVII.

Volodyovski and Zagloba found all the forces of the Crown assembled at Zbaraj, and waiting for the enemy. The cup-bearer of the Crown, Ostrorog, who had come from Konstantinoff, was there, and Lantskoronski, castellan of Kamenyets, who had gained the first victory at Bar; the third commander, Pan Firlei of Dombrovitsa, castellan of Belsk, and Andrei Serakovski, secretary of the Crown; Konyetspolski, the standard-bearer, and Pshiyemski, commander of the artillery, a warrior specially expert in the capture and defence of towns; and with them ten thousand troops, not counting a number of Prince Yeremi's squadrons previously quartered at Zbaraj.

Pan Pshiyemski, on the southern side of the town and the castle and the two ponds, had laid out a strong camp, which he fortified in foreign fashion, and which it was only possible to capture in front; for at the rear and two sides it was defended by the ponds, the castle, and the river. In this camp the commanders intended to offer resistance to Hmelnitski, and delay his avalanche till the king, with the rest of the forces and the national militia of all the nobility, should come. But was that plan possible of execution in view of the power of Hmelnitski? There was much doubt, and there were reasonable causes for the doubt,--among them the disorder in the camp itself. First of all, secret contention was raging among the leaders. The commanders had come against their will to Zbaraj, yielding in this to the desires of Prince Yeremi. They wished at first to make their defence at Konstantinoff; but when the news went forth that Yeremi would appear in his own person only in case Zbaraj should be the point of defence, the soldiers declared immediately to the leaders of the Crown that they would go to Zbaraj, and would not fight elsewhere. Neither persuasion nor the authority of the baton availed; and in short the commanders discovered that if they should continue in longer resistance, the army, from the heavy hussar regiments to the last soldier of the foreign companies, would leave them and go over to the banners of Vishnyevetski. This was one of those sad cases of military insubordination of increasing frequency in that time, and caused by the incapacity of the leaders, their mutual disagreements, the unexampled terror before the power of Hmelnitski, and the defeats unheard of till then, especially the defeat of Pilavtsi.

So the commanders had to march to Zbaraj, where the command, in spite of the appointments made by the king, had by the force of circumstance passed into the hands of Yeremi; for the army would obey only him,--fight and perish under him alone. But that leader *de facto* was not in Zbaraj yet; therefore unrest was increasing in the army, discipline was relaxed to the last degree, and courage fell. For it was already known that Hmelnitski, together with the Khan, was approaching with forces the like of which the eyes of men had not seen since the days of Tamerlane. Fresh tidings kept flying to the camp like ill-omened birds,--reports, each more recent and more terrible than the preceding,--and weakened the manhood of the soldiers. There were fears that a panic like that of Pilavtsi might break out suddenly and scatter that handful of an army which stood between Hmelnitski and the heart of the Commonwealth. The leaders themselves had lost their heads. Their contradictory orders were not carried out, or if carried out, with unwillingness. In fact Yeremi alone could avert the catastrophe hanging over the camp, the army, and the country.

Zagloba and Volodyovski dropped at once into the vortex of army life. They had barely appeared on the square when they were surrounded by officers of various regiments, interrupting one another in their inquiries for news. At sight of the Tartar captives, confidence entered the hearts of the curious. "The Tartars are plucked! Tartar prisoners! God gave a victory!" repeated some. "The Tartars are here, and Burlai with them!" cried others. "To arms! To the walls!" The news flew through the camp, and Kushel's victory was magnified along the road. An increasing throng gathered around the prisoners. "Kill them! What are we to do with them?" Questions fell thick as flakes in a snow-storm. Kushel would give no answer, and went with a report to the quarters of Firlei, the castellan of Belsk. Volodyovski and Zagloba were greeted at once by their acquaintances of the Russian squadron; but they escaped as well as they could, for they were in haste to see Pan Yan.

They found him in the castle with Zatsvilikhovski, two Bernardine priests of the place, and Pan Longin Podbipienta. Skshetuski grew a little pale on seeing them, and half closed his eyes, for he was reminded of too much to see them without pain; still he gave a calm and even joyful greeting, inquired where they had been, and was satisfied with the first convenient answer. Since he looked on the princess as dead, he wished for nothing, hoped for nothing, and not the slightest suspicion entered his soul that their long absence related to her. They made no mention of the object of their journey, though Pan Longin looked first on one and then on the other with an inquiring glance, sighed, and turned in his place, wishing to read even a shadow of hope on their faces. But both were occupied with Pan Yan, whom Volodyovski seized by the shoulders repeatedly; for his heart grew soft at the sight of that old and trusty friend, who had passed through so much and lost so much that he had almost nothing to live for.

"We shall have all the old comrades together again," said he to Skshetuski, "and you will be happy with us. A war too will come, I see, such as has not been yet, and with it great delights for every soldier soul. If God gives you health, you will lead the hussars many a time to come."

"God has already returned me my health, and I wish nothing more for myself than to serve while my service is needed."

Skshetuski was in fact well, for youth and his sturdy strength had conquered the illness within him. Grief had bitten his spirit, but it could not bite his body. He had merely grown spare and pallid, so that his forehead, cheeks, and nose seemed formed of church wax. The former austerity had settled firmly on his face, and there was in it the rigid repose that we note in the visage of the dead. An increasing number of silver threads wound through his dark beard. In other regards he differed in nothing from the rest of men, except, contrary to soldier custom, he avoided crowds, noise, and drinking. He conversed more readily with monks, to whose discourse on the life of the cloister and the life to come he listened with eagerness; but he performed his service with diligent care, for the expected siege occupied him equally with all the others.

Soon conversation touched on this subject, for no one in the camp, castle, and town thought of aught else. Old Zatsvilikhovski asked about the Tartars and Burlai, with whom he had an acquaintance of ancient date.

"That's a great warrior," said he. "It is too bad that he should rise against the country with others. We served together at Khotím. He was still a youth, but already gave promise of ripening into an uncommon man."

"But he is from the Trans-Dnieper, and leads men of that region," said Skshetuski. "How is it, father, that he is now marching from the south, from the direction of Kamenyets?"

"It seems," answered the old man, "that Hmelnitski fixed winter quarters for him there on purpose, since Tugai Bey remained on the Dnieper, and that great murza has a hatred for him from former times. No one has cut up the Tartars like Burlai."

"And now he will be a comrade to them?"

"Yes," said Zatsvilikhovski, "such are the times. But Hmelnitski will watch and keep them from devouring each other."

"When do they expect Hmelnitski here, father?" asked Volodyovski.

"Any day. But who can tell? The commanders should send out scout after scout; but they do not. I was barely able to prevail on them to send Kushel to the south and Piglovski to Cholganski Kamen. I wished to go myself, but there are counsels without end. They should send also the secretary of the Crown with some squadrons. They would better hurry, lest it be too late. God give us the prince at the earliest moment, or we shall be met by disgrace like that of Pilavtsi."

"I saw those soldiers as we rode through the square," said Zagloba, "and I think there are more fools among them than good men. They should be market-boys, not comrades to us who are enamoured of glory, esteeming it beyond our own lives."

"What are you talking about?" blurted out the old man. "I do not belittle your bravery, though once I was of another mind. But all the knights here are the first soldiers that the Commonwealth has ever had. Only a head is needed,--a leader! Lantskoronski is a good skirmisher, but no general; Firlei is old, and as to the cup-bearer, he and Prince Dominik made a reputation for themselves at Pilavtsi. What wonder that no one wants to obey them! A soldier will shed his blood freely if sure that he will not be destroyed without need. But now, instead of thinking of the siege, they are disputing about positions."

"Are there provisions enough?" asked Zagloba, in alarm.

"Not so many as are necessary; but we are still worse off for provender. If the siege should last a month, there will be only shavings and stones for the horses."

"There is still time to get provender," said Volodyovski.

"Then go and tell them so. God give us the prince! I repeat."

"You are not the only one who is sighing for him," interrupted Pan Longin.

"I know that," answered the old man. "Look out on the square! All at the walls look with longing eyes toward Old Zbaraj; others in the town have climbed the towers; and if any one cries in a joke, 'He is coming,' they are mad with joy. A thirsty stag is not so eager for water as we for the prince. Oh, if he could only get here before Hmelnitski! But I think he must have been delayed."

"We too pray, whole days at a time, for his coming," said one of the Bernardines.

The prayers and wishes of all the knighthood were soon to gain their object, though the following day brought still greater fears and was full of ominous prophecies. On Thursday, July 8, a terrific storm raged over the town and the freshly raised ramparts of the camp. Rain fell in torrents. A part of the earthworks was swept away. Gnyezna and the two ponds overflowed. In the evening lightning struck the infantry under command of Firlei, castellan of Belsk, killed a number of men, and tore the banner to pieces. This was considered of evil omen,--an evident sign of the anger of God, the more since Firlei was a Calvinist. Zagloba proposed that a deputation be sent to him with the request and prayer to become a Catholic, "for there could be no blessing of God for an army whose leader was living in disgusting errors hateful to Heaven." Many shared this opinion; and only the dignity of the castellan's person and the command prevented the sending of the deputation. But their courage fell all the more. The storm raged without interruption. The bulwark, though strengthened with stones, willows, and stakes, became so soft that the cannon began to sink. They were obliged to put planks under the howitzers, mortars, and even under the eight-pounders. In the deep ditches the water roared to the height of a man. Night brought no rest. The storm drove to the east new gigantic piles of clouds which, concentrating and discharging with terrific noise in the heavens, cast out on Zbaraj their whole stock of rain, thunder, and lightning. Only the servants remained in the tents at the camp; soldiers, officers, and commanders, with the exception of the castellan of Kamenyets, took refuge in the town. If Hmelnitski had come with the storm, he would have taken the camp without a blow.

Next day it was a little better, though rain was still falling. About five o'clock in the afternoon the wind drove away the clouds, the blue sky opened above the camp, and in the direction of Old Zbaraj a splendid seven-colored rainbow was shining. The mighty arc with one arm extended beyond Old Zbaraj, while the other, seeming to drink in the moisture of the Black Forest, glittered, changed, and played on the background of fleeing clouds. That moment confidence entered all hearts. The knights returned to the camp and stood on the slippery bulwark to gladden their eyes with the sight of the rainbow. Immediately they began to talk loudly and to guess what this favorable sign might announce, when Volodyovski, standing with others over the very ditch, covered his panther eyes with his hand and cried,--

"Troops are coming from under the rainbow!"

There was a stir as if a whirlwind had moved the human mass, and then a sudden murmur. The words "Troops are coming!" flew like an arrow from one end of the rampart to the other. The soldiers began to crowd and push, gathering in groups. Murmurs rose and fell; still all hands rested above the eyes; all eyes were turned, strained with effort, into the distance; hearts were throbbing; and all, holding the breath in their breasts, were suspended between hope and fear. Then something began to sway, and swayed still more definitely, and rose out of the distance, and approached still nearer, and became still more distinctly visible, till at last the banners, flags, and bunchuks appeared, later a forest of streamers. The eyes doubted no longer,--it was an army. Then one gigantic shout rose from the breasts of all, a shout of inconceivable joy,--

"Yeremi! Yeremi! Yeremi!"

The oldest soldiers were simply seized with frenzy. Some threw themselves from the ramparts, waded through the ditch, and hurried on foot through the water-covered plain to the advancing regiments; others rushed to their horses; some laughed; others wept, placing their hands together and crying: "Our father is coming,--our savior, our chief!" It might have seemed that the siege was raised, Hmelnitski finished, and the victory won.

Meanwhile the regiments of the prince had drawn so near that the banners could be distinguished. In advance came, as usual, the light regiments of the prince's Tartars, the Cossacks, and the Wallachians, after them Makhnitski's foreign infantry, then the cannon of Vershul, the dragoons, and the heavy hussar regiments. The rays of the sun reflected on their armor and on the points of their upraised lances. All marched in unusual splendor, as if the halo of victory were around them.

Skshetuski, standing with Pan Longin on the ramparts, recognized from afar his own squadron, which he had left in Zamost, and his faded cheeks colored a little; he drew several deep breaths, as if he had thrown some great weight from his breast, and his eyes grew glad; for days of superhuman toil were near him too, as well as heroic struggles which heal the heart better than all, and hurl down painful memories deeper and deeper somewhere into the bottom of the soul.

The regiments continued to approach, and barely a thousand yards separated them from the camp. The officers too had hurried up in order to witness the entrance of the prince; the three commanders also, and with them Pan Pshiyemski, Pan Konyetspolski, Pan Marek Sobieski, starosta of Krasnostav, Pan Korf, and all the other officers, as well of Polish as foreign command. All shared in the universal joy; and especially Lantskoronski, one of the commanders, who was more a knight than a general, but enamoured of military glory. He stretched his baton in the direction from which Yeremi was coming, and called in a voice so loud that all heard him,--

"There is our supreme chief, and I am the first to give him my command and my office."

The regiments of the prince began to enter the camp. They were three thousand men in all; but the courage of the garrison increased by a hundred thousand, for they were the victors from Pogrébische, Nyemiroff, Makhnovka, and Konstantinoff. Then acquaintances and friends greeted one another. After the light regiments Vershul's artillery came in at last with difficulty, bringing twelve cannon. The prince, who had sent his regiments from Old Zbaraj, entered after sunset. All that was living assembled to greet him. The soldiers, taking lamps, candles, torches, bits of pitch-pine, surrounded the prince's steed and barred his advance. The horse was caught by the bridle, so that the warriors might sate their eyes with the sight of the hero; they kissed his garments, and almost bore him away on their shoulders. The excitement rose to that degree that not only soldiers of his own regiments but of foreign companies declared they would serve three months without pay. The throng became denser each moment, so that he was unable to move a step. He sat then on his white steed, surrounded by the soldiery as a shepherd by his flocks, and there was no end to shouts and applause. The evening was calm and clear, thousands of stars glittered in the dark sky, and then appeared favorable omens. Just as Lantskoronski approached the prince to deliver the baton into his hand, one of the stars, torn away from the sky and drawing after it a stream of light, fell with a noise, and was quenched in the direction of Konstantinoff, from which Hmelnitski had to come. "That is Hmelnitski's star!" shouted the soldiers. "A miracle! a miracle!" "An evident sign!" "Vivat Yeremi victor!" repeated a thousand voices. Then Lantskoronski approached and gave a sign with his hand that he wanted to speak. Immediately there was silence, and he said,--

"The king gave me this baton, but into your more worthy hands do I yield it, wishing to be first to obey your orders."

"And we are with him," repeated two other commanders.

Three batons were extended to the prince; but he drew back his hand, saying, "It was not I that gave them, and I will not receive them."

"Let there be a fourth with the three," said Firlei.

"Vivat Vishnyevetski! vivat the commanders!" shouted the knights. "We will die together!"

At that moment the prince's steed raised his head, shook his purple-stained mane, and neighed mightily, so that all the horses in the camp answered him in one voice.

This too was considered prophetic of victory. The soldiers had fire in their eyes; their hearts were hot with thirst for battle; the quiver of eagerness ran through their bodies. The officers shared the universal ecstasy. Prince Ostrorog wept and prayed. Lantskoronski and the starosta of Krasnostav began first to wave their sabres, encouraging the soldiers, who, running to the edge of the rampart and stretching out their hands in the darkness, shouted in the direction from which they expected the enemy,--

"Come on, dog-brothers! You will find us ready for you!"

That night no man slept in the camp, and till daybreak there was thunder of shouts with the rushing to and fro of lamps and torches.

In the morning Pan Serakovski, secretary of the Crown, came with a scouting-party from Cholganski Kamen, and brought news that the enemy were twenty-five miles from the camp. The party had a battle with a superior force of Tartars, in which the two Mankovskis and Pan Oleksich had fallen, with a number of good soldiers. The informants brought in declared that behind this body the Khan and Hmelnitski were marching with all their forces. The day passed in waiting and preparations for defence. The prince, having taken the command, without further delay put the army in order; he showed each part where to stand, how to defend itself, and how to give succor to the rest. The best spirit reigned in the camp, discipline was restored, and instead of the former confusion, antagonism of authority, and uncertainty, accuracy and order were everywhere present. Before mid-day all were in their places. The pickets thrown out before the camp reported at intervals what was doing in the neighborhood. The camp attendants despatched to the adjacent villages brought in provisions and forage, whatever was yet to be found. Soldiers standing on the ramparts chatted merrily and sang, and they passed the night slumbering by the fires, sabre in hand, with the same readiness as if the assault might begin at any moment.

At daylight something dark began to appear in the direction of Vishnyovets. The bells in the town rang en alarm, and in the camp the prolonged plaintive sound of the trumpets roused the soldiers to wakefulness. The infantry regiments mounted the ramparts, the cavalry took position in the intervals, ready to rush forward at the signal of attack, and through the whole length of the ditch ascended slender streaks of smoke from the lighted matches.

At this moment the prince appeared on his white steed. He was in silver armor, but without a helmet. Not the least concern was visible on his forehead, but gladness shone out of his eyes and his face.

"We have guests, gentlemen, we have guests!" he repeated, riding along the ramparts.

Silence followed, and then could be heard the waving of banners, which the light breath of air now raised and now wound around the staffs. Meanwhile the enemy came so near that it was possible to take them in with the eye.

This was the first wave; not Hmelnitski himself, with the Khan, but a reconnoitring party made up of thirty thousand chosen Tartars, armed with bows, muskets, and sabres. Having captured fifteen hundred men sent out for provisions, they went in a dense mass from Vishnyovets; then, stretching out in a long crescent, they began to ride around from the opposite side toward Old Zbaraj.

The prince, satisfied that this was merely a party, ordered the cavalry out of the intrenchments. The voices of command were heard; the regiments began to move and issue from behind the ramparts like bees from a hive. The plain was soon filled with men and horses. From a distance could be seen the captains riding around the squadrons and putting them in line of battle. The horses snorted playfully, and sometimes their neighing went through the ranks. Then from out this mass pushed forth two squadrons of Tartars and Cossacks, and advanced on a light trot; their bows shook on their shoulders, and their caps glittered. They rode in silence: and at their head was the red Vershul, whose horse reared under him as though wild, throwing his front hoofs in the air as if wishing to escape the bit and spring at once into the tumult. The blue of heaven was unspotted by a cloud; the day was clear, transparent, and the assailants were visible as on the palm of the hand.

Now there appeared from the side of Old Zbaraj a small wagon-train of the prince, which had not succeeded in entering with the army, and was hurrying with all its might to escape capture at a blow by the Tartars. Indeed it had not escaped their glance, and the long crescent moved swiftly toward it. Cries of "Allah!" flew to the ears of the infantry on the ramparts; the squadrons of Vershul shot on like a whirlwind to the rescue.

But the crescent arrived at the train sooner, and engirdled it in a moment as if with a black ribbon; and simultaneously several thousand of the horde turned with an unearthly howl to surround Vershul in like manner. Here might be noted the experience of Vershul and the skill of his soldiers. Seeing that they were flanking him on right and left, he divided his forces into three parts and sprang to the sides; then he divided them into four, then into two; and each time the enemy had to turn with his whole line, for he had no opponent in front and his wings were already broken. The fourth time they met breast to breast; but Vershul struck with all his force in the weakest part, burst through, and immediately found himself in the rear of the enemy, whom he left, and rushed like a tempest to the train, regardless of pursuit.

Old soldiers, beholding this from the ramparts, stood with armored hands on their hips, crying: "May the bullets strike them, only the prince's captains lead in that style!"

Then Vershul struck in the form of a sharp wedge the ring surrounding the tabor, and pierced it as an arrow pierces a man. In the twinkle of an eye he was in the centre. Now instead of two battles there raged one, but all the more stubborn. It was a marvellous sight. In the centre of the plain was a small tabor, like a moving fortress, throwing out long streaks of smoke and vomiting fire; without, a black and wildly moving swarm, as one gigantic eddy followed another, horses fleeing without riders; within, noise, uproar, and the thunder of guns. In one place some were rushing through others, in another they struggled unbroken. As a wild boar at bay defends himself with his white tusks and tears the raging dogs, so that tabor in the midst of the cloud of Tartars defended itself desperately, hoping that assistance greater than Vershul's would come from the camp.

The red coats of the dragoons of Kushel and Volodyovski soon twinkled on the field. You would have said they were red leaves of flowers driven by the wind. They rushed to the cloud of Tartars and disappeared in it as in a black forest; so for a time they were invisible, but the uproar increased. The troops wondered why the prince did not send force enough at once to the succor of the surrounded; but he delayed, wishing to show exactly what he sent, and in this way to raise their courage and prepare them for still greater perils.

However, the fire in the tabor grew weak; it was evident they had no time to load, or the barrels of the muskets had grown hot. The shouts of the Tartars increased continually; the prince therefore gave a signal, and three hussar squadrons--one (his guard) under Skshetuski, the second under the starosta of Krasnostav, the third a royal squadron under Piglovski-- rushed to the battle from the camp. They struck them as an axe strikes; they broke the ring of Tartars at once, threw them back, scattered them, pressed them to the woods, re-dispersed and drove them more than a mile from the camp. The little tabor entered the intrenchments in safety, amidst joyous shouts and the thunder of cannon.

The Tartars, however, feeling that Hmelnitski and the Khan were following, did not disappear altogether, but came again, and shouting "Allah!" galloped around the whole camp, occupying at the same time the roads, highways, and villages, from which pillars of black smoke were soon rising to the sky. Many of their skirmishers came near the trenches; against these the soldiers of the prince and the quarter-soldiers rushed out at once, singly and in parties, especially from the Tartar, Wallachian, and dragoon squadrons.

Vershul was unable to take part in the skirmishes; for, struck six times in the head while defending the tabor, he lay as if dead in the tent. Volodyovski, red as a lobster, though untouched, still unsatisfied, took his place, and moved first to the field. These skirmishes, at which the infantry and heavy cavalry looked from the camp as at a spectacle, lasted till evening. Sometimes one side excelled, sometimes the other; they fought in groups or singly; captives were taken alive. But Pan Michael, as soon as he struck any one and finished him, turned again, and his red uniform circled over the whole field of battle. At last Skshetuski pointed him out from a distance to Lantskoronski as a curiosity, for as often as he met with a Tartar it might be said that lightning had struck that man. Zagloba, though beyond the hearing of Pan Michael, encouraged him with shouts from the ramparts. From time to time he turned to the soldiers standing around, and said,--

"Look, gentlemen! I taught him to use the sabre. Well done! If he goes on, with God's help, he will equal me soon."

But now the sun had gone down, and each skirmisher began to withdraw slowly from the field, on which remained only bodies of horses and men. From the town the first sounds of the "Ave Maria" were heard.

Night fell gradually; still darkness did not come, for fires in the country about gave light. Zalostsitse, Barzyntse, Lublyanki, Striyovka, Kretovitse, Zarudzie, Vakhlovka were burning; and the whole vicinity, as far as the eye could reach, was blazing in one conflagration. The smoke in the night became red; the stars were shining on the rosy background of the sky. Clouds of birds rose from the forests, thickets, and ponds with a tremendous noise, circled in the air lighted by the burning, and looked like flying flames. The cattle in the camp, terrified by the unusual spectacle, began to bellow plaintively.

"It cannot be," said old soldiers to one another in the trenches, "that the Tartars of that party have set such fires; surely Hmelnitski, with the Cossacks and the whole horde, are advancing."

These were not empty surmises, for Pan Serakovski had brought intelligence on the preceding day that the Zaporojian hetman and the Khan were in the rear of that party. They were expected therefore with certainty. The soldiers were in the trenches to a man; the citizens were on the roofs and towers; all hearts were unquiet; women were sobbing in the churches, stretching out their hands to the most holy sacrament. Uncertainty, worse than all, oppressed with immeasurable weight the town, the castle, and the camp.

But it did not last long. Night had not fallen completely when the first ranks of the Cossacks and Tartars appeared on the horizon; then the second, third, tenth, hundredth, thousandth. You would have said all the forests and groves had torn themselves suddenly from their roots, and were marching on Zbaraj. In vain did the eye seek the end of those ranks; as far as the eye reached swarms of men and horses were blackening, vanishing in the smokes and fires of the distance. They moved like clouds, or like locusts which cover the whole country with their terrible moving mass. Before them went the threatening rumble of human voices, like wind in a forest among the branches of the ancient pines; then, halting about a mile and a quarter away, they began to settle down and make fires for the night.

"You see the fires," whispered the soldiers; "they extend farther than a horse could go in one journey."

"Jesus and Mary!" said Zagloba to Skshetuski. "I tell you there is a lion in me and I feel no alarm; but I would that a blazing thunderbolt might crush them all before morning. As God is dear to me, there are too many of them. Unless perhaps in the valley of Jehoshaphat there will not be a greater crowd. And tell me, what do those scoundrels want? Would not every dog-brother of them be better at home, working his serfage peaceably for his land? What fault is it of ours if God has made us nobles and them trash, and commanded them to obey? Tfu! I am beside myself with rage. I am a mild-mannered man, soft as a plaster; but let them not rouse me to anger! They have had too much freedom, too much bread; they have multiplied like mice in a barn; and now they are dying to get at the cats. Ah, wait! There is one cat here called Yeremi, and another called Zagloba. What do you think, will those two enter upon negotiations? If the rebels had surrendered with obedience, then their lives might be granted, might they not? One thing disturbs me continually,--are there provisions enough in the camp? Oh, to the devil! Look, gentlemen; fires beyond fires, and still fires! May black death fall on such a crowd!"

"Why talk about treaties," said Skshetuski, "when they think they have us all under their hands, and will get us to-morrow?"

"But they won't get us, will they?" asked Zagloba.

"Well, the will of God for that. In any case, since the prince is here, it won't come easy to them."

"You have consoled me indeed. I do not care that it should not come easy to them, but that it should not come at all."

"It is no small pleasure for a soldier not to yield his life for nothing."

"True, true! But may lightning strike the whole affair, and your consolation with it!"

At that moment Podbipienta and Volodyovski approached.

"They say that the Cossacks with the horde are half a million strong," said the Lithuanian.

"I wish that you had lost your tongue," said Zagloba; "you have brought good tidings."

"It is easier to kill them in assault than in the field," continued Pan Longin, mildly.

"Now that our prince and Hmelnitski have met at last, there will be no talk about negotiations. Either master or monk.[18] To-morrow will be the day of judgment," said Volodyovski, rubbing his hands.

He was right. In that war the two most terrible lions had not yet stood eye to eye. One had crushed the hetmans and the commanders; the other powerful Cossack atamans. On the footsteps of both followed victory; each was a terror to his enemies. But whose side will be weightiest in a direct encounter? This was to be decided now. Vishnyevetski looked from the intrenchments on the countless myriads of Tartars and Cossacks, and strove in vain to embrace them with the eye. Hmelnitski looked from the field on the castle and camp, thinking in his soul: "My most terrible enemy is there; when I have finished with him, who can oppose me?"

It was easy to guess that the conflict between these two men would be long and stubborn, but the result could not be doubtful. That prince in Lubni and Vishnyovets stood at the head of fifteen thousand troops, counting the camp-servants; while the peasant chieftain was followed by mobs, from the Sea of Azoff and the Don to the mouth of the Danube. The Khan too marched with him at the head of the Crimean, Bélgorod, Nogai, and Dobrudja hordes; men marched with him who dwelt on the tributaries of the Dniester and the Dnieper, men from the lower country, and a countless rabble from the steppes, ravines, woods, towns, hamlets, villages, and farms, and all who had formerly served in private regiments or those of the Crown; Cherkes,[19] Wallachians, Silistrians, Rumelians, Turks, bands of Serbs and Bulgarians were also in that host. It might appear that a new migration of nations had abandoned the dreary abodes on the steppes, and were moving westward to win fresh lands and found a new kingdom.

This was the relation of the struggling forces,--a handful against legions, an island against the sea. No wonder then that many a heart was beating with alarm. Not only in that town, not only in that corner of the land, but in the whole Commonwealth they looked on that lonely trench, surrounded by a deluge of wild warriors, as the tomb of great knights and their mighty chief.

Hmelnitski too looked on it in just the same way; for scarcely were the fires well kindled in his camps, when a Cossack envoy began to wave a white flag before the trenches, to sound a trumpet, and cry out not to shoot.

The guards went and brought him in at once.

"From the hetman to Prince Yeremi," said he to them.

The prince had not yet dismounted, and was on the bulwark with face as calm as the sky. The flames were reflected in his eyes, and invested his delicate white countenance with rosy light. The Cossack standing before the face of the prince lost his speech; his legs trembled under him, and a shiver went through his body though he was an old wolf of the steppes and had come as an envoy.

"Who are you?" asked the prince, fixing his calm glance upon him.

"I am the sotnik Sokol,--from the hetman."

"And why have you come?"

The sotnik began to make bows as low as the stirrups of the prince. "Pardon me, lord! I tell what has been commanded me. I am to blame in nothing."

"Speak boldly!"

"The hetman commanded me to inform you that he has come as a guest to Zbaraj, and will visit you in the castle to-morrow."

"Tell him that not to-morrow, but to-day I give a feast in the castle," answered the prince.

In fact an hour later the mortars were thundering salutes, joyous shouts were raised; all the windows of the castle shone with a thousand gleaming lights.

The Khan, hearing the salutes of the cannon and the sound of trumpets and drums, went out in front of the tent in company with his brother Nureddin, the Sultan Galga, Tugai Bey, and many murzas, and later sent for Hmelnitski.

The hetman, though he had been drinking, appeared at once. Bowing and placing his fingers to his forehead, his beard, and his breast, he waited for the question.

The Khan looked long at the castle, shining in the distance like a gigantic lantern, and nodded his head slightly. At last he passed his hand over his thin beard, which fell in two long tresses upon his weasel-skin shuba, and asked, pointing to the gleaming windows,--

"Zaporojian hetman, what is that?"

"Most mighty Tsar," answered Hmelnitski, "that is Prince Yeremi giving a feast."

The Khan was astonished. "A feast?"

"He is giving a feast for the slain of to-morrow," said Hmelnitski.

That moment new discharges thundered from the castle, the trumpets sounded, and mingled shouts reached the worthy ears of the Khan. "God is one!" muttered he. "There is a lion in the heart of that infidel." And after a moment of silence he added: "I should rather be with him than with you."

Hmelnitski trembled. He paid for the indispensable Tartar friendship, and besides was not sure of his terrible ally. Any whim of the Khan, and all the hordes might turn against the Cossacks, who would be lost beyond redemption. Hmelnitski knew this, and knew too that the Khan was aiding him really for the sake of plunder, gifts, and unfortunate captives, and still looking upon himself as a legitimate monarch, was ashamed in his soul to stand on the side of rebellion against a king, on the side of such a "Hmel" against such a Vishnyevetski. The hetman of the Cossacks often got drunk, not from habit alone, but from desperation.

"Great monarch," said he, "Yeremi is your enemy. It was he who took the Trans-Dnieper from the Tartars; he hanged, murdered murzas like wolves on the trees, as a terror; he intended to visit the Crimea with fire and sword."

"And have you not done damage in the uluses?" asked the Khan.

"I am your slave."

The blue lips of Tugai Bey began to quiver. He had among the Cossacks a deadly enemy, who in his time had cut a whole chambul to pieces and almost captured him. The name of that man was pressing to his mouth from the implacable power of revengeful memories; he did not restrain himself, and began to snarl in a low voice: "Burlai! Burlai!"

"Tugai Bey," said Hmelnitski, immediately, "you and Burlai, at the exalted and wise command of the Khan, poured water on your swords the past year."

A new salvo of artillery from the castle interrupted further conversation.

The Khan stretched out his hand and described a circle with it enclosing Zbaraj, the town, the castle, and the trench. "To-morrow will that be mine?" asked he, turning to Hmelnitski.

"To-morrow they will die there," answered Hmelnitski, with eyes fastened on the castle. Then he bowed again, and touched with his hand his forehead, beard, and breast, considering the conversation ended.

The Khan wrapped himself in his weasel-skin shuba,--for the night was cool, though in July,-- and said, turning toward the tent: "It is late already!"

Then all began to nod as if moved by one power, and he went to the tent slowly and with dignity repeating in a low voice: "God is one!"

Hmelnitski withdrew also, and on the road to his quarters muttered: "I'll give you the castle, the town, booty, and captives; but Yeremi will be mine, even if I have to pay for him with my life."

Gradually the fires began to grow dim and die, gradually the dull murmur of thousands of voices grew still; but here and there was heard the report of a musket, or the calling of Tartar herdsmen driving their horses to pasture. Then those voices were silent, and sleep embraced the countless legions of Tartars and Cossacks.

But at the castle there was feasting and revelry as at a wedding. In the camp all expected that the storm would take place on the morrow. Indeed the throngs of the mob, Cossacks, Tartars, and other wild warriors marching with Hmelnitski had been moving from early morning, and approached the trenches like dark clouds rolling to the summit of a mountain. The soldiers, though they had tried in vain the day before to count the fires, were benumbed now at the sight of this sea of heads. This was not yet a real storm, but an examination of the field, the intrenchments, the ditch, the ramparts, and the whole Polish camp. And as a swollen wave of the sea, which the wind urges from afar, rolls, advances, rears itself, foams, strikes with a roar and then falls back, so did they strike in one place and another, withdraw, and strike again, as if testing the resistance, as if wishing to convince themselves whether the very sight of them by numbers alone would not crush the spirit of the enemy before they would crush the body.

They fired cannon too, and the balls began to fall thickly about the camp, from which answer was given with eight-pounders and small arms. At the same time there appeared a procession on the ramparts with the most holy sacrament in order to freshen the benumbed soldiers. The priest Mukhovetski carried the gilded monstrance; holding it with both hands above his face and sometimes raising it on high, he moved on under a baldachin, calm, with closed eyes and an ascetic face. At his side walked two priests supporting him under the arms,--Yaskolski, chaplain of the hussars, a famous soldier in his time, in military art as experienced as any chief; and Jabkovski, also an ex-soldier, a gigantic Bernardine, second in strength only to Pan Longin in the whole camp. The staffs of the baldachin were supported by four nobles, among whom was Zagloba; before the baldachin walked sweet-faced young girls scattering flowers. They passed over the whole length of the ramparts, and after them the officers of the army. The hearts of the soldiers rose, daring came to them, fire entered their souls at the sight of the monstrance shining like the sun, at the sight of the calmness of the priest, and those maidens clothed in white. The breeze carried about the strengthening odor of the incense burned in the censers; the heads of all were bent down with humility. Mukhovetski from time to time elevated the monstrance and his eyes to heaven, and intoned the hymn, "Before so great a sacrament."

The powerful voices of Yaskolski and Jabkovski continued, "We fall on our faces;" and the whole army sang, "Let the old give place to the new law with its testament!" The deep bass of the cannon accompanied the hymn, and at times the cannon-balls flew past, roaring above the baldachin and the priests; sometimes the balls striking lower in the ramparts scattered earth on the people, so that Zagloba wriggled and pressed up to the staff. Fear affected especially his hair. When the procession halted for prayer there was silence, and the balls could be heard distinctly flying like great birds in a flock. Zagloba merely reddened the more; the priest Yaskolski looked to the field, and unable to restrain himself muttered, "They should rear chickens and keep away from cannon!" for in truth the Cossacks had very bad gunners, and he, as a former soldier, could not look calmly on such clumsiness and waste of powder. Again they went on till they reached the other end of the ramparts, where there had been no great pressure from the enemy. Trying here and there, especially from the western pond, to see if they could not create a panic, the Tartars and Cossacks drew back at last to their own positions, and remained in them without sending out even skirmishers. Meanwhile the procession had freshened the minds of the besieged completely.

It was evident that Hmelnitski was waiting for the arrival of his tabor; still he felt so sure that the first real storm would be sufficient, that he barely ordered a few trenches to be made for the cannon and did not undertake other earthworks to threaten the besieged. The tabor arrived the following day, and took its place near the camp, wagon after wagon, in a number of tens of rows a mile in length, from Vernyaki to Dembini. With it came also new forces; namely, the splendid Zaporojian infantry, almost equal to the Turkish janissaries in storms and attacks, and far more capable than the Cossacks or the mob.

The memorable day, Tuesday, July 13, was passed in feverish preparations on both sides. There was no doubt that the assault would take place, for the trumpets, drums, and kettle-drums were sounding the alarm from daybreak in the Cossack camp; among the Tartars a great sacred drum, called the balt, was roaring like thunder. The evening came, calm and clear, but from both ponds and the Gnyezna thin mists were rising; at length the first star began to twinkle in the sky.

At that moment sixty Cossack cannon bellowed with one voice; the countless legions rushed with a terrible cry to the ramparts, and the storm began. It appeared to the soldiers standing on the ramparts that the ground was quivering under their feet; the oldest remembered nothing like it.

"Jesus and Mary! what is that?" asked Zagloba, standing near Skshetuski among the hussars, in the interval of the rampart; "those are not men coming against us."

"Of course you know they are not men; the enemy are driving oxen ahead, so that we may spend the first shots on them."

The old noble became as red as a beet, his eyes were coming out of his head, and from his mouth burst one word, in which all the rage, all the terror, all that he could think at that moment was included: "Scoundrels!"

The oxen, as if mad, urged by wild, half-naked herdsmen with clubs and burning brands, were insane from fear; they ran forward with an awful bellowing, now crowding together, now hurrying on, now scattering or turning to the rear; urged with shouts, burned with fire, lashed with rawhides, they rushed again toward the ramparts. At last Vurtsel's guns began to vomit iron and fire; then smoke hid the light, the air was red, the terrified cattle were as if cut by a thunderbolt. Half of them fell, and over their bodies went the enemy.

In front ran captives with bags of sand to fill the ditch; they were stabbed from behind with pikes and scorched with musketry fire. These were peasants from around Zbaraj, who had been unable to take refuge in the town before the avalanche came,--young men as well as old, and women. All ran forward with a shriek, a cry, a stretching of hands to heaven, and a wailing for mercy. Hair stood on end from the howl, but pity was dead upon earth at that hour. On one side the pikes of Cossacks were entering their shoulders; on the other the balls of Vurtsel mashed the unfortunates, grape-shot tore them to pieces, dug furrows among them. They ran on, fell, rose again, and went forward; for the Cossack wave pushed them,--the Cossack, the Turk, and the Tartar. The ditch was soon filled with bodies, blood, and sand-bags; at last it was evened, and the enemy rushed over with a shout.

The regiments pushed on, one after another; by the light of the cannon-fire were to be seen the officers urging forward new regiments to the ramparts. The choicest men rushed to the quarters and troops of Yeremi, for at that point Hmelnitski knew the greatest resistance would be. The kurens of the Saitch therefore came up; after them the formidable men of Pereyasláv, with Loboda. Voronchenko led the regiment of Cherkasi, Kulak the Karvoff regiment, Nechai the Bratslav, Stepka the Uman, Mrozovetski the Korsún regiment; also the men of Kalnik went, and the strong regiment of Belotserkoff,--fifteen thousand men in all, and with them Hmelnitski himself, in the fire, red as Satan, exposing his broad breast to the bullets, with the face of a lion and the eye of an eagle,--in chaos, smoke, confusion, slaughter, and tempest, in flames, observant of everything, ordering everything.

After the Zaporojians went the wild Cossacks of the Don; next, Cherkes fighting with knives; Tugai Bey led chosen Nogais; after them Subahazi, Bélgorod Tartars; then Kurdluk, swarthy men of Astrakhan, armed with gigantic bows and arrows, one of which was almost equal to a spear. They followed one another so closely that the hot breath of those behind was blown on the necks of those in front.

How many of them fell before they reached the ditch filled with the bodies of the captives, who shall tell, who shall relate? But they reached and crossed it, and began to clamber on the ramparts. Then you would have said that that starry night was the night of the Last Judgment. The cannon, unable to strike the nearest, bellowed unceasing fire on the farther ranks. Bombs, describing arcs of fire through the air, fell with a hellish laughter, making bright day in the darkness. The German infantry with the Polish land regiments, and at their side the dismounted dragoons of Vishnyevetski poured fire and lead into the faces and breasts of the Cossacks.

The first ranks wished to fall back, but pressed from behind they could not; they died in their tracks. Blood spattered under the feet of the advancing. The rampart grew slippery; hands, feet, and breasts went sliding upon it. Men grasped it, and again fell covered with smoke, black from soot, stabbed, cut, careless of wounds and death. In places they fought with cold weapons. Men were as if beside themselves from fury, with grinning teeth and blood-covered faces. The living battled on top of the quivering mass of wounded and dying. Commands were not heard; nothing was heard but a general and terrible roar, in which all sounds were merged,--the thunder of guns, the cough of the wounded, the groans, and the whistling of bombs.

This gigantic struggle without quarter lasted whole hours. Around the rampart rose another rampart of corpses, which hindered the approach of the assailants. The Zaporojians were cut almost to pieces, the men of Pereyaslav were lying side by side around the ramparts; the Karvoff, Bratslav, and Uman regiments were decimated; but others pressed on, pushed forward themselves from behind by the guard of the hetman, the Rumelian Turks and Tartars of Urum Bey. But disorder rose in the ranks of the assailants when the Polish land infantry, the Germans, and the dragoons drew back not a step. Panting, dripping with blood, carried away with the rage of battle, streaming in sweat, half mad with the smell of blood, they tore over one another at the enemy, just as raging wolves rush to a flock of sheep. At that juncture Hmelnitski pressed on again with the remnants of his first regiments and with the whole force, as yet intact, of the Belotserkoff Tartars, the Turks and Cherkes.

The cannon from the ramparts ceased to thunder, and the bombs to flash; hand-weapons alone were heard through the whole length of the western rampart. Discharges flashed up anew. Finally, musketry fire also stopped. Darkness covered the combatants. No eye could see what was doing there, but something was turning in the darkness like the gigantic body of a monster cast down in convulsions. Even from the cries it could not be told whether it gave forth the sounds of triumph or despair. At times these sounds also ceased, and then could be heard only one measureless groan, as if it were going out on every side, from under the earth, over the earth, in the air, higher and higher, as if spirits were flying away with groans from that field of conflict. But these were short pauses: after such a moment the uproar and howls rose with still greater power, ever hoarser and more unearthly.

Then again thundered the fire of musketry. Makhnitski with the rest of the infantry was coming to aid the wearied regiments. The trumpets began to sound a retreat in the rear ranks of the Cossacks.

Now came a pause; the Cossack regiments withdrew a furlong from the ramparts, and stood protected by the corpses of their own men. But a half-hour had not passed when Hmelnitski rushed on again and hurried his men to the assault a third time.

But this time Prince Yeremi appeared on the rampart himself, on horseback. It was easy to know him, for the banner and bunchuk of the hetman were waving above his head, and before and behind him were borne a number of tens of torches, shining with blood-colored gleams. Immediately they opened the artillery on him; but the awkward cannoneers sent the balls far beyond the Gnyezna, and he stood calm and gazed upon the approaching clouds.

The Cossacks slackened their gait as if bewitched by the sight. "Yeremi! Yeremi!" passed in a low murmur, like the sound of a breeze, through the deep ranks. Standing on the rampart in the midst of the blood-colored torches, that terrible prince seemed to them like a giant in a myth tale of the people; therefore a quiver ran over their wearied limbs, and their hands made signs of the cross.

He stood motionless. He beckoned with the gilded baton, and immediately an ominous flight of bombs sounded in the air, and fell into the advancing ranks. The host twisted like a mortally wounded dragon; a cry of terror flew from one end of the line to the other.

"On a run! on a run!" commanded the Cossack colonels.

The dark mass rushed with all its impetus to the ramparts under which refuge from the bombs could be found; but they had not passed half the interval when the prince, ever visible as on the palm of the hand, turned somewhat to the west and again beckoned with his baton.

At this signal, from the side of the pond, through the space between it and the ramparts, the cavalry began to push forth, and in the flash of an eye they poured out on the edge of the shore-level. By the light of the bombs were perfectly visible the great banners of the hussars of Skshetuski and Zatsvilikhovski, the dragoons of Kushel and Volodyovski, with the prince's Tartars, led by Roztvorovski. After them pushed out still new regiments of the prince's Cossacks and the Wallachians of Bykhovets. Not only Hmelnitski, but the last camp-follower of the Cossacks, knew in one moment that the daring chief had determined to hurl his entire cavalry into the enemy's flank.

That moment the trumpets sounded a retreat in the ranks of the Cossacks. "Face to the cavalry! Face to the cavalry!" was heard in alarmed voices. Hmelnitski endeavored simultaneously to change the front of his troops and defend himself from cavalry with cavalry. But there was no time. Before he could arrange his ranks the prince's regiments had started, moving as if on wings, shouting "Kill! slay!" with rustling of banners, whistling of plumes, and the iron rattle of arms. The hussars thrust their lances into the wall of the enemy, and followed themselves, like a hurricane, overturning and crushing everything on the road. No human power, no command, no leader could hold the infantry on which their first impetus came. Wild panic seized the picked guard of the hetman. The men of Belotserkoff threw down their muskets, pikes, scythes, sabres, and shielding their heads with their hands in helplessness of terror, with the roar of beasts, they rushed against the Tartars in the rear. But the Tartars received them with a storm of arrows. So they rushed to the flank, and ran along the tabor under the infantry fire and the cannon of Vurtsel, covering the ground so thickly that it was rare when one did not fall upon another.

But now the wild Tugai Bey, aided by Subahazi and Urum Murza, struck with rage on the onrush of hussars. He did not hope to break; he wished merely to restrain them till the Silistrian and Rumelian janissaries might form in a quadrangle and protect the men of Belotserkoff from the first panic. He sprang at them as if into smoke, and flew on in the front rank, not as a leader, but as a simple Tartar; he cut and killed,--exposed himself with the others. The crooked sabres of the Nogais rang upon chain-mail and breastplates, and the howl of the warriors drowned all other voices. But they could not hold out. Pushed from their places, crushed with the terrible weight of the iron horsemen, against whom they were unaccustomed to stand with open front, they were driven toward the janissaries, hacked with long swords, whirled from their saddles, thrust through, beaten down, twisted like poisonous reptiles; but they defended themselves with such venom that in fact the onset of the hussars was stopped. Tugai Bey rushed like a destroying flame, and the Nogais went with him, as wolves with their female.

Still they gave way, falling more frequently on the plain. When the cry of "Allah!" thundering from the field, announced that the janissaries had formed, Skshetuski rushed on the raging Tugai Bey, and struck him on the head with, a double-handed sword. But it was evident either that the knight had not regained his whole strength, or perhaps the helmet forged in Damascus withstood the blow; it is enough that the blade turned on the head, and striking with the side was shivered to fragments. But that instant darkness covered the eyes of Tugai Bey; he dropped into the arms of his Nogais, who, seizing their leader, hurried away on two sides with a terrible uproar, like a cloud blown by a mighty wind. All the prince's cavalry was then in front of the Silistrian and Rumelian janissaries and Mohammedanized Serbs, who together with the janissaries formed one great quadrangle, and were withdrawing slowly to the tabor with their front to the enemy, bristling with muskets, lances, javelins, battle-axes, and swords.

The squadrons of armored dragoons and the Cossacks of the prince rushed on like a whirlwind; and in the very front, with a roar and heavy tramp, Skshetuski's hussars. He flew on himself in the first rank, and at his side Pan Longin on his Livonian mare, his terrible broadsword in his hand.

A red ribbon of fire flies from one end of the quadrangle to the other; bullets whistle in the ears of the riders; here and there a man groans, here and there a horse falls. The line of cavalry is broken, but pushes on,--is approaching. The janissaries now hear the snorting and blown breath of the horses; the quadrangle forms more closely still, and inclines its wall of spears, held by sinewy arms, against the furious chargers. How many points are in that wall? With how many deaths does it threaten the knights?

Just then a certain hussar of gigantic size rushes upon the wall of the quadrangle with an irresistible impulse; in a moment the forefeet of his great horse are in the air; and the knight with his steed falls into the middle of the throng, splintering lances, overturning men, breaking, mashing, destroying. As an eagle swoops on a flock of white partridges, and they, crouching before him in a timid group, become the prey of the robber, who grasps them in his talons and his beak, so Pan Longin Podbipienta, falling into the midst of the enemy, rages with his broadsword. And never has a whirlwind made such destruction in a young and thick forest as he is making in the throng of janissaries. He is terrible; his form assumes superhuman proportions. His mare becomes a species of dragon, snorting flame from her nostrils; and the double-handed sword triples itself in the hands of the knight. Kislar-Bak, a gigantic aga, hurls himself upon him and falls, cut in two. In vain do the strongest men put forth their hands, stopping him with their spears. They die as if struck by lightning. He tramples them, pushes on to the densest throng, and when he strikes they fall, like grass beneath the scythe. An open space is made; the uproar of terror is heard,--groans, the thunder of blows, the biting of steel on the helmets, and the snorting of the infernal mare.

"A div! a div!" cried terrified voices.

That instant the iron mass of the hussars, with Skshetuski at the head of it, bore down the gate opened by the Lithuanian. The walls of the quadrangle burst, like the walls of a falling house, and the masses of janissaries rushed fleeing in every direction.

It was not a moment too soon, for the Nogais under Subahazi were returning to the fight like bloodthirsty wolves, and from the other side Hmelnitski, rallying the men of Belotserkoff, was coming to the aid of the janissaries; but now everything was in confusion. Cossacks, Tartars, renegade Serbs, janissaries, fled in the greatest disorder and panic to the tabors, giving no resistance. The cavalry pressed on them, cutting as they came. Those who did not perish in the first furlong perished in the second. The pursuit was so envenomed that the squadrons went ahead of the rear ranks of the fugitives; their hands grew weary from hewing. The fugitives threw away arms, banners, caps, and even coats. The white caps of the janissaries covered the field, like snow. The entire chosen force of Hmelnitski's infantry, cavalry, artillery, the auxiliary Tartar and Turkish divisions formed one disorderly mass; distracted, wild, blinded with terror, whole companies fled before one man. The hussars, having broken the infantry and cavalry, had done their work; now the dragoons and light squadrons emulated them, and with Volodyovski and Kushel at their head extended this catastrophe, passing human belief. Blood covered the terrible field, and plashed like water under the violent blows of the horse-hoofs, sprinkling the armor and faces of the knights.

The fleeing crowds were resting in the centre of their tabors when the trumpets called back the cavalry of the prince. The knights returned with singing and shouts of joy, counting on the way with their streaming sabres the corpses of the enemy. But who could with a cast of his eye estimate the extent of the defeat? Who could count all when at the trench itself bodies were lying to the height of a man? Soldiers were as if dizzy from the odor of the blood and the sweat. Fortunately from the side of the ponds there was rather a strong breeze, which carried the odor to the tents of the enemy.

Thus ended the first meeting of the terrible Yeremi and Hmelnitski.

But the storm was not ended; for while Vishnyevetski was repulsing the attacks directed against the right wing of the camp, Burlai on the left barely missed becoming master of the ramparts. Having surrounded the town and the castle in silence at the head of his warriors of the Trans-Dnieper, he pushed on to the eastern pond, and fell violently upon Firlei's quarters. The Hungarian infantry stationed there were unable to withstand the attack, for the ramparts at that pond were not yet completed; the first squadron fled from its banner; Burlai sprang to the centre, and after him his men, like an irresistible torrent. The shouts of victory reached the opposite end of the camp. The Cossacks, rushing after the fugitive Hungarians, scattered a small division of cavalry, captured a number of cannon, and were coming to the quarters of the castellan of Belsk, when Pan Pshiyemski at the head of a number of German companies hurried to the rescue. Stabbing the flag-bearer with a single thrust, he seized the flag, and hurled himself on the enemy. Then the Germans closed with the Cossacks. A fearful hand-to-hand struggle raged, in which on one side the fury and crushing numbers of Burlai's legions, on the other the bravery of the old lions of the Thirty Years' War, were contending for superiority. In vain Burlai pressed into the densest ranks of the combatants, like a wounded wild boar. Neither the contempt of death with which the Cossacks fought nor their endurance could stop the irresistible Germans, who going forward in a wall, struck with such force that they swept them out of their places, pushed them against the trenches, decimated them, and after half an hour's struggle drove them beyond the ramparts. Pshiyemski, covered with blood, first planted the banner on the unfinished bulwark.

Burlai's position was now desperate,--he had to retreat on the same road by which he had come; and since Yeremi had crushed the assailants on his right wing, he could easily cut off Burlai's whole division. It is true that Mrozovetski had come to his aid with his mounted Cossacks of Korsún; but at that moment the hussars of Konyetspolski, supported by Skshetuski returning from the attack on the janissaries, fell upon Burlai, hitherto retreating in order.

With a single onset they scattered his forces, and then began a fearful slaughter. The Cossacks, having the road to the camp closed, had open to them only the road to death. Some without asking for quarter defended themselves with desperation, in groups or singly; others stretched forth their hands in vain to the cavalry, thundering like a hurricane over the field. Then began pursuit, artifice, single struggles, search for the enemy hidden in holes or uneven places. Tar-buckets were now thrown out from the trenches to light up the field. These flew like fiery meteors with flaming manes. By the aid of these red gleams they finished the remainder of the Trans-Dnieper Cossacks.

Subahazi, who had shown wonders of valor that day, sprang to the aid of the Cossacks; but the brave Marek Sobieski, starosta of Krasnostav, stopped him on the spot, as a lion stops a wild buffalo, Burlai saw now that there was no salvation for him from any side. But, Burlai, thou didst love thy Cossack glory beyond life; therefore thou didst not seek for safety. Others escaped in the darkness, hid themselves in openings, slipped out between the feet of horses; but he still sought the enemy. He cut down with his own hand Pan Dombka and Pan Rusitski, and the young lion Pan Aksak, the same who had covered himself with undying glory at Konstantinoff; then Pan Savitski; then he stretched out together two winged hussars upon their native earth. At last, seeing a noble enormous in size coursing over the field and roaring like an aurochs, he sprang forward and went at him like a glittering flame.

Zagloba, for it was he, bellowed still louder from fear, and turned his horse in flight. What hair he had left stood straight on his head; but still he did not lose his presence of mind. Stratagems were flashing through his head like lightning, and at the same time he roared with all his power: "Whoever believes in God!" and he drove like a whirlwind toward the thickest mass of Polish cavalry. Burlai was heading him off from the side, as a bow the string. Zagloba closed his eyes, and in his head a voice was roaring, "I shall perish now with my fleas!" He heard behind him the rushing of the horse, saw that no one was coming to his aid, that there was no escape, and that no other hand but his own could tear him from the grasp of Burlai. But in that last moment, almost in the agony of death, his despair and terror suddenly turned to rage; he bellowed as no wild bull has ever bellowed, and wheeling his horse in his tracks, turned against his opponent.

"You are pursuing Zagloba!" cried he, pushing on with drawn sabre.

At that moment a new lot of burning tar-buckets was thrown from the trenches, and there was light. Burlai saw and was astounded. He was not astounded at hearing the name, for he had never heard it in his life before; but he was astounded when he recognized the man whom a short time before he had feasted in Yampol as the friend of Bogun. But just that unfortunate moment of surprise destroyed the brave leader of the Cossacks, for before he recollected himself Zagloba cut him on the temple, and with one blow rolled him from his horse.

This was in view of the whole army. A joyful shout from the hussars answered a cry of terror from the Cossacks, who seeing the death of their old lion of the Black Sea, lost the rest of their courage, and abandoned all resistance. Those who were not rescued by Subahazi perished to a man; no prisoners were taken in that night of terror.

Subahazi fled to the camp, pursued by Sobieski and the light cavalry. The assault along the whole line of trenches was repulsed; only near the Cossack tabor was the cavalry sent out by the prince in pursuit still at work.

A shout of triumph and joy shook the whole camp of the attacked, and mighty cries went up to heaven. The bloody soldiers, covered with sweat, dust, black from powder, with raging faces and brows still contracted, with fire still unquenched in their eyes, stood leaning on their weapons, catching the air with their breasts, ready again to rush to the fight if the need should come. But the cavalry too returned gradually from the bloody harvest near the tabor. Then the prince himself rode out on the field, and behind him the commanders, the standard-bearer, Marek Sobieski, and Pshiyemski. All that brilliant retinue moved slowly along the intrenchment.

"Long live Yeremi!" cried out the army. "Long live our father!"

The prince, without helmet, inclined his head and his baton on every side. "I thank you, gentlemen, I thank you!" repeated he, in a clear, ringing voice. Then he turned to Pshiyemski. "This trench," said he, "encloses too much space."

Pshiyemski nodded his head in sign of agreement.

The victorious leaders rode from the western to the eastern pond, examining the battle-field, the injuries done to the ramparts by the enemy, and the ramparts themselves.

Immediately after the retinue of the prince, the soldiers, carried away by enthusiasm, bore Zagloba in their arms to the camp, as the greatest conqueror of the day. Borne aloft by twenty sturdy arms, appeared the form of the warrior, who, purple, sweating, waving his arms to keep his balance, cried with all his power,--

"Ha! I gave him pepper. I pretended to flee, so as to lure him on. He won't bark at us any more, the dog-brother! It was necessary to show an example to the younger men. For God's sake, be careful, or you will let me fall and kill me! Hold on tight; you have something to hold! You may believe me, I had work with him. To-day every trash was thrusting itself on nobles; but they have got their own. Be careful! Devil take it, let me down!"

"Long life to him, long life!" cried the nobles.

"To the prince with him!" repeated others.

"Long life to him! long life to him!"

The Zaporojian hetman, rushing into his camp, roared like a wounded wild beast; he tore the coat on his breast and disfigured his face. The officers who had escaped the defeat surrounded him in gloomy silence, without bringing a word of consolation, and madness almost carried him away. Foam was on his lips; he drove his heels into the ground, and with both hands tore his hair.

"Where are my regiments, where are my heroes?" asked he, in a hoarse voice. "What shall I tell the Khan, what Tugai Bey? Give me Yeremi! Let them put my head on the stake!"

The officers were gloomily silent.

"Why have the soothsayers promised victory? Off with the heads of the witches! Why have they said that I should get Yeremi?"

Generally when the roar of that lion shook the camp the colonels were silent; but now that the lion was conquered, trampled, and fortune seemed to be forsaking him, defeat gave insolence to the officers.

"You cannot withstand Yeremi," muttered Stepka.

"You are destroying us and yourself," added Mrozovetski.

The hetman sprang at them like a tiger. "And who gained Jóltiya Vodi, who Korsún, who Pilavtsi?"

"You!" answered Voronchenko, roughly, "but Vishnyevetski was not there."

Hmelnitski tore his hair. "I promised the Khan lodgings in the castle to-night!" howled he, in despair.

To this Kulak replied: "What you promised the Khan concerns your head. Have a care lest it drop from your neck; but do not push us to the storm, do not destroy servants of God! Surround the Poles with trenches, put ramparts round your guns, or woe to you!"

"Woe to you!" repeated gloomy voices.

"Woe to you!" answered Hmelnitski.

And thus they conversed, terrible as thunders. At last Hmelnitski staggered, and threw himself on a bundle of sheepskins covered with carpet in the corner of the tent. The colonels stood around him with hanging heads, and silence lasted for a long time. At length the hetman looked up, and cried hoarsely: "Gorailka!"

"You will not drink!" said Vygovski, "The Khan will send for you."

At that time the Khan was about five miles from the field of battle, without knowledge of what was passing. The night was calm and warm. He was sitting at the tent in the midst of mullahs and agas in expectation of news; while waiting, he was eating dates from a silver plate standing near. At times he looked at the starry heavens and muttered, "Mohammed Rosulla!"

Meanwhile Subahazi, on a foaming horse, rushed in, breathless, and covered with blood. He sprang from the saddle, and approaching quickly, began to make obeisance, waiting for a question.

"Speak!" said the Khan, with his mouth full of dates.

The words were burning Subahazi's mouth like flame, but he dared not speak without the usual titles. He began therefore in the following fashion, bowing continually,--

"Most mighty Khan of all the hordes, grandson of Mohammed, absolute monarch, wise lord, fortunate lord, lord of the tree commended from the east to the west, lord of the blooming tree--"

Here the Khan waved his hand and interrupted. Seeing blood on Subahazi's face, and in his eyes pain, sorrow, and despair, he spat out the uneaten dates on his hand and gave them to one of the mullahs, who took them as a mark of extraordinary honor and began to eat them. The Khan said,--

"Speak quickly, Subahazi, and wisely! Is the camp of the unbeliever taken?"

"God did not give it."

"The Poles?"

"Victorious."

"Hmelnitski?"

"Beaten."

"Tugai Bey?"

"Wounded."

"God is one!" said the Khan. "How many of the Faithful have gone to Paradise?"

Subahazi raised his arm and pointed with a bloody hand to the sparkling heavens. "As many as of those lights at the foot of Allah," said he, solemnly.

The heavy face of the Khan became purple; rage seized him by the breast. "Where is that dog," inquired he, "who promised that I should sleep to-night in the castle? Where is that venomous serpent whom God will trample under my foot? Let him stand before me and give an account of his disgusting promises."

A number of murzas hurried off for Hmelnitski. The Khan calmed himself by degrees, and at last said: "God is one!" Then he turned to Subahazi. "There is blood on thy face!"

"It is the blood of the unbeliever," answered the warrior.

"Tell how you shed it, and console our ears with the bravery of the believers."

Here Subahazi began to give an extended account of the whole battle, praising the bravery of Tugai Bey, of Galga, of Nureddin; he was not silent either of Hmelnitski, but praised him as well as the others,--the will of God alone and the fury of the unbelievers were the causes of the defeat. But one circumstance struck the Khan in the narrative; namely, that they did not fire at the Tartars in the beginning of the battle, and that the cavalry of the prince attacked them only when at last they stood in the way.

"Allah! they did not want war with me," said the Khan, "but now it is too late."

So it was in reality. Prince Yeremi, from the beginning of the battle, had forbidden to fire at the Tartars, wishing to instil into the soldiers that negotiations with the Khan were already commenced, and that the hordes were standing on the side of the mob merely for show. It was only later that it came to meeting the Tartars by the force of events.

The Khan shook his head, thinking at that moment whether it would not be better yet to turn his arms against Hmelnitski, when the hetman himself stood suddenly before him. Hmelnitski was now calm, and came up with head erect, looking boldly into the eyes of the Khan; on his face were depicted daring and craft.

"Approach, traitor!" said the Khan.

"The hetman of the Cossacks approaches, and he is not a traitor, but a faithful ally, to whom you have pledged assistance not in victory alone," said Hmelnitski.

"Go pass the night in the castle! Go pull the Poles out of the trenches as you promised me!"

"Great Khan of all the hordes!" said Hmelnitski, with a powerful voice, "you are mighty, and except the Sultan the mightiest on earth; you are wise and powerful, but can you send forth an arrow from your bow to the stars, or can you measure the depth of the sea?"

The Khan looked at him with astonishment.

"You cannot," continued Hmelnitski, with still more force; "so can I not measure all the pride and insolence of Yeremi! If I could dream that he would not be terrified at you, O Khan, that he would not be submissive at sight of you, would not beat with his forehead before you, but would raise his insolent hand against your person, shed the blood of your warriors, and insult you, O mighty monarch, as well as the least of your murzas,--if I could have dared to think that, I should have shown contempt to you whom I honor and love."

"Allah!" said the Khan, more and more astonished.

"But I will tell you this," continued Hmelnitski, with increasing assurance in his voice and his manner: "you are great and powerful; nations and monarchs from the east to the west incline before you and call you a lion; Yeremi alone does not fall on his face before your beard. If then you do not rub him out, if you do not bend his neck and ride on his back, your power is in vain, your glory is empty; for they will say that one Polish prince has dishonored the Tsar of the Crimea and received no punishment,--that he is greater, that he is mightier than you."

Dull silence followed; the murzas, the agas, and the mullahs looked on the face of the Khan, as on the sun, holding the breath in their breasts. He had his eyes closed, and was thinking. Hmelnitski was resting on his baton and waiting confidently.

"You have said it," answered the Khan at last. "I will bend the neck of Yeremi; I will sit on his back as on a horse, so it may not be said from the east to the west that an unbelieving dog has disgraced me."

"God is great!" cried the murzas, with one voice.

Joy shot from the eyes of Hmelnitski. At one step he had averted destruction hanging over his head, and turned a doubtful ally into a most faithful one. At every moment that lion knew how to turn himself into a serpent.

Both camps till late at night were as active as bees warmed by the spring sun in the swarming-season, while on the battle-field slept--an endless and eternal sleep--the knights thrust through with spears, cut with swords, pierced with arrows and bullets. The moon rose, and began her course over the field of death, was reflected in pools of stiffened blood, brought forth from the darkness every moment new piles of slain, passed from some bodies, came quietly to others, looked into open and lifeless eyeballs, lighted up blue faces, fragments of broken weapons, bodies of horses; and her rays grew pale, at times very pale, as if terrified with what they saw. Along the field there ran here and there, alone and in little groups, certain ominous figures,-- camp-followers and servants, who had come to plunder the slain, as jackals follow lions. But superstitious fear drove them away at last. There was something awful and mysterious in that field covered with corpses, in that calmness and quiet of human forms recently alive, and in that silent harmony with which Poles, Turks, Tartars, and Cossacks lay side by side. The wind at times rustled in the bushes growing over the field, and to the soldiers watching in the trenches it seemed that those were the souls of the slain, circling above their bodies. It was said in fact that when midnight had struck in Zbaraj, over the whole field, from the bulwark of the Poles to the tabor of the Cossacks, there rose with a rustle as it were a countless flock of birds. Wailing voices were heard also in the air, enormous sighs, which made men's hair stand on end, and groans. Those who were yet to fall in that struggle, and whose ears were more open to cries from beyond the earth, heard clearly the Polish spirits, when flying away, cry: "Before thy eyes, O Lord, we lay down our sins;" and the Cossacks groan: "O Christ, O Christ, have mercy on us!" As they had fallen in a war of brothers, they could not fly straight to light eternal, but were predestined to fly somewhere in the dark distance, and hover in the wind over this vale of tears, to weep and groan by night, till the full remission of their offences,--till they should receive pardon at the feet of Christ, and oblivion for their sins.

But at that time the hearts of men grew harder yet, and no angel of peace flew over the field.

CHAPTER LVIII.

Next morning, before the sun had scattered its golden rays over the sky, a new protecting rampart encircled the Polish camp. The old ramparts included too much space. Defence and the giving of mutual assistance were difficult within them. The Prince and Pan Pshiyemski, in view of this, decided to enclose the troops within narrower intrenchments. They worked vigorously, the hussars as well as all the other regiments, and the camp-servants. Only at three o'clock in the morning did sleep close the eyes of the wearied knights, but at that hour all save the guards were sleeping like stones. The enemy labored also, and then was quiet for a long time, after the recent defeat. No assault was looked for that day.

Skshetuski, Pan Longin, and Zagloba sat in their tent drinking beer, thickened with bits of cheese, and talked of the labors of the past night with that satisfaction peculiar to soldiers after victory.

"It is my habit to lie down about the evening milking, and rise with the dawn, as did the ancients," said Zagloba, "but in war it is difficult! You sleep when you can, and you rise when they wake you. I am vexed that we must incommode ourselves for such rubbish; but it cannot be helped, such are the times. We paid them well yesterday; if they get such a feast a couple of times more, they won't want to wake us."

"Do you know whether many of ours have fallen?" asked Podbipienta.

"Oh, not many; more of the assailants always fall. You are not so experienced in this as I am, for you have not been through so many wars. We old soldiers have no need to count bodies; we can estimate the number from the battle itself."

"I shall learn from you, gentlemen," said Pan Longin, with amiability.

"Yes, if you have wit enough; but I haven't much hope of that."

"Oh, give us peace!" said Skshetuski. "This is not Podbipienta's first war. God grant the foremost knights to act as he did yesterday."

"I did what I could," said the Lithuanian, "not what I wanted."

"Still your action was not bad," said Zagloba, patronizingly; "and that others surpassed you [here he began to curl his mustaches] is not your fault."

The Lithuanian listened with downcast eyes and sighed, thinking of his ancestor Stoveiko and the three heads.

At that moment the tent door opened and Pan Michael entered quickly, glad as a goldfinch on a bright morning.

"Well, we are here," said Zagloba; "give him some beer."

The little knight pressed the hands of his three comrades, and said: "You should see how many balls are lying on the square; it passes imagination! You can't pass without hitting one."

"I saw that too," said Zagloba, "for when I rose I walked a little through the camp. All the hens in the province of Lvoff won't lay so many eggs in two years. Oh, I only wish they were eggs! Then we should have them fried; and you must know, gentlemen, that I consider a plate of fried eggs the greatest delicacy. I am a born soldier, and so are you. I eat willingly what is good, if there is only enough of it. On this account too I am more eager for battle than the pampered youngsters of to-day who can't eat anything unusual without getting the gripes."

"But you scored a success yesterday with Burlai," said Volodyovski. "To cut down Burlai in that fashion! As I live I did not expect that of you, and he was a warrior famous throughout the Ukraine and Turkey."

"Pretty good work, wasn't it?" asked Zagloba, with satisfaction. "It's not my first, it's not my first, Pan Michael. I see we were all looking for poppyseed in the bottom of the bushel; but we have found four, and such another four you could not find in the whole Commonwealth. If I should go with you, gentlemen, and with our prince at the head, we could reach even Stamboul! Just think! Skshetuski killed Burdabut, and yesterday Tugai Bey."

"Tugai Bey is not killed," interrupted the colonel. "I felt that the sabre was turning in my hand; then they separated us."

"All one; don't interrupt me, Pan Yan! Pan Michael cut up Bogun at Warsaw, as we have said--"

"It is better not to mention that," interrupted the Lithuanian.

"What is said is said," answered Zagloba, "though I should prefer not to mention it. But I go further: Here is Pan Podbipienta from Myshekishki, who finished Pulyan, and I Burlai. I will not hide from you, however, that I would give all these for Burlai alone; and this perhaps because I had terrible work with him. He was a devil, not a Cossack. If I had sons like him legitimately born, I should leave them a splendid name. I am only curious to know what his Majesty the King and the Diet will say when they reward us,--who live more on brimstone and saltpetre than anything else."

"There was a knight greater than all of us," said Pan Longin; "and no one knows his name or mentions it."

"I should like to know who he was,--one of the ancients?" asked Zagloba, offended.

"No; he was that man, brother, who at Tshtsiana brought the king Gustavus Adolphus to the ground with his horse, and took him prisoner."

"I heard it was at Putsek," interrupted Volodyovski.

"But the king tore away from him, and escaped," said Skshetuski.

"He did," said Zagloba, closing his eyes. "I know something about that matter, for I was then under Konyetspolski, father of the standard-bearer. Modesty did not permit that knight to mention his own name, therefore no one knows it; and believe me, Gustavus Adolphus was a great warrior,--almost equal to Burlai; but in the hand-to-hand conflict with Burlai I had heavier work. It is I who tell you this."

"That means that you overthrew Gustavus Adolphus?" said Volodyovski.

"Have I boasted of it, Pan Michael? Then let it remain unremembered. I have something to boast of to-day; no need of bringing up old times! This horrid beer rattles terribly in the stomach, and the more cheese there is in it the worse it rattles. I prefer wine, though God be praised for what we have! Soon perhaps we shall not have even the beer. The priest Jabkovski tells me that we are likely to have short rations; and he is all the more troubled, for he has a belly as big as a barn. He is a rare Bernardine, with whom I have fallen desperately in love. There is more of the soldier than the monk in him. If he should hit a man on the snout, then you might order his coffin on the spot."

"But," said Volodyovski, "I have not told you how handsomely the priest Yaskolski acted last night. He fixed himself in that corner of the tower at the right side of the castle, and looked at the fight. You must know that he is a wonderfully good shot. Said he to Jabkovski: 'I won't shoot Cossacks, for they are Christians after all, though their deeds are disgusting to the Lord; but Tartars,' said he, 'I cannot stand;' and so he peppered away at the Tartars, and he spoiled about a score and a half of them during the battle."

"I wish all priests were like him," sighed Zagloba; "but our Mukhovetski only raises his hands to heaven and weeps because so much Christian blood is flowing."

"But give us peace," said Skshetuski, earnestly. "Mukhovetski is a holy man, and you have the best proof of it in this, that though he is not the senior of these two, they bow down before his worthiness."

"Not only do I not deny his holiness," retorted Zagloba, "but I suppose he would be able to convert the Khan himself. Oh, gentlemen, his Majesty the Khan must be so mad that the lice on him are standing on their heads from fright. If we have negotiations with the Khan, I will go with the commissioners. The Khan and I are old acquaintances. Once he took a great fancy to me. Perhaps he will remember me now."

"They will surely choose Yanitski to negotiate," said Skshetuski, "for he speaks Tartar as well as Polish."

"And so do I. The murzas and I are as well acquainted as white-faced horses. They wanted to give me their daughters when I was in the Crimea so as to have beautiful grandchildren, as I was young in those days, and had made no *pacta conventa* with my innocence like Podbipienta. I played many a prank."

"Ah, it is disgusting to hear him!" said Pan Longing dropping his eyes.

"And you repeat the same thing like a trained starling. It is clear that the Botvinians are not well acquainted with human speech yet."

Further conversation was interrupted by a noise beyond the tent. The knights went out therefore to see what was going on. A multitude of soldiers were on the ramparts looking at the place round about, which during the night had changed considerably and was still changing before their eyes. The Cossacks had not been idle since the last assault; they had made a breastwork and placed cannon in it, longer and carrying farther than any in the Polish camp; they had begun traverses, zigzags, and approaches. From a distance these embankments looked like thousands of gigantic mole-hills; the whole slope of the field was covered with them; the freshly dug earth lay black everywhere in the grass, and every place was swarming with men at work. The red caps of the Cossacks were glittering on the front ramparts.

The prince stood on the works with Sobieski and Pshiyemski. A little below, Firlei was surveying the Cossack works through a field-glass, and said to Ostrorog,--

"The enemy are beginning a regular siege. I see we must abandon defence in the trenches and go to the castle."

Prince Yeremi heard these words, and said, bending from above to the castellan: "God keep us from that, for we should be going of our own choice into a trap. Here is the place for us to live or die."

"That's my opinion too, even if I had to kill a Burlai every day," put in Zagloba. "I protest in the name of the whole army against the opinion of the castellan of Belsk."

"This matter does not pertain to you!" said the prince.

"Quiet!" whispered Volodyovski, jerking him by the sleeve.

"We will exterminate them in those hiding-places like so many moles," said Zagloba, "and I beg your serene Highness to let me go out with the first sally. They know me already, and they will know me better."

"With a sally!" said the prince, and wrinkled his brow. "Wait a minute! The nights are dark in the beginning now." Here he turned to Sobieski, Pshiyemski, and the commanders, and said: "I ask you, gentlemen, to come to counsel."

He left the intrenchment, and all the officers followed him.

"For the love of God, what are you doing?" asked Volodyovski, "What does this mean? Why, you don't know service and discipline, that you interfere in the conversation of your superiors. The prince is a mild-mannered man, but in time of war there is no joking with him."

"Oh, that is nothing, Pan Michael! Konyetspolski, the father, was a fierce lion, and he depended greatly on my counsels; and may the wolves eat me up to-day, if it was not for that reason that he defeated Gustavus Adolphus twice. I know how to talk with magnates. Didn't you see now how the prince was astonished when I advised him to make a sally? If God gives a victory, whose service will it be,--whose? Will it be yours?"

At that moment Zatsvilikhovski came up. "What's this? They are rooting and rooting, like so many pigs!" said he, pointing to the field.

"I wish they were pigs," said Zagloba. "Pork sausage would be cheap, but their carrion is not fit for dogs. Today the soldiers had to dig a well in Firlei's quarters, for the water in the eastern pond was spoiled from the bodies. Toward morning the bile burst in the dog-brothers, and they all floated. Now next Friday we cannot use fish, because the fish have eaten their flesh."

"True," said Zatsvilikhovski; "I am an old soldier, but I have not seen so many bodies, unless at Khotím, at the assault of the janissaries on our camp."

"You will see more of them yet, I tell you."

"I think that this evening, or before evening, they will move to the storm again."

"But I say they will leave us in peace till to-morrow."

Scarcely had Zagloba finished speaking, when long white puffs of smoke blossomed out on the breastwork, and balls flew over the intrenchment.

"There!" exclaimed Zatsvilikhovski.

"Oh, they know nothing of military art!" said Zagloba.

Old Zatsvilikhovski was right. Hmelnitski had began a regular siege. He had closed all roads and escapes, had taken away the pasture, made approaches and breastworks, had dug zigzags near the camp, but had not abandoned assaults. He had resolved to give no rest to the besieged; to harass, to frighten, to keep them in continual sleeplessness, and press upon them till their arms should fall from their stiffened hands. In the evening, therefore, he struck upon the quarters of Vishnyevetski, with no better result than the day before, especially since the Cossacks did not advance with such alacrity. Next day firing did not cease for an instant. The zigzags were already so near that musketry fire reached the ramparts; the earthworks smoked like little volcanoes from morning till evening. It was not a general battle, but a continual fusillade. The besieged rushed out sometimes from the ramparts; then sabres, flails, scythes, and lances met in the conflict. But scarcely had a few Cossacks fallen in the ranks, when the gaps were immediately filled with new men. The soldiers had no rest for even a moment during the whole day; and when the desired sunset came, a new general assault was begun. A sally was not to be thought of.

On the night of the 16th of July two valiant colonels--Gladki and Nebaba--struck upon the quarters of the prince, and suffered a terrible defeat. Three thousand of the best Cossacks lay on the field; the rest, pursued by Sobieski, escaped to the tabor, throwing down their arms and powder-horns. An equally unfortunate result met Fedorenko, who, taking advantage of the thick fog, barely failed to capture the town at daybreak. Pan Korf repulsed him at the head of the Germans; then Sobieski and Konyetspolski cut the fugitives almost to pieces.

But this was nothing in comparison with the awful attack of July 19. On the previous night the Cossacks had raised in front of Vishnyevetski's quarters a lofty embankment, from which guns of large calibre vomited an uninterrupted fire. When the day had closed, and the first stars were in the sky, tens of thousands of men rushed to the attack. At the same time appeared some scores of terrible machines, like towers, which rolled slowly to the intrenchment. At their sides rose bridges, like monstrous wings, which were to be thrown over the ditches; and their tops were smoking, blazing, and roaring with discharges of small cannon, guns, and muskets. These towers moved on among the swarm of heads like giant commanders,--now reddening in the fire of guns, now disappearing in smoke and darkness.

The soldiers pointed them out to one another from a distance, whispering: "Those are the 'travelling towers.' We are the men that Hmelnitski is going to grind with those windmills."

"See how they roll, with a noise like thunder!"

"At them from the cannon! At them from the cannon!" cried some.

In fact the prince's gunners sent ball after ball, bomb after bomb, at those terrible machines; but since they were visible only when the discharges lighted the darkness, the balls missed them most of the time.

Meanwhile the dense mass of Cossacks drew nearer and nearer, like a black wave flowing in the night from the distant expanse of the sea.

"Uf!" said Zagloba, in the cavalry near Skshetuski, "I am hot as never before in my life. The night is so sultry that there is not a dry thread on me. The devils invented those machines. God grant the ground to open under them, for those ruffians are like a bone in my throat,--amen! We can neither eat nor sleep. Dogs are in a better condition of life than we. Uf! how hot!"

It was really oppressive and sultry; besides, the air was saturated with exhalations from bodies decaying for several days over the whole field. The sky was covered with a black and low veil of clouds. A storm or tempest was hanging over Zbaraj. Sweat covered the bodies of soldiers under arms, and their breasts were panting from exertion. At that moment drums began to grumble in the darkness.

"They will attack immediately," said Skshetuski. "Do you hear the drum?"

"Yes. I wish the devils would drum them! It is pure desperation!"

"Cut! cut!" roared the crowds, rushing to the ramparts.

The battle raged along the whole length of the rampart. They struck at the same time on Vishnyevetski, Lantskoronski, Firlei, and Ostrorog, so that one could not give aid to the other. The Cossacks, excited with gorailka, went still more ragingly than during the previous assaults, but they met a still more valiant resistance. The heroic spirit of their leader gave life to the soldiers. The terrible quarter infantry, formed of Mazovians, fought with the Cossacks, so that they became thoroughly intermingled with them. They fought with gun-stocks, fists, and teeth. Under the blows of the stubborn Mazovians several hundred of the splendid Zaporojian infantry fell. The battle grew more and more desperate along the whole line. The musket-barrels burned the hands of the soldiers; breath failed them; the voices of the commanders died in their throats from shouting. Sobieski and Skshetuski fell with their cavalry upon the Cossack flank, trampling whole regiments.

Hour followed hour, but the assault relaxed not; for Hmelnitski filled the great gaps of the Cossack ranks, in the twinkle of an eye, with new men. The Tartars increased the uproar, at the same time sending clouds of arrows on the defending soldiers; men from behind drove the mob to the assault with clubs and rawhide whips. Rage contended with rage, breast struck breast, man closed with man in the grip of death. They struggled, as the raging waves of the sea struggle with an island cliff.

Suddenly the earth trembled; the whole heavens were in blue flames, as if God could no longer witness the horrors of men. An awful crash silenced the shouts of combatants and the roar of cannon. The artillery of heaven then began its more awful discharges. Thunders rolled on every side, from the east to the west. It seemed as though the sky had burst, together with the cloud, and was rolling on to the heads of the combatants. At moments the whole world seemed like one flame; at moments all were blind in the darkness, and again ruddy zigzags of lightning rent the black veil. A whirlwind struck once and again, tore away thousands of caps, streamers, and flags, and swept them in the twinkle of an eye over the battle-field. Thunders began to roll, one after another; then followed a chaos of peals, flashes, whirlwind, fire, and darkness; the heavens were as mad as the men.

The unheard-of tempest raged over the town, the castle, the trenches, and the tabor. The battle was stopped. At last the flood-gates of heaven were open, and not streams, but rivers of rain poured down upon the earth. The deluge hid the light; nothing could be seen a step in advance. Bodies were swimming in the ditch. The Cossack regiments, abandoning the assault, fled one after the other to the tabor; going at random, they stumbled against one another, and thinking that the enemy was pursuing, scattered in the darkness; guns and ammunition wagons followed them, sticking and getting overturned on the way. Water washed down the Cossack earthworks, roared in the ditches and zigzags, filled the covered places, though provided with ditches, and ran roaring over the plain as if pursuing the Cossacks.

The rain increased every moment. The infantry in the trenches left the ramparts, seeking shelter under the tents. But for the cavalry of Sobieski and Skshetuski there came no order to withdraw; they stood one by the other as if in a lake, and shook the water from their shoulders. The tempest began gradually to slacken. After midnight the rain stopped entirely. Through the rents in the clouds here and there the stars glittered. Still an hour passed, and the water had fallen a little. Then before Skshetuski's squadron appeared the prince himself unexpectedly.

"Gentlemen," inquired he, "your pouches are not wet?"

"Dry, serene prince!" answered Skshetuski.

"That's right! dismount for me, advance through the water to those machines, put powder to them and fire them. Go quietly! Sobieski will go with you."

"According to orders!" replied Skshetuski.

The prince now caught sight of the drenched Zagloba. "You asked to go out on a sally; go now with these," said he.

"Ah, devil, here is an overcoat for you!" muttered Zagloba. "This is all that was wanting."

Half an hour later, two divisions of knights, two hundred and fifty men, wading to their waists in the water with sabres in hand, hastened to those terrible moving towers of the Cossacks, standing about half a furlong from the trench. One division was led by that "lion of lions," Marek Sobieski, starosta of Krasnostav, who would not hear of remaining in the trench; the other by Skshetuski. Attendants followed the knights with buckets of tar, torches, and powder. They went as quietly as wolves stealing in the dark night to a sheepfold.

Volodyovski went, as a volunteer with Skshetuski, for Pan Michael loved such expeditions more than life. He tripped along through the water, joy in his heart and sabre in hand. At his side was Podbipienta, with his drawn sword, conspicuous above all, for he was two heads higher than the tallest. Among them Zagloba pushed on panting, while he muttered with vexation and imitated the words of the prince,--

"'You asked to go on a sally; go now with these.' All right! A dog wouldn't go to a wedding through such water as this. If ever I advise a sally in such weather may I never drink anything but water while I live! I am not a duck, and my belly isn't a boat. I have always held water in horror, and what kind of water is this in which peasant carrion is steeping?"

"Quiet!" said Volodyovski.

"Quiet yourself! You are not bigger than a gudgeon, and you know how to swim, it is easy for you. I say even that it is unhandsome on the part of the prince to give me no peace. After the killing of Burlai, Zagloba has done enough; let every one do as much, and let Zagloba have peace, for you will be a pretty-looking crowd when he is gone. For God's sake, if I fall into a hole, pull me out by the ears, for I shall fill with water at once."

"Quiet!" said Skshetuski. "The Cossacks are sitting in those dark shelters; they will hear you."

"Where? What do you tell me?"

"There in those hillocks, under the sods."

"That is all that was wanting! May the bright lightning smash--"

Volodyovski stopped the remaining words by putting his hand on Zagloba's mouth, for the shelters were barely fifty yards distant. The knights went silently indeed, but the water spattered under their feet; happily rain began to fall again, and the patter deadened the noise of their steps.

The guards were not at the shelters. Who could have expected a sally after an assault in such a tempest, when the combatants were divided by something like a lake?

Volodyovski and Pan Longin sprang ahead and reached the shelter first. Volodyovski let his sabre drop, put his hand to his mouth and began to cry: "Hei, men!"

"What?" answered from within the voices of Cossacks, evidently convinced that some one from the Cossack tabor was coming.

"Glory to God!" answered Volodyovski; "let us in!"

"Don't you know the way?"

"I do," replied Volodyovski, and feeling for the entrance he jumped in. Podbipienta, with a few others, rushed after him.

At that moment the interior of the shelter resounded with the terrified shout of men; at the same instant the knights rushed with a shout to the other shelter. In the darkness were heard groans and clash of steel; here and there some dark figures rushed past, others fell on the ground, then came the report of a shot; but all did not last longer than a quarter of an hour. The Cossacks, surprised for the most part while in a deep sleep, did not even defend themselves, and were destroyed before they could seize their weapons.

"To the marching towers! to the marching towers!" cried Sobieski.

They hurried to the towers.

"Fire them from within, for they are wet outside!" shouted Skshetuski.

But the command was not easy of execution. In these towers built of pine planks there was neither door nor opening. The Cossack gunners mounted them on ladders. The guns, since only those of the smaller calibre could be carried, were drawn up with ropes. The knights therefore ran around the towers some time yet, cutting the planks in vain with their sabres or grasping with their hands on corners.

Happily the attendants had axes; they began to cut. Sobieski ordered them to place boxes underneath with powder, prepared on purpose. The buckets with tar, as well as the torches were lighted; and flame began to lick the planks, wet outside but full of pitch within.

Before, however, the planks had caught fire or the powder had exploded. Pan Longin bent down and raised an enormous stone, dug out of the ground by the Cossacks. Four of the strongest men could not move it from its place; but he raised it, and only through the light of the tar-buckets could it be seen that the blood came to his face. The knights grew dumb with amazement.

"He is a Hercules! May the bullets strike him!" cried they, raising their hands.

Pan Longin approached the still unkindled machine, bent and hurled the stone at the very centre of the wall.

Those present bent their heads, so loud was the whistle of the stone. The mortises were broken by the blow; a rattle was heard all around; the tower twisted as if broken in two, and fell with a crash. The pile of timber was covered with pitch and fired in a moment.

Soon gigantic flames illuminated the whole plain. Rain fell continually; but the fire was too strong, and those moving towers were burning, to the astonishment of both armies, since the night was so wet.

Stepka, Kulak, and Mrozovetski hurried from the Cossack tabor with several thousand men, to quench the fire. Pillars of flame and red smoke shot up toward the sky, with power increasing each moment, and were reflected in the lakes and ponds formed by the tempest on the battle-field.

The knights began to return in serried ranks to the rampart. They were greeted even at that distance with shouts of joy. Suddenly Skshetuski looked around, cast his eyes into the heart of the company, and called with a thundering voice: "Halt!"

Pan Longin and the little knight were not among the returning. It was evident that, carried away by ardor, they had remained too long at the last tower, and perhaps found Cossacks hidden somewhere; it was enough that, seemingly, they had not noticed the retreat.

"Return!" commanded Skshetuski.

Sobieski, at the other end of the line, did not know what had happened and ran to inquire. At that moment the two knights showed themselves as if they had risen out of the earth, half-way between the towers and the other knights. Pan Longin with his gleaming broadsword strode with gigantic steps, and at his side ran Pan Michael on a trot. Both had their heads turned to the Cossacks, who were chasing them like a pack of dogs. By the red light of the flames the whole pursuit was perfectly visible. One would have said that an enormous elk with her young was retreating before a crowd of hunters ready to hurl herself at any moment on the enemy.

"They will be killed! By the mercy of God, forward!" cried Zagloba, in a heart-rending voice; "they will be shot with arrows or muskets! By the wounds of Christ, forward!" And not considering that a new battle might begin in a moment he flew, sabre in hand, with Skshetuski and others, to the succor; he thrust, twisted, sprang up, panted, cried, was shaking all over, and rushed on with what legs and breath remained to him.

The Cossacks, however, did not fire, for their muskets were wet, and the strings of their bows damp; they only pressed on. Some had pushed to the front and were about to run up, when both knights at bay turned to them and giving an awful shout, raised their sabres on high. The Cossacks halted. Pan Longin, with his immense sword, seemed to them some supernatural being.

As two tawny wolves pressed overmuch by hounds turn and show their white teeth, and the dogs whining at a distance do not dare to rush on, so these turned repeatedly, and each time their pursuers halted. Once only a man, evidently of bolder nature, ran up to them with a scythe in his hand; but Pan Michael sprang at him like a wildcat and bit him to death. The rest waited for their comrades, who were coming on the run in a dense body.

But the line of Cossacks came nearer and nearer, and Zagloba flew with his sabre over his head, shouting with an unearthly voice: "Kill! slay!"

Then there was a report from the bulwarks, and a bomb screaming like a screech-owl described a red arc in the sky and fell in the dense crowd; after it a second, a third, a tenth. It seemed that battle would begin anew. Till the siege of Zbaraj, projectiles of that kind were unknown to the Cossacks, and when sober they feared them terribly, seeing in them the sorcery of Yeremi. The crowd therefore stopped for a moment, then broke in two; the bombs burst, scattering death and destruction.

"Save yourselves! save yourselves!" was shouted in tones of terror.

All fled. Pan Longin and Volodyovski dropped into the saving ranks of the hussars. Zagloba threw himself on the neck of one and the other, and kissed them on the cheeks and eyes. Joy was choking him; but he restrained it, not wishing to show the softness of his heart, and cried,--

"Oh, the ox-drivers! I won't say that I love you, but I was alarmed about you! Is that the way you understand service, to lag in the rear? You ought to be dragged behind horses over the square by your feet. I shall be the first to tell the prince, that he may think of a punishment for you. Now we'll go to sleep. Thank God for that too! Those dog-brothers were lucky to run away before the bombs, for I should have cut them up like cabbage. I prefer fighting to seeing my friends die. We must have a drink to-night. Thank God for that too! I thought we should have to sing the requiem over you to-morrow. But I am sorry there was no fight, for my hand is itching awfully, though I gave them beans and onions in the shelters."

CHAPTER LIX.

The Poles had to raise new ramparts to render the earthworks of the Cossacks useless and make defence easier for their own reduced forces. They dug therefore all night after the storm. On this account the Cossacks were not idle. Having approached quietly in the dark night between Thursday and Friday, they threw up a second and much higher wall around the camp. All shouted at dawn, and began to fire at once, and four whole days and nights they continued firing. Much damage was done on both sides, for from both sides the best gunners emulated one another.

From time to time masses of Cossacks and the mob rushed to attack, but did not reach the ramparts. Only the musketry fire became hotter. The enemy, having strong forces, changed the divisions in action, leading some to rest and others to fight. But in the Polish camp there were no men for change; the same persons had to shoot, rush to the defence at any moment under danger of assaults, bury the dead, dig walls, and raise the ramparts for better defence. The besieged slept, or rather dozed, on the ramparts under fire, while balls were flying so thickly that every morning they could be swept from the square. For four days no one removed his clothing. The men got wet in the rain, dry in the sun, were burning in the daytime and chilled at night. During four days not one of them had anything warm in his mouth; they drank gorailka, mixing powder with it for greater strength; they gnawed cakes, and tore with their teeth hard dried meat; and all this in the midst of smoke and fire, the whistling of balls and the thunder of cannon. It was nothing to get struck on the head or body; a soldier tied a nasty bit of cloth around his bloody head and fought on. They were wonderful men,--with torn coats, rusty weapons, shattered muskets in their hands, eyes red from sleeplessness; ever on the alert, ever willing day and night, wet weather or dry; always ready for battle.

The soldiers were infatuated with their leader, with danger, with assaults, with wounds and death. A certain heroic exaltation seized their souls; their hearts became haughty, their minds callous. Horror became to them a delight. Different regiments strove for pre-eminence in enduring hunger, sleeplessness, toil, daring, and fury. This was carried to such a degree that it was difficult to keep the soldiers on the walls; they were breaking out against the enemy as wolves ravenous from hunger against sheep. In all the regiments reigned a kind of wild joy. If a man were to mention surrender, he would be torn to pieces in the twinkle of an eye. "We want to die!" was repeated by every mouth.

Every command of the leader was carried out with lightning rapidity. Once it happened that the prince, in his evening tour of the ramparts, hearing that the fire of the quarter-regiment of Leshchinski was weakening, came to the soldiers, and asked: "Why don't you fire?"

"Our powder is gone; we have sent to the castle for more."

"You have it nearer!" said the prince, pointing to the enemy's trench.

He had scarcely spoken when the whole body sprang from the rampart, rushed to the enemy, and fell like a hurricane on the intrenchment. The Cossacks were clubbed with muskets and stabbed with pikes, four guns were spiked; and after half an hour the soldiers, decimated but victorious, returned with a considerable supply of powder in kegs and hunting-horns.

Day followed day. The Cossack approaches enclosed the Polish rampart with an ever-narrowing ring, and pushed into it like wedges into a tree. The firing was so close that without counting the assaults ten men a day fell in each battalion; the priests were unable to visit them with the sacrament. The besieged sheltered themselves with wagons, tents, skins, and suspended clothing. In the night they buried the dead wherever they happened to lie; but the living fought the more desperately over the graves of their comrades of the day before. Hmelnitski expended the blood of his people unsparingly, but each storm brought him only greater loss. He was astonished himself at the resistance. He counted only on this,--that time would weaken the hearts and strength of the besieged. Time did pass, but they showed an increasing contempt for death.

The leaders gave the example to their men. Prince Yeremi slept on bare ground at the rampart, drank gorailka, and ate dried horse-flesh, suffering changes of weather and toils beyond his lordly position. Konyetspolski and Sobieski led regiments to the sallies in person; in time of assault they exposed themselves without armor in the thickest rain of bullets. Even leaders who, like Ostrorog, were lacking in military experience, and on whom the soldiers looked with distrust, appeared now, under the hand of Yeremi, to become different men. Old Firlei and Lantskoronski slept also at the ramparts; and Pshiyemski put guns in order during the day, and at night dug under the earth like a mole, putting counter-mines beneath the mines of the enemy, throwing out approaches, or opening underground roads by which the soldiers came like spirits of death among the sleeping Cossacks.

Finally Hmelnitski determined to try negotiations, with the idea too that in the mean while he might accomplish something by stratagem. On the evening of July 24 the Cossacks began to cry from the trenches to the Poles to stop firing. The Zaporojians declared that the hetman wanted to see old Zatsvilikhovski. After a short consultation the commanders agreed to the proposition, and the old man went out of the camp.

The knights saw from a distance that caps were removed before him in the trenches; for Zatsvilikhovski, during the short period that he was commissioner, succeeded in gaining the good-will of the wild Zaporojians, and Hmelnitski himself respected him. The firing ceased. The Cossacks with their approaches were close to the ramparts, and the knights went down to them. Both sides were on their guard, but there was nothing unfriendly in those meetings. The nobles had always esteemed the Cossacks more than the common herd, and now, knowing their bravery and endurance in battle, they spoke with them on terms of equality as cavaliers with cavaliers. The Cossacks examined with wonder that impregnable nest of lions which checked all their power and that of the Khan. They began to be friendly, therefore, to talk and complain that so much Christian blood was flowing; finally they treated one another to tobacco and gorailka.

"All, gentlemen," said the old Zaporojians, "if you had stood up like this always, there would have been no Jóltiya Vodi, Korsún, or Pilavtsi. You are real devils, not men, such as we have not seen yet in the world."

"Come to-morrow and the day after; you will always find us the same."

"We'll come; but thank God now for the breathing-spell! A power of Christian blood is flowing; but, anyhow, hunger will conquer you."

"The king will come before hunger; we have just eaten a hearty meal."

"If provisions fail us, we will go to your tabors," said Zagloba, with his hand on his hip.

"God grant Father Zatsvilikhovski to make some agreement with our hetman! If he doesn't, we shall have an assault this evening."

"We are already tired of waiting for you."

"The Khan has promised that you'll all get your 'fate.'"

"And our prince has promised the Khan that he will drag him by the beard at his horse's tail."

"He is a wizard, but he can't do that."

"Better for you to go with our prince against the Pagans than to raise your hands against the authorities."

"H'm! with your prince! Nice work indeed!"

"Why do you revolt? The king will come; fear the king. Prince Yeremi was a father to you too--"

"Such a father, as Death is mother. The plague has not killed so many brave heroes as he."

"He will be worse; you don't know him yet."

"We don't want to know him. Our old men say that whatever Cossack looks him in the eye is given to death."

"It will be so with Hmelnitski."

"God knows what will be. This is sure, that it is not for them both to live in the white world. Our father says if you would give him up Yeremi he would let you all go free, and bow down to the king with all of us."

Here the soldiers began to frown and grit their teeth.

"Be silent, or we'll draw our sabres!"

"You Poles are angry, but you'll have your 'fate.'"

And so they conversed, sometimes pleasantly and sometimes with threats, which, in spite of them, burst out like thunder-peals. In the afternoon Zatsvilikhovski returned to the camp. There were no negotiations, and a cessation of arms was not obtained. Hmelnitski put forth monstrous demands,--that the prince and Konyetspolski should be given up to him. Finally he told over the wrongs of the Zaporojians, and began to persuade Zatsvilikhovski to remain with him for good; whereupon the old knight was enraged, sprang up, and went away. In the evening followed an assault, which was repulsed with blood. The whole camp was in fire for two hours. The Cossacks were not only hurled from the walls, but the infantry captured the first intrenchment, destroyed the embrasures, the shelters, and burned fourteen moving towers. Hmelnitski swore that night to the Khan that he would not withdraw while a man remained alive in the camp.

The next day at dawn brought fresh musketry-firing, digging under the ramparts, and a battle till evening with flails, scythes, sabres, stones, and clods of earth. The friendly feeling of the day before, and regret at the spilling of Christian blood gave way to still greater obstinacy. Rain began to fall in the morning. That day half-rations were issued to the soldiers, at which Zagloba complained greatly, but in general empty stomachs redoubled the rage of the Poles. They swore to fall one after the other, and not to surrender to the last breath. The evening brought new assaults from the Cossacks, disguised as Turks, lasting, however, but a short time. A night full of uproar and cries followed, "a very quarrelsome night." Firing did not cease for a moment. Both sides challenged each other; they fought in groups and pairs. Pan Longin went out to the skirmish, but no one would stand before him; they merely fired at him from a distance. But Stempovski covered himself with great glory, and also Volodyovski, who in single combat killed the famous partisan Dundar.

At last Zagloba himself came out, but only to encounters of the tongue. "After killing Burlai," said he, "I cannot meet every common scrub!" But in the encounter of tongues he found no equal among the Cossacks, and he brought them to despair; when covered with a good embankment he cried, as if under the ground, with a stentorian voice,--

"Sit here at Zbaraj, you clowns, but the Lithuanian soldiers are going down the Dnieper. They are saluting your wives and young women. Next spring you will find crowds of little Botvinians in your cottages, if you find the cottages."

The Lithuanian army was really descending the Dnieper, under Kadzivil, burning and destroying, leaving only land and water. The Cossacks knowing this fell into a rage, and in answer hailed bullets on Zagloba, as a man shakes pears from a tree. But Zagloba took good care of his head behind the embankment, and cried again,--

"You have missed, you dog-spirits, but I didn't miss Burlai. I am alone here; come to a duel with me! You know me! Come on, you clowns! shoot on while you have a chance, for next winter you'll be taking care of young Tartars in the Crimea, or making dams on the Dnieper. Come on, come on! I'll give a copper for the head of your Hmel. Give him a whack on the snout from me, from Zagloba, do you hear? Hei! you filthy fools, is it little of your carrion that lies on the field smelling like dead dogs? The plague sends her respects to you. To your forks, to your ploughs, to your boats, you scurvy villains! It is for you to tug salt and dried cherries against the current of the Dnieper, not to stand in our way."

The Cossacks had their laugh too at the "Panowie[21] who have one biscuit for three," and they were asked why they did not collect their taxes and tithes. But Zagloba got the upper hand in the disputes. These conversations rattled on, interrupted by curses and wild outbursts of laughter for whole nights, under fire and with more or less fighting. Then Pan Yanitski went out to negotiate with the Khan, who repeated again that all would meet their "fate," till the impatient envoy said: "You promised that long ago, but nothing has happened to us yet! Whoever comes for our heads will leave his own!" The Khan asked Prince Yeremi to meet his vizier in the field; but that was simply treachery, which was discovered, and the negotiations were finally broken off. All this time there was no intermission in the struggle,--assaults in the evening, during the day cannonading and musketry fire, sallies from the ramparts, encounters, hand-to-hand conflict of battalions, and wild attacks of cavalry.

A certain mad desire of fighting, of blood, and danger upheld the soldiers. They went to battle with songs, as if to a wedding. They had indeed become so accustomed to uproar and tumult that those divisions which were detailed to sleep slept soundly under fire, amidst thickly falling bullets. Provisions decreased every day, for the commanders had not supplied the camp sufficiently before the coming of the prince. The price of everything was enormously high, but those who had money and bought bread or gorailka shared it gladly with others. No one cared for the morrow, knowing that one of two things would not miss them,--either succor from the king, or death! They were equally ready for either, but more ready for battle. An unheard-of case in history, tens meeting thousands with such resistance and such rage that each assault was a new defeat for the Cossacks! Besides, there was no day in which there were not several attacks from the ramparts on the enemy in his own trenches. Those evenings when Hmelnitski thought that weariness must overcome the most enduring and was quietly preparing an assault, joyful songs would come to his ears. Then he struck his hands on his legs with wonder, and thought, "In truth Yeremi is a greater wizard than any in the Cossack camp." Then he was furious, hurried to the fight, and poured out a sea of blood; for he saw that his star was beginning to pale before the star of the terrible prince.

In the tabor they sang songs about Yeremi, or in a low voice related things of him, which made the hair stand on the heads of the Cossacks. They said that he would appear at times in the night on the ramparts, and would grow up before one till his head was higher than the towers of Zbaraj; that his eyes were then like two moons, and the sword in his hand like that star of ill omen which God sometimes sends out in the sky for the destruction of men. It was said that when he shouted, the Poles who had fallen in battle rose up with clanking armor and took their places in the ranks with the living. Yeremi was in every mouth,--they sang about him, minstrels spoke of him, the old Zaporojians, the ignorant mob, and the Tartars; and in those conversations, in that hatred, in that superstitious terror there was a certain wild love with which that people of the steppes loved their bloody destroyer. Hmelnitski paled before him, not only in the eyes of the Khan and the Tartars, but in the eyes of his own people; and he saw that he must take Zbaraj, or the spell which he exercised would be dissipated, like darkness before the morning dawn,--he must trample that lion, or perish himself.

But the lion not only defended himself, but each day he issued more terrible from his lair. Neither stratagem, nor treachery, nor evident preponderance availed. Meanwhile the mob and the Cossacks began to murmur. It was difficult for them to sit in smoke and fire, in a rain of bullets, with the odor of corpses, in rain, in heat, before the face of death. But the valiant Cossacks did not fear toil, nor bad weather, nor storms with fire and blood and death; they feared "Yarema."

CHAPTER LX.

Many a simple knight covered himself with undying glory on that memorable rampart of Zbaraj; but the lyre will celebrate Pan Longin Podbipienta among the first, since the greatness of his gifts could be equalled only by his modesty. The night was gloomy, dark, and wet; the soldiers, wearied with watching at the ramparts, dozed, leaning on their weapons. After the recent ten days of firing and assaults, this was the first moment of quiet and rest. From the neighboring trenches of the Cossacks--for they were scarcely thirty yards distant--there were neither cries, curses, nor the usual uproar. It appeared as though the enemy, wishing to weary the Poles, had grown weary themselves. Here and there only glittered the faint light of a fire, covered under a mound; from one place came the sweet, low sound of a lute, on which some Cossack was playing; far away in the Tartar camp the horses neighed; and on the embankments, from time to time, was heard the voice of the guards.

The armored cavalry of the prince was on infantry duty that night. Skshetuski, Podbipienta, Volodyovski, and Zagloba on the bulwark were whispering quietly among themselves; in the intervals of the conversation they listened to the sound of the rain falling into the ditch.

"This quiet is strange to me," said Skshetuski. "My ears are so accustomed to thundering and uproar that silence rings in them; but I hope treachery is not hidden in this silence."

"Since I am on half-rations it is all one to me," muttered Zagloba, gloomily. "My courage demands three things,--to eat well, to drink well, and to sleep well. The best strap, if not oiled, will grow dry and break; what if, in addition, you soak it in water, like hemp? The rain soaks us, the Cossacks hackle us, and why should not strips fall from us? Beautiful conditions!--a biscuit costs a florin, and a measure of vudka five. A dog would not take this foul water in his mouth, for in the wells is the essence of the dead; and I am as thirsty as my boots, which have their mouths open like fish."

"But your boots drink water without extravagant talk."

"You might keep your mouth shut, Pan Michael! You are no bigger than a titmouse; you can live on a grain of millet and drink out of a thimble. But I thank God that I am not so delicate, and that a hen did not scratch me out of the sand with her hind legs, but a woman gave me birth; therefore I must live by eating and drinking, like a man, not like a May-bug; and as I have had nothing in my mouth but spittle since yesterday noon, your jokes are not at all to my taste."

Here Zagloba began to puff with anger, and Pan Michael put his hand on his side and said,--

"I have in my pocket a flask, which I got of a Cossack to-day; but if a hen scratched me out of the sand, I think gorailka from such an insignificant person would not be to your taste. Here's to you, Yan!" said he, turning to Skshetuski. "Give it here," said Skshetuski, "for the air is cold."

"Drink to Pan Longin."

"You are a rogue, Pan Michael," said Zagloba, "but you are one in a hundred; you take from yourself and give to others. A blessing on hens that scratch such soldiers from the sand! But there are none such, and I was not thinking of you."

"Then take it after Podbipienta. I have no wish to offend you."

"What are you doing? Leave some to me!" cried Zagloba in alarm, when he saw the Lithuanian drinking. "Why do you throw your head back so far? God grant it to remain in its usual place. You are too long; it is no small task to moisten you. May you burst!"

"I've barely touched it," said Podbipienta, handing him the flask.

Zagloba turned over the flask completely, and drank to the bottom; then he snorted, and said,--

"The only consolation is that if our miseries come to an end, and God lets us take our heads out of these dangers in safety, we'll reward ourselves for all. They will be sure to prepare some loaves for us. The priest Jabkovski has fine skill in eating, but I'll make a ram's-horn of him."

"And what word of truth have you and Jabkovski heard to-day from Mukhovetski?"

"Silence!" said Skshetuski; "there is some one coming in the square."

They were silent; and soon a dark figure stood near them, and asked in a hushed voice: "Are you watching?"

"We are," answered Skshetuski, straightening himself.

"Give careful attention; this calm is of evil augury."

The prince passed on to see if sleep had overcome the wearied soldiers anywhere. Pan Longin clasped his hands: "What a leader! what a warrior!"

"He takes less rest than we do," said Skshetuski. "He examines the whole rampart in this way every night as far as the second pond."

"God grant him health!"

"Amen!"

Silence followed. All looked with strained eyes into the darkness, but nothing could be seen. The Cossack trenches were quiet, the last light in them quenched.

"They might be caught napping now, like susliks," muttered Volodyovski.

"Who knows?" answered Skshetuski.

"Sleep torments me," said Zagloba, "so that my eyes are coming out, and sleep is not permitted. I am curious to know when it will be permitted. Whether there is firing or not, one must stand under arms and nod from weariness, like a Jew on the Sabbath. It's a dog's service! I don't know myself what has got hold of me,--whether it's the gorailka, or the irritation from that blow which I with the priest Jabkovski was forced to endure without reason."

"How was that?" asked Podbipienta; "you began to tell us, and didn't finish."

"I'll tell you now. Maybe we'll shake off sleep somehow. I went this morning with Jabkovski to the castle, hoping to come upon something to gnaw. We search and search, look everywhere, find nothing; we return in bad humor. In the yard we meet a Calvinist minister who had been giving the last consolation to Captain Shenberk, of Firlei's battalion, who was shot yesterday. I opened on him: 'Haven't you,' said I, 'strolled around about long enough, and displeased the Lord sufficiently? You will draw a curse on us.' But he, relying evidently on the protection of the castellan of Belsk, answered: 'Our faith is as good as yours, if not better!' And he spoke in such a way that we were petrified from horror. But we kept silent. I thought to myself: 'Jabkovski is here; let him do the arguing.' But my Jabkovski snorted, and whacked him under the ribs with arguments. He made no answer to this strongest of reasons, for he went spinning around till he was brought up standing against the wall. That moment the prince came in with Mukhovetski and fell upon us; said that we were making an uproar and disturbance; that it was neither the time nor the place, nor were ours the arguments. They washed our heads for us, as if we had been a couple of boys. I wish they were right; for unless I am a false prophet, these ministers of Firlei will bring misfortune to us yet."

"And did not that Captain Shenberk renounce his errors?" asked Volodyovski.

"What, renounce! He died, as he had lived, in abomination!"

"Oh that men should yield up their salvation rather than their stubbornness!" sighed Pan Longin.

"God is defending us against Cossack predominance and witchcraft," continued Zagloba; "but these heretics are offending him. It is known to you, gentlemen, that yesterday, from this very intrenchment before us, they shot balls of thread into the square; and the soldiers say that immediately on the place where the balls fell the ground was covered with a leprosy."

"It's a known fact that devils wait on Hmelnitski," said the Lithuanian, making the sign of the cross.

"I saw the witches myself," added Skshetuski, "and I'll tell you--"

Further conversation was stopped by Volodyovski, who pressed Skshetuski's arm suddenly, and whispered: "Silence!" Then he sprang to the very edge of the rampart, and listened attentively.

"I hear nothing," said Zagloba.

"Ts! the rain drowns it," answered Skshetuski.

Pan Michael began to beckon with his hand not to interrupt him, and he listened carefully for some time. At last he approached his comrades. "They are marching!" whispered he.

"Let the prince know; he has gone to Ostrorog's quarters," whispered Pan Yan. "We will run to warn the soldiers."

Straightway they hurried along the ramparts, stopping from moment to moment and whispering everywhere to the soldiers on guard: "They are coming! they are coming!"

The words flew like silent lightning from mouth to mouth. In a quarter of an hour the prince, already on horseback, was present, and issuing orders to the officers. Since the enemy wished, evidently, to spring into the camp while the Poles were asleep and off guard, the prince enjoined on all to maintain this error. The soldiers were to remain in immovable stillness and let the assaulters come to the very rampart, and when cannon-shot was given as a signal, to strike unexpectedly.

The soldiers were ready. They dropped the muzzles of their guns, bent forward noiselessly, and deep silence followed. Skshetuski, Pan Longin, and Volodyovski drew long breaths, side by side. Zagloba stayed near them, for he knew by experience that most balls fell on the square, and that it was safest on the ramparts near three such sabres. They merely drew back a little, that the first onrush might not strike them. Podbipienta knelt somewhat to one side with his double-handed sword; Volodyovski crouched near Skshetuski, and whispered in his very ear,--

"They are coming, surely."

"With measured tread."

"That's not the mob, nor the Tartars."

"Zaporojian infantry."

"Or janissaries; they march well. We could strike them better with cavalry."

"It is too dark for cavalry to-night."

"Do you hear them now?"

"Ts! Ts!"

The camp seemed sunk in deepest sleep. In no place movement, in no place life; everywhere the most profound silence, broken only by the rustle of rain fine as if scattered from a sieve. Gradually, however, there rose in this another rustle, low, but more easily caught by the ear, for it was measured, drawing nearer, growing clearer; at last, a few steps from the ditch, appeared a sort of prolonged dense mass, visible in so far that it was blacker than the darkness, and halted.

The soldiers held their breaths; but the little knight punched Skshetuski in the side, as if wishing in this way to show his delight. The assailants reached the ditch, let down their ladders into it, descended on them, and moved toward the rampart. The rampart was as silent as if on it and behind it everything had expired; a silence of the grave succeeded. Here and there, in spite of all the care of the assailants, the ladder-rounds squeaked and trembled.

"You'll get beans!" thought Zagloba.0

Volodyovski stopped punching Skshetuski, Pan Longin pressed the hilt of his double-handed sword, and distended his eyes, for he was nearest the edge of the rampart and expected to give the first blow.

Three pairs of hands appeared on the outer rim, and grasped it firmly; after them began to rise slowly and carefully three helmet points, higher and higher.

"Those are Turks!" thought Pan Longin.

At that moment was heard the awful roar of several thousand muskets; it was clear as day. Before the light had gone out Pan Longin had drawn his weapon and cut terribly, so that the air whined under his sword-edge. Three bodies fell into the ditch, three heads in helmets rolled to the knees of the kneeling knight. Then, though hell was raging on earth, heaven opened before Pan Longin; wings grew from his shoulders; choirs of angels were singing in his breast, and he was as if caught up to heaven; he fought as in a dream, and the blows of his sword were like thanks giving prayers. All the Podbipientas, long since dead, beginning with Stoveiko, the founder of the line, were rejoicing in heaven that the last surviving, Zervikaptur Podbipienta, was such a man.

This assault, in which auxiliary forces of Rumelian and Silistrian Turks, with guards from the janissaries of the Khan, took a preponderant part, received a more terrible repulse than others, and drew a fearful storm on Hmelnitski's head. He had guaranteed in advance that the Poles would fight with less rage against the Turks, and if those companies were given him he would capture the camp. He was obliged therefore to mollify the Khan and the enraged murzas, and at the same time win them with presents. He gave the Khan ten thousand thalers; Tugai Bey, Korz Aga, Subahazi, Nureddin, and Galga, two thousand each.

Meanwhile the camp-servants drew the bodies out of the ditch. In this they were not hindered by firing from the intrenchment. The soldiers rested till morning, for it was certain that the assault would not be repeated. All slept uninterruptedly, except the troops on guard and Podbipienta, who lay, in the form of a cross, all night on his sword, thanking God, who had permitted him to accomplish his vow and cover himself with such renown that his name had gone from mouth to mouth in the camp and the town. Next morning the prince summoned him, and praised him greatly, and the soldiers came in crowds all day to congratulate him and look at the three heads which the attendants had brought before his tent, and which were already blackening in the air. There was wonder and envy not a little, and some would not believe their eyes, for the heads and the capes of the helmets were cut off as evenly as if some one had cut them with shears.

"You are an awful tailor!" said the nobles. "We knew that you were a good knight; but the ancients might envy such a blow, for the best executioner could not give a better."

"The wind does not take off caps as those heads were taken!" said another.

All pressed the palms of Pan Longin; but he stood with downcast eyes, sunshiny, sweet, timid as a maiden before marriage, and said as if in explanation: "They were in good position."

Then they tested the sword; but since it was the double-handed sword of a crusader, no man could move it freely, not excepting even the priest Jabkovski, though he could break a horse-shoe like a reed.

Around the tent it grew noisier; and Zagloba, Skshetuski, and Volodyovski did the honors to the visitors, treating them with stories, for they had nothing else to give them since the last biscuits in the camp had been eaten; they had long had no other meat than dried horse-flesh. But valor gave them meat and drink. Toward the end, when the others began to disperse, Marek Sobieski appeared with his lieutenant, Stempovski. Pan Longin ran out to meet him; the starosta greeted him with thanks, and said,--

"It is a holiday with you?"

"In truth it is a holiday," answered Zagloba, "for our friend has fulfilled a vow."

"Praise be to the Lord God!" answered the starosta. "Then it is not long, brother, till we may congratulate you on your marriage. And have you any one in mind?"

Pan Longin was extremely confused, grew red to his ears; and the starosta continued,--

"I see by your confusion that you have. It is your sacred duty to remember that such a stock should not perish."

Then he pressed the hands of Pan Longin, Skshetuski, Zagloba, and the little knight; and they were rejoiced in their hearts to hear praise from such lips, for the starosta of Krasnostav was the mirror of bravery, honor, and every knightly virtue,--he was an incarnate Mars. All the gifts of God were richly united in him, for in remarkable beauty he surpassed even his younger brother Yan, who was afterward king. He was equal in fortune and name to the very first, and the great Yeremi himself exalted his military gifts to the skies. He would have been a wonderful star in the heaven of the Commonwealth, but that by the disposition of God, the younger, Yan, took his glory to himself, and Marek vanished before his time in a day of disaster.

Hitherto our knights had rejoiced greatly at the praises of this hero; but he did not stop at that, and continued,--

"I have heard much of you from the prince himself, who loves you beyond others. I do not wonder that you serve him without reference to promotion, which comes more readily in the regiments of the king."

"We are all," answered Skshetuski, "really enrolled in the hussar regiment of the king, except Pan Zagloba, who is a volunteer from native valor. We serve under the prince, first, out of love for his person, and, secondly, because we wish to have as much as we can of the war."

"If such be your wish, you have chosen well. Surely Pan Podbipienta could not have found his heads under any other command so easily. But as to war in these times, we all have enough of it."

"More than of anything else," said Zagloba. "Men have been coming here from early morning with praises; but if any one would ask us to a bite of food and a drink of gorailka, he would honor us best."

Having said this, Zagloba looked diligently into Sobieki's eyes, and muttered unquietly; but the starosta sighed, and said,--

"Since yesterday noon I have taken nothing into my mouth. A gulp of gorailka, however, I think can be found somewhere. I am at your service, gentlemen, for that."

Skshetuski, Pan Longin, and Volodyovski began to draw back and scold Zagloba, who extricated himself as he could and explained matters as he was able.

"I did not press myself," said he, "for it is my ambition rather to give away my own than touch what belongs to another; but when such a distinguished person invites, it would be churlish to refuse."

"Well, come on!" said the starosta. "I like to sit in good company, and while there is no firing we have time. I do ask you to eat, for it is difficult to get horse-flesh,--for each horse killed on the square a hundred hands are stretched forth; but there are two flasks of gorailka which certainly I shall not keep for myself."

The others were unwilling, and refused; but when he insisted urgently, they went. Pan Stempovski hurried on in advance, and exerted himself so that a few biscuits and some bits of horse-flesh were found as a bite after the gorailka. Zagloba was in better spirits immediately, and said,--

"God grant the king, to liberate us from this siege, then we will go at once to the wagons of the general militia. They always carry a world of good things with them, and care more for their stomachs than they do for the Commonwealth. I'd rather eat with them than fight in their company; but being under the eye of the king, perhaps they will fight fairly well."

The starosta grew serious. "Since we have sworn," said he, "to fall one after another without surrender, we shall do so. We must be ready for still harder times. We have scarcely any provisions, and what is worse, our powder is coming to an end. I should not say this to others, but to you I can speak. Soon we shall have nothing but desperate determination in our hearts and sabres in our hands, readiness for death, and nothing more. God grant the king to come at the earliest moment, for this is our last hope! He is a military man, and is sure not to spare life, health, or comfort in rescuing us; but his forces are too few, and he must wait,--you know how slowly the general militia muster. Besides, how is the king to know the conditions in which we are defending ourselves, and that we are eating the last fragments?"

"We have sacrificed ourselves," said Skshetuski.

"But couldn't we let him know?" asked Zagloba.

"If there could be found a man of such virtue as to undertake to steal through," said the starosta, "he would win immortal glory in his lifetime,--he would be the savior of the whole army, and would avert defeat from the fatherland. Even if the general militia has not all appeared yet, perhaps the nearness of the king might disperse the rebellion. But who will go, who will undertake it, since Hmelnitski has so possessed every road and exit that a mouse could not squeeze through from the camp? Such an undertaking is clear and evident death!"

"But what are stratagems for?--and one is now entering my head."

"What is it, what is it?" asked the starosta.

"This. Every day we take prisoners: bribe one of these; let them feign escape from us, and run to the king."

"I must mention this to the prince," said the starosta.

Pan Longin fell into deep thought; his brows were covered with furrows, and he sat a whole hour in silence. Suddenly he raised his head, and spoke with his usual sweetness: "I will undertake to steal through the Cossacks."

The knights, hearing these words, sprang from their seats in amazement. Zagloba opened his mouth, Volodyovski's mustaches quivered, Skshetuski grew pale; and the starosta, striking himself on the breast, cried: "Would you undertake to do this?"

"Have you considered what you say?" asked Pan Yan.

"I considered it long ago," answered the Lithuanian; "for this is not the first day that the knights say that notice must be given the king of our position. And I, hearing this, thought to myself: 'If the Most High God permits me to fulfil my vow, I will go at once. I am an obscure man; what do I signify? What harm to me, even am killed on the road?'"

"But they will cut you to pieces, without doubt!" cried Zagloba, "Have you heard what the starosta says,--that it is evident death?"

"What of that, brother? If God wishes, he will carry me through; if not, he will reward me in heaven."

"But first they will seize you, torture you, give you a fearful death. Have you lost your reason, man?" asked Zagloba.

"I will go, anyhow," answered the Lithuanian, mildly.

"A bird could not fly through, for they would shoot it from their bows. They have surrounded us like a badger in his hole."

"Still I will go!" repeated the Lithuanian. "I owe thanks to the Lord for permitting me to fulfil my vow."

"Well, look at him, examine him!" said Zagloba, in desperation. "You would better have your head cut off at once and shoot it from a cannon over the tabor, for in this way alone could you push through them."

"But permit me, my friends," said Pan Longin, clasping his hands.

"Oh, no; you will not go alone, for I will go with you," said Skshetuski.

"And I with you both!" added Volodyovski, striking his sword.

"And may the bullets strike you!" cried Zagloba, seizing himself by the head. "May the bullets strike you with your 'And I,' 'And I,' with your daring! They have not had enough of blood yet, not enough of destruction, not enough of bullets! What is doing here is not sufficient for them; they want more certainty of having their necks twisted. Go to the dogs, and give me peace! I hope you will be cut to pieces." When he had said this he began to circle about in the tent as if mad. "God is punishing me," cried be, "for associating with whirlwinds instead of honorable, solid men. It serves me right." He walked through the tent awhile longer with feverish tread; at last he stopped before Skshetuski; then, putting his hands behind his back and looking into his eyes, began to puff terribly: "What have I done that you persecute me?"

"God save us!" exclaimed the knight. "What do you mean?"

"I do not wonder that Podbipienta invents such things; he always had his wit in his fist. But since he has killed the three greatest fools among the Turks he has become the fourth himself--"

"It is disgusting to hear him," interrupted the Lithuanian.

"And I don't wonder at *him*," continued Zagloba, pointing at Volodyovski. "He will jump on a Cossack's bootleg, or hold to his trousers as a burr does to a dog's tail, and get through quicker than any of us. The Holy Spirit has not shone upon either of the two; but that you, instead of restraining their madness, should add excitement to it, that you are going yourself, and wish to expose us four to certain death and torture,--that is the final blow! Tfu! I did not expect this of an officer whom the prince himself has esteemed a valiant knight."

"How four?" asked Skshetuski, in astonishment. "Do you want to go?"

"Yes!" cried Zagloba, beating his breast with his fists, "I will go. If any of you go, or all go together, I will go too. My blood be on your heads! I shall know next time with whom to associate."

"Well may you!" said Skshetuski.

The three knights began to embrace him; but he was angry in earnest, and puffed and pushed them away with his elbows, saying: "Go to the devil! I don't want your Judas kisses." Then was heard on the walls the firing of cannon and muskets. "There it is for you, go!"

"That is ordinary firing," remarked Pan Yan.

"Ordinary firing!" repeated Zagloba, mocking him. "Well, just think this is not enough for them. Half the army is destroyed by this ordinary firing, and they turn up their noses at it."

"Be of good cheer," said Podbipienta.

"You ought to keep your mouth shut, Botvinia. You are most to blame; you have invented an undertaking which if it is not a fool's errand then I'm a fool."

"But still I'll go, brother," said Pan Longin.

"You'll go, you'll go; and I know why. Don't exhibit yourself as a hero, for they know you. You have virtue for sale, and are in a hurry to take it out of camp. You the worst among knights, not the best,--simply a drab, trading in virtue. Tfu! an offence to God,--that's what you are. It is not to the king you want to go, but you would like to snort through the villages like a horse through a meadow. Look at him! There is a knight with virtue for sale! Vexation, vexation, as God is dear to me!"

"Disgusting to hear him!" cried the Lithuanian, thrusting his fingers in his ears.

"Let disputes rest," said Skshetuski, seriously. "Better let us think about this question."

"In God's name," said the starosta, who had listened hitherto with astonishment to Zagloba, "this is a great question, but we can decide nothing without the prince. This is no place for discussion. You are in service and obliged to obey orders. The prince must be in his quarters; let us go to him and see what he will say to your offer."

"I agree to that," answered Zagloba; and hope shone in his face. "Let us go as quickly as possible."

They went out and crossed the square on which already the balls were falling from the Cossack trenches. The troops were at the ramparts, which at a distance looked like booths at a fair, so overhung were they with many-colored clothing sheepskin coats, packed with wagons, fragments of tents, and every kind of object which might become a shelter against the shots which at times ceased neither day nor night. And now above those rags hung a long bluish line of smoke, and behind them ranks of prostrate red and yellow soldiers, working hard against the nearest trenches of the enemy. The square itself was like a ruin; the level space was cut up with spades, or trampled by horses; it was not made green by a single grass-blade. Here and there were mounds of earth freshly raised by the digging of walls and graves; here and there lay fragments of broken wagons, cannon, barrels, or piles of bones, gnawed, and whitening before the sun. Bodies of horses were nowhere visible, for each one was removed immediately as food for the soldiers; but everywhere were piles of iron,--mostly cannon-balls, red from rust, which fell every day on that piece of land. Grievous war and hunger were evident at every step. On their way our knights met greater or smaller groups of soldiers,--some carrying wounded or dead, others hurrying to the ramparts to relieve their overworked comrades. The faces of all were black, sunken, overgrown with beard; their fierce eyes were inflamed, their clothing faded and torn; many had filthy rags on their heads in place of caps or helmets; their weapons were broken. Involuntarily came the question. What will happen a week or two later to that handful hitherto victorious?

"Look, gentlemen," said the starosta; "it is time to give notice to the king."

"Want is showing its teeth, like a dog," said the little knight.

"What will happen when we have eaten the horses?" asked Skshetuski.

Thus conversing, they reached the tents of the prince, situated at the right side of the rampart, before which were a few mounted messengers to carry orders through the camp. Their horses, fed with dried and ground horse-flesh and excited by continual fire, reared restively, unable to stand in one place. This was the case too with all the cavalry horses, which in going against the enemy seemed like a herd of griffins or centaurs going rather by air than by land.

"Is the prince in the tent?" asked the starosta of one of the horsemen.

"Yes, with Pan Pshiyemski," answered the orderly.

The starosta entered first without announcing himself, but the four knights remained outside. After a while the canvas opened, and Pshiyemski thrust out his head. "The prince is anxious to see you," said he.

Zagloba entered the tent in good humor, for he hoped the prince would not expose his best knights to certain death; but he was mistaken, for they had not yet bowed when he said,--

"The starosta has told me of your readiness to issue from the camp, and I accept your good will. Too much cannot be sacrificed for the country."

"We have only come for permission to try," said Skshetuski, "since your Highness is the steward of our blood."

"Then you want to go together?"

"Your Highness," said Zagloba, "they want to go, but I do not. God is my witness that I have not come here to praise myself or to make mention of my services; and if I do mention them, I do so lest some one might suppose that I am afraid. Pan Skshetuski, Volodyovski, and Podbipienta of Myshekishki are great knights; but Burlai, who fell by my hand (not to speak of other exploits), was also a famous warrior, equal to Burdabut, Bogun, and the three heads of the janissaries. I mean to say by this that in knightly deeds I am not behind others. But heroism is one thing, and madness another. We have no wings, and we cannot go by land; that is certain."

"You will not go then?" said the prince.

"I have said that I do not wish to go, but I have not said that I will not go. Since God has punished me with their company, I must remain in it till death. If we should be hard pressed, the sabre of Zagloba will be of service yet; but I know not why death should be put upon us four, and I hope that your Highness will avert it from us by not permitting this mad undertaking."

"You are a good comrade," answered the prince, "and it honorable on your part not to wish to leave your friends; you are mistaken in your confidence in me, for I accept your offer."

"The dog is dead!" muttered Zagloba, and his hands dropped.

At that moment Firlei, castellan of Belsk, entered the tent. "Your Highness, my people have seized a Cossack who says that they are preparing an assault for to-night."

"I have received information too," answered the prince. "All is ready, only let our people hurry with the ramparts."

"They are nearly finished."

"That is well! We will occupy them in the evening." Then he turned to the four knights. "It is best to try after the storm, if the night is dark."

"How is that?" asked Firlei; "are you preparing a sally?"

"The sally in its own order,--I will lead it myself; but now we are talking about something else. These gentlemen undertake to creep through the enemy and inform the king of our condition."

The castellan was astonished, opened his eyes, and looked at the knights in succession. The prince smiled with delight. He had this vanity,--he loved to have his soldiers admired.

"In God's name!" said the castellan; "there are such hearts then in the world? As God lives, I will not dissuade you from the daring deed."

Zagloba was purple from rage; but he said nothing, he only puffed like a bear. The prince thought awhile, then said,--

"I do not wish, however, to spend your blood in vain, and I am not willing that all four should go together. One will go first; if the enemy kill him, they will not delay in boasting of it, as they have once already boasted of the death of my servant whom they seized at Lvoff. If they kill the first, the second will go; afterward in case of necessity the third and the fourth. But perhaps the first will pass through; in such an event I do not wish to expose the others to a useless death."

"Your Highness," interrupted Skshetuski.

"This is my will and command," said Yeremi, with emphasis. "To bring you to agreement, I say that he shall go first who offered himself first."

"It was I!" cried Pan Longin, with a beaming face.

"To-night, after the storm, if it is dark," added the prince. "I will give no letters to the king; you will tell what you have seen,--merely take a signet-ring as credential."

Podbipienta took the signet-ring and bowed to the prince, who caught him by the temples and held him awhile with his two hands; then he kissed him several times on the forehead, and said in a voice of emotion,--

"You are as near to my heart as a brother. May the God of Hosts and our Queen of Angels carry you through, warrior of the Lord! Amen!"

"Amen!" repeated Sobieski, the castellan of Belsk, and Pan Pshiyemski.

The prince had tears in his eyes, for he was a real father to the knights. Others wept, and a quiver of enthusiasm shook the body of Pan Podbipienta. A flame passed through his bones; and rejoiced to its depth was his soul, pure, obedient, and heroic, with the hope of coming sacrifice.

"History will write of you!" cried the castellan.

"Non nobis, non nobis, sed nomini tuo, Domine, da gloriam (Not to us, not to us, but to thy name, Lord, give the glory)," said the prince.

The knights issued from the tent.

"Tfu! something has seized me by the throat and holds me," said Zagloba; "and it is as bitter in my mouth as wormwood, and there they are firing continually. Oh, if the thunders would fire you away!" said he, pointing to the smoking trenches of the Cossacks. "Oh, it is hard to live in this world! Pan Longin, are you really going out? May the angels guard you! If the plague would choke those ruffians!"

"I must take farewell of you," said Podbipienta.

"How is that? Where are you going?" asked Zagloba.

"To the priest Mukhovetski,--to confess, my brother. I must cleanse my sinful soul."

Pan Longin hastened to the castle; the others returned to the ramparts. Skshetuski and Volodyovski were silent, but Zagloba said,--

"Something holds me by the throat. I did not think to be sorrowful, but that is the worthiest man in the world. If any one contradicts me, I'll give it to him in the face. Oh, my God, my God! I thought the castellan of Belsk would restrain the prince, but he beat the drums still more. The hangman brought that heretic! 'History,' he says, 'will write of you.' Let it write of him, but not on the skin of Pan Longin. And why doesn't he go out himself? He has six toes on his feet, like every Calvinist, and he can walk better. I tell you, gentlemen, that it is getting worse and worse on earth, and Jabkovski is a true prophet when he says that the end of the world is near. Let us sit down awhile at the ramparts, and a go to the castle, so as to console ourselves with the company of our friend till evening at least."

But Pan Longin, after confession and communion, spent whole time in prayer. He made his first appearance at the storm in the evening, which was one of the most awful, for the Cossacks had struck just when the troops were transporting their cannon and wagons to the newly raised ramparts. For a time it seemed that the slender forces of the Poles would fall before the onrush of two hundred thousand foes. The Polish battalions had become so intermingled with the enemy that they could not distinguish their own, and three times they closed in this fashion. Hmelnitski exerted all his power; for the Khan and his own colonels had told him that this must be the last storm, and that henceforth they would only harass the besieged with hunger. But after three hours all attacks were repulsed with such terrible losses that according to later reports forty thousand of the enemy had fallen. One thing is certain,-- after the battle a whole bundle of flags was thrown at the feet of the prince; and this was really the last great assault, after which followed more difficult times of digging under the ramparts, capturing wagons, continual firing, suffering, and famine.

Immediately after the storm the soldiers, ready to drop from weariness, were led by the tireless Yeremi in a sally, which ended in a new defeat for the enemy. Quiet then soothed the tabor and the camp.

The night was warm but cloudy. Four black forms pushed themselves quietly and carefully to the eastern edge of the ramparts. They were Pan Longin, Zagloba, Skshetuski, and Volodyovski.

"Guard your pistols well, to keep the powder dry," whispered Pan Yan. "Two battalions will be ready all night. If you fire, we will spring to the rescue."

"Nothing to be seen, even if you strain your eyes out!" whispered Zagloba.

"That is better," answered Pan Longin.

"Be quiet!" interrupted Volodyovski, "I hear something."

"That is only the groan of a dying man,--nothing!"

"If you can only reach the oak grove."

"Oh, my God! my God!" sighed Zagloba, trembling as if in a fever.

"In three hours it will be daylight."

"It is time!" said Pan Longin.

"Time! time!" repeated Skshetuski, in a stifled voice. "Go with God!"

"With God, with God!"

"Farewell, brothers, and forgive me if I have offended any of you in anything."

"You offend? O God!" cried Zagloba, throwing himself into his arms.

Skshetuski and Volodyovski embraced him in turn. The moment came. Suppressed gulping shook the breasts of these knights. One alone, Pan Longin, was calm, though full of emotion. "Farewell!" he repeated once more; and approaching the edge of the rampart, he dropped into the ditch, and soon appeared as a black figure on the opposite bank. Once more he beckoned farewell to his comrades, and vanished in the gloom.

Between the road to Zalostsitse and the highway from Vishnyovets grew an oak-grove, interspersed with narrow openings. Beyond and joining with it was an old pine-forest, thick and large, extending north of Zalostsitse. Podbipienta had determined to reach that grove. The road is very perilous, for to reach the oaks it was necessary to pass along the entire flank of the Cossack tabor; but Pan Longin selected it on purpose, for it was just around the camp that most people were moving during the whole night, and the guards gave least attention to passers-by. Besides, other roads, valleys, thickets, and narrow places were set by guards who rode around continually, by essauls, sotniks, and even Hmelnitski himself. A passage through the meadows and along the Gnyezna was not to be dreamt for the Cossack horse-herders were watching there from dusk till daylight with their herds.

The night was gloomy, cloudy, and so dark that at ten paces not only could a man not be seen, but not even a tree. This circumstance was favorable for Pan Longin; though on the other hand he was obliged to go very slowly and carefully, so as not to fall into any of the pits or ditches, occupying the whole expanse of the battle-field and dug by Polish and Cossack hands. In this fashion he made way to the second Polish rampart, which had been abandoned just before evening, and had passed through the ditch. He stopped and listened; the trenches were empty. The sally made by Yeremi after the storm had pushed the Cossacks out, who either fell, or took refuge in the tabor. A multitude of bodies were lying on the slopes and summits of these mounds. Pan Longin stumbled against bodies every moment, stepped over them, and passed on. From time to time a low groan or sigh announced that some one of the prostrate was living yet.

Beyond the ramparts there was a broad expanse stretching to another trench made before the arrival of Yeremi, also covered with corpses; but some tens of steps farther on were those earth-shelters, like stacks of hay in the darkness. But they were empty. Everywhere the deepest silence reigned,--nowhere a fire or a man; no one on that former square but the prostrate.

Pan Longin began the prayer for the souls of the dead, and went on. The sounds of the Polish camp, which followed him to the second rampart, grew fainter and fainter, melting in the distance, till at last they ceased altogether. Pan Longin stopped and looked around for the last time. He could see almost nothing, for in the camp there was no light; but one window in the castle glimmered weakly as a star which the clouds now expose and now conceal, or like a glow-worm which shines and darkens in turn.

"My brothers, shall I see you again in this life?" thought Pan Longin; and sadness pressed him down like a tremendous stone. He was barely able to breathe. There, where that pale light was trembling, are his people; there are brother hearts,--Prince Yeremi, Pan Yan, Volodyovski, Zagloba, the priest Mukhovetski; there they love him and would gladly defend him. But here is night, with desolation, darkness, corpses; under his feet choruses of ghosts; farther on, the blood-devouring tabor of sworn, pitiless enemies. The weight of sadness became so great that it was too heavy even for the shoulders of this giant. His soul began to waver within him.

In the darkness pale Alarm flew upon him, and began to whisper in his ear: "You will not pass, it is impossible! Return, there is still time! Fire the pistol, and a whole battalion will rush to your aid. Through those tabors, through that savageness nothing will pass."

That starving camp, covered every day with balls, full of death and the odor of corpses, appeared at that moment to Pan Longin a calm, peaceful, safe haven. His friends there would not think ill of him if he returned. He would tell them that the deed passed human power; and they would not go themselves, would not send another,--would wait further for the mercy of God and the coming of the king. But if Skshetuski should go and perish! "In the name of the Father, Son, and Holy Ghost! These are temptations of Satan," thought Pan Longin. "I am ready for death, and nothing worse can meet me. And this is Satan terrifying a weak soul with desolation, corpses, and darkness; for he makes use of all means." Will the knight return, cover himself with shame, suffer in reputation, disgrace his name, not save the army, renounce the crown of heaven? Never! And he moved on, stretching out his hands before him.

Now a murmur reached him again, not from the Polish camp, however, but from the opposite side, still indefinite, but as it were deep and terrible, like the growling of a bear giving sudden answer in a dark forest. Disquiet had now left Pan Longin's soul; sadness had ceased, and changed into a mere sweet remembrance of those near to him. At last, as if answering that menace coming up from the tabor, he repeated once more in spirit: "But still I will go."

After a certain time he found himself on that battle-field ere on the first day of the storm the prince's cavalry had defeated the Cossacks and janissaries. The road here was more even,-- fewer pits, ditches, shelters, and no corpses, those who had fallen in the earlier struggles had been buried by the Cossacks. It was also somewhat clearer, for the ground was not covered with various obstacles. The land inclined gradually toward the north. But Pan Longin turned immediately to the flank, wishing to push through between the western pond and the tabor.

He went quickly now, without hindrance, and it seemed him already that he was reaching the line of the tabor, when some new sound caught his attention. He halted at once, and after waiting a quarter of an hour heard the tramp and breathing of horses. "Cossack patrols!" thought he. The voices of men reached his ears. He sprang aside with speed, and searching with his foot for the first depression in the ground, fell to the earth and stretched out motionless, holding his pistol in one hand and his sword the other.

The riders approached still nearer, and at last were abreast of him. It was so dark he could not count them; but he heard every word of their conversation.

"It is hard for them, but hard for us too," said some sleepy voice. "And how many good men of ours have bitten the dust!"

"Oh, Lord!" said another voice, "they say the king is far. What will become of us?"

"The Khan got angry with our father; and the Tartars threaten to take us, if there will be no other prisoners."

"And in the pastures they fight with our men. Father has forbidden us to go to the Tartar camp, for whoever goes there is lost."

"They say there are disguised Poles among the market-men. I wish this war had never begun."

"It is worse this time than before."

"The king is not far away, with the Polish forces. That is the worst!"

"Ha, ha! You would be sleeping in the Saitch at this hour; now you have got to push around in the dark like a vampire."

"There must be vampires here, for the horses are snorting."

Their voices receded gradually, and at last were silent. Pan Longin rose and went on.

A rain fine as mist began to fall. It grew still darker. On the left side of Pan Longin gleamed at the distance of two furlongs a small light; after that a second, a third, and a tenth. Then he knew he was on the line of the tabor. The lights were far apart and weak. It was evident that all were sleeping, and only here and there might they be drinking or preparing food for the morrow.

"Thank God that I am out after the storm and the sally," said Pan Longin to himself. "They must be mortally weary."

He had scarcely thought this when he heard again in the distance the tramp of horses,--another patrol was coming. But the ground in this place was more broken; therefore it was easier to hide. The patrol passed so near that the guards almost rode over Pan Longin. Fortunately the horses, accustomed to pass among prostrate bodies, were not frightened. Pan Longin went on.

In the space of a thousand yards he met two more patrols. It was evident that the whole circle occupied by the tabor was guarded like the apple of the eye. But Pan Longin rejoiced in spirit that he was not meeting infantry outposts, who are generally placed before camps to give warning to mounted patrols.

But his joy was of short duration. Scarcely had he advanced another furlong of the road when some dark figure shifted before him not more than twenty yards distant. Though unterrified, he felt a slight tremor along his spine. It was too late to withdraw and go around. The form moved; evidently it had seen him. A moment of hesitation followed, short as the twinkle of an eye. Then a suppressed voice called,--

"Vassil, is that you?"

"I," said Pan Longin, quietly.

"Have you gorailka?"

"I have."

"Give me some."

Pan Longin approached.

"Why are you so tall?" asked the voice, in tones of terror.

Something rustled in the darkness. A scream of "Lor--!" smothered the instant it was begun, came from the mouth the picket; then was heard the crash as it were of broken bones, heavy breathing, and one figure fell quietly to the earth. Pan Longin moved on.

But he did not pass along the same line, for it was evidently a line of pickets; he turned therefore a little nearer to the tabor, wishing to go between the pickets and the line of wagons. If there was not another line of pickets, Pan Longin could meet in that space only those who went out from camp to relieve those on duty. Mounted patrols had no duty here.

After a time it became evident that there was no second line of pickets. But the tabor was not farther than two bow-shots; and wonderful! it seemed to grow nearer continually, though he tried to go at an equal distance from line of wagons.

It was evident too that not all were asleep in the tabor. At the fires smouldering here and there sitting figures were visible. In one place the fire was greater,--so large indeed it almost reached Pan Longin with its light, and he was forced to draw back toward the pickets so as not to pass through the line of illumination. From the distance he distinguished, hanging on cross-sticks near the fire, oxen which the butchers were skinning. Disputing groups of looked on. A few were playing quietly on pipes for butchers. It was that part of the camp occupied by herdsmen. The more distant rows of wagons were surrounded by darkness.

But the line of the tabor lighted by the smouldering fires again appeared as if nearer to Pan Longin. In the beginning he had it only on his right hand; suddenly he saw that he had it in front of him. Then he halted and meditated what to do. He was surrounded. The tabor, the Tartar camp, and the camps of the mob encircled all Zbaraj like a ring. Inside this ring sentries were standing and mounted guards moving, that no one might pass through.

The position of Pan Longin was terrible. He had now the choice either to go through between the wagons or seek another exit between the Cossacks and the Tartars. Otherwise he would have to wander till daylight along that rim, unless he wished to return to Zbaraj; but even in the latter case he might fall into the hands of the mounted patrol. He understood, however, that the very nature of the ground did not permit that one wagon should stand close to another. There had to be intervals in the rows, and considerable ones. Such intervals were necessary for communication, for an open road, for necessary travel. He determined to look for such a passage, and with that object approached still nearer to the wagons. The gleam of fires burning here and there might betray him, but on the other hand they were useful, for without them he could see neither the wagons nor the road between them.

After a quarter of an hour he found a road, and recognized it easily, for it looked like a black belt between the wagons. There was no fire on it; there could be no Cossacks there, since the cavalry had to pass that way. Pan Longin put himself on his knees and hands, and began to crawl to that dark throat like a snake to a hole.

A quarter of an hour passed, half an hour; he crawled continually, praying at the same time, commending his body and soul to the protection of the heavenly powers. He thought that perhaps the fate of all Zbaraj was depending on him then, could he pass that throat; he prayed therefore not for himself alone, but for those who at that moment in the trenches were praying for him.

On both sides of him all was silent,--no man moved, no horse snorted, no dog barked; and Pan Longin went through. The bushes and thickets looked dark before him; behind them was the oak-grove; behind the oak-grove the pine-woods, all the way to Toporoff; beyond the pine-woods, the king, salvation, and glory, service before God and man. What was the cutting of three heads in comparison with this deed, for which something was needed beyond an iron hand? Pan Longin felt the difference, but pride stirred not that clean heart; it was only moved like that of a child with tears of thankfulness.

Then he rose and passed on. Beyond the wagons there were either no pickets or few easily avoided. Now heavier rain began to fall, pattering on the bushes and drowning the noise of his steps. Pan Longin then gave freedom to his long legs, and walked like a giant, trampling the bushes; every step was like five of a common man,--the wagons every moment farther, the oak-grove every moment nearer, and salvation every moment nearer.

Here are the oaks. Night beneath them is as black as under the ground; but that is better. A gentle breeze sprang up; the oaks murmured lightly,--you would have said they were muttering a prayer; "O great God, good God, guard this knight, for he is thy servant and a faithful son of the land on which we have grown up for thy glory!"

About seven miles and a half divided Pan Longin from the Polish camp. Sweat poured from his forehead, for the air was sultry, as if gathering for a storm; but he went on, caring nothing for the storm, for the angels were singing in his heart. The oaks became thinner. The first field is surely near. The oaks rustle more loudly, as if wishing to say: "Wait; you were safe among us." But the knight has no time, and he enters the open field. Only one oak stands on it, and that in the centre; but it is larger than the others. Pan Longin moves toward that oak.

All at once, when he was a few yards from the spreading branches of the giant, about a dozen figures push out and approach him with wolf-springs: "Who are you? who are you?" Their language is unknown; their heads are covered with something pointed. They are the Tartar horse-herders, who have taken refuge from the rain. At that moment red lightning flashed through the field, revealing the oak, the wild figures of the Tartars, and the enormous noble. A terrible cry shook the air, and the battle began in a moment.

The Tartars rushed on Pan Longin like wolves on a deer, I seized him with sinewy hands; but he only shook himself, and all the assailants fell from him as ripe fruit from a tree. Then the terrible double-handed sword gritted in scabbard; and then were heard groans, howls, calls for aid, the whistle of the sword, the groans of the wounded, the neighing and the frightened horses, the clatter of broken Tartar swords. The silent field roared with all the wild sounds that can possibly find place in the throats of men.

The Tartars rushed on him repeatedly in a crowd; but he put his back to the oak, and in front covered himself with the whirlwind of his sword, and slashed awfully. Bodies lay dark under his feet; the others fell back, impelled by panic terror. "A div! a div!" howled they, wildly.

The howling was not without an answer. Half an hour had not passed when the whole field swarmed with footmen and horsemen. Cossacks ran up, and Tartars also with poles and bows and pieces of burning pitch-pine. Excited questions began to fly from mouth to mouth. "What is it, what has happened?" "A div!" answered the Tartars. "A div!" repeated the crowd. "A Pole! A div! Take him alive, alive!"

Pan Longin fired twice from his pistols, but those reports could not be heard by his comrades in the Polish camp. Now the crowd approached him in a half-circle. He was standing in the shade, gigantic, supported by the tree, and he waited with sword in hand. The crowd came nearer, nearer. At last the voice of command shouted: "Seize him!"

They rushed ahead. The cries were stopped. Those who could not push on gave light to the assailants. A whirl of men gathered and turned under the tree. Only groans came out of that whirl, and for a long time it was impossible to distinguish anything. At last a scream of terror was wrested from the assailants. The crowd broke in a moment. Under the tree remained Pan Longin, and at his feet a crowd of bodies still quivering in agony.

"Ropes, ropes!" thundered a voice.

The horsemen ran for the ropes, and brought them in the twinkle of an eye. Then a number of strong men seized the two ends of a long rope, endeavoring to fasten Pan Longin to the tree; but he cut with his sword, and the men fell on the ground on both sides. Then the Tartars tried, with the same result.

Seeing that too many men in a crowd interfere with one another, a number of the boldest Nogais advanced once more, wishing absolutely to seize the enormous man alive; but he tore them as a wild boar tears resolute dogs. The oak, which had grown together from two great trees, guarded in its central depression the knight; whoever approached him from the front within the length of his sword perished without uttering a groan. The superhuman power of Pan Longin seemed to increase with each moment. Seeing this, the enraged hordes drove away the Cossacks, and around were heard the wild cries: "Bows! bows!"

At the sight of the bows, and of the arrows poured out at the feet of his enemies from their quivers, Pan Longin saw that the moment of death was at hand, and he began the litany to the Most Holy Lady.

It became still. The crowds restrained their breath, waiting for what would happen. The first arrow whistled, as Pan Longin was saying, "Mother of the Redeemer!" and it scratched his temple. Another arrow whistled, as he was saying, "O glorious Lady," and it stuck in his shoulder. The words of the litany had mingled with the whistling of arrows; and when Pan Longin had said, "Morning Star," arrows were standing in his shoulders, his side, in his legs. The blood from his temples was flowing into his eyes; he saw as through a mist the field and the Tartars; he heard no longer the whistle of the arrows. He felt that he was weakening, that his legs were bending under him; his head dropped on his breast. At last he fell on his knees. Then he said, with a half groan: "Queen of the Angels--" These words were his last on earth. The angels of heaven took his soul, and placed it a clear pearl at the feet of the "Queen of the Angels."

CHAPTER LXI.

Zagloba and Volodyovski were standing on the rampart next morning among the soldiers, looking carefully toward the tabor, from the side of which masses of peasants were approaching. Pan Yan was in counsel with the prince; but they, taking advantage of the moment of quiet, were talking about the preceding day and the present movement in the enemy's tabor.

"That forebodes no good for us," said Zagloba, pointing at the dark masses moving like an enormous cloud. "They are surely coming to an assault again, and here our hands will not move in their joints."

"Why should there be an assault in the clear day? They will do nothing more this time," said the little knight, "than occupy our rampart of yesterday, dig into our new one, and fire from morning till evening."

"We might stir them up nicely with our cannon."

Volodyovski lowered his voice. "We haven't much powder. With our present use it will not last six days probably; but by that time the king will come surely."

"Let him do what he likes. If only our Pan Longin, poor man, has got through in safety! I could not sleep the whole night. I was thinking only of him, and whenever I dozed I saw him in trouble; and such sorrow seized me that sweat stood out on my body. He is the best man to be found in the Commonwealth, looking with a lantern for three years and six weeks."

"And why did you always jeer at him?"

"Because my lip is worse than my heart. But don't make it bleed, Pan Michael, with remembrances, for as matters are I reproach myself; and God forbid that anything should happen to Pan Longin! I should have no peace till my death."

"Don't grieve so much. He never had any ill feeling against you, and I have heard him say himself, 'An evil mouth, but a golden heart.'"

"God give him health, the worthy friend! He never knew how to talk in human fashion, but he made up for a hundred such deficiencies by great virtue. What do you think, Pan Michael, did he pass through?"

"The night was dark, and the peasants after the defeat were terribly tired. We had not a good watch; what must it have been with them?"

"Praise God for that! I told Pan Longin to inquire carefully whether our poor princess had been seen anywhere, for I think Jendzian must have taken her to the king's headquarters. Pan Longin will be sure not to rest; he will not come back without the king. In that case we shall have news again soon."

"I have faith in the wit of that lad Jendzian, and think that he saved her somehow. I should know no peace if harm met her. I did not know her intimately, and I believe if I had a sister she would not have been dearer to me."

"She was a sister to you, but to me a daughter. From these troubles my beard will grow white altogether, and my heart break from sorrow. When you love some one,--one, two, three, and that one is gone; then you sit, console yourself, worry, grieve, meditate,--having besides an empty stomach, and holes in your cap through which the water is falling on your bald head like rain through a broken thatch. Dogs have at present a pleasanter life in the Commonwealth than the nobles, and we four are the worst off of all. It is time to go to a better world, Pan Michael, what do you think?"

"I have thought more than once whether it would not be better to tell Skshetuski all; but this restrains me, that he himself never speaks of her, and when any one utters a word he just quivers as if something pierced his heart."

"Tell him, open the wounds dried up in the fire of this war, while now some Tartar maybe is leading her by the hair through Perekop! Flaming fires stand in my eyes when I think of such a thing. It is time to die, it cannot be otherwise; for there is torture alone in this world, nothing more. If only Pan Longin gets through!"

"He must have more favor in heaven than others, for he is virtuous. But look! what are the rabble doing?"

"There is such a glitter from the sun to-day that I cannot see."

"They are cutting up our rampart of yesterday."

"I said there would be an assault. Let us go, Pan Michael; we have stood here long enough."

"They are not digging to make an assault; they must have an open road to return, and besides they will surely bring machines to shoot from. Just see how the shovels are working; they have levelled the ground about forty yards already."

"I see now; but there is a terrible glare to-day." Zagloba covered his eyes with his hand, and looked.

At that moment through the cut made in the rampart rushed a stream of people who scattered in the twinkle of an eye along the space between the ramparts. Some fell to firing; others, digging the ground with spades, began to raise a new mound and trenches to enclose the Polish camp with a third ring.

"Oh, ho!" cried Volodyovski, "the word is scarcely out of my mouth, and they are rolling in the machines."

"Well, there will be an assault soon. Let us leave this place," said Zagloba.

"No; this is another kind of tower," said the little knight.

Really, the machines which appeared in the cut were built differently from the ordinary moving-tower. The walls were composed of ladders fastened together with hasps, covered with cloth and skins, from behind which the best marksmen, sitting from half the height of the machine to the top, struck the enemy.

"Come away! Let the dogs gnaw on where they are!"

"Wait!" answered Volodyovski. They began to count the machines, as new ones appeared in the cut.

"One, two, three--it is evident they have no small supply--four, five, six--they are coming yet--seven, eight--they can kill a dog on our square, for there must be splendid marksmen there--nine, ten--evident as on your hand, for the sun shines on it--eleven--" All at once Pan Michael stopped counting. "What is that?" he asked, in a voice of amazement.

"Where?"

"There on the highest one--a man is hanging!"

Zagloba strained his glance. Indeed, on the highest machine the sun was shining on the naked body of a man, swaying on a rope with the movement of the machine, like a great pendulum.

"True," said Zagloba.

Then Volodyovski grew pale as a sheet, and cried with a terrified voice: "Almighty God! it is Podbipienta!"

A murmur rose on the ramparts like wind through the leaves of trees, Zagloba bent his head, covered his eyes with his hands, and whispered with blue lips, groaning: "Jesus, Mary! Jesus, Mary!"

The murmur changed into a noise of confused words, and then into a roar as of a stormy sea. The men on the ramparts saw that by that infamous cord was hanging the comrade of their sufferings, a knight without reproach. All knew that that was Pan Longin Podbipienta, and terrible anger began to raise the hair on the heads of the soldiers.

Zagloba at last took his hands from his eyes. He was a terror to look at. On his mouth was foam, his face was blue, his eyes bursting from his head. "Blood! blood!" roared he, with such a voice that a quiver passed through those standing near him.

He sprang into the ditch. After him rushed everything that had life on the ramparts. No power--not even the commands of the prince--could have restrained that outburst of rage. They climbed out of the ditch, one over the shoulders of the other; they seized the bank of the ditch with their hands and with their teeth, and when one sprang out he ran without looking, not turning to see whether others were following. The machines were smoking like tar-factories, and trembled from the roar of musketry, but nothing availed. Zagloba rushed on in advance, his sabre above his head, raging like a mad bull. The Cossacks sprang forward too with scythes and flails on the assailants. Two walls, as it were, struck with a crash. But fat dogs cannot defend themselves long against hungry and raging wolves. Pushed from their place, cut with sabres, torn with teeth, beaten, crushed, the Cossacks could not withstand the fury; they were soon confused, and then fled to the cut. Zagloba, raging, rushed into the thickest crowd, like a lioness whose cubs are gone. An opening was made before him; and at his side went, like another devouring flame, Volodyovski, wild as a wounded leopard. The marksmen in the machines were cut to pieces; the rest pursued to the cut in the ramparts. Then the soldiers mounted the machine and freed Pan Longin, letting him down carefully to the ground.

Zagloba fell on his body. Volodyovski's heart was rent in like degree, and he was covered with tears at the sight of his dead friend. It was easy to see how Pan Longin had perished, for his whole body was covered with spots from the wounds inflicted by arrows. But the arrows had not injured his face, except one, which had left a long line on his temple. The few drops of blood had grown dry on his cheek; his eyes were closed, and on his pale face was a quiet smile, and had it not been for the azure paleness of the visage, the chill of death in the features, it might have seemed that Pan Longin was sleeping calmly. His comrades took him at last and bore him on their shoulders to the rampart, and then to the chapel of the castle.

Before evening a coffin was made, and the funeral celebrated by night at the Zbaraj cemetery. All the clergy were present except the priest Jabkovski, who, shot in the back during the last assault, was near death. Having given the command to Sobieski, the prince had come; also Konyetspolski, Pshiyemski, Skshetuski, Volodyovski, Zagloba, and the officers of the squadron in which the dead man had served. The coffin was placed at the newly dug grave, and the ceremony began.

It was a starry night. The torches burned with an even flame, gleaming on the yellow planks of the freshly made coffin, on the figure of the priest, and the stern faces of the knights standing in a circle. The smoke from the censer rose slowly, spreading the odor of myrrh and juniper. The silence was broken only by the stifled sobs of Zagloba, the deep sighs of the strong breasts around, and the distant roar of discharges on the ramparts. But the priest Mukhovetski raised his hand in sign that he was about to speak. The knights therefore held their breaths. He was silent a little longer; then fixing his eyes on the starry heights, he began at length as follows:--

"'What knocking do I hear at night on the door of heaven?' asks the hoary warden of Christ, springing up from sweet slumber. 'Open, holy Peter, open! I am Podbipienta.' But what deeds, what offices, what services embolden you, O Podbipienta, to trouble so important a doorkeeper? By what right do you wish to enter where neither birth, though as honorable as your own, nor senatorial dignity, nor offices of the Crown, nor the majesty even of the purple, of themselves alone give free entrance, since men cannot drive there by the broad highway in a carriage and six, with haiduks, but must climb by the steep and thorny path of virtue? Ah, open, holy Peter, open quickly, for by just such a steep and thorny path did our fellow-soldier and dear comrade Podbipienta pass, till he came to your presence like a dove wearied after long flight; came naked, like Lazarus; came like Saint Stephen, torn with Pagan arrows; like poor Job; like the virgin who has never known a husband,--pure, obedient as a lamb, patient and quiet, without a spot of sin, with a sacrifice of blood joyfully shed for his earthly fatherland. Admit him, holy Peter; for if you do not admit him, whom will you admit in these days of corruption and ungodliness? Admit him, holy warden! admit this lamb; let him pasture in the heavenly meadow; let him nip its grass, for he came hungry from Zbaraj."

In this manner the priest Mukhovetski began his discourse; and then he depicted the whole life of Pan Longin with such eloquence that every one acknowledged himself wicked in the presence of the silent coffin of the knight without reproach, who had surpassed the lowliest in modesty and the loftiest in virtue. All then beat their breasts. Every moment greater sadness seized them, and they saw more clearly what the country had suffered and Zbaraj had lost. The priest took a lofty flight, and when at last he described the passage through the enemy and the martyr death of Pan Longin, he forgot altogether his rhetoric and quotations; and while taking leave of the mortal remains in the name of the clergy, the officers, and the army, he broke into weeping himself, and said, sobbing like Zagloba: "Give us your blessing, brother; give us your blessing, comrade! Not to an earthly, but to a heavenly king--to the surest tribunal--have you carried our groans, our famine, our misery and sufferings. You will gain for us there a more certain salvation. But you will never return yourself; therefore do we weep, therefore do we pour tears upon your coffin,--for we loved you, dearest brother!"

All wept with the worthy priest,--the prince, the commanders, the army, and most of all the friends of the deceased; but when the priest intoned for the first time, "Requiem æternam dona ei Domine! (Grant him eternal rest, Lord!)," there was a universal outburst, though all were men hardened against death, and long accustomed to it, through their daily service.

When the coffin was placed on the ropes it was as difficult to tear Zagloba away as if his father or brother had died. But at last Skshetuski and Volodyovski drew him aside. The prince approached and took a handful of earth; the priest began to say, "Anima ejus;" the ropes rattled; the earth began to fall,--it was thrown in with hands, with helmets; and soon above the remains of Pan Longin rose a lofty mound, shone on by the pale sad light of the moon.

Three friends were returning from the town to the square, from which came an uninterrupted sound of firing. They walked in silence, for neither wished to speak the first word; but other groups were speaking of the deceased, giving him unanimous praise.

"It was a splendid funeral," said an officer passing at the side of Skshetuski; "they did not give a better to Serakovski, the secretary of the Crown."

"For he deserved it," answered another officer; "who else would have undertaken to break through to the king?"

"But I heard," added the third, "that among Vishnyevetski's men there was a number of volunteers; but after such a terrible example the desire will surely desert them all."

"Besides, the thing is impossible. A snake could not creep through."

"As I live, it would be pure madness."

The officers passed on. A new moment of silence followed. Suddenly Volodyovski said: "You heard, Yan, what they said?"

"Yes," answered Skshetuski; "it is my turn now."

"Yan," said Volodyovski, seriously, "you know me of old, and you know that I am not quick to withdraw before peril; but peril is one thing, and downright suicide is another."

"And you, Michael, say this?"

"Yes, for I am your friend."

"And I am your friend. Give me your word of honor that you will not go third if I perish."

"Impossible!" cried Volodyovski.

"Ah, you see, Michael! How can you ask that of me which you will not do yourself? Let the will of God be done."

"Then let me go with you."

"The prince has prohibited that,--not I. You are a soldier, and you must obey."

Pan Michael was silent, for he was a soldier first of all; then his mustaches only quivered violently by the light of the moon. At last he said: "The night is very clear; don't go now."

"I should prefer a darker one, but delay is impossible. The weather is, as you see, settled for a long time, our powder is almost gone, our provisions are at an end. The soldiers are digging through the square, looking for roots; the gums of some of them are rotting from the rubbish they have eaten. I will go to-night,--at once; I have taken farewell of the prince already."

"I see that you are simply desperate."

Skshetuski smiled gloomily. "God guard you, Michael! It is certain that we are not swimming in luxury, but I shall not seek death of my own will, for that is a sin; besides, it is not a question of perishing, but of getting through, going to the king, and saving the camp."

Volodyovski was suddenly seized with such a desire to tell Skshetuski all about the princess that he almost opened his mouth; but he thought to himself, "His head will be turned by the news, and they will catch him the more easily," He bit his tongue therefore, was silent, and then asked: "Which way are you going?"

"I told the prince that I should go through the pond, and then by the river till I passed far beyond the tabor. He said that this was a better road than others."

"There is no help, I see," said Volodyovski. "Since death is predestined to a man, it is better on the field of glory than in bed. God attend you, God attend you, Yan! If we do not meet in this world we shall in the other, and I shall surely keep my heart for you."

"As I shall mine for you. God reward you for all the good you have done! And listen to me, Michael! If I die, they will perhaps not put me up as they did Pan Longin, for they have received too severe a lesson; but they will be sure to boast of it in some way, in which case let old Zatsvilikhovski go to Hmelnitski for my body, for I do not wish that dogs should drag me through their camp."

"Rest assured!" said Volodyovski.

Zagloba, who from the beginning had listened in semiconsciousness, understood the conversation at last, but he felt unable to restrain or dissuade; he only groaned deeply: "Yesterday that one, to-day this one. My God, my God, my God!"

"Have faith," said Volodyovski.

"Pan Yan--" began Zagloba, and he could go no further. His gray, suffering head rested on the breast of the knight, and he drew up to him like a helpless little child.

An hour later Skshetuski sank into the water of the western pond.

The night was very clear, and the middle of the pond looked like a silver shield; but Skshetuski vanished straightway from the eye. The shore was thickly overgrown with rushes and reeds; farther on, where the reeds were thinner, was a rich growth of pond-weed and plants. That mixture of wide and narrow leaves, slippery stalks, snaky stems winding around the legs and body to the waist hindered his advance greatly, but at least concealed him from the patrol. To swim across the clear centre of the pond was out of the question, for any dark object would have been seen easily. Skshetuski determined therefore to pass along the shore of the pond to the swamp at the other side, through which the river entered the pond. Patrols of Cossacks or Tartars were likely to be there; but the place was overgrown with a whole forest of reeds, only the edge had been cut down to make cabins for the mob. The swamp once attained, it would be possible to push on through the reeds, even in the daytime, unless the quagmire should be too deep. But that road also was a terrible one. Under the sleeping water, not farther than a yard from the shore, the mud was an ell or more in depth. After every step Skshetuski took there rose to the surface of the water bubbles, the gurgling of which could be heard distinctly in the stillness. Besides, in spite of the slowness of his movements, ripples were formed which ran every moment farther from their source to the open water, in which the light of the moon was reflected. In time of rain Skshetuski would have swum straight across the pond, and in half an hour, at most, would have come to the swamp; but there was not a cloud in the sky. Whole torrents of greenish light fell upon the pond, changing the leaves of the lily into silver shields, and the tufts on the reeds to brushes of silver. No breeze was blowing. Happily the gurgling of the bubbles was lost in the noise of the guns, noticing which, Skshetuski moved only when the discharges on the ramparts and trenches became more lively. But that calm, pleasant night caused another difficulty,--legions of mosquitoes rose from the reeds and swarmed over the head of the knight, fastening on his face and eyes, biting him, buzzing and singing above his ears their mournful vespers.

Pan Yan in selecting this road did not deceive himself as to its difficulties, but he did not foresee everything. He did not foresee, for instance, its terrors. Every depth of water, even the best known, has in it something mysterious and terrifying, and involuntarily urges the question, What is down at the bottom? And this pond of Zbaraj was simply awful. The water in it seemed to be thicker than common water, and exuded the odor of corpses, for hundreds of Cossacks and Tartars had decayed there. Both sides had drawn out corpses, but how many of them might be hidden among the reeds, the plants, and the thick growth! The cold of a wave embraced Pan Yan, and sweat stood on his forehead. What if some slippery arm should seize him suddenly, or if greenish eyes should look at him from under the leaves? The long stems of the water-lily wound around his knees, and the hair stood on his head, because that may be the spirit of a drowned man to keep him from going farther. "Jesus, Mary! Jesus, Mary!" whispered he unceasingly, pushing ahead. At times he raised his eyes, and at the sight of the moon, the stars, and the silence of the sky he found a certain rest. "There God is," repeated he, in an undertone, so that he might hear himself. Then he would look on the shore, and it seemed to him that he was looking on the ordinary world of God from some condemned world beyond the earth,--a world of swamps, black depths, pale moonlight, ghosts, corpses, and night. Yearning took such hold of him that he wanted immediately to rush forth from that net of reeds.

But he pushed along the shore unceasingly, and he had already gone so far from the camp that on that God's world (outside) he saw at some paces distant from the shore a Tartar on horseback; he stopped then and looked at the figure, which, nodding with uniform motion toward the neck of the horse, seemed to be sleeping.

It was a strange sight. The Tartar nodded continually, as if bowing in silence to Skshetuski, and the latter did not take his eye from him. There was something terrible in this; but Skshetuski breathed with satisfaction, for in presence of that definite fear fancies a hundred times more difficult to be borne disappeared. The world of ghosts fled somewhere, his coolness returned at once; and only questions like these began to crowd into his head: "Does he sleep, or not? Must I go on, or wait?"

At length he went on, moving still more quietly, still more cautiously than at the beginning of his journey. He already half-way to the swamp and the river when the first breath of a light wind rose. The reeds moved therefore, and gave forth a strong sound by striking one another; and Skshetuski was rejoiced, for in spite of all his care, in spite of the fact that sometimes he lost several minutes in taking a step, an involuntary movement, a stumble, a splash might betray him. Now he advanced more boldly, covered by the loud noise of the reeds with which the whole pond was filled; and everything grew vocal about him, the water on the bank began to plash with its rocking wave.

But this movement evidently roused not the plants along the shore alone, for at that time some dark object appeared before Pan Yan and began to move toward him as if preparing for a spring. He almost screamed at first; but fear and aversion restrained the voice in his bosom, and at the same time a terrible odor came to him. But after a while, when the first idea that this might be a drowned person barring his road on purpose disappeared, and there remained only aversion, the knight passed on. The talk of the reeds continued and increased every moment. Through, their moving tufts Skshetuski saw a second and a third Tartar patrol. He passed these, passed a fourth also. "I must have gone around half the pond," thought he; and he raised himself a little to look through the reeds and see where he was. Something pushed his legs; he looked around and saw there at his knees a human face. "This is the second," thought he.

This time he was not frightened, for the second body lay on its back, without signs of life or movement. Skshetuski merely hastened his steps so as not to become dizzy. The reeds grew thicker, which on the one hand gave him a safe shelter, but on the other greatly impeded his advance. Half an hour passed, an hour; he went on unceasingly, but grew more and more weary. The water in some places was so shallow that it just reached above his ankles, but in others it came almost to his waist. He was tortured beyond measure by the slow dragging of his feet out of the mud. His forehead was streaming with perspiration, and from time to time a quiver went through him from head to foot.

"What is this?" thought he, with terror in his heart; "is delirium seizing me? Somehow the swamp does not appear; I don't recognize the place among the reeds. Shall I miss it?"

It was a terrible danger; for in that way he might circle about the pond all night, and in the morning find himself at the same point from which he had started, or fall into the hands of the Cossacks at another place.

"I have chosen a bad road," thought he, failing in spirits; "it is impossible to get through the pond. I will return, and in the morning go as Pan Longin did. I might rest till morning."

But he went on, for he saw that by promising to return and rest he was tempting himself; it also occurred to him that by going so slowly and halting every moment he could not have reached the swamp yet. Still the thought of rest grew on him more and more. At moments he wished to lie down somewhere in the reeds, just to draw breath. He struggled with his own thoughts and prayed at the same time. The trembling passed over him oftener; he drew his legs out of the mud with less force. The sight of the Tartar patrol sobered him; but he felt that his head as well as his body was tormenting him, and that a fever was coming upon him.

Again half an hour passed; the swamp was not visible yet. But bodies of drowned men appeared more frequently. Night, fear, corpses, the noise of reeds, toil, and sleeplessness benumbed his thoughts. Visions began to come to him. Now Helena is in Kudák; and he is sailing with Jendzian in a boat down the Dnieper. The reeds are rustling; he hears the boatmen sing. The priest Mukhovetski is waiting in his stole; Pan Grodzitski takes the place of a father. The girl is there looking day after day on the river, from the walls. Suddenly she sees something, claps her hands, and cries: "He is coming! he is coming!" "My master," says Jendzian, pulling him by the sleeve, "the lady is here--"

Skshetuski wakes. It is the tangled reeds that stop him on the way. Visions disappear; consciousness returns. Now he does not feel such weariness, for the fever lends him strength.

"Oh, is not this the swamp yet?" But around him the reeds were still the same as if he had not stirred from the spot. Near the river there must be open water; therefore this is not the swamp yet.

He goes on, but his thoughts return with invincible stubbornness to the pleasant vision. In vain he defends himself; in vain he begins to say, "Oh, Venerable Lady!" in vain he tries to retain all his consciousness. Again he is sailing down the Dnieper; he sees the boats, the skiffs, Kudák, the Saitch; only this time the vision is more disordered, there is a multitude of persons in it. At the side of Helena are the prince and Hmelnitski, the koshevoi ataman, Pan Longin, Zagloba, Bogun, Volodyovski,--all in gala attire for his wedding. But where is the wedding? They are in some strange place,--neither Lubni nor Rozlogi nor the Saitch nor Kudák,--in unknown waters among floating corpses.

Skshetuski wakes a second time, or rather he is roused by a loud rustling coming from the direction in which he is going; he halts therefore, and listens. The rustling approaches; a kind of grating and plashing is heard,--it is a boat, visible already through the reeds. Two Cossacks are sitting in it,--one is pushing with an oar; the other holds in his hand a long pole gleaming in the distance like silver, and he pushes the water-plants aside with it.

Skshetuski sank in the water up to his neck, so that only his head was sticking out above the lilies, and he looked. "Is that an ordinary picket," thought he, "or are they already on the trail?" But soon he concluded by the quiet and careless motions of the Cossacks that it must be an ordinary picket. There must be more than one boat on the pond, and if the Cossacks were on his trail a number of boats would be assembled and a crowd of men. Meanwhile they passed by, the noise of the reeds deafened their words; he caught only the following snatch of conversation:--

"Devil take them, they have given orders to patrol this filthy water."

The boat pushed on behind bunches of reeds; but the Cossack standing at the prow struck continually with measured blows of his pole among the water-plants, as if he wished to frighten the fish.

Skshetuski hurried on. After a time he saw a Tartar picket standing at the bank. The light of the moon fell straight on the face of the Nogai, which was like the snout of a dog. But Skshetuski feared these pickets less than loss of consciousness. He exerted all his will, therefore, to give himself a clear account of where he was and whither he was going. But the struggle only increased his weariness, and soon he discovered that he was seeing double and treble, and at moments the pond seemed to him the square and the camp, and the bunches of reeds tents. At such moments he wished to call Volodyovski to go with him, but he had sufficient consciousness to restrain himself. "Don't call, don't call!" repeated he to himself; "that would be death."

But the struggle with himself was more and more difficult. He left Zbaraj tormented with hunger and terrible sleeplessness, from which soldiers there were dying already. That night-journey, the cold bath, the odor of corpses in the water, weakened him completely. Added to this were the excitement of fear, and pain from the biting of mosquitoes which pierced his face so that it was covered with blood. He felt therefore that if he did not reach the swamp soon he would either go out on the shore and let what might meet him meet him quickly, or he would fall among the reeds and be drowned.

That swamp and the mouth of the river seemed to him a port of salvation, though in fact new difficulties and dangers began there. He defended himself feverishly, and went on, taking less care each moment. In the rustle he heard the voices of men,--conversation; it seemed to him that the pond was talking about him. Will he reach the swamp or not? Will he go on shore or not? The mosquitoes sang with their thin voices more sadly. The water became deeper; soon it reached to his belt, then to his breast. He thought that if he should have to swim, he would be entangled in the thick web and drown.

Again an almost irrestrainable, unconquerable desire of calling Volodyovski seized him. He had already put his hand to his mouth to cry: "Michael! Michael!" Fortunately some kind reed struck him with its wet, dripping brush in the face. He came to his mind, and saw in front but a little to one side a dim light. He looked steadily at the light, and went straight toward it for a while. He stopped suddenly; he saw a belt of clear water lying athwart him. He drew breath. It was the river, and on both sides of it a swamp.

"I will stop going by the shore, and will go into that wedge," thought he.

On both sides of the wedge extended two strips of reeds. The knight entered that one to which he had come. After a while he saw he was on a good road. He looked around. The pond was already behind him. He moved parallel with the narrow strip of water, which could be nothing but the river. The water there was cooler also. But after a time terrible weariness possessed him. His legs trembled, and before his eyes rose as it were a dark fog.

"It cannot be helped; I will go to the shore and lie down. I will not go farther; I will rest."

Then he fell on his knees. His hands felt a dry tuft covered with moss; it was like a little island among the rushes. He sat down and began to wipe his bloody face with his hands, and then to draw long breaths.

After a while the odor of smoke reached his nostrils. Turning to the shore, he saw, about a hundred paces from the brink, a fire, and around it a knot of people. He was directly in front of this fire, and at moments when the wind bent the reeds he could see everything perfectly. At the first glance he recognized the Tartar horse-herds, who were sitting at the fire eating.

Then he felt a fearful hunger. Yesterday morning he had eaten a bit of horse-flesh which would not have satisfied a wolf-whelp two months old; since then he had had nothing in his mouth. He began to pluck the round stems growing about him and suck them greedily. He allayed his thirst as well as his hunger,--for thirst tormented him too. At the same time he looked continually at the fire, which grew paler and dimmer. The people near it began to be hidden by a mist, and seemed to go into the distance.

"Oh, sleep torments me! I will sleep here on the mound," thought the knight.

But there was a noise by the fire. The horse-herds rose. Soon there came to Skshetuski's ears the cries: "Losh! losh!" They were answered by a short neigh. The fire was deserted and went out. After a time he heard whistling and the dull thump of hoofs on the moist meadow.

Skshetuski could not understand why the horse-herds had ridden away. Then he saw the tops of the reeds and the broad leaves of the lilies were somewhat pale; the water received a different light from that of the moon; the air was shrouded with a light of joy. He looked around. The day was breaking. He had spent the whole night in going around the pond before reaching the river and the swamp. He was barely at the beginning of the road. Now he must go by the river and pass through the tabor in the day. The air was filled more and more with the light of dawn. In the east the sky took on a pale sea-green color.

Skshetuski slipped down again from the tuft into the swamp, and pushing toward the shore, after a short interval thrust his head out of the reeds. At the distance of five hundred yards, perhaps, a Tartar picket was visible; with this exception the meadow was empty,--only the fire shone with a dying light on a dry place at some little distance. Skshetuski determined to crawl to it through the high grass interspersed here and there with tall rushes.

Having crawled to the place, he looked carefully to find some remnants of food. He found in fact freshly picked mutton bones with bits of sinew and fat, then some pieces of roasted turnips thrown into the hot ashes. He began to eat with the greed of a wild beast, and ate till he saw that the pickets stationed along the road which he had passed were approaching him through the meadow on their way to the tabor.

Then he began to retreat, and in a few minutes disappeared in the wall of reeds. Having found his tuft, he put himself on it without a rustle. The pickets rode by at the same time. Skshetuski began at once on the bones which he had brought with him, and which he broke in his jaws, powerful as those of a wolf. He gnawed off the fat and the sinews, sucked out the marrow, chewed the bone-fat,--allayed his first hunger. Such a morning feast he had not had for a long time in Zbaraj.

He felt stronger now. The food, as well as the rising day, strengthened him. It became brighter every moment. The eastern side of the sky from greenish became rosy and golden. The cool of the morning troubled him greatly, it is true; but he was comforted by the thought that the sun would soon warm his wearied body. He examined the place carefully. The tuft was pretty large, rather short, because round, but wide enough for two persons to lie side by side with ease. The reeds stood around like a wall, hiding it completely from the eyes of men.

"They will not find me here," thought he, "unless they go fishing in the reeds; and there are no fish, for they have died of infection. Here will I rest and think what further to do." And he began to think whether he should go on by the river or not. Finally he determined to go if the wind should rise and the reeds tremble; if not, the noise and rustle might betray him,-- especially as most likely he would have to pass near the tabor.

"Thanks to thee, O Lord, that I am alive till now," whispered he quietly; and he raised his eyes to Heaven. Then his thoughts flew away to the Polish ramparts. The castle was visible from that tuft, especially since it was gilded by the first rays of the rising sun. Maybe some one is looking from the tower to the pond and reeds through a field-glass. Volodyovski is there surely; and Zagloba will pass the whole day in looking from the ramparts to see if he can find him hanging on some moving tower.

"They will not see me," thought the knight, and his breast was full of the happy feeling of security. "They will not see me, they will not see me," he repeated several times. "I have passed only a short road, but it had to be passed. God will help me to go farther."

Here he saw, with the eyes of his imagination, beyond the tabor, in the forest, behind which stand the armies of the king, the general militia of the whole country,--hussars, infantry, foreign regiments. The earth groaned under the weight of men, horses, and cannon, and in the midst of this swarm of people is the king himself. Then he saw an immense battle, broken tabors, the prince with all his cavalry flying over piles of bodies, the greetings of armies. His eyes, aching and swollen, closed beneath the excess of light, and his head bent under the excess of thought; a kind of pleasant weakness began to embrace him. At last he stretched himself at full length and fell asleep.

The reeds rustled. The sun rose high in the sky, warmed with its burning glance the knight, and dried the clothing on his body. He slept soundly without motion. Whoever should see him lying thus on the tuft with bloody face, would think that a corpse thrown up by the water was lying there. Hours passed; still he slept. The sun reached the zenith, and began to descend the other side of the sky; he was sleeping yet. He was roused by the piercing cry of horses feeding on the meadow, and the loud calls of the herdsmen lashing the stallions with whips.

He rubbed his eyes, remembered where he was, looked in the sky; stars were twinkling in the red and still unquenched gleams of the sunset. He had slept the whole day. He felt neither refreshed nor stronger; all his bones were aching. He thought, however, that new toil would restore the activity of his body, and putting his feet into the water he moved on his journey without delay.

He went now through clear water by the reeds, so as not to rouse the attention of the horse-herds on shore by the rustle. The last gleams had disappeared and it was quite dark, for the moon had not risen yet from behind the woods. The water was so deep that Skshetuski lost bottom in places and had to swim, which was difficult to do, for he was dressed, and he swam against the current, which, though slow, still pushed him back toward the pond. But as a recompense the sharpest Tartar eyes could not see that head advancing along the dark wall of reeds. He pushed on therefore rather boldly, swimming at times, but for the greater part wading to his waist and armpits, till at last he reached the place from which his eyes beheld, on both sides of the river, thousands upon thousands of lights.

"These are the tabors," thought he; "now God aid me!" And he listened.

The bustle of mingled voices reached his ear. Yes, these were the tabors. On the left bank of the river stood the Cossack camp with thousands of wagons and tents; on the right the Tartar camp,--both noisy, uproarious, full of conversation, wild sounds of drums and flutes, bellowing of cattle, camels, neighing of horses, shouts. The river divided them, forming a barrier against disputes and fights; for the Tartars could not remain in peace at the side of the Cossacks. The river was widest at this place, and perhaps dug out on purpose. On one side the wagons, on the other reed huts were near the bank, judging by the fires, within a few score of yards; but at the water itself there were surely pickets.

The reeds and rushes became thinner; opposite the camps the banks were evidently bare. Skshetuski pushed on some yards farther, and halted. A certain power and terror came out against him from those swarms. At that moment it seemed to him that all the watchfulness and rage of those thousands of human beings were turned upon him, and in presence of them he felt perfectly helpless. He was alone.

"No one can pass them," thought he; but he pushed on still, for a certain painful, irrestrainable curiosity attracted him. He wished to look more nearly on that terrible power.

Suddenly he stopped. The forest of reeds ended as if cut with a knife; perhaps they had been cut to make cabins. Farther on the clear water was red from the reflection of the fires. Two great and clear flames were blazing there at the banks. Before one stood a Tartar on horseback; before the other a Cossack with a long lance in his hand. Both looked at each other and at the water. In the distance were to be seen others standing on guard in the same way and looking. The gleam of the piles threw as it were a fiery bridge across the river. Under the banks were to be seen rows of small boats used by the guards on the pond.

"An impossibility!" muttered Skshetuski.

Despair seized him at once. He could neither go backward nor forward. The time had been passing as he was pushing through the swamps and reeds breathing the infected air and soaked in water, only to discover after he had come to those very camps through which he had undertaken to pass, that it was impossible.

But it was impossible to go back; the knight knew that he might find sufficient strength to drag himself ahead, but he could not find it to go back. In his despair there was at the same time a dull rage; for the first time he wished to emerge from the water, throttle the guard, then rush on the crowd and perish.

Again the wind began to move along the reeds with a wonderful whisper, bringing with it the sound of bells from Zbaraj. Skshetuski began to pray ardently and beat his breast, imploring aid from heaven with the strength and the desperate faith of a drowning man; he prayed, but the two camps roared ominously as if in answer to his prayer. Black figures and figures red from fire pushed around like herds of devils in hell. The guards stood motionless; the river flowed on with its blood-colored water.

"The fires will go down when deep night comes," said Pan Yan to himself, and waited.

One hour passed, and another. The noise decreased; the fires really began to smoulder, except the two fires of the guards, which blazed up more brightly. The guards were changed, and it was evident that the fresh ones would remain till morning. The thought came to Skshetuski that perhaps he might be able to slip through more easily in the daytime; but he soon abandoned that idea. In the daytime they took water, watered the cattle, bathed; the river must be full of people. Suddenly his glance fell upon the boats. On both banks of the river there was a number of them in a line, and on the Tartar side the rushes extended to the first boat.

Skshetuski sank in the water to his neck, and pushed slowly toward the boats, keeping his eyes fastened on the Tartar guard as on a rainbow. At the end of half an hour he was at the first boat. His plan was simple. The sterns of the boats were raised over the water, forming above it a kind of arch through which the head of a man might pass easily. If all the boats stood side by side there, the Tartar guard could not see a head pushing under them. There was more danger from the Cossack; but he might not see it, for under the boats, notwithstanding the opposite fire, it was dark. Anyhow there was no other passage.

Skshetuski hesitated no longer, and soon found himself under the sterns of the boats. He crawled on his hands and feet, or rather dragged himself, for the water was shallow. He was so near the Tartar standing on the bank that he heard the breathing of his horse. He stopped a moment and listened. Fortunately the boats were placed side by side. He had his eyes then fastened on the Cossack guard, whom he saw as on the palm of his hand. The Cossack was looking at the Tartar camp. Skshetuski had passed fifteen boats, when suddenly he heard steps on shore and Tartar voices. He stopped immediately and listened. In his journeys to the Crimea he had learned Tartar. Now a shiver ran through his whole body when he heard the words of command: "Get in and go!"

He grew feverish, though he was in the water. If they should take the boat under which he was hiding, that moment he was lost; if they should take the one before him he was lost too, for there remained an open lighted space. Each second seemed to him an hour. Soon steps sounded on the planks. The Tartars sat in the fourth or fifth boat behind him, pushed it out and began to sail in the direction of the pond. But that movement directed the eyes of the Cossack guard to the boats. Skshetuski did not stir for something like half an hour. Only when the guards were changed did he resume his onward movement.

In this way he reached the end of the boats. After the last boat began the rushes again, and farther on the reeds. When he reached the rushes the knight, breathless, dripping with perspiration, fell upon his knees and thanked God with his whole heart.

He hastened on somewhat more boldly, taking advantage of every breeze which filled the banks with rustling. From time to time he looked around. The guard-fires began to retreat, to be hidden, to glimmer, to weaken. The lines of rushes and reeds became darker and thicker, for the shores were more swampy. The guards could not stand close to one another; the noise of the camp grew less. A kind of superhuman power strengthened the limbs of the knight. He pushed through reeds, clumps of earth, sank in the swamp, went under water, swam, and rose again. He did not dare yet to go on shore; but he almost felt that he was saved. He could not render account to himself of how long he advanced, wading in this way; but when he looked around again the watch-fires seemed like little points gleaming in the distance. A few hundred yards farther, and they vanished altogether. The moon went down; around about was silence. Now a noise was heard louder and more solemn than the rustle of the reeds. Skshetuski came near screaming with joy,--the woods were on both sides of the river.

He turned then to the bank and came out of the reeds. The pine-forest began here, beyond the rushes and reeds. The odor of rosin came to his nostrils; here and there in the depths shone the fern, like silver. He fell a second time on his knees, and kissed the earth in prayer. He was saved!

Then he entered the forest darkness, asking himself where he should go, where those forests would take him, where the king and the army were. His journey was not finished; it was not easy, it was not safe; but when he thought that he had come out of Zbaraj,--that he had stolen through the guards, swamps, tabors, and almost half a million of enemies,--then it seemed to him that all dangers were passed, that that forest was a clear highway which would lead him straight to his Majesty the King; and that wretched-looking, hungry, shivering man, bespattered with his own blood, with red filth, and black mud, passed on with joy in his heart, and hope that he would soon return in different circumstances and with greater power.

"They will not be left hungry and hopeless," thought he of his friends in Zbaraj, "for the king will come."

His heart rejoiced at the near rescue of the prince, the commanding officers, Volodyovski, Zagloba, and all those heroes confined in the ramparts. The forest depths opened before him and covered him with their shade.

CHAPTER LXII.

In the drawing-room of the Court at Toporoff sat three magnates one evening in secret consultation. A number of bright lights were burning on a table covered with maps of the surrounding country; near them lay a tall cap with a dark plume, a field-glass, and a sword with hilt set in pearls, on which was thrown a handkerchief embroidered with a crown, and a pair of elk-skin gloves. Near the table, in a high-armed chair, sat a man about forty years of age, rather small and slender, but powerfully built. He had a swarthy, sallow, wearied face, black eyes, and a Swedish wig of the same color, with long locks falling on his neck and shoulders; a thin black mustache, trimmed upward at the ends, adorned his upper lip. His lower lip with his beard protruded strongly, giving his whole physiognomy a characteristic mark of pride and stubbornness. It was not a beautiful face, but unusually lofty. A sensuous expression, indicating an inclination to pleasure, was combined in it with a certain sleepy torpor and coldness. The eyes were as if smouldering; but it was easy to guess that in a moment of exaltation, joy, or anger they could cast lightnings which not every eye might meet. At the same time kindness and affability were depicted on his countenance.

The black dress, composed of a satin doublet with lace ruffles, from under which a gold chain was visible, increased the distinction of this uncommon figure. On the whole, in spite of sadness and anxiety evident in the face and form, there was something majestic in them. In fact it was the king himself, Yan Kazimir Vaza, who had succeeded his brother Vladislav somewhat less than a year before.

A little behind him, in the half-shade, sat Hieronim Radzeyovski, the starosta of Lomjin, a thick, corpulent, low-set, red-visaged man with the unblushing face of a courtier; and opposite him, at the table, a third personage, leaning on his elbow, looking at the maps representing the country around, raising from time to time his eyes to the king. His face had less majesty, but almost more official distinction, than that of the king. The cool and reasoning face of the statesman was furrowed with cares and thought, the severity of which had not marred his unusual beauty. He had penetrating blue eyes; his complexion was delicate, in spite of his age; a magnificent Polish dress, a beard trimmed in Swedish fashion, and the lofty tuft above his forehead, added still something of senatorial dignity to his features, regular as if chiselled from stone.

This was Yerzy Ossolinski, chancellor of the Crown, a prince of the Roman Empire, an orator, and a diplomat admired by the courts of Europe,--the famous opponent of Yeremi Vishnyevetski.

His unusual abilities turned upon him early in life the attention of preceding reigns, and soon raised him to the highest offices, in virtue of which he guided the ship of state, at the present moment near its final wreck.

But still the chancellor was as if created to be the helmsman of such a ship. Laborious, enduring, wise, looking to the distant future, calculating for long years, he would have directed any other State but the Commonwealth to a safe harbor with a sure and steady hand; for every other State he would have secured internal power and long years of strength,--if he had only been the absolute minister of such a monarch, for example, as the King of France or Spain.

Reared beyond the boundaries of his own country, furnished with foreign models, in spite of all his innate quickness of mind, in spite of long years of practice, he was unable to accustom himself to the helplessness of government in the Commonwealth; and all his life he could not learn to reckon with it, though that was the rock on which all his plans, designs, and efforts were wrecked, though by reason of this he saw now in the future a precipice and ruin, and later died with despair in his heart.

He was a genial theorist who did not know how to be genial in practice, and he fell into a circle of errors without issue. Possessing an idea which might give fruit in the future, he went to the realization of it with the stubbornness of a fanatic, not observing that that idea, saving in theory, might, in view of the actual condition of affairs, bring terrible disasters.

Wishing to strengthen the government and the State, he let loose the terrible Cossack element, not foreseeing that the storm would turn not only against the nobles, the great estates of the magnates, the abuses, license of the nobility, but against the most vital interests of the State itself.

Hmelnitski rose out of the steppes and grew into a giant. On the Commonwealth fell the defeats of Jóltiya Vodi, Korsún, Pilavtsi. At the first step this Hmelnitski joined with the enemy, the Crimean power. Thunderbolt followed thunderbolt; there remained only war and war. The terrible element should have been crushed first of all, so as to use it in the future; but the chancellor, occupied with his idea, was still negotiating and delaying, and still believed even Hmelnitski.

The power of events crushed his theories; it became clearer every day that the results of the chancellor's efforts were directly opposed to his expectations, till at last came Zbaraj and confirmed it most convincingly.

The chancellor was staggering under the burden of regrets, bitterness, and universal hatred. He did that therefore which in times of failure and disaster people do whose faith in themselves is greater than all disasters,--he looked for the guilty.

The whole Commonwealth was to blame, and all the estates,--the past, and the aristocratic structure of the State; but he who fearing lest a rock lying on the incline of a mountain might fall to the bottom, wishes to roll it to the top without calculating the necessary force to do this, only hastens its fall. The chancellor did more and worse, for he called in the rushing and terrible Cossack torrent, not considering that its force could only wash out and carry off the foundation on which the rock was resting.

When he sought then for persons to blame, all eyes were turned upon himself as the cause of the war, the calamities and misfortune. But the king believed in him yet, and believed in him the more because the voice of all without sparing his Majesty accused him in an equal degree with the chancellor.

The king sat therefore in Toporoff suffering and sad, not knowing well what to do, for he had only twenty-five thousand troops. The conscript writs had been sent out too late, and barely a part of the general militia had assembled up to that time. Who was the cause of this delay, and was it not one more mistake of that stubborn policy of the chancellor?--the mystery was lost between the king and the minister; it is enough that both felt disarmed at that moment before the power of Hmelnitski.

What was more important yet, they had no accurate information concerning him. In the camp of the king it was still unknown whether the Khan with all his forces was with Hmelnitski, or only Tugai Bey and a few thousands of the horde were accompanying the Cossacks. This was a matter as important as life or death. With Hmelnitski himself the king might in extremities try his fortune, though the rebellious hetman disposed of ten times greater power. The magic of the king's name meant much for the Cossacks,--more perhaps than the crowds of the general militia of unformed and untrained nobles; but if the Khan were present, it was an impossibility to meet such superior force.

Meanwhile there were the most varied reports on this head, and no one knew anything accurately. The careful Hmelnitski had concentrated his forces; he had not let out a single party of Cossacks or Tartars on purpose, that the king might not capture an informant. The rebellious hetman had another plan,--it was to shut in with a part of his forces Zbaraj, already dying, and appear himself unexpectedly with the whole Tartar and remaining Cossack force before the king, surround him and his army, and deliver him into the hands of the Khan.

It was not without reason then that a cloud covered the royal face, for there is no greater pain for a king than a feeling of weakness. Yan Kazimir leaned impotently on the back of the chair, threw his hands on the table and said, pointing to the maps,--

"These are useless. Get me informants."

"There is nothing I wish for more," answered Ossolinski.

"Have the scouts returned?"

"They have returned, but brought no one."

"Not a single prisoner?"

"Only neighboring peasants who know nothing."

"But Pan Pelka, has he returned? He is a splendid partisan."

"Your Majesty," said the starosta of Lomjin, from behind the chair. "Pan Pelka has not returned, and he will not, for he is killed."

A moment of silence followed. The king fixed his gloomy look on the flickering light, and began to drum with his fingers on the table. "Have you no help?" asked he at length.

"Wait!" said the chancellor, with importance.

The forehead of Yan Kazimir was covered with wrinkles, "Wait?" repeated he; "and Vishnyevetski and the commanders will be in worse condition under Zbaraj."

"They will hold out awhile yet," said Radzeyovski, carelessly.

"You might be silent if you have nothing good to offer," said the king.

"I have my own counsel, your Majesty."

"What is it?"

"To send some one as if to negotiate with Hmelnitski at Zbaraj. The envoy will discover whether the Khan is there in his own person, and will report when he returns."

"Impossible!" said the king. "Now when we have proclaimed him a rebel and laid a price on his head, have given the baton of the Zaporojians to Zabuski, it is not becoming our dignity to enter into negotiations with him."

"Then send to the Khan," said the starosta.

The king turned an inquiring glance on the chancellor, who raised upon him his blue, severe eye, and after a moment's thought answered: "The counsel would be good were it not that Hmelnitski, beyond a doubt, would detain the envoy, and for this reason it would serve no purpose."

Yan Kazimir waved his hand. "I see," said he, slowly, "that you have no plan; then I will tell you mine. I will order to horse, and move with the whole army to Zbaraj. Let the will of God be done! There we shall discover whether the Khan is present or not."

The chancellor knew the daring of the king, restrainable by nothing, and he doubted not that he was ready to do this. On the other hand he knew from experience that when the king had something in view and was opposed in the undertaking, no dissuasion was of avail. Therefore he did not oppose him at once, he even praised the idea; but he dissuaded from haste, explained to the king that it could be done to-morrow or the day after. In the mean while favorable news might come. Every day would increase the dissension of the rabble, weakened by disasters at Zbaraj and by the news of his Majesty's approach. The rebellion might dissolve from the presence of the king, as snow from the rays of the sun, but time was necessary.

"The king bears within himself the salvation of the whole Commonwealth, and responsibility before God and posterity. He should not expose himself, especially since, in case of misfortune, the forces at Zbaraj would be lost beyond redemption."

"Do what you like, if I only have an informant tomorrow."

Again a moment of silence. An enormous golden moon shone in through the window; but it was darker in the room, for the tapers needed trimming.

"What o'clock?" asked the king.

"Almost midnight," answered Radzeyovski.

"I will not sleep to-night. I will go around the camp, and do you go with me. Where are Ubald and Artsishevski?"

"In the camp. I will go and order the horses," answered the starosta.

He approached the door. At that moment there was some movement in the antechamber; a lively conversation was audible, the sound of hurried steps; then the doors opened half-way, and Tyzenhauz, the personal attendant of the king, rushed in panting.

"Your Majesty," cried he, "an officer has come from Zbaraj!"

The king sprang from his chair; the chancellor rose too, and from the mouths of both came the cry: "Impossible!"

"Yes, he is standing in the antechamber."

"Bring him here!" cried the king, clapping his hands. "Let him end our anxiety. This way with him, in the name of the Most Holy Mother!"

Tyzenhauz vanished through the door, and after a moment there appeared instead of him some tall, unknown form.

"Nearer!" cried the king, "nearer! We are glad to see you."

The officer pushed up to the table; and at sight of him, the king, the chancellor, and the starosta of Lomjin drew back in astonishment. Before them stood a kind of frightful-looking man, or rather an apparition. Rags torn to shreds barely covered his emaciated body; his face was blue, covered with mud and blood, his eyes burning with feverish light; his black tangled beard fell toward his breast; the odor of corpses went forth from him round about, and his legs trembled to such a degree that he was forced to lean on the table.

The king and the two dignitaries looked on him with staring eyes. At that moment the doors opened and a crowd of dignitaries, military and civil, came in; and among them, the generals Ubald and Artsishevski, with Sapieha, vice-chancellor of Lithuania. All stood behind the king, looking at the newly arrived.

The king asked: "Who are you?"

The miserable-looking man tried to speak, but a spasm seized his jaw; his beard began to tremble, and he was able only to whisper: "From--Zbaraj!"

"Give him wine!" said a voice.

In the twinkle of an eye a goblet was filled; he drank it with difficulty. By this time the chancellor had taken off his own cloak and covered the man's shoulders with it.

"Can you speak now?" inquired the king after a time.

"I can," he answered, with a voice of more confidence.

"Who are you?"

"Yan Skshetuski, colonel of hussars."

"In whose service?"

"The voevoda of Rus."

A murmur spread through the hall.

"What news have you, what news have you?" asked the king, feverishly.

"Suffering--hunger--the grave--"

The king covered his eyes. "Jesus of Nazareth! Jesus of Nazareth!" said he in a low voice. After a while he asked again: "Can you hold out long?"

"There is lack of powder. The enemy is on the ramparts."

"In force?"

"Hmelnitski--the Khan with all his hordes."

"Is the Khan there?"

"He is."

Deep silence followed. Those present looked at one another; uncertainty was on every face.

"How could you hold out?" asked the chancellor, with an accent of doubt.

At these words Skshetuski raised his head, as if new power entered him. A flash of pride passed over his face, and he answered with a voice strong beyond expectation: "Twenty assaults repulsed, sixteen battles in the field won, seventy-five sallies."

Again silence followed.

Then the king straightened himself, shook his wig as a lion would his mane, on his sallow face came out a blush, and his eyes flashed. "As God lives!" cried he, "I've enough of these councils, of this halting, of this delay! Whether the Khan is there or not, whether the general militia has come or not, I have enough of this! We will move to-day on Zbaraj."

"To Zbaraj! to Zbaraj!" was repeated by a number of powerful voices.

The face of the newly arrived brightened like the dawn. "Your Majesty, we will live and die with you."

At these words the noble heart of the king grew soft as wax, and without regarding the repulsive appearance of the knight, he pressed his head with his hands and said: "You are dearer to me than others in satin. By the Most Holy Mother, men for less service are rewarded with starostaships. But what you have done will not pass unrewarded. I am your debtor."

Others began immediately to call out after the king: "There has been no greater knight!" "He is the first among the men of Zbaraj!" "You have won immortal glory!"

"And how did you push through the Cossacks and Tartars?"

"I hid in the swamp, the reeds, went through the woods--got astray--ate nothing--"

"Give him to eat!" cried the king.

"To eat!" repeated others.

"Clothe him!"

"They will give you horses and clothing to-morrow," said the king again. "You shall want for nothing."

All, following the king, surpassed one another in praises of the knight. Then they began again to hurl questions at him, to which he answered with the greatest difficulty, for growing weakness had seized him; he was barely half-conscious. Meanwhile they brought him refreshments; and at the same time entered the priest Tsetsishovski, the chaplain of the king.

The dignitaries made way for him, for he was a very learned man, and respected. His word had almost more weight with the king than that of the chancellor, and from the pulpit he gave utterance to words such as few would dare to say at the Diet. The priest was surrounded then, and they began to tell him that an officer had come from Zbaraj; that the prince was there, though in hunger and wretchedness, and was still beating the Khan, who was present in his own person, as well as Hmelnitski, who during the whole past year had not lost so many men as at Zbaraj; finally, that the king was going to move to his succor, even if he had to lose his whole army.

The priest listened in silence, moving his lips and looking every moment at the emaciated knight, who was eating at the time, for the king had commanded him not to mind his presence; and he even waited on him himself, and from time to time drank to him from a little silver goblet.

"What is the name of this knight?" asked the priest at last.

"Skshetuski."

"Yan?"

"Yes."

"Colonel with the voevoda of Rus?"

"Yes."

The priest raised his wrinkled face, prayed again, and said: "Let us praise the name of the Lord, for undiscoverable are the ways by which he brings a man to happiness and peace. Amen! I know this officer."

Skshetuski heard, and involuntarily turned his eyes to the face of the priest; but his face, form, and voice were completely unknown to him.

"You are the man out of the whole army who undertook to pass through the enemy's camp?" asked the priest.

"A worthy man tried before me, but he perished."

"The greater is your service, since after him you dared. I see by your suffering that the road must have been an awful one. God looked on your sacrifice, on your virtue, on your youth, and he led you through."

Suddenly the priest turned to Yan Kazimir. "Your gracious Majesty," said he, "it is then your unchangeable decision to march to the rescue of the voevoda of Rus?"

"To your prayers, father," answered the king, "I commit the country, the army, and myself, for I know it is an awful undertaking. But I cannot permit that the prince should perish behind those unfortunate ramparts, with such knights as this officer."

"God send down victory!" cried a number of voices.

The priest raised his hands to heaven, and silence followed in the hall. "I bless you in the name of the Father, Son, and Holy Ghost."

"Amen!" said the king.

"Amen!" repeated all the voices.

Peace was spread over the face of Yan Kazimir after his previous suffering; but his eyes shot forth unusual gleams. Among all assembled rose the buzz of conversation about the impending campaign, for it was much doubted yet whether the king could move at once. He took his sword, however, from the table, and nodded to Tyzenhauz to gird him.

"When does your Majesty think of marching?" asked the chancellor.

"God has granted a pleasant night," said the king; "the horses will not be heated. Commander of the camp," he added, turning to the dignitaries, "order the march to be sounded!"

The commander of the camp left the room at once. Ossolinski, the chancellor, said with quiet dignity that all were not ready; that they could not move the wagons before day. But the king answered immediately: "Let that man remain to whom the wagons are dearer than the country."

The hall grew empty. Each man hastened to his standard, put everything in order, and prepared for the march. Only the king, the chancellor, the priest, with Skshetuski and Tyzenhauz, remained in the room.

"Gentlemen," said the priest, "you have learned already from this officer what you had to learn. He should now get rest, for he is barely able to stand on his feet. Allow me, your Majesty, to take him to my quarters for the night!"

"All right, father," replied the king. "Your demand is just. Let Tyzenhauz and some one else conduct him, for surely he cannot walk alone. Go, go, dear friend," said he; "no one has earned his rest better than you. And remember that I am your debtor; henceforth I shall forget myself rather than you."

Tyzenhauz caught Skshetuski under the arm and they passed into the antechamber. They met Sapieha, who supported the tottering knight on the other side. The priest went in advance, before him a boy with a lantern; but the boy carried it to no purpose, for the night was clear, calm, and warm. The great golden moon sailed over Toporoff like a boat. From the square of the camp came the bustle of men, the creaking of wagons, the noise of trumpets sounding the tattoo. At some distance, in front of the church lighted by the gleams of the moon, were already visible crowds of soldiers, infantry and cavalry. Horses were neighing in the village. To the creaking of wagons was joined the clatter of chains and the dull thump of cannon. The uproar increased every moment.

"They are moving already!" said the priest.

"On Zbaraj--to the rescue--" whispered Pan Yan. And whether from joy or from the toils he had endured, or from both together, he grew so weak that Tyzenhauz and the starosta were obliged almost to drag him along.

When they were turning to the priests' house they went among the soldiers standing in front of the building. These were the cavalry of Sapieha and the infantry of Artsishevski. Not in rank yet for the march, they stood without order, crowded in places and hindering the passage.

"Out of the road, out of the road!" cried the priest.

"Who wants the road?"

"An officer from Zbaraj--"

"With the forehead to him! with the forehead to him!" cried many voices.

A way was opened at once; but some crowded the more to see the hero. They looked with astonishment on that suffering, on that terrible face, lighted by the gleam of the moon, and they whispered in wonder: "From Zbaraj! from Zbaraj!"

The priest brought Skshetuski to the house with the greatest difficulty. After he had been bathed and washed from the mud and blood, he had him put in the bed of the priest of the place, and went out himself at once to the army, which was moving to the march.

Skshetuski was half conscious. Fever did not let him sleep immediately; he knew not where he was, or what had happened. He heard only the noise,--the tramp, the rumble of wagons, the thundering tread of infantry, the shouts of soldiers, then the blare of trumpets; and all this was mingled in his ears in one enormous sound. "The army is moving," he muttered. That sound began to retreat, to weaken, to vanish, to melt, till at last silence embraced Toporoff. Then it seemed to Skshetuski that together with the bed he was flying into some bottomless abyss.

CHAPTER LXIII.

Skshetuski slept a number of days, and when he woke he had a violent fever, and suffered long. He talked of Zbaraj, of the prince, of the starosta of Krasnovstav; he talked with Pan Michael, with Zagloba; he cried, "Not this way!" to Pan Longin; of the princess alone he spoke not a word. It was clear that the great power with which he had confined in himself the memory of her did not desert him a moment even in weakness and pain. At that moment, he seemed to see hanging over him the chubby face of Jendzian, precisely as he saw it when the prince after the battle of Konstantinoff sent him with troops to Zaslav to cut down lawless bands, and Jendzian appeared to him unexpectedly at his night quarters. This face brought confusion to his mind; for it seemed to him that time halted in its flight, and that nothing had changed from that period. So he is again at Khomor, is sleeping in the cottage, is marching to Tarnopol to give over his troops; Krívonos, beaten at Konstantinoff, has fled to Hmelnitski; Jendzian has come from Gushchi, and sits with him. Skshetuski wanted to talk,--wanted to order the lad to have the horse saddled,--but could not. And again it comes into his head that he is not at Khomor; that since that time too was the taking of Bar. Here Skshetuski halted in his pain, and his unfortunate head sank in darkness. He knows nothing now, sees nothing; but at times out of that chaos comes the heroism of Zbaraj, the siege. He is not at Khomor then? But still Jendzian is sitting over him, bending toward him. Through an opening in the shutters a narrow bright ray comes into the room, and lights completely the face of the youth, full of care and sympathy.

"Jendzian!" cried Skshetuski, suddenly.

"Oh, my master! do you know me already?" cried the youth, and fell at the feet of his master. "I thought you would never wake again!"

A moment of silence followed; only the sobbing of the youth could be heard as he continued to press the feet of his master.

"Where am I?" asked Skshetuski.

"In Toporoff. You came from Zbaraj to the king. Praise be to God!"

"And where is the king?"

"He went with the army to rescue the prince.'"

Silence followed. Tears of joy continued to flow along the face of Jendzian, who after a while began to repeat with a voice of emotion: "That I should look on your body again!" Then he opened the shutters and the window.

Fresh morning air came into the room, and with it the bright light of day. With this light came all Skshetuski's presence of mind. Jendzian sat at the foot of the bed.

"Then I came out of Zbaraj?"

"Yes, my master. No one could do that but you, and on your account the king went to the rescue."

"Pan Podbipienta tried before me, but he perished--"

"Oh, for God's sake! Pan Podbipienta,--such a liberal man, so virtuous! My breath leaves me. How could they kill such a strong man?"

"They shot him with arrows."

"And Pan Volodyovski and Zagloba?"

"They were well when I came out."

"Praise be to God! They are great friends of yours, my master--But the priest won't let me talk."

Jendzian was silent, and for a time was working at something with his head. Thoughtfulness was expressed on his ruddy face. After a while he said: "My master?"

"Well, what is it?"

"What will be done with the fortune of Pan Podbipienta? Very likely he has villages and every kind of property beyond measure--unless he has left it to his friends; for, as I hear, he has no relatives."

Skshetuski made no answer. Jendzian knew then that he did not like the question, and began as follows:--

"But God be praised that Pan Zagloba and Pan Volodyovski are well. I thought that the Tartars had caught them. We went through a world of trouble together--But the priest won't let me talk. Oh, my master, I thought that I should never see them again; for the horde so pressed upon us that there was no help."

"Then you were with Pan Volodyovski and Zagloba? They did not tell me anything about that."

"For they didn't know whether I was dead or alive."

"And where did the horde press on you so?"

"Beyond Ploskiri, on the road to Zbaraj. For, my master, we travelled far beyond Yampol--But the priest Tsetsishovski won't let me talk."

A moment of silence.

"May God reward you for all your good wishes and labors," said Skshetuski; "for I know why you went there. I was there before you to no purpose."

"Oh, my master, if only that priest-- But this is how it is. 'I must go with the king to Zbaraj, and do you,' says he, 'take care of your master; don't you tell him anything, for the soul will go out of him.'"

Pan Yan had parted long since from every hope to such a degree that even these words of Jendzian did not rouse in him the least spark. He lay for a time motionless, and then inquired: "Where did you come from to Tsetsishovski and the army?"

"The wife of the castellan, Pani Vitovska, sent me from Zamost to inform her husband that she would join him at Toporoff. She is a brave lady, my master, and wishes to be with the army, so as not to be away from her husband. I came to Toporoff the day before you. She will be here soon,--ought to be here now. But what if he has gone away with the king?"

"I don't understand how you could be in Zamost when you went with Volodyovski and Zagloba beyond Yampol. Why didn't you come to Zbaraj with them?"

"You see, my master, the horde pressed us sorely. There was no help. So they two alone resisted a whole chambul, and I fled and never drew bridle till I reached Zamost."

"It was happy they were not killed; but I thought you were a better fellow. Was it manly of you to leave them in such straits?"

"But, my master, if there had been only three of us, I should not have left them, you may be sure; but there were four of us; therefore they threw themselves against the horde, and ordered me to save--if I were sure that joy wouldn't kill you--for beyond Yampol we found--but since the priest--"

Skshetuski began to look at the youth, and to open and shut his eyes like a man waking from sleep. Suddenly it seemed as though something had broken within him, for he grew pale, sat up in the bed, and cried with a thundering voice: "Who was with you?"

"My master, my master!" called the youth, struck with the change that had come on the face of the knight.

"Who was with you?" cried Skshetuski; and seizing Jendzian by the shoulder, he shook him, began himself to tremble as in a fever, and press the youth in his iron hands.

"I'll tell anyhow," shouted Jendzian, "let the priest do what he likes. The princess was with us, and she is now with Pani Vitovska."

Pan Yan grew rigid; he closed his eyes, and his head fell heavily on the pillow.

"Help!" cried Jendzian. "Surely, my master, you have breathed your last. Help! What have I done? Better I had been silent. Oh, for God's sake! my master, dearest master, but speak! For God's sake! the priest was right. My master, my master!"

"Oh, this is nothing!" said Skshetuski at length. "Where is she?"

"Praise be to God that you have revived! Better for me to say nothing. She is with Pani Vitovska; you will soon see them here. Praise be to God, my master! only don't die; you will see them soon. The priest gave her to Pani Vitovska for safe keeping, because there are libertines in the army. Bogun respected her, but misfortune is easily found. I had a world of trouble; but I told the soldiers, 'She is a relative of Prince Yeremi,' and they respected her. I had to give away no small money on the road."

Skshetuski lay motionless again; but his eyes were open, turned to the ceiling, and his face very serious. It was evident he was praying. When he had finished, he sprang up, sat on the bed, and said: "Give me my clothes, and have the horse saddled."

"If you knew, my master, what a plenty of everything there is; for the king before going gave much, and others gave. And there are three splendid horses in the stable--if I only had one like them--but you would better lie and rest a little, for you have no strength yet."

"There is nothing the matter with me. I can sit on a horse. In the name of the living God, make haste!"

"I know that your body is of iron; let it be as you say! But defend me from the priest! Here are your clothes; better cannot be had from the Armenian merchants. You can choose, and I'll tell them to bring wine, for I told the priest's servant to heat some."

Jendzian occupied himself with the food, and Skshetuski began to put on hastily the clothes presented by the king and others. But from time to time he seized the youth by the shoulders and pressed him to his bosom. Jendzian told him everything from the beginning,--how Bogun, stricken down by Volodyovski, but already partly recovered, had met him in Vlodava, and how he had learned of the princess from him, and received the baton; how he had gone subsequently with Volodyovski and Zagloba to Valadinka, and having killed the witch and Cheremís, had taken away the princess; and finally, what peril they were in while fleeing before the forces of Burlai.

"Pan Zagloba killed Burlai," interrupted Skshetuski, feverishly.

"He is a valiant man," answered Jendzian. "I have never seen his equal; for one is brave, another eloquent, a third cunning, but all these are sitting together in Zagloba. But the worst of all that happened was in those woods behind Ploskiri, when the horde pursued us. Pan Volodyovski with Zagloba remained behind to attract them and stop the pursuit, I rushed off sidewise toward Konstantinoff, leaving Zbaraj; for I thought this way,--that after they had killed the little man and Zagloba they would pursue us to Zbaraj. Indeed, I don't know how the Lord in his mercy rescued the little man and Pan Zagloba. I thought they were cut to pieces. Meanwhile I with the princess slipped through between Hmelnitski, who was marching from Konstantinoff, and Zbaraj, to which the Tartars were marching."

"They did not go there, for Pan Kushel stopped them. But hurry!"

"Yes, if I had known that! But I did not know it; therefore I pressed through with the princess between the Tartars and the Cossacks, as through a defile. Happily the country was empty; nowhere did we meet a living man, neither in the villages nor in the towns, for all had fled, each where he could, before the Tartars. But my soul was sitting on my shoulders from terror, lest that should catch me which I did not escape in the end."

Skshetuski stopped dressing and asked: "What was that?"

"This, my master. I came upon the division of the Cossack Donyéts, brother of that Horpyna with whom the princess was lodged in the ravine. Fortunately I knew him well, for he saw me with Bogun. I brought him a greeting from his sister, showed him Bogun's baton, and told him all, how Bogun had sent me for the lady, and how he was waiting for me beyond Vlodava. But being Bogun's friend, he knew that his sister had been guarding the lady. As a matter of course, I thought he would let me go and give me provisions and money for the road; but, said he: 'Ahead there the general militia is assembling; you'll fall into the hands of the Poles. Stay with me. We'll go to Hmelnitski, to his camp; there the girl will be safest of all, for there Hmelnitski himself will take care of her for Bogun.' When he told me this I thought I should die, for what could I say to it? I said then: 'Bogun is waiting for me, and my life depends on bringing her at once.' But he said: 'We'll tell Bogun; but don't you go, for the Poles are on that side.' Then I began to dispute, and he disputed, till at last he said: 'It is a wonder to me that you are afraid to go among the Cossacks. Ho! ho! are you not a traitor?' Then I saw there was no other help but to slip away by night, for he had already begun to suspect me. Seven sweats came out on me, my master. I had prepared everything for the road, when Pan Pelka, from the armies of the king, fell upon us that night."

"Pan Pelka?" asked Pan Yan, holding his breath.

"Yes, my master. A splendid partisan,--Pan Pelka, who was killed the other day. May the Lord light his soul! I don't know whether there is any one who could lead a detachment better and creep up to the enemy better than he, unless Volodyovski alone. Pan Pelka came then, and cut up the detachment of Donyéts so that not a foot got away. They took Donyéts himself prisoner. They drew him on a stake with oxen a couple of weeks ago,--served him right! But with Pan Pelka I had trouble not a little, for he was a man desperately intent on the virtue of women,--God light his soul! I was afraid that the princess, who had escaped harm from the Cossacks, would be worse treated by her own. But I told Pan Pelka that the lady was a relative of our prince. And I must tell you that he, whenever he mentioned our prince, removed his hat, and was always preparing to enter his service. He respected the princess therefore, and conducted us to Zamost to the king; and there the priest Tsetsishovski--he is a very holy priest, my master--took us in care, and gave the lady to Pani Vitovska, wife of the castellan of Sandomir."

Skshetuski drew a deep breath, then threw himself on the neck of Jendzian. "You shall be a friend to me, a brother, not a servant. When was Pani Vitovska to come here?"

"The week after I left, but it is now ten days. You lay eight days without consciousness."

"Let us go, let us go!" exclaimed Skshetuski, "for joy is tearing me to pieces."

But before he had finished speaking the tramp of horses was heard outside, and the window was suddenly darkened by horses and men.

Skshetuski saw through the glass, first the old priest Tsetsishovski, and then the emaciated faces of Zagloba, Volodyovski, Kushel, and other acquaintances among the red dragoons of the prince. A shout of joy was given forth, and in a moment a crowd of knights with the priest at the head of them burst into the room.

"Peace concluded at Zborovo, the siege raised!" cried the priest.

But Skshetuski inferred this immediately by the look of his companions of Zbaraj; and at once he was in the embraces of Zagloba and Volodyovski, who disputed for him with each other.

"They told us that you were alive," cried Zagloba, "but the joy is the greater that we see you so soon in health. We have come here for you, purposely. Yan, you don't know with what glory you have covered yourself, and what reward awaits you."

"The king has rewarded you," said the priest, "but the King of Kings has provided something better."

"I know already," said Skshetuski. "May God reward you! Jendzian has told all."

"And joy did not kill you? So much the better! Vivat Skshetuski! vivat the princess!" shouted Zagloba. "Well, Yan, we didn't whisper a word to you about her, for we didn't know that she was alive. But Jendzian is a cunning rogue; he escaped with her, *vulpes astuta!* The prince is waiting for you both. Oh, we went for her to Yagorlik. I killed the hellish monster that was guarding her. Those twelve boys got out of your sight, but now you'll see them, and more. I'll have grandchildren, gentlemen! Jendzian, tell us if you met great obstacles. Imagine to yourself that I with Pan Michael checked the whole horde. I rushed first on the Tartar regiment. They were trembling before us; nothing could help them. Pan Michael stood up well too. Where is my daughter? Let me see my daughter."

"God give you happiness, Yan!" said the little knight, taking Skshetuski again by the shoulders.

"God reward you for all you have done for me! Words fail me. My life and blood would not suffice to repay," answered Skshetuski.

"Enough of this!" cried Zagloba. "Peace is concluded,--a fool's peace, gentlemen, but the position was difficult. It is well that we have left that pestilent Zbaraj. There will be peace now, gentlemen. It is by our labors, especially mine; for if Burlai had been living the negotiations would have come to nothing. We'll go to the wedding. After that, Yan, keep your eyes open. But you cannot guess what a wedding present the prince has for you! I'll tell you some other time; but where the hangman is my daughter? Let me have my daughter. Bogun won't get her this time; first he'll have to break the rope that binds him. Where is my dearest daughter?"

"I was just getting into the saddle to meet Pani Vitovska," said Skshetuski. "Let us go, for I am losing my senses."

"Come on, gentlemen! Let us go with him, not to lose time. Come on!"

"The lady of Sandomir cannot be far distant," said the priest.

"To horse!" added Pan Michael.

But Skshetuski was already outside the door, and sprang on his horse as lightly as if he had not just risen from a bed of sickness. Jendzian kept close to his side, for he preferred not to be alone with the priest. Volodyovski and Zagloba joined them, and they rode as fast as their horses could gallop in advance of all. The whole party of nobles and red dragoons flew along by the Toporoff road like poppy leaves borne by the wind.

"Come on!" cried Zagloba, beating his horse with his heels.

And so they flew on about ten furlongs, till at the turn of the highway they saw before them a line of wagons and carriages surrounded by a number of attendants. Seeing armed men in front of them, some of these hurried with all speed to inquire who they were.

"Ours, from the king's army!" cried Zagloba. "And who is coming there?"

"The lady of Sandomir," was the answer. Such emotion seized Skshetuski that not knowing what he did, he slipped from the horse and stood tottering at the roadside. He removed his cap, his temples were covered with drops of perspiration, and he trembled in every limb in presence of his happiness. Pan Michael sprang also from the saddle, and caught his enfeebled friend by the shoulder.

Behind them all the others formed with uncovered heads at the side of the highway. Meanwhile the line of wagons and carriages had come up and begun to pass by. In company with Pani Vitovska were travelling a number of other ladies, who looked with astonishment, not understanding what this military procession at the roadside could mean.

At last, in the centre of the retinue, appeared a carriage richer than the rest. The eyes of the knights beheld through its open windows the dignified countenance of the gray-haired lady, and at her side the sweet and beautiful face of the princess.

"Daughter!" roared Zagloba, rushing straight to the carriage, "daughter! Skshetuski is with us, my daughter!"

They began to cry, "Stop! stop!" along the line. Hurry and confusion followed; then Kushel and Volodyovski conducted or rather drew Skshetuski to the carriage; he had weakened altogether, and became heavier every moment in their hands. His head hung upon his breast; he could walk no farther, and fell on his knees at the steps of the carriage.

But a moment later the strong and beautiful arms of the princess held his weakened and emaciated head.

Zagloba, seeing the astonishment of the lady of Sandomir, cried: "This is Skshetuski, the hero of Zbaraj. He worked through the enemy; he saved the army, the prince, the whole Commonwealth. May God bless them, and long may they live!"

"Long may they live! Vivant! vivant!" cried the nobles.

"Long may they live! Long may they live!" repeated the Vishnyevetski dragoons, till the thunder of their voices was heard over the fields of Toporoff.

"To Tarnopol, to the prince, to the wedding!" cried Zagloba. "Well, daughter, your sorrows are over, and for Bogun the executioner and the sword."

The priest Tsetsishovski had his eyes raised to heaven, and his lips repeated the wonderful words: "They sowed in tears, and reaped in joy."

Skshetuski was seated in the carriage at the side of the princess, and the retinue moved on. The day was wonderfully bright; the oak-groves and the fields were floating in sunlight. Low down on the fallow land, and higher above them, and still higher in the blue air drifted here and there silver threads of spider-web, which in the later autumn cover the fields in those parts as if with snow. And there was great stillness all around; but the horses snorted distinctly in the retinue.

"Pan Michael," said Zagloba, knocking his stirrup against that of Volodyovski, "something has caught me by the throat, and holds me as in that hour when Pan Longin--eternal rest to him!--went out from Zbaraj. But when I think that these two have found each other at last, it is as light in my heart as if I had drunk a quart at a draught. If the accident of marriage does not strike you, in old age we'll nurse their children. Every one is born for something special, Pan Michael, and both of us it seems are better for war than wedlock."

The little knight made no answer, but began to move his mustaches more vigorously than usual.

They were going to Toporoff and thence to Tarnopol, where they were to join Prince Yeremi, and thence with his troops to the wedding at Lvoff. On the way Zagloba told the lady of Sandomir what had happened recently. She learned therefore that the king, after a murderous, indecisive battle, had concluded a treaty with the Khan, not over favorable, but securing peace to the Commonwealth, for some time at least. Hmelnitski in virtue of the treaty remained hetman, and had the right to select for himself forty thousand registered Cossacks, for which concession he swore loyalty and obedience to the king and the estates.

"It is an undoubted fact," said Zagloba, "that it will come to war again with Hmelnitski; but if only the baton does not pass by our prince, all will go differently."

"Tell Skshetuski the most important thing," said Volodyovski, urging his horse nearer.

"True," answered Zagloba, "I wanted to begin with that, but I couldn't catch my breath till now. You know nothing, Yan, of what has happened since you came out,--that Bogun is a captive of the prince."

Skshetuski and the princess were astonished at this unexpected news to such a degree that they could not speak a word. Helena merely raised her hands, a moment of silence followed; then she asked: "How? In what manner?"

"The finger of God is there," answered Zagloba,--"nothing else but the finger of God. The negotiations were concluded, and we were just marching out of that pestilent Zbaraj. The prince hurried with the cavalry to the left wing to watch lest the horde should attack the army, for frequently they do not observe treaties; when suddenly a leader with three hundred horse rushed upon the cavalry of the prince."

"Only Bogun could do such a thing," said Skshetuski.

"It was he too. But it is not for Cossacks to fall upon soldiers of Zbaraj. Pan Michael surrounded and cut them to pieces; and Bogun, wounded by him a second time, went into captivity. He has no luck with Pan Michael, and he must be convinced of it now, since that was the third time he tried him; but he was only looking for death."

"It appeared," added Volodyovski, "that Bogun wished to reach Zbaraj from Valadinka; but the road was a long one. He failed; and when he learned that peace was concluded, his mind was confused from rage, and he cared for nothing."

"Who draws the sword will perish by the sword, for such is the fickleness of fortune," said Zagloba. "He is a mad Cossack, and the madder since he is desperate. A terrible uproar arose on his account between us and ruffiandom. We thought that it would come to war again, for the prince cried first of all that they had broken the treaty. Hmelnitski wanted to save Bogun; but the Khan was enraged at him, for, said he, 'he has exposed my word and my oath to contempt.' The Khan threatened Hmelnitski with war, and sent a messenger to the king with notice that Bogun was a private robber, and with a request that the prince would not hesitate, but treat Bogun as a bandit. It is probable too that it was important for the Khan to get the captives away in quiet. Of these the Tartars have taken so many that it will be possible to buy a man in Stamboul for two hob-nails."

"What did the prince do with Bogun?" inquired Skshetuski, unquietly.

"The prince was about to give orders to shave a stake for him at once, but he changed his mind and said: 'I'll give him to Skshetuski; let him do what he likes with him.' Now the Cossack is in Tarnopol under ground; the barber is taking care of his head. My God, how many times the soul tried to go out of that man! Never have dogs torn the skin of any wolf as we have his. Pan Michael alone bit him three times. But he is a solid piece; though, to tell the truth, an unhappy man. But let the hangman light him! I have no longer any ill-feeling against him, except that he threatened me terribly and without cause; for I drank with him, associated with him as with an equal, till he raised his hand against you, my daughter. I might have finished him at Rozlogi. But I know of old that there is no thankfulness in the world, and there are few who give good for good. Let him--" Here Zagloba began to nod his head. "And what will you do with him, Yan?" asked he. "The soldiers say you will make an outrider of him, for he is a showy fellow; but I cannot believe you would do that."

"Surely I shall not. He is a soldier of eminent daring, and because he is unhappy is another reason that I should not disgrace him with any servile function."

"May God forgive him everything!" said the princess.

"Amen!" answered Zagloba. "He prays to Death, as to a mother, to take him, and he surely would have found it if he had not been late at Zbaraj."

All grew silent, meditating on the marvellous changes of fortune, till in the distance appeared Grabovo, where they stopped for their first refreshments. They found there a crowd of soldiers returning from Zborovo; Vitovski, the castellan of Sandomir, who was going with his regiment to meet his wife, and Marek Sobieski, with Pshiyemski and many nobles of the general militia who were returning home by that road. The castle at Grabovo had been burned, as well as all the other buildings; but as the day was wonderful,--warm and calm,--without seeking shelter for their heads, all disposed themselves in the oak-grove under the open sky. Large supplies of food and drink were brought, and the servants immediately set about preparing the evening meal. Pan Vitovski had tents pitched in the oak grove for the ladies and the dignitaries,--a real camp, as it were. The knights collected before the tents, wishing to see the princess and Pan Yan. Others spoke of the past war; those who had not been at Zbaraj asked the soldiers of the prince for the details of the siege; and it was noisy and joyous, especially since God had given so beautiful a day.

Zagloba, telling for the thousandth time how he had killed Burlai, took the lead among the nobles; Jendzian, among the servants who were preparing the meal. But the adroit young fellow seized the fitting moment, and drawing Skshetuski a little aside, bent obediently to his feet. "My master," said he, "I should like to beg a favor."

"It would be difficult for me to refuse you anything," answered Skshetuski, "since through you everything that is best has come to pass."

"I thought at once," said the youth, "that you were preparing some reward for me."

"Tell me what you want."

Jendzian's ruddy face grew dark, and from his eyes shot hatred and stubbornness. "One favor I ask,--nothing more do I want. Give me Bogun, my master."

"Bogun!" said Skshetuski, with astonishment. "What do you want to do with him?"

"Oh, my master, I'll think of that. I'll see that my own is not lost, and that he shall pay me with interest for having put me to shame in Chigirin. I know surely that you will have him put out of the way. Let me pay him first."

Skshetuski's brows contracted. "Impossible!" said he, with decision.

"Oh, for God's sake! I'd rather die," cried Jendzian, piteously. "To think that I have lived for disgrace to fasten to me."

"Ask what you like, I'll refuse you nothing; but this cannot be. Ask your grandfather if it is not more sinful to keep such a promise than to abandon it. Do not touch God's punishing hand with your own, lest you suffer. Be ashamed, Jendzian! This man as it is prays to God for death; and besides he is wounded and in bonds. What do you want to be to him,--an executioner? Do you want to put shame on a man in bonds, to kill a wounded man? Are you a Tartar or a Cossack man-slayer? While I live I will not permit this, and do not mention it to me!"

In the voice of Pan Yan there was so much power and will that the youth lost every hope at once; therefore he added with a tearful voice: "When he is well he could manage two like me, and when he is sick it is not becoming to take vengeance. When shall I pay him for what I have suffered?"

"Leave vengeance to God," said Pan Yan.

The youth opened his mouth. He wished to say something more, inquire about something; but Pan Yan turned away and went to the tents, before which a large assembly had collected. In the centre sat Pani Vitovska, at her side the princess, around them the knights. In front of them stood Zagloba, cap in hand. He was telling those who had been only at Zborovo of the siege of Zbaraj. All listened to him with breathless attention; their faces moved with emotion, and those who had not taken part in the siege regretted that they had not been there. Pan Yan sat near the princess, and taking her hand, pressed it to his lips: then they leaned one against the other and sat quietly. The sun was already leaving the sky, and evening was gradually coming. Skshetuski was lost in attention, as if hearing something new for himself. Zagloba wiped his brows, and his voice sounded louder and louder. Fresh memory or imagination brought before the eyes of the knights those bloody deeds. They saw therefore the ramparts as if surrounded by a sea, and the raging assaults; they heard the tumult and the howling, the roar of cannon and musketry; they saw the prince, in silver armor, standing on the ramparts, amidst the hail of bullets; then suffering, famine; those red nights in which death circled like a great ill-omened bird over the intrenchments; the departure of Podbipienta, of Skshetuski. All listened, sometimes raising their eyes to heaven or grasping their swords, and Zagloba finished thus:--

"It is now one tomb, one mighty mound; and if beneath it are not now lying the glory of the Commonwealth, the flower of its knighthood, the prince voevoda, I, and all of us, whom the Cossacks themselves call the lions of Zbaraj, it is owing to him!" And he pointed to Skshetuski.

"True as life!" cried Marek Sobieski and Pan Pshiyemski.

"Glory to him,--honor, thanks!" strong voices began to cry. "Vivat Skshetuski! vivat the young couple! Long life to the hero!" was cried louder and louder.

Enthusiasm seized all present. Some ran for the goblets; others threw their caps in the air. The soldiers began to rattle their sabres, and soon was heard one general shout: "Glory! glory! Long life!"

Skshetuski, like a true Christian knight, dropped his head obediently; but the princess rose, shook her tresses, a glow came in her face, her eyes were gleaming with pride,--for this knight was to be her husband, and the glory of the husband falls on the wife like the light of the sun on the earth.

Late at night the assembly parted, going in two directions. Vitovski, Pshiyemski, and Sobieski marched with their regiments toward Toporoff; but Skshetuski, with the princess and the squadron of Volodyovski, to Tarnopol. The night was clear as day. Myriads of stars shone in the sky; the moon rose and illuminated the fields covered with spider-webs. The soldiers began to sing. Then white mists rose from the meadows and turned the land as it were into one gigantic lake, shining in the light of the moon.

On such a night Skshetuski once went forth from Zbaraj, and on such a night now he felt the heart of Kurtsevichovna beating near his own.

EPILOGUE.

But this tragedy of history was finished neither at Zborovo nor Zbaraj, and not even the first act of it. Two years later all Cossackdom rushed forth to do battle with the Commonwealth. Hmelnitski rose mightier than ever before; and with him marched the Khan of all the hordes, attended by the same leaders who had fought at Zbaraj,--the wild Tugai Bey, Urum Murza, Artimgirei, Nureddin, Galga, Amurat, and Subahazi. Pillars of flame and groans of men went on before them; thousands of warriors covered the fields, filled the forests; half a million of mouths sent forth shouts of war, and it seemed to men that the end of the Commonwealth had come.

But the Commonwealth had risen from its lethargy, had broken with the past policy of the chancellor, with treaties and negotiations. It was seen at last that the sword alone could win enduring peace. When the king therefore marched against the hostile inundation, there went with him an army of one hundred thousand soldiers and nobles, besides legions of irregulars and attendants.

No one living of the personages in the foregoing narrative was absent. Prince Yeremi Vishnyevetski was there with his whole division, in which were serving, as of old, Skshetuski and Volodyovski, with the volunteer Zagloba; both hetmans, Pototski and Kalinovski, were there, ransomed at that time from Tartar captivity. There were present also Stephen Charnetski, later on the crusher of Karl Gustav, the Swedish king; Pan Pshiyemski, commander of all the artillery; General Ubald: Pan Artsishevski; Marek Sobieski, starosta of Krasnostav, with his brother, Yan Sobieski, starosta of Yavorov, afterward King Yan III.; Ludvik Weyher, voevoda of Pomorie; Yakob, voevoda of Marienburg; Konyetspolski, the standard-bearer; Prince Dominik Zaslavski; the bishops, the dignitaries of the Crown, the senators,--the whole Commonwealth, with its supreme leader the king.

On the fields of Berestechko those many legions met at last, and there was fought one of the greatest battles of history,--a battle the echoes of which thundered through all contemporary Europe. It lasted for three days. During the first two the fates wavered; on the third a general engagement decided the victory.

Prince Yeremi began that engagement; and he was seen in front of the entire left wing as, armorless and bareheaded, he swept like a hurricane over the field against those gigantic legions, formed of all the mounted heroes of the Zaporojie, and all the Tartars,--Crimean, Nogai, and Bélgorod,--of Silistrian and Rumelian Turks, Urumbalis, Janissaries, Serbs, Wallachians, Periotes, and other wild warriors assembled from the Ural, the Caspian, and the swamps of Mæotis to the Danube. As a river vanishes from the eye in the foaming waves of the sea, so vanished from the eye the regiments of the prince in that sea of the enemy. A cloud of dust moved on the plain like a mad whirlwind and covered the combatants.

The whole army and the king stood gazing on this superhuman struggle. Leshchinski, the vice-chancellor, raised aloft the wood of the Holy Cross, and with it blessed the perishing.

Meanwhile, on the other flank, the army of the king was approached by the whole Cossack tabor, two hundred thousand strong, bristling with cannon, which vomited fire. It was like a dragon pushing slowly out of the woods his gigantic claws.

But before the bulk of the enemy had issued from the dust in which Vishnyevetski's regiments had disappeared, horsemen began to drop away from their ranks, then tens, hundreds, thousands, and tens of thousands of them, and rush to the height on which stood the Khan surrounded by his chosen guard. The wild legions fled in mad panic and disorder, pursued by the Poles. Thousands of Cossacks and Tartars strewed the battle-field; and among them lay, cut in two by a double-handed sword, the sworn enemy of the Poles but the trusty ally of the Cossacks, the wild and manful Tugai Bey.

The terrible prince had triumphed.

But the king looked with the eye of a leader on the triumph of the prince, and determined to break the hordes before the Cossacks could come up. All the forces moved, all the cannon thundered, scattering death and disorder. Soon the brother of the Khan, the lordly Amurat, fell struck in the breast with a bullet. The hordes roared with pain. Wounded in the very beginning of the battle, the Khan looked on the field with dismay. From the distance came Pshiyemski in the midst of cannon and fire, and the king with the horse; from both flanks the earth thundered beneath the weight of the cavalry rushing to the fight.

Then Islam Girei quivered, left the field, and fled; and after him fled in disorder all the hordes,--the Wallachians, the Urumbali, the mounted warriors of the Zaporojie, the Silistrian Turks, and the renegades,--as a cloud before a whirlwind.

The despairing Hmelnitski caught up with the fugitives, wishing to prevail on the Khan to return to the battle; but the Khan, bellowing with rage at the sight of the hetman, ordered the Tartars to seize, bind him to a horse, and bear him away.

Now there remained but the Cossack tabor. The leader of that tabor, colonel of Krapivna, Daidyalo, knew not what had happened to Hmelnitski; but seeing the defeat and shameful flight of all the hordes, he stopped the advance, and pushing back with the tabor, halted in the marshy forks of the Pleshova.

Now a storm burst in the heavens, and measureless torrents of rain rushed down. "God was washing the land after a just battle." The rain lasted some days, and some days the armies of the king rested, wearied from struggles; during this time the tabor surrounded itself with ramparts, and was changed into a gigantic movable fortress.

With the return of fair weather began a siege, the most wonderful ever seen in life. The hundred thousand warriors of the king besieged the twice one hundred thousand Zaporojians. The king needed cannon, provisions, ammunition. The Zaporojians had immeasurable supplies of powder and all necessaries, and besides seventy cannon of heavier and lighter calibre. But at the head of the king's armies was the king, and the Cossacks had not Hmelnitski. The armies of the king were strengthened by a recent victory; the Cossacks were in doubt of themselves.

Several days passed; hope of the return of Hmelnitski and the Khan disappeared. Then negotiations began. The Cossack colonels came to the king, and beat the forehead to him, asking for pardon; they visited the senators' tents, seizing them by their garments, promising to get Hmelnitski even from under the earth and deliver him to the king.

The heart of Yan Kazimir was not opposed to forgiveness. He wished to let the rabble return to their homes if all the officers were surrendered; these he determined to keep till Hmelnitski should be rendered up. But such an agreement was not to the mind of the officers, who, from the enormity of their offences, had no hope of forgiveness. Therefore in time of negotiations battles continued, desperate sallies, and every day Polish and Cossack blood flowed in abundance. The Cossacks fought in the daytime with bravery and the rage of despair; but at night whole clouds of them hung round the camp of the king, howling dismally for pardon.

Daidyalo was inclined to compromise, and was willing to give his head as a sacrifice to the king, if he could only ransom the army and the people. But dissension rose in the Cossack camp. Some wished to surrender, others to defend themselves to the death; but all were thinking how to escape from the tabor. To the boldest, however, this seemed impossible. The tabor was surrounded by the forks of the river and by immense swamps. Defence was possible for whole years, but to retreat only one road was open,--through the armies of the king. Of that road no one in the camp thought.

Negotiations, interrupted by battles, dragged on lazily. Dissensions among the Cossacks became greater and more frequent. In one of these Daidyalo was deposed from leadership, and a new man chosen. His name gave fresh strength to the fallen spirits of the Cossacks, and striking a loud echo in the camp of the king, roused in some hearts forgotten memories of past sorrows and misfortunes. The name of the new leader was Bogun. He had already occupied a lofty position among the Cossacks in council, and in action the general voice indicated him as the successor of Hmelnitski.

Bogun, foremost of the Cossack colonels, stood with the Tartars at Berestechko at the head of fifty thousand men. He took part in the three days' cavalry fight, and defeated with the Khan and the hordes by Yeremi, he succeeded in bringing out of the defeat the greater part of his forces and finding shelter in the camp. Then after Daidyalo the party opposed to conciliation gave him chief command, hoping that he was the one man able to save the tabor and the army.

In truth the young leader would not hear of negotiations. He wanted battle and blood, even if he had to drown in that blood himself. But soon he saw that with his troops it was vain to think of passing with armed hand over the bodies of the king's army. Therefore he grasped after other means.

History has preserved the memory of those matchless efforts which to contemporaries seemed worthy of a giant, and which might have saved the army and the mob.

Bogun determined to pass through the bottomless swamp of the Pleshova, and build over those quagmires a bridge of such make that all the besieged might cross. Whole forests began then to fall under the axes of the Cossacks and sink in the swamp. Wagons, tents, coats, sheepskins were thrown in, and the bridge extended day by day. It appeared that there was nothing impossible to that leader.

The king deferred the assault, from aversion to bloodshed. But seeing these gigantic works, he recognized that there was no other way, and ordered the trumpets to sound in the evening for the final struggle.

No one knew of that intention in the Cossack camp, and the bridge lengthened all night as before. In the morning Bogun went forth at the head of the officers to examine the work.

It was Monday, July 7, 1651. The morning of that day rose pale, as if from fright; the dawn was bloody in the east; the sun appeared, red, sickly; a sort of bloody reflection lighted the woods and forests. From the Polish camp they were driving the horses to pasture; the Cossack tabor sounded with the voices of awakened men. Fires were lighted, the morning meal prepared. All saw the departure of Bogun, his retinue and the cavalry going with him, by the aid of which he intended to drive away the voevoda of Bratslav, who had occupied the rear of the tabor and was injuring the Cossack works with his cannon.

The crowd looked on the departure quietly, and even with hope in their hearts. Thousands of eyes followed the young commander, and thousands of mouths said: "God bless thee, my falcon!"

The leader, the retinue, and the cavalry receded gradually from the tabor, came to the edge of the forest, glittered once more in the early sunlight, and began to disappear in the thicket. Then some awful, terrified voice shouted, or rather howled, at the gate of the tabor: "Save yourselves, men!"

"The officers are fleeing!" roared hundreds and thousands of voices. The roar passed through the crowd, as when a whirlwind strikes a pine-wood; and then a terrible, unearthly cry burst forth from two hundred thousand throats: "Save yourselves! Save yourselves! The Poles! The officers are fleeing!" Masses of men rose at once, like a mad torrent. Fires were trodden out, wagons and tents overturned, palings broken to pieces, men trampled and suffocated. Piles of bodies barred the road. They rushed over corpses, amidst howls, shouts, uproar, groans. Crowds poured from the square, burst on to the bridge, stuck in the swamp; the drowning seized one another with convulsive embraces, and crying to heaven for mercy, sank in the cold moving swamp. On the bridge began a battle and slaughter for place. The waters of the Pleshova were filled with bodies. The Nemesis of history took terrible payment for Pilavtsi with Berestechko.

The awful shouts came to the ears of the young leader, and he knew at once what had happened. But in vain did he return at that moment to the tabor; in vain did he turn to meet the crowd with hands raised to heaven. His voice was lost in the roar of thousands. The terrible river of fugitives bore him away, with his horse, his retinue, and all the cavalry, and carried him on to destruction.

The armies of the king were amazed at the sight of this movement, which some mistook at first for a desperate attack. But it was difficult not to believe the eyes of all. A few moments later, when their amazement had passed, all the regiments, without waiting even for command, rushed upon the enemy. First went like a whirlwind the dragoon regiment; in the front of it Volodyovski, with sabre above his head.

The day of vengeance, defeat, and judgment had come, Whoever was not trampled or drowned went under the sword. The rivers were so filled with blood, that it could not be told whether blood or water flowed in them. The bewildered crowds, still more disordered, began to trample and push one another into the water, and drown. Death filled those awful forests, and reigned in them the more terribly since strong divisions began to defend themselves with rage. Battles were fought in the swamp, on the stumps, in the field. The voevoda of Bratslav cut off retreat to the fugitives. In vain did the king give orders to restrain the soldiers. Mercy had perished; and the slaughter lasted till night,--a slaughter such as the oldest warriors did not remember, and at the recollection of which the hair rose on their heads in later times.

When at last darkness covered the earth, the victors themselves were terrified at their work. No "Te Deum" was sung, and not tears of joy, but of regret and sorrow, flowed from the eyes of the king.

So ended the first act in the drama of which Hmelnitski was the author.

But Bogun did not lay down his head with others in that day of horror. Some say that, seeing the defeat, he was the first to save himself by flight; others, that a certain knight of his acquaintance saved him. No one was able to reach the truth. This alone is certain, that in succeeding wars his name came out frequently among the names of the most noted leaders of the Cossacks. A shot from some vengeful hand struck him a few years later, but even then his last day did not come. After the death of Prince Vishnyevetski, from military toils, when the domains of Lubni fell away from the body of the Commonwealth, Bogun obtained possession of the greater part of their area. It was said that at last he would not recognize Hmelnitski over him. Hmelnitski himself, broken, cursed by his own people, sought aid from abroad; but the haughty Bogun refused every guardianship, and was ready to defend his Cossack freedom with the sword.

It was said, too, that a smile never appeared on the lips of this strange man. He lived not in Lubni, but in a village which he raised from its ashes, and which was called Rozlogi.

Intestine wars survived him, and continued for a long time; then came the plague and the Swedes. The Tartars were almost continual visitors in the Ukraine, carrying legions of people into captivity. The Commonwealth became a desert; a desert the Ukraine. Wolves howled on the ruins of former towns, and a land once flourishing became a mighty graveyard. Hatred grew into the hearts and poisoned the blood of brothers.

NOTES.

POLISH ALPHABET.

Since the Polish alphabet has many peculiar phonetic combinations which are difficult to one who does not know the language, it was decided to transliterate the names of persons and places in which such combinations occur in this book. The following are the letters and combinations which are met with most frequently;--

Polish Letters.	English Sounds.
c	ts
cz	*ch* in "chief"
sz	*sh* in "ship"
szcz	shch
rz	*r* followed by the French *j*
w	v
ż	*j* in French

In this transliteration *ch* retains its ordinary English sound. *Kh* is used as the German *ch*, or the Gaelic *ch* in "loch;" so is *h*, as in Hmelnitski, and a few names in which it is used at the beginning and preceding a consonant, where it has the power of the German *ch*. *J* is the French *j*; the vowels *e, i, u*, are, respectively, *ai* in "bait," *ee* in "beet," *oo* in "pool," when long; when short, "bet," "bit," "put" swould represent their values.

The following names will illustrate the method of this transliteration:--

Polish Form of Name.	Form in Transliteration.

Potocki	Pototski
Kulczinski	Kulchinski
Gdeszinski	Gdeshinski
Leszczinski	Leshchinski
Rzendzian	Jendzian
Woronczenko	Voronchenko
Żabkowski	Jabkovski

In Jendzian the initial R has been omitted, on account of the extreme difficulty of its sound to any one not a Pole. In Skrzetuski, a very difficult name also, *sh* has been used instead of the French *j*, because in this word the two sounds are almost identical, and the sound of *sh* is known to all, while *j* is not.

ACCENT.

All Polish words, with few exceptions, are accented on the syllable next the last, the penult. The exceptions are foreign names, some compounds, some words with enclitics. Polish names of men and places are generally accented on the penult. In Russian--both of the Ukraine and the North, or of Little and Great Russia--there is much freedom in placing the accent. In this book there are many Russian names of men and places; but the majority of names are accented on the penult. It has been thought best, therefore, to state this fact, and place accents only on words accented on syllables other than the penult. Some of these were accented in the body of the book; the rest are accented here. The following names of men are accented on the last syllable:--

Balaban	Burdabut
Barabash	Chernota
Bogun	

The following names of places are accented as indicated:--

Bakche	Seraí Korovái
Bazalúk	Mírgorod
Bél	Per

gorod	ekóp
Bóguslav	Sekírnaya
Gálata	Sléporod
Hassan Pashá	Volochísk
Kámenyets	Yagorlík

Polish names in *ski* and *vich* are adjectives, regularly declined, with masculine and feminine endings. The titles of address *Pan, Pani, Panna*, refer respectively to a gentleman, a married lady, an unmarried lady. The following are examples:--

Pan Kurtsevich,	Pani Kurtsevichova,

Panna Kurtsevichovna.

These three forms when applied to one family refer to the father, mother, and an unmarried daughter.

The ending in *ski* is not so complicated; for instance,--

Pan Pototski,	Pani Pototska,

Panna Pototska.

The names in *vich* denote descent; those in *ski*, origin in, or lordship over, a place.

Nikolai Pototski, Grand Hetman, captured at Korsún, was Pan Pototski, which means lord of Potok (Potok being the name of the place which he inherited); he was also Pan Krakovski, lord of Krakov (Cracow), because he was castellan of Krakov (Cracow), an office to which he was appointed by the king.

The names of villages which Zagloba mentions as belonging to Podbipienta are curious enough, whether real or invented by the whimsical narrator; as is also the name Povsinoga, which he gives the tall Lithuanian, and which means "tramp." The villages--taken in the order in which he gives them on page 540--Myshikishki, Psikishki, Pigvishki, Sirutsiani, Tsiaputsiani, Kapustsiana glowa, Baltupye, are--excluding the first two, the meanings of which are given on page 20--Crabapple town, Homespunville, Simpletown, Cabbagehead, and Slabtown.

The soup botvinia, mentioned in connection with Podbipienta and Pan Kharlamp, which is made of vegetables and fish in eastern Russia, may be made, it seems, without fish in Lithuania. The word is used figuratively to designate a rustic or stay-at-home villager.

OFFICES AND THINGS.

Balalaika, a stringed instrument used in southern Russia, resembling the guitar.

Cástellan, the chief of a town or city under Polish rule, as well as the district connected with it. The castellan was always a senator, and was appointed by the king.

Chambul, a party of mounted Tartars.

Koshevói, chief of a Cossack camp.

Kurén, a company or group of Cossacks as well as the barracks in which they lived.

Sotnik, a captain of Cossacks. This word is exactly equivalent to "centurion," and is derived from *sto*, "one hundred," with the nominative ending *nik*.

Stanitsa, a Cossack village.

Stárosta, chief of a town under Polish control.

Starshiní, elders. This word meant for the Cossacks the whole body of their officers.

Telega, the ordinary springless wagon of Russia, smaller than the country wagon in the United States.

Teorbán, or *Torbán*, a large musical instrument of twenty strings or more.

Voevoda, governor and commander of troops in a province, corresponding to the military governor of modern times. This office was common to the Poles and the Russians of the East or Moscow.

FOOTNOTES:

Footnote 1: The author uses Skshetuski, the family name of his hero, oftener than Yan, his Christian name, prefixing Pan = Mr. in both cases. I have taken the liberty of using Yan oftener than Skshetuski because more easily pronounced in English.

Footnote 2: Tear-trousers.

Footnote 3: Tear-cowl.

Footnote 4: Dog entrails.

Footnote 5: Mouse entrails.

Footnote 6: This is the popular form in Little Russian; therefore it is quoted.

Footnote 7: The right bank of the Dnieper was called Russian; the left, Tartar.

Footnote 8: Hmelnitski is made to apply the title Tsar to the Khan, either to give him more importance in the eyes of the Cossacks or because Tugai Bey was present.

Footnote 9: The author uses sometimes the word *vudka* and sometimes *gorailka*. The first is Polish; the second Little Russian. Both mean a liquor distilled generally from rye. When *vudka* is used it might mean that the liquor was from Poland, and when *gorailka* that it was of Ukraine origin; but here the words are used indifferently.

Footnote 10: *Krívonos* signifies "crooked nose;" *Prostonos*, "straight nose."

Footnote 11: "Holota" (Nakedness) was used as a nickname in those days to designate a poor nobleman. Abstract nouns were used by the Cossacks also as names; e. g., Colonel Chernota, which means "blackness."

Footnote 12: City of the Tsar = Constantinople.

Footnote 13: A pun on "Pulyan," which in Polish means "half Yan," or John.

Footnote 14: "Hmel," a nickname for Hmelnitski among the Poles, = "hops."

Footnote 15: Holota (Nakedness) was often given as a nickname to a poor noble.

Footnote 16: Nicknames given by Hmelnitski to the three Polish commanders.

Footnote 17: *Kapustsiani*, "of cabbage," the masculine form of the adjective. *Kapustsiana glowa* means "a cabbage head; a stupid fellow." *Glowa* is the ordinary word for *head* in Polish, and takes the feminine adjective ending in *a*: hence *Kapustsiana*. For explanation of the other names see list of names and places.

Footnote 18: This means, "Everything or nothing;" "Carry the day or go to a monastery."

Footnote 19: Circassians from the Caucasus.

Footnote 20: *Div* is a Persian word for "demon" or "evil spirit." This word meant "a divinity" in times anterior to Zoroaster, and is identical with the root *div* in our word "divine." In India and Europe it retained its original signification, and became of evil import only in Persia, in consequence of the triumph of Zoroastrianism.

Footnote 21: "Panowie" is the plural of Pan.

CPSIA information can be obtained at www.ICGtesting.com
Printed in the USA
LVOW09s1324300816

502483LV00023B/343/P